Network Administrator's Reference

Tere' Parnell
Christopher Null

Osborne/**McGraw-Hill**

Berkeley New York St. Louis San Francisco
Auckland Bogotá Hamburg London Madrid
Mexico City Milan Montreal New Delhi Panama City
Paris São Paulo Singapore Sydney
Tokyo Toronto

Osborne/**McGraw-Hill**
2600 Tenth Street
Berkeley, California 94710
U.S.A.

For information on translations or book distributors outside the U.S.A., or to arrange bulk purchase discounts for sales promotions, premiums, or fund-raisers, please contact Osborne/**McGraw-Hill** at the above address.

Network Administrator's Reference

1234567890 AGM AGM 90198765432109

ISBN 0-07-882588-1

Publisher	**Copy Editor**
Brandon A. Nordin	Dennis Weaver
Associate Publisher and	**Proofreader**
Editor in Chief	Laurie Stewart
Scott Rogers	**Indexer**
Acquisitions Editor	Jack Lewis
Gareth Hancock	**Computer Designer**
Project Editor	Roberta Steele
Ron Hull	**Illustrators**
Editorial Assistant	Beth Young
Stephane Thomas	Brian Wells
Technical Editor	**Series Design**
Dick Hol	Peter F. Hancik

For my children, Claire and Elliot: Mom's home.
And for my husband, Jeff: Let's go skiing.
Tere' Parnell

For my wife, Ashley, who put up with lost evenings and weekends so I
could finish this project, and who had to suffer through months of
incessant rambling about clock speeds and cache sizes. Also for my
collaborator Tere', who got me into this business in the first place.
Christopher Null

CONTENTS

Part II

The Applications

Part III

The Infrastructure

Part IV

The 'Nets

ACKNOWLEDGMENTS

This project was cursed. If you don't believe it, consider that during the course of writing this book:

- ▼ My then-fiancé-now-husband was injured while stationed 4,000 miles away
- ■ Four different contract writers and an assistant quit before completing their commitments to this book
- ■ I moved my household 2,000 miles
- ■ I lost my job
- ■ I contracted severe bronchitis
- ■ We experienced a mid-project change in editorial assistants
- ■ I had to make an emergency trip to India
- ■ I became the first person in the United States to catch the 1999 Asian flu
- ■ Three different nannies quit with less than a week's notice
- ▲ Got engaged, disengaged, re-engaged, and married

And this is just the stuff I care to make public.

However, the finished product—the book itself—is far from cursed. So how did this experiment in misery become a great book? Through the help of some very sharp and dedicated people. I want to thank them here.

Many thanks to Gareth Hancock, my acquisitions editor at Osborne/McGraw-Hill. Without his dedication, good cheer, and unwavering moral support, I would have ditched this project long ago. The wonderful thing about Gareth is that no matter how viciously I treated him, he always responded with elegant tact and boundless kindness.

And I do not want to forget Osborne's own answer to The Shadow, Ron Hull. Working tirelessly behind the scenes, Ron knows the evil that has lurked throughout this project, yet has championed it to the end. You may never see him, but rest assured, The Shadow *knows.*" Thank you, Ron.

Stephane Thomas, editorial assistant at Osborne, stepped in and saved the day when this book was floundering in chaos. Stephane, this book could not possibly have gone to print without you. You are the U.S. Cavalry and all three of Charlie's Angels rolled into one.

And speaking of the U.S. Cavalry, I would like to thank them—more precisely, the Fourth Squadron of the Seventh Cavalry—for providing me with shelter (and enough material to fill several books) at Camp Garry Owen, near Munsan, Republic of Korea, while I developed the concept of this book. Guys, if it were in my power, I'd *send* you Charlie's Angels.

At the same time, I must thank the U.S. Army for allowing me to *leave* Camp Garry Owen, while requiring that my fiancé remain behind. Had they not done so, this book would never have been written.

I would also like to thank my good friend, collaborator, and one of the brightest people I know, Christopher Null. Chris was the only one of five writers who made good on his commitment to coauthor this book. As he did at *LAN Times* and does now at *PC Computing*, Chris delivered outstanding material on time, for which there is no adequate way to express my gratitude. He also coined the term, "oxygen thief," for which I am eternally in his debt.

Many thanks to David D. Bezar, who provided the material for Chapter 18, "The Internet." David D. Bezar received his Bachelor of Science Degree in Computer Information Systems from Cal Poly, Pomona. He has over 13 years of diversified telecommunications experience, including network planning and management of medium to large telecommunications systems. David started his career in telecommunications back in 1985 where he worked for Computer Technology Consultant, Inc. In 1988 David became a principal in Telemanagement Systems Group, a company that specialized in providing telecommunications management solutions to colleges, universities, banks, hospitals, and local governments. In early 1995 David became cofounder of Top-Net, a computer consulting firm specializing in the Internet. He is currently a consultant in many areas of telephony, including, but not limited to: the Internet, desktop video conferencing, switch procurement, network planning, optimization, and troubleshooting. Some of the clients he has worked for in the past and present include: Spring Long Distance, Carson Productions, Warner Brothers, the United States Army and Air Force, Pepperdine University, Villanova University, Home Savings and Loan, Scripps Medical Clinic, Nissan Motor Corporation, and Jet Propulsion Laboratories.

If you are in need of telecommunications or Internet consulting services, David can be contacted at:

Top-Net
Attn: David Bezar
1114 Flintlock Road
Diamond Bar, CA 91765
Voice (909) 444-3020, Video (909) 444-3017
Fax (909) 612-0313, E-mail dbezar@primenet.com

As always, my children, Claire and Elliot, have been champions during the year this project took. They not only endured but thrived despite the four nannies, three simultaneously homes, multiple schools and tutors, ever-changing time zones and continents, countless airplanes, and long separations—not to mention my occasional foul humor. Someday, kids, when I grow up, I want to be just like you.

And let's not forget those who not only provided me with professional insight on this project, but also talked me off the ledge more than once: my sisters, Valerie Libby and Seema Varghese, as well as J. C. Pletcher, Carol Grissom, Kelli Weaver, and especially Kathy Palmer (who is the greatest thing ever to hit Meade County, Kentucky—if only its residents could recognize it—but really needs to stop referring to herself as Ms. Lieutenant Palmer). Thank you, thank you, thank you.

Finally, I want to express my appreciation, gratitude, and love for 1Lt. Jeffrey Bracco, who married me anyway.

Tere' Parnell

Tere' has covered the genesis of this book with surprising accuracy and candor. I hope the rest of the book provides as much enlightenment and amusement as her opus. In addition to her acknowledgments, I would be remiss without mentioning *LAN Times*, the magazine which spawned my career, well, writing stuff like this. I learned a lot about journalism from the good folks at *LAN Times* (may she rest in peace), and a fair amount about technology, too. Thanks also to Tere' for letting me swirl my hand in this masterpiece of technical knowledge, and thanks to my wife Ashley for putting up with said swirling (she'll get used to it someday). Even more thanks to the tireless staff at Osborne who kept all the details in check and never let a single ball drop. And of course, thanks to all the high-tech companies and innovators who dreamt up all this stuff... so we could give you the lowdown on how it really works.

Christopher Null

INTRODUCTION

▼

"My boss told me to build an intranet."

"We need to put our business on the Web."

"Sales needs access to accounts receivable information."

"Now what?"

While at the *LAN Times* Testing Center, we receive hundreds of letters, e-mails, and telephone calls asking for help in designing and building computer networks. The questions range from the precise,

"Can you recommend a 155Mbps ATM adapter for our servers?"

to the very broad,

> "We are implementing SAP globally in approximately 85 remote sites. This is a central network design based out of our headquarters. These remote sites will access all file and print services (SAP, Office 97, etc.) from a Novell 4.11 SMP fileserver located in headquarters using Wyse terminals running Citrix. We expect 2000 simultaneous users. The infrastructure is pretty much a mainframe design for PCs. Let me know if you know of any companies I can speak with who have (successfully or unsuccessfully) done this."

to the overwhelming,

> "I can connect the router directly to the Web server which supplies the LAN server and the terminal server with the connection to the Internet, and the router is connected to the CSU/DSU device, which is the direct feed to the T1 line, right? So what kind of router and CSU/DSU devise will I need? What is the best solution, and how much will it cost? What kind of protocol do need? I know that my LAN will be based on an IP protocol, but what if I want a TCP/IP protocol for my dial-in users? Do you have any suggestions?"

While reading through these "letters from the lovelorn," we have realized that *all* networking professionals, regardless of expertise or experience, run into situations in which they need some help. Some need training, some need advice or suggestions, some need confirmation—some just need a drink. We have written this book for all of them.

After all, building a network means connecting different parts of your business so that the whole is greater than the sum of the parts. Unfortunately, most network architecture strategies don't clarify the business objective. And they're often vague on the tactics. No wonder networks grow haphazardly and network managers don't know which way to turn.

We designed *Network Administrator's Reference* for every network professional—from the newly drafted administrator to the veteran application developer to the IS director. It will help you clearly define your business objectives, develop cohesive strategies to meet those objectives, and outline appropriate tactics *in detail*. From installing the first network cable to selecting appropriate data encryption to developing custom network applications, this book will help you determine what you need to build, what you need to buy, who you need to hire, and how to manage it all.

We realize there is no cookbook for building a network. Each computer network has a unique set of business goals, obstacles, users, and physical parameters. However, there is a common set of design principles, devices, services, and tools from which any network professional can draw to help solve his or her particular problem. The goal of this book is to provide a directory of these tools and a blueprint for using them.

Most networking books try to draw this blueprint by explaining each stage through a tedious review of the International Standards Organization's Open Systems Interconnect (ISO/OSI) model. Maybe you've had this experience: After painstakingly reading through a description of each of the model's seven layers—starting with layer 1 and building to a crescendo with layer 7—you begin to wonder what the theoretical model has to do with your real-world network.

Actually, a lot.

Familiarity with the relationship between the ISO/OSI model and the functions performed by each component of your network is vital to understanding your network and troubleshooting common network problems.

Oddly, though, other books rarely relate the ISO/OSI layers to the business tasks of networks. But that's the easiest way to understand what each protocol layer does, why it's important, and what you need to consider at each layer. Therefore, Part I of this book starts with your business. What do you want to do? What are the unique characteristics of your business and operating environment? In short, where are you, and where do you want to go? This part covers the functions that the different departments in your company must perform. For example, it discusses front-office functions such as document production, back-office functions like accounting, and electronic commerce—business on the 'net. In each chapter, we describe the ultimate business goal of the function and the means available to accomplish it.

Part II describes the various computer applications that can help you perform the functions covered in Part I. It describes what applications do, their relationship to each other and the network, and how they interact and communicate with one another, as well as the types of applications that will best serve your particular environment. Part II also discusses the issues of keeping information as close as possible to the users of that information—without risking data security. This part will help you determine where your applications should be installed and how they should be designed to meet your business needs.

Part III discusses the network infrastructure on which the applications operate—the computers, cables, operating environments, and other devices that together make the most visible portion of your network. In Part III we discuss all the software systems necessary to provide a solid and secure environment for running you chosen applications. We also include information on desktop computers, network servers, and the devices that connect them. We go into very detailed explanations of network protocols and how they are switched and routed. This part will help you select the appropriate hardware for running the infrastructure software you must have to support your chosen applications.

It seems all the world is talking about different types of 'nets: intranets, extranets, and the mac-daddy of them all, the Internet. But what exactly are these different types of networks, how do you build them, and how do you connect to them? Part IV addresses all of these questions for each different type of network, showing you what services, software, and equipment to add to enable your network to connect to and become one of the great 'nets. In this part we also discuss unified messaging—where it is today and where it's headed.

In the appendix, we conclude the book with a discussion of how to keep your network running smoothly, how to stay ahead of trends, and how to prepare your network for its inevitable expansion and continuous metamorphosis. The appendix includes hints on hiring consultants, keeping your staff in a constant state of readiness, avoiding burnout, and being prepared for change.

Whatever your experience and skill level, we hope this book will keep you company during the dark hours of network planning and troubleshooting. We also hope it will keep those hours to a minimum.

PART I

Building a Network

CHAPTER 1

Front-Office Functions

The front office at Boyce Clubb is a busy place. Yet from the minute a client walks in the door, the client feels important. The sleek receptionist greets the valued client by name and directs him to Conference Room A, where a pile of file folders containing neatly bound documents, a large video monitor, and a delicious blend of French roast coffee (black, two sugars) await him.

Unfortunately, when the client opens the folders, he notices the documents aren't his (but they make interesting reading, anyway, because they belong to his ex-partner). Then an unidentified young man enters the room and asks if he is here for the staff meeting. It sounds as though Boyce Clubb does indeed need some refinement of its *front-office systems*.

IT'S THE (SEEMINGLY) LITTLE THINGS THAT COUNT

Generally speaking, front-office systems are those activities that generally involve the way the enterprise deals with its customers. They help the enterprise "put its best face forward" with its clients, from initial contact through the repeat sale. Let's go over some of the most important front-office functions that Boyce Clubb could improve using network applications.

Scheduling and Time Management

The appointment book is probably the oldest business tool still in existence. Being able to keep track of where you are supposed to be at each hour of the day is a basic need for conducting business. Of course, it's not sufficient simply for each individual to monitor his or her own time. It's important to coordinate schedules with coworkers and clients, resolving conflicts and using time as efficiently as possible.

As a result, a good group scheduling application is the foundation of useful front-office applications. It ranges from shrink-wrapped, off-the-shelf packages from large companies such as Microsoft and Novell to custom software designed specifically for your type of business. The shrink-wrapped software has the benefit of being less expensive (usually) and having a large base of trained technicians available to assist in installation and support. Many packages are also customizable to some degree. However, it may lack essential features that the custom software can provide. This is critical, because group scheduling software has evolved into more than a series of calendars for each person in the company. It can be an important link to other systems and resources. Below are some important features to consider.

Check In/Check Out

One component of group scheduling software is a module for employees and/or customers checking in and out of the office. In a firm like Boyce Clubb, the group scheduling package only needs to keep track of where employees are. When employees "check out" in the group scheduling program before leaving the office, no one has to waste time searching the premises for someone who has left. Instead, when trying to locate an employee, the seeker can simply check the group scheduling software, which includes not only the employee's whereabouts, but also how to contact him or her.

In another type office—a dental practice, for example—the check-in/check-out feature is vital for keeping track of customers. When a customer checks in, the group scheduling program can generate necessary paperwork such as insurance and health history forms, as well as accounts receivable information noting any balances due from that patient. In such an environment, the check-out program will likely be tied to a back-office program such as accounts receivable, recording balances due, and amounts paid.

Conference Scheduling

An important feature of a group scheduling program is its ability to schedule conferences and all the resources needed for a conference. Anyone who has ever tried to schedule a meeting knows that it can be nearly impossible to find a time when all necessary participants *and* a conference room, video projector, and Internet connection are available simultaneously. A good conference scheduling system can help with this by allowing you to check the availability of—and reserve—people, rooms, and equipment. After reserving the necessary resources, these packages send invitations to the potential attendees, giving them an opportunity to confirm or decline participation.

Teleconferences (Audio and Video)

Despite the best-laid plans, there are always times when necessary conference participants are not in the office. When teleconferences are necessary, front-office applications can refer the conference coordinator to a list of preferred teleconference vendors, and schedule a reminder to ensure that the teleconference has been set up. These packages may even have features that determine which conference rooms may be scheduled for a meeting depending upon the type of conference being set up. For example, the package wouldn't allow you to schedule a multimedia teleconference in a room that was not equipped with videoconferencing capabilities.

People

How much control you can afford to give your employees is an important consideration in selecting a group scheduling package. Some packages enable users to conceal their schedules from other users. Others allow users to decline invitations to meetings, while some do not. If you don't want employees—or at least certain employees—to be able to hide their schedules and/or decline invitations to meetings, you need to be able to configure this in the scheduling package.

Personal Information Management

If the appointment book is the oldest business tool, the address book is the most widely used. Contact information is the lifeblood of any organization. It's no surprise, therefore, that managing personal information is a key front-office function.

Personal information ranges from contact information (the name, address, e-mail address, and telephone number) to full dossiers. Birthdays, anniversaries, names of family members, notes on past meetings, and favorite foods can all be important and very valuable information about our clients and other important business associates. But to be truly valuable, this information must be at your fingertips, so you can refer to it instantly should that person call.

At Boyce Clubb the partners understand how vital this personal information is to their business relationships. Therefore, they want this information maintained on their network rather than in each individual's *personal data assistant*, or PDA. With the information on the network, the network manager can back it up, archive it, and keep it safe from accidental or intentional deletion. As well, other employees within Boyce Clubb can access this data in the event that the original collector of the data is unavailable (whether on vacation, sick, or—oh no!—defected to another firm).

Contact Management

Sales organizations have special client information management needs. They need to maintain information about the needs, complaints, and past ordering history of current clients. They also need to keep track of the progress they are making with prospective clients. Information on the dates, topics, and tone of past meetings is vital. In fact, it is one of the greatest assets of almost any company. Monitoring and controlling this type of information is called *contact management*, and it is a critical front-office function.

Call Management

No one likes to be kept on hold—least of all the upscale clientele of Boyce Clubb. Company policy is to pick up an incoming call within three rings. And when a client calls, he or she wants answers. After all, they're being billed by the hour. So, the pertinent files should be at the answerer's fingertips. *Call management software* identifies voice calls and links them to the caller's files stored on the network, making them available to the callee, the person who picks up the telephone handset.

If the callee isn't available, the caller should have the option to leave a message either on a voice mail system or with a live person. To ensure that clients' calls don't go unanswered for long, Boyce Clubb partners would like to be able to pick up their messages using either telephones or their notebook computers.

Order Entry

Although this isn't an issue with Boyce Clubb order entry is an important front-office function. Being able to enter orders quickly and accurately is obviously critical to the success of any product-oriented business.

Not only can order entry be an important function of networked front-office systems, it can be linked to call management that can pull customer information from databases based on the calling customers' telephone numbers. As well, these systems can—and definitely should—be linked to back-office systems to streamline billing and accounts receivable functions.

Of course, once an order is entered, the company should be able to track it. Therefore, easy order tracking is an important adjunct to your order entry system.

Customer Service

The most visible front-office function is customer service. Because it requires fast and accurate delivery of customer data, this is the true testing ground for front-office systems. Some customer service functions are described below.

Customer Profiles

A good customer service application keeps detailed information on each customer. This information should be linked from contact information, order entry information, and personal information gathered by individual employees and stored on a central database on the network. Together, all of this information builds a current snapshot of the client and the work in progress for that client.

ANI Is Your Friend

Automatic Number Identification, or ANI, is a feature available through local exchange carrier telephone companies that allows you to identify the telephone number of a calling party. By linking ANI information with a customer profile database, you can have very detailed customer information ready and waiting *before* you lift the receiver to answer that customer's call.

Technical Support

A customer support application can do far more than just identify your clients and their order histories. Customer support systems can also include modules that compile databases of technical information and problem resolution. This makes it easy to look up a probable solution for a technical problem based on a few key descriptions of the problem. Such a database also allows you to track technical problems to ensure that none "slip through the cracks," then catalog the problem and its ultimate resolution for future reference should the problem occur again.

Complaints and Resolution

Problem tracking systems are a part of customer service applications. Just like systems that track technical problems, these systems keep track of all customer communications (which are generally order tracking or complaints, to be honest), making sure they are all properly recorded and ultimately resolved.

Document Preparation

Probably the most familiar front-office function is document preparation. In fact, the first network application most people ever used is the trusty word processing package. Document preparation now involves far more than typing and formatting documents. It also includes compiling documents from multiple document types, such as spreadsheets and databases, and multiple media types, such as video and sound, then routing them through various departments and employees for editing and approval.

Research

Compiling these documents requires research, and now with the advent of fast and easy Internet connectivity, the network is equipped to support that research. Browser software is obviously the enabling application for this type of corporate research. Therefore, selecting, installing, and maintaining browser software is key to implementing this particular front-end function.

Document Management And Retrieval

Once the professionals at Boyce Club, PC have prepared a document, they need to ensure that it's filed accurately and safely so that all the appropriate parties can retrieve it when necessary. Conversely, they must ensure that the wrong parties *cannot* access it. All of these functions are handled by document management and retrieval software packages.

Electronic Mail

No one at Boyce Clubb, in fact, no one on the planet, would know how to survive without e-mail. What was a novelty just a few years ago is now as indispensable to daily business as the telephone. Electronic mail is without a doubt the most widely used front-office application today. To make it as useful as possible, however, Boyce Clubb would like to integrate it with its other front-office functions, such as document preparation and group scheduling, to ensure the smooth flow of information throughout the firm.

Internal News Management

The bulletin board has been replaced by Web pages on the corporate intranet. But designing, managing, and updating these pages requires a lot more skill than its wood-and-cork predecessor. And determining who should have access to do what on the intranet pages can require the wisdom of Solomon. Therefore, implementing this particular front-end system on your network usually requires expertise that is as much political as it is technical.

Timekeeping

The partners at Boyce Clubb charge by the hour. This means that they have to keep painstakingly accurate and detailed records of the time they spend working on each client's files. However, partners can't bill the time they spend recording their time. Therefore, timekeeping applications, which automatically record how much time users spend on applications and documents, would make life much easier (and more profitable) for Boyce Clubb's employees. Another benefit of such applications is that they can feed directly into the accounts receivable system in the back office, streamlining the billing and collections process.

Preparing Expense Reports

Like preparing time sheets, preparing expense reports is a necessary but loathesome job to the timekeepers of Boyce Clubb. Filling out the forms by hand, then printing, signing, and delivering them is a major hassle every month. Luckily for them, expense report preparation software is available that simplifies the completion and validation of the report and electronically routes the completed report to accounts payable in the back office for payment.

ON TO THE BACK DOOR

Of all the possible enhancements to the front-office systems, the partners at Boyce Clubb are most enthusiastic about the addition of timekeeping software and expense report preparation software. Not only would these make their jobs a little easier, but they would also provide an important electronic link between the workings of the front office and the workings of the back office. But what exactly is this back-office function, and how can an improved network better support it? This is the topic we discuss in the next chapter.

CHAPTER 2

Back-Office Functions

The back office at Boyce Clubb is hopping, too. From the accounting systems to the records management systems to the Web and databases servers that support them all, the information supporting back-office operations is flowing furiously through the firm.

WHERE IS THE BACK END?

Back-end systems has two main definitions:

▼ Systems that support the operation of an enterprise

▲ Information systems that provide services to users

Because these two systems are related, but distinctly different, we will discuss each of these in turn.

Systems That Support Operations

These are the systems such as the accounting system, the records management system, and the human resources system. Boyce Clubb has a sophisticated accounting system that can produce any type of report. Want to know your top 10 billing accountants? The system can produce it. In which industries does Boyce Clubb have its most lucrative clients? The accounting system can provide a report.

Alas, the accounting system runs on a midrange computer, and it is currently inaccessible via the firm's PC network—which, according to the firm's controller, isn't altogether bad, because she isn't sure how adequate security can be implemented to protect sensitive financial data from unauthorized users. However, the accountants at Boyce Clubb want to have immediate access to this information, and they want to be able to pull reports based on *ad hoc queries*—that is, reports that they have designed to answer a unique and specific question. Therefore, one of the main challenges that faces Boyce Clubb is the integration of its accounting system with its local area network.

Another problem with the accounting system is that it isn't integrated with the firm's network-based timekeeping software. The accountants keep track of their billable hours using their timekeeping software, entering their time in the system throughout the day. Then, every Friday, the data processing staff must extract the data from the timekeeping software and load it into the host accounting database. The entire process is tedious, time-consuming, processor-taxing, and redundant. It would be so much easier if data from the timekeeping system were automatically entered into the accounting system without human intervention.

The firm's human resources system is also midrange-based, and it is tightly integrated with the accounting system. Again, however, it would be much more convenient for managers in the firm if HR performance, tenure, and salary data for their employees were available over the PC network. As it is now, the managers have to request that the data processing staff create and run such a report, delivering a paper report to them several hours (or days) later.

Other supporting systems that Boyce Clubb plans to make accessible over its network are as follows:

▼   Office administration

■   Document management

■   Purchasing

▲   Recruiting

Each of these systems would be more effective if it were more tightly integrated into other back-end systems *and* searchable via the PC network.

Systems That Provide Services to Users

Over its long history, Boyce Clubb has had several different computer systems. As a result, it has stored a lot of important historical data on a variety of computers—very few of which communicate directly with one another. Therefore, another of the many projects Boyce Clubb plans to undertake is to make this wealth of historical data available to its current PC network users. In other words, Boyce Clubb needs to make legacy back-end data systems more accessible.

This brings us to the other definition of "back end," which is the servers (which can be PC servers, midrange computers, and/or mainframes) that provide information services to users. An example of the second would be Web servers, database servers, and e-mail. Other common back-end systems are database management systems (DBMS), network management systems, messaging systems (such as Lotus Notes), and communication gateways to other, dissimilar systems such as mainframes and midrange computers.

These servers may be physically located on a departmental network where the data they contain is used most frequently. However, it's now more common for these servers to be located together in a *server farm*, as illustrated in Figure 2-1.

As we will discuss in Part II of this book, back-end systems are based on *client/server architecture*, in which the system divides the processing between a front-end, or *client*, portion of the system and the back-end, or *server*, portion. Users interact with the client part of the system, using client applications to request data from the server systems. The server systems then process the requests for information by searching databases, sorting search results, then responding to the client with the requested data. These back-end server systems are usually located on the same computing platform as the data they are searching, so responses are quick and data traffic is minimal.

As we will see in Chapters 5 and 6, client/server systems often add a middle system that handles some of the request processing. For example, a Web server may receive requests from clients and determine to which back-end system to forward the request. The Web server may then receive the response to the request from the back-end server, then

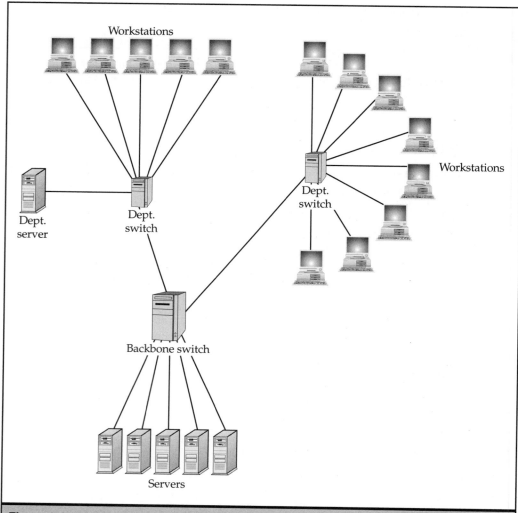

Figure 2-1.   A server farm configuration and a departmental server configuration

format the response into a Web page before sending the requested data on to the client. This arrangement, called a *three-tiered* or *multitiered system*, is extremely scalable because it lets the middle system determine to which back-end system to send the data. Thus the middle system can distribute processing evenly among back-end servers. Furthermore, as we will also see in Chapter 6, the middle system can maintain the *business logic* (rules, procedures, and/or operational sequences) for the enterprise, allowing it to be managed at a single point, yet shared by all users.

NOTE: As we will see in Chapter 6, there is a special form of multitiered system called a *data warehouse* that allows data from back-end servers to be extracted, sorted, summarized, and stored on middle systems so that users can access data from back-end servers more easily.

THE FUTURE

It sounds as though overhauling the front-end and back-end systems should keep the Information Services staff at Boyce Clubb busy. And it will. But upgrading and integrating these systems will only bring their information technology up to date. It won't prepare it for the future. And Boyce Clubb has big plans for the future: They want to enter the world of electronic commerce, which we will describe in the next chapter.

CHAPTER 3

Electronic Commerce

The Internet has changed everything we know about the way business works. Geographical boundaries, language barriers, and even currency restrictions are falling right and left, and electronic commerce technology is to thank—or to blame.

Depending on which side of the fence you're on, *e-commerce*, as it's commonly known, can be a great boon or a real pain. If you're a casual user of the Web, you've probably browsed sites like CDNow or Amazon.com and maybe purchased an item or two. As of 1998, the portion of consumers who had purchased products online was about five percent. By the end of 1999, that will at least double to ten percent. For that small fraction of us, online shopping has become an absolute necessity, and physical music and bookstores never seem to have the selection or the convenience of their online counterparts.

If your business is considering putting up an electronic storefront, you've got an uphill road to climb. Deciding how to integrate your existing business with a Web-based commerce solution is only the first step. After that, you'll need to consider what packages you want to use in setting up your online presence, how to process payments, what to do about new electronic money and online banking offerings, how to advertise, and, most important, how to manage the security for all of this.

If you thought securing your intranet was a daunting task, wait until your company's livelihood—and its financial transactions—are on the Web.

But don't be discouraged. An online business has a plethora of benefits, including the following:

▼ Storefront and inventory requirements are lessened, resulting in lower cost of operations.

■ You have access to a potentially unlimited customer base.

■ Changing or adding to your sales inventory is much quicker and easier.

■ You can achieve better integration with your accounting, manufacturing, and/or fulfillment applications.

▲ Finally, you can effectively locate your business anywhere in the world.

But before you have an ISDN line installed on your favorite lounge chair or ski lodge, you need to take an inventory of the resources you have. You can then use that information to build a strategy to figure out what additional resources you need to get your business online.

USING WHAT YOU'VE GOT

Depending on the size of your company, your adventure with electronic commerce begins in your server room. If you already have a Web site that is hosted on a machine in your offices, you're well on your way already.

Your first step is to consider the platform you're using. If you're using Windows NT and running a Microsoft or Netscape Web server, you won't run into nearly as many compatibility issues as you will with a lesser-known platform. While some packages use CGI scripts to speak to your Web server, many are geared toward specific servers and use NSAPI or ISAPI to process queries. While using these APIs will give you a speed boost, you lose compatibility.

E-commerce packages are still fairly new phenomena. Unless you're interested in coding your own commerce applications, you're going to be limited to a handful of better-known e-commerce solutions. Because of the market's immaturity, sticking to a more robust and widely implemented Web server platform will server you well.

Also of primary concern: How is your company's sales and production information currently managed? If you use, for example, a custom Microsoft SQL Server database to house your production database, it will be much easier to tie it together with a Microsoft Internet Information Server Web platform and a third-party Web commerce package that supports IIS. On the other hand, if you have a large enterprise IS solution from a company like SAP or Oracle, Web commerce packages are available as extensions to the base system. Or, you may have an old mainframe or minicomputer-based inventory and accounting system, and an e-commerce system may have to be developed from scratch. Still, you'll probably be surprised at the depth and breadth of e-commerce packages currently on the market.

It goes without saying that the market for e-commerce suites is rapidly changing, and no one can promise whether the solution you buy today will be around tomorrow.

EDI

Finally, consider who your customer is. You may already have some form of electronic data interchange (EDI) system in-house, especially if you work with behemoth companies that insist on using it and can command a great deal of your attention.

The old-style EDI consisted of two dedicated machines: one at your site, and one at the site of a very large and important customer, for example. When the customer's stock ran low, its systems would note this fact, then issue a command to your dedicated terminal over a standard modem connection. Your system would spit out an order and automatically generate shipping and billing information for you.

This way, people (and subsequently, errors) were cut out of the loop as much as possible. This was also a great way to speed up the order fulfillment process under a just-in-time (JIT) production plan.

Dial-up EDI has been around for decades. In later years, the dial-up gave way to the leased line (usually a fractional T1 line) that your "partner" would install on your premises. Sometimes the partnering company would even provide the equipment.

Thanks to improved security (or at least, the perception of such) on the Internet, these costly arrangements can be avoided through an EDI system that runs over the Net with the aid of a secure virtual private network (VPN). While the Internet is a wild and woolly place, a VPN encrypts traffic to and from a trusted site (like your partner company), making your transactions safe from potential tampering and prying eyes. We'll cover

Internet security issues in depth in Chapter 12, and VPNs specifically in Chapter 15. Figure 3-1 shows how EDI systems have evolved.

Today's EDI system is much cheaper, easier to implement, and just as fast as a traditional EDI platform. As secure VPNs and tamper-proofing techniques continue to advance, EDI over the Net will continue to be implemented at a company near you.

Making the Jump to the Consumer

So, if your EDI system is moving to the Internet, this presents a perfect opportunity for you to move more of your business to the Web, by setting up an electronic storefront where you can take orders from anywhere. But you won't be able to count on a business partner to set this up for you. That's where this reference comes in.

GETTING WHAT YOU NEED

Getting what you want from EDI and the Internet starts with determining what you really need. The principal types of commercial Web sites are described next:

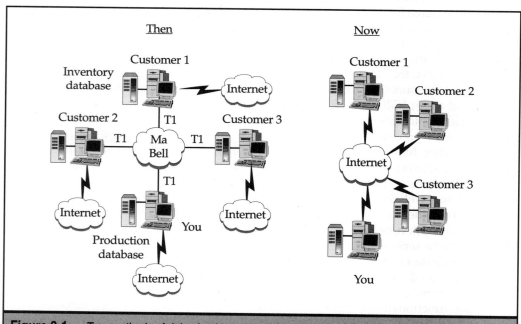

Figure 3-1.   Two methods of doing business over the wire

Electronic Storefronts

Selecting an electronic storefront is largely a component of your company's individual needs. If you sell only a few items, a few simple pages that act as a virtual brochure will most likely suffice. You may not even need search functionality. If this is the case, you can probably build your own Web pages from scratch without investing in a commerce server or electronic storefront. The only concern you will have is security for your customers' transactions, which you can probably have forwarded to you over e-mail.

If doing it solo isn't your bag, there are several low-end electronic storefront software packages on the market. For less that $1,000, you can have a fully functional set of Web pages to handle all your Web commerce needs. They also offer built-in payment systems so you don't have to worry about finding another way to secure transactions. Look at Open Market's ShopSite for an example of a low-cost solution. Open Market (which acquired ICentral to obtain ShopSite) is online at www.openmarket.com. The company produces a wide range of e-commerce solutions.

On the other hand, if you offer a large range of items, you'll need a higher-end solution. iCat's electronic commerce suite (www.icat.com) is a good starting point. It costs up to $10,000, but the package is substantially more advanced than systems like ShopSite, and it even handles sales promotions and has a slew of third-party add-ons Microsoft Site available to help you do just about anything. For an all-in-one solution, Server Commerce Edition offers full electronic commerce services for about $3,500 and is definitely worth a look.

For the ultrahigh-end, like Amazon.com, which carries over 2.5 million book titles, you will probably need to look at a solution like IBM's Net.Commerce PRO, which starts at almost $20,000 for your first processor and runs on NT and higher-end platforms. (See Figure 3-2.) Of course, to run a shop like Amazon, you'll need servers with serious RISC power and about 1GB of RAM apiece.

An electronic storefront package typically includes database connectors, HTML templates for your catalog pages, and some kind of payment system support (also known as "back-office functionality"). You may also get customer information management tools with your system, and some have basic accounting functionality as well. Again, the state of e-commerce tools is far from fully developed, so whether or not you get these tools and how well they actually work is really up in the air. Expect the market to change radically over the next few years.

The final option, of course, is doing all of this yourself with an in-house programming staff. If you're serious about Web commerce, this is probably not as bad an idea as it sounds, because of the complexity of handling security and day-to-day maintenance of the gargantuan databases that will power your site. Also, you'll probably be adding and removing items, changing prices, announcing sales and promotions, and changing the look and functionality of your site often. All of this requires extensive on-the-fly reprogramming, and unless you want to spend a fortune on contractors, an in-house staff is really the only way to go.

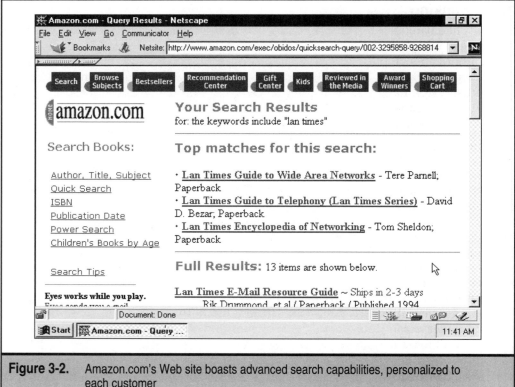

Figure 3-2.   Amazon.com's Web site boasts advanced search capabilities, personalized to each customer

Electronic Payment Systems

If you anticipate under a few hundred transactions per day, the ironic truth is that it's easier and more cost-effective to manually perform payment transactions than invest in an automated solution. This can be as simple as using encrypted e-mail to forward your customers' credit card numbers to you, then running the numbers through your own credit check and billing system.

If your transaction needs get serious, you can start to automate some of the work. Solutions from companies like Payment Processing Inc. and Internet Commerce Services let you offload the drudgery of order taking and/or payment processing to a third party. They simply send you an e-mail when it's time to fill an order. This type of service is quite inexpensive and can actually be found for under $100 a month.

More advanced solutions are available, of course, depending on how much you want to spend. Pandesic LLC is a company (jointly owned by Intel and SAP) that sells complete, fully automated, turnkey e-commerce solutions, hardware included. Other companies like ICVERIFY/Cybercash and CheckFree provide payment processing products and services that integrate with your existing e-commerce platform.

Online Banking

Big banks like Bank of America are rolling out Internet merchant services as well. This development essentially lets you eliminate the middleman by letting your bank do all the credit authorization, billing, and payment processes for you.

Unfortunately, banks are not the most technically current organizations around, so merchant services may be slow in coming. Over the next few years, and especially, as personal online banking catches on, expect the larger banks to enter the electronic commerce market in a big way.

Electronic Money

Electronic money never really took off like some people had hoped, and it is, for all practical purposes, a dead technology. Digicash's ecash is the only reasonably serious virtual money technology still around, and it basically works like this. Your bank, which must be one of only a half-dozen *worldwide*, must support ecash. You then apply for an ecash account from that bank, and then set up an "ecash Purse" on your Windows PC.

You must then withdraw cash from your bank in exchange for ecash that resides on your PC. You can then use this ecash in exchange for goods and services, but only from companies that also support ecash transactions (of which, there are not too many).

The drawbacks with ecash are obvious. Having cash on your PC that does not bear interest and is very illiquid is not a very efficient use of funds. Also, no American bank currently issues ecash. From both the customer and the merchant standpoint, ecash simply doesn't make a lot of sense right now.

The Next Generation

Electronic money may find an application yet, if companies like Transactor have any say. Transactor Networks is designing commerce technologies for the buying and selling of intangible "digital objects" that exist only in the digital world. Another interesting concept is the "virtual economy" being built in Origin Systems' Ultima Online gaming world. Here, users (who pay for software and monthly access fees) can interact in real time with other users, through combat, cooperation, or trading of some sort. Players can buy and sell items that have value, even if the item isn't real—and neither is the currency—but the system treats it as if all of it were. Ultima Online is the first time a multiuser economy of this scale (there are tens of thousands of players) has been attempted, and it's only a first step toward some big changes on the horizon. Its degree of success is yet to be determined.

Security

The most serious concern for Web commerce, as mentioned earlier, is making sure your customers' payment information (in most cases, a credit card number) gets to you safely and securely.

The problem is that most traffic going across the Internet and your LAN is notoriously insecure, and a skilled hacker can easily intercept any unencrypted information sent over the Net. It is also possible for a hacker to impersonate you, creating a need for some sort of electronic proof that you are who you say you are.

Certificate Authorities and Digital Certificates

Currently, the most widely implemented means of confirming the identity of someone (be that a Web page or the author of an e-mail) over the Net is the use of a digital certificate. Digital certificates are sold (or rather, leased) to you as a pair of "keys," one of which is *public* for the world to know, one of which is *private* to you and protected by a passphrase. Each key can perform a one-way manipulation of data, which the other key can undo. In this way, you can sign a file with your private key as proof that you authored it and that the message has not been altered in transit. Or, you can encrypt a file with your intended recipient's public key, so that it can only be decrypted by that person if he or she indeed has the matching private key. Public keys can be simply exchanged through e-mail. Figure 3-3 shows how authentication works with key pairs. Encryption works in a similar fashion.

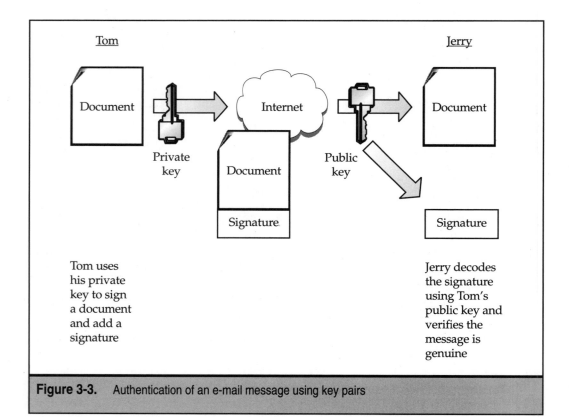

Figure 3-3. Authentication of an e-mail message using key pairs

The weak link with this arrangement is that you can't really know who a public key belongs to without some third party to verify it. That's where certificate authorities (CAs) come in. VeriSign is by far the largest and most well-known CA and issuer of digital certificates in the world. You can obtain a personal certificate for about $10 a year.

These principles can help you secure your Web site with Netscape's Secure Sockets Layer (SSL), the current standard for WWW protection, which basically works along the same lines outlined above. VeriSign's Server ID, which costs about $350 a year for basic needs, even comes with a $100,000 protection plan in the event your certificate is compromised.

The problem with SSL is that it isn't quite as secure as most of us would like. SSL is based on the RC4 block-encryption algorithm, which is believed to be secure, but is really unknown because the actual algorithm is secret and cannot be widely tested by the cryptographic community, unlike most other encryption algorithms. SSL has also been experimentally hacked by several people, leaving further doubt as to its future. Suddenly, that VeriSign guarantee looks awfully appealing.

SET

SET, or Secure Electronic Transaction, is a next-generation protocol designed specifically to handle e-commerce and, ultimately, to replace SSL. Unlike digital certificates, which are general-purpose encryption and authentication tools, SET is being marketed as the end-all, be-all of online shopping.

SET was developed in 1996 by a host of major players, including Visa, MasterCard, Microsoft, IBM, and Netscape (and now managed by SETCo, a company built specifically to govern its use). It works much like a two-person digital signature scheme, only a merchant bank is added to the mix, creating a three-way transaction.

Figure 3-4 shows a basic SET transaction. Note that each transaction among the three parties is encrypted through a public key algorithm as described earlier.

Believe it or not, SET is still quite controversial despite almost three years in the making. The reason hinges on the "Digital Wallet" kept on your PC. The Digital Wallet houses a user's credit card information on his or her PC. This information is encrypted and password-protected, so there shouldn't be a problem, right?

Well, it's not that easy. Any encryption scheme is only as strong as the password behind it, and poor password choices by the vast majority of people make cracking files a simpler task than it seems. If a thief can obtain your Digital Wallet through physical theft, or more to the point, through a malicious Java or ActiveX applet, you may be robbed without ever knowing it.

It takes a lot of skill to pull off a heist like this, and credit card companies have been quick to guarantee any losses from such activities. Still, people are paranoid, and only time will change their minds. But the truth is that your credit card is probably much safer on your computer than it is in your back pocket.

Smart Cards

Here's a technology not too many of us are thrilled about.

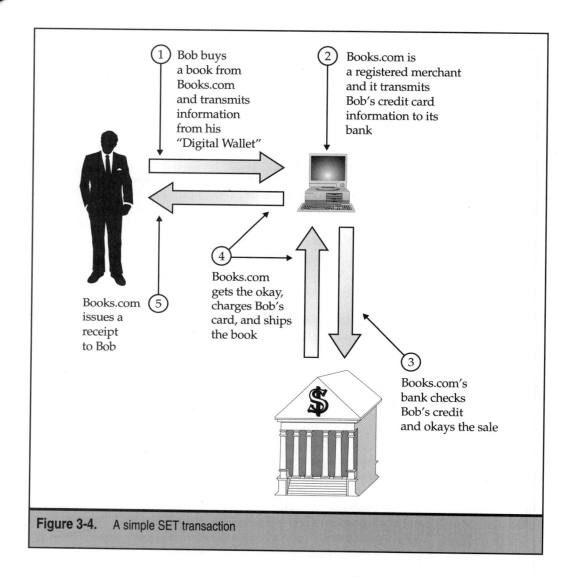

Figure 3-4. A simple SET transaction

Smart cards store cash electronically, on a coded card, supposedly making bills and coins less necessary. They are preloaded with funds over phone lines, and they are used, in practice, like a debit card. The trick is that you don't need to call a bank to ensure it's valid. You swipe the smart card and the transaction is completed instantly; the money leaves your smart card and ends up in the merchant's computers, to be transferred to its bank at the end of the day.

The problems with smart cards are enormous. First, there is absolutely no security to them, not even a PIN, so if the card is stolen or lost, you're out of luck. Once the money is transferred to the card, it stays there until spent. And once the cash is taken out of your bank account, it ceases to accrue interest.

Credit card companies are skittish, although Visa Cash and MasterCard's Mondex are slowly making their rounds. The problem is that Visa and co. really don't want smart cards to exist, because they get a nice two to four percent of each transaction made with a credit or check card, not to mention service charges on consumers' balances.

So the customer saves 30 seconds in the checkout line? That's what the big fuss is over?

Well, no. The third part of the commerce chain is also the largest and most powerful: the millions of merchants who would love to be able to accept money that's as good as cash but can't really be stolen at gunpoint, would be thrilled to save all those credit card transaction fees, and don't need special phone lines or expensive equipment to do credit checks. Still, keeping your money and identity on a card feels a bit too Orwellian to most, and only time will tell if smart cards will catch on.

In the meantime, the credit card companies will probably duke it out to be the big fish (the supplier of the equipment and back-end services) in a small pond.

Outsourcing... and Doing Without

SET, smart cards, certificate authorities? Sound like too much to deal with?

You're not alone. The world of electronic commerce can be a hairy place; for a few hundred dollars a month, your ISP will probably host your Web site on its servers, eliminating some of your security problems.

One recent phenomenon is the rapid acceptance of hosted commerce. Yahoo! Store is one of the most popular ways to outsource your e-commerce initiative, starting at only $100 a month. For a third party will completely take care of payment processing. You can also outsource the design and maintenance of your electronic storefront, wherever it resides.

The problem is that all of this costs money, and with each function you hand to another party, you also hand a portion of your profits.

Suddenly, online business doesn't look all that spectacular, and it's easy to see why the mad rush of businesses to the Net still hasn't quite caught on with consumers who are as equally frustrated with security and privacy issues as merchants are. Do you absolutely *need* an online presence? Probably not. In three to five years? You'd better be online.

We're entering a golden age of information technology, and the bumps we're hitting now are inevitable. Early adopters will be rewarded, so you are encouraged to start planning to take your business virtual. In time, buying a book, a computer, or even a car over the Web will be commonplace. It might even be passé.

If you want to keep up with the ever-changing world of e-commerce, check out Wilson Internet Services' in-depth *Web Commerce Today* newsletter (samples are available on its Web site at www.wilsonweb.com). Ferris Research's messaging analyzer information service (www.ferris.com) also regularly includes more general updates on e-commerce standards, mergers, and other news. (Be sure to look for the free subscription offer.)

PART II

The Applications

CHAPTER 4

Layer 7 and What It Means to You

The purpose of computers is to do work. This work could be preparing a document, calculating a loan amortization, or determining the climactic effects of detonating a 35 megaton atomic bomb over the North Pole. And this work is all performed by computer *applications*. Without applications, there would be no reason to use computers (which would, were this the circumstance, no doubt please some of you). Therefore, we're going to devote this chapter to discussing what applications are, taking a high-level look at how they work, and learning a little about how applications connect to the lower-level functions of computers.

WHAT'S AN APPLICATION?

Let's start at the beginning. *Applications* are software. And software, as you no doubt know, is any form of information that you can store electronically. There are two main types of software:

▼ Systems software

▲ Application software

Systems software is all the software necessary to make computer software run. Systems software works very closely with the computer's hardware, telling it how to interact with electronic data. Therefore, systems software is also sometimes called *low-level* software. Examples of systems software are the operating system, such as Microsoft Windows 98 or Sun Microsystem's Solaris, as well as supporting utilities and drivers.

Application software is the software that performs the tasks for which people buy and use computers. Database software, word processors, and accounting software are all examples of applications. Application software is therefore often called *high-level* or *end-user* software.

The relationship between systems software and application software is illustrated in Figure 4-1. Application software sits on top of systems software, relying on the function of systems software to do its job.

Application software	Word processing	Spreadsheets	Games
Systems software	Operating system	File manager	Compiler
Hardware			

Figure 4-1.   How application and systems software interact

Taking Instruction

More specifically, an application is a set of *instructions*, or ordered operations, for a computer to complete. An instruction is the most basic form of computer command. Applications consist of sequences of instructions that computers execute. The computer receives an instruction, completes it, then receives the next instruction, and so on, until the application program is complete.

You can think of applications as recipes in which you can make a lot of ingredient substitutions. For example, instead of saying "take two eggs and mix well," the application may say, "take whatever is on the dairy shelf and mix well." Figure 4-2 draws the analogy.

The application program consists of a list of data or *variables*, which are like ingredients, and a list of *statements*, which are like recipe directions, that tell the computer what to do with each of the variables.

NOTE: We will discuss program instructions in more detail in our discussion of microprocessors in Chapter 13, "The Desktop."

<u>Recipe</u>	<u>Instructions</u>
1. Take contents of carton labeled "milk."	1. Take value in Register 1.
2. Place in mixing bowl.	2. Place in main memory.
3. Take contents of box labeled "flour."	3. Take value in Register 2.
4. Add to milk already in mixing bowl.	4. Add to value from Register 1 already in main memory.

Figure 4-2.   An application is like a recipe with variable ingredients

Speaking the Language

Application developers write programs using *programming languages*. There are many programming languages, but they all fall into three categories:

▼ **High-level programming languages**   These are languages that are somewhat similar to human languages. Some examples are BASIC, C++, and COBOL.

■, **Low-level programming languages**   These are programming languages closer to the language used by a computer. Low-level programming languages are also known as *assembly language*. Programming in assembly languages is more difficult than programming in high-level languages, because assembly languages have virtually no similarity to human languages.

▲ **Machine languages**   These are the programming languages used by computers. Machine languages are comprised entirely of numbers. Except for programmable microcode (which we will discuss in Chapter 13), which is utilized by only some newer computers, machine languages are the lowest-level programming language. They are also nearly impossible for humans to understand, much less use efficiently.

Whichever programming language a developer uses, the statements he or she writes in this language are called the *source program* or *source code*. After the source code is complete, it must be translated into machine language so that the computer can interpret the instructions and correctly execute them, as illustrated in Figure 4-3.

Performing the translation is the function of *compilers*, *interpreters*, and *assemblers*. Figure 4-4 illustrates the translation process.

Compilers

For programs written in high-level languages, translation from source code into machine language is performed by compilers and interpreters.

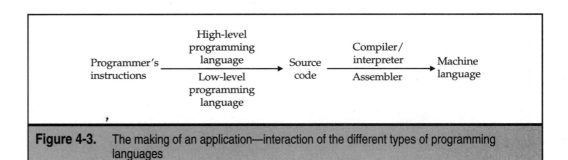

Figure 4-3.   The making of an application—interaction of the different types of programming languages

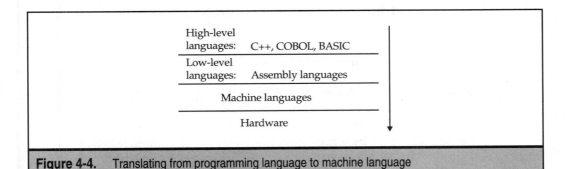

Figure 4-4. Translating from programming language to machine language

A compiler is a specialized program that reorganizes the instructions in a piece of source code written in a high-level programming language. It then translates the high-level instructions into commands that a computer can understand and execute, as shown in Figure 4-5. Using a specific and predefined set of rules, the compiler sorts through the source code, determining whether the instructions are valid, then putting them in a format a computer can understand.

A compiler looks at the entire set of instructions as a single piece. As we will see, this all-of-a-piece handling is what differentiates a compiler from an interpreter. Because the compiler looks at the source code as one big chunk of instructions, compilers require quite a bit of time to translate source code into an executable program, called *object code*. However, as we'll see, object code produced by compilers usually runs faster than that produced by an interpreter.

Compilers are unique to each type of programming language. Therefore, source code written in C needs a different compiler than source code written in COBOL. Because compilers translate source code into object code, which is unique for each type of computer, many compilers are available for the same language. As well, different vendors market compilers for each language on each microprocessor. Therefore, application developers usually have a wide selection of compilers from which to choose, each with its unique advantages—and disadvantages.

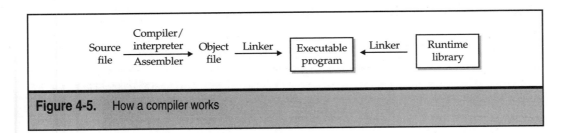

Figure 4-5. How a compiler works

NOTE: As we will see in Chapter 13, every microprocessor employs its own unique machine language. Therefore, to run on different types of microprocessors, application programs must be written and/or compiled to run on each specific type of microprocessor.

Interpreters

Interpreters differ from compilers in the way they handle source code. Unlike compilers, interpreters don't look at the entire chunk of source code. Instead, they read, interpret, and execute each individual line of source code separately. It does this by translating the source code not into final object code, but into a kind of "middle" code that it then executes immediately. Therefore, it takes much less time to interpret source code than it does to compile it. However, interpreted programs run much more slowly than compiled programs.

Interpreters and compilers fill their own unique functions in application development and use. Interpreters are most commonly used by developers while they are writing an application. Interpreters provide them a quick way to run, test, and troubleshoot individual lines of code. Completed applications run by end users are usually compiled, although this isn't always the case. For example, some programming languages, such as BASIC, are actually designed to be interpreted rather than compiled.

Assemblers

Assemblers are to low-level source code what compilers are to high-level source code. They are specialized programs that translate source code written in low-level languages into machine language.

Don't Fret

The preceding discussion was strictly for your enlightenment. You can live a long and happy life as a network manager without having to deal directly with source code and compilers. That's because the applications you purchase—whether off-the-shelf or custom-developed—are almost always the executable version. In other words, the source code is already compiled, interpreted, or assembled in machine language, and is ready to use.

HOW APPLICATIONS WORK

Now that you know what an application is and how it is built, it's time to take a look at how they do the work you want them to. From a system analysis perspective, there are six basic functions performed by any piece of software:

- ▼ Capture
- ■ Transmit
- ■ Store

- ■ Retrieve
- ■ Manipulate
- ▲ Display

Capture

The first job of an application is to *capture* data from the appropriate source. This means the program pulls the data it needs to perform the job from the appropriate input device.

Transmit

Once data is captured, the application must be able to deliver the data to a storage place, called a *memory buffer*, where it will be held until the program needs it. As well, once data has been manipulated and a result calculated, the application must be able to transmit the result to the appropriate display device.

Store

An application must also be able to store data until it's time to work with it. An application generally stores data in memory buffers until it begins executing an instruction that involves that data. Take the example of editing a document with a word processor. When you edit the document, the word processor copies the document—or pieces of it—into a temporary storage space in main memory called a memory buffer. Unless you then save your files to permanent storage on a disk drive, all the changes you made to the document will disappear when you exit the application or turn off the computer. This is why some applications can be configured to save files automatically at regular intervals. We'll talk more about registers and data storage in Chapter 13, "The Desktop."

Retrieve

Applications must also retrieve data from storage places. When the application begins executing an instruction that involves a particular value, referred to as an *operand*, it must be able to locate that value in the storage facility and retrieve it.

Manipulate

Manipulating data is what application programs are all about. This is the heart of application work. These are the logic *operations* performed on data (the operands we mentioned in the preceding paragraph) to produce the work the application is supposed to do. Operations are specific actions that the computer performs on operands. For example, in the expression

$8 - x$

8 and x are operands and $-$ is an operator instructing the computer to subtract x from 8. There are four basic operations, as shown here:

Operation	Symbol
Addition	+
Subtraction	−
Multiplication	*
Division	/

Applications use more complex operations. For example, relational operations compare one value to another. However, they are all based on these basic operations.

Display

An application must be able to display both the values being manipulated and results of the operations. The application can display data either on a computer monitor or a printer, or both.

WHAT DOES THIS HAVE TO DO WITH LAYER 7?

Now that we've talked about what applications do and what they are, it's time to talk about how the application layer of the Open Systems Interconnection (OSI) model affects the workings of these applications.

First, let's talk about the purpose of the OSI model and why it's important. The OSI model is a set of guidelines for computer network product developers that sets the rules, or *protocols*, for how computer systems communicate. Each layer of the model represents a network communication task that must be performed, and the model lays out the rules for accomplishing that task. When two computer systems need to communicate, they must use the same protocols in each of the seven layers. Layer 7, the highest layer in the model, establishes the protocols for how an application on one computer system can talk to an application on another system over a network. Therefore, applications that run on networks must conform to the protocols established in this layer. These protocols define a uniform way to access communication protocols in the underlying six layers. Examples include print services, file access, and resource sharing over the network.

NOTE: Later in this book, we'll discuss the functions of the other six layers of the OSI model in turn.

Applications and the Internet

In the TCP/IP model, on which Internet functions are defined, the application layer resides directly on top of the TCP/IP protocol stack. The TCP/IP model lacks the presentation layer and session layer found in the OSI model. See Figure 4-6. Instead, the application layer communicates directly with the transport layer. Therefore, applications meant to function over the Internet must conform to a different set of protocols than applications designed to run in an OSI-compliant environment. Examples of Internet applications are Telnet and File Transfer Protocol.

APPLICATIONS ARE BORN STUPID

Despite all the sophisticated mathematical functions that applications can perform, by themselves they are essentially stupid. Unless their design adheres to the OSI or TCP/IP models, they don't know much beyond their own home computer system. For example, they don't know how to talk with other applications or computers systems across a network, they don't know where to find data on a network, and they don't know where to print.

Luckily, a great deal of work has gone into designing architectures that can support applications spread out across a network. In fact, pieces of applications can be located in different places across a network and function together as though the entire application resided on a single computer. In the next four chapters, we will discuss these distributed computing architectures and give you tips on how to implement them in your own network.

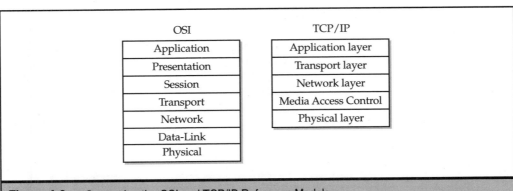

Figure 4-6. Comparing the OSI and TCP/IP Reference Models

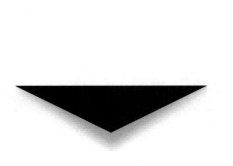

CHAPTER 5

Where Applications Live

Applications live on *application servers*. An application server is just that: a server on a network that runs an application or database program. An application may live on a single application server, or parts of the application—as well as the data it accesses—may be spread among several servers. Distributing applications among servers has its good points:

▼ No single server need be overburdened with application processing.

▲ Application updates are easier because they take place in a central location.

However, distributing applications also has its bad points: The second most likely place to have a bandwidth crunch (after the backbone) is among the networked servers, an area often called a *server farm*. Let's take a minute to look at where applications live, and address some structural concerns.

SERVER FARMING

If you have one of these, you're probably not experiencing the network throughput your users need. However, because the term is used so loosely, you're probably not even sure whether you have one, much less how to improve its performance. We'll begin by defining the structure of the server farm, illustrated in Figure 5-1, and then discuss the specific

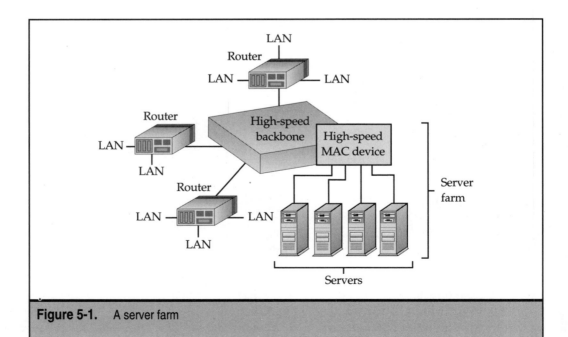

Figure 5-1. A server farm

requirements it demands of its transport protocol. Next, we'll discuss the indications of insufficient bandwidth in a server farm environment and how to alleviate it.

Do Servers Grow on Farms?

Many manufacturers of high-speed networking devices recommend their products for use in server farms. However, rarely do these same manufacturers define what they mean by "server farm." Often, they mean anything from a backbone to a UNIX workgroup. For the purposes of this book, however, let's define a server farm as a group of servers that share processing responsibility for a common information system. This type of environment is often called a distributed computing system, or, more recently, a distributed information access architecture. Before you can design a network to support a distributed computing system, you first need to understand the function of this architecture and the tools used to implement it.

A distributed computing environment, such as the one shown in Figure 5-2, generally has two goals:

▼   Allow enterprise-wide access to information

▲   Distribute processing load across specialized platforms

Enterprise-Wide Access to Information

Enabling all users throughout the enterprise to access corporate information is truly the most important goal of a distributed computing environment. It is the driving force behind developing a distributed computing environment, and so we will address this goal first.

How It All Began

For decades now, companies have developed and maintained databases—at times huge and very expensive—containing vital corporate information of all kinds. These databases were developed independently on a variety of computing platforms using many different development tools and programming languages. All of these databases fulfilled their intended functions (some better than others), but they existed for the most part as islands of information. The users who needed access to the information had to have specialized software loaded on their specialized workstations, which were in turn connected by specialized cables to the specialized host computing platform that held the database.

During the past decade or so of mergers, takeovers, consolidations, and downsizing, however, maintaining these large, expensive, and disparate databases has become both unwieldy and uneconomical. Executive managers wanted fast, seamless, integrated access to all corporate information. MIS managers wanted to be able to access all databases from one desktop platform rather than having to support a terminal, a UNIX workstation, and a PC for each user so that he or she could access all the various corporate databases. Users didn't want to have to learn how to work on three different work-

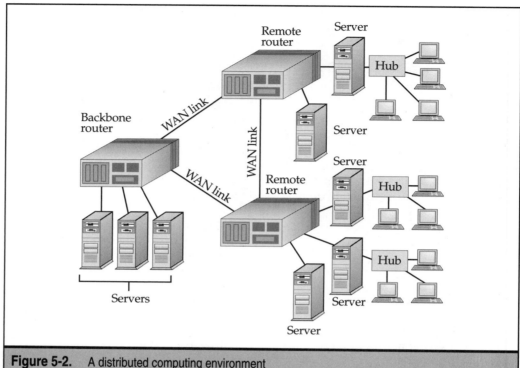

Figure 5-2. A distributed computing environment

stations and six different host platforms to pull their daily reports, then have to spend hours manually consolidating them. Furthermore, as companies discovered that many of their databases could be moved from expensive mainframe platforms to more economical local area and wide area networks, they began pressuring their data processing departments to port applications and databases to these less expensive platforms.

The result of these different forces—corporate mergers, downsizing, the emergence of local area networks, and plain old economic pressures—is the emergence of distributed computing systems. A distributed computing system is a logical evolutionary step from centralized computer systems and even client/server computer systems, as shown in Figure 5-3.

Issues and Concerns About Distributed Computing Systems

A distributed computing system is really client/server computing on a grander scale. While in a client/server system data is located on one server, in a distributed computing system the data is located on many servers. Furthermore, these servers can be located anywhere—in the next room or in the next state.

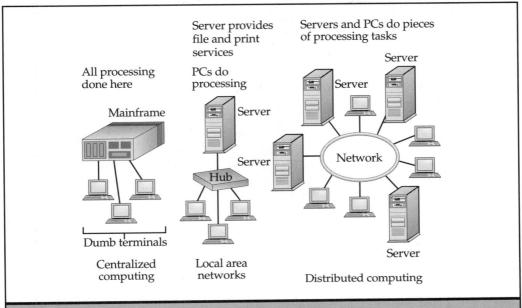

Figure 5-3. The evolution of distributed computing systems

Obviously, a distributed computing system has a lot of advantages over the old centralized computing systems, including fault tolerance. Because data is replicated on several servers, users are protected from loss or downed systems. A distributed computing system also makes more computing power available as it is needed. However, there are some problems associated with implementing a distributed computing system. Among these are

▼ **Management** Because distributed computing systems by definition include multiple platforms, the time required to manage them increases exponentially over that required for a centralized system. Also, distributed computing systems are often the result of merging existing systems, which involves finding and resolving integration problems.

■ **Data synchronization** Keeping all data updated and consistent across all computing platforms is a major management challenge.

■ **Time synchronization** The system must have some means of resolving updates when more than one user creates a transaction to change the same field in the same record at the same time.

▲ **Security and control** "Multiple platforms" means multiple points of access, and general concerns about data location, content, control, and management.

Distribute Processing Load Across Specialized Platforms

A distributed computing system is very similar to a client/server environment except that rather than a single server with many clients, there are many servers and many clients who can—and do—access any one of those servers at any time. This opens up many possibilities for efficient use of computing hardware, but also presents challenges as to how to make the best use of each platform.

In some ways, distributed computing is similar to multiprocessing. A multiprocessing computer system divides processing functions into multiple discrete tasks, then assigns these tasks to each of its multiple processors. The multiprocessing computer balances the load so that no one processor becomes overwhelmed. Distributed application processing does the same thing, except that it balances processing across computers rather than just across processors in the same computer platform. Furthermore, there are, theoretically at least, more kinds of computing resources available in the distributed computing system, such as random access memory and disk storage space. For example, in many offices around the world, thousands of megabytes of memory lie idle every evening as workers turn off their desktop systems and leave for the day. It is possible, however, for a distributed application to use this idle memory.

Distributed systems have some clear advantages. First, in a client/server environment, inexpensive personal computers can relieve the server of many tasks. In the same manner, relatively inexpensive local area network servers can handle some of the processing that once required CPU cycles from a mainframe. Furthermore, using multiple server platforms allows network managers a flexibility in hardware upgrades, moves, and changes that simply wasn't possible in centralized mainframe systems.

However, as we mentioned, distributed computing systems present their share of challenges, mostly in the area of network design. For example, distributed computing systems theoretically allow a client system to locate other computer systems on the network to process all or part of a task. The criteria for delegating processing tasks might include load balancing or processing power. Developing applications that can seek out appropriate computer platforms and take advantage of them is a challenge in and of itself. However, these distributed applications must be supported by a network that is fast enough, manageable enough, and fault-tolerant enough to make such distributed processing possible. For example, the only way to make our scenario of using workstation memory during idle periods possible is by using extremely high-speed links to make memory of one platform available for use by another.

IMPLEMENTATIONS OF DISTRIBUTED COMPUTING SYSTEMS

In the move to consolidate corporate data and port it to the most efficient and economic platforms available, certain types of distributed computing systems have become standard for commercial environments. These different types of systems determine the design of the networks that support them, so we'll take some time to describe these tools and their requirements.

Distributed Application Processing

As we mentioned earlier, distributed computing environments can employ distributed applications. A distributed application is one that can take advantage of multiple computing platforms by running different processes on different computers attached to the same network. Groupware applications, for example, are distributed applications because they let users work with the same data at the same time or take advantage of the network to share information easily. Document processing, scheduling, electronic mail, and workflow software are examples of groupware. Some applications automatically integrate data from systems attached to the network. For example, Windows NT lets users take information stored in other places on the network and "paste" it in their own documents. The original source of the information can still be updated by other users. When the original data is changed, the copies of that data that are pasted in other users' documents are automatically changed as well.

Distributed Databases

By definition, a distributed computing system has data located at multiple sites. Users everywhere should be able to access all data no matter where it is located. Users should therefore only have to concern themselves with the data, not with the design of the network.

These distributed databases generally reside in server-based database management systems (DBMS) and mainframe-based information systems. In the centralized computing model, users accessed only their local database server. However, in the new distributed computing model, users can—and do—access any server in the enterprise. The network challenge here is providing transparent access from any user on the network to any database. Furthermore, distributed databases may also require some level of local control so that managers at the local site can secure the data.

Data Warehousing

While data warehousing is not itself a distributed computing system—and is actually the antithesis of distributed computing—it is a practice that often enables distributed computing systems to exist. Data warehousing is the practice of extracting working copies of databases and storing these copies on a database warehouse server or servers— usually large multiprocessor computers. The data is extracted from various distributed databases, cleansed, and transformed in the information warehouse, making distributed access quicker and easier (as well as often providing more accurate results). This practice allows users to access actual, current corporate data, running involved and processor-intensive queries, without affecting the production systems. This not only protects the integrity of vital data and production systems, but also is often the most efficient way of allowing access to multiple databases of differing designs. It is also one of the more practical ways of storing and managing historical information, accounting detail, and other data that may be too unwieldy to manage on local systems.

Many companies have used data warehousing successfully to preserve their distributed computing systems while simultaneously allowing users "one-stop shopping" for all the data contained in the various distributed databases. As a result, data warehouses are becoming increasingly popular.

To keep the data in the warehouse sufficiently current to meet the needs of its users, data may have to be transferred from the production databases to the warehouse (after cleansing and normalization) many times a day. This frequent transfer of data places special demands on the network, because the data will need to be transferred quickly enough to keep the warehouse up to date (if you need to update the warehouse every six hours, but a data transfer takes eight hours, you've a real problem on your hands) while not bringing the network traffic for the production databases to a standstill.

One thing to keep in mind when you are designing a network to support a data warehouse is that usually the primary reason for implementing data warehousing is cost. Therefore, any additional cost incurred to develop a network for a data warehouse system will likely be closely scrutinized by corporate management. As a result, a lower-cost, high-speed networking alternative is probably the best choice for this environment.

BUILDING BLOCKS OF DISTRIBUTED COMPUTING SYSTEMS

So far we have discussed the goals of distributed computing systems as well as some of the ways these systems are implemented. All of these systems are designed and built using a common set of database tools and techniques. Understanding these basic "building blocks" of distributed computing systems will help you better understand their networking requirements, so we'll describe them in some detail.

Relational Databases

The relational database has become the data structure of choice for most corporate distributed computing systems. One reason is that its structure is, by definition, transparent to its users. Here's how it's designed: All relational databases consist of only two-dimensional tables with rows. The rows are not in any particular order. Rows are, however, supposed to have a unique primary key that defines a sort order or other criteria. A single column is common to every row in the table, as shown in Figure 5-4.

The model doesn't specify exactly how tables are represented physically, so they could take pretty much any form—indexed files, for example. However, all the users see is a table with rows and columns.

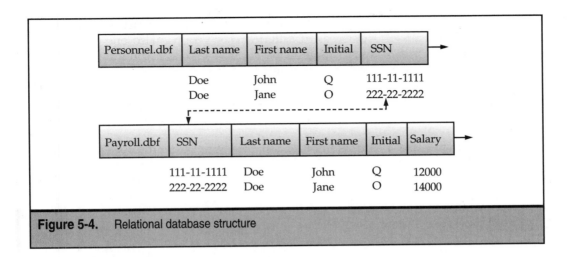

Figure 5-4. Relational database structure

Structured Query Language

Almost every relational database product available supports a Structured Query Language (SQL) interface. SQL, invented by IBM and now standardized by the American National Standards Institute (ANSI), started life as a database query language for the VM/370 and MVS/370 operating systems. Today, SQL is used to access data on all different types of database systems, including mainframes, midrange systems, UNIX systems, and network servers.

SQL is both a data definition language and a data manipulation tool that can be used to develop complex queries. SQL takes advantage of the inherent strengths of relational databases: efficient optimizers that make all the decisions about data access at the time the database is compiled or at execution. Therefore, SQL specifies the targeted values of the queries or updates, but specifies nothing about how the data is to be accessed. For example, in SQL you can't save a pointer or select indices.

SQL plays a key role in a client/server environment. It provides a standard interface between the user's front-end application and the DBMS engine. This interface can be implemented through application programming interfaces embedded in the programming language (embedded application program interfaces—APIs) or called externally (call-level APIs). In either case, SQL effects the communication between the front-end application—which usually resides on the user's desktop computer—and the back-end database—which usually runs on a server located elsewhere on the network.

Middleware

Middleware is software that lets users access data on a server using a wide variety of front-end applications. Using middleware is now a well-established practice in client/server networks, because it lets users select any front-end application they want to access any back-end server on the network, hiding the underlying network from applications. This allows users and programmers to use and develop applications without having to know anything about the networks on which they will run or the communication protocols that will be used on those networks. This lets the programmers concentrate on the applications and the users concentrate on doing their work. It also provides a mechanism for integrating legacy database applications with new ones. Clearly, middleware is especially helpful for programmers developing applications that will run on networks that use different network communication protocols.

Caught in the Middle

Like its name suggests, middleware acts as an intermediary between front-end applications and back-end engines, as shown in Figure 5-5.

Its role is something like that of a diplomat mediating an agreement among countries that don't share common cultures or languages. The diplomat provides language translation services as well as a standard etiquette by which all parties agree to conduct themselves. Therefore, citizens of Country A may know nothing about the culture of Country W, but they know if they conduct themselves by the standard etiquette, or protocol, they will be able to carry on trade with them successfully. Likewise, middleware translates between the APIs of front-end and back-end applications and provides a standard interface to which developers of both types of applications can write for successful interaction.

Middleware is crucial to client/server computing for a couple of reasons. First, it hides the differences among various vendors' SQL. Although SQL is supposed to provide a standard interface between front-end applications and back-end data, each vendor has slight differences in how they have implemented SQL. Thus, middleware plays an important role in making back-end data available to all vendors' SQL.

Second, it keeps application development generic. For example, without middleware, a programmer developing an application for a multiprotocol environment would have to

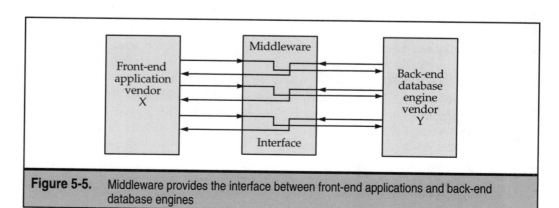

Figure 5-5. Middleware provides the interface between front-end applications and back-end database engines

develop a variation of the application to work with each of the protocols present in the network. Middleware, however, was developed to negotiate the multiprotocol environment, so all the programmer has to do is write the application to work with the middleware interface and middleware takes care of the rest.

Types of Middleware

Middleware comes in three flavors. Each has a different impact on network traffic, so we'll briefly discuss each of them. The three types of middleware are

- ▼ Conversations
- ▦ Messaging systems
- ▲ Remote procedure calls

CONVERSATIONS   A conversation is a continuous stream of requests and replies between two or more systems. Because of its continuous nature and many-to-many orientation, conversations are generally used in situations where full synchronization of databases is critical.

MESSAGING SYSTEMS   Messaging systems are store-and-forward systems that can be likened to a voice mail system. They allow applications to leave messages—in the form of commands and data—for other applications to pick up and process at a later time.

Because messaging systems aren't real-time and require no synchronization among systems, messaging systems are connectionless. Because messaging systems don't operate in real time, they are generally deployed in widely dispersed networks and/or networks with low transfer rates. Obviously, therefore, middleware based on messaging systems is not crying out for a high-speed network to support it.

REMOTE PROCEDURE CALLS   Remote procedure calls (RPCs) are requests from one machine to another over a network, as shown in Figure 5-6. In an RPC, the requester waits for a response before issuing the next request. Consequently, RPCs are usually real-time calls that take place over connection-oriented interfaces. The Open Software Foundation has written specifications for an environment called the Distributed Computing Environment (DCE) that includes a set of middleware RPCs that can break processing tasks down into smaller routines, any of which can then be run on any server on a network.

Developing Standards in Middleware

As middleware becomes more prevalent and more crucial in the development of distributed computing environments, different organizations and companies are attempting to develop standards that will allow interoperability among all front-end and back-end systems. Currently, the major standards seem to be Microsoft's Open Database Connectivity (ODBC) standard and the Independent Database Application Program Interface (IDAPI), which was jointly developed by IBM, Novell, and Borland. At the time of this writing, Microsoft's ODBC appears predominant.

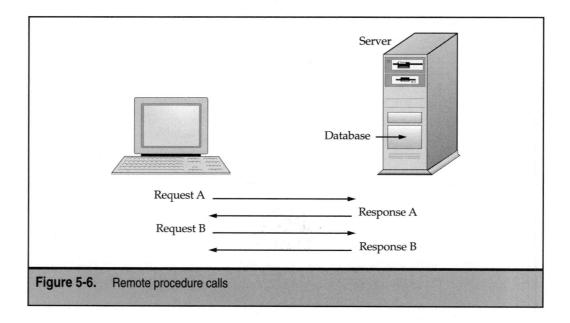

Figure 5-6. Remote procedure calls

Data Propagation

Data propagation is really just copying data in whole or in part. As well as copying, data propagation may also involve some level of data processing, such as summarizing or aggregating. The concept of data propagation plays a key role in designing a distributed computing system because it is the means by which the data is distributed to various platforms around the network.

A carefully planned system of data propagation, such as the one shown in Figure 5-7, allows database administrators to divide processing tasks among the server platforms that are best able to perform them. It lets administrators break large processing tasks into several smaller tasks and distribute them throughout the network. It also allows them to maintain security by providing users with only those parts of the data absolutely necessary to perform their jobs. This explains why it is so popular for financial analysis and decision support systems.

Data propagation has many costs associated with it. As a result, you must carefully plan your data propagation strategy. Data propagation obviously increases network traffic, data storage requirements, data communications facilities, and management time. Management is especially crucial because maintaining the consistency of the directories, synchronizing data, and providing adequate storage on the various server platforms require careful planning and frequent review. As well, the security of data both over the wire as it is being propagated and on the hard drives of the server platform may be critical.

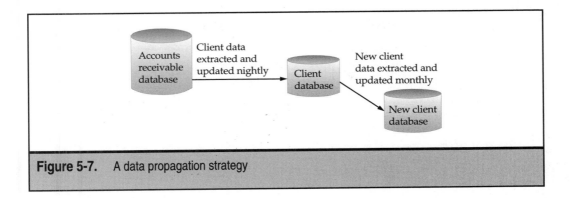

Figure 5-7.   A data propagation strategy

NETWORK REQUIREMENTS OF A SERVER FARM

Now that we've had a fairly thorough discussion of the what, why, and how of a server farm, it's time to translate that into network needs. From the preceding discussion, we can see that a network that connects a distributed computing environment like the one illustrated in Figure 5-8 must support

- ▼ A wide variety of communications protocols
- ■ Real-time connection-oriented requests to servers
- ■ Quick updates to a directory naming service
- ■ High-speed replication of data to various servers
- ■ High-speed transfers of extracted data to data warehouse computers
- ■ Database connectivity
- ■ Security
- ■ Rapid synchronization of data
- ■ Transparency to users
- ■ Quick response to users, even during extract transfer replications and backups
- ■ Fault tolerance
- ■ Easy installation and configuration, because you will probably be moving it around frequently to balance the load on servers
- ■ Driver support for many different server platforms
- ▲ Support for fiber-optic cabling and other high-speed, high-security media

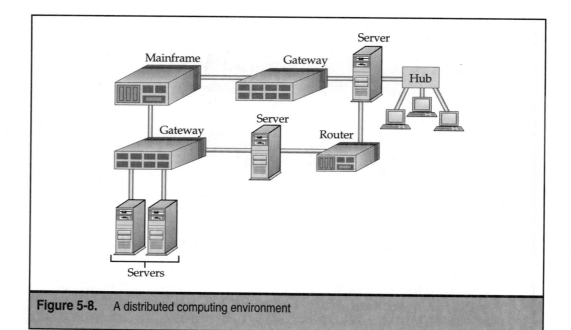

Figure 5-8. A distributed computing environment

TIP: Security may be far more important on a server farm than on other portions of the network. This is because distributed computing systems are most frequently used to handle accounting systems and decision support systems that include sensitive financial data.

INDICATIONS OF BANDWIDTH DROUGHT ON THE FARM

The empirical evidence that your server farm is suffering from insufficient bandwidth includes the following:

- ▼ Delayed replication of databases
- ■ Corrupted databases caused by poor synchronization
- ■ Slow response time to users during data extract transfers
- ▲ Slow updates to directory naming service

OTHER CAUSES AND CURES FOR SLOW PERFORMANCE ON THE SERVER FARM

Even if the network supporting your server farm is suffering from one or more of the problems listed above, it is still premature to conclude that implementing a high-speed network is the solution. There are other situations that can cause slow performance on a server farm. And there certainly may be other—often less expensive—solutions.

Location of Data and Applications

Before you conclude that you need more bandwidth on the server farm, however, ask yourself whether it's possible to balance the load more equitably among the servers. If you can move databases and/or applications from busier servers to more idle servers, you may notice performance problems alleviating or disappearing altogether. Also, whenever possible, be sure all users are as close as possible—both physically and logically—to the databases they use most frequently. Although the point of a distributed computing system is that users anywhere can effectively access data anywhere, you can sometimes spot trends in data usage and keep users as close to their data as possible. This helps keep network traffic to a minimum.

TIP: Balancing server load and keeping users close to their data is much more efficient—and much less expensive—than implementing a high-speed protocol on your server farm. The problem is that today's traffic patterns (80 percent of traffic now leaves the local area) make it almost impossible to keep users close to their applications and data.

Inadequate Hardware

You should also check your workstation hardware configuration. Client/server application front ends tend to demand a lot of processing power from workstations, so be sure that they are up to the task. Ensure that your workstations have sufficient memory and processing power for the job.

Also, check servers to make sure that they are not the bottleneck. Database engines can put a strain on disk input/output. If your servers are waiting on disk input/output, that's probably the cause of the network slowdown, and it can be alleviated by installing a faster disk subsystem. Likewise, insufficient memory (often indicated by memory swapping to disk), low throughput to and from the network adapter (resulting in dropped packets and retransmissions), and inadequate processors can all slow your servers and cause them to be a bottleneck on your server farm.

Buying the Farm

Of course, the true and indisputable determination of where your server farm's bottleneck lies comes from in-depth analysis of your network traffic with a protocol analyzer. A protocol analyzer will help you determine whether packets are being dropped, resulting in retransmissions, and pinpoint where those packets are being dropped. It will also help you confirm whether your network has heavy internetwork traffic (data packets addressed to a node not on the same segment on which the packets originated). You can also use the protocol analyzer to determine bandwidth utilization, or the average percentage of bandwidth being used, on your server farm's network.

If you are experiencing slow network performance and dropped packets, and if your network's bandwidth utilization over the server farm's segment(s) consistently averages over 50 percent, it's fairly safe to say that the problem is too much network traffic being generated by your distributed applications.

CHAPTER 6

Application Neighborhoods

Applications are neighborly things. They constantly interact with different components of the network on which they are operating, making and filling requests for data and resources located on the network. In this chapter, we'll discuss the "neighborhood" in which an application lives, how applications navigate their neighborhoods, and how they locate the resources they need in those neighborhoods.

THE APPS IN THE 'HOOD: DISTRIBUTED APPLICATIONS

A *distributed application* is designed to take advantage of a network. These applications run optimally in a networked environment, using each system in the network to its best advantage. In fact, implementing distributed applications is often the motivation for building an enterprise network. These applications function among the various computer systems attached to the network, letting users access programs, data, and other resources on multiple systems simultaneously.

A distributed application has two major components: the *client*, which performs front-end functions, and the *server*, which performs back-end operations. This structure is referred to as the *client/server model*. This model distributes the application processing duties among clients and servers, ensuring a balanced division of processing work and therefore optimal performance.

Intranets and the Internet have taken the definition of distributed applications to a new level by providing a universal client, called a *browser*. A browser provides a uniform interface to access all applications and other resources on the network, whether local or remote. To facilitate access to resources over intranets and the Internet, the *multitiered architecture* for distributed applications has been developed. This architecture places reusable component software on servers in the middle of the network, between front-end clients and back-end server systems. We talk more about multitiered systems later in this chapter.

NOTE: Although in this chapter we will focus on client application suites designed for distributed networks, such as Microsoft BackOffice and Office 95, Lotus Notes, and Novell's GroupWise, there are also distributed management applications. Management applications are designed to take advantage of distributed computing. The Simple Network Management Protocol (SNMP), which we discuss in Chapter 11, uses management clients to gather data from remote systems and transmit it to a management console for analysis.

Distributed Databases

A distributed application uses data residing on multiple systems at multiple locations. A distributed database system allows distributed applications to find and use this distributed data. Synchronizing data across a network is tricky: the database must ensure that a change in one part of the database is reflected in all other associated parts. As well, the database must ensure that there are backup copies of each piece of the database to prevent failure. Therefore, distributed databases must include sophisticated partitioning, replication, and transaction tracking features.

To ensure data integrity, a distributed database includes a master database located at a single site. This master database is partitioned and replicated to other sites. *Partitioning* means splitting a database into related chunks that will reside on different systems, while *replication* means copying those blocks to other systems where they will reside. The reasons for partition and replication are threefold:

▼ To protect data by making copies of it

■ To increase performance by keeping data as close to its users as possible

▲ To aid in disaster recovery by providing multiple locations for data

When data is distributed over many database servers, it must be able to keep all copies of the database synchronized. For example, suppose an order entry system is updated at three separate remote databases: at the point of sale system, at the warehouse inventory system, and at the accounts receivable system. If a connection to any of these databases fails before the transaction is written to all of the databases, they will not be in synchronization. Therefore, distributed databases must incorporate transaction tracking mechanisms to monitor the changes and ensure that they are made to all associated databases. If any one of the databases is not updated, then the transaction tracking feature must back them all out.

In a network, with its variety of computer platforms, applications, and operating environments, establishing and maintaining database connections between clients and servers can be difficult. Luckily, there are several connectivity schemes available to ensure communication among these systems. We will discuss these schemes in detail in Chapter 7.

Some of the characteristics that define a distributed database system are as follows:

▼ There is no centralized data site that presents a single point of failure.

■ Data is partitioned, or split, and the pieces stored at multiple sites across the network.

■ Each site maintains its data independently.

■ The location of the data is transparent to users.

■ Distributed databases are hardware, operating system, database management system, and network protocol independent, and therefore run on a variety of computers, database management systems, and networks.

■ The pieces of the database are copied, or replicated, to multiple servers on the network.

■ Users can query remote sites via distributed query processing.

▲ Distributed databases use distributed transaction tracking to synchronize the updating of all database components.

The Nuts and Bolts of Client/Server Computing

As we mentioned, client/server computing is an architecture for developing applications that distribute their processing among client computers, server computers, and sometimes middleware computers.

Client/server computing started out as a way to take advantage of the powerful desktop computers that began appearing in the early 1990s. Rather than burdening the server with all the processing load, reasoned application developers, why not develop programs that would let these high-powered machines do as much of the processing as possible? This original architecture had only two parts: the client and the server, as shown in Figure 6-1. This was called a *two-tier* model, and the design made sense both in theory and in practice. The clients made requests of the servers, and the servers responded to these requests by locating the resources, processing the data as requested, and replying to the clients with the results.

Although it makes sense at it makes to use client processing power, it's impractical if the back-end server containing necessary data is located across a WAN link. Thus, the model shown in Figure 6-2 was developed. In this model, a database is copied to a remote system so that users at the remote site don't have to cross a WAN link to access the data. To ensure data integrity, the two servers periodically synchronize their databases.

With the increasing use of the Internet, however, client/server computing outgrew its two-tier model. In the new *multitiered* model, clients communicate with a Web server or servers, which then query back-end servers. New application architectures are also being

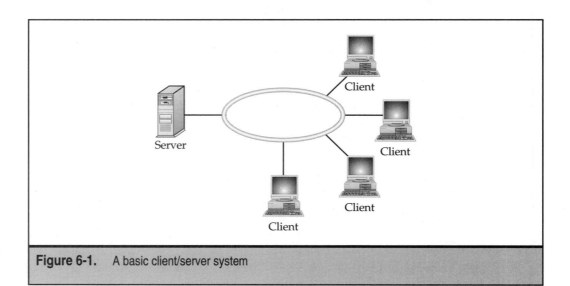

Figure 6-1.　A basic client/server system

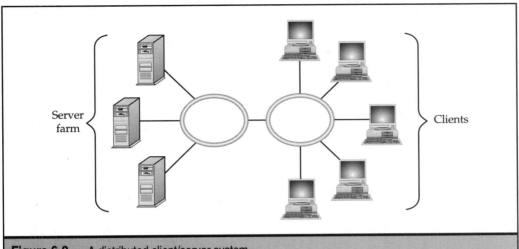

Figure 6-2.   A distributed client/server system

developed to facilitate distributed computing. In these new systems, a client downloads *objects*, such as ActiveX controls and Java applets, to run on the local client processor. In other words, applications exist as a collection of discrete component parts that run as services—such as data presentation or application logic—on different computers. Where the component runs is determined by the location of the data it uses, or where the user of the result is located, or where the systems themselves are managed. Each of these services can run on different computers on the network, which in turn provides the transmission infrastructure over which the components communicate. Despite the components' being spread across the network, to the end user the application appears to be located all on one platform. Furthermore, server programs can run multiple processing requests, or *threads*, simultaneously via a process called *concurrent execution*. Once a thread completes its tasks, any results are returned to the client, if necessary.

NOTE: Objects are abstractions of real-world entities such as orders in an order entry system. Object-oriented systems provide an elegant mechanism for storing data and creating applications in distributed environments.

A special type of client/server system, called a *data warehouse*, is shown in Figure 6-3. Notice that clients don't access the warehouse data directly. Instead, a *staging server* stores frequently requested data and/or makes queries to the back-end data server on behalf of the clients. We will discuss data warehouses in more detail when we discuss multitiered systems later in this chapter.

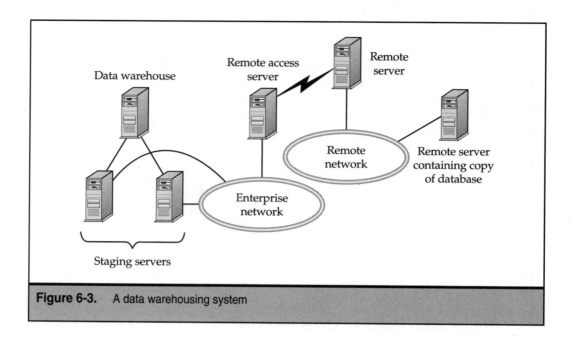

Figure 6-3.   A data warehousing system

The client/server application model has many advantages over the single-platform application model. Among them are the following:

▼ **Parallel processing**   Multiple computer systems can work together in the completion of a processing task, speeding performance and balancing the processing load.

■ **Increased security**   Because data is stored in one location, it is more secure. In fact, data warehousing provides a means of maintaining control of data while allowing it to remain available at intermediate workgroup servers. Also, because the data is centralized on back-end servers, stricter security controls and monitoring systems can be implemented more easily and cost-effectively.

■ **Minimized network traffic**   Data can be stored close to servers where it is processed, thus minimizing the amount of data transmitted over the network. Also, the server transmits only the specific data requested by a client, rather than the entire contents of an application or data file.

■ **Load balancing**   Large server systems can offload applications that are better handled by personal workstations.

▲ **More efficient use of memory**   Data is cached once in the server's memory rather than separately in the memory of each workstation that accesses it.

The Component Approach

Component technology is **the** distributed applications environment on intranets. In fact, a distributed computing environment such as an intranet is an ideal place to deploy component technology. In a component application environment, applications are split up into smaller components (also known as *objects* or *applets*), which are then distributed to users. These smaller components are easy to download and update as needed. They also have an interface that allows programmers to combine them with one another to build complete applications. They are kept in sync with each other by *object request brokers* that coordinate the components throughout the network.

Component technology has a lot of advantages over traditional application development technology. For example:

▼   **Ease of enhancement**   You can add new components any time to enhance and expand application functions and features.

■   **Ease of updating**   Rather than updating an entire application, you can update only individual components.

■   **Shorter development cycles**   You can reuse existing components to build new applications, reducing development time.

▲   **Efficient use of resources**   Users don't have to install an entire application. They can install only the components they need. In addition, by using standard languages like Java, you can combine components from different vendors to make new applications.

Component software has changed the face of most corporate intranets as well as the Internet. You can get components from Web sites to expand the functionality of enterprise applications and utilities, making it quick and easy to get the latest technology. More important, component technology makes it possible to design multitiered environments in which applications are broken up into different pieces that run on different computers and operating environments. For example, application services such as information retrieval, transaction monitoring, and application logic can run on different computing platforms, yet communicate across the network to present a unified application interface.

Component Development Languages

The two common development languages for component technology are Java, from Sun Microsystems, and ActiveX from Microsoft. The Web is chock full of components available for download for both languages. Some are simple components, such as three-dimensional spinning logo components. Others are more complex, such as financial or scientific calculation components. When you download a component to your Web browser, the component stays on your computer. It executes when you access the server containing the information it was designed to process. If the component ever needs to be updated, the new components are downloaded automatically the next time you access that server.

How the Pieces Fit Together

The component software development model consists of five pieces:

▼ Components

■ Containers

■ Scripts

■ Transaction monitors

▲ Object request brokers (ORBs)

COMPONENTS Components are pieces of applications. More specifically, they are the programming code that makes up a piece of an application.

CONTAINERS *Containers* are programming "shells" where components are assembled. The most popular containers are ActiveX for the ActiveX component development language and JavaBeans for the Java component development language. When a component is placed in a container, the component registers its interfaces so that other components within the same system know about it. Then, the component publishes its interfaces so that other objects know how to interact with it.

SCRIPTING LANGUAGES Scripts are the languages in which component programmers write instructions that make components interact in a particular way. Again, the most popular scripting languages are ActiveX Script for the Active X component development environment and JavaScript for the Java component development environment.

TRANSACTION MONITORS In transaction-based applications, such as financial applications, it's critical that the components are coordinated to ensure that the transaction is completed successfully. For example, transferring money from one account to another is a two-step transaction. First, funds are withdrawn from one account. Second, funds are deposited in the other account. Suppose, that the first step is completed, but due to a network error the second is not. Unless the first step is "rolled back," there is no money in either account. Transaction monitoring systems keep track of such multipart transactions and ensure that failed transactions are returned to their original state.

An example of a transaction monitoring system is Microsoft's Transaction Server. It both processes and monitors transactions in a component application environment. Therefore, it operates as a transaction-based object request broker.

OBJECT REQUEST BROKERS (ORBs) Components communicate with one another in object environments through *object request brokers* (ORBs). ORBs coordinate the registration, publishing, and execution of components, keeping them synchronized with one another across the network. An example of a common ORB is the one used in *Common Object Request Broker Architecture* (CORBA). CORBA is a cross-platform architecture that allows components written for different operating environments to work together.

Multitiered Architectures

As we mentioned, in a traditional client/server environment, clients access servers and servers reply to clients. Most of the processing is done at the server, although the client performs some processing as well. In the n-tier model, however, most of the processing is done on a server that sits logically between the client and the back-end server, called a *middle-tier server*. This middle-tier server not only does much of the processing, but also serves as the repository for the logic—the procedures and rules governing the processing of and access to data. By storing logic in a central shared system, all the rules and procedures are located on a single server, so they are easier to access, secure, and manage.

There are several examples of multitier systems in widespread use, such as:

▼ **Data warehousing**   Data warehousing uses a multitier model in which a client requests data from back-end servers. Before the data is even requested, however, it has been retrieved from the back-end servers, then summarized, scrubbed, and placed on middle-tier servers called *staging systems*, where clients can more easily access the information.

■ **The World Wide Web**   The World Wide Web is another example of a network built on a multitier model. The client tier is composed of the Web browser, and Web servers—performing various functions of storing, sorting, or staging data—act as the middle tier. Back-end database servers function as the server tier. Figure 6-4 illustrates how this works. The browser sends requests to the Web server. In turn, the Web server sends these requests in Structured Query Language (SQL) format to back-end database servers. When the back-end server responds, the Web server repackages the result and transmits it to the client browser.

▲ **Enterprise networks**   As shown in Figure 6-5, an enterprise network may consist of clients connecting with middle-tier systems. Enterprise networks can use either connection-oriented protocols such as remote procedure calls

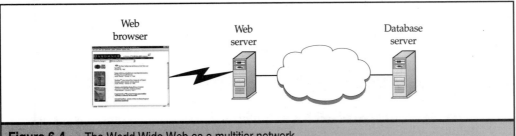

Figure 6-4.   The World Wide Web as a multitier network

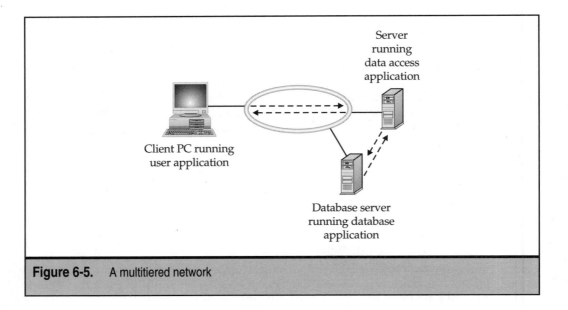

Figure 6-5.   A multitiered network

(RPCs), or connectionless protocols such as message-oriented middleware, which we will discuss in the next section.

PLANNED NEIGHBORHOODS

So how do you build a suitable neighborhood for a distributed application? How will components communicate and interact? There's no one answer. In fact, there are several models:

▼ **Remote procedure call (RPC)**   As we mentioned earlier, an RPC is a connection- and session-oriented protocol that computers use to communicate across networks. Because it is connection oriented and ensures transmission delivery, RPCs are used for real-time communication among components.

■ **Message-oriented middleware (MOM)**   Message-oriented middleware is a store-and-forward means of transferring information among application components via message queues. Due to its store-and-forward nature, MOM isn't suitable for real-time transmissions.

▲ **Object request broker (ORB)**   Think of an ORB as a coordinator that manages communications and plots the path objects will use to communicate with one another over the network. For example, an object running on a client will communicate with an object running on the server via the client's *stub*, or ORB interface. The client object's stub will communicate directly with the server object's stub.

Living in the Warehouse District

One perfect place for an application network is the warehouse district—the *data warehouse* district, that is. *Data warehouses* are specialized data storage and retrieval systems that were designed to overcome a basic problem: data unavailability.

An average company has billions of bytes of data that it can't use because the format of the data prevents easy access, presentation, or use. Data warehousing is a system of rules for unlocking this data and making it available for a variety of uses.

One of the reasons that corporate data has traditionally been difficult to access is because in the past, system developers saw data as being immutably belonging to one of two distinct systems:

▼ Operational systems, which handle the daily information processing of an organization. These systems include accounting, billing, and order entry applications.

▲ Decision support systems, which are the stores of data and applications that managers analyze to make strategic business decisions and plans.

Operational data is, in fact, a subset of the data used for decision support systems. Decision support systems use the data provided by operational systems—for example, inventory or sales figures—to make decisions about business strategy. But decision support systems don't deal exclusively with operational data; they pull information from many enterprise information sources, including the following:

▼ **External data**   This is information gathered from systems outside the enterprise. For example, Web servers and external databases can provide information to decision support systems.

▲ **Legacy data**   This is data that has been gathered and stored over the life of the enterprise. For example, information collected and stored on old mainframes or legacy minicomputer systems is considered legacy data. This information is generally not in a format that microcomputer-based applications can access, thus causing accessibility problems.

Data gathered from these various sources is formatted, encoded, and even stored in many different ways. For example, dates from different databases may be in a variety of formats (MMDDYY, YYMMDD, or Julian). In addition, because much of this data has been accumulated over time, the database developers that built the databases probably used their own—often poorly documented—conventions in building data structures.

Because all of this data is in different formats as well as in different locations, it is difficult for a user of a decision support system to access it and manipulate it. Therefore, after data is drawn from the external, operational, and legacy sources, it must be "scrubbed," or cleaned up and put in a consistent format. Data scrubbing can be done either by people or by special applications. The data is extracted from back-end systems and then summarized using online analytical processing (OLAP) and/or other "data mining" tools that uncover relationships amongst the data. This data cleanup can involve combining, formatting, altering, renaming, and manipulating data, as well as data integrity checking to ensure that the data is accurate and up-to-date.

When the data extraction and "scrubbing" is complete. This data is then made available via a middle-tier "staging" system that provides decision support system users with secure access to data in a usable format. Figure 6-6 shows a typical data warehouse configuration.

A data warehouse is made up of the following components:

▼ **Client, or front end**   The client is the interface for the user of the decision support system. These are usually PC applications like Lotus 1-2-3 or Microsoft Excel, or a specialized decision support application. The front end lets the user analyze and display the decision support data.

▲ **Middleware**   This is the point of access for the client system. The middleware is software that makes the data from the back-end servers appear to all clients to be all in the same accessible format. Because a network has a variety of platforms, operating environments, and clients, it needs middleware to coordinate data access among these different components, as shown in Figure 6-7. Think of middleware as software that lets data warehouse developers hide the differences among various systems and applications and provide seamless connections for all clients.

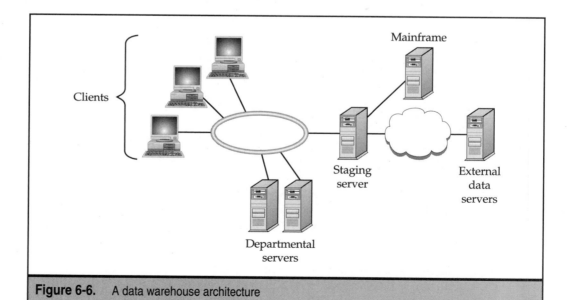

Figure 6-6.   A data warehouse architecture

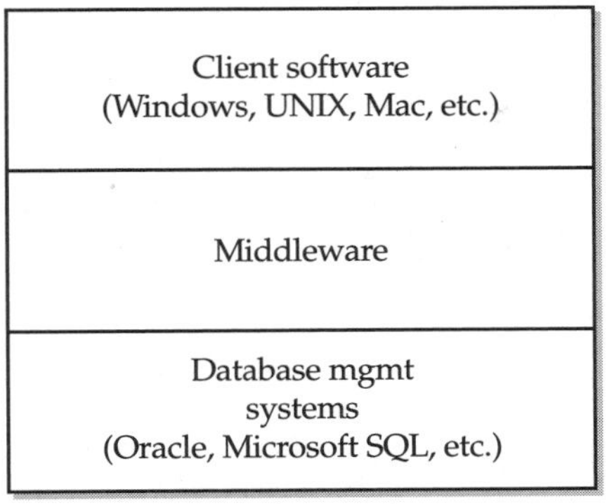

Figure 6-7.   The job of middleware illustrated

There are many types of middleware to fit different environments. There is middleware that hides the differences in databases and middleware that provides transaction processing to ensure that multiple servers coordinate their activities. Middleware also provides a communication system in the form of a messaging system or a direct real-time link between client and server.

▼ **Data mart**   This is a staging location for the information extracted from back-end systems. Data is stored here after it has been "scrubbed," or cleaned up, and formatted in a way that makes it accessible to clients via middleware. A data warehouse can have several data marts. The data mart has only the latest information, and that information is read-only—users can't alter or delete the information in the data mart.

■ **Back-end data repositories**   These are the mainframes, minicomputers, and operational databases that contain the information to be used in the decision support system.

■ **Messaging system**   This is the system that transmits and receives the requests for data and the responses to those requests. The messaging system uses the network infrastructure to transport data.

▲ **Metadata store**   This is the system that contains all the information about the location and format of the data in the data warehouse. The metadata store is "data about data" that lets users have access to data anywhere, even if they don't know the precise location of the data they want.

Of course, clients can access data on the legacy systems directly, as shown in Figure 6-8. However, as much as possible, it's best to direct client traffic through the data mart to ensure security and data integrity.

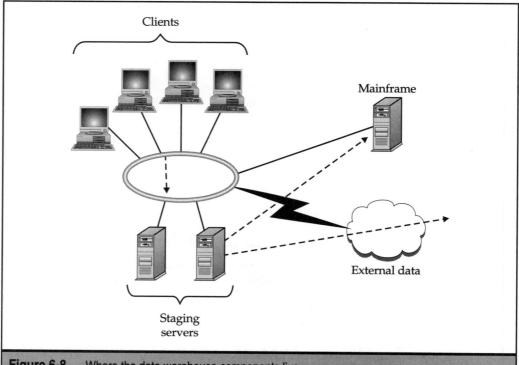

Figure 6-8. Where the data warehouse components live

Ordering from the Data Warehouse

A data warehouse contains a summary of the data available from the external, legacy, or operational data sources—not the "live" data. The real data is still located on the operational systems, where all data updates occur. The data in the data mart is refreshed at set intervals to ensure that the information being accessed is the latest.

There are different levels of data summarization, depending upon the detail stored in the data warehouse. For example, Prism Solutions (www.prismsolutions.com), describes four levels of data summary, as illustrated in Figure 6-9:

▼ Older detail data is historical or legacy data.

■ Current detail data (typically operational data) is the most recent data. It is voluminous and requires extensive summarization to make it easily accessible.

■ Lightly summarized data is data that has been distilled from the current detail data by a database or analyst or some other process.

▲ Highly summarized data is compact and easily accessible by end users within specific departments.

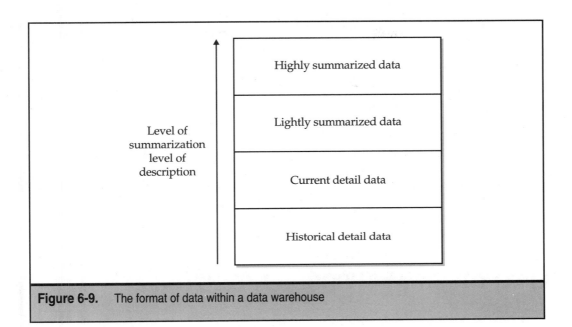

Figure 6-9.   The format of data within a data warehouse

How to Build a Sound Data Warehouse

Building a data warehouse is not for the faint of heart. Nor is it for the inexperienced. You may have heard some horror stories about organizations that set out to build data warehouses, but ended up with expensive, unusable "data shacks" instead. There are many potential pitfalls associated with designing and building a data warehouse, not the least of which is building a data warehouse full of outdated and/or inaccurate information.

When planning a data warehouse, be sure to allow ample time for planning. Before a single piece of hardware is purchased, database analysts and developers should spend a great deal of time studying the current information systems of your enterprise, reviewing information flows within your organization, and working with your company's users to ensure that the data warehouse will provide them with all of the information they need in the format in which they will need it.

The next step for building a data warehouse is to develop a prototype system. While these prototypes should not function in a production environment at first, once you have perfected them, they can be moved onto your production network and grown as needed.

Getting Professional Help

As we mentioned, designing and building a data warehouse isn't a task for a novice. It's best to bring experienced vendors of data warehousing tools and systems into your data warehouse project. Different vendors have developed different systems for data warehousing, and spending some time exploring each may provide you with options you didn't know you had. For example, IBM has developed what it calls its "Information Warehouse," which uses mainframes and minicomputers as back-end data repositories. If your network includes such platforms, using them as a part of your data warehouse may help you leverage your investment. Other vendors of data warehousing tools and systems are Pyramid Technology (www.pyramid.com), Prism Technology (www.prism.com), and D2K, Inc. (www.d2kinc.com).

Data Warehousing and the Web

The latest trend in data warehousing is to equip the system with a World Wide Web interface. This enables data from the data mart to be delivered to and displayed by Web browsers. Furthermore, developers are implementing push technologies with Web interfaces to deliver up-to-the-minute data to users who subscribe to the push data warehousing service. This makes data even more universally available, so that any user on any system using any Web browser can access information from the data warehouse.

FINDING YOUR WAY THROUGH THE 'HOOD

Now that you know where applications live and how these neighborhoods look, you're probably wondering how applications communicate across them and find the data they need to do their jobs. That is the subject of the next chapter, so read on!

CHAPTER 7

What Every Application Should Know

W hile distributed applications can increase performance and data accessibility on your enterprise network, they can also cause problems if they don't play together nicely. For example, how can you be sure that all users are working with the latest data? How can you ensure that all portions of a multipart transaction complete properly? And how do you correct the problem if they don't? In this chapter, we will explore the mechanisms and architectures that solve these problems and enable distributed applications to work together properly in a network environment.

PROBLEMS WITH DISTRIBUTED DATA

When several users are working with the same data simultaneously, potential problems arise. For example:

▼ When more than one user wants to change the same data at the same time, which user's changes should take priority?

■ When more than one user is accessing the same data, and one user changes the data, should all users be notified of the change?

■ How often should data be updated?

■ How often should databases be replicated?

▲ Where should remote database users' changes be recorded—in the master database or in a replicated database?

Clearly, applications must contain mechanisms that resolve these questions, as well as other logistical issues.

The first two questions can be resolved by locking mechanisms, which prevent one user from accessing data until another user has finished making changes. Of course, this solution can present its own problems in a time-sensitive environment. In some situations, investment banking, for example, waiting for one user to complete changes before releasing a block of records for others to use is unacceptable. In this instance, interleaved updates, which are updates interspersed among data reads and writes, can help the server keep track of changes on an ongoing basis.

Transaction Tracking Essentials

Another problem that may arise concerns multipart transactions, such as check clearing operations. Check clearing involves at least two transactions—one to take money from the payer's account, and another to add that money to the payee's account. If the first transaction is completed but the server crashes or the communication link fails before the second is completed, the entire transaction must be voided.

Furthermore, should a server crash during a transaction update, all of its data will have to be restored after it is repaired and brought back online. At the same time, incomplete multipart transactions will have to be voided on all databases involved in the transaction.

These problems are compounded when the transaction takes place in real time. Systems that process transactions in real time, called online transaction processing (OLTP) systems, immediately write changes to shared databases and other data files.

The first, most important safety mechanism in transaction processing is *transaction rollback*, which is the ability to roll back a transaction that can't be completed for any reason. If a transaction isn't fully completed, the portion of the transaction that *was* completed must be backed out, and all the databases involved in the transaction must be returned to their original state. A program that monitors transactions and determines whether each completes is called a *transaction monitor*. The transaction monitor also backs out incomplete transactions in the event of a transaction failure.

The ACID Test

To work successfully in a distributed environment, a transaction processing system must meet the following four requirements. Collectively these are called ACID, and appear here—along with a discussion of a two-phase commit—as described in *The Encyclopedia of Networking* (Sheldon; Osborne, 1998):

▼ **Atomicity**   This defines individual units of work. If a transaction is distributed, all the subtransactions that affect data at separate sites must execute together as a single transaction, either to completion or rolled back if incomplete. To keep data at multiple sites consistent, a two-phase commit procedure is used, as described later in this section.

■ **Consistency**   This is basically a requirement that databases move from one state to another in coordination. The transaction monitor must verify that all affected data is consistent.

■ **Isolation**   Transactions must execute in isolation until completed, without influence from other transactions.

▲ **Durability**   This property has to do with the final commitment of a transaction. Once a transaction is verified to be accurate on all affected systems, it is committed and from then on cannot be rolled back.

Two-Phase Commit

Two-phase commits separate the writing of data into two phases, each ending with a verification of completeness. In the following steps, assume that no faults occur during the transaction:

1. The database systems involved in the transaction hold the data to commit to the database in memory.

2. The transaction monitor sends a "precommit" command to the database systems.

3. The database systems reply that they are ready to commit.

4. On hearing back from every database system, the transaction monitor sends a "commit" command.

5. The database systems reply that they successfully committed the data.

6. The transaction monitor completes the transaction when it receives a response from all database systems that data was successfully committed.

If the transaction monitor fails to hear a response from every database system in steps 3 and 5, the transaction monitor alerts the systems to roll back their transactions.

Transaction Processing on the Web

As it has everything else, the Internet has changed the nature of transaction processing. We mentioned in the preceding chapter that software developers are now writing distributed applications that use component technology, in which components and data reside in different physical locations throughout an enterprise network or throughout the Internet.

While the benefits of better performance, load balancing, and greater accessibility are obvious, distributed components also present some interesting challenges. For example, what happens if a component necessary to complete a transaction is unavailable—either through system failure or simply heavy traffic? As well, how do you roll back a failed transaction if the component that successfully completed its part of the transaction has already distributed the results of its portion of the transaction throughout the network? Where is the list of related systems that must be contacted to roll back the failed transaction?

Enter middleware, another vital skill that every distributed application should master. To ensure that component-technology-based transactions have the same degree of integrity as traditional transaction applications, programmers have developed *transaction middleware* products for component technology environments.

MIDDLESPEAK

As we mentioned in the preceding chapter, *middleware* is the point of access to back-end data for the client system. The middleware is software that makes the data from the back-end servers appear to all clients to be in the same accessible format. It acts something like a translator, letting client and server systems with different interfaces exchange data readily.

Because a network has a variety of platforms, operating environments, and clients, it needs middleware to coordinate data access among these different components, as shown in Figure 7-1. Think of middleware as software that lets data warehouse developers hide the differences among various systems and applications and provide seamless connections for all clients. Developers write applications to talk to the standard

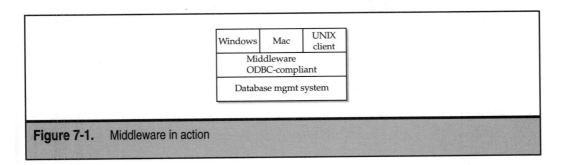

Figure 7-1.   Middleware in action

middleware interface rather than writing unique interfaces between each client and each server they need to access.

How does middleware work this magic? Messaging is one means that middleware uses to allow the easy flow of information among systems with different interfaces.

One Size Does Not Fit All

There are several different types of middleware available to aid in the construction and communication of distributed applications. Among them are the following:

▼ **Transaction processing monitors**   Yes, the faithful transactions processing monitors that we discussed earlier in this chapter are a form of middleware. Developers write client and server interfaces to the transaction monitor.

■ **Remote procedure calls (RPCs)**   As we mentioned in Chapter 6, an RPC is a connection- and session-oriented protocol that computers use to communicate across networks. Because it is connection oriented and ensures transmission delivery, RPCs are used for real-time communication among components.

■ **Database middleware**   This is software such as Microsoft's Open Database Connectivity (ODBC), which allows clients access database server systems from nearly any operating system or application.

■ **Object request brokers**   As discussed in Chapter 6, an ORB is a coordinator that manages communications and plots the path objects will use to communicate with one another over the network. For example, an object running on a client will communicate with an object running on the server via the client's *stub*, or ORB interface. The client object's stub will communicate directly with the server object's stub.

■ **E-mail**   How do different types of e-mail systems exchange messages? By writing interfaces to e-mail middleware.

■ **Message-oriented middleware**   Message-oriented middleware is a store-and-forward means of transferring information among application components via message queues. Due to its store-and-forward nature, MOM isn't suitable for real-time transmissions.

▲   **Web middleware**   This is software that provides a common interface for both new and existing applications and systems to interoperate across the Web.

For purposes of this section, we're most interested in Web middleware that facilitates transaction tracking.

Web Middleware

In the beginning, all an application had to do to be "Web-enabled" was to include support for Hypertext Transfer Protocol (HTTP) and Hypertext Markup Language (HTML). For Web publishing, that's enough. However, HTTP and HTML aren't really adequate for running sophisticated distributed applications, especially those that require transaction monitoring. This is largely because HTTP doesn't support *state management*. That means that a client doesn't establish a session with the server and maintain the connection after sending it a request. And that means that right after a client receives a Web page, the client no longer has any contact with the server. If the user should click on a button on the Web page just downloaded, the client makes another connection to the server to send this request. This connection lasts only as long as it takes to send the request.

You can imagine how inappropriate this "out of sight, out of mind" connection scheme is for transaction processing, in which all parts of the transaction must be monitored until completion. In transaction processing applications, the client must establish a connection with the server, and both client and server exchange status data until all portions of the transaction are complete.

Therefore, transaction application developers often bypass HTTP, either by using proprietary remote procedure calls (RPCs) or object request brokers (ORBs). The RPC method works something like this:

1. A Web browser client contacts a Web server.

2. The Web server downloads some components to the client.

3. The new components enable the client to make direct program calls to the data server without having to use HTTP and HTML.

This solution is neat, but proprietary—which means that an interface has to be written specifically for each client-server combination.

Object request brokers (ORBs), on the other hand, are capable of finding other objects that can fulfill requests. In fact, the ORB is the crucial communication coordinator among the services, applications, and network infrastructure. This communication is illustrated in Figure 7-2. Here's how it works:

1. An object sends a request to its ORB interface, or *stub*.

2. The ORB locates the requested object and establishes a connection between the client and server.

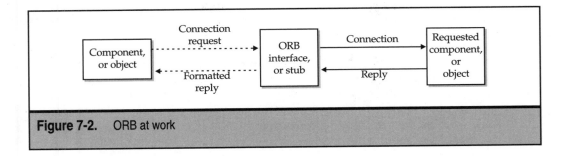

Figure 7-2.   ORB at work

3. The requested object responds to the ORB.

4. The ORB formats the response and forwards it to the requester.

In fact, much of the literature on ORBs refers to the ORB as a kind of software bus that provides a common interface that multiple objects of different kinds can use to communicate with each other, as illustrated in Figure 7-3.

Common Object Request Broker Architecture (CORBA) is the basis of most vendors' ORB implementations. Because CORBA is a critical architecture for building robust transaction processing applications for the Internet and intranets, we will spend some time investigating it in detail.

Common Object Request Broker Architecture (CORBA)

Common Object Request Brokering Architecture, or CORBA, was originally defined and developed by the Object Management Group (OMG) in a specification it called the Object Management Architecture (OMA). CORBA has since been adopted by The Open Group.

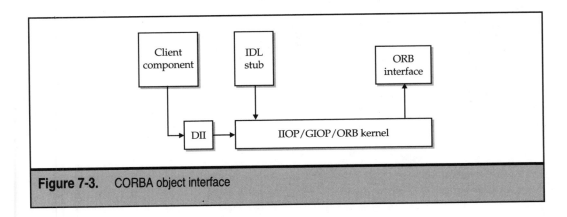

Figure 7-3.   CORBA object interface

CORBA is a *distributed component technology*, which, you will remember from Chapter 6, is an environment in which applications are split up into smaller components (also known as *objects* or *applets*) that are then distributed to users. These smaller components are easy to download and update as needed. They also have an interface that allows programmers to combine them with one another to build complete applications. They are kept in sync with each other by *object request brokers* that coordinate the components throughout the network.

As with all computer technologies, different companies and organizations soon began developing theories and models to determine the best way to implement component technology. The Object Management Group (OMG) put forth its vision of the future of component technology, called *The Object Management Architecture*, which describes both system-level and application-level components. The OMG set out to create a standard schema for building distributed object applications that would support products from multiple vendors and would run across all networks, including the Internet. The OMA is the result of the OMG's efforts. CORBA adheres to this model, illustrated in Figure 7-4.

Figure 7-5 shows a higher-level view of CORBA and where it fits in relationship to both the Open Systems Interconnection and TCP/IP protocol stacks.

As you can see, the top layers of CORBA function as the interface to the General Inter-ORB Protocol (GIOP) or Environment-Specific Inter-ORB Protocol (ESIOP) layer. GIOP is the interface to CORBA's TCP-mapped protocol, IIOP, which we will discuss later. ESIOP is the interface for application-specific connections. For example, Distributed Computing Environment (DCE) is supported through CORBA with DCE Common-Inter-ORB Protocol (DCE-CIOP), which binds DCE to TCP.

The other components that make up CORBA are as follows:

▼ **Object request brokers (ORBs)**   Components communicate with one another in object environments through *object request brokers* (ORBs). ORBs are agents that coordinate the registration, publishing, and execution of components, keeping them synchronized with one another across the network.

■ **Object services**   These are the security, authorization, and transaction processing services provided to components or objects.

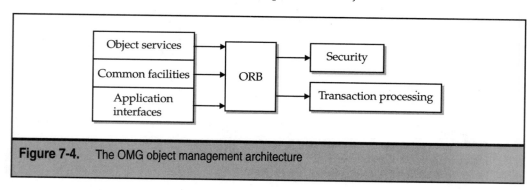

Figure 7-4.   The OMG object management architecture

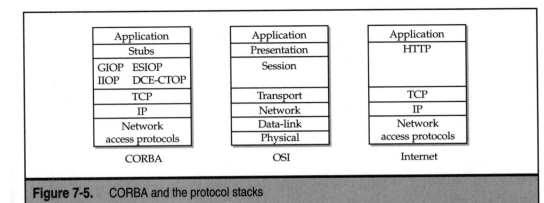

Figure 7-5. CORBA and the protocol stacks

- ■ **Application interface** This is the interface for application-specific objects.
- ▲ **Common facilities** This is the interface for objects that are shared by multiple applications.

CORBA is a messaging technology defined by the OMG for Object Messaging Architecture. It uses a standard protocol, the Internet Inter-ORB Protocol (IIOP),which bypasses HTTP. In CORBA, the only time a Web server with its HTTP interface is part of the transaction is when a user first contacts the Web site. After this initial contact, the user downloads the necessary components and then the client initiates a connection-oriented session.

Inner Workings of CORBA

When a CORBA client wants to communicate with another object, the client sends a request either through its ORB interface or through one of two special interfaces, the IDL Stubs Interface or the Dynamic Invocation Interface, determined by the type of target object the client wants to contact:

- ▼ **The IDL Stubs Interface** This is the OMG's Interface Definition Language (IDL), which provides a programming-language-independent interface for objects. This interface is accessed when IDL is used to coordinate between different client and server object implementations.
- ▲ **The Dynamic Invocation Interface (DII)** This allows inter-ORB interoperability, letting a client access the ORB even if it hasn't used IDL to specify the ORB.

This is illustrated in Figure 7-6.

CORBA and the Future

CORBA has been well received by distributed application vendors. It has been successfully implemented by multiple vendors, and has become an important standard for building distributed applications across the Internet. Netscape is even incorporating IIOP in its browsers. CORBA and IIOP have been so successful, in fact, that some day IIOP may replace HTTP as the fundamental client/server protocol on the Web. Furthermore, although to date CORBA has been mapped only to TCP/IP through IIOP, it could also be mapped to other transport protocols such as IPX, OSI, and SNA.

Alternatives to CORBA

CORBA isn't the only object-oriented architecture in town. It competes directly with Microsoft's Distributed Component Object Model (DCOM), introduced in 1996, and ActiveX technology. DCOM is Microsoft's Windows-based object technology. It is a technology of, for, and by Microsoft, although in an attempt to have DCOM recognized as a standard rivaling CORBA, the company has turned both it and ActiveX over to The Open Group. In addition, Microsoft has developed its Microsoft Transaction Server to support object transactions over intranets and the Internet.

DCOM is a strong competitor to CORBA, thanks largely to the market dominance of Microsoft's Windows. However, CORBA has better multivendor support, and many application developers believe it is better for networks that include a variety of operating environments. For instance, as we mentioned, Netscape has incorporated CORBA into its Web browsers. As well, a new technology called "ORBlets" has been developed to allow Java applets to interact with objects that comply with the CORBA model. Of course, only time will tell which model—if either—prevails on the wide open frontier of the Internet.

And speaking of the Internet, it's time to talk in more detail about how applications navigate its uncharted and constantly changing byways. The next chapter deals with how applications interact with network infrastructures, both locally and over the Internet.

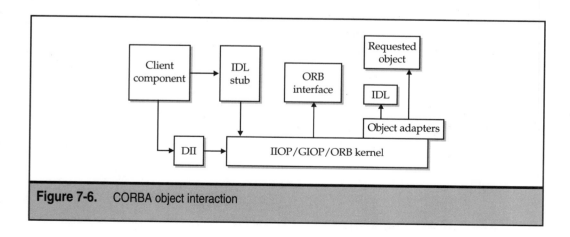

Figure 7-6. CORBA object interaction

CHAPTER 8

Applications Going the Distance

In the preceding two chapters, we have discussed how networked applications are constructed and how their distributed components interact with one another across the network. But how do these distributed applications find the resources they need when those resources are scattered across the enterprise—and sometimes across the world?

DIRECTORY ASSISTANCE, PLEASE

To find the resources an application wants to use, an application does what you and I often do: it looks it up in the "phone book." Actually, the "phone book" that applications use is called *directory services*. This is a listing of all available resources—people, devices, applications, and services—available on the network. Directory services can function as either white pages—letting applications look up specific resources by name—or as yellow pages—letting applications know about available services whether or not the applications call them by name. Therefore, applications that are *directory service enabled* can take advantage of directory services to find what they need.

Directory services provide a wide array of information to the applications and people that use them. For example, directory services on a *names server* would respond to queries about how to access network resources by their appropriate names using the established resource naming conventions. Directory services on a security server, on the other hand, would answer queries about access rights to various network resources. A basic "white pages" server would handle questions about the names and addresses of people listed in that server's database.

You can imagine how vital good directory services are to distributed network applications, especially in large enterprises and on the Internet. In fact, nearly every distributed network operating environment incorporates a directory service. However, these directory services are largely proprietary and not always interoperable. While network operating system vendors have based their proprietary directory services on the X.500 standard developed by the International Telecommunication Union, this standard has not been fully adopted. This is largely because X.500 is based on the OSI Reference Model, yet operating environment vendors have supported their traditional proprietary protocols and/or the TCP/IP protocol on which the Internet is based. The good news is that most vendors are planning to implement directory services using Lightweight Directory Access Protocol (LDAP).

LIGHTWEIGHT DIRECTORY ACCESS PROTOCOL (LDAP)   Lightweight Directory Access Protocol (LDAP) is a directory service protocol designed on a client/server architecture that runs over Transport Control Protocol/Internet Protocol (TCP/IP). LDAP organizes information about a network object, called an *attribute,* into records called *entries*. Attributes all have a type, which identifies what kind of object it is—such as an e-mail address or a compressed video file—and at least one value. In the example of an e-mail address, the value would be the actual e-mail address of the object. Each entry is identified by its *distinguished name* (DN).

All of this information is arranged in a hierarchical tree. The tree is built to represent geographical as well as organizational structure. For example, the object at the top of the LDAP tree is the country in which the object resides. Below that would be the state or enterprise in which the object resides. Below that might be the department or functional area. Below that would be the individual entry for the objects.

Because it is designed to run on a client/server model, the actual LDAP database can be located on one or more servers. When an LDAP client wants to find information on an object in the LDAP directory, it connects to an LDAP server and queries it. The server either replies by sending the client the requested information or it sends the client a pointer to another server on which the requested data resides.

While LDAP is an Internet Engineering Task Force (IETF) standard directory service that has its roots in X.500, it is still on the TCP/IP protocol rather than the OSI protocol. However, the widespread adoption of LDAP as a standard directory service hasn't yet taken place. Therefore, while there are several good directory service options available for an enterprise, there currently is no single, standard, universal, interoperable directory service available for the Internet as a whole.

Getting on the List

Directory services are really just a database—or listing—containing all the resources available at all locations across the network. The list is available to all users—both people and applications—of resources on the network. This sounds simple, and it often is, depending upon the interface of the directory services. If an application is designed to be able to access the directory services via its application program interface (API), it is called directory service enabled.

Users can also access directory services via the user interface. The user interface is the key to the success of a directory service. Even the most comprehensive directory service in the world is all but worthless if it is too difficult for people to use. Therefore, a good deal of thought and planning should go into the design of the user interface. There are several basic designs for a directory system's user interface, including the following:

▼ **Address book**   In this model, the directory services provide each user with a software version of an address book that contains the resources that particular user is allowed to use.

■ **Graphical user interface (GUI)**   For this model, each user is presented with a hierarchical *directory tree* that shows the network resources available to that user. An example of such a tree is shown in Figure 8-1.

■ **Query model**   In this model, users actually enter a request for services that match keywords or classes of services. For example, a user could enter a search for printer resources, and the user interface would return a list of printers that particular user may access.

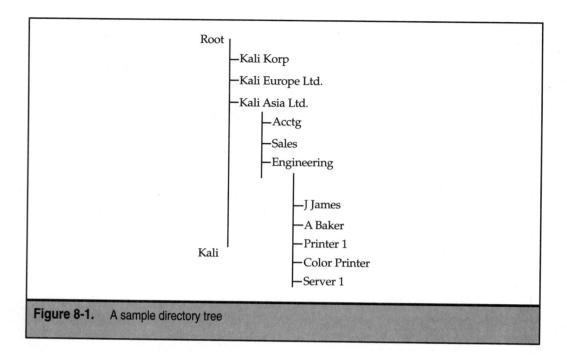

Figure 8-1.   A sample directory tree

▲   **Search agent model**   This method is similar to the query model, except that special components called *search agents* perform the search across the network (or the Internet) to find the resources that meet the criteria specified in the search query.

Containing the List

As you can imagine, constructing a usable directory service requires a great deal of planning. The organization of the directory service is critical to its usability, and luckily there are some standard schemes used to build them. To learn more about them, let's look again at the directory tree in Figure 8-1 above. Notice that the directory structure consists of three types of objects:

▼   Root directory

■   Container objects

▲   Leaf objects

A typical directory service is organized as a hierarchical tree structure as shown in Figure 8-1. At the base of the tree is the *root directory* (clever, no?). All other resources branch out from this root directory. Branching from the root directory are *container objects*, which are also called *organizational units* (OUs). True to their name, container objects are structures that contain other objects, either other *containers* or *leaf objects.* Leaf objects are not containers—that is, they don't contain other objects. Instead, leaf objects represent the actual resources available on the network, such as printers or other users.

SAFEGUARDING THE DIRECTORY: REPLICATION AND PARTITIONING

Clearly directory services are vital to the smooth operation of a network—especially a large one. Therefore, the designers of directory services have taken steps to ensure that these services are constantly available. Two key mechanisms that ensure the availability of directory services are *replication* and *partitioning*.

To understand replication and partitioning, we must first take a look at where the directory services database is stored. The main, or *master*, database is kept in one place on a single server. This is the "master copy" of the database that is the most accurate and current. This master database can be partitioned, or broken into pieces. These pieces can be stored on different servers, ensuring that these portions of the database will be available in the event that the server containing the master database goes down. Partitioning also increases performance, because it breaks large databases down into smaller, more quickly searchable parts.

Furthermore, the pieces of the partitioned database can be *replicated* to servers in other locations. This not only increases security and ensures disaster recovering, it also improves performance in remote locations. Remote users access the directory services database over fast local connections rather than over slow wide area network links. Therefore, for wide area networks, it makes sense to partition and replicate a database by geographic location. For example, a company's Dallas branch network server should maintain the portion of its directory services database that contains information on the Dallas office, while the master copy of the whole database should be maintained at headquarters—wherever headquarters may be.

Keeping in Sync

Obviously, partitioning and replicating directory services databases can cause problems with keeping all parts of the database accurate and current. This means that changes made in one copy of the database should be made in all copies of the database as soon as possible. Otherwise, users won't be working with the latest information. However, it's important not to burden the network with constant database updates, or the only traffic that crosses the network will be the traffic that synchronizes the database!

Most directory services databases set their own synchronization schedules. These schedules are optimized to limit the burden on network traffic, yet still keep the database acceptably accurate. Fortunately, for the most part it isn't crucial that every portion of a directory services database be strictly up-to-date. A delay of a few seconds—or even a few minutes—generally won't compromise the effective functioning of the network.

Locking It Down

Because currently most directory services are for internal company use only, securing the directory services isn't a major concern right now. However, the increasing need to have a universal directory service for finding resources on the Internet—and hence throughout the world—is pressing companies to open their network directories to the world. Furthermore, the purpose of the ITU X.500 standard is to provide global access to all network resources through directory services.

On the other hand, few companies are prepared to invite the world into their directory services. After all, what company would want their competitors to know what resources they have, who their key employees are, and how to contact them? In addition, why would they want to make it easy for mass marketers to flood their enterprise networks with junk e-mails and unsolicited advertisements? For these reasons, there is both growing demand for and strong resistance to universal directory services.

The fact that there isn't a single, universal directory service has prompted many enterprises to cobble together their various directory services into *metadirectories*. Metadirectories are actually directories of directory services. They integrate and coordinate multiple directory services, making them interoperable. Metadirectories provide a de facto universal directory service—if only for those directory services used by a single enterprise and its affiliates—by making all directory services information available from a single registry. This not only makes it easier to find resources and information, but also makes it easier to update this information as it changes. A change made in the metadirectory is replicated across all the directory services it coordinates.

A DIRECTORY OF DIRECTORY SERVICES

Now that we've discussed what directory services are and what they do, it's time to discuss the individual directory services that are available and functioning in network operating environments today. Currently these are as follows:

- ▼ X.500
- ■ Banyan StreetTalk
- ■ Novell Directory Services
- ■ Windows NT Server Directory Services
- ■ Active Directory
- ■ DCE Directory Services
- ▲ Netscape Directory Server

X.500

We've talked a great deal about X.500 in this chapter. Now it's time to get to know it a little better. X.500 is a set of OSI standards developed jointly by the International Standards Organization and the International Telecommunications Union. Although

X.500 was the first standard for implementing "network white pages," it doesn't support TCP/IP and is therefore not usable on the Internet. This lack of support for the de facto Information Superhighway has limited its acceptance. However, it still remains a model for developing interoperable directory services.

Information in the X.500 database, called a *data information base*, is organized in a hierarchical directory tree as shown in Figure 8-2. A truly international standard, the top level of the tree defines the countries in which the resources are located. Container objects (organizational units) and leaf objects branch from the countries.

NOTE: Originally, the root of the tree was to be an international authority such as the ITU that would manage the entire X.500 structure. However, this concept has yet to be accepted, and may never be given X.500's limited popularity.

X.500 addresses generally take a five-part form similar to this:

CN=user, OU=department, OU=division, O=company, C=country

However, don't think that X.500 is only useful as a multination directory service. You can also implement it within an enterprise as a private directory service. Of course, this inherently bears the double-edged sword of enabling easy connection to a global X.500 directory service.

X.500 is a comprehensive directory service, but as a result it can also be complex and unwieldy. In fact, most organizations have found that the thoroughness of the X.500

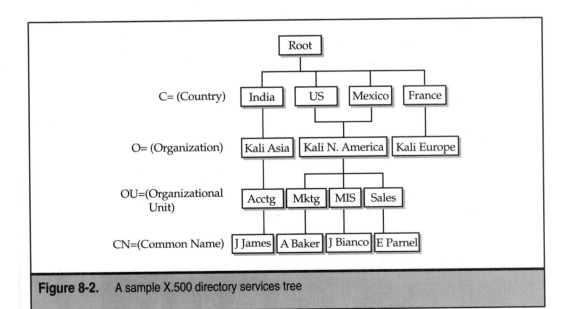

Figure 8-2.   A sample X.500 directory services tree

directory service isn't worth the trade-off in performance and complexity—not to mention the security risks of having an "open" directory service structure. Add to that the fact that X.500 doesn't support the TCP/IP protocol suite used on the Internet, and you can understand why X.500 is not widely used. Nonetheless, as we mentioned, it has served as a model for some very successful and widely used directory services, such as Novell's Network Directory Services, which we will discuss shortly.

Banyan StreetTalk

Banyan StreetTalk is the grandfather of directory services. It allows network users to locate and access resources quickly, without their having to know the physical location of the resources. An elegant, proprietary directory service developed by Banyan Systems, Inc., originally it was a part of the Banyan VINES network operating system. In fact, for many years VINES was the only operating environment that StreetTalk supported. However, versions of StreetTalk are now available that support other operating environments such as SCO UNIX, Novell NetWare, and Windows networks.

StreetTalk has a simpler naming convention than X.500. Instead of X.500's five-part naming convention, StreetTalk uses a three-part naming convention:

resource@group@organization

StreetTalk is able to provide meaningful information about resources without requiring lengthy descriptive names because it attaches properties, which it calls *attributes*, to every resource on the network. Attributes are defined by the network administrator using the standard property types described in the X.500 specification.

StreetTalk has become a favorite of both network managers and users because it includes tools to help both do their jobs more easily. It includes a GUI-based management application that makes it easy to find and manage network resources. Furthermore, StreetTalk integrates with network core services so that all network services and applications know the physical location and security privileges of every user. This means that users can log on anywhere, yet their network environment and access rights are always the same.

StreetTalk also offers StreetTalk Directory Assistance (STDA), which provides distributed directory services. It gathers data about services throughout the network and stores it in databases that users can search when looking for resources on the network. STDA is powerful and easy-to-use directory assistance service that makes finding resources quick and easy.

Despite all the advantages of StreetTalk, this directory service enjoyed limited popularity at first because it initially supported only VINES. This slowed its growth for awhile. Therefore, while StreetTalk is popular and gaining market share, it isn't as widely used as it might have been had it originally supported more widely used network operating environments.

Novell Directory Services (NDS)

Novell Directory Services (NDS) first appeared in NetWare version 4.x, and has since been adapted for the Windows NT and UNIX operating environments. NDS employs distributed directory services using the hierarchical directory tree structure defined in the X.500 standard, as was shown in Figure 8-1.

NDS includes a GUI-based management utility called the NetWare Administrator (NETADMIN). Like Banyan StreetTalk, NDS allows network managers to define properties for its resources. All network users and resources are stored in NDS as objects with properties. This information is entered when the client account is created. NETADMIN lets network administrators view all properties of all resources while at the same time allowing them to restrict the types of information that garden-variety users can view. The NETADMIN management utility lets users expand or collapse the view of the directory tree, allowing managers to "drill down" to finer and finer levels of detail about each network resource.

The entire directory service entry—consisting of a resource and its properties—exists as an object in the NDS database. Like X.500, NDS defines three basic types of objects:

▼   The root object

■   Container objects

▲   Leaf objects

However, within each of these three broad types of objects, NDS defines specific types of objects unique to NDS. A few of these specific object types are as follows:

▼   **Country container**   A container object that defines the country in which a branch of the directory tree is located.

■   **Organization**   A container object that names the enterprise.

■   **Organizational unit**   A container object used to organize departments, regions, or functions within an enterprise.

■   **Organizational role**   A container that defines a particular role or position in the enterprise, such as a director or supervisor.

■   **Group**   A container object that holds a group of user leaf objects.

■   **NetWare server**   A leaf object that defines a NetWare server.

▲   **Volume**   A leaf object that defines a physical volume of data storage, such as a hard drive on a server.

As we discussed earlier, it makes sense to plan a directory service around the geography of the physical network, and this is fairly easy to accomplish with NDS. Figure 8-3

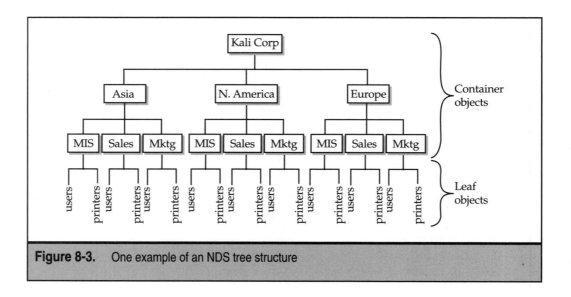

Figure 8-3.   One example of an NDS tree structure

shows how a physical topology could be mapped into an NDS directory tree. The tree has container objects to represent the entire company, as well as its regional divisions and local offices. The container object for each local office contains departmental container objects, which in turn hold the leaf objects representing the network resources at that location.

NetWare Directory Services are widely used, in part thanks to its inclusion with the very popular NetWare operating environment. However, it is also a flexible, easy-to-administer directory service that is gaining in popularity as it expands the number and types of operating environments it supports.

Windows NT Server Directory Services

Microsoft has developed a directory service to run on Windows NT Server 4.0 and subsequent versions of the Windows NT operating environment. Based on LDAP, Windows NT Server Directory Services combines features of X.500 and the Internet's DNS locator service. It's LDAP foundation lets it operate across operating environments and support multiple name spaces—for example, it supports both Internet and OSI naming formats. This means that network managers can use Windows NT Server Directory Services to administer other types of directory services.

The Windows NT Directory Services doesn't use a hierarchical tree structure the way Novell's NDS does. Instead, it uses Microsoft's old domain model from earlier versions of Windows NT. Like directory trees, however, domains can be arranged by organizational unit (OU) container objects, as shown in Figure 8-4.

Within each domain, network managers can assign security and management of portions of the domain to different network administrators. This is new to Microsoft

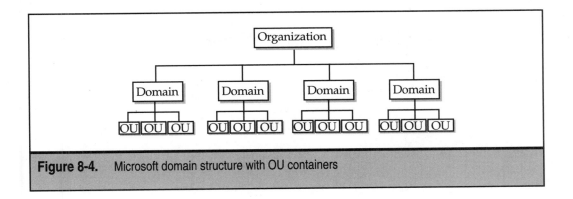

Figure 8-4.   Microsoft domain structure with OU containers

Windows NT—in the past, the security and administration rights had to be assigned for the entire domain, not just to a portion of it. With Windows NT Directory Services, management and security can be assigned separately within each domain, within a subtree of OUs within a domain, or for a single OU.

Microsoft's directory services includes many helpful features. Among these are the following:

▼ **Programmability**   You can program Microsoft's directory services using a variety of scripting languages.

■ **Multimaster replication**   This replication scheme updates servers closest to the users in question instead of strictly at a master server.

▲ **NetWare support**   Microsoft's Directory Services supports NetWare version 4.x as well as being backward compatible with Windows NT Domain Services.

Active Directory

Application access to Microsoft's Windows NT Directory Services is provided through the Active Directory API, based principally on the LDAP protocol. Active Directory offers a single set of interfaces for accessing, searching, and managing multiple directories. To allow this unified directory management, Microsoft developed a suite of Windows Open System Architecture (WOSA) application programming interfaces called Open Directory Services Interface (ODSI). Applications written to communicate with these application programming interfaces can interoperate with various directory services.

Thanks to Active Directory, Windows NT Directory Services can enable an enterprise to integrate multiple directory services that may be used within its network. It also enables Windows NT Directory Services to access application-specific directory services, such as Lotus Notes and Web browser addresses.

Active Directory components are available not only for Windows NT, but also for Novell NetWare and most other directory services that support LDAP. Once fully implemented, Active Directory's interoperability may make it the directory service of choice, although it still has a long way to go—and some very stiff competition to overcome.

DCE Directory Services, The Open Group

The Open Group's Distributed Computing Environment (DCE), which we discussed in Chapter 7, includes its own directory services, called Distributed Directory Services (DDS), which is integrated with other DCE components. DDS offers a single naming model that reaches across the DCE environment. It incorporates the X.500 naming system, and recently has added LDAP support.

Netscape Directory Server

As part of its ongoing goal to make the Internet accessible to all, Netscape has developed its Directory Server as a central administration point for user information. Based on LDAP, Netscape Directory Server distributes and coordinates directory information across multiple servers on an intranet. You can incorporate these directory services into Netscape's SuiteSpot, thus implementing a uniform information structure for all SuiteSpot applications. Netscape Directory Server offers tools for writing directory-enabled applications, as well as program enhancements for nonstop processing, disaster recovery, and heterogeneous replication—among LDAP-compliant servers only.

MOVING ON DOWN THE CHAIN

We've now discussed applications: what they are, why they are, and how they do what they do. So what's next? It's time that we took a look at the protocol layer on which applications rest. In the next chapter, we'll discuss—and hopefully demystify—that most misunderstood of all OSI layers, the presentation layer.

CHAPTER 9

Layer 6 and What It Means to You

The presentation layer, layer 6 of the Open Systems Interconnection (OSI) Reference Model, is probably the most misunderstood layer of the protocol stack. Lying just below the application layer (as shown in Figure 9-1) supporting it, preparing data for it, the presentation layer gets no respect—and receives very little attention. In fact, the presentation layer is often considered just a "pass-through protocol" for data traveling from the application layer to the session layer.

But some very important things actually do take place at layer 6. The presentation layer has the crucial job of preparing incoming data for the application layer so that once it arrives at layer 7, the application user can actually view the data.

That being said, unless you are a developer of distributed applications, or simply extremely interested in what developers do, you can live a long and happy life without knowing any of the workings of layer 6. So unless the preceding description fits you, it's safe for you to skip this chapter and move on.

HAPPENINGS AT LAYER 6

The presentation layer is a busy place. Some of the things that take place here are as follows:

▼   Request session establishment

■   Transfer data

■   Select data syntax

■   Translate data syntax

▲   Request session termination

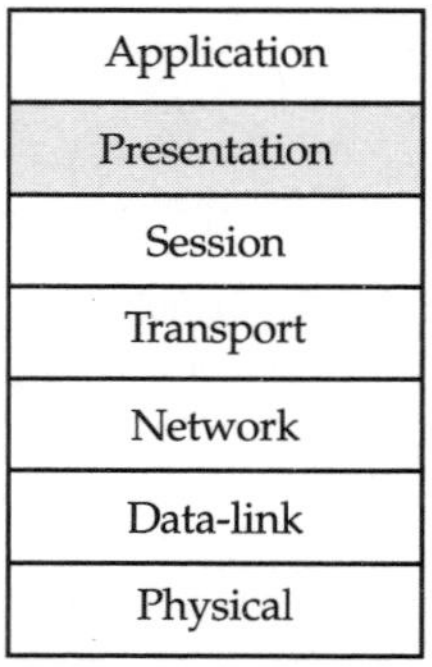

| Application |
| Presentation |
| Session |
| Transport |
| Network |
| Data-link |
| Physical |

Figure 9-1.   The presentation layer in the OSI Reference Model

Think of the presentation layer as the translator for the application layer. The application layer speaks its native language, or *data format*, which is called its *abstract syntax*. However, two nodes that want to communicate may speak in different abstract syntaxes. The presentation layer establishes a common "language," or data format, between communicating nodes on a network. So its main job is to ensure that two communicating network nodes that use two different formats for the same data can talk to each other successfully. The presentation layer accomplishes this by translating the data format at the sending node into one common data format, called the *transfer syntax*, then presenting the data to the receiving end to be translated into that node's data format.

This layer is responsible for taking the data from the sending node and translating it into a format that the receiving node can understand. Often, this involves translating from one data format to another. For example, the presentation layer may change the byte ordering from left to right to right to left. It may also change the character set from EBCDIC to ASCII.

Layer 6 provides the protocols for the translation of data, it defines the format for data, and it provides the *data syntax* for incoming data. For outgoing data, layer 6 translates data from the application layer format into a format that is suitable for transmission over the network. In fact, syntax translation is probably the most important role played by the presentation layer. It accomplishes this translation using embedded encoding rules for data translations.

Figure 9-2 illustrates the workings of the presentation layer. It selects a transfer syntax to use on the presentation connection between the two nodes.

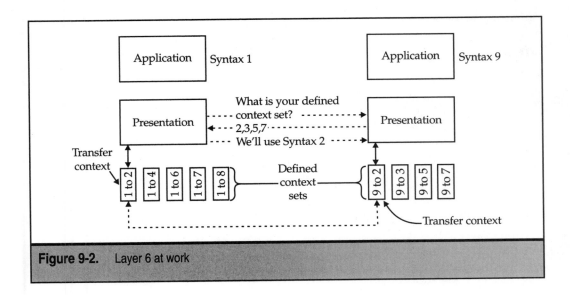

Figure 9-2.   Layer 6 at work

NOTE: The transfer syntax may change during the duration of the connection.

Data Encryption and Data Compression

Another important job done at the presentation layer is data encryption and compression. Because data compression and encryption is a form of data presentation, it seems natural that compression would take place here.

In fact, it makes sense that these functions take place here because they can have a dramatic impact on the meaning of the data being transmitted, and the presentation layer is the last layer in the OSI protocol stack that is concerned with preserving that meaning. The five layers beneath the presentation layer don't know and aren't concerned with what the information they are transmitting means—or whether it means anything at all. So, they're probably not the best place to be performing delicate operations such as encryption and compression. We will talk about data encryption and compression processes in Chapter 22.

Minding Your (Data) Grammar

In its role as official data translator, the presentation layer is a stickler for data grammar, known as *data syntax*. This means that layer 6 ensures that the two communicating nodes either use the same rules to organize their data communications or have an accurate translation between two differing sets of data organization rules.

To make the job of the presentation layer a bit easier, the International Standards Organization (ISO) has defined several open, standard abstract data syntax formats. These are defined in the ISO's Abstract Syntax Notation 1 (ASN.1). Applications written to these standards will transmit data that translates easily from one platform to another so the poor presentation layer isn't overworked.

NOTE: Contrary to popular belief, the ASN.1 is *not* synonymous with the OSI's layer 6 protocol. Rather, the ASN.1 defines standard protocols used within the presentation layer for representing machine-independent data formats so that applications on different types of computing platforms can communicate.

In practice, the only transfer syntax notation of the ASN.1 that currently exists in the OSI Reference Model is the *Basic Encoding Rules* (BER). Of course, as with everything else in the world of distributed network applications, we expect this to change.

Presentation Layer Functional Units

The services provided by the presentation layer are divided into functional units, each unit performing a distinct job to ensure data transfer syntax selection and translation.

Applications may request the use of these functional units separately. The functional units are as follows:

▼ Presentation kernel

■ Context management

■ Context restoration

■ Connection establishment

■ Connection termination

■ Connection management

■ Information transfer

▲ Dialog control

Presentation Kernel

The *presentation kernel* is the core service of the presentation layer. Its job is simply to send outgoing data down to the session layer and incoming data up to the application layer. If two applications are using the same syntax for all the data they want to exchange, then the only functional unit called into service will be the presentation kernel.

Context Management

Layer 6 often has to coordinate multiple *presentation contexts*. Each presentation context defines the abstract syntax of the application data and the transfer syntax that will be used to transmit that application data to the receiving node.

An analogy would be the United Nations. Suppose the Indian ambassador wants to talk to the Pakistani ambassador (not highly likely, but it's a dream of mine, and this is my book, so that's the example I'm going to use). Let's assume that the Indian ambassador speaks only Hindi (again, not likely, but it's just an example) and the Pakistani ambassador speaks only Urdu. The ambassadors contact the Director of Translators at the UN to find appropriate translators. The Director of Translators discovers that there are no translators available who speak both Hindi and Urdu, but there are translators who speak Hindi and French, Hindi and Spanish, Urdu and French, and Urdu and Spanish. The Director of Translators first sends the Hindi-French translator to translate the Indian ambassador's words into French. As well, she sends the Urdu-French translator to convert the French translation of the Indian ambassador's words into Urdu. In this instance, the *abstract syntaxes* are Hindi and Urdu. The *transfer syntax* is French. And the *presentation context* for the Indian ambassador is Hindi-French, while for the Pakistani ambassador the presentation context is French-Urdu. And the Director of Translators, who organized the whole thing, is acting as the *context manager*.

Suppose, however, that the Hindi-French translator becomes ill and can't work any longer (too much French food will do that). In this instance, the Director of Translators has to do something quickly or communications will break down. Of course, she has a backup plan. She calls in the Hindi-Spanish and the Urdu-Spanish translators. Now, while the *abstract syntaxes* remain Hindi and Urdu, the *transfer syntax* has changed to Spanish. So the *transfer contexts* have changed to Hindi-Spanish for the Indian ambassador and Spanish-Urdu for the Pakistani ambassador. And the context manager, the Director of Translators, is a hero.

This is similar to what takes place at the presentation layer. The two communicating nodes agree on a presentation context via the negotiations of the presentation layer. If for some reason the initial presentation context fails, hopefully there is another presentation context that can work. The entire set of presentation contexts available to the presentation layer is called the *defined context set*. The *default context* is the presentation context that is always available to presentation layer is therefore used initially, as well as when the defined context set is empty.

Context Restoration

In our preceding example at the UN, when the Hindi-Spanish and Urdu-Spanish translators were brought in, they obviously had to be briefed on the status of the negotiations, the logistics of the conference, and the duration of the session. "Now, Ms. Bleeth, please be sure that your skirt covers your knees at all times and that you don't show the soles of your feet to the Pakistani ambassador. Mr. Dloor, we're at a very sensitive point in the negotiations, so stay alert and be extremely careful not to add any inflection that might be misinterpreted. It's going to be a long session, so everyone get a drink of water and get comfortable. Dinner will be brought in at 8:00 P.M., and that's probably when your next 10-minute break will be. Now, the Indian ambassador had just told the Pakistani ambassador that he admired his tie. We can resume from that point." In this capacity, the Director of Translators has taken on the *context restoration* function. This brings senders, receivers, and translators of data up to speed and ready to resume communication, and synchronizes the transmission of information.

Connection Establishment, Termination, and Management

The presentation layer is responsible for setting up, managing, and tearing down the communication session with the presentation layer on the communicating node. These functional units handle the connection-oriented tasks.

Information Transfer

The *information transfer* functional unit is the unit that actually transmits data in the transfer syntax down to the session layer. This is also the functional unit that sets the priority of transmitted data.

Dialog Control

This functional unit manages the transfer of data between the presentation layer and the session layer. The transmission flow control and restoration are handled within this functional unit.

BUT WHAT DOES IT *MEAN*?

As you can see, some vital tasks are performed by layer 6. The whole ability of your applications to understand data received from other places hinges on the efforts of layer 6. But as we mentioned, as a network manager, the workings of the presentation layer mean little in your daily life. These tasks and the challenges they present (no pun intended) are the concern of the developers of distributed applications, not the managers of the networks on which they run.

Better to move on to the next chapter, to layer 5 and a world that involves you intimately.

PART III

The Infrastructure

CHAPTER 10

Operating Environments

Whether you're running Microsoft NT, Novell NetWare, Banyan VINES, IBM OS/2 Warp Server, or a flavor of UNIX, a thorough understanding of the processes that take place at the session layer (layer 5) of the International Standards Organization's (ISO) Open Systems Interconnect (OSI) Reference Model is essential. There are a number of native and open protocols that operate at layer 5, controlling the network session of each application.

Additionally there are session layer application programming interfaces (APIs) that, while they are not protocols, do operate at layer 5. Session layer APIs are in essence a workaround for NOS environments that lack specific application support. By developing a product based on an API, vendors can offer their products to a wider NOS community. APIs require special software on both ends of the session. In this chapter, we'll discuss the function, operation, protocols, and APIs encompassing layer 5. Working in tandem, the protocols and APIs of the OSI Reference Model's upper layers (5, 6, and 7—session, presentation, and application) allow dissimilar systems to effectively communicate.

LAYER 5 AND WHAT IT MEANS TO YOU

If you were to set out to search for information specific to layer 5, chances are you wouldn't turn up much. In fact, most of our discussion about layer 5 includes protocols from layers below and above it. This is due in part to the fact that each layer utilizes information that has been provided to it from the previous layer and passes its information to the next layer. An additional factor in discussing other layers of the OSI model here is that network protocols aren't always an exact fit to the OSI Reference Model. That is, NOS protocols span multiple layers of the OSI Reference Model.

If there's a problem at layer 5, you'll know it pretty quick. As an upper layer of the OSI Reference Model, the session layer is responsible for establishing, managing, and ceasing communications between hosts. Layer 5 of the OSI Reference Model loosely maps to the host-to-host layer of the Department of Defense (DoD) model and to the data flow control layer of the Standard Network Architecture (SNA) model. Examples of session layer operations include users logging in, drive mappings, printer attachments, file transfers, and the like.

Layer 5 utilizes a variety of control mechanisms, including dialog control, synchronization, and token management to regulate communications. Additionally, layer 5 provides provisions for mapping of names to addresses, error condition reporting, and separating conversations into manageable sessions.

The session layer operation can be broken into three distinct phases: connection establishment, data transfer, and connection termination. While establishing the connection, the session layer authenticates the connection, negotiates protocols, and determines dialog control. During the data transfer phase, services for data expedition, token management, session synchronization, and exception reporting are provided. And, during the connection termination phase, services are provided for handling both abnormal and normal disconnects. A user-requested termination is handled through the presentation layer.

Ever receive the "Abort, Retry or Ignore" message? Those successful retries are one of layer 5's services: synchronization. It allows for a connection to be resumed rather than reestablished in the event of a failed or abnormally terminated connection. Layer 5 handles this by inserting checkpoints into the data stream (a controlled flow of data between two processes), so that the only data to be retransmitted is the data after the last checkpoint.

Dialog control is established by utilizing simplex, half-duplex, or full-duplex communications. Simplex is a one-way, no round-trip type of communication. An example of simplex communication is printing. With half-duplex connections, hosts transmit and receive; however, they just can't do both at the same time. Half-duplex is like a walkie-talkie—you must wait until the other party has stopped talking. Finally, full-duplex allows the hosts to communicate at the same time, like a telephone.

Another important service provided by layer 5 is token management. When critical operations are being performed, a conversation can be controlled by token management. In order to prevent both hosts from performing the same operation simultaneously, layer 5 utilizes token management so that only the host with the token may perform the operation.

As part of its management function, layer 5 is also responsible for the allocation and deallocation of resources like memory and CPU time. Prior to successful establishment, a session must be authenticated. Authentication is achieved via the transmission of login, password, and access right information.

When a user requests a network service—whether it's a file or other network device—the client and server must have adequate memory to service the request. In other words, the requesting host must have an adequate buffer size to "pull" all of the requested information. If adequate buffer sizes haven't been configured on the workstation shell software or on the server's NOS software, the session will fail. At the establishment of a connection, layer 5 assigns session identifiers, creates the communications process, and authenticates the hosts. When the conversation is complete, each host releases its resources.

Layer 5 expects streaming data, but has the ability to determine an early connection loss. (When data is continuously sent, or "streaming," the receiving host must have adequate resources or communication buffers to process the data.) Session layer protocols have the ability to handle idle time during a connection by what are referred to as "tickle" packets. Simply stated, "tickle packets" are "Are you there?" requests and "Yes, I am." responses. The transmission of tickle packets assures layer 5 that the connection is intact. If one end of the session hasn't received a packet within a specified period of time, it will perform a normal termination on its respective end of the session, but only after attempting to locate its conversation partner. It is this feature that allows a host to free its resources.

Many times, an abnormally terminated session can present problems. An abnormally terminated session occurs when one of the hosts either crashes or is powered off. Although the unheard from host may become available after the session has closed, sometimes the session cannot be recovered. In a networking environment, when a session is abnormally terminated, the other end of the session consumes valuable resources waiting to hear from the terminated side. Although the time the connection remains open is minimal, on a busy network, time is money. Also, it is possible for users to overwrite files with partial files as a result of an abnormally terminated session. Worse yet are open files. Most of the time a server can efficiently close files, but many times it can't. When a server is unable to efficiently close files, locks and corruption can occur. It is important that employees be cautioned about the method in which they terminate a session. Unfortunately, not all applications have been developed to efficiently handle abnormally terminated sessions.

In summary, layer 5 is responsible for establishing communication sessions between processes on two hosts. It provides the following services:

▼ Unique process address registration such as that for NetBIOS names

■ Establishes, monitors, and terminates virtual circuit sessions

■ Delimits messages appending header information that prevents the receiving layer from transmitting data to the application until the entire message is received

■ Informs the receiving application when buffer space is insufficient or that the message is incomplete

▲ Performs authentication and other security functions required for processes to communicate

NETWARE CORE PROTOCOL (NCP)

The NetWare Core Protocol (NCP) is NetWare's proprietary protocol used at the upper layers of the OSI Reference Model. There is some controversy over which layers of the OSI Reference Model that NCP is distributed across. Some of the confusion is attributed to Novell's reluctance to disclose detailed information about NCP. Actually, NCP spans layers 5, 6, and 7 of the OSI Reference Model. And since NCP performs functions relative to layer 5, we've included it in our discussion.

NCP is used for all requests for services by the clients and for the server's responses to the requests. NCP establishes a connection between the workstation and server and communicates requests and responses between the two hosts. NCP is implemented as a shell that resides on top of the client. Network requests are redirected through NCP to the server. Although NCP uses the Internetwork Packet Exchange (IPX) datagram service, it utilizes its own session control, error detection, and retransmission.

Here's how NCP works. When the NetWare shell is loaded, SAP and RIP packets are transmitted to locate a server. Once a server is located, NCP establishes and maintains the connection. When an application requests a network service, the request is encapsulated within the NCP message and transmitted to the server. The server responds to the workstation request by returning a response NCP packet. For every IPX packet, NCP requires an acknowledgement packet. The NCP packet is encapsulated within the IPX packet and the well-known socket number of 451h is inserted into the destination socket field of the IPX packet. The NCP request header is a 6-byte packet and the NCP response header is an 8-byte packet.

Their header data is detailed below:

▼   The Request Type field is the type of NCP service request, and the valid values are 1111 for Connection Creation, 2222 for General Service Request, 5555 for Connection Termination, and 7777 for Burst Mode Transfer Request.

■   The Sequence Number field is an incremental value for the number of connections created.

■   The Connection Number Low field is the number assigned to the host at login. Connection numbers can be displayed by executing USERLIST from a client.

■   The Task Number field indicates the host requesting NCP services. A zero indicates all tasks are complete and the connection may be terminated.

■   The Connection Number High field is not currently used and will have a value of 00h.

■   The NCP response header is identical to the NCP request header, but includes an additional 2 bytes for the Completion Code and Connection Status fields.

■   The Reply Type field in the response header can be 3333 for Service Response, 7777 for Burst Mode Connection, or 9999 for Request Being Processed.

■   The Completion Code field is used to indicate the status of request, and the valid values are 0 for Successful and 1 for Error Encountered.

▲   The Connection Code field can indicate the status of a connection. A downed server is indicated by a 1 in the fourth bit.

NCP services are further defined by function and subfunction codes in addition to service request and service response codes.

BURST MODE PROTOCOL (BMP)

The Burst Mode Protocol (BMP) was designed to more efficiently handle file reads and writes. Where NCP requires a response for every request, BMP allows multiple responses to a single service request. One major advantage of burst mode is that large amounts of data can be transferred from a single request regardless of the application. A host can receive up to 64K from a single request. Burst mode is transparent to applications since the workstation shell handles the request. In order to utilize BMP, the source and destination host must utilize BMP software. This is accomplished by running the BMP NLM on the server, the burst mode shell on the workstation, and by including the BMP parameter in the NET.CFG file. While establishing the connection, packet size is negotiated. If the host server isn't BMP-enabled, it will respond with a connection code of 251 (No Such Property), and the standard request/response method of NCP will be used. The BMP header is 52 bytes in length.

▼   The Request Type field is the NCP type, and the valid value for burst mode is 7777h.

- The Flags field indicates the status of the session, and valid values are SYS for a system packet without burst data, EOB for the end of the burst data, and ABT for an abnormally terminated session. In the initial implementation of BMP, two other flags were available but not in use: SAK indicates a request to transmit missing fragments and BSY indicates the host server is busy.

- The Stream Type field utilized by the host server indicates Big Send Burst, and the only valid value is 02h.

- The Source Connection ID field is a random number generated by the sending host that provides a unique identifier for the burst connection.

- The Destination Connection ID field is a random number generated by the receiving host that provides a unique identifier for the burst connection.

- The Packet Sequence field tracks the number of packets in each connection.

- The Send Delay Time field is the delay time, specified in 100-microsecond units, between the sender's transmissions.

- The Burst Sequence Number field is the number of successful bursts sent during the connection.

- The ACK Sequence Number field is the next burst sequence number expected. It is used to determine successful transmission of the last burst.

- The Total Burst Length field is the total length in bytes of the burst being transmitted.

- The Burst Offset field specifies the sequencing of the packet in the burst.

- The Burst Length field is the length of the burst transaction.

- The Fragment List Entries field specified the number of missing elements, and a 0 indicates no missing fragments.

▲ The Function field indicates whether the burst is a read or a write.

REMOTE PROCEDURE CALL (RPC)

Many operating environment manufacturers have implemented the RPC model as a means to allow integration of third-party products that are not natively supported. RPC is a session layer protocol and is used in many network protocol stacks. Working in conjunction with a transport layer protocol, RPC uses XDR (library routines for External Data Representation) for data representation. XDR routines allow programmers to define data structures in a machine-independent fashion. This is accomplished by encoding and decoding data for remote procedure calls (RPCs) within XDR.

RPC includes a three-layer application programming interface (API). Control is provided for from the highest layer to the lowest, with maximum control being available at the lowest layer.

The uppermost layer of the RPC API is the area between the client procedure and the client stub (a small program substituting for a larger program). RPC programs are compiled with stubs. Stubs are, so to speak, the "middleman" for RPC calls. RPC client- and server-specific applications are implemented at the middle layer, and they are used for the development of client and server stubs.

The lowest layer is required for authentication, time-outs, or transport layer selection. Library routines can be integrated with RPCs to provide communication and synchronization services. RPCs can support multiple authentication and security methods, including UNIX-style and Data Encryption Standard (DES) authentication.

With UNIX-style authentication, user and group identification must be supplied to the RPC server and the user must have access to the RPC server. Authentication on UNIX can be handled in one of two styles. One style requires the client's user and group ID to be supplied with each RPC request, whereupon the server must subsequently check its password file with each request. The other style eliminates the subsequent password file checking by returning a unique short ID. By maintaining an ID lookup table, the server can quickly validate further requests.

The use of DES authentication allows for non-UNIX authentication. DES supplies users with a unique network name. Authentication is made on the unique name for each request. The initial request requires a DES key, referred to as the conversation key. The conversation key is used in all subsequent requests. The key provides an encrypted time stamp that is supplied with each request. After the key is decrypted, if the server verifies the time stamp to be later than the last requests' time stamp, authentication is complete and the request is honored.

BANYAN VINES REMOTE PROCEDURE CALL (NetRPC)

Banyan's Virtual Integrated Networking System's (VINES) socket communications are transparently handled by layer 5. In VINES, layer 5 manages the conversion between ordinary local procedure calls and VINES Interprocess Communications Protocol (IPC) reliable messages at the transport layer. VINES' Remote Procedure Call Utility (NetRPC) is utilized at layers 5 and 6 to provide a network interface to the transport layer.

Like NetBIOS, NetRPC is an API that simplifies the development of distributed applications. By utilizing NetRPC, programmers can develop transport-layer-independent software. In VINES, NetRPC provides both session and presentation layer functions. NetRPC got its start as a compiler of the XNS Courier Protocol, an early remote procedure call protocol. NetRPC was later enhanced and adhered to the ISO American National Standards Institute (ANSI) model. Simplifying service and client communications, the ANSI model uses the request/reply method. With the ANSI model NetRPC, parameter and message packaging is automatic.

NetRPC's function at the session level is to provide a network interface to the transport layer. With NetRPC managing transport layer sockets, VINES applications use RPCs and IPC port addresses to exchange IPC-reliable messages of up to 5,800 bytes.

NETWORK BASIC INPUT/OUTPUT SYSTEM (NetBIOS)

Network Basic Input/Output System (NetBIOS) is an application programming interface (API) that enhances the disk operating system (DOS) basic input/output system (BIOS). NetBIOS integrates special network functions to interoperate with the DOS BIOS. It provides support for name management, session services, and datagram services. LANs originated utilizing NetBIOS, and many network operating system (NOS) vendors have improved the original NetBIOS by enhancing its network functionality.

For identification on a network, hosts are assigned alphanumeric names and groups. Network names can be no more than 16 characters in length; however, the sixteenth character is reserved, so only 15 characters are usable. The host workstation name must be unique, like a login. The group name allows users within the same group to share information; however, a group name cannot be used as a workstation name.

The NetBIOS name management services ensure the uniqueness of NetBIOS names. That is, they verify that no other host on the network is using the name that the host is attempting to register. It accomplishes this task by broadcasting the name. If the broadcast is unanswered, the name is successfully registered. It is a NetBIOS function that performs the broadcast and response for network names. Resolution of network names to network addresses is performed by NetBIOS through broadcasts.

Both connectionless and connection-oriented communications are used with NetBIOS. Connectionless communications are a datagram service. Datagrams are packets of encapsulated data that don't require session establishment for delivery. Delivery is achieved by the bottom layers sifting through the packets for the destination. The caveat to this type of delivery is that there is no assurance the data will arrive intact or at all.

Datagrams can be addressed in one of two forms: specific or broadcast. Specific addressing provides for multiple specific recipients, whereas broadcast allows the user to communicate with a group or groups of hosts. Regardless of the datagram addressing scheme utilized, message receipt is handled in the same fashion. Other hosts on the network are constantly polling the network for datagrams intended for themselves.

Connectionless communications don't utilize handshaking or acknowledgment. It's sort of like sending a letter and hoping that who it's been addressed to has received it. If you are concerned about acknowledgment of the receipt of the message, you'll send it certified or registered.

With connection-oriented communications, a session is established between two hosts, and this is where layer 5 comes in. As mentioned earlier, connection-oriented communications are the guaranteed method of message delivery. If a message is not successfully transmitted to the recipient, an error is returned. NetBIOS session services are what categorize it as a layer 5 protocol, although NetBIOS is not a protocol. NetBIOS session services ensure reliable, guaranteed data transmissions through connection-oriented services.

In correlation with layer 5 of the OSI Reference Model, NetBIOS is responsible for establishing, managing, and terminating a session. During session establishment, the Internet Protocol (IP) address and Transmission Control Protocol (TCP) port are determined. Once the session is established, NetBIOS monitors the state of the session, and the session is subsequently closed when the hosts have requested a session close or when NetBIOS determines the session has been abnormally terminated.

There are three NetBIOS operational modes: broadcast (B-node), point-to-point (P-node), and mixed (M-node). The B-node mode identifies the destination host and subsequently establishes a P-node session between hosts. P-node implementations are complex and require a NetBIOS Name Server in addition to a NetBIOS Datagram Distribution Server. Lastly, M-nodes are P-node implementations with support for B-nodes. The most commonly used operational mode is B-node; TCP/NetBIOS supports this mode operation.

Since TCP/IP addresses are 32 bits and NetBIOS names are alphanumeric 16-character names, conversions are necessary for name resolution. Additionally since NetBIOS names can legally contain blanks, they are not compatible with TCP/IP addresses. In order to avoid potential naming conflicts, *scopes* can be specified.

Scopes are strings of characters used when network applications communicate using NetBIOS over TCP/IP. Scope identifiers must be the same for all computers on a NetBIOS network using TCP/IP as the transport. If you have different scope identifiers on your computers, NetBIOS assumes they are part of a different logical network and cannot connect to them.

Hosts can have the same names if the scopes are different. By appending the scope to the host name, uniqueness can be maintained. In other words, SJONES can be used for several hosts if their working areas or scopes are different. With the use of scopes, there can be an SJONES.SALES, SJONES.MIS, and so on. Although scopes are transparent to the users, users cannot communicate across scopes.

NetBIOS utilizes the server message block (SMB) format. SMB is a DOS and Windows message format for sharing network services, files, directories, printers, and so forth. Since NetBIOS uses the SMB format, PC-based LANs utilize SMB for access to heterogeneous networks.

SERVER MESSAGE BLOCK PROTOCOL (SMB)

Server Message Block Protocol (SMB) is a protocol for sharing files, printers, serial ports, and communications abstractions such as named pipes and mail slots between computers. SMB was first defined in a Microsoft/Intel document called "Microsoft Networks/OpenNET-FILE SHARING PROTOCOL" in 1987, and was subsequently developed further by Microsoft and others. Many of the documents that define the SMB protocol(s) are available at ftp.microsoft.com in the SMB documentation area.

SMB is a client/server, request/response protocol. The only exception to the request/response nature of SMB (that is, where the client makes requests and the server sends back responses) is when the client has requested opportunistic locks (oplocks) and the server subsequently has to break an already granted oplock because another client has requested a file open with a mode that is incompatible with the granted oplock. In this case, the server sends an unsolicited message to the client signaling the oplock break.

Servers make file systems and other resources (printers, mail slots, named pipes, APIs) available to clients on the network. Client computers may have their own hard disks, but they also want access to the shared file systems and printers on the servers. Clients connect to servers using TCP/IP (actually NetBIOS over TCP/IP as specified in RFC1001 and RFC1002), NetBEUI, or IPX/SPX. Once they have established a connection, clients can then send commands (SMBs) to the server that allow them to access shares, open files, read and write files, and generally do all the sort of things that you want to do with a file system. However, in the case of SMB, these things are done over the network.

As mentioned, SMB can run over multiple protocols. SMB can be used over TCP/IP, NetBEUI, and IPX/SPX. If TCP/IP or NetBEUI are in use, the NetBIOS API is being used. NetBIOS over TCP/IP seems to be referred to by many names. Microsoft refers to it as NBT in some places and NetBT in others (specifically in their Windows NT documentation and in the Windows NT registry). Others refer to it as RFCNB. NetBEUI is sometimes referred to as NBF (NetBIOS frame format) by Microsoft.

NetBIOS Names

If SMB is used over TCP/IP or NetBEUI, NetBIOS names must be used in a number of cases. NetBIOS names are up to 15 characters long, and are usually the name of the computer that is running NetBIOS. Microsoft, and some other implementers, insist that NetBIOS names be in uppercase, especially when presented to servers as the CALLED NAME.

SMB Protocol Variants

Since the inception of SMB, many protocol variants have been developed to handle the increasing complexity of the environments that it has been employed in. The actual protocol variant client and server will use is negotiated using the negprot SMB, which must be the first SMB sent on a connection. Some variants introduced new SMBs, some simply changed the format of existing SMBs or responses, and some variants did both.

The first protocol variant was the Core Protocol, known to SMB implementations as PC NETWORK PROGRAM 1.0. It could handle a fairly basic set of operations that included the following:

▼ Connecting to and disconnecting from file and print shares

■ Opening and closing files

■ Opening and closing print files

■ Reading and writing files

■ Creating and deleting files and directories

■ Searching directories

■ Getting and setting file attributes

▲ Locking and unlocking byte ranges in files

Security

The SMB model defines two levels of security:

▼   **Share level**   Protection is applied at the share level on a server. Each share can have a password, and a client only needs that password to access all files under that share. This was the first security model that SMB had and is the only security model available in the Core and CorePlus protocols. Windows for Workgroups' vserver.exe implements share-level security by default, as does Windows 95.

▲   **User level**   Protection is applied to individual files in each share and is based on user access rights. Each user (client) must log in to the server and be authenticated by the server. When it is authenticated, the client is given a UID that it must present on all subsequent accesses to the server. This model has been available since LAN Manager 1.0.

Browsing the Network

Having lots of servers out in the network is not much good if users cannot find them. Of course, clients can simply be configured to know about the servers in their environment, but this does not help when new servers are to be introduced or old ones removed. To solve this problem, browsing has been introduced. Each server broadcasts information about its presence. Clients listen for these broadcasts and build up browse lists. In a NetBEUI environment, this is satisfactory, but in a TCP/IP environment problems arise. The problems exist because TCP/IP broadcasts are not usually sent outside the subnet in which they originate (although some routers can selectively transport broadcasts to other subnets). Microsoft has introduced browse servers and the Windows Internet Name Service (WINS) to help overcome these problems.

CIFS: The Latest Incarnation?

Microsoft and a group of other vendors (Digital Equipment, Data General, SCO, Network Appliance Corp., and so on) are engaged in developing a public version of the SMB protocol. It is expected that CIFS 1.0 will be essentially NT LM 0.12 with some modifications for easier use over the Internet.

An Example SMB Exchange

The protocol elements (requests and responses) that clients and servers exchange are called SMBs. They have a specific format that is very similar for both requests and responses. Each consists of a fixed-size header portion, followed by a variable-sized parameter and data portion.

After connecting at the NetBIOS level—either via NBF, NetBT, etc.—the client is ready to request services from the server. However, the client and server must first identify which protocol variant they each understand. The client sends a negprot SMB to the server listing the protocol dialects that it understands. The server responds with the index of the dialect that it wants to use, or 0xFFFF if none of the dialects was acceptable.

Dialects more recent than the Core and CorePlus protocols supply information in the negprot response to indicate their capabilities (max buffer size, canonical filenames, and so on). Once a protocol has been established, the client can proceed to logon to the server, if required. They do this with a sesssetupX SMB. The response indicates whether or not they have supplied a valid username password pair and, if so, can provide additional information. One of the most important aspects of the response is the UID of the logged on user. This UID must be submitted with all subsequent SMBs on that connection to the server.

Once the client has logged on (and in older protocols—Core and CorePlus—you cannot log on), the client can proceed to connect to a tree. The client sends a *tcon* or *tconX* SMB specifying the network name of the share that they wish to connect to, and if all is kosher, the server responds with a TID that the client will use in all future SMBs relating to that share.

Having connected to a tree, the client can now open a file with an open SMB, followed by reading it with read SMBs, writing it with write SMBs, and closing it with close SMBs.

NAMED PIPES

Named Pipes is an Interprocess Communication (IPC) function that provides communication service between multiple host processes. Named Pipes, another API like NetBIOS, provides layer 5 functionality. However, Named Pipes works in conjunction with NetBIOS for name resolution. Hosts that will use Named Pipes for communication are required to register with a NetBIOS name service.

Named Pipes is typically found in client/server environments and provides guaranteed, reliable session services. Its functions include creating the session, transferring data, and closing the session. Named Pipes works by forming a unique connection to another host. A Named Pipes server creates a named pipe and keeps one end of that pipe open for client connections. The unique connection is monitored and reliable packet delivery is guaranteed through a Named Pipe.

Basically, Named Pipes allows programs on one host to communicate with programs on another host. Most LANs are able to achieve this functionality through NetBIOS alone. However since Named Pipes is a higher-level API, developers can more easily implement it rather than NetBIOS. Also, Named Pipes can be a more expedient method of communication since the session is maintained through multiple transactions, better known as multithreading.

Windows NT enhances Named Pipes services through the use of an "impersonation" feature. Impersonation allows the server to assume the client's identity. In this manner, the server stands-in or proxies for the client requests. It can make requests on behalf of the client for services that the client may not have access to. By assuming the client's ID, authentication is based on the client's ID rather than the ID of the server. Although

Named Pipes is robust and easily implemented from a development standpoint, it isn't a popular service for network administrators to support.

TCP

Transmission Control Protocol/Internet Protocol (TCP/IP) is based on the Department of Defense's (DoD) four-layer network model. The TCP/IP protocols cannot be mapped one-for-one to the OSI Model. As we mentioned, layer 5 of the OSI Reference Model loosely corresponds to layers 3 and 4, the host-to-host and process/application layers of the DoD model.

Actually, TCP and UDP are both transport layer, layer 4 of the OSI Reference Model, protocols. The major functional difference between TCP and UDP is reliability. Because TCP is connection-oriented, it is a reliable delivery mechanism. Conversely, UDP is a connectionless, unreliable delivery service. The difference between the two protocols is a result of the varying uses of the DoD's layer 3, the host-to-host layer.

Transmission Control Protocol (TCP) is a reliable protocol for communications between interconnected hosts. However, the price of reliability is overhead. TCP doesn't concern itself with routing, leaving that responsibility to the Internet Protocol (IP). Like NetWare's NCP, TCP uses network addresses to identify hosts; however, it doesn't care about a host's hardware or MAC address.

The communication between TCP and a local process is referred to as a port. A port allows TCP and the local process to communicate. Many common processes have predefined port numbers assigned by the Internet Assigned numbers Authority (IANA). IANA's predefined port numbers are referred to as "well-known ports." An efficient connection method is established through the use of ports. During connection establishment, the port number and the host IP address are concatenated, forming a "socket." The creation of a socket gives the connection a unique network identifier. Upon creation of the sockets, the connection is established as a full-duplex connection via the two sockets. Sockets create an application program interface (API) for TCP, processes, and applications. The TCP header includes the following information:

▼ The Source Port field identifies the transmitting port number.

■ The Destination Port field identifies the receiving port number.

■ The Sequence Number field identifies the position of the data byte in the data stream.

■ The Acknowledgment Number identifies the expected sequence number of the next data stream.

■ The Data Offset field specifies the length of the header in 32-bit words.

■ The Control Bits Field is a referral to other fields of the header.

　　■ URG refers to the Urgent Pointer field.

　　■ ACK refers to the Acknowledgment Number field.

- ■ PSH initiates a push function.

- ■ RST forces a connection reset.

- ■ SYN synchronizes sequencing counters and is enabled when a request is made to open the connection.

- ■ FIN indicates there is no more data and that the connection should be closed.

■ The Window field specifies the number of bytes the transmitter can accept.

■ The Checksum field is an error control mechanism that provides a count of the number of bits in the transmission unit that are included with the unit. If the counts match, it's assumed that the complete transmission was received.

▲ The Urgent Pointer field is the sequence number of the frame following urgent data.

FTP, SMTP, SNMP, AND TELNET

File Transfer Protocol (FTP), Simple Mail Transfer Protocol (SMTP), Simple Network Management Protocol (SNMP), and Telnet are part of the TCP/IP protocol suite. These applications more closely map to layers 6 and 7 of the OSI Reference Model. Also, they are categorized as process/application layer protocols of the DoD model. However, some of their functionality and services are indicative of layer 5 protocols.

File Transfer Protocol (FTP)

The File Transfer Protocol (FTP) allows hosts to exchange files. Like NetWare's BMP, FTP requires client and server software components. When an FTP client establishes a connection to an FTP server, a two-socket connection, or a virtual circuit is established. Two connections, a control connection and a data connection, are used for the transmission of FTP data, which is encapsulated within a TCP header. By utilizing two connections, a differentiation between the control information and the actual data can be made, expediting the transmission. The data connection is terminated once the data has been transmitted; however, the control connection is not terminated until the client requests the session be closed.

Simple Mail Transfer Protocol (SMTP)

Simple Mail Transfer Protocol (SMTP) is the protocol that supports Internet e-mail. Most Internet e-mail systems utilize SMTP for message transmission. SMTP also requires the execution of client and server processes. SMTP transmissions utilize a 7-bit character compatible encoding format for binary data, which must be decoded on the receiving end.

Simple Network Management Protocol (SNMP)

Simple Network Management Protocol is a device management protocol. It was designed to facilitate management of equipment such as hubs, concentrators, switches, bridges, and routers. In addition to providing traffic statistics and errors, it provides a utility to configure and reset equipment. Configuration can include the establishment of triggers and thresholds for which the user wishes to be notified.

Like other protocols that span the upper layers, SNMP requires software on both ends of the connection. The client utilizes the SNMP "manager" and the server runs an SNMP "agent" process. Both the manager and agent portions of SNMP are in essence APIs that allow the formation and transmission of packets. The agent gathers information based on how it's been configured by the manager.

Telnet

Telnet, a terminal emulation protocol, is the Internet standard for remote terminal access. It is a mechanism that allows users to log in to a remote host. Like BCP, NetBIOS, and Named Pipes, Telnet requires client and server software. Telnet and telnetd are the programs required on the respective hosts. Telnet is a TCP-based service—that is, its data is encapsulated within TCP (connection-oriented) packets. Telnet uses the TCP destination port or "well-known" port of 23. Since Telnet transmissions are unencrypted, it is a very unsecured method of remote access.

A Telnet server runs a process that remains idle until it receives an inbound connection. Connections are established by execution of the client-side Telnet process. Telnet provides services for a remote host to read and write to the Telnet server and to transmit acknowledgments.

WHAT LAYER 5 TELLS YOU ABOUT YOUR NETWORK

Utilizing your NOS logs or results from protocol analyzers, you can examine the effects of layer 5 resource usage on your network. By understanding layer 5 protocols and their headers, you can determine the types of requests being made on your network. Equipped with the information you've gathered, you'll have the ability to make educated adjustments for tuning and optimizing your network. Effects of layer 5 protocols can be realized from the monitoring of your communication buffer utilization.

Communication buffer usage is affected by a variety of factors—the number of messages being sent and received by a service; if the server performs routing, the amount of traffic being routed; the number of open sockets and Sequenced Packet Protocol (SPP) connections; serial line communications and TCP connections occurring from other application layer processes.

Messages being transmitted to and from a server affect buffer usage. Part of a server's communication buffer is utilized to process a message. Once a message has been processed, the resources can be released. And since messages vary in size, resource allocation will vary. You need your communication buffers to accommodate normal and heavy load conditions.

If your LAN is experiencing noise, or during heavy traffic periods, communication buffer utilization can quickly soar. A communication buffer utilization range of 20 percent to 35 percent is acceptable for a busy server that is not too heavily loaded.

Drops are requested buffers that cannot be serviced. Drops occur when a server is unable to respond quickly enough to the messages being generated by services. An example of this would be during large file transfers, extensive searching, or numerous program executions. Additionally, if you've got a noisy LAN, the repeated requests for the server to process LAN card interrupts for bogus packets can result in drops.

Another reason drops occur is due to inadequate buffer space as a result of the server maintaining synchronous high-speed communications such as HDLC. Where possible, offload high-speed communications responsibilities to a dedicated server.

Optimally, you want to tune your server to see no more than 200 drops per 100,000 messages. If your drops exceed this recommended threshold, the problem is either a heavily loaded server or hardware problems. Review the server's hardware interface statistics to determine if there is a high error number count. A high error number count is indicative of NIC or cabling trouble. Otherwise, your server is too heavily loaded. You can remedy the problem by offloading users, increasing communication buffers, or by relocating services.

ISO TECHNICAL DOCUMENTS

The following ISO technical documents detail specifications for network operating environments:

▼ **ISO 8326**   Information Processing Systems—Open Systems Interconnection Basic Connection Oriented Session Service Definition, First Edition, 1987

■ **ISO 8326/DAD2**   Information Processing Systems—Open Systems Interconnection Basic Connection Oriented Session Service Definition Addendum 2: Incorporation of Unlimited User Data, June 1988

■ **ISO 8327**   Information Processing Systems—Open Systems Interconnection Basic Connection Oriented Session Protocol Specification, First Edition, 1987

▲ **ISO 8327/DAD2**   Information Processing Systems—Open Systems Interconnection Basic Connection Oriented Session Protocol Specification Addendum 2: Incorporation of Unlimited User Data. Systems Data Communications—Network Service Definition, First Edition, 1988

RFCS

The following *Requests for Comment* (RFCs) include detailed information on proposed standards for network operating environments:

▼ **RFC 0060**   A Simplified NCP, 1970

■ **RFC 0062**   A System for Interprocess Communication in a Resource Sharing Computer Network, 1970

■ **RFC 0091**   A Proposed User-User Protocol, 1970

■ **RFC 0129**   A Request for Comments on Socket Name Structure, 1971

■ **RFC 0793**   Transmission Control Protocol DARPA Internet Program Protocol Specification, 1981

■ **RFC 0854**   Telnet Protocol Specification, 1983

■ **RFC 0959**   File Transfer Protocol Specification, 1985

■ **RFC 1001**   Protocol Standard for a NetBIOS Service on a TCP/UDP Transport: Concepts and Methods, 1987

■ **RFC 1002**   Protocol Standard for a NetBIOS Service on a TCP/UDP Transport: Detailed Specifications, 1987

▲ **RFC 1594**   FYI on Questions and Answers, Answers to Commonly asked "New Internet User" Questions, 1994

WEB SITES

The following Web sites are good sources of information on network operating environments and standards:

▼ **http://www.iso.ch**   International Organization for Standardization

■ **http://www.ietf.org**   Internet Engineering Task Force

■ **http://www.iana.org**   Internet Assigned Numbers Authority

■ **http://www.isoc.org**   Internet Society

■ **http://www.irtf.org**   Internet Research Task Force

■ **http://www.iab.org**   Internet Architecture Board

▲ **http://www.nist.gov**   National Institute of Standards and Technology

CHAPTER 11

Managing and Monitoring Software

An essential part of planning your network infrastructure is designing and implementing methods for managing it. "Network management" is certainly a broad term, which can and does encompass everything from determining the amount of traffic on a particular segment to monitoring how an application uses memory on a network client to tracking whether certain devices are functioning properly.

In this chapter we will take a look at three very broad areas of network management and the various management systems used for each. The areas of management are

▼ Traffic management

■ Application management

▲ Device management

TRAFFIC MANAGEMENT

When most people talk about network management, they are really talking about *traffic management*. The purpose of traffic management is to determine how much of what type of data traffic is traveling over your network infrastructure at any given time. Upon determining this, you can decide whether your network infrastructure can handle that amount of traffic, and make changes in bandwidth or access method or protocol type to ensure optimum throughput.

Traffic management systems fall generally into three categories:

▼ Packet generators

■ Network analyzers

▲ Application testers

Packet Generators

Packet generators operate at the network and data-link layers of the OSI model. They load a network with "synthetic traffic." Synthetic traffic is composed of packets that the packet generator created (rather than packets from real network production traffic). These packets are sent in huge volume from a central location on the network. The goal of packet generators is to "stress-test" a network, or find its maximum traffic limits. Packet generators are able to flood a network, while normal production traffic is rarely able to do so.

The downside of packet generators is that the traffic patterns it produces aren't real. Ordinary network traffic doesn't come as fast, as constant, or as uniformly shaped and directed as the traffic produced by packet generators. Therefore, while packet generators are great for determining the maximum theoretical limits of traffic that your network can handle, they don't tell you much about how your network will perform under day-to-day traffic loads. A well-known packet generator is SmartBits from Netcom Systems, Inc.

Network Analyzers

Network analyzers monitor actual network traffic. They allow you to take a sample of traffic and analyze its content and composition. For example, if you are having slow response times on a particular segment of your network, you could place a network analyzer on that segment to monitor it for several hours—or even several days. The network analyzer would record the type of traffic (10Base-T, token ring, and so on), the network protocol (IP, IPX, router protocols, and others), how much of the available bandwidth is being used, and information about collisions, incomplete packets, and packet retransmissions. This information can help you locate "chattering" cards (cards that are malfunctioning and flooding the network with bad packets), overloaded segments, and "top talkers"—users who take up most of the network's traffic resources.

Some examples of network analyzers are Internet Advisor from Hewlett-Packard and Sniffer from Network Associates.

Application Testers

Application testers model and measure node-to-node traffic patterns from the application layer. They simulate real-world traffic associated with using specific types of distributed network applications such as databases and document preparation packages. The packages allow you to test the impact that adding a given application would have on your network so that you can plan infrastructure changes accordingly. Some examples of application testers are Chariot from Ganymede Software, Inc., and Dynameasure from Bluecurve, Inc.

APPLICATION MANAGEMENT

While traffic management devices are great for helping you locate problems and bottlenecks in the infrastructure, they don't tell you anything about the resources that are being used by network applications, nor the resulting availability and response time of those applications. This is the venue of application management systems, which have arrived fairly recently on the scene.

In fact, application management systems are so new that at the time of this writing, there are no standards for application management. Right now, application vendors are using proprietary technology to implement management and monitoring systems. For example, Oracle Corporation has enabled SNMP support for its database, and has developed its own proprietary management console. This works well in a single-vendor situation, but in reality, most enterprise environments will have multiple mission-critical applications from a variety of vendors. Each of these applications should be monitored—and a separate management system for each critical application simply isn't workable. The ideal application management product should be able to monitor a wide range of applications with an open and scalable architecture.

Therefore, the Desktop Management Task Force (DMTF) is working on developing such standards. Currently the Distributed Application Performance (DAP) working group of the DMTF has been charged with defining a standard model for the behavior of distributed applications. This model will define the runtime behavior for applications for *each unit of work*. A unit of work could be a transaction, a database query, or even an input/output event.

The stated goals of the DAP working group are as follows:

▼ Extend the core/meta schema if necessary to model runtime performance and incorporate quality of service objects.

■ Relate these models to the common schemas of the other management domains: Systems/devices, network, applications, service, support, and user.

▲ Evolve standard methods to populate the model, developed independent of operating system or performance agent availability.

For more information on the DMTF DAP working group (WG), please contact the chairperson at chair-dap@dmtf.org.

DEVICE MANAGEMENT

One of the most widespread needs in network management is to monitor devices to determine whether they are functioning properly. This is called *device management*.

Most device management packages gather information from devices by using *agents* to collect information from devices all over the network, then send it back to a centralized *management console*. At the management console, the network manager can use the information to create reports on the health of the network.

Device management systems also use agents to send alerts about trouble on the network such as device failures or performance problems. Agents reside throughout the network on servers, routers, switches, and client computers. Agents gather information about the device on which they are installed and send it back to the management console. Management console functions include network topology mapping, event reporting, traffic monitoring, network diagnostic functions, trend analysis, and report generation.

The most widely used management applications that employ agents use the Simple Network Management Protocol (SNMP). SNMP is a management protocol for TCP/IP networks. Due most likely to the UNIX roots of TCP/IP networks, most SNMP management systems are UNIX based, although Windows NT systems are becoming more popular. In any event, SNMP was developed by the Internet community, and it defines how agents and management consoles interact through request and response messaging.

Simple Network Management Protocol (SNMP)

SNMP is a communication protocol for gathering information from network devices. Each network device hosts an agent that gathers information about the performance of the device, then sends that information to a management console. Each piece of information gathered about a device is defined by a *managed object*. A managed object is a logical representation of a real physical entity on the network. Each managed object gathers some information from the device hosting it. The managed object then maintains that information for use by the management system.

All of these managed objects are organized as a management information base (MIB). A *MIB* is just a hierarchical database of managed objects. There are both generic and vendor-specific MIBs. Individual vendors must design managed objects for each piece of information they want to monitor on their devices. The vendors must provide these managed objects in the form of a MIB that adheres to SNMP standards.

How SNMP Works

Figure 11-1 shows the components of a typical SNMP management environment and how these components work together. The components are as follows:

▼ **Devices**   Network devices such as hubs, switches, and routers hosting agents that gather information about the devices and send it to the management console.

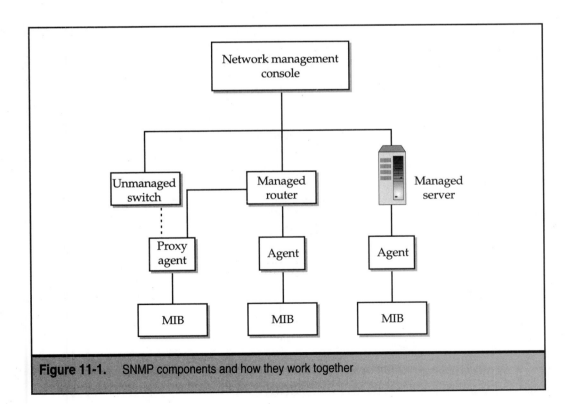

Figure 11-1.   SNMP components and how they work together

- ■ **Proxy agent**   In devices that aren't able to host an agent, a proxy agent can be run by another device on behalf of the SNMP-incapable device.

- ■ **Management systems**   The application that assembles the information gathered by agents.

- ▲ **SNMP**   The protocol that provides both the query language for gathering information from as well as the transport protocol for sending the information to the agents that run in the devices.

Most SNMP management systems discover the topology of the network automatically, then display the network topology in the form of a graphic. Administrators can choose a particular segment to view in more detail. They can then select a particular device to monitor, and view all information collected from it.

The agents running on the managed devices constantly collect information. Each agent collects only that information it is specifically charged with collecting. For example, an agent on a switch may count each packet received on each port. Collecting this information and sending it to the management system is the sole job of the SNMP agent.

Back at the central collection point, the management system continuously contacts the various agents to obtain the information they have collected. SNMP uses UPD, which is part of the TCP/IP suite, to carry its messages across the network. Because SNMP uses this connectionless transport protocol and a simple command set, it is fairly efficient and can usually operate over the busiest networks without causing noticeable stress. The agents send this information to the management system upon request.

NOTE: The management system knows only about those pieces of information listed in its management information bases for the managed object. Therefore, it's important that every time a new device is added to the network, the management system's MIBs must be updated to include all the pieces of information that the agent running on the device can collect.

SNMP Alarms

Network administrators can set alarms to alert them to device failures or other problem spots on the network. Alarms are triggered when predefined *events* occur on the network. Events occur when limits specified in MIBs are exceeded—for example, when the number of bad packets received on a switch port exceed a fixed amount. When an event occurs, the device that identifies the event "traps" the event, then sends a report to all management consoles.

SNMP is simple, robust, and—most important—it does its job well. However, it's not without its shortcomings. For example, an SNMP management console constantly polls agents to gather information. This increases both the network traffic and the management console.

RMON to the Rescue

To alleviate some of this stress, the Internet Engineering Task Force developed RMON to let agents collect information only about their own network segments. Actually, RMON is a MIB extension that collects information about entire network segments rather than just about individual devices.

Like SNMP, RMON uses agents, called *probes*, which are software processes—running on devices—that collect data. However, with RMON, the collected information is stored in a local MIB rather than at the central management console.

Figure 11-2 shows how this works. Probes located in network devices such as hubs and switches collect and maintain historical information in a MIB located on the same segment as the device. The network management console does not need to constantly poll probes and receive information from them to ensure that historical management information is properly collected. In fact, in RMON, the relationship between probes and the management console is reversed. The probes function as servers and the management console acts as a client in a client/server relationship.

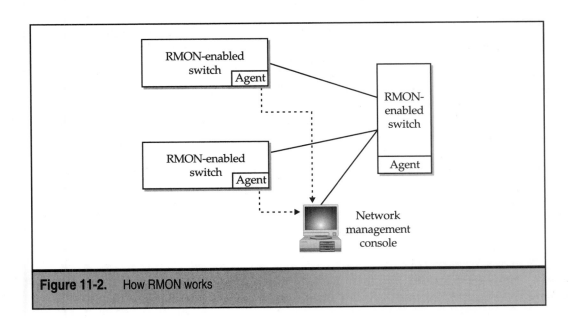

Figure 11-2.   How RMON works

Just like SNMP, RMON can send alarms when events occur. When a manager receives an alarm, she or he can assess network conditions by analyzing the information provided in the nine RMON *groups*:

- ▼ **Statistics**   Gathers and maintains traffic statistics and errors
- ■ **History**   Collects statistics at specified intervals for historical analysis
- ■ **Alarms**   Sends alerts when events occur
- ■ **Hosts**   Gathers information and calculates statistics based on MAC addresses
- ■ **HostTopN**   Gathers data about which hosts are generating the most traffic
- ■ **Matrix**   Gathers data about which devices are communicating with each other
- ■ **Events**   Triggers actions based on alarms
- ■ **Packet capture**   Lets you capture packets by type
- ▲ **Filter**   Lets you view only selected packets

For example, a manager receives an alarm about excessive traffic. The manager could then collect information from the HostTopN and Matrix groups to find out which nodes are transmitting the most information and to whom they are talking. Once the busiest transmitters are located, the manager can analyze traffic from those transmitters to see whether there are errors—indicating a device that needs to be repaired—or whether more bandwidth can be added to that segment to accommodate the traffic.

RMON is not a replacement for SNMP, but rather an extension of it. SNMP, via UDP, still provides the communication mechanism for transmitting data from the RMON probes to the management consoles.

Basing RMON's architecture on that of network analyzers, the IETF's goal in developing the RMON standard was to allow open monitoring of all networks from any vendor's network management system. It also provides network analyzer functionality on remote networks. For example, RMON also supports packet filtering and capturing on specific network segments. It also lets network managers remotely analyze traffic at all seven layers of the protocol stack. This means that running RMON on a remote network will obviate traveling to a network site to attach a network analyzer.

Son of RMON: Merging with Application Management

At the time of this writing, the current RMON RFC is 1757. This RFC was released in 1995, which means that an update is both inevitable and imminent.

The current RMON RFC has two Ethernet-specific monitoring groups and seven monitoring groups that apply to both token ring and Ethernet. The next RMON standard is RFC 1513, which defines additional token ring extensions. In addition, RMON 2 provides monitoring support all the way up to the application layer. It will allow managers to monitor the amount of traffic that is generated by applications running in workstations and servers. This should be a big boost to the application management initiative, because it gives information about the actual usage of the network, not just traffic flows. RMON 2 will also provide information about end-to-end traffic flows.

Evolving SNMP

Nothing stays the same, and SNMP is no exception. The IETF began work on SNMPv2 in 1992. The goal of the next incarnation of SNMP was better security, enhanced management features, and more efficient information retrieval. Unfortunately, the developers of SNMPv2 soon found that adding security would make it incompatible with the original SNMP. As a result, SNMPv2 development ground to a halt, and the IETF disbanded the SNMPv2 group in 1996. Later, however, the SNMP revision group reemerged and development soon began on SNMPv3.

While a new official version of SNMP was trying to develop, a trend emerged that used the HTTP protocol to transport management information, making each managed device a Web server of sorts. This makes management information available via Web browsers modified to function as management consoles. This takes us into the world of *web-based network management*.

Web-Based Network Management

As mentioned above, Web-based network management lets network managers monitor their networks using Web technologies like browsers and HTTP. It lets administrators monitor devices remotely, in real time, and collect information about systems. It also lets them troubleshoot systems and create reports about network problems or trends. Web-based network management uses the TCP/IP protocols, which is the coin of the realm on the Internet and corporate intranets. Therefore, the same Web management tools can be used to manage a switch in the same room or anywhere in the world via the worldwide Internet. This trend is becoming so popular that many vendors of network management systems have already added Web browser interfaces to their management systems.

Web-Based Enterprise Management (WBEM)

In July of 1996, five companies formed the Web-Based Enterprise Management (WBEM) Consortium with the express goal of integrating disparate management protocols, management information, and management systems. The five companies are

▼ BMC Software

■ Cisco Systems

■ Microsoft

■ Intel

▲ Compaq

While WBEM was founded by these five companies, its initiative is now supported by over 50 vendors.

So, what is the WBEM initiative all about? While SNMP is still the most widely used management protocol, WBEM would like to see new Internet standards such as Hypermedia Management Protocol (HMMP) and Common Information Model (CIM) take the forefront in network management. The HMMP advantage, says the WBEM Consortium, is that it lets network management system vendors build systems that use all the same protocols and provide access through the same user interface. As well, the WBEM Consortium is interested in developing a common data structure to facilitate easier, more uniform access to corporate data.

HYPERMEDIA MANAGEMENT PROTOCOL (HMMP)   Hypermedia Management Protocol (HMMP) is an Internet protocol used to access and publish data across the Internet, as well as to exchange management and control messages between HMMP nodes. As a client/server protocol, it is similar to Hypertext Transfer Protocol (HTTP). HMMP clients request data from HMMP servers. However, unlike HTTP, HMMP clients can be management processes running in standard Web browsers or management and monitoring processes hosted by managed devices.

When HMMP servers receive requests from clients, they either respond to those requests with information or pass the request on to another server. In the latter instance, the requesting server is now a client of the server to which it is passing the request. As you can see, HMMP doesn't require that every client know how to manage every device it needs to use directly. Instead, clients can make requests to servers that manage groups of devices. The devices it manages may in fact use proprietary management mechanisms and protocols unknown to the client. This doesn't affect the client making the request, because the servers always respond to the clients' requests for information using HMMP.

COMMON INFORMATION MODEL (CIM)   Common Information Model (CIM) is also part of the WBEM initiative. CIM is a data structure that uses HMMP to access and manipulate data held by HMMP management hosts. The CIM structure is a set of standard classes and types that represent hardware devices and other such managed objects in the network management environment.

Where Is WBEM?

WBEM really hadn't made much headway at the time of this writing. Two years after its inception, the WBEM Consortium was still developing its initiatives and garnering support for them. Will WBEM ever become the Internet-wide force for uniform management that its founders hoped? That remains to be seen.

Java Management API

As an alternative to WBEM, Sun Microsystems and some 15 other companies developed and presented the Java Management API (JMAPI). JMAPI is an environment for developing Web-based management applications using the Java programming language. JMAPI uses a simple ODBC database to store collected management information. To access and analyze the management data, developers can write applets that will run on any system that has a Java-enabled operating system. Any Java-enabled browser can then access the management information. It supports SNMP, so JMAPI applications can access information collected by SNMP agents.

While JMAPI sounds like an elegant and much-needed solution for IP network management, we're not sure that it will ultimately succeed. Unfortunately, at the time of this writing we haven't seen any JMAPI applications, so it is difficult to know whether this far-reaching solution will actually take hold.

MANAGEMENT PLATFORMS

All of the various types of network management systems we have discussed represent a substantial investment in money, time, and staff—so much of an investment, in fact, that running separate management systems for each type of system is prohibitively expensive. With limited resources, you may feel you must select which one of the management systems to implement, and therefore have to choose which of the types of systems is most crucial to your network.

Fortunately, this isn't the case. All of these systems can be integrated into one of several comprehensive network management platforms that act as a framework for building, operating, and—yes—*managing* network management systems. The six major network management platforms are listed in Table 11-1, along with the Web site addresses of the manufacturers.

The networking world refers to these products as "platforms" because they have extensive features, they can manage entire enterprise networks, and they have the ability to manage other network management systems.

Company	Product	URL
Cabletron	Spectrum	ctron.com/spectrum
Computer Associates	Unicenter TNG	cai.com/products.htm
Hewlett-Packard	OpenView	hp.com/openview
Microsoft	Systems Management Server	microsoft.com/smsmgmt
Novell	ManageWise	novell.com/managewise
Sun Microsystems	Solstice	sun.com/solstice

Table 11-1.   Network Management Tools

IETF NETWORK MANAGEMENT DEVELOPMENTS

As you may have guessed from the preceding sections, the most influential standards body in developing management system standards is the Internet Engineering Task Force. The IETF has a number of working groups that are developing methods for using SNMP and other protocols to access management information for a wide variety of devices on intranets and the Internet. Its primary goal is to advance management initiatives for Web servers and the HTTP MIB, but the IETF also—at least officially—states an interest in expanding its standards work to include many other devices.

To keep abreast of the IETF and its many RFCs (Requests for Comment) related to network management, check out the IETF Web site at http://www.ietf.org/html.charters/wg-dir.html.

CHAPTER 12

Security

Ever since a young Matthew Broderick fired up an old TRS-80 Model I in 1983's *WarGames*, a misguided paranoia has reigned supreme over the world that malicious hackers (sometimes called crackers) are out to destroy every computer in existence. The hacker witch-hunts began in earnest in 1990 with Operation Sundevil, a nationwide crackdown on illicit computer activity. Computer hacking was in the doldrums for a few years after that, but when the Internet became a phenomenon in the mid-1990s, a new wave of computer hackers took the stage.

Hackers are out there. But should you be concerned? The truth is that, while so-called "dark side" hackers do exist, the incidence of electronic break-ins from unknown outsiders is relatively small, provided we're not talking about government or telco computers, which are still the Holy Grail for teenage prowlers. Provided you are running an average business with no exciting video games under development or controversial fur coats for sale, your primary concern should be protecting your network against hostile acts by people already inside your system.

Whether it's an angry person with a grudge against the CEO or a simple, honest accident, someone who already has access to the system—electronically and/or physically—represents a much greater risk to your network security. Still, the risk of a malicious break-in from the outside is a real one, and you should take measures to protect your networks by using the tools outlined in this chapter.

SOFTWARE VS. HARDWARE SECURITY

The debate will probably never end over whether you should implement security in hardware (such as having a firewall implemented in a router) or software (using an application to filter IP packets for you). While hardware implementations of just about any security product are generally considered more secure, their software counterparts are cheaper—and are often easier to configure properly.

Fortunately, software security products are getting better and better, particularly those written for the Windows NT platform. Hardware products are also harder to come by, and unless you're a large company with a number of far-flung sites, they often don't justify their expense. Further, most hardware security products are only available through VARs, who also perform the installation and maintenance of the units (at even greater cost). For smaller outfits, this is even more unrealistic.

Ultimately, the decision is yours to make. Because the majority of you will probably lean toward implementing at least part of your security solution in software, though, we have focused this chapter on the security applications you'll want to examine, with briefer coverage of hardware security solutions.

HOW SECURE IS YOUR OPERATING SYSTEM?

You wonder how secure your operating system is? Not very.

Put simply, the PC was never meant to be a secure computing platform. In the old days, if you needed security, you got the biggest iron you could afford and locked it behind three levels of steel doors. In today's computing environment, information has to be widely distributed, and a locked-up resource is essentially useless. Data has to be available to everyone who needs it, and those people may not be in the same building, or even the same country. Of course, the problem is that there are competitors and criminals out there who would love to get their hands on your data as well, and there's not really an operating system that's been built to withstand their attacks.

The Big Three network operating systems (Microsoft Windows NT, Novell NetWare, and UNIX) are all the equivalent of Swiss cheese when it comes to counting security holes. UNIX has problems because, as an open system, source code for most of its flavors is freely available to everyone. This makes poking around for holes much easier than in closed environments, which must be hacked through trial and error. Also, UNIX exists in many different versions and each has its own flaws, which in turn compounds the sheer number of security bugs. And let's not forget that UNIX has been around for decades, and some UNIX installations out there are still running 20-year-old versions of the operating system, some of which are completely insecure systems that are accessible through a simple Telnet session.

Microsoft's Windows NT platform has been plagued by a mountain of security problems, and the company releases patch after patch in the hopes of finally resolving the issue. It doesn't seem likely that Windows will ever be a completely secure computing platform, though, and most systems out there aren't running the latest patches in any event. The problem is that security has always been an afterthought at Microsoft, and the company has some catching up to do.

Novell NetWare is moderately secure, but each version has some well-known holes that experienced hackers can penetrate. Of course, NetWare has a lesser presence on Internet-connected machines because of its devotion to IPX/SPX as a primary protocol, so the main threat to your NetWare servers is the internal one.

Microsoft

It's safe to say that from Microsoft's humble beginnings with MS-DOS, the company could never have expected to be a leader in network operating systems. While Windows NT has been a phenomenal success for the company, Microsoft finds itself embroiled in the same problems that have plagued it for years: Its operating systems aren't secure.

While DOS has absolutely no security measures built in to it, the company's first windowing software package, Windows for Workgroups 3.11 (in its final incarnation) was little more than a GUI that helped you work with DOS. As a result, WfW is almost as unsecure as DOS is, the only safeguards being basic password protection. Each encrypted password is stored separately with a .PWL extension, and all any half-witted hacker has to do in order to beat this security is simply delete the file, which otherwise has no security associated with it. If that's too brutish, the hacker can always resort to a widely available utility like Glide to crack the password file.

Microsoft tried for security again with Windows 95, and while its scheme for managing user profiles and their associated passwords was clever, it is still essentially an unsecure OS. All hackers have to do to bypass Windows 95 security is boot into DOS or Safe Mode. The former gives them complete file access; the latter does the same, plus allows them to hack the registry and basically do whatever they please.

The only real solution to fix the problem is a third-party encryption tool and/or a utility that radically interferes with the system at boot time—refusing to boot from floppy and so on. If this seems a bit extreme, that's because it is. But it is the unfortunate price that must be paid if you really want security on a Windows machine.

Windows NT was built for networking, and by the mid-1990s Microsoft had apparently worked out some of its security bugs. With a base NT system, there is no DOS, and there is no Safe Mode. There's no inherent way to bypass the login, although a malicious hacker who has physical access could easily reformat your system from scratch—a problem inherent to virtually every known OS.

But even with a DOS boot disk, a hacker will be stumped by the Windows NTFS file system, which is incompatible with DOS. Then again, with a free utility called NTFSDOS, a DOS boot disk can become a tool to let you browse any NTFS-formatted drive, although the authors wisely disabled file copying and deletion from the utility's feature set.

As with any OS, it is critical to stay abreast of the service packs and security patches that Microsoft releases in response to security hole discoveries. Proper use of NT's permission features is also key, and again, encryption tools will help defeat any boot utility, but they may also frustrate the users who need access to those files. As an administrator, you have to be disciplined and knowledgeable to use these security tools, and, as always, physical security is imperative.

The proper implementation of a firewall and the frequent use of intrusion detection tools (both are discussed later in this chapter) can both be lifesavers.

Novell

As stated earlier, Novell NetWare has always had fairly good security, especially against attacks coming in over the wire. But as with any NOS, the internal attack is the one you must fear the most, and it's especially true with NetWare.

A savvy hacker inside your company can easily compromise security by intentionally corrupting the bindery on NetWare 3.x systems, thus causing all password information to be automatically rebuilt from scratch, including default Supervisor passwords. Also, on older systems, the loading of hostile NLMs from the server console can open the door to outsiders.

Possibly of greatest importance, plain old bad security practices can be an enormous problem, and NetWare has plenty of nooks and crannies where key passphrases are often hard-coded in clear text. (Be sure to check any and all scripts for them!)

Finally, the various NetWare NOSs have been the subject of a great many password-cracking utilities, and there are probably more available for the Novell environment than for any other platform. Again, it is highly advisable to seek out a definitive reference on security software and patches specific to your NetWare OS version.

UNIX

Finally, we come to the grandfather of all insecure operating systems, where tales of bad security begin and end.

UNIX probably gets a worse rap than it deserves because of its widespread use (along with DEC's VAX/VMS) in academic installations, which during the 1970s and 1980s were widely known as the path of least resistance for any aspiring hacker. A university is supposed to spread knowledge by letting people in, not locking people out, right?

Unfortunately, at the time, most universities were connected to the ARPANET, the infant version of today's Internet that was spawned from the U.S. military network. It doesn't take a genius to figure out the best way into classified military systems is through the wide-open college down the street.

Many colleges of the day were not overly concerned about, or even aware of, the hackers' presence. Even when hackers were caught, they were usually released with little more than a warning. For years, the university scene was literally crawling with hackers trying every trick in the book to break into military systems.

It all seemed harmless enough until 1988, when systems admin Clifford Stoll discovered an intruder hacking military systems through his network at a research lab under the University of California at Berkeley. After months of tirelessly tracking him, an enormous conspiracy was revealed, involving a German hacker who was working under the payroll of the KGB. The world was stunned.

Stoll's network ran UNIX. After all, Berkeley *made* UNIX. At least one version, anyway, and BSD UNIX from Berkeley Software Distributions remains a widely implemented version of the OS. If Berkeley can't keep people from playing in its own backyard, what hope do you have?

Okay, it's not that bad. But the existence of many flavors of UNIX means there are that many more security holes to worry about. Some are the same from version to version, such as the grand history of decrypting unprotected (or unshadowed) password files by brute force dictionary attacks. There is also the peril of buggy or insecure remote services like rlogin and rsh. Essentially every Internet protocol or service on UNIX OSes has been painfully broken at one time or another. Even holes in the innocuous finger utility could let an intruder wreak all kinds of havoc.

UNIX is an open operating system, meaning the source code is freely available to all takers. This makes it an even simpler matter to seek out and exploit security bugs like the ones outlined above. Then again, as a side note, having a closed system does not necessarily make it any more secure. VMS was Digital's prized OS, and a totally closed one, yet the tales of hacking VAX systems are as common as UNIX hacks. In fact, one widely publicized break-in was against DEC itself, when hackers (reportedly, Kevin Mitnick and co.) actually made off with the VMS source code itself, suddenly making VMS a very open system whether DEC liked it or not. As one DEC security memo put it, "When sources are outlawed, only outlaws will have sources." Clearly, the debate over security and open-source computing has no easy resolution.

You could write an entire book about UNIX security alone, and, indeed, many have. Put simply, if you have any illusions of using a UNIX server to connect to the Internet or any remote access service, you absolutely have to know what you're doing. The cryptic innards of the OS will not be any help, and you'll absolutely need a dedicated security manual, and probably a consultant, specific to your chosen UNIX flavor.

FIREWALLS

In November 1996, the Web site for Kriegsman Furs was hacked by a group of animal rights activists, unhappy with the company's line of business. Instead of the usual home page, visitors were greeted with a manifesto and links to animal rights pages. The official site for the movie *Hackers* was hacked immediately after the film opened, by a group of hackers who didn't much care for the picture. MGM was so impressed it even archived the hacked page on its site.

Nethosting Corp., a Web page hosting service, had its page hacked shortly after the Kriegsman incident . . . along with all 1,500 of its clients' pages, all in one day. Virtually every government home page has been hacked at one point or another, and when Telia (Sweden's biggest telecommunications company) had its Web site hacked, it went on public radio to announce that its security problems had been fixed. It was hacked again the very same day.

These organizations have nothing in common except that their Internet security was vulnerable. And while many hackers posture that no site is completely secure, having a solid firewall is the best first line of defense.

Types of Internet Attacks

By the time you read this, there will probably be a dozen new varieties of Internet attacks that have yet to be conceived. Staying abreast of the latest trends and techniques is almost a full-time job, but being familiar with the current hacker MOs is well worth a little research.

The Front Door

By far, the most common attack for computer networks is intruders coming through the front door. Whether they are curious kids, disgruntled employees, malicious hackers, or foreign spies, they will take advantage of weak and/or default passwords to gain admittance to your network. All it takes is one unprotected guest account to pave the way for all kinds of havoc, from altering your Web site to stealing confidential files to permanently deleting information.

The best way to combat this is proactively: Make sure your users change their passwords regularly, and set strict limits on password length and composition. Delete guest and other default accounts as soon as the server is out of the box. Finally, a number of intrusion detection tools (discussed later) will help you analyze overall password strength.

Denial of Service

The Denial of Service (DoS) attack really came into the public eye on November 2, 1988, when Robert T. Morris's infamous Internet worm, the elder grandmaster of DoS hacks, was unleashed over the infant network. (The worm exploited a hole in, of all things, BSD UNIX, but that's another story.)

The RTM worm didn't really *do* anything; it just copied itself over and over to as many machines as it could find. Allegedly, Morris didn't intend for the worm to go as obscenely out of control as it inevitably did, but in the end, thousands of systems were rendered inoperable. The little stunt eventually earned Morris a felony conviction.

Fortunately today, the DoS attack is one of the less prevalent forms of malice on the Internet (because it is not very elegant and can be recovered from quickly), but it's also one of the easiest hacks to pull off. DoS is simply the disruption of your ability to use your computer or your network.

A DoS attack can take a variety of forms. (See Figure 12-1.) Mail bomb attacks (a particularly noisome one involves signing the user up on an endless number of Internet mailing lists) were probably the first incarnation of DoS on the Net, the electronic version of the crank phone call. Programs like Up Yours, Avalanche, and Unabomber make mail bombing simple.

So-called SYN flooding, which takes advantage of a weakness in the TCP three-way handshake, essentially prevents any clients from making a successful connection to the target server. This effect ends whenever the hacker breaks off the attack. DNS attacks, the fabled "Ping of Death," the Solaris suicidal ping, and numerous other techniques allow a malicious hacker to either busy-out a networked computer or crash it altogether.

The Computer Emergency Response Team (CERT) is a well-known central repository for up-to-the-moment information on security breaches and viruses. They also have a popular security mailing list you can subscribe to. You can visit its Web site at www.cert.org.

If you prefer your security information from the other side of the fence, check out Hackers.Com at www.hackers.com.

More Sophisticated Attacks

The more high-profile cases involve hackers who manipulate NOS holes (mainly in UNIX and VAX/VMS, as described earlier) to gain root, or supervisor, access to your network. For example, Windows NT was once vulnerable to "man in the middle" attacks, where clear text passwords could be captured during transmission.

Other advanced hacks include manipulation of data at the packet level: IP spoofing is the best example of this. Unlike the first two types of attacks, these hacks are extremely difficult to pull off, and they require advanced knowledge about the OS in question, or, at least, an experienced teacher. The details are beyond the scope of this book, but many advanced security texts will give you the full story.

If you discover signs of tampering with your OS, your best bet is to bring in a savvy computer security consultant, because your problem is likely quite severe. Of course, it's best to protect yourself before the problem gets that bad, and here's how.

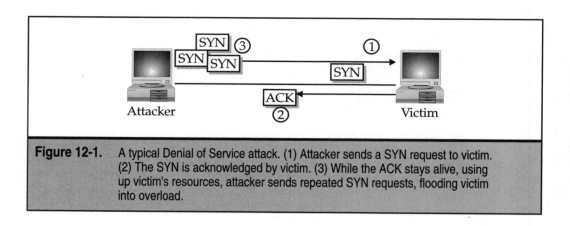

Figure 12-1. A typical Denial of Service attack. (1) Attacker sends a SYN request to victim. (2) The SYN is acknowledged by victim. (3) While the ACK stays alive, using up victim's resources, attacker sends repeated SYN requests, flooding victim into overload.

How Firewalls Work

The Internet firewall is probably the first and best line of security in protecting your network from intruders. Firewalls work as a gateway through which all traffic must pass while going between the Internet and your network. This can be a hardware device that sits between your LAN and the Internet or any of a dozen other configurations in hardware and/or software, several of which are outlined below. They all have the common goal of filtering data packets to determine whether or not they can pass through the firewall. Firewalls are also generally able to log activity and provide some degree of monitoring on the status of the system.

Most firewall products also include Network Address Translation (NAT) services, which let you assign IP addresses from a different subnet to your LAN than you use for the firewall itself. The idea is that the IP addresses on the other side of the firewall remain a mystery to those on the outside, and since these IP addresses are usually invalid on the Internet anyway (in the 192.168.xxx.xxx range), the inside of your firewall is theoretically invisible. Bear in mind that NAT services traditionally put a heavy burden on the firewall, and performance will often be seriously hampered if they are implemented.

Some firewalls are also configurable to include proxy services, which run dangerous Internet services on the behalf of client machines, forwarding the requests and responses back and forth. This way, the proxy server runs the risk of malicious TCP attacks instead of the client, something like a sacrificial lamb for the LAN. Packet filters and proxy servers both have substantial advantages and disadvantages, but both are useful in preventing unauthorized entry to your LAN. (Be aware, however, that proxy services require some configuration on the client side, and an above average user will quickly learn how to bypass your proxy server unless more stringent security measures are taken.)

On the other hand, firewalls cannot protect you from malicious intruders who have obtained access by coming in the front door, as described earlier, or by careless or angry employees who have legitimate access. A firewall is also not an antivirus device, although implementations are popping up that attempt to address both of the above threats in addition to doing packet filtering.

The way a standard firewall works is very simple. You can think of it as an electronic hall monitor: No data gets by without being examined by the firewall, packet by packet. And the firewall can be as strict (no inbound traffic allowed at all) or as loose (only marginal impositions on traffic) as the administrator would like. Packets can be filtered based on inbound/outbound status, source IP address, destination IP address, TCP type, and port number. Depending on your familiarity with the intricacies of TCP/IP, this can get pretty complex, fast. While a properly configured packet filter can offer comfortable security, enterprising hackers are always finding loopholes that administrators have overlooked.

Today's firewalls bristle with advanced configuration options, remote management and deployment strategies, detailed logging features, and continual improvements in security and performance. But in the end, the bottom line is simple: The firewall keeps potentially hostile traffic out of your LAN.

Router-Based Firewalls

The simplest firewall architecture involves a router that sits between your LAN and the Internet, and serves as the only gateway between the two. Cisco, Ascend, and many other vendors equip their hardware with the ability to filter packets instead of simply routing them, if you so desire. While this is an elegant way to protect your LAN, it often involves working with complex configuration utilities.

Another version of a router-based firewall is the use of a proprietary OS on your host machine that has firewall-type services built in. With these OSes, you simply specify which IP addresses the host will accept a connection from. If the incoming IP is out of that range, the connection is denied.

Depending on the size of your network, a router doesn't necessarily have to be sold to you as such. You can use a converted PC, loaded with routing software and a packet filter application, to do the work instead. The problem with this is the operating system security, as outlined above. For simplicity's sake, we assume you're using a dedicated router in the following examples, as shown in Figure 12-2.

Dual-Homed Hosts

Very similar in design to the router-based firewall is the dual-homed host. Put simply, a dual-homed host is a computer with two network connections: one to the Internet and one to your LAN. It is not possible for traffic to pass directly between the two; it must go through the dual-homed host.

It's up to the administrator how much traffic to allow through, and the only way it can provide connectivity services is by proxying them. For example, an HTTP request to view a Web site is sent by a user to the dual-homed host. The host examines the request to determine if it is acceptable, then resends the request to the Internet. When a response is returned, the host resends this data on to the client that requested it. In the client's eyes (in theory, anyway), the proxy server is invisible; as far as the user can tell, the information

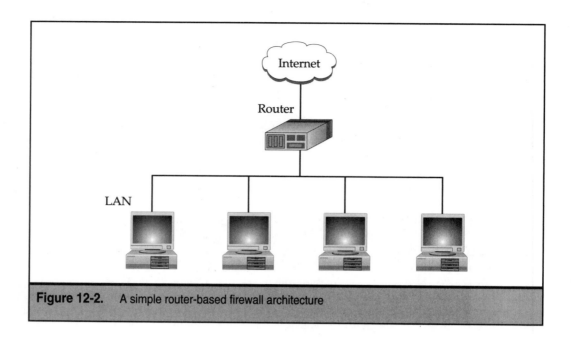

Figure 12-2.   A simple router-based firewall architecture

was sent directly to and from the Internet. Unfortunately, because of the Web's popularity, a dozen simultaneous users can quickly overpower a low-end proxy server, making the "seamlessness" of the process something less than perfect. Also, the dual-homed host architecture, as shown in Figure 12-3, is limited in its range of features; for the provision of new and untrusted services, you will need to look at one of the following architectures.

Bastion Hosts

A bastion host architecture is something of a combination of the two previous architectures. Sometimes called a "screened host architecture," the bastion host architecture has a screening router as the only pipeline to the Internet, backed up by a machine (the bastion host) that sits on your LAN to provide needed services.

The router is set up to allow connections only to and from the bastion host; clients on the LAN cannot see through it (although this can be modified at the administrator's judgement); Internet hosts cannot see any other systems on your LAN aside from the bastion host. The bastion host again serves as a proxy for any services that you wish to deny direct access to.

This configuration gives you the best of both worlds: the added security of a bastion host plus the extensibility of a router-based firewall, as shown in Figure 12-4.

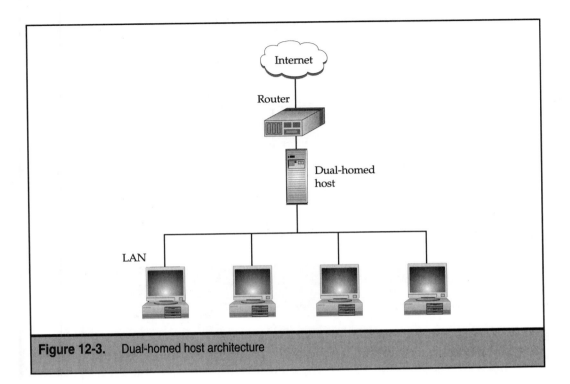

Figure 12-3.   Dual-homed host architecture

Multiple Router Configurations

Firewall configurations can become more and more complex by adding more and more routers to the system (often called a "screened subnet" architecture). The idea is that each router between the Internet and the LAN is set to be progressively more secure. (Each segment between two routers is referred to as a perimeter network.) This way, a hacker who gets past one router will have a more difficult time with the next. (The hope is that he or she will eventually give up.) Figure 12-5 shows the simplest configuration, involving two routers.

Configurations like this can take on dozens of forms, and, obviously, the more complex the system becomes, the easier it becomes to misconfigure. There is also, as always, the ever-increasing cost to consider. If you are this concerned with your security, your best bet—and probably your only bet—is to call in a seasoned security professional to do the dirty work.

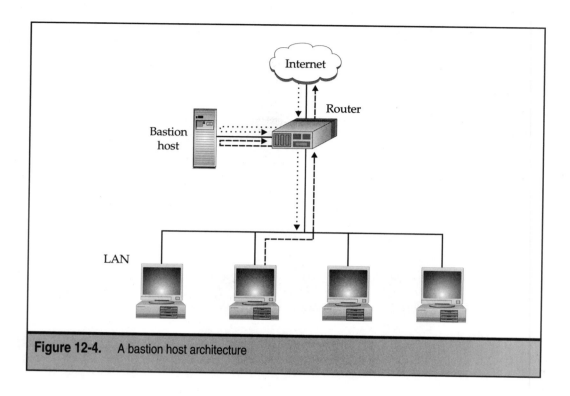

Figure 12-4.   A bastion host architecture

The Pack

There are over 40 firewall products on the market today, and choosing one for your enterprise can be a mind-boggling affair. The unavowed leader of the firewall pack is Check Point's Firewall-1, long established as an industry leader (but also subject to much criticism in Usenet debates). NetGuard's Guardian, Cyberguard's Cyberguard Firewall, DEC's AltaVista Firewall, Microsoft's Proxy Server, and Watchguard's Firebox are all also well known in the industry. Cisco, IBM, and AXENT also make solid firewalls.

Universally, firewall products are getting better and better, and they are also starting to offer added services, like VPN integration, S/MIME features, Java and ActiveX security, antivirus protection, and more. For example, BGP-4 (Border Gateway Protocol 4) is an emerging router protocol that provides information about the security of remote hosts. Keep an eye open; this long-established market is still far from maturity.

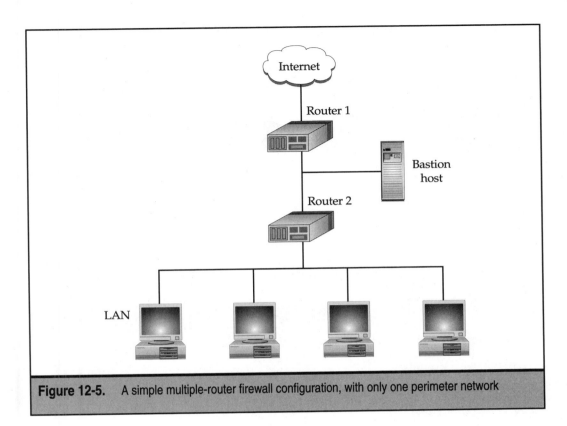

Figure 12-5. A simple multiple-router firewall configuration, with only one perimeter network

CRYPTOGRAPHY

Secrecy is key to just about every business.

The problem with putting your business on the Web is that the Internet is a cold and impersonal place. Dealing with another company or another person is largely a function of trusting they are who they claim to be, and without security, any information you transmit over the Net is an open book.

Authentication and Encryption

The Internet is probably the most appealing place to do business you can imagine. Its reach is worldwide, startup costs are very low, and there is virtually no regulation.

Unfortunately, the Internet has at its roots a military and research network, not the type of computers that lend themselves to transacting business. In the very early days of the Net—if you had access to it at all—you automatically had full access to virtually any machine you could reach, with the exception of a few classified military computers. There were no differing levels of privilege, and access rights were either all or nothing. Adding to that, the IP protocol has no built-in security features at all (although IPv6 promises to change that). Security wasn't even an afterthought; it wasn't a thought at all.

Those days are over. The Internet isn't only attractive to legitimate businesses. It's just as attractive to more nefarious sorts who hope to make a quick buck off of unsuspecting Net surfers. For example, the real problem with spam e-mail isn't just that it's a nuisance, it's that it is also usually filled with any number of get-rich-quick scams, pyramid schemes, and outright frauds that less-seasoned Internet users may not be wise to. This problem has been enough to scare off a large part of the potential e-commerce market, and it will be an uphill road to bring those potential buyers back.

The central dilemma is: Who can you trust? On the Internet, there are no photo IDs, no physical credit cards, no fingerprints, and no face to put a name to. The solution can be found in cryptography.

Cryptography goes a long way toward curing the problems of Internet anonymity and data snooping. The basic goal of cryptography is helping you, the user, decide who you can and cannot trust, and providing a means for trusted parties to communicate. This is done through the use of authentication and encryption tools.

We'll discuss authentication in depth in Chapter 23. Chapter 22 will expand upon those ideas and delve further into the topic of encryption.

Virtual Private Networks

The next generation of cryptography tools goes beyond simple user-to-user or buyer-to-merchant authentication and encryption. Many companies are now adopting virtual private networks, or VPNs, as a way to use the Internet as a replacement to expensive leased lines for internal communications. (VPN technology is occasionally referred to as "IPSec support" or "IP Encapsulating Security Payload (ESP) support," but the ultimate meaning is essentially the same.)

Leased lines are as secure as they come; they offer, in effect, a two-way communications pipe that cannot be breached (at least, not without some extremely complicated computer hacking). The Internet offers no such promises. It's a wild no-man's-land, and if you want to use the Net for something beyond simple e-mail, you better start thinking about securing your data in transit.

A VPN provides a secure tunnel from one physical site to another, or from your headquarters to your remote users. VPNs can be implemented in hardware or software, the former being a much pricier option, but one that promises better security and, especially, performance. Either way, a VPN allows you to use the Internet as a secure communications conduit, while eliminating the expense and configuration problems of leased lines.

We will discuss VPNs in detail in Chapter 24.

SECURE MESSAGING

Never mind the Web; some 80 percent of all Internet traffic is in the form of simple e-mail. For almost every business and any technologically savvy individual, electronic messaging is more than just a tool, it's a lifeline to the world. In fact, for many of us, e-mail is the de facto preferred method of communication, as its flexibility, archiving features, ability to be easily shared or forwarded, and universal reach combine to make e-mail easier than a fax machine and less intrusive than a telephone.

Of course, there's a catch. Unless you're using a VPN and are not communicating with the outside world at all, all of that Internet traffic is sent in clear text, easily intercepted and decoded. While you can probably trust the administrators of the four to ten links a typical e-mail message passes through from sender to receiver, if you want your e-mail to be even remotely secure from tampering, you need to implement an authentication and/or encryption strategy.

PGP

PGP, or Pretty Good Privacy, was the first messaging encryption utility, and it is still quite popular today. PGP was developed in 1991 by Phil R. Zimmerman as a form of protest to a then-pending crime bill that would have legislated that all encryption products contain a "trap door" to allow easy decryption by the government. (The bill did not pass, although so-called "key escrow" is still a hot debate topic.)

PGP enjoyed a lively and colorful history. It was spread through underground bulletin board systems by ultraparanoid computer and civil rights enthusiasts. It was the subject of a near-lawsuit from RSA, which claimed patent infringement. It roused the ire of the U.S. government when it was illegally exported, and almost got Zimmerman indicted under International Traffic in Arms Regulations violations. MIT eventually took over its distribution, and Zimmerman also formed a company around PGP called, of all things, PGP Inc. (PGP Inc. has since been acquired by Network Associates.)

Contrary to what you may have heard and what many people believe, PGP is perfectly legal and is now free of any patent uncertainties, provided you use the proper version (depending on whether you are inside or outside the United States). It is widely available in both freeware and commercial versions.

How PGP Works

Until recently, PGP has been strictly a client-side affair. You install PGP software on your machine or on the machines of your network users who need secure e-mail. The PGP utility works as a simple plug-in for several popular e-mail packages. The recipient must also have PGP installed in order to decode the encrypted message.

PGP is a simple form of public key cryptography, as described in Chapters 3 and detailed in Chapters 22 and 23. To exchange secure e-mail, you obtain the public, or asymmetric, key of your intended recipient. You use that key as the code to encrypt the message. When she receives it, she uses her private, or symmetric, key, which is safely stored on her machine and is protected by a passphrase, to decrypt it. It may sound simple and insecure, but the billions of key permutations make brute-force attacks on decrypting an encoded message nearly impossible, provided the private key length is long enough. (Currently, 128 bits is the accepted "unbreakable" private key length.)

This is what an actual PGP public key looks like:

```
-----BEGIN PGP PUBLIC KEY BLOCK-----
Version: PGP for Personal Privacy 5.0

mQGiBDNJc8URBADySyB/T3Kfcq2+Ee1uv85xnSx1I13TfOhMTeeIhwSNXE4aY/Yr
Fmu8kpc41GxmaO8xmKeKFT22i+Ahu1xukynFnGIdaw41JaCSd1mT7H1SVwQnP0Hw
2PNOvfYGWwc4XFp43ry0bgrQu2/5sF5yDxu1yht8OYj/nyMwUsxUjVIUewCg/+4w
g1RbT58+iQBCMeIIjRPFp4kD/2quMOz+V8P4Xxj2+OILjVIAmrNrqNmZFlqwvrkJ
HAGNho0tCYbekATTvKgdBYcNeErxJm8f+hGXLKef/GScVgEEMrRjI34F8Q6LmqhU
fEyaLhq4T/mo5jh2bC6sUDYrAYPSSVTWlIT4DCb9VR4u30AEqliX40V8v5SsDQlZ
jjb0A/9nbt1h6GjoZ2rvE50d92t1pcotFUZKz2jqkOckzgOYST5ZixKs8nSdcc82
jOMJ2BXHuEx7Tb9Z9TXpmMfRIWIqfoAlR8CE9XhzC021PIdSdXrRTBH3/AksfZVv
0dTGXUVG+vsWxKpq41tUYjbSXYhkkEkXrBoY02rLzn40Meb3LbQiUGhpbGlwIFIu
IFppbW1lcm1hbm4gPHBByekBwZ3AuY29t PokASwQQEQIACwUCM0lzxQQLAwECAAoJ
EGPLaR3669X8EYYAoI/npyskFaP8uBbrRTEMw01xfq0wAJwJ1P2jkUIfWtaKZI8X
k0DPIw1HgokAlQMFEDNJdItleYS4x61m3QEBiZgD/0vhIcNAkbomAzbX4Q3Llb6A
glbaX+9BlBmBzZSVf3DyogKKPH/1Fo5N01PNyIcyaJuJHzWRJoajCqVqj77Ijw+a
fjdy6+dMZhh/q3pajtSmgivvuCqlxChPBPFPQ6qGwdF9Nmsf5JEwl5vGSrHSxCrP
VqA4+ExLCee77FYMz1GjiQA/AwUQM5S+SBe2aTQFJUGbEQKs/wCg0dv0B6xvv7+x
bNygVdQDvNaMBPAAn0bzhh22EeciiQB7hhXSR711DPOsiQA/AwUQM5TiKBs4EMXQ
J6CgEQKNjQCghC3d1uTV8MPYkv7XT19VKuWyRrAAn2zf3kS+4qb7R2tDLKozmfiU
rxa1iQA/AwUQM5H1o13oAGhBPj0zEQJPwACfZF4XfII3KGmQfmYhH17LOjVRce8A
oM//jTaLxMsExfZvfC1HgRyKYJhNpiQA/AwUQM45uim2DbAjiym+LEQKqNgCffT6I
ubkpFHdH4QZM4RvqfVpWZYgAoNfizire9S7qn91u4f2N28QtM8aYiQA/AwUQM5T4
yay7FkvPc+xMEQKtagCfUKCE7ZsX5ayuZyL9eNo0Bl+8/MUAmwfwut1VxTgscZc9
njOOS0WX1+EKiQA/AwUQM5HkkLCaT/N8WqvxEQKQVgCgkEu/wjMydDMsabqswIwT
aKAjqtAAn1l+Sm9rnohT1ord1O2GNCiEkYKduQINBDNJdHAQCADKiTNKDUVbHxFM
H0z2tgxvpmdY/4H48vPHwi2KgwRD29g4Sybj4/YXP8QuUbANADUyhVzKuxscyMsj
RINIqnDCPzQU9Pk0tipVWPATewKs+gcIGnOaOOn/dRsAHAdy0u10pVY2DNO7rLpB
GtmFQP/JWSBjx9Qo//U2Hyt4d7lzb84V2t8EuzVkM7wUwco+remXDX2NBtmov4kA
tN4fKbdxAYMNDuLWSyhBJhtgovNgJr3C0xIMwrRle44nOgSyyL8rdiJE2Zdcup Nt
4k/fZFGhywaitlxoEi3aoZ0996/03rzIO8VhOgpjYfkxGtUGtAvrhJhpY85Xgdcu
+WuuEtnzAAICB/wOK/AAlZsF049BGTY3FrpjAVIyU7uu6ro9XosEiKLUiKDJIh7K
IqtKYmsFxltSxoTb3LLQALoL9gnrDMlnsct1e3y2EURh+Br/n7eWzaNcMkGKYifs
osErYS/OaLq8de81OSx2yMTm+mwxEkooEIZ3R8xzR+MlWhnU4y4kUegSVM3W0S3c
MdBz2I21QEppj3dNqae+SCuzEfoLxGeUI8hRcwEmMABEU6Ewl S4k5JrM+PDg70zJ
SZicA9pipCf9daU9aNIXZ5N2W4kv9KV9EWhb7hpGh7kskVMZE8hWIcywOeh/gwhs
ZaZxhB+dOrMTiPwo1KRffU3S8Nfkb/JfBNrciQA/AwUYM010cGPLaR3669X8EQI7
4wCfdUcaxo7zsZxfkI1gA3k+opzg67MAoPOk41vvIBlwA9sTKc8O2eJRtuyV
=maAF
-----END PGP PUBLIC KEY BLOCK-----
```

As a matter of fact, the above key belongs to Phil Zimmerman himself. You can use the code to send a secure message to Phil, and only he will be able to decode its contents.

So where do you get these keys, and how do you exchange them with others? Therein lies the trouble inherent with PGP.

Your public key is built from the passphrase of your choice, based on your specified key length. Passphrases should be exactly that: long strings of text that would be extremely difficult to hack through brute force. Your private key is then generated from the public key you have just created.

Then, it's up to you to get the public key into the hands of the right people. You can append it to your e-mail messages, as many people do. You can post it on a Web site, another popular choice. You can even put it on your business card, although we don't recommend it. Commercial public key servers are also becoming available for users to house their key information, although this generally entails using a commercial version of the product.

Regardless of the method you choose, the point is that, like its name, it's a *public* key, and if it has been generated properly, it can't do you any harm if the whole world knows it. Only with the corresponding private key can messages be encrypted.

Is PGP for You?

The problem with PGP is that this key exchange method is a bit informal and suspect. The many flavors and versions of PGP have fragmented it much like the UNIX operating system, although it is generally still possible to communicate even if users have different versions installed. The informality of exchanging public keys also makes the process completely insecure and public key tampering is an easy matter. While this probably won't compromise security, an incorrect public key can leave you with a box full of unreadable e-mail. Finally, PGP is simply, at its very core, a user's security tool, not an enterprise security tool. Although this is slowly changing, and building a PGP-based infrastructure is possible, other secure messaging solutions already work much better at the enterprise level.

If you want to build a personal "web of trust" with a few close associates, PGP is indeed a "pretty good" solution. But if you want a serious, business-grade secure messaging solution, you'll be better served looking elsewhere.

S/MIME

Besides a few fundamental flaws, PGP was designed in the pre-Windows days of MS-DOS, and it is starting to show its age. By all accounts, the heir apparent to the throne of secure messaging is S/MIME.

The appeal of S/MIME is twofold. First, it is standards-based, building on the well-established MIME (Multipurpose Internet Mail Extension) messaging protocol by adding encryption and digital signature capabilities to it. Second, it was developed by RSA Data Security and has the full backing of Microsoft, Netscape, Lotus, Novell, and just about every other messaging software vendor, so it certainly has the appearance and capability of sticking around for awhile. Netscape Communicator has S/MIME functionality built in, as shown next.

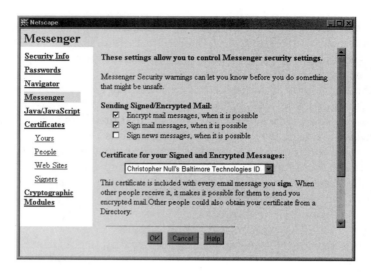

Also, S/MIME is just more secure than PGP. While PGP will probably live on for decades in limited use, the future is in S/MIME.

How S/MIME Works

S/MIME is very similar to PGP in its usage, but it is a bit more complex. We will only cover it here in general terms. Basically, S/MIME messages can be any of three types: clear-signed, opaque-signed (aka PKCS#7-signed), and encrypted. Encrypted messages can also be signed, and they usually are.

Clear-signed messages are sent with their contents in clear text. The message is freely readable by any mail reader, and a digital S/MIME signature is attached to the message. The recipient of the message uses this information to verify that the sender is who he or she claims to be and that the message has arrived intact. If your mail reader does not support S/MIME, the signature can effectively be discarded without compromising the integrity of the message.

Opaque-signed messages are similar to clear-signed messages, but their contents are entirely encoded in MIME. Thus, opaque-signed messages are only readable through MIME-capable mail readers, even though the contents are not encrypted in any way. (Most mail readers are MIME-capable, but a few are not.)

Finally, encrypted messages are entirely encoded in MIME and are largely encrypted. They can only be decrypted with a MIME-capable mail reader *and* if the correct private key is used. As stated earlier, encrypted messages can also be signed by either of the above methods.

The Certificate Authority

What truly differentiates S/MIME from PGP is the use of the certificate authority, or CA, to issue, manage, and revoke keys. This gives internal users and external visitors a secure and easy way to obtain and verify public keys for authentication and encryption services. A CA can be built within your organization (this is called building a public key infrastructure, or PKI) or you can outsource some or all of the CA services.

Unless you are planning to deploy S/MIME on a grand scale, outsourcing the complicated CA services to a company like VeriSign will give you a cheaper and easier way to roll out S/MIME. Not only will your security be far easier to manage, but you will find yourself under the aegis of the same company that provides security to many other organizations. Most likely, many of these organizations will be your customers and suppliers, allowing you to forgo the building of your own web of trust.

Again, building your own PKI is a daunting task, but sometimes it is unavoidable. For starters, outsourcing some of your security functions places you in a position of legal liability if something goes awry. Also, you have to have complete trust in the provider of your CA, because you will essentially be giving them the keys to your company. Note that VeriSign offers monetary assurances if your security is compromised.

We'll examine in-house CAs and PKIs in greater detail in Chapters 22 and 23.

Enterprise Solutions

Both PGP and traditional S/MIME security have one common flaw, and that is that they are both client-based implementations of a security tool. This means that, as an administrator, you have to go from machine to machine to install the utilities, and you will spend many hours training users on the admittedly complex and inaccessible topic of cryptography.

Wouldn't it be easier if a solution existed that allowed you to implement secure messaging without having to worry about these problems? Well, it's not quite that simple, but a few solutions are getting close.

Enterprise-based security works much the same way a messaging content filter, antivirus tool, or antispam utility works: at the server. With an application like Worldtalk's WorldSecure Server, you build a second gateway between your messaging server and the Internet, often called an "e-mail firewall." This gateway can automatically encrypt and decrypt anything that passes through it. WorldSecure also provides content, virus, and spam filtering as well.

The flaw is that none of this protection is valid for internal, non-Internet communications. It generally works best with other companies that have a similar encryption scheme, with which you transact a large volume of e-mail and that you trust implicitly. Finally, while this eases the complexity placed on the user, it greatly increases the complexity given to the administrator. Installing and administering systems like these is no piece of cake, and it will require a great investment of time and energy on your part to ensure the system is working properly. And, because more processing is done and the mail is transferred through another system, performance will be necessarily slowed a bit.

In a nutshell, secure messaging is possible today, but setting it up may be more than you bargain for. Until enterprise solutions become more manageable and extensible, we recommend you roll out a client-based S/MIME package to the users on your network who really need it. Just don't forget to train them how to use it!

WEB SECURITY

The idea of complete client security when browsing the Web is a full-blown fantasy, and it's a situation that's poised to get much, much worse.

World Wide Web attacks are not widely publicized because they are not very common. For now. But when the hacker community embraces hostile Java applets, malicious ActiveX controls, and the exploitation of the numerous holes that Netscape Communicator and Microsoft Internet Explorer contain, expect to see a huge eruption in the small market of "personal firewalls," or client-side Internet security tools.

Browsers

Netscape Communicator and Microsoft Internet Explorer are the only Web browsers you're likely to come in contact with, and we'll deal with each in turn.

Netscape was first on the scene, has been through more revisions, and (for the time being) has a larger market share. It has also been subject to the relentless testing of security professionals and computer hackers, each looking for a way to circumvent its security, enabling an outsider to wreak havoc on the Web surfer's system.

As discussed in Chapter 3, Netscape was the developer of SSL, Secure Sockets Layer, which provides secure two-way communications between a browser and a secure Web site. SSL has been widely implemented in browsers and Web servers alike, and its use does not pose any well-known security threat. S-HTTP (Secure HTTP) is another well-known secure Web protocol, and it too is not the subject of any known security breaches.

In fact, the underlying code of Communicator is what is at risk, not any front-door security algorithm. Savvy programmers have found subtleties in Communicator that can give an intruder unthought-of power on your system. For example:

▼   A number of bugs allowed malicious Web site operators to read a user's Preferences file, which contains account information.

■   The Tracker bug allowed a malicious Web site to find out where a user visits after leaving the malicious site, as well as see cookie (q.v.) information.

▲   The Singapore bug allowed a hacker to observe a user's Web activity through a LiveConnect exploitation.

Numerous other bugs have been found in Communicator, and all have been fixed, but these repairs require users to constantly upgrade their software. Downloading an 8MB patch file is not something users with slow modems enjoy doing on a monthly basis, so the problem is real and difficult to solve.

Microsoft Internet Explorer

While Microsoft has made every attempt to build security into Internet Explorer, Netscape's security problems seem laughable in the face of the holes and bugs in Microsoft IE.

Some of IE's holes include the following:

▼ One bug allowed a hacker to write files to the user's hard disk without his knowledge or permission. The file content could be extremely damaging.

■ IE could allow executables to be launched by viewing a hostile Web page. These executables could in turn delete files or perform other hostile acts.

▲ IE could be coaxed into giving out your password file or encryption keys.

The problems go on and on, and a permanent solution has not been forthcoming. Short of disconnecting your business from the Web, any administrator serious about Web browser security should install Netscape Communicator over IE in the enterprise.

Cookies

Cookies do not present so much a security threat as they do a privacy risk. Still, they bear some mentioning here. A cookie file is automatically generated by your browser. Its purpose is to hold a large listing of preferences for various Web sites you visit.

Cookies are generally harmless, but it is possible to take advantage of a cookie file to gather information about a user through an accumulation of cookie file entries. To see your own cookies file just search your hard drive for cookies.txt. You may be surprised what you find inside.

Both browsers contain mechanisms for turning cookies off or for warning you before cookies are written. Turning the warning mechanism on is a useful step, but you may find yourself so inundated with cookie requests that you, like most of us, just set the browser to accept all cookies without warning. As this is presently not a huge security hole, it is probably acceptable to enable cookies, at least for the time being.

Java, JavaScript, and ActiveX

Imbuing Web browsers with the ability to execute code in the form of Java/JavaScript or ActiveX makes matters much worse than we've already discussed.

Java is Sun Microsystems's powerful object-oriented programming language that has been embraced by the Internet community. It is the basis for Netscape's JavaScript, a very simple scripting language that allows a browser to execute an actual application without leaving the browser. Never content to let another company do something new, Microsoft developed ActiveX as a competitor.

As seen with browsers, JavaScript and ActiveX are horrendously insecure scripting tools that can wreak havoc on your system in the hands of a hostile Web site operator. And again, Microsoft's ActiveX is much more dangerous.

Weaknesses in the Java language can be used to build scripts that generate Denial of Service attacks in a number of ways: through overloading a PC's memory, disabling or rerouting DNS services, and locking critical files. JavaScript has also been used in privacy attacks like those mentioned for the Netscape browser.

As bad as that sounds, ActiveX is much worse, and Microsoft has had to answer for some overwhelmingly bad press because of it. ActiveX is at the heart of the idea behind the link between the Web browser and the operating system, an integration that Microsoft has really been pushing (and that has earned them the attention of the Department of Justice). Of course, the idea of somehow linking the Internet to your OS becomes a bit ridiculous if you give it any thought, but Microsoft has not been daunted.

ActiveX was rushed out the door and into the arms of a waiting sea of critics. Within months, ActiveX controls were used to transfer bank account funds through Quicken, delete files on users' hard disks, corrupt registry entries, and crash systems. In fact, ActiveX has so much leeway, malice doesn't actually have to be involved to do any of this: All it really takes to corrupt your registry with ActiveX is bad programming.

Consider yourself warned, and consider disabling ActiveX in your browser, if you decide to go with IE. (ActiveX is, quite wisely, not supported by Netscape.)

Web Security Tools

Our intention is not to throw you into a panic over browser insecurity, but you do need to be informed. With that said, products are starting to show up on the market that offer some protection from Web-based security threats, especially Java and ActiveX holes.

At the client level, you can install a so-called "personal firewall." These utilities (from the likes of Network Associates, eSafe, and Finjan) run on top of your browser and monitor traffic for suspicious behavior. There are also a number of more comprehensive server-level utilities that work much like a real firewall does. These utilities sit on a dedicated machine between your network and the Internet, and they filter out hostile code before it ever reaches the network. Obviously, these are much more expensive and complex.

Do you need one of these? To be honest, while Java and ActiveX are dangerous, the threat of you actually being the victim of a hostile applet or control is minimal. Other attacks are more in vogue, and you should be more worried about viruses, low-level DoS attacks, and front-door hacking attempts than problems like these. In addition, our testing shows that these tools just don't work that well. While you may stop some hostile processes, you'll have no assurances that you are completely protected. We recommend you only install a product like this if you truly feel Java and ActiveX security is an immediate and serious problem.

VIRUSES

Viruses are a problem that have plagued IS Managers since their advent in 1986, and the tools that are built to catch them have become an enormous industry. New computer viruses now pop up at the astounding rate of about four per day, and as a network administrator, you need to stay on top of the problem.

Most viruses are merely annoying, but some can cause serious damage, from slowing your system to a halt to deleting system files, reformatting your hard disk, or even making a hard disk completely unreadable (and thus, useless). Viruses exist in a dozen basic types, from traditional file viruses that infect executables, to boot sector viruses that toy with low-level disk operations, to macro viruses that infect documents (most notably, Microsoft Word documents). Surprisingly, most OSes are very safe from viruses, but Microsoft DOS, Windows, and NT are notoriously susceptible. And in virtually any network, Windows-based PCs are rampant, and some form of antivirus protection is mandatory.

Here are a few things to think about when working with antivirus software:

▼ Almost 90 percent of viruses are transmitted through infected floppy diskettes, not over the Internet or through e-mail.

■ About half of the viruses found on corporate networks are transmitted by employees bringing in disks they use at home.

■ Six percent of virus infections are traced back to shrink-wrapped commercial software.

▲ Rumors of "dead viruses" are completely false. Some of today's most common infections continue to be variants on a few of the first viruses ever released.

The bottom line is simple: You can't trust anyone or anything when it comes to security against viruses. User education is critical, and you should insist that any employees bringing in outside disks screen them first with your IS staff.

Antivirus Software

Fighting viruses is done half through education and half through an antivirus software package. There are a number of companies making antivirus software now, including Network Associates, Symantec, and Computer Associates. There are pros and cons to each, but overall, any of them is an adequate choice.

You'll have to decide whether to install virus security at the client, on your file servers, or on messaging/groupware servers. Most environments will be completely secure with just file server and client-based antivirus software. Unless your organization is a heavy groupware user or corresponds with outsiders whose security is questionable, an e-mail virus filter is probably not necessary. Some organizations can probably get away with only client-based antivirus protection, but this should be a consideration only if file servers are not heavily used and you find server protection too expensive (which it certainly can be).

It's impossible to stress too heavily how critical the education process is regarding viruses. Monthly or biweekly data file updates should be distributed to users along with a warning about the dangers of viruses and how they are transmitted. If a virus outbreak does occur, contain it as quickly as possible, and find out where the virus originated. If a user brought in an infected floppy, make an example of it by publicly destroying the disk for all to see.

Be aware that antivirus tools have their critics. One controversial study found all antivirus packages to be completely useless, letting hundreds of known viruses go by undetected. While no antivirus tool will be completely perfect, some protection will be better than none, and in our personal experience, we've found these tools to be quite reliable against all reasonably common virus strains.

INTRUSION DETECTION

Say a hacker gets around your firewall, bypasses your VPN, or skirts your PKI. How would you know? The goal of intrusion detection tools is to tell you when just such an event occurs, either constantly monitoring your system for break-ins or analyzing your network to help you find and plug the holes.

Security Auditing Tools and Scanners

Getting started with a security analysis generally means obtaining a security auditing tool. These tools range from fairly simplistic (like the UNIX host command) to extremely in-depth, as we'll discuss below.

One of the best stand-alone security auditors is Intrusion Detection's Kane Security Analyst. KSA is available for Windows NT and NetWare, and it lets you run a full audit to test security in about 20 areas, including file permissions, event logging, and password strength. A number of other utilities are on the market that do all or some of these functions. (And there are many stand-alone password crackers.) It's definitely worth the money to invest in a tool like this, especially since many are available as freeware or shareware.

If you want to get a little more sophisticated, you can obtain a security monitor to constantly run on your network and watch for intrusions. The monitor will then alert you via e-mail or a page if something is amiss. Kane Security Monitor is the monitoring extension of the KSA product, and it watches for any suspicious activity, including hack attempts, password guessing, DoS attacks, and other basic intrusion attempts. Many firewall vendors are starting to build functionality like this into their base product, extending their range.

If you want to get even more sophisticated in your quest to harden your network, you can look into an advanced scanner. Scanners are the kings of intrusion detection tools, and they can be much more complex than their friendlier brethren.

The current lead scanners are the multiplatform Internet Security Systems Internet Scanner and the UNIX-based SATAN (Security Administrator's Tool for Analyzing Networks). As you might imagine, Internet Scanner is the corporate product with a fancy GUI and extensive security precautions built in. SATAN is the underground scanner preferred by hackers.

Both SATAN and Internet Scanner take the functionality of a tool like KSA to its limit. Every aspect of your network is stressed and tested, especially TCP ports ("port scanner" is a synonymous term), which is where most savvy hackers will look to search for machines on a network and then exploit their weaknesses. Both SATAN and Internet Scanner will give you pages (sometimes hundreds) of reports about potential weaknesses on your network. In the wrong hands, this can be a blueprint for breaking in.

In many locales, unauthorized use of a scanner constitutes a real crime. Because scanners can attempt to crash systems or steal password files, you are responsible for the consequences if they are successful.

The bottom line: By all means, look into a scanner for auditing your network, but be sure it doesn't fall into the wrong hands, and be sure you know what you're doing before you use it.

Packet Sniffers

At the lowest level of your network, a packet sniffer is the ultimate tool for security analysis. It's also the most complex. Simply, a sniffer analyzes traffic as it passes through a point on your network. Most network traffic is useless to analyze—it's just insecure data being transferred from client to server. Ostensibly, a sniffer is supposed to help you look at network traffic. In reality, a sniffer is more likely to be used by a hacker to look at network traffic he or she shouldn't be seeing.

In capable hands, a packet sniffer can reveal everything about your network: specifically, usernames, host IDs, and passwords being transmitted across the LAN. Obviously, an experienced hacker with a sniffer running on your network is a considerable threat. How he or she gets the sniffer there in the first place is irrelevant, be it a physical break-in or a surreptitious ftp upload to one of your PC's hard drives. Regardless, once it's inside, sensitive data can be gathered with little effort on the hacker's part. All he or she needs to do is pick it up at a later time for analysis.

A sniffer can be either a hardware device or an application process running on a machine. In either case, a sniffer is virtually invisible to you. The only real security against it is a solid encryption scheme to protect confidential data and passwords. After that, some network topology changes, like segmenting your network with switches, can be made, but those issues are really beyond the scope of this book.

The most important thing you can do, however, to protect your network against a sniffer or any other security threat will be covered posthaste.

PHYSICAL SECURITY

Computer hacking is no easy feat. It involves skill, patience, experience, and some measure of luck. It can take decades to learn to be a crack computer hacker, but it doesn't take much skill at all to break down the back door.

Location, Location, Location

All the firewalls, VPNs, and scanners in the world won't do you a lick of good if your network is physically insecure. The time to start thinking about security is at the beginning, when you first build your network. Given that it's probably too late for that, you can still work on your network's physical security after the fact.

Here are some key points to remember:

▼ **Lock everything up!** You can't have too many levels of physical security between the outside world and your network. But it's not just your file servers that need protecting. Networks can be compromised at any point from the most remote client to the network core (this includes your PBX and wiring closets). Make sure your buildings are adequately protected, have video surveillance where warranted, and make sure you are insured in case of loss.

■ **Have a written security policy.** This should include everything from required password length to approved software packages to antivirus data file update procedures. Distribute an abbreviated version of the policy to your users and make sure it is read. The point of a written security policy isn't to browbeat your users into submission; it's to stress that good security habits are in everyone's best interest . . . and to let them know that you're watching.

■ **Prepare for the worst.** You should also write a disaster recovery plan in the event a security breach does occur (and someday, it will). Also, it won't hurt to run through practice drills with your IS staff on containing damage from viruses or hack attempts.

■ **Insist on background checks for personnel with sensitive network access.** Too many security breaches could have been avoided if a paroled hacker had not been hired to do the job.

■ **Backups are critical.** Tape backups should be done daily at least, and you should store tapes at numerous points on- and off-site. Be sure to keep a solid three to six months of backup tapes for worst-case scenarios.

▲ **Trust no one.** More on this in the following section.

Social Engineering

Even if your network is locked up tight both electronically and physically, a hacker still has one way in, and it's often the weakest link in the chain. Social engineering is the art of exploiting that link: people.

In fact, many of the great hackers of history have been skilled social engineers first and foremost. Actual technical ability often runs a close second. Here's how a typical social engineering stunt works: A hacker calls the receptionist and asks for the name of the CEO's secretary. The receptionist gladly obliges and the hacker in turn calls up that secretary. The hacker then assumes the identity of a network admin. The hacker tells the secretary that the CEO's account is somehow locked up, that system maintenance is about to occur, or some other bogus story—in any event, the hacker/network admin needs the CEO's password to fix the problem so everyone can get back to doing their job. Sprinkled throughout this little speech are personal touches—the name of the CEO's dog, the color of the secretary's hair, "memories" of the company party from two weeks ago—something that subconsciously affirms that the person on the phone is who he or she claims to be. Of course, this knowledge is easy to come by and is obtained through similar means as this.

When the hacker hangs up the phone, he or she has the username and password of the CEO. No hacking is needed, just a dial-up number or URL to the intranet and the hacker has free rein to run largely undetected on your network.

Once a hacker has a privileged account on your network, tracking him or her down can be murder. Defeating social engineering feats like this is 100 percent a matter of education, and only through written and verbal training will your users learn to never, *ever* give a password out over the phone.

Make sure you communicate this well and often, and leave your door open to users who feel they've been the victim of a social engineering stunt. As with any type of security attack, knowing it's underway solves half of the problem.

THE FUTURE

Like the contents of any other section of this book, the security market is an evolving thing. In a few years, this information will largely be outdated. So here are a few things to keep your eyes open for in the near future.

Security Consolidation

Corporate acquisitions are a daily event, and security companies are no exception to the rule. Big players like Network Associates and AXENT are expanding their security product lines by buying the technology they haven't developed themselves. Even Microsoft is expanding its security product line (as the security community rolls its eyes at the thought).

Whatever the company behind it, the idea is that security will eventually become a one-stop shopping decision: you can get a firewall, VPN, CA, secure messaging, and scanner in one package, and you can administer all of it centrally.

This is fine and good, but the potential hazards are greater than with a multitude of disparate security systems. Sure, administration will be easier, but a single point of failure is often introduced into the mix, so if an intruder bypasses security on one of those pieces or your admin tool, he or she may be able to compromise them all. The point to remember is that, as security consolidations continue, make sure you're comfortable with the company you choose as your one-stop security provider.

The New IP

One of these days, IPv6 is going to stop being something we're merely threatened with and start being a reality. While IPv4 is the 32-bit standard we've all become familiar with, IPv6 (aka IPng) actually became an official proposed standard back in 1994.

The problem, of course, with IPv4 is that 32 bits just doesn't provide for enough unique IP addresses. That, combined with a ridiculous manner for handing them out, has made it virtually impossible (or at least, very expensive) to obtain a legitimate IP address. IPv6 was designed to fix that and more.

IPv6 is a 128-bit addressing scheme, and it will create some insanely large number of addresses so that the entire galaxy could never possibly run out. (We thought that about IPv4, but who's keeping score?) Not only will IPv6 give us an exhaustive number of addresses, but it will also provide for better multicasting, quality of service, built-in authentication, and be much simpler from a header standpoint. It will also fully support old IPv4 addresses.

In other words, IPv6 is going to be a good thing . . . if we ever get around to implementing it for real. Why the delay? Well, there are a lot of IPv4 networks out there, and bringing even one IPv6 device into the picture basically means upgrading your entire infrastructure. It also means all of your IPv4-based filters and VPNs are going to be useless. And it will open your network up to a new generation of IP-based attacks.

What are you going to do? Not upgrading is probably not an option in the medium-term, but, fortunately, unless your IP network needs to grow by leaps and bounds, IPv6 is a technology you can keep socked away in the back of your mind for a little while longer. IPv4, like DOS, is going to stick around for quite some time. If you really don't want to upgrade, no one is going to make you.

CHAPTER 13

The Desktop

The desktop in and of itself is a brain, processing and storing information. If the desktop is inoperable or malfunctioning, business operations become paralyzed. If businesses are to avoid paralysis, IT departments must have surgeons skilled in the practice of desktop computing.

FINDING YOUR DESKTOP

Take a look at a business desk. Better yet, look at your desk. It's well equipped with the items necessary to perform business tasks. Items found on the desk might include pens, pencils, highlighters, sticky notes, stapler, scissors, paper clips, tape, glue, paper, folders, books, manuals, telephone, personal organizer, calendar, personal recorder, and maybe a clock radio. Most of these items are standard-issue office supplies, but they're necessary for productivity. And, you're familiar with your desk. But the desk has never been necessarily a physical desk. It's an environment. The environment requires tools for productivity.

Successful business operations have been and will continue to be conducted from anywhere. In addition, hardware technology is paving the way for businesses to become more efficient regardless of the location.

Automating business meant reengineering employees. The manner in which employees performed tasks was about to change and would continue to do so. Fear of the unknown coupled with the black art of technology didn't facilitate automation. Though familiarity breeds contempt—and desktops are no exception—the ability to easily personalize desktop computing proved to be the redeeming quality of automation for employees.

Automation is a work in progress (WIP). It's all about conversions, migrations, cut-overs, upgrades—constant change. Parallel systems, redundancy, and disaster recovery weren't given a great deal of thought when it came to the desktop. Employees have become intimate with their new environment and subsequently dependent on the desktop.

Reengineering didn't stop with employees. The way software applications work has changed as well. Instead of an entire application loading and executing on a single computer—usually a network server—applications were broken into discrete pieces. Each piece could and often did run on a different computer. A good example of this type of application architecture is called the *Distributed Computing Environment (DCE)*.

The Distributed Computing Environment (DCE)

Distributed Computing Environment (DCE) was developed by the Open Software Foundation (OSF), an organization founded in 1998 for the express purpose of developing a distributed computing environment. In February of 1996, OSF merged with X/Open Company Ltd., a company founded in 1984 with the mission of providing compliance to open systems specifications. The goal of the new merged company, called the Open Group (http://www.opengroup.org), is to facilitate end-user choice in the implementation of multivendor information systems.

True to its purpose, DCE is a suite of software services that enable distributed processing and distributed data across the enterprise. In effect, DCE provides an intermediary service platform that negotiates the differences among the products and technologies of different vendors. Therefore, no changes need be made among the products and technologies themselves to enable interoperability. It provides an open development environment in which developers can easily write applications for distributed applications without having to know anything about the network itself. Thus, DCE offers freedom of choice among operating systems and network protocols. As well, DCE offers end users access to data from legacy systems, distributed file replication, and single login capability.

Figure 13-1 illustrates the DCE architecture. As you can see, DCE is a layered development model that seamlessly combines a well-defined set of services and technologies, which we'll describe shortly. The foundation of the architecture consists of basic services like operating systems and file access systems. Applications are the top of the architecture.

DCE provides two kinds of services:

▼   Development tools

▲   Data-sharing services

DCE Development Tools

Software developers use the development tools to build the end-user services necessary for distributed computing. Examples of these end-user services are *remote procedure calls (RPCs)*, *time services*, *directory services*, *thread services*, and *security services*.

REMOTE PROCEDURE CALLS (RPCs)   Developers use remote procedure calls to build client/server applications that can run processes on other computers connected to the same network. RPCs both enable servers to handle the requests of multiple clients simultaneously and enable clients to interact with multiple servers.

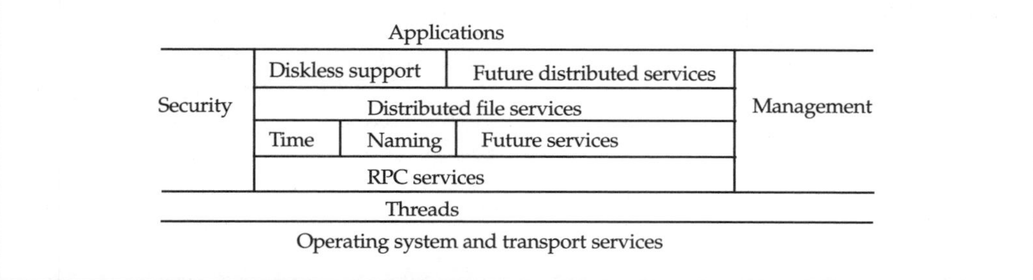

Figure 13-1.   The DCE architecture

TIME SERVICES   Developers use time services to create applications that can schedule activities. Time services also enable applications to determine event sequences and event length. These time services also coordinate the synchronization of clocks in network devices.

DISTRIBUTED DIRECTORY SERVICES (DDS)   Distributed directory services offer a single naming scheme throughout the distributed computing environment. This enables users to request resources by name, and therefore they don't have to know the location or network address of these resources. The DCE directory service has integrated both the X.500 global naming system and LDAP.

THREAD SERVICES   DCE's thread services have support for concurrent processing, meaning that it enables applications to perform many tasks simultaneously. This lets a server handle multiple clients.

SECURITY SERVICES   Security services consist of authentication, authorization, and user account management. These three security services can be trusted by all network hosts regardless of operating system, and are provided through secure communication that ensures both integrity and privacy.

DCE Data-Sharing Services

DCE data-sharing services offer distributed data access capabilities. These services currently consist of diskless workstation and distributed file system support.

DISTRIBUTED FILE SYSTEM (DFS)   The DCE distributed file system is a data-sharing component that enables file access across the enterprise network. DFS offers both file location transparency and a uniform name space. It is also very scalable, performing well all across large networks that span great distances and have lots of users. To prevent loss of data access in the event of a file server failure, DFS replicates files and directories on multiple hosts.

Desktop Impact of Distributed Computing Environment

The ability to distribute pieces of applications, along with the metamorphosis of the office desk into a computer screen, has changed the nature of desktop computing. We've had to change our mindset about hardware clients. The hardware client is no longer just a PC or workstation. The hardware client and accessories have become a virtual desk. As a result, business operations are no longer solely dependent on employees. They're at the mercy of the machine.

FUNCTIONS OF THE DESKTOP

Hardware wanted: Powerful, stable, easily used, fast, portable, 24-hour availability, interoperability with any device or mechanism, unlimited simultaneous multiple tasks, must include lifetime warranty, service and maintenance agreement at no additional cost, and be reasonably priced.

Not an advertisement you're likely to see. But it's exactly what businesses are asking of the technology industry. And, IT departments are struggling, attempting to meet unrealistic demands of "the perfect desktop."

As businesses have become more dependent on the desktop computer to fulfill business operations, the functionality of the hardware and accessories has increased.

We're now utilizing hardware for a comprehensive set of functions. By understanding the functions of the desktop, you'll be better prepared to procure adequate hardware and maintain the desktop. However, interoperability is an obstacle that just can't be worked around. Hardware and software are both culprits. Trying to isolate a hardware problem can be like searching for the Holy Grail—obsessive.

TYPES OF DESKTOPS

The technology *quickening* has brought business a long way since the launch of the IBM PC in 1981 and Compaq Computer Corporation's first IBM PC clone in 1982. However, antiquated desktop hardware is still abundant and must be supported. Better yet, it's incredible that up until 1997 vendors were still supplying hardware that wasn't Y2K compliant. As for high-end, state-of-the-art hardware clients, expect a desktop lifetime of three years. Hence, the disposable desktop.

Desktop hardware runs the gamut: dumb terminals, PCs, Macintoshes, UNIX workstations, diskless workstations (affectionately referred to as "pizza boxes"), notebook computers, docking stations, handheld computers, the network computer, digital cameras, video cameras, scanners, multimedia monitors, printers, and modems.

The heterogeneous nature of desktop hardware and the varying brands, makes, and models of like hardware are the challenges for the desktop. However, there are several steps you can take to alleviate some, but not all, of the desktop woes:

▼   Conduct and maintain hardware inventory

■   Develop and implement IT hardware standards

■   Develop and implement IT desktop policies

■   Develop and institute service level agreements

■   Institute a training program

▲   Determine total cost of ownership (TCO)

Inventory

Conducting a detailed inventory of all hardware and software is a major undertaking. If maintained, it can be a valuable insight tool. If you don't have a disaster recovery plan, now is the time to start developing one.

▼ There are a variety of desktop inventory products that may be helpful to you. Regardless of the product you choose, be sure to obtain all pertinent inventory information.

■ Consider every department. There may be dumb terminals and line printers in accounting, several managers with handheld computers, and don't forget about the variety of gateway computers with DSUs. It's not a project you'll want to take on again.

■ Choose classifications for hardware types like PC, NC, Monitor, Terminal, Monitor, Modem, CSU/DSU. For hardware with essential peripheral equipment like notebooks, you may want to separate entries for batteries and power packs.

■ Include circuit numbers, network service names, and modem numbers for gateways, printers, and the like.

▲ Where applicable, back up boot information such as configuration, batch, registry, and drivers. If hardware is being used as a gateway, include the gateway software and configuration files as well.

Standards

Contrary to popular belief, distributed computing hasn't off-loaded the responsibilities of IT departments. In fact, it has increased the workload and promulgated the need for IT standards.

Departmentalized hardware and software selections are still the responsibility of the IT department to install, configure, and maintain. In addition, the support for road warriors and telecommuters has made matters worse.

Be proactive in developing and maintaining standards. If possible, conduct an electronic survey to assess desktop needs. The assessment can give you a better understanding of the following:

▼ Low- and high-end desktop requirements

▲ Service and warranty needs

Once you've established the requirements and needs, you should do the following:

▼ Locate a vendor that can accommodate your spectrum of needs

■ Define a minimum hardware configuration

▲ Include hardware specifications and vendor information in standards documentation

Service-Level Agreements

For years, businesses have maintained contractual agreements with third parties. Staffing, support, and training requirements to maintain office equipment were met.

When desktop problems arise, everyone gets involved. It's extremely inefficient when coworkers, people on the help desk, hardware technicians, network administrators, application developers, and telecommunication staff are involved in resolving a desktop problem.

Meanwhile, deadlines are missed, projects are delayed, files are corrupted or lost, and the frustration level is at an all-time high—and in cases where desktop decisions and support are provided by everybody but the IT department, the residual effects can be much worse.

Regardless of the problem, the resolution must be smooth and swift. It's not just a label-maker program, or an unofficial database—it's the desk. Replacing the desktop is analogous to moving to a new desk. Items on the desk are personalized and customized. The desk items shouldn't be moved, but if they must, they need to be put back exactly as they were. It's no longer just a computer—it's the desk. End users want it just like they had it, and you would too.

Service-level agreements specifically define support services. You can establish reasonable yet acceptable service levels by considering the following:

▼   Nature of business functions (critical, sensitive, remote, client-based)

■   Deadlines of business functions (processing cutoffs, maintenance shutdowns)

▲   Location of business functions (remote sites, telecommuters, mobile users)

Finally, be specific in what the user should do to prepare for the service (remove pictures and notes from hardware, and so on).

Training

Training doesn't have to be costly, and it doesn't have to be termed "training." It's communicating with the business about their business. It's just as beneficial to the IT department as it is to the employees. The IT department learns and their rapport with the user community can be improved.

Have IT staff conduct sessions or seminars specific to their area of desktop responsibility. For example, the network administrator can provide a high-level overview of the desktop activity that takes place when a user accesses the network. Application developers could discuss the application's effect and resource usage on the desktop:

▼   Form user groups

■   Develop a desktop FAQ

▲   Create a desktop mailing list

Cost of Ownership

Realizing the true cost of the desktop can greatly assist IT departments in effectively implementing desktop solutions. All costs associated with the desktop are referred to as TCO, the total cost of ownership.

In addition to the hardware, TCO accounts for the less obvious costs such as staffing, training, and support—the maintenance and service costs. If you can obtain an inventory, and establish standards and service-level agreements, you'll be better prepared to estimate desktop TCO.

Don't forget to consider the following:

▼ Service contracts on out-of-warranty desktops

■ Special spare parts (notebook batteries and power pack spares, special cables, and connectors)

■ Supplies (surge protectors, cables, diskettes, tapes, CDs, toner and ink cartridges, paper, equipment cleaning supplies, compressed air, and tool kits)

■ NOS/OS/software (increased user licensing)

■ Upgrades and technical support programs

■ Backup equipment and media

▲ Ergonomic office furniture

Assume any hardware you purchase today will be obsolete within three to five years. Purchase the latest technology. Ensure the hardware you purchase can scale to business needs over the next three to five years.

Although many IT departments have distributed the responsibility of the desktop to individualized departments, ultimately it is an IT responsibility. By establishing standards, policies, and guidelines, desktop decisions and support can be better made.

HEART OF HARDWARE: MICROPROCESSORS

Now that we've discussed the implications and requirements of the desktop in today's business computing environment, it's time to take a closer look at the hunk of metal that dominates your workday.

We're not going to enter into an exhaustive discussion of each of the hardware components that make up a desktop computer. There are several excellent computer hardware manuals on the market that will guide you step by step through trouble-shooting and upgrading. Rather, we are going to continue to discuss the desktop computer from a strategic perspective. To that end, we're going to focus our discussion of desktop hardware on the one component that determines who uses a particular type of desktop computer, how, and why: the *microprocessor*.

The microprocessor is the heart and soul (and brain, obviously) of every desktop computer. It is the component that determines pretty much everything worth knowing about the computer: its speed, power, and the types of applications is can handle. This is because the microprocessor does almost all the data processing for the desktop computer.

Microchips and Salsa: A Primer

We're now going to discuss the development and function of microprocessors. This explanation is by no means exhaustive, but will give you the information necessary to determine the following:

▼   Types of microprocessors available

■   How they differ from each other

▲   The strengths and weaknesses of each

Microprocessors begin life as silicon that has been artificially grown through methods that provide very pure crystals. This pristine silicon crystal is then carefully sliced very thin and baked. It isn't baked in just any old oven, but rather in specially designed ovens that contain a gaseous blend of substances. These substances bake into the pure silicon and change its electrical properties, making it suitable for transmitting and storing electrical impulses. In other words, it gives the silicon the ability to react to electrical impulses and "remember" their patterns. It is therefore capable of extremely rudimentary "thinking."

Don't get scared. Although microprocessors can "think," they can't reason. They aren't self-aware. And they weigh consequences. In fact, microprocessor thinking is more akin to a human reflex than a human thought process. Just as your knee kicks out in the same exact way each time it's hit with a rubber mallet, a microprocessor reacts by doing the same exact thing every time it's hit with a specific sequence of electrical impulses. These electronic knee jerks can be strung together in sequence to accomplish very complex tasks. From these humble beginnings mighty computers grow.

Everything that a computer does involves one of two operations:

▼   Decision making, or reacting

▲   Memory, or remembering

And because you can control one electrical signal with another electrical signal, you can perform both operations with simple electrical circuits.

Let's take a look at how this works using an electromechanical example, the familiar and nearly extinct telegraph. When a telegraph operator in location A presses down on the telegraph key, the contact between the key and the contact plate closes an electrical circuit, as shown in Figure 13-2.

Once the electrical circuit is closed, an electrical impulse travels along the circuit to location B, where it activates the electromagnet in the key of the remote telegraph unit. The electromagnet, now active, quickly draws the key of the remote unit to the contact plate. The key and the contact plate collide with a "smack." This series of smacking noises

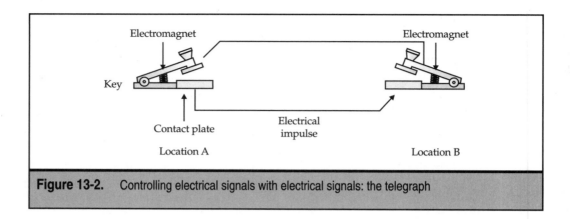

Figure 13-2. Controlling electrical signals with electrical signals: the telegraph

is interpreted as data. So an electrical signal at one location has just controlled an electrical signal at another location with the result of transmitting data.

However, you can do more with a telegraph than simply create a "smack" sound at a remote location. You could, for example, connect the telegraph arm to a light switch with a rigid wire so that every time the telegraph key smacked the contact plate, the light flashed on. Or, as a rudimentary means of data validation, you could require that data be received simultaneously from two separate locations, and link the two receiving telegraph arms to a "stiff" switch so that the force of both arms was necessary to flip the light switch. Or, as a kind of redundancy, you could connect the two telegraphs to the light switch so that a signal on either one would turn on the light. And just to be perverse, you could even install the light switch upside down so that when the telegraph arm pulled down, the light would turn off.

Logic Gates

These three examples provide more than rudimentary data validation, redundancy, and perversion. They are also examples of the AND, OR, and NOT *logic gates* used in microprocessors. These special types of circuits are known as *gates* because they control the electrical impulses, allowing them to pass or shutting them off. By using the AND, OR, and NOT logic gates, the microprocessor gains a type of decision-making ability. By carefully sequencing electrical impulse flows through a series of logic gates, simple electrical "reflexes" can be transformed into complex computations that result in logical decision-making ability.

BOOLE WHO? The concepts underlying logic gates are the brainchild of English mathematician George Boole. Boole developed the system of modern symbolic logic that we call Boolean logic, which reduces logical propositions to formulas that use the same rules and operators used to solve problems in mathematics. Properly applied and sequenced, the three logic gates AND, OR, and NOT can perform the functions of all the operators in Boolean logic. Therefore, these three logic gates together are the foundation on which all logic circuitry is based.

LOGIC AND MEMORY   These same logic gates are the basis of microprocessor memory as well. If the switch feeds back voltage so that the electrical impulses the switch controls also power the switch itself, the switch will stay in the "on" position. In other words, it "remembers" that it has been turned on. Even when the electrical signal is no longer supplied to the switch, it will stay on because at that point it is self-sustaining. Clearly, this presents the problem of how to turn a switch off once it's been turned on. After all, you don't want to have to turn your computer off after each instruction is executed!

The problem of resetting logic gates is solved by using a form of memory that has two electrical signals. One signal switches the gate on, while the other switches it off. This type of circuitry is often called *set-reset memory*.

Instruction Sets

In practice, computers have millions of logic gates controlled by electrical signals. The sequential presence or absence of an electrical signal at one of the microprocessor's pins is a coded *command*. These signals, each representing either a 0 or a 1 bit, make up a bit pattern. Some bit patterns have been assigned unique and specific meanings by microprocessor designers, and are designated as microprocessor *instructions*. For example, a bit pattern may tell a microprocessor to add or subtract, or move bits around, or simply to wait for the next instruction.

The entire set of commands that a given microprocessor understands is known as an *instruction set* for that microprocessor. Different types of microprocessors have different instruction sets.

Every task performed by a microprocessor is simply a sequence of these very narrow instructions. In fact, a computer program is nothing more than a sequence of microprocessor instructions, just as a novel is created from a sequence of words.

Registers

For a microprocessor to perform mathematical operations on numbers, it must know the following:

▼ Which operations to perform

■ The order in which to perform the operations

▲ The numbers on which to perform the operations

The most direct way of providing this information would be to provide signals encoding the numbers simultaneously with the signals that represent the operations to perform. For example, to divide the number 8 by the number 11, you could submit signals representing 8 and 11 along with the instruction to divide. But how will the microprocessor know whether you want to divide 8 by 11 or 11 by 8?

Just as you distinguish the numbers in a subtraction problem by where you put them in the equation, a microprocessor distinguishes the numbers on which it works by where they are found in memory. In other words, the microprocessor determines which number to perform operations on by the location of the numbers. Unfortunately, microprocessors have only one interface to memory, so they can only see only one number in memory at a time. Therefore, a microprocessor must load one or more numbers into internal storage areas called a *registers*. The microprocessor can then see and act on multiple numbers in its register as well as a number held in memory. A register holds bit patterns until they can be worked on or output, but it is far from a static memory receptacle. Changes resulting from the execution of instructions appear in the register because it is connected to the microprocessor's processing circuits.

NOTE: One function of microprocessor instructions is to tell the chip which registers to use for data. Another function is to tell the chip into which registers to load which data, as well as where to put the answers it comes up with.

SIZE MATTERS   Today's microprocessors contain varying numbers of registers, some dedicated to specific functions, such as remembering which instruction is currently being executed, and some designed for general purposes. Not only do different microprocessors have different numbers of registers, but the register size varies among microprocessors. The size of a register determines the number of bits a microprocessor can work on at one time. Therefore, a 32-bit microprocessor has one or more registers that each hold 32 bits of data.

SIZE DOES NOT EQUAL SPEED   Unless the microprocessor can simultaneously perform more multiple mathematical operations, adding more registers to a microprocessor does not make it faster. Because older microprocessors could only perform one operation at a time, more than two registers seemed unnecessary. Furthermore, most mathematical operations either involve no more than two numbers or can be reduced to a series of operations involving only two numbers. Nonetheless, designing microprocessors with more registers enabled software developers to write more efficient programs. This is because with more places to put data inside the microprocessor, the program had to move bits in and out of the microprocessor less frequently, which could save both programming steps and clock cycles.

Modern microprocessor designs, however (particularly those influenced by RISC research), require more than two registers. This is because microprocessors run far faster than memory. Therefore, the microprocessor has to slow down each time it accesses memory to get information. Repeated memory access slows down the processor dramatically. Therefore, systems with microprocessors that let you store more data in registers run faster than systems that require that most data be stored in memory.

But incorporating multiple registers into the microprocessor increases the complexity of the microprocessor, because this design essentially incorporates memory technology into the microprocessor. After all, having a lot of registers in the microprocessor is the same as having main memory located in the microprocessor.

Therefore, the key to top microprocessor performance is to have just the right number of registers—not too many and not too few. In current microprocessor technology—especially RISC technology—64 registers seems to be the optimal number. As a result, nearly all of today's RISC microprocessors have 64 registers.

The width of the microprocessor's registers also has a significant effect on the speed of performance. The more bits that a single register can handle, the more data a microprocessor can handle in a single operation. But if the computer program being run doesn't take advantage of the full register width, you won't realize any performance gains. For example, if the program you are running instructs the microprocessor to work only with data 32 bits at a time, you won't be able to take advantage of the full 64-bit capability. Therefore, to realize the full performance of a microprocessor, you must run software written to take advantage of the width of the registers.

Clocked Logic

Microprocessors don't execute instructions the instant they receive them. This is because electrical signals carrying these encoded instructions don't change state instantly. They always go through a transition period, and if the microprocessor tried to act on instructions during this change of state period, the microprocessor would probably be unable to interpret the instruction properly and so it would crash. Furthermore, not all signals change state at the same rate, so at any given time some signals would be at their correct values while others would still be in transition. Consequently, microprocessors experience significant periods of electronic confusion during which its signals are meaningless.

So how does the microprocessor know when to carry out an instruction? It's all in the timing. The chip waits for a signal that there is a valid command to carry out. This signal is provided by the *system clock*. Each time the microprocessor receives a clock pulse, it checks the computer instructions—unless, of course, it isn't already carrying out an instruction. And, in fact, most microprocessors can't carry out an entire instruction each clock cycle. This is because the number of cycles needed to complete an instruction is a function of the microprocessor design. And some microprocessor designs are more efficient than others.

NOTE: Clock speed is generally expressed as a frequency in megahertz (MHz).

Because the number of clock cycles doesn't directly correspond to the number of instructions completed, clock speed alone isn't a reliable indicator of performance. This is especially true when comparing the speed of two microprocessors. For example, suppose a microprocessor takes an average of 12 clock cycles to complete an instruction. Another microprocessor needs only 4. Even if the clock speed of the first microprocessor is twice that of the second one, the first will be 50 percent slower. In fact, the only time that clock speed only is a true indication of relative performance is if the microprocessors are otherwise identical, for example, two Pentium II microprocessors, one running at 230MHz and the other running at 300MHz.

CLOCKWORKS   Microprocessor clocked logic has three components:

▼   Input/output unit (I/O unit)

■   Control unit

▲   Arithmetic logic unit (ALU)

NOTE: The control unit and the arithmetic logic unit together are often referred to as the microprocessor's central processing unit (CPU).

The three parts interact as shown in Figure 13-3. The results of calculations performed by the ALU govern the control unit, which in turn directs the I/O unit. How these three parts interact determines the speed and capabilities of the microprocessor.

For example, the control unit actually runs the internal clock of the microprocessor, which establishes the microprocessor's operating speed. Furthermore, the microprocessor's bus width is determined by the I/O unit. Finally the ALU's registers determine how much data the microprocessor can handle at one time.

THE INPUT/OUTPUT UNIT (I/O UNIT)   The I/O unit connects the microprocessor to the rest of the computer's circuitry. The I/O unit can be composed of just a few buffers, or it may perform many sophisticated functions. For example, in today's popular Intel microprocessors, the I/O unit has cache memory, as well as clock-doubling logic that enables the slower external memory to match the operating speed of the microprocessor. It transmits program instructions and data to the registers of both the control unit and arithmetic logic unit. One of the key jobs of the I/O unit is to align the signal levels and clock timing of the microprocessor's internal circuitry with that of the other components inside the computer. This is because the circuits inside the microprocessor require low

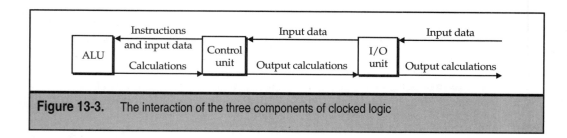

Figure 13-3.   The interaction of the three components of clocked logic

operating voltages so that they can run fast yet remain cool. However, computer components outside the microprocessor require higher currents. To match these differing power needs, each signal leaving the microprocessor enters a *signal buffer* in the I/O unit that increases its current capacity.

Intel and Intel-compatible microprocessors have two kinds of external connections to their I/O units:

▼   Address buses

▲   Data buses

The *address bus* is a connection that transmits the address of memory locations to or from which the microprocessor will send or receive data or program instructions. The width of the address bus determines how much memory a microprocessor can address. For example, a microprocessor with 16 address lines can directly work with 216 addresses; that's 65,536 (or 64K) different memory locations. Over the history of their development, microprocessors have had address bus widths ranging from 20 to 64 bits. The current development takes the address bus to 128 bits.

The *data bus* is the connection through which the actual data or program instructions are sent. The speed of the data bus is directly related to its width. Obviously, the more bits that a microprocessor can use at a time, the faster that microprocessor will operate. The latest production microprocessors go all the way to 64 bits.

THE CONTROL UNIT   The control unit is an internal clocked logic circuit that controls the operation of the entire microprocessor. The control unit's function is fairly flexible—unlike integrated circuits, whose function is fixed by the hardware design. In its most basic form, the control unit gets its instructions from an external program—the I/O unit—and in turn the control unit directs the operation of the ALU. The control unit also keeps track of which step of the program is being executed. In Pentium microprocessors, the control unit also determines the routing of signals between the two processing units that make up the Pentium microprocessor's design.

THE ARITHMETIC LOGIC UNIT (ALU)   The ALU performs all the mathematical and logical operations that comprise the decision-making function of the microprocessor. The ALU receives instructions that the control unit has interpreted, then executes either the instructions themselves or the microcode that modifies the data contained in ALU's registers. The results of this computation is then passed back out of the microprocessor through the I/O unit.

Microcode

As we mentioned, an instruction tells a microprocessor what to do. To complete an instruction, a microprocessor often has to complete more than one step. Therefore, the instruction is in essence a list of steps. These instruction sets and the steps that comprise them are called *microcode*.

Microcode enables programmers to write low-level computer programs that perform operations such as moving data into and out of registers and performing mathematical operations on that data.

Each manufacturer of microprocessors can develop a different microcode for its microprocessors—simple or complex, depending upon the requirements for the system the chip will power. And indeed, there is a trade-off in writing microcode: the more comprehensive the instruction set, the easier it is to write programs for the microprocessor. However, the more comprehensive the microcode set, the slower the performance. How these steps are controlled marks a monumental schism in microprocessor design.

How to Go Faster: Do Less

Constantly increasing microprocessor clock speeds has some negative effects. It makes computer circuitry more difficult—and hence more expensive—to design and manufacture. Therefore, a lot of energy has gone into developing microprocessors that increase speed by processing more instructions at a given clock speed, rather than increasing the clock speed. This means that the microprocessor gains performance through efficiency rather than through a raw increase in clock speed.

One way to achieve this efficiency is to reduce the number of steps required to complete a program. There are two ways to accomplish this:

▼   Combine steps into fewer, more complex instructions

▲   Simplify instructions so that fewer steps are required in the first place

Microprocessor development engineers have pursued both ideas. Both camps have succeeded in producing workable solutions. The first camp has produced the *complex instruction set computer (CISC)*, and the second has produced the *reduced instruction set computer (RISC)*.

COMPLEX INSTRUCTION SET COMPUTERS (CISC)   Microprocessors whose microcode adheres to the former principle are called complex instruction set computers. Most desktop micro- processor designs, such as those for Intel and Motorola microprocessors, are CISC designs.

In CISC designs, a single, complex instruction might do the job of several simple instructions. These complex instructions take longer to execute than simple instructions, but because the programs would need fewer instructions overall, the system would run fast. In addition to high speed, CISC designs offer a rich variety of operations, allowing CISC systems the ability to perform elaborate computations. For example, it's not unusual for a CISC desktop system to have seven or eight different types of subtraction commands.

REDUCED INSTRUCTION SET COMPUTERS (RISC)   RISC microprocessors adhere to the second approach to microprocessor design: simplify instructions so that microcodes execute faster. The trade-off is that these microprocessors require more difficult and complex external programming of the microcode.

RISC designs are a result of work done at IBM by John Cocke, who discovered that about 20 percent of a computer's instructions did about 80 percent of the work. His discovery that microcode execution adheres to the familiar 80/20 rule led to the development of RISC architecture. RISC limits the number of instructions to only those that are used most. The other instructions must be implemented in external software—hence the more difficult programming required for RISC microprocessors.

RISC designs have been adopted by most workstation manufacturers, such as DEC for its Alpha and the IBM RS line.

CISC VS. RISC   Today, CISC architecture microprocessors dominate the market. This is in part due to the falling cost of hardware, which makes it increasingly cost-effective to add more instructions into the computer's architecture. In fact, many CISC manufacturers have become so efficient that for most practical purposes the advantage of RISC evaporates.

Today, the effective difference between RISC and CISC systems is that most CISC systems run Windows and most RISC systems run UNIX (which we will discuss later). And even this differentiation is governed more by tradition than hardware design. In fact, as processor-independent operating systems (which we will discuss later in this chapter) have come into widespread use, even this difference between RISC and CISC has begun to evaporate.

Other Ways to Rev Processor Speed

Another way to speed up microprocessors is to design them to operate on more than one instruction simultaneously. There are a couple of ways to accomplish this:

▼   Pipelining

▲   Superscalar architecture

Pipelining

Originally, microprocessors worked on one instruction at a time. The microprocessor read an instruction from memory, executed each step in turn, then moved on to the next instruction. Pipelining designs allow a microprocessor to read an instruction, begin processing, and—as soon as processing begins on the first instruction—read the next instruction. Because an instruction requires multiple steps performed in different parts of the microprocessor, pipelining allows the microprocessor to work on several instructions simultaneously. The instructions are passed through the chip like a car on an assembly line.

As long as each instruction is executing steps that use the resources in a different part of the microprocessor, the steps will execute without a hitch. However, the different instruction streams have to be coordinated carefully. If one step fails or delays, all the other instructions in the pipeline will suffer.

An example of microprocessor pipelining is the Pentium from Intel. These microprocessors have four levels of pipelining, which means that it can execute as many as four different instructions at once.

SUPERSCALAR ARCHITECTURES   The steps in an instruction don't always have to be carried out in the order they are listed in the program. Some steps can be performed simultaneously. *Superscalar* microprocessors allow the system to do that. It can process multiple steps simultaneously because it has multiple, pipelined execution paths. However, note that these parallel execution paths aren't the only requirement for successful implementation of a superscalar design. The microprocessor also has to be able to determine which instructions can be split up without skewing results, as well as exactly how to split them up.

The name "superscalar" derives from the fact that this design provides more than the linear incremental increase in speed gained by the traditional means of decreasing, or "downscaling," microprocessor circuitry. Formerly, microprocessor speed was improved by reducing the size of microprocessor circuitry, thus reducing the distance electrical signals travel within the microprocessor. Superscalar architectures, on the other hand, increase microprocessor performance more substantially by increasing, or "superscaling," the microprocessor circuitry.

Both of these designs—pipelining and superscaling—have the number of microprocessor clock cycles needed to execute most instructions. In fact, most microprocessors, whether RISC or CISC, process an instruction in less than one clock cycle.

Microprocessors in Practice: What You'll Find on Desktops

So what do all these advances in microprocessor technology mean to you? Now that we've spent some time delving into the bowels of microprocessor technology, we can show you how advances in chip design translate into products that you can put to work on the desktops of your enterprise. As we look at the best-known types of desktop systems, keep in mind that the amount of memory and storage, and the types of peripheral devices, vary. However, as we will discuss, it is the *microprocessor designs* they employ that determine which type of system is best suited for a particular purpose.

Intel and Intel-Compatible Processors

Today, Intel Corporation, the inventor of the microprocessor, is also the largest manufacturer of these microchips. Intel and the companies whose products emulate Intel designs dominate the market for microprocessors for desktop computers. Therefore, we'll take a little time to explore the company's current family of microprocessor products, including the following:

▼   Pentium

■   Pentium Pro

■   Pentium MMX

■   Pentium II

▲   Celeron and Xeon

NOTE: Although the Intel (and Intel-compatible) product line was founded with the 8088/8086 microprocessor and spans the 80286, 80386, and 80486, we'll forego a description of these because they are no longer in production. In fact, it's difficult to find a Pentium system these days, with desktop and server-class production having now focused on the Pentium II (and to some degree, Pentium Pro) processors.

PENTIUM When Intel introduced the Pentium processor in 1993, its name came as something of a shock. The name "Pentium" was a departure from Intel's usual naming convention dating back to its introduction of the 8086 microprocessor. Since then, each successive generation of chip had been designated as 80*x*86, with *x* being the generation designator.

NOTE: Intel probably changed its product nomenclature as a result of a federal court ruling that determined that the numeric "name" 386 did not designate a unique product, but rather a type of product, and was therefore not eligible for trademark. As a result, Intel probably determined to create trademarkable names that other companies couldn't use for their clones of Intel microprocessors.

Another departure for the Pentium was that Intel incorporated a few elements of RISC into the design of this line. Although Intel's chips are more complex than RISC chips, they offer performance that rivals RISC designs.

Further, the Pentium differs drastically from the old 386/486 microprocessor design in its address and memory interfaces. For example, instead of the 32-bit host address interface employed by the 386 and 486 microprocessors, the Pentium has a 64-bit address bus. This lets the Pentium access and save data twice as fast as the old 386/486 microprocessors. However, the Pentium uses the same 32-bit internal memory addressing scheme that the older microprocessors use, which means it can reach 4GB of system memory directly. What's unusual is that internally the Pentium uses familiar technology. In fact, its internal processing is done by two 486 microprocessors— collocated on the same microchip—that are connected by circuitry to distribute work among them. The Pentium's two microprocessors contain 3.1 million transistors, which is a major increase in circuit density of the 486 microprocessor.

To help coordinate the speed of the Pentium microprocessor to the bus speed of standard desktop computers, the Pentium has a 16K internal cache built into it. However, only half of this cache buffers data. The other 8K of the internal buffer manages program instructions. This highly efficient split cache buffer design is also very different from the 8K cache buffer design of the old Intel 486 family of microprocessors. The Pentium carries on the Intel tradition of backward compatibility.

Although its internal design is very different, Pentium microprocessors run all the same programs that 386 and 486 microprocessors can run. And it runs them in the very same operating modes. It works like this: After the Pentium boots up in *real mode*, it can switch back and forth between *protected* and *virtual 8086* modes. Furthermore, while the

Pentium instruction set has unique new instructions, it also includes all the same commands used in the 486 microprocessor family.

> **NOTE:**   The Pentium microprocessor was designed to work with multitasking operating systems. Therefore, it wasn't very speedy when running DOS applications. Realizing the full benefits of the Pentium design required redesign of both system and application software.

All these innovations would be meaningless, however, if the Pentium didn't have one very important advantage over its predecessors: speed. And yes, the Pentium is faster. While the initial Pentium microprocessors operated at a clock speed of only about 66MHz, faster Pentium processors—with clock speeds of up to 166MHz—were introduced in rapid succession.

PENTIUM PRO   If Intel had maintained its 80*x*86 naming convention, the Pentium Pro would have been called the 80686. Released in 1995, it is the company's sixth-generation microprocessor, and thus is also known as the P6 microprocessor.

Designed for multiuser systems and systems that run multimedia applications, the architecture of the Pentium Pro is again a significant departure from that of the Pentium. It includes such innovative features as superpipelining, dynamic execution, and an on-chip L2 cache. It also implements a multichip design that features the microprocessor on one chip and the cache memory on another. With its 5.5 million transistors, the Pentium Pro also represents another increase in microprocessor circuit density. All of these design features enable the Pentium Pro to perform nearly twice as fast as the older Pentium microprocessors.

PENTIUM MMX   The Intel Pentium MMX is a microprocessor specially designed to run multimedia applications faster. Intel claims that not only does the MMX microprocessor run most applications approximately 10 percent faster than non-MMX microprocessors of identical clock speed, it also executes multimedia applications more than 50 percent faster.

So what's the magic in MMX? Three major technological advances make this increased speed possible:

▼ **Larger memory cache**   The MMX memory cache was expanded to 32KB, which means that it doesn't have to access external memory as often as a non-MMX microprocessor.

■ **New program instructions**   The MMX microprocessor has 57 new instructions to handle multimedia data more efficiently.

▲ **Single instruction multiple data (SIMD)**   This is a new process that enables one instruction to perform the same operation on multiple data items simultaneously.

MMX core technology also uses newly designed algorithms that increase microprocessor performance. It does this by performing operations on bigger chunks of data. It also enables parallel processing of information. This works together with the SIMD process to speed up microprocessor performance on all types of applications. In fact, while this technology was designed specifically to boost performance on multimedia applications, it also enables better performance for—and is fully compatible with—all current applications and operating systems.

PENTIUM II The Pentium II is the successor of the Pentium Pro microprocessor. You may have heard the Pentium II being described as merely a Pentium processor with MMX support, but it is so much more than that. The Pentium II builds on the basic design improvements of the Pentium Pro, but it also brings more raw horsepower to the track. For example, the Pentium II includes 2 million more transistors than the Pentium Pro microprocessor, for a total of 7.5 million. This increase in transistors, along with a new memory bus design that operates at 100MHZ, gives the Pentium II its biggest advantage over the Pentium Pro: speed. Current versions of the chip run at clock speeds of over 400MHz.

But MMX support, more transistors, and higher clock speeds are not the only improvements offered by the Pentium II. This new microprocessor has several innovative features, including the following:

- ▼ **Single Edge Contact Cartridge (SECC)** This lets the Pentium II fit into slot 1 of a desktop computer.

- ■ **More Level Two (L2) memory cache** The Pentium II has a 512KB L2 memory cache—twice as much as the Pentium Pro. This L2 memory cache can support error-corrected code (ECC).

- ▲ **More Level One (L1) memory cache** The Pentium II also has twice as much L1 memory cache as the Pentium Pro—32KB.

What makes something different can also be a liability. The SECC design allows the Pentium II to fit into slot 1, but this design allows for only two CPUs. Therefore, unlike Pentium Pros, Pentium II microprocessors do not support four-way and greater multiprocessing. Therefore, until such time as Intel develops slot 2 support for the Pentium II, you won't find them in large multiprocessor servers.

CELERON AND XEON The Pentium II design has continued to evolve. The newest incarnations of this speedy microprocessor are

- ▼ **Celeron** This is a Pentium II without the L2 cache, or with a smaller L2 cache. This microprocessor is targeted for low-end desktop computers.

- ▲ **Xeon** This Pentium-based design will likely replace the Pentium Pro microprocessor in high-end deployments such as enterprise servers and workstations.

DESCHUTES   This is a small, fast, low-power-consumption variation on the Pentium II design. The Deschutes incorporates the Single-Edge Contact Cartridge (SECC), 512KB L2 memory cache, and MMX instruction set of the Pentium II. The small size and low power consumption are due largely to the fact that the transistors in the Deschutes micro-processors are only 0.25 microns, as opposed to the 0.35-micron transistor size of the standard Pentium II. This means that the Deschutes can hold many more transistors per square millimeter than older Pentium II chips. Other than that, the Deschutes design is identical to the Pentium II.

While Deschutes microprocessors are small and power-thrifty, they aren't currently as fast as standard Pentium II microprocessors. The first Deschutes processors, announced in January of 1997, have a clock speed of 333MHz. The reason for the standard clock speed—despite the ability to incorporate more transistors—is the bottleneck created by the memory bus, which runs at only 60 or 66MHz—the same bus designed used for the initial Pentium microprocessor introduced five years ago. Therefore, for the performance of the Deschutes to reflect its increased processing power, the memory bus must be redesigned to operate at higher speeds.

Intel has promised a bright future for Deschutes. First of all, the company plans to introduce a Deschutes microprocessor with a high-speed memory bus, allowing it to run at clock speeds of 350 to 400MHz. However, we have yet to see this version of the Deschutes. In fact, we haven't seen much in the way of Deschutes development for some time, causing speculation on Intel's commitment to this particular microprocessor.

Sun Microsystems Scalable Performance Architecture (SPARC)

Sun Microsystems' SPARC microprocessors are reduced instruction set computer (RISC) microprocessors that can scale from desktop computer systems to supercomputer systems. The SPARC product family has three members:

▼   **MicroSPARC**   This is the SPARC line of microprocessors for desktop computer systems. It is also being developed for portable computer use.

■   **SuperSPARC**   This line of microprocessors is designed for high-end workstations and network servers. It features a 32-bit architecture with clock speeds up to the 90MHz range.

▲   **UltraSPARC**   This is the premium 64-bit SPARC processor. It has clock speeds ranging from 200MHz to 300MHz.

The SPARC microprocessor was originally developed for computer workstations: high-end desktop systems that ran 3-D, scientific, and engineering design applications. However, the design has expanded to include everything from low-end desktop computer systems to server systems. In fact, Sun also has a mainframe-class system, the Ultra Enterprise 10000, which is based on the UltraSPARC microprocessors.

PowerPC

Once all the rage—and heralded as the future of desktop computers—the PowerPC is a RISC-based computer developed jointly by IBM, Motorola, and Apple Computer. This microprocessor's name is a cute acronym of the IBM designation for this design: Performance Optimization With Enhanced RISC (POWER).

The PowerPC is the result of RISC workstation development efforts that began with the IBM Personal Computer RT, and continued with the Motorola RISC System/6000 system microprocessor. The PowerPC microprocessors are a direct descendant of this RS/6000 technology, which in essence combines the functionality of many microprocessors into one.

In 1994, Apple became the first company to introduce a product based on the PowerPC design, the Power Mac. Other manufacturers soon followed suit. The claim to fame for the PowerPC is its ability to be somewhat "operating environment agnostic." That is, the microprocessor—through software emulation—can run DOS, UNIX, and Apple PowerPC programs, despite the fact that the PowerPC is not code-compatible Intel microprocessors. Today, most popular operating systems, including Windows NT, OS/2, and Apple's Macintosh OS (System 7.5 and higher) run on the Power PC microprocessor.

THE RISC OF POWER   The PowerPC is based on such standard RISC features as the following:

▼   Compact instructions

■   Consistent encoding system

■   Simple, consistent three-operand format

▲   Superscalar design

The PowerPC architecture also adds new features to the world of RISC microprocessors, such as integral handling of floating point numbers and instruction sets that perform multiple operations in each instruction. Because it supports these complex instruction sets, the PowerPC design looks a lot like complex instruction set computers.

Unfortunately, although the technical reviews of products have been good, the PowerPC hasn't set the computing world on fire. The market seems to be divided firmly between traditional RISC and CISC designs, leaving little room for adoption of this hybrid architecture.

Lightweight Clients

A new breed of simpler, less powerful desktop network hardware has surfaced. These new devices have different names and come in a variety of architectures, but they have all been developed with three goals:

▼   Lower costs

■   Simplify management

▲   Increase security

These products aren't designed to do independent computing, but rather to function in conjunction with network servers—in much the same way that old-fashioned terminals functioned with mainframe computers. The configuration for each device is stored on a network server. Then, regardless of a user's physical location, when that user logs on to the network, the user downloads his or her familiar desktop configuration. Dial-up services allow users to dial a number local to them and access remote servers over the Internet in a secure way while reducing long-distance charges.

These systems have a lot of advantages. They reduce the cost of desktop systems by decreasing the resources each device needs. They simplify management by minimizing maintenance and centralizing control and management by letting network administrators "lock down" desktop configurations, deny users access to certain executable files, and prevent users from accessing system files and installing unapproved applications. Also, they increase security by providing features that prevent theft of hardware, software, and data.

Currently, there are three broad categories of lightweight desktop hardware devices:

▼ Diskless workstations

■ Network computers (NCs)

▲ NetPCs

DISKLESS WORKSTATIONS   A diskless workstation is exactly what the name implies: a computer without a floppy or hard disk drive. Its lack of storage and computing power make it both a secure and relatively inexpensive network access device. As a result, diskless workstations are ideal for temporary employees or for use in unsupervised areas.

There are, however, a couple of things to consider before you opt for diskless workstations. First, keep in mind that you'll need a network interface card that supports the use of a remote boot PROM (programmable read-only memory) chip. It is this boot PROM that allows the diskless workstation to log in to a network server when it is turned on, and continue its boot procedures from a boot file located on that server. Most interface cards have a boot PROM option available for an additional charge.

Second, remember that a diskless workstation will access the server for all of its data. If the server goes down, there won't be any place to store the data currently being processed by the diskless workstation. With improvements in network hardware, software, and availability, this isn't as big a concern as it used to be—but it's still a consideration.

NETWORK COMPUTERS   *Network computers* are similar to diskless workstations in that they are inexpensive network access devices that do not have floppy drives or hard drives. They use network servers for their disk and storage requirements. Just like diskless workstations, they can only operate when the network is up and running. Often called *thin clients*, NCs are in fact just a specific type of diskless workstation. The characteristics that define a network computer are

▼ TCP/IP network connection

▲ Support for terminal emulation, X-Windows, Java, and Web browser software

Actually, it's probably most accurate just to think of an NC as an Internet terminal. NCs are perfect for providing secure, inexpensive Internet access in places in which you don't need much local computing power. NCs execute Java applets that have been downloaded from servers on the Internet or intranet. Most of the application runs on the server, so the client device doesn't need a lot of computing power. In the multitiered Internet model illustrated in Figure 13-4, the user runs a browser on an NC to connect to a Web server. The Web server then connects with data located on back-end server systems.

The beauty of an NC is that it can be based on nearly any kind of microprocessor. That's because it runs Java and Web software, which are processor independent.

The Sun Microsystems JavaStation is probably the most well-known NC, as well as one of the truest to the original NC concept. After booting from a boot file on a Sun server, the JavaStation downloads Java applets and executes them in memory. You can also purchase NC-like network access devices from vendors such as Boundless Technologies and Neoware Systems. These devices either operate as Windows terminals or run X-Windows applications.

NETPCS The NetPC is the Microsoft/Intel-based version of the network computer (NC). These two companies, along with other manufacturers of Intel-compatible computers, developed a model they called the NetPC Reference Platform. This model defines an industry-standard, Intel-based terminal that runs Windows applications but doesn't allow end users to modify the system hardware. This design provides the cost, management, and security benefits of NC products, but without forcing Windows-based networks to convert to new applications and operating environments.

The requirements outlined by the NetPC Reference Platform are

▼ Minimum 16MB memory

■ Hard drive for boot and caching

■ Minimum 100MHz Pentium microprocessor

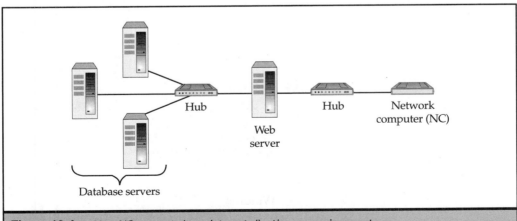

Figure 13-4. How NCs operate in an Internet client/server environment

- Support network connections via 10Base-T, Token Ring, 28.8Kbps modems, ISDN, T1, or ATM
- Sealed case with no expansion slots
- VGA display adapter
- Audio support
- Unique machine ID
- Plug-and-Play support, with each system and add-on device having its own unique device ID
▲ Require minimal user configuration

Notice that, unlike the NC, the NetPC requires a hard disk. NetPCs can therefore boot from these local hard drives, so they don't have to connect to a network server to access their boot files. The NetPC designers believe this speeds up both the boot procedure and overall network performance, because it reduces traffic on the network during the desktop boot procedure. However, note that the NetPC does not have floppy disks or CD-ROMs, so it offers the same security benefits as the NC-type devices.

WINDOWS TERMINAL   The Windows Terminal is similar in concept to the NetPC. A Windows Terminal provides familiar terminal services in which a Windows client executes applications on a Windows NT server. However, the Windows Terminal also lets users access Java applications.

The enabling technology behind the Windows Terminal is Winframe, developed by Citrix Systems. WinFrame, as we will see in the next section, is a multiuser Windows *application server*. An application server puts most of the burden of processing Windows applications on the server rather than the Windows client. Microsoft and Citrix developed WinFrame support within Windows itself.

THE SOFTER SIDE OF THE DESKTOP: SOFTWARE CLIENTS

Now that we have discussed the hardware options that you have for your desktop devices, it's time to take a look at the various operating environments available for these devices.

Traditionally, the type of operating environment you selected determined the type of hardware you selected. This was because, until not too long ago, UNIX ran only on RISC processors and Windows ran only on Intel processors. In fact, the type of UNIX you selected mandated a specific type of RISC microprocessor.

Now, however, there are versions of UNIX that run on Intel microprocessors. And Windows NT runs on some RISC processors. This opens many new options, but it also implies an important caveat: *Be sure that the microprocessor supports the intended operating environments, and vice versa.*

UNIX

UNIX is robust, open, and highly regarded operating system. Because it has had such a profound impact on the development of high-end workstations, a little history of this operating system is in order.

UNIX Roots

UNIX was developed in the late 1960s and early 1970s by Ken Thompson and Dennis Ritchie while they were working at Bell Laboratories. The first versions of UNIX were developed to run on DEC midrange computers. The unusual name of this operating system is a sort of acronym for Uniplexed Information and Computer System, which is derived in turn from a play on the word Multics, which was a time-sharing operating system developed in the early 1960s. Multics was probably the first operating system that implemented multitasking through time-sharing.

In the early 1970s, three events took place that revolutionized UNIX and gave it a major technological edge. In 1973, UNIX was rewritten in the C programming language by workers at Bell Labs. The C language is known for its ability to be recompiled to run on just about any hardware platform, so this new version of UNIX made the operating system highly portable. It now contains system components written in a common, well-known programming language that is easily recompiled to work on a variety of systems. About the same time, developers integrated *pipes*, a means of accessing and combing data gathered from different programs, into UNIX. Piping provides a way to send the data output of one command directly into another command. In 1975, AT&T, then owners of Bell Labs, made the operating system freely available to universities and colleges for their internal use. The result was a solid, open operating system that could run on just about any hardware platform and access data from just about any application, and had a built-in base of enthusiastic and technologically sophisticated users.

When college researchers and students began experimenting (as college students are known to do) with UNIX, the resulting variations of the operating system produced some very important technical breakthroughs. Probably the best known and most significant of these efforts is from the University of California at Berkeley. For example, it was at Berkeley that TCP/IP networking protocols were incorporated into UNIX. It was also the place where UNIX was first ported to the DEC VAX. The versions of UNIX developed at Berkeley were so significant that they have their own name: the *Berkeley Software Distributions*, or *BSDs*.

NOTE: The version of UNIX stemming from AT&T's original work is now called the System V Release or SRV.

MARRIAGES OF CONVENIENCE (AND INCONVENIENCE) As UNIX development gained more significance and momentum, AT&T concentrated its UNIX development resources into a unit called UNIX System Laboratories (USL). In the early 1990s, AT&T entered into a joint venture with Novell, Inc., called Univell, to develop a desktop UNIX system with built-in

Novell NetWare support. This product was called UnixWare. Only a couple of years after the founding of this joint venture, Novell purchased USL and used it as the basis of its UNIX Systems Group (USG) whose function was to manage the development and marketing of UnixWare.

Novell thereby gained both ownership of USL and control over the UNIX trademark, which in turn gave the company a great deal of control over UNIX products. Novell immediately began to promote a single UNIX operating system, to which its trademark authority lent force. To that end, Novell gave the UNIX trademark to the X/Open organization, a group founded in the mid-1980s to ensure open UNIX standards through product testing. Unfortunately, developers of UNIX and developers of NetWare were unsuccessful in designing an operating system that incorporated the best of both. Unable to compromise on features and functionality, Novell began to fear that UNIX would rival—rather than complement—NetWare. Therefore, in 1995, the company sold UNIX to the Santa Cruz Operation.

How UNIX Works

Whether deployed on a desktop or in a server, UNIX is a multiuser system. It supports distributed file systems such as Sun Microsystems' Network File System (NFS). Because of its unique design, UNIX is very easy for a user to customize.

> **NOTE:**   Sun Microsystems' NFS is the most commonly used distributed file-sharing system included with UNIX, although the Andrew File System (AFS), developed by the Open Group, is also used.

The core of UNIX is a small *kernel* of code with the sole job of executing and managing *processes*. Examples of processes are print services and user applications. The UNIX kernel doesn't change much from one computing platform to another. On the other hand, even users with just a little UNIX knowledge can add processes at will. Therefore, a user can add new services that he or she needs, and remove services that he or she doesn't use. This makes UNIX more useful and efficient for each individual user. In fact, users access the operating system through a special type of process called a *shell*, which the user can customize to meet his or her particular needs and tastes.

UNIX employs a hierarchical file system, meaning it is designed with a root directory and subdirectories beneath it. Individual files are located beneath directories and/or subdirectories. Peripheral devices are managed as though they were files.

UNIX includes networking capability as an integral part of the operating system. Largely as a result of some of the development work done at Berkeley, TCP/IP protocols are tightly integrated with UNIX. In fact, every UNIX implementation currently available incorporates TCP/IP as well as support for the Ethernet network access method.

As you can see, UNIX is a form of one-stop shopping. It's a powerful, flexible, multiuser operating system that runs on virtually any hardware platform and lets users share files and execute processes on other computers. However, as we have said, there are several different "flavors" of UNIX available. So it's probably best at this point to take a look at some of the most popular.

Solaris

Probably the most popular version of UNIX on the planet is Sun Microsystems' Solaris. It is a Berkeley Software Distribution version of UNIX, although it has many of the features of the AT&T System V Releases. In fact, Solaris based on UNIX System V Release 4, which Sun optimized for distributed network environments. In addition, Solaris is now Java-enabled, includes the HotJava browser, and supports Java Virtual Machine (VM).

Solaris runs on both SPARC and Intel platforms, and a PowerPC version is planned. It also supports multiprocessing—which means a single server uses multiple processors—and multithreading—which enables the processor to break applications into separate processes that are executed in parallel on different processors.

COMMON DESKTOP ENVIRONMENT   The latest release of Solaris also includes Common Desktop Environment (CDE) as the default desktop. CDE is a set of UNIX specifications defining a standard desktop interface to provide a consistent look and feel across UNIX platforms. It was developed and is overseen by the Open Group, and is based on the X Windows System Motif desktop.

NOTE: The Open Group was founded in 1996 when X/Open merged with the Open Software Foundation (OSF). The Open Group grants the UNIX trademark to UNIX products that comply with accepted specifications designed to promote portability of applications among operating systems. In addition to CDE, the Open Group also manages the Motif graphical user interface and other UNIX standards. For more information on the Open Group, visit www.opengroup.org.

The goal of CDE is to offer a common programming interface for developing shrink-wrapped UNIX software that looks and acts the same on all versions of UNIX. It is also intended to provide a common graphical user interface for both users and system administrators that will help UNIX compete more effectively with Windows NT. Among the administrative aims of CDE is to make desktop operating systems simpler for "power users" to manage and use, as well as to give system administrators more control over high-end desktops.

THE SOLARIS UNIVERSE   Solaris is designed for Web networking, as evidenced by the fact that it includes WebNFS, a Web-enabled version of Network File System. Solaris also includes all of the networking you would expect from a UNIX operating system, such as TCP/IP service and distributed naming services. These are included in a package of services incorporated into Solaris called Open Network Computing (ONC). Solaris also comes with NIS+ Global Directory Services for a distributed data management, as well as DCE.

FreeBSD

Another member of the Berkeley UNIX family is FreeBSD, which like Solaris can run on Intel processors. As its name implies, FreeBSD is free. All you have to do is download it from the Internet at www.frebsd.org.

Linux

Judging by its recent surge in popularity, Linux is more than an operating system, but something only slightly less than a cult. Like FreeBSD, it is available at no charge. Version 2.2 of Linux is a 64-bit version of UNIX that runs on almost any hardware platform, including SPARC, Intel, PowerPC, and DEC Alpha processors. It also supports multi-processing hardware platforms. It adheres to the standards set forth by the Open Group. It supports Java (naturally), and will run applications written for the SVR4 and SCO UNIX systems without modification or recompilation. Also, it has recently gained a lot of popularity as a platform for Web servers and firewalls.

While the kernel of this operating system was developed by Linus Torvalds as a college assignment, many of the features and functionality of his namesake operating environment were developed as freeware by its users. While the price is certainly right, the catch is that critical drivers, features, and patches may not be available because no one has seen fit to develop them. And even if you can locate the patch or fix you need, you may not be able to find support for it. (For all you know, the user who developed it is on six-month sabbatical in Antarctica.)

Therefore, before you decide to put Linux in your production environment, do some research to make sure that your intended applications run on Linux and that you have all the necessary patches, features, drivers, and fixes you need. A good place to begin is the Web site for the Linux Documentation Project at sunsite.unc.edu/LDP. You may also want to find yourself a reliable Linux specialist.

Windows

When Microsoft first introduced Windows, the product was little more than a graphical user interface (GUI) for the company's Disk Operating System (DOS). However, when Microsoft shipped Windows 3.0, it marked a significant advance in desktop operating system environments because this product took advantage of the multitasking possibilities of the 386 microprocessor. This meant that users were able to run more than one application at a time. However, Windows 3.0 was still not a full operating system, but rather a GUI for DOS.

That has changed, however. Beginning with Windows 95 (shipped, as the name implies, in 1995), Windows became a true operating system, and no longer required DOS. In fact, Microsoft Windows is now an entire product family, including the following desktop and palm-top products:

▼ **Windows 95**   Currently, this is probably the most widely used version of Windows. Windows 95 is a 32-bit multitasking operating system with integrated networking, electronic messaging, Internet access, and fax support. It can also support mobile computing. Although Windows 95 performs best when running applications that have been written for it—and many thousands of applications have been—it can also run DOS applications.

■ **Windows 98**   This newest version of Windows is designed to support desktop computers that function in a Web environment. Not only does it fully support Web application and browser technologies such as Internet Explorer, it also has fully integrated support for the multimedia hardware needed to view much of the Web content, technologies, and entertainment platforms.

■ **Windows NT Workstation 4.0**   Microsoft intended its NT Workstation product as the operating system of choice for high-end desktop computers. This product is a 32-bit operating system with extra security features and enhanced performance. However, adoption of Windows NT Workstation, even among high-end clients, hasn't been nearly as widespread as that of Windows 95. Microsoft is planning to release its Windows NT Workstation 5.0 (now called Windows 2000) sometime in 1999. Perhaps this new version of NT will begin to replace Windows 95/98 as the preeminent high-end desktop operating system.

▲ **Windows CE**   This is a scaled-back version of Windows for small, highly specialized devices such as mobile telephones and palm-top computers.

WinFrame

We mentioned WinFrame earlier in this chapter during our discussion of NetPCs. As we mentioned, WinFrame is a product of Citrix Systems, although its current version is very much a result of collaboration between Microsoft and Citrix. WinFrame increases and extends the multiuser functionality of Windows to allow NetPCs and diskless work-stations to run Windows NT remotely, executing the code on a server itself rather than locally on the desktop hardware. In essence, WinFrame enables a Windows NT server to host multiple client sessions and perform most of the processing. This relocation of Windows processing is transparent to the users, who see the same Windows GUI they would see if the processing were done locally.

The core of WinFrame technology is a presentation service protocol for Windows developed by Citrix called the *Independent Computing Architecture* (ICA), a terminal-mainframe type model that runs locally over PPP, IPX/SPX, and TCP/IP. It also operates remotely over frame relay, ATM, and ISDN.

ICA operates on much the same principle as X-Windows in UNIX. It turns the client computer into a terminal that sends and receives only displays and keystrokes between the client and the server, while the applications are run on the server. This has several advantages, including the following:

▼ Clients don't have to be powerful machines.

■ Network traffic is limited to narrow-bandwidth transmissions of screens and keystrokes.

▲ Older desktop computers can run 32-bit applications on servers.

MANAGING THE DESKTOP

We've got the desktop hardware. We've selected the desktop operating environment. Now how do we manage it?

Management of the desktop environment and desktop assets is probably one of the most difficult challenges facing network administrators. By their very nature, these network assets are scattered throughout the enterprise and vulnerable to tampering, abuse, and theft. In the remainder of this chapter, we discuss some of the latest initiatives and products aimed at helping network administrators monitor desktop systems and keep them working efficiently.

Zero Administration for Windows Initiative

Microsoft's Zero Administration for Windows (ZAW) initiative is actually a suite of technologies that

▼ Centralizes the administration of Windows desktops

■ Automates installation and configuration of Windows-based desktop systems

■ Allows Windows desktops to be "locked" so that end users can't change configurations

■ Stores users' desktop configurations on the network server, so users can log in to any desktop on the network and still access their unique desktop configuration

▲ Supports caching on the network client to improve performance and reduce network traffic

ZAWS is an important part of Microsoft's management architecture for multiuser systems such as WinFrame and Hydra Server.

Wired for Management (WfM) Initiative

Microsoft's ZAW is largely implemented in software. Complementing ZAW on the hardware side is Intel's Wired for Management (WfM) architecture. Together, the two management schemes create a flexible system for building and managing desktops in a distributed environment.

WfM specifies a standard set of requirements for managing hardware, such as:

▼ Remote wake-up

■ Boot capability

■ Power management

- Remote configuration
- Remote troubleshooting
- Centralized, automated software distribution and upgrades
- ▲ Centralized system management

Furthermore, Intel's WfM supports *Desktop Management Interface* (DMI), which we will discuss in the next section.

Desktop Management Interface (DMI)

Desktop Management Interface (DMI) is both a programming and reporting standard to facilitate the management of computers. Defined by the Desktop Management Task Force (DMTF), DMI is an application programming interface designed to give network managers specific data about desktop computers connected to their networks, as well as to assist network managers with remote configuration of these computers. DMI defines the specifications agents that manufacturers of desktop hardware and software products can build into their products. These agents collect information about the desktop system and its components, then report that information back to a DMI management console, providing network managers with information about remote desktops. The DMI console also allows network managers to perform management and configuration tasks remotely, based on the information gathered by the DMI agents. Among the types of information that DMI agents can gather about desktop systems are

- ▼ Hardware components, such as processor type and speed, amount of memory, and available disk storage space
- Software components
- Hardware configuration
- Software configuration information
- Troubleshooting and status reports on hardware and software components
- ▲ Version of hardware and software components, and information on whether these are the most current and/or the network standard version

As you can clearly see, having this information collected and available in one place is vital to enabling network managers to solve desktop problems quickly—and relatively painlessly.

Because DMI is based on standard specifications, it is open and interoperable with any management protocol. Furthermore, all applications that adhere to DMI can access the same interface. DMI can also be integrated in desktop peripherals such as modems and printers.

DMI Architecture Components

The components involved in the DMI architecture are illustrated in Figure 13-5. DMI presents a standard means for accessing the Management Interface (MI). Applications make requests to the MI via DMI. These requests are then forwarded to the Component Interface (CI). The CI enable remote management via the DMI, and the CI allows the vendor of a product to set the level of remote management needed and allowed for their products.

Another component defined in the DMI is the Management Information Format File (MIFF). This is simply a text file in which DMI records data about the desktop systems. Management applications that comply with DMI know to check the MIFF for information about the component.

DMTF (Desktop Management Task Force)

Founded in 1992, the Desktop Management Task Force is a forum composed of companies such as Intel, Hewlett-Packard, and Microsoft for the purpose of developing products and technologies to facilitate the management of desktop computer systems. DMI is the first and most far-reaching result of this collaboration, but its work did not stop there. In 1996, the DMTF started developing a common information model for management information based on an object-oriented architecture.

Where It Begins and Ends

As you can see, while the familiar desktop computer seems to be the least intimidating of all network components, selecting the appropriate desktop systems involves several

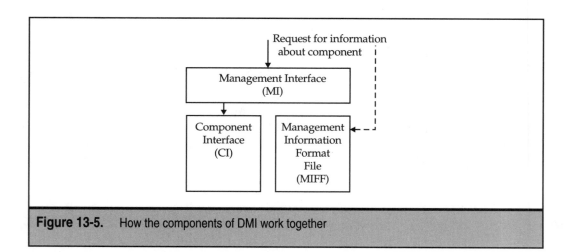

Figure 13-5.   How the components of DMI work together

critical technology choices. What type of work the user must accomplish, the resources available to that user, and the environment in which the user must work are all considerations. And there is another critical factor in determining the type of desktop system: the type of server on which the applications and data the user needs are located. And that is the subject of our next chapter.

CHAPTER 14

The Server

No matter the size of your network—from a five-computer home office to the thousands of machines in a multinational conglomerate—the heart of your network is the file server. Sure, mainframes and minis still exist and are humming along quite nicely, but even the staunchest of Big Iron shops have fallen victim to the rush in recent years of client/server computing.

Unfortunately, while file servers are readily available from dozens of manufacturers, choosing the configuration that's right for you is not a simple task. In fact, the server purchase is likely to be one of the most agonizing decisions you'll have to make as an IS manager. We present this chapter to help you make sense of the acronyms and to better make an informed buying, upgrading, or redeployment decision.

SERVER FUNCTIONS

File servers perform a variety of tasks, depending on the specific implementation of the machine as well as its capabilities. In general, servers provide some or all of the following services:

▼ Centralized storage, management, and backup of user files

■ Centralized storage of applications (and now, Web pages)

■ Management of user security and rights

■ Management of the company's electronic mail

■ Monitoring of the network, servers, and clients for performance, security, and troubleshooting

▲ Centralized printing or fax services

Clearly, the more of the above tasks that you want your server to do, the more you're going to have to pay for it. If file servers were clearly marketed giving their fitness for each of the above processes, choosing one would be a snap. Unfortunately, categorization of servers is nowhere near standardized, so you'll have to carefully analyze the features of any server you're considering, and weigh that against the price you're willing to pay.

Take, for example, the recently discontinued line of Prioris servers by Digital Equipment Corp. (now Compaq). The Prioris family was divided into four categories: Workgroup, Mainstream, Applications, and Enterprise. While it's clear that a Workgroup server offered limited performance at a budget price, and the Enterprise server was the high-end offering (about $30,000), exactly what a "Mainstream" server was good for was decidedly unclear. While the Prioris line was overall of very high quality, deciding from the six major models and hundreds of possible configurations was a very daunting task.

Even worse, Sun Microsystems offers a line of servers called Sun Enterprise. The line includes a whopping 15 models (at current count), which run the gamut from the very affordable, bottom-of-the-line, PC-sized Sun Enterprise 1 (under $5,000) to the gargantuan, up-to-64-processors, 1,400-pound Sun Enterprise 10000. The Enterprise 10000 typically lists for about $3 million.

As you can see, even choosing from among the array of "Enterprise" systems will often leave you baffled at the range of options.

So where do you start? First, let's look at the different functions of servers along with the general requirements you'll need to fulfill those tasks.

File Servers

File servers, in the purest sense of the term, are used to centrally store documents and data files of the users on the network. Centrally locating these files allows them to be easily shared among other users, and more important, provides a single point for backing up data. With any reasonably fast file server, data access speed will be indistinguishable as to whether the file is coming over the LAN or is located on the user's hard drive.

I/O is the critical subsystem for pure file servers. Look for a server with a fast RAID (redundant array of inexpensive disks) controller and speedy drives. You'll also want a large amount of storage plus the ability to grow; data files, more than anything, have a way of rapidly ballooning in size. With most file servers, the actual CPU isn't as important as the amount of memory the server has. Because RAID slows the system down, I/O transactions will back up into RAM during periods of heavy usage. The more memory you can load on to your system, the better off you'll be.

Application Servers

The ability to centrally store applications is one benefit of servers, although it is inappropriate in many situations. For example, storing a copy of Microsoft Word on the server, which is then used by all of the clients on the network, has some advantages. You only have to install the application once; when a new version comes out, you only have to update it once; and permissions for each application can be managed from one central point. This allows you to get away with less processing power on the client machines, because the server does more of the work.

Unfortunately, unlike storing data files, serving applications across the LAN can cause some serious bottlenecks. First, most applications are large and memory-hungry executables. Running one copy on the server isn't a problem, but running 10, 20, or 30 copies of it might be. This is where extra memory, extra CPUs, *and* faster I/O processing will be required. You'll also likely need a 100Base-T network infrastructure to handle all of the traffic this can generate.

As the server does more and more of the work, the clients can be less sophisticated. Ultimately, this can culminate in a so-called "thin client" computing paradigm, where the client machines are stripped-down terminals that do very little processing on their own. What this requires, though, is a gargantuan server that can do the processing for all of the clients simultaneously. This type of power does not come cheap.

With the continued advances of Microsoft Terminal Server, Citrix MetaFrame, and Oracle's network computing platforms, building a system like this may not be such a bad idea. However, be prepared to pay dearly for the hardware to build it, as well as the software that makes it run.

Database Servers

A database server looks a lot like a file server, in theory: it simply stores a large amount of information and gives it to the clients that request it. However, a database server typically does a vastly larger amount of processing because, rather than just picking and choosing files to send to the client, the database server is often called on through a query to provide a more intelligent selection of database records that are filtered or manipulated into a more useful format.

Database servers not only require good I/O and lots of RAM, but they easily benefit from better and faster CPUs. The "TPC" benchmarks you read about in server advertisements are all based on database transaction speeds.

Web Servers

Web servers have been a rapidly growing market segment over the last few years, much in keeping with the growth of the Internet. A Web server can fall into one of several categories: it can serve up static HTML pages (the Web server functioning much like a file server); it can perform complex searches and lookups; or it can serve Java applets (the Web server functioning more like a database or application server). Choosing a Web server is largely contingent on these specifics.

Probably of more importance, however, is the software you use to implement your Web server. Most high-end Web servers are currently UNIX-based Apache servers. While Microsoft and Netscape produce very popular Web servers for the Windows NT market, UNIX is still the dominant Web player. Typically, a Sun Microsystems server is the platform of choice. However, Intel-based machines running the free Linux operating system are also quite popular.

Mail Servers

The single most-used application in any office is typically e-mail. From the receptionist to the CEO, just about every employee in today's office environment relies on e-mail to get his or her job done. With the expansion of messaging systems into full-fledged "groupware" applications, performing scheduling, conferencing, and workflow management duties, mail servers have had to grow in their capabilities.

If your e-mail is limited to simple messaging, memory and I/O will be key, especially if large messages or attachments are commonly sent in and out of the organization. If you use some of the groupware functions discussed above, you'll also need a powerful CPU. Thankfully, most mail server applications like Microsoft Exchange include performance-monitoring tools to let you know what subsystems are lacking. Don't forget to make sure you have a fast Internet connection, too, if much of your e-mail leaves your network.

Print Servers

We all know that one user in the office who prints a copy of *everything*, from the most menial e-mail to the README file on his or her new application. Because it makes much more sense to centralize printing services, users like this can dominate the printer for a workgroup of only a few people.

Print servers generally handle loads like this much better than the printers themselves, but it's important to make sure that the server has plenty of disk space to hold the print queue. A fair amount of RAM (32MB usually suffices) is fine for even heavy print jobs. Most printers can get by without a print server at all, using a device that costs just a few hundred dollars to interface with the network on the printer's behalf. These devices (HP's JetDirect is a good example) work quite well and are recommended for users who don't have spare machines lying around to work as print servers. Many file servers also work fine doing double duty as a print server.

Fax Servers

Why install a modem in every PC (and a direct phone line in every office) when you can do PC-based faxing from a central point? No reason, really. Fax servers make a lot of sense, and while you can usually build one out of your e-mail server without additional software, the more sophisticated applications like GFI FAXmaker (www.gfifax.com) or RightFAX Enterprise (www.rightfax.com) can provide inbound and outbound fax services, with incoming faxes delivered to the user's e-mail inbox. These applications also provide sophisticated usage reports, backup features, and management utilities.

Remote Access Servers

Remote access is of growing importance to most networks; remote access servers, however, are *not*. That's because with the growth of Internet connectivity and virtual private networking, the days of having a large bank of modems to support your remote users are rapidly coming to a close.

Even when remote access does require direct dial-in access, this can generally be accomplished more effectively by using a remote access appliance like the Shiva LanRover (www.shiva.com). These appliances interface with your network and have four, eight, or more dial-in ports that you simply connect to your POTS lines. It is certainly a more elegant solution than a wall full of modems that must be individually troubleshot.

Backup Servers

While many IS shops connect a backup device directly to the server that needs to be backed up, sometimes it makes more sense to have a dedicated machine perform backup duties. This is especially true if you have multiple servers and don't want the hassle of multiple tape drives and multiple copies of backup software (Computer Associates ARCServe (www.cai.com) and Seagate BackupExec (www.seagatesoftware.com/products) are the market leaders). We'll cover more of the details of data backups in a later section in this chapter.

As with file servers, backup servers are simply copying files from a hard disk (or the network) to the tape drive. Fast I/O and RAM are important, but in general, the speed of the tape drive will be the bottleneck unless you invest in an expensive, high-end backup device.

SERVER MARKETING CATEGORIES

As mentioned earlier, it would be nice to know at a glance which of the above tasks a given server is good for. While the following guide to server marketing categories is by no means definitive (as we've seen, Sun crosses all of these lines with its "Enterprise" machines), it's a place to start when looking at product descriptions.

Workgroup/Department Servers

Some server vendors differentiate these two categories, with department servers being a slightly higher-end system, but for all intents and purposes they are identical.

In the first half of 1999, a typical workgroup server includes one or two high-speed Pentium II or Pentium III processors, 128MB to 256MB of RAM, three to six 4GB or 8GB disk drives, a CD-ROM drive, a standard 100Mbps NIC, and a copy of Intel LANDesk or some other server management software. Hot-swap drives and a RAID controller may or may not be included. If neither is included, the price should run around $6,000. With both, and with a better combination of the above features, prices creep into the $12,000 and $13,000 range. Performance will vary greatly depending on the amount of RAM and the specs of the drives and/or RAID card.

Workgroup servers will almost always make excellent file and print servers, and with speedy processors and lots of RAM, they can work as Web, application, and database servers as well. In the archetypal workgroup, the workgroup server does all of these things, just not for many people. As your headcount increases, you'll need to add more servers, splitting the employee load among each system, or (more likely) dividing the duties among different servers, each of which is optimized for its particular task.

Often, older servers tend to find uses when demoted to providing secondary services like Domain Name Services (DNS), or working as backups in case a primary server fails. Remember that you may be able to extend the life of old hardware significantly by reevaluating its use as it ages.

Midrange Servers

Traditionally, midrange systems have been either souped-up workgroup servers or stripped-down enterprise systems. Because workgroup servers have advanced so much, so quickly, and because prices of enterprise systems have fallen considerably, the midrange market is starting to disappear. Some midrange servers still exist: a few dual

Pentium Pro systems, department systems with high-end RAID controllers, or servers with advanced management features that don't quite match the enterprise servers, all priced around $15,000 to $18,000. As server prices continue to fall, however, expect these types of systems to continue to disappear.

Enterprise Servers

The enterprise server typically starts at $25,000 and goes nowhere but up. As mentioned before, Sun's Enterprise 10000 runs up to $3 million.

Today's Intel-based enterprise server is typically something like the Dell Computer 6300, a four-way Pentium II Xeon system with 1GB of RAM, six or eight hot-swappable Ultra2/LVD SCSI drives, dual 100Mbps NICs with hot-swap features built in, redundant power supplies, and advanced management tools. Servers like Axil Computer's (now defunct) Northridge system contained eight Pentium Pro processors, 2GB of RAM, over 20 disk drives, a touchscreen for instant server diagnostics, and more (the Northridge ran from about $50,000 up to $120,000 or more). As you can probably tell, the upper price boundary for enterprise systems is undefined.

The point of an enterprise server is to do anything you want. Typically, this involves being the back-end for a database-heavy application suite like SAP/R3 or Oracle Financials, or powering a mammoth Web site. The server may also do triple or quadruple duty as a file/print server and e-mail server as well.

When you're looking for a server that can "do everything," remember to keep in mind the growth of your company, your plans for the Internet and e-commerce, and the technology that's on the horizon. The server that fits today's needs perfectly might be out-of-date in six short months. With a purchase of this magnitude, it's crucial to look to the future.

No one ever said it would be easy!

SERVER ARCHITECTURE

In our general discussion of server architecture, we're going to assume a few things. First, we assume you are buying an Intel-based machine, or at least a machine that can run Windows NT or Novell NetWare. While the discussion herein is largely appropriate to machines with other chipsets designed to run UNIX, their architecture is generally proprietary to a given manufacturer and is outside the scope of our discussion.

We also assume you're not looking to spend more than about $35,000 on a server. If you want a higher-end system, and plenty exist, the architecture again creeps into proprietary design, even on Intel-based systems. We cover systems like eight-way Pentium Pro servers only briefly herein, and as they relate to their lower-end brethren.

Other than that, we'll hit all the bases of each important component and subsystem of a file server, and we'll try to give you an idea of what to expect in today's server offerings.

Server Design: The Big Picture

By and large, a file server looks, and acts, like an overgrown PC. Figures 14-1 and 14-2 show the externals of a generic file server. Keep in mind that the actual design of any server will

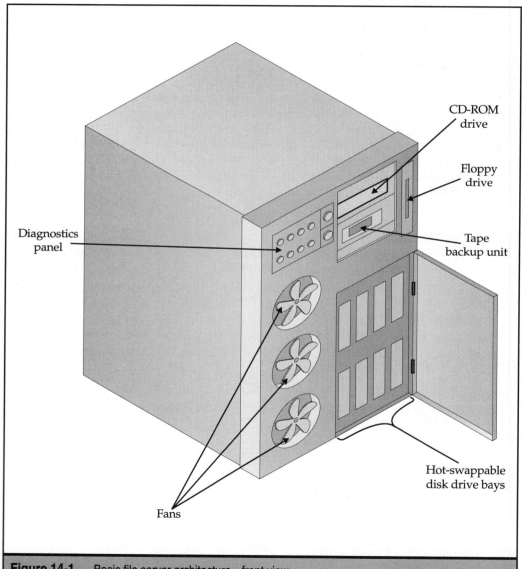

Figure 14-1.   Basic file server architecture—front view

vary from manufacturer to manufacturer, but by and large, the same components will be present: you'll probably just have more or less of each.

With the exception of the hot-swappable disk drive bays, the front of a file server should look very familiar. CD-ROM and floppy drives, as well as tape backup units or additional fixed drives normally sit in one of the upper corners. Diagnostic LEDs or LCD diagnostic screens are generally found next to these bays.

In the lower half of the server, or running in a horizontally mounted column, are the disk drive bays. Some servers have as few as three drive bays; higher-end servers have up to 12. Pictured in Figure 14-1 is a server with eight bays, mounted vertically in two rows.

The total number of bays can depend in part on the form factor of the drives: obviously, 1"-high drives take up less space than 1.6"-high, higher-capacity drives. Some servers, like Dell's PowerEdge line, allow you to adjust the backplane (the circuit board to which the drives are connected) based on the form factor of the drives you want to use.

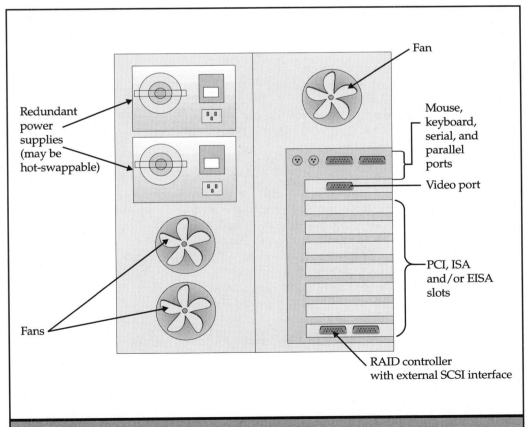

Figure 14-2. Basic file server architecture—rear view

This way, if you use 1" drives instead of 1.6" drives, you can usually squeeze two additional disks into the system.

Again, the rear of a file server will look much like that of an average PC. The main difference you'll likely notice are multiple power supplies. Power supplies in file servers are typically redundant, since power supplies are not the most reliable component in any given system. They may also be hot-swappable, although we've never actually seen anyone install a new power supply on a running server (and don't recommend it unless absolutely necessary).

In addition to the standard mouse, keyboard, serial, and parallel ports, most servers will have an array of slots for expansion use. Typically, a few ISA or EISA slots are included for supporting legacy devices (this is especially common if you have an old tape drive that has its own controller card). However, since PCI is the current standard, and 64-bit PCI is rapidly taking standard PCI over, most of the slots will be of this variety. (Expect ISA and EISA slots to vanish by the end of 1999.) More modern servers will have hot-swap capabilities built in to the PCI slots as well.

You will also see USB ports on a few new servers, even though server-grade USB devices are still hard to find.

Server Motherboard Design

As with PCs, motherboards vary quite a bit from server to server. Figure 14-3 shows a typical dual Pentium II motherboard.

With the exception of a few extra expansion card connectors, the now-standard Intel i960 chip, and the additional Pentium II slot, the basic server motherboard is of very familiar design. We'll discuss each of the components in turn.

MICROPROCESSORS

Any server purchase is likely to start with the central component of every computer system: the microprocessor, or CPU. The reigning king of PC and server processors is, of course, Intel. The 80x86 and Pentium series of CPUs have now become household names, and even though other CPUs (notably, Motorola's PowerPC) have regularly trounced the Pentium and its kin in independent tests, the Intel chips are still the rulers of the roost. We mentioned CPUs in Chapter 13 and will expand that discussion here.

Intel

The history of the modern Intel microcomputer CPU starts back in 1979, with the release of the 8088 chipset. However, Intel had been dabbling with processors even earlier, with the 4004, a 2,300-transistor chip it introduced in 1971. The 4004 operated at 108KHz, could address all of 640 bytes of memory, and was typically used in calculators at the time.

That's a far cry from today's CPUs, but you'd be surprised how useful a 10-year-old 486, or even a 15-year-old 386 machine, can be in certain situations.

So before you toss that old hardware, read through the substantially abbreviated history of Intel's chips shown in Table 14-1 and see if there isn't something you can use that old PC for, other than a doorstop.

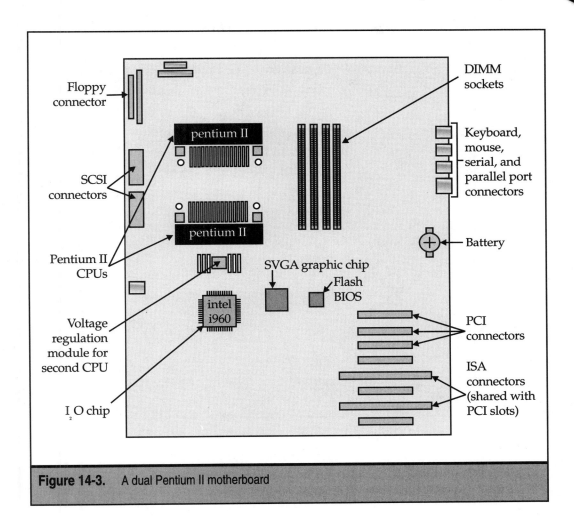

Figure 14-3.   A dual Pentium II motherboard

8088

In 1979, the original IBM PC was equipped with a single Intel 8088 processor. The 8088 instantly became the standard for PCs and clones of the day.

A scaled-down version of the more costly 8086, released a year earlier, the 8088 ran at 4.77MHz and could address 1MB of memory, although 384KB of this was reserved for BIOS and expansion cards. The 8088 is a 16-bit chip and uses an 8-bit instruction bus. For comparative purposes, the original 8088 is about 200 times slower than a high-end 486 processor.

You can still find plenty of 8088-based machines in existence today, and you can probably pick them up for free. (Then again, you won't want to, as a typical PC of the day

Processor	Year Introduced	Clock Speed	Scalability	Transistors
8088	1979	5MHz to 8MHz	One only	29,000
286	1982	6MHz to 12MHz	One only	134,000
386DX	1985	16MHz to 33MHz	One only	275,000
486DX	1989	25MHz to 120MHz	One only	1.2 million
Pentium	1993	60MHz to 233MHz	Up to 2	3.1 million+
Pentium Pro	1995	150MHz to 200MHz	Up to 8	5.5 million
Pentium II and Pentium III*	1997	233MHz to 600MHz+	Up to 2	7.5 million
Pentium II Xeon and Pentium III Xeon*	1998	400MHz to 700MHz+	Up to 8	7.5 million
Merced/IA-64**	2000	500MHz to 1GHz	Unknown	About 30 million

* The Pentium II, Pentium III, and Xeon have not yet reached their terminal speed or scalability specifications.

** Details on Merced have not been disclosed; these figures are based on industry speculation.

Table 14-1.   A Selected History of Intel CPUs

weighed well over 50 pounds.) Unfortunately, there is little use for any 8088-based system in today's computing environment. Not only does the chip's speed make it incapable of doing anything of value beyond basic word processing and spreadsheet calculations, but the 1MB memory limit leaves it unable to run any application built in the last 15 years.

8088s are great for nostalgia, but that's about it.

80286

Intel's first attempts at a successor to the successful but aging 8088 were met with frustration. The 80186 and 80188 chips did not provide the desired results, and although they were still used on controller cards and other adapters, these chips were quickly supplanted by 1982's 80286, commonly referred to as the 286. By this time, the slower x88 series had been dropped in favor of the x86, which remained the standard for the next 11 years.

IBM chose the 286 for its IBM AT computer, and the clones followed suit. While the chip was fully compatible with 8088-based software, it promised performance gains of 300 to 1,000 percent.

The leap from the 8088 to the 286 is probably one of the greatest single-generation performance gains in computing history. For the growing world of PCs, this was a critical evolution, and the 286's architecture enhancements, from streamlined instruction handling, support (in theory, anyway) for multitasking, and the ability to access virtual memory, were much-needed developments.

Unfortunately, you don't see a whole lot of 286-based computers still in existence. The 286 promised such impressive new features, yet it never really caught on. Why? Because no software had been written to take advantage of these new innovations. The 8088 was firmly entrenched, and PCs of the day were quite expensive. Convincing people to upgrade to an entirely new chipset for which no new software was available was difficult at best.

By the time software did start to show up on the market, Intel had already announced the 386. Consumers and businesses waited for the new machines with the new chips.

80386

If you don't think you have a 386-based system lying around in your spare parts room or sitting under someone's desk, you aren't looking hard enough. The 386 was such a phenomenon and an amazing success that it alone is likely responsible for a decade of Intel's good fortune.

The 386 was so well received because it continued the trend of improved performance and additional features. The original 386DX improved clock speed to 16MHz, and provided better memory management and much more robust virtual memory operation (called virtual real mode). The 386DX could also run on less power than any of its predecessors, could address up to 4GB of physical memory, and could utilize up to 64TB of virtual memory (not that you'd ever see these levels on a real PC!). The 386 just happened to be the standard chip during the release of Microsoft Windows 3.0, another factor that accounts for its presence in many still-running computers.

The 386 was Intel's first with an internal register size of 32 bits, which is still the standard in today's Pentium III Xeon. The 386's 32-bit data bus was also the first of its kind, and this remained the high end until the Pentium's 64-bit data bus emerged in 1993. The 386SX, a crippled (and much cheaper) version of the 386DX was also quite successful, and in many cases, its performance was indistinguishable from its big brother.

By today's standards, the performance of the 386 is nothing to write home about, but you'd be surprised how useful a 386 can be. Many portable computers of the day were based on the 386 chip (the 386SL was specifically designed for portables), and these are perfect for roaming data collection purposes, especially when the risk of loss or damage is high. 386 desktops can also be useful as data entry stations, fax servers, or dedicated print servers. In any hazardous situation, like a shipping dock or warehouse, where low-end, brute-force computing power is required, a 386 is perfect, because you won't get too upset when it gets covered in coffee, is stolen, or is destroyed.

80486

Another chip that remained a standard for four years, the 486 was the final chip in Intel's numeric series before it switched to words (like Pentium) for trademark purposes.

The original 486DX was two to four times faster than the 386DX and at least 50 times faster than the 8088. Again, the 486 improved on the number of clock cycles it required to perform an instruction, included a built-in high-speed memory cache (known as the Level 1 or L1 cache) right on the CPU, and on the DX version had an integrated floating-point unit (FPU) for faster math processing. Unlike its predecessors, the 486 also promised an upgrade path (to the DX2, DX4, and various OverDrive chips), although this was not altogether a success. In any case, soon after the arrival of the 486, the 386 all but vanished from the market.

The 486 offered such improved performance that, as opposed to the old 386 days, running Windows on your PC didn't seem so slow. Windows sales took off simultaneously with that of the 486, and many 486 systems came with Windows preinstalled. Intel even marketed a 486SX chip (a 486DX with no FPU) for "low-cost entry-level PCs," hastening the demise of the 386.

As mentioned earlier, the 486 was designed to be upgradable to a newer, faster processor. This is great—in theory—but because of the wildly differing socket sizes for various versions of the 486 and Pentium (eight in total, through the Pentium Pro), figuring out the upgrade path for a given system was often a nightmare. Some of Intel's so-called OverDrive chips had compatibility problems, including physical spacing and cooling issues (a major concern), BIOS problems, and even 486 chips that had been soldered to the motherboard (a frustrating and quite common problem). Clearly, while Intel wanted upgradable CPUs, PC manufacturers were not necessarily in agreement. These problems are still common, even on recently produced PCs (particularly un-branded PCs). To resolve some of the confusion, Intel maintains a very complete index of upgrade paths on its Web site at www.intel.com/overdrive/upgrade/index.htm.

So what can you do with a 486? Quite a lot, really. Properly configured, a latter-day 486 with plenty of RAM can do anything. The performance of a 100MHz 486DX4 is indistinguishable from a low-end Pentium system, and as a PC or server can handle any chore that doesn't involve heavy data manipulation. In our experience, 486 systems that are deployed as database servers traditionally get into trouble under heavy loads and are prone to crashes.

Can you use a 486 as a heavy-duty file server? Absolutely—just up the RAM and the RAID controller. For print, fax, and light-use e-mail services, a 486 will typically work well, also. Don't overlook the deployment option of your older 386 and 486 systems. They may not be glamorous, but they are certainly much cheaper than buying a new server!

Pentium

In early 1993, Intel released the Pentium into the world, and in one brilliant move made possible the unheard-of idea that a chip company could directly market its products to consumers. "Intel Inside" was born alongside a snazzy chip with a newfangled name . . . and some powerful new features that earned it a place as the market standard for almost six years—and it's still going.

The Pentium's primary innovation is an up-to-fourfold increase in raw processing speed, thanks to the chip's dual data pipelines. With these pipes, referred to as "superscalar technology," the Pentium can execute two sets of instructions simultaneously. Combined with the internal clock multiplier technology introduced with the 486DX2 and 486DX4, the performance gains were impressive, with even early Pentiums doubling the speed of high-end 486 chips.

Contrary to many commonly held opinions, the Pentium is not a RISC chip at all. Despite Intel's claims of revolutionizing microchip design, the Pentium is simply the next generation in the x86 line. It just has a different name, but Intel even designed a new compiler to take advantage of the Pentium's added features, continuing the propagation of the myth. On the other hand, the Pentium does include technology that was, at the time, uncommon in CISC chips like its predecessors, although the underlying instruction set was really no different.

Other features new to the Pentium included a 64-bit data bus (though, internally, the Pentium is still a 32-bit chip). Intel also developed "branch prediction," which attempts to forecast the upcoming instructions in an application in order to execute them faster. A second 8KB cache was added to give the L1 cache double its previous firepower. The cache can also operate in write-back mode, allowing it to cache both write and read operations.

Much to Intel's chagrin, the original Pentium's FPU shipped with a bug that caused certain floating-point division operations to yield incorrect results. Earlier versions of the 100MHz and slower Pentium were all produced with the flaw.

After a mammoth public outcry, Intel finally relented and agreed to unconditionally replace any Pentium chips that contained the FPU bug. This was quite a pie in the face for the chip company, as its chips regularly exhibit erratic behavior under specific circumstances, and Intel had never been forced to recall a chip in the past. Regardless, Intel still honors this commitment today, and if you boot up an old PC or server and find it to have the flaw, Intel will replace the chip with one of comparable speed. It is nigh impossible to find the instructions to do this on Intel's Web site, so we provide that URL here: www.intel.com/procs/support/pentium/fdiv/replqa3.htm.

You can test for the flaw with any spreadsheet or with a utility called CPUID (available at the above URL), and Windows NT will automatically find the flaw during installation. Windows NT can also perform a software workaround for you if you don't want to bother with replacing the chip.

With the FPU bug a thing of the distant past, next-generation Pentiums grew smaller and drew less power, while increasing the clock speed and internal clock multiplier. MMX technology was introduced into what looked to be the Pentium's final version in 1997, which added another million or so transistors, 16KB caches, and even lower power requirements. Of course, the MMX hype was all about multimedia support, including about 60 new instructions specifically for audio/video applications and other instruction processing enhancements. (Note that Intel now sometimes calls MMX "Katmai New Instructions" (KNI), at least in its following generations of the instruction set.)

The MMX versions of the Pentium are also able to scale to two processors on one motherboard, the first Intel CPUs able to grow beyond "one-way" systems. By 1997, though, the Pentium Pro had long since become the standard for scalability, and you are not likely to find many dual Pentium systems on the market.

Pentium desktops are probably ubiquitous on your network, and any Intel servers you still have in operation are likely to be Pentium-based. In usage, consider a standard Pentium server to be a faster version of a 486 server. With enough RAM and fast storage, any Pentium will be up to the common task. If you plan to use your server as an application server for CAD, video streaming, or other multimedia application, and you don't want to invest in a new Pentium II system, consider a fast, MMX-enhanced Pentium motherboard; you'll probably find it more than adequate.

Pentium Pro

The Pentium Pro, introduced in 1995, is not a simple revision of the original Pentium. Actually, it's a quite different chip with some interesting features that made it the processor of choice for highly scalable enterprise servers, until the introduction of the Pentium II Xeon in 1998.

The Pentium Pro is designed in two parts—the actual processing unit and a separate, but integrated, Level 2 (L2) cache of static RAM (previous chips' L2 caches were external to the CPU altogether). The Pentium Pro also advances the Pentium's dual instruction pipe technology by expanding it to three pipes, allowing the chip to perform multiple operations within one clock tick. The Pro is also more advanced in its branch prediction technology and can execute instructions even if they aren't in the proper order. Intel calls this technology combination "dynamic execution."

The Pentium Pro is optimized for 32-bit computing, particularly Windows NT, which is a fully native 32-bit OS. Of course, the big selling point of the Pentium Pro is in its ability to scale up to eight processors on one motherboard. This provided Intel-based computers the ability to greatly expand their processing power simply by adding chips. For this reason, virtually every high-end server produced between 1995 and mid-1998 has been based on multiple Pentium Pro chips.

You'll see the Pentium Pro in a number of systems, including some desktop machines, although it never really took off as a client CPU. That's because you really need to run Windows NT to take advantage of the Pro's features, and because most desktop users prefer (or are forced to use) Windows 95 or Windows 98, the chip just doesn't do much good. For a server, however, a Pentium Pro solution will work well in just about any implementation, and if you need the heavy transaction processing power for a database or application server, you can simply add more CPUs and additional RAM.

Put simply, Pentium Pro servers are excellent at running Windows NT. A six- or eight-way Pentium Pro system will typically run $30,000 to $60,000, so it is really not outrageously more expensive than lower-end servers. In multiprocessor servers like these, you will also usually find advanced management capabilities, making them quite savvy in enterprise settings where 100 percent uptime is mandatory. Pentium Pro systems have just about vanished except in second-hand markets.

Pentium II

If nothing else, 1997's Pentium II introduced the idea that you could sell a whole lot of chips with guys in colorful, metallic jumpsuits, dancing to old disco tunes. Intel's ad campaign didn't really do justice to the Pentium II, a substantially advanced chip that is primarily characterized by its new Single Edge Contact Cartridge. Pentium II chips, unlike their predecessors, come in little black cartridges that simply plug into slots on the motherboard. This eliminated the hassles of aligning pins to do chip replacements and upgrades by giving the CPU its own carrying case.

The Pentium II's architecture is similar to the Pentium Pro, including its integrated L2 cache. In some ways, the Pentium II outpaces the Pro by including the MMX/KNI instruction set, being able to handle up to 64GB of memory (prior chips could only address 4GB), and independent buses for the L2 cache and primary RAM.

On the other hand, the Pentium II drew a lot of fire because, although it was marketed as a high-end chip, it could only scale to two processors. The Pentium Pro could scale to eight, casting serious doubt that the Pentium II would displace the Pro in enterprise servers. It did not. While the Pentium II was embraced in workstation and midrange servers, and is currently the definitive standard in PCs and laptops, the Pro continued to dominate the enterprise market until the introduction of the Xeon. The Pro is now finally being phased out. The Pentium II is really a phenomenal chip, and its cartridge packaging will certainly remain a standard for some time. But put simply, the Pentium II is just plain fast, and servers based on it can be deployed in any capacity.

Pentium II Xeon

Currently, the Pentium II Xeon (often just referred to as the Xeon) is Intel's top of the line. Packaged in a Single Edge Contact Cartridge, a Xeon processor module is instantly distinguishable from a Pentium II because it is about three times the size (about 30 square inches on its face) of the earlier model.

Xeon processors are enormous, and they need an even bigger heat sink to cool properly. Although the Xeon has the same number of transistors as the Pentium II, and is similarly architected, the Xeon has more new features that make it run very hot. In addition to the standard Pentium II features, the Xeon also includes a faster system bus (100MHz instead of 66MHz) and the ability to include up to 2MB of L2 cache. (Later-model Pentium Pro CPUs could be configured with 1MB of L2 cache.) The cache, unlike previous chips, operates at the full speed of the bus, as well.

Xeon's biggest selling point is its scalability, however. At introduction, the chip could scale four ways, and eight-way scalability was promised soon after. With clock speeds starting at 400MHz, this is a chip designed solely with the high end in mind. That's a good thing, because the Xeon is very expensive—a 400MHz/2MB cache version was introduced at a price of about $4,500, twice the cost of the Pentium Pro and five times the cost of a high-end Pentium II.

Of course, server vendors pass this expense on to you, and while the Xeon does offer unprecedented performance, it may not be worth the price unless you need high-end transaction processing abilities and scalability is a concern. Watch for prices to fall considerably over the next 18 months.

Pentium III and Pentium III Xeon

Intel's latest revision of the Pentium II series of chips is the Pentium III. What bold new changes does Intel deliver with this chip? Not much.

The Pentium III, at its core, is not much different than the Pentium II. Starting at 450MHz where the Pentium II leaves off, the Pentium III adds support for "Streaming SIMD (single instruction, multiple data) Extensions," which are designed to boost the multimedia performance of the chip.

Same story with the Pentium III Xeon: a bump in clock speed and support for SIMD are the main features. However, the Pentium III Xeon will scale to eight processors, whereas the Pentium II Xeon only goes to four. Watch for the new Xeon to make a serious run at grabbing share from RISC-based servers.

The Pentium III line also promises a slight boost in TCP/IP performance, in the range of five to ten percent. Be aware, however, that a SIMD-enabled operating system is needed to give the Pentium III its juice. As of yet, only Microsoft has such a project in the works.

Watch the Pentium III to continue its evolution as new, .18 micron fabrication technology is perfected and these CPUs get even faster.

Merced

Intel's hush-hush new chip will be its first with true 64-bit architecture (called IA-64). It is under development with Hewlett-Packard, and Microsoft is also collaborating with Intel to build a version of Windows NT specifically for the Merced chip.

Details are sketchy, but the chip will likely at least start at 500MHz speeds and inch its way up to a full 1GHz. It will contain four times as many transistors as any previous chip, and will basically be the best thing since, well, the Xeon.

Keep your eyes open for details until the year 2000 (or later) release. Intel's Web site is at www.intel.com.

AMD

Advanced Micro Devices, a well-known hanger-on of Intel, is a company that largely makes its living by producing its own proprietary versions of comparable Intel chips. Unfortunately, because of differences in CPU design (all microprocessor designs are patented, so copying them is illegal), there are generally a few vagaries between the features of what would otherwise be the same chip. Because software, and in particular the operating system, has to be designed specifically for the CPU for which it was intended, there are usually a few, often minor, things that don't work quite right when using an AMD chip as your CPU, despite AMD's assurances of 100-percent compatibility.

Of course, the AMD version of a comparable Intel CPU will almost always be far less expensive than its big brother. Performance tests have generally shown the AMD versions of a chip to be roughly the same as an Intel version, to boot. Of course, because AMD has to develop its processors based on what Intel has already released, the latest products from AMD tend to lag about 12 to 18 months behind Intel. As a result, you'll rarely find AMD chips in servers; instead, they are usually found in lower-cost PC clones. You can, however, buy the chips yourself and do your own installation as an upgrade from a lower-end CPU. Of course, as with any microprocessor upgrade, be careful to ensure that the slot type and number of the system you're upgrading is compatible.

AMD currently has two major chips on the market. First is the AMD-K6, a direct competitor to the Pentium and Pentium II. The K6 includes the MMX instruction set. The K6 is a RISC-based CPU, and it is available in clock speeds from 200MHz to 300MHz. Performance is slightly lower than a similarly clocked Pentium II.

AMD's latest chips are the AMD-K6-2 and K6-3, which includes technology AMD calls 3DNow! Obviously, these CPUs are marketed toward 3D applications, particularly 3D gaming, which can make use of the chip's 3D instruction set. Unfortunately, most applications are not able to take advantage of this, so performance on typical server applications will lag a bit behind a similar Pentium II. However, if you are looking for 3D power and don't want to buy an add-on 3D accelerator, the K6-2 or K6-3 is a good choice. AMD's K7 should arrive sometime in late 1999, which promises un-precedented performance for the x86 architecture. We'll see.

The bottom line is that if you are looking to implement a low-end server where 100 percent compatibility is not a concern (say, a print server or a workhorse file server), an AMD CPU is an excellent low-cost solution. However, if you plan to do any serious transaction processing, where the OS is going to be heavily involved in data manipulations, you should probably accept no imitation. You can find more information about AMD at its Web site: www.amd.com.

Cyrix

Same story as AMD. Cyrix is another Intel clone chipmaker, and the company lags a bit behind AMD in development time and market acceptance.

Cyrix' current high-end chip offerings include the 6x86MX, a MMX-enabled processor that falls somewhere between the Pentium and the Pentium II for chips of equal speed. Cyrix also recently introduced the M II chip, an inexpensive competitor to the Pentium II that offers slightly worse performance at a dramatically lower price.

You will rarely find Cyrix CPUs on a server motherboard, but evaluate any upgrade decision the same way you would with an AMD chip. Full details on Cyrix chips are available at www.cyrix.com.

Sun Microsystems

Perhaps the biggest threat to Intel's chip hegemony is Sun Microsystems' UltraSPARC. The UltraSPARC is a RISC chip, is very scalable, and is openly architected, unlike most chip development processes. The SPARC was originally introduced in 1987, and the chip has advanced considerably since. The current version of the SPARC is a 64-bit chip, and it incorporates high-speed memory transfer capabilities (above 1GB per second). The SPARC equivalent of the L2 cache scales up to 4MB in size. Multimedia and graphics instructions are also included with the chip.

All of the SPARC's technological advances combine to make it a *very* fast chip. Pound for pound, it smokes anything Intel's got. So what's the catch? Unfortunately, the only place you can buy a SPARC chip is inside a Sun Microsystems machine. And although the chip is developed openly, it is really only designed to do one thing: run Solaris, Sun's version of the UNIX OS—unlike an Intel chip, which can run Windows, NetWare, and several versions of UNIX. All the performance in the world won't do you any good if you can't run your applications on it.

For UNIX gurus who need a platform for a heavy-duty database back-end, like an Oracle server, a Sun machine is often a perfect solution, as it provides the raw transaction processing speed that Windows and NetWare can't. But for serving Microsoft Office applications to your Windows 9x users or providing simple file storage, a SPARC will either be unable to do the task or will simply be overkill.

While this is certainly a simplified argument, the long and tedious discussion over what is the best operating system is left to the reader as an exercise.

Sun Microsystems is online at www.sun.com.

Digital Equipment Corp. (R.I.P.)

In mid-1998, immediately before the chaos of DEC's merger with Compaq, DEC sold its semiconductor manufacturing and marketing operation to its old rival, Intel. DEC's chief semiconductor product was the Alpha, a 64-bit RISC chip that remains the only major non-Intel (or compatible) chip that will run the Windows NT operating system.

DEC fought a valiant battle against Intel for years, but it finally quit. With DEC now under Intel's control, it's unclear what the future of the Alpha will be, although Intel has stated it intends to continue production and further development of the Alpha. It will be a surprise if certain elements of the Alpha don't end up in Intel's upcoming Merced chip.

Like the SPARC, the Alpha is blazingly fast (at speeds of up to 600MHz), RISC-based, and filled with new technology. The Alpha has four parallel instruction pipelines and it even runs Windows and Digital's version of UNIX, so why didn't the Alpha eat Intel's lunch? First, the Alpha runs very hot, consuming up to 40 watts of power (a Pentium II consumes about 30 watts). Alpha-equipped servers need special heat sinks and mother-board designs to maximize airflow across the chip, making the server much more fragile in general due to its propensity for heat damage. The chip itself and the servers that use it are also more expensive than their Intel counterparts. The Alpha is also incompatible with earlier DEC chips, making many users of old chipsets reluctant to upgrade.

So where can you find Alpha chips? Only in DEC servers, and only in a few of those; most DEC servers have been Pentium-based, and this will likely become more the norm as the Compaq acquisition is digested. The Alpha, already the lowest-volume RISC chip on the market, looks to be headed even further down in market share.

You can find bare-bones details about the chip at the following URL: www.digital.com/
semiconductor/alpha/alpha.htm.

Silicon Graphics

Silicon Graphics (SGI) spun off its microprocessor division (for its MIPS product) into a
company called MIPS Technologies in June 1998. SGI heralds the MIPS chip as the
number one selling RISC chip on the market. While true, this is a little misleading. The
MIPS CPU is used not only in SGI's servers and workstations, it's also used in routers,
Windows CE devices, and even Nintendo gaming machines.

Microsoft supported MIPS for some time, but the company began phasing out
Windows NT support for MIPS in 1996. MIPS and Microsoft currently work together on
Windows CE-based handhelds.

This leaves MIPS with no place to go but SGI's own line of servers, running SGI's IRIX
UNIX—not the most widely supported flavor of UNIX you'll find. Put simply, the MIPS
chip does not have the muscle in mathematical calculations that its brethren have. Best
implemented only if you can find servers at a bargain price. SGI is turning to Intel CPUs
now, but full details on MIPS and SGI are online at www.sgi.com/MIPS/ (the URL is
case-sensitive).

Motorola

One of the grandest designs and biggest fumbles in recent computing history has been
the checkered development of the PowerPC. Motorola, Apple, and IBM formed an
unlikely alliance to develop the chip. The trio succeeded, and as a successor to the
M680x0 series of chips, Motorola found itself as the developer of the first RISC chip to
gain mainstream acceptance by consumers. In fact, the PowerPC is still the only RISC
chip in wide use in desktop PCs. However, because virtually all of those PCs are
Macintoshes, the future of the PowerPC is not rosy.

While the PowerPC was intended to run everything from Windows NT to Solaris, the
only real OS support for the PowerPC came from the MacOS. IBM's AIX will run on
PowerPC, as well, and IBM markets several AIX servers that use PowerPC chips.

PowerPC's big feature is low cost and very low power consumption, making it a good
choice for mobile computing. Performance has been very good in comparison to the
Pentium series of chips, but other RISC chips are typically faster.

Without a doubt, MacOS networks will rely on the PowerPC for server and clients; in
fact, it's really the only choice. Read all the gory details at Motorola's PowerPC site (mot-
sps.com/sps/General/chips-nav.html) and IBM's PowerPC site (www.chips.ibm.com/
products/ppc/).

Hewlett-Packard

HP's PA-RISC series of microprocessors are, like many RISC chips, specifically designed
for the company's own SMP servers running HP's own variety of UNIX (HP-UX). The

PA-RISC is a monster of scalability, and it can scale to up to hundreds of processors for enterprise data center machines.

With the HP/Intel collaboration on IA-64 technology, the PA-RISC series is nearing the end of its lifetime. At the same time, it remains a very capable and quite expensive platform for UNIX computing. With HP's servers being some of the biggest and most scalable on the market, a PA-RISC chip may be the one of the only choices for meeting the highest of high-end computing needs.

Oddly, details on the PA-RISC are hard to come by on HP's Web site. Here's a starting point, though: www.hp.com/esy/technology/unix_news/.

IBM

Much like HP's strategy with the PA-RISC, IBM's RS-series (currently the RS/6000) is a homegrown RISC chip for running homegrown UNIX, in this case, IBM's AIX. The scalability (up to 512 processors) and price of the RS/6000 are similar to the PA-RISC. Some RS/6000 servers also support adding PowerPC chips for additional processing power. You can read more about the PowerPC in the section titled "Motorola," earlier in this chapter.

Full details on the RS/6000 are available at www.rs6000.ibm.com.

One Chip or More?

With all this talk of scalability, it's logical to ask, "How many processors does my server need?"

Like all good questions about technology, the answer depends on how you use it. In most cases, a file server's processor is largely idle. Client/server technology, by default, loads the burden of processing on the client, leaving the server often twiddling its proverbial thumbs. The CPU scaling issue really only becomes an issue when you start to load the server up with tasks that it has to think about.

In a nutshell, a file server will get by fine on one fast processor. Obviously, since the CPU runs the operating system, the faster the CPU, the faster just about everything is going to be. However, we typically see dual processor units perform slightly better than single processor servers on throughput tests, although this is nowhere near a universal truth.

Once you start loading up your server with applications like e-mail services, Web site hosting, and database back-ending, CPU requirements start to grow. Determining the growth pattern in advance is largely impossible. It's a function of the application in question and the average number of connections or processes that are going on simultaneously. Of course, this applies to all subsystems of the server, not just the CPU. Performance monitoring is key to finding bottlenecks and planning for upgrades, but that doesn't help you get started.

Determining your requirements in advance is a difficult task. Make use of your IS colleagues who have similar infrastructures. Find out what equipment they have and how well it solves the IS problem. If you've decided on a platform and vendor, your salesperson may also be a good resource for capacity planning, but don't hold your breath: the average salesperson's technical ability varies widely.

If at all possible, leave room to grow. Buy servers that can be upgraded, not just in chip speed but in the number of chips supported. Of course, this goes for RAM and hard drive space as well.

Finally, draw on your experience as time goes on. As you work with more and more servers, different operating systems, and different chipsets, you'll get an intuitive feel for a server's breaking point. More often than not, you'll find your hunches are correct.

MEMORY

RAM, your server's main memory area, is a common bottleneck on many file servers. Fortunately, RAM technology has matured quite rapidly over the last several years, and thanks to a worldwide glut of RAM chips on the market, prices have fallen to the point where upgrading system RAM is a no-brainer decision. On many older servers, upgrading RAM is a cheap and easy way to boost system performance.

Why is a lack of RAM a bottleneck? Every OS command, every file transfer, every print request passes through RAM. Every network adapter, PC card, and RAID controller needs RAM space as well in order to provide base functionality. While the CPU processes the data and executes the instructions, the system's main memory is a short-term storage area for everything that the CPU deals with.

The only alternative to RAM would be to use a hard disk or some other physical storage medium for storing current data. With "virtual memory," this is still true, as virtual memory arrangements swap infrequently used data to the hard disk (to a place called the "swap file"), while keeping more frequently used files in actual RAM. In systems with insufficient RAM, these swap functions occur constantly. Because hard disk access is extremely slow in comparison to the all-electronic operations of the CPU and RAM, systems that have to constantly swap data with the hard disk's virtual memory quickly bog down with all the extra processing and I/O overhead.

Because your operating system, open applications, and active files are all maintained in RAM, small RAM spaces can get filled up in a hurry. OSes, application executables, and data files are all getting larger, and RAM requirements have grown as a result. It's critical your server have plenty of RAM on it. Of course, figuring out which of the dozen or more types of RAM you need is not always so simple.

Table 14-2 is a (very) rough guide to how much memory your system needs, based on usage patterns and use of the Windows 9x or Windows NT operating systems.

The Two Basic Memory Types

At the highest level of categorization, there are two types of RAM: DRAM and SRAM. We'll cover each in brief.

Use	Recommended RAM
Light administrative	12MB
Heavy administrative	32MB
Knowledge worker	32–64MB
Heavy graphics/Web design	64–128MB
Heavy CAD design	256MB–1GB+
Single CPU file server	64MB
Medium-use mail server	128MB
Dual-CPU database/application server	256MB–1GB
4-way and up CPU enterprise server	1GB+

Table 14-2.   Suggested Memory Requirements

DRAM

DRAM, or dynamic RAM, is what is commonly referred to as simply RAM. You can expand your system's DRAM by adding relatively inexpensive chips into the server's dedicated sockets. The CPU communicates with DRAM through the data bus and address bus. When you read about a CPU's bus length, this is what is being discussed. (The 8088 had an 8-bit data bus; the Pentium II has a 64-bit data bus.) The bigger the bus, the more information can be simultaneously sent between RAM and the CPU, in turn increasing the overall speed of the CPU subsystem.

DRAM performance is typically measured by the amount of time that passes from the moment the CPU sends an instruction to RAM to the moment the CPU receives the response. A few years ago, this time was 120 nanoseconds. Today's RAM chips have this down to about 6 or 8 nanoseconds, and it continues to fall.

DRAM is "dynamic" because of the way it works. In DRAM, information is stored in charges on capacitors on the RAM chips (SIMMs and DIMMs, discussed below). These capacitors discharge every millisecond or so, and must be immediately recharged. This charging and recharging process is why it is referred to as dynamic. It is also what causes DRAM to be slow in comparison to SRAM.

SRAM

For much faster access, modern CPUs have access to cache memory, as discussed earlier. The L2 cache is the best example of SRAM, or static RAM, in modern computing. SRAM doesn't need to be refreshed like DRAM does, taking the discharge/recharge loop out of the process. SRAM access speeds are typically in the range of 12 to 20 nanoseconds and can be as low as 4.5 nanoseconds.

If SRAM is so fast, why not dump DRAM altogether and have the entire system use SRAM? The problem is that SRAM is frighteningly expensive. A mere 2MB of SRAM adds about $3,000 to the price of a Pentium II Xeon chip, and 2MB of DRAM, if you can find such a small card, costs about $15. Today, 32MB of DRAM can be obtained for about $50. SRAM chips are also much larger, byte for byte, than DRAM chips. A typical DRAM chip is one-fourth the size of an SRAM chip of the same storage capacity.

SRAM currently comes in three varieties:

▼ **Async SRAM (Asynchronous SRAM)**   Async SRAM is the original version of SRAM, which filled the cache of the original L2 since Intel's 80386 chip. Async SRAM is called asynchronous because it is not synchronized with the system clock. This makes Async SRAM comparatively slower than other SRAM varieties (at 12, 15, or 20 nanosecond versions), although it is still much faster than DRAM.

■ **Sync SRAM (Synchronous Burst SRAM)**   Sync SRAM is similar to Async SRAM, but it is synchronized with the system clock, eliminating some of the CPU waiting time that you get with Async SRAM. Sync SRAM operates at delays of up to 8.5 nanoseconds and has not commonly been used in L2 caches. That's because the synchronization of Sync SRAM breaks down at a bus speed of about 66MHz, which Intel passed with its 350MHz Pentium II and the Pentium II Xeon (these chips have 100MHz system buses). Because of its relative incompatibility and expensive production costs, Sync SRAM should be largely off the market by the time you read this.

▲ **PB SRAM (Pipelined Burst Static RAM)**   PB SRAM overcomes the limitations of Sync SRAM by using output registers to get a head start on address location during data transfer requests. At bus speeds of 75MHz to 133MHz, PB SRAM is the only way to provide very fast RAM access, at access speeds from 4.5 to 8 nanoseconds. PB SRAM is the current standard for L2 caches and should remain so, at least until the release of Merced.

Memory Cards

Your SRAM decision will have been made for you by the manufacturer of your CPU, as L2 caches are normally embedded on the processor. DRAM is another matter. While your system will come preinstalled with some amount of RAM, in almost every server's life there comes a time when it needs an upgrade.

You'll find two major kinds of DRAM module packages on the market—SIMMs and DIMMs—and several varieties of each of those. SIPPs (single inline pinned packages) and DIPs (dual inline packages) also used to be available for expanding memory much less conveniently, but those days have long since passed.

SIMMs

SIMMs, or single inline memory modules, are probably well known to most PC users, because they have been standard on systems basically since the dawn of computers.

A SIMM looks like a small circuit board with several chips soldered on it on one or both sides of the board. Depending on the card and your system, a common SIMM will have either 30 or 72 pins on it, as shown in Figures 14-4 and 14-5, though there are variations on this standard. The 30-pin SIMMs offer an 8-bit data path with one parity bit; 72-pin SIMMs have 32-bit data paths with four parity bits. You won't find 30-pin SIMMs on many modern units, because of their slow speed due to their small 9-bit data path.

SIMMs were the standard for years, until the Pentium's 64-bit data path made using them a problem. Because the Pentium has a 64-bit data bus, 32-bit SIMMs have to be installed in groups of two on a Pentium motherboard. Because many systems only have four expansion slots, this was very inefficient and more expensive than it should have been, so the new standard became DIMMs.

With SIMMs on the way out, you'll usually find them fairly cheap. It is usually a good idea to buy a bulk quantity of SIMMs to keep on hand for cheaply upgrading older 486 servers and client PCs. (Memory chips also fail more often than other electronic components; keeping a stash on hand for repairs a good idea.)

DIMMs

As can be seen in Figure 14-6, DIMMs are 168-pin memory modules (although 200-pin, 144-pin, and many other versions also exist) that provide a data path of 64 bits, with or without eight bits of parity. DIMMs can be added one at a time, and you can mix and match DIMM sizes on a system (with SIMMs, you had to use matched pairs to upgrade a

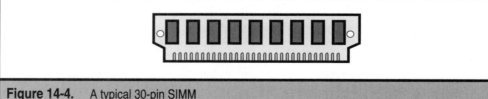

Figure 14-4.   A typical 30-pin SIMM

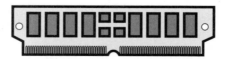

Figure 14-5.   A typical 72-pin SIMM

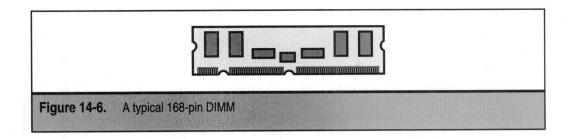

Figure 14-6. A typical 168-pin DIMM

Pentium system). In general, DIMMs are much more efficient than SIMMs, have higher capacities, run faster, and will certainly displace SIMMs completely in the near future. (Ironically, DIMMs have been a standard on the Macintosh for about a decade.)

Other than these advantages, a DIMM is functionally the same as a SIMM.

RAM Technologies

Too bad it's not as simple as SIMM or DIMM. FPM, EDO, BEDO, SDRAM, ECC? All these acronyms and more typically precede the SIMM or DIMM module type classification, and each of them has an important meaning that you need to be aware of.

FPM

For a long while, the only type of RAM you could by was FPM, or *fast page mode RAM*. Actually a revision of the original page mode, you rarely hear FPM as a modifier because it's assumed unless the DIMM is labeled otherwise.

FPM RAM has dropped from a 120-nanosecond access time to 60 nanoseconds today. This is plenty fast for most applications, and until the advent of the Pentium, no one complained. However, FPM proved unable to handle bus speeds of greater than 66MHz, and memory speed began to cause a performance problem on Pentium-class machines. This is part of the reason why the L2 cache was enlarged, and most of the reason why a next generation of RAM was introduced.

EDO

EDO (*extended data out*) RAM is regularly touted as superior to FPM, but it's hardly a revolutionary change. The 66MHz limit is still in place with EDO. Instead, EDO boosts performance by up to 40 percent by simply remembering the location of the last memory access. Because, as with hard disk access, the next memory poll is likely to be near the location of the previous poll, it makes sense to wait there for instructions instead of starting from the beginning and trying to locate that instruction from scratch.

To be sure, EDO RAM is faster, and it does offer access speeds as low as 50 nanoseconds. Unfortunately, the quick fix of providing location memory doesn't do a lot at the high end, and EDO's 66MHz limit will eventually place it in the dead technology section next to FPM.

BEDO

BEDO, or *burst extended data out*, RAM is a relatively new technology, which uses "bursting" to quickly process sequential sections of RAM space. Another evolutionary step up the FPM/EDO chain, BEDO processes four addresses in one burst, meaning there is no processing delay (or almost no delay; about 10 nanoseconds) for the last three addresses.

While this does indeed speed RAM access considerably, the 66MHz thorn still haunts BEDO RAM. The technology is also not supported by many chipsets yet, as SDRAM is currently the memory technology of choice. However, BEDO RAM is less expensive than SDRAM, so it may yet find support.

SDRAM

Synchronous DRAM (SDRAM) is to DRAM what Sync SRAM is to SRAM. SDRAM is a true change in the fundamental way RAM works, and it is already finding its way into high-end Pentium Pro and Pentium II servers. SDRAM with an 8-nanosecond access time is often called PC100 RAM (an Intel spec).

For starters, SDRAM supports bus speeds up to 100MHz. Like Sync SRAM, it is synchronized with the system clock, which was impossible up until its advent. SDRAM also has the capability of having two memory pages open at the same time. Finally, SDRAM can also operate in burst mode like BEDO. These abilities are nothing short of revolutionary, and, as a result, SDRAM has taken the computer industry by storm. Already it is the memory choice *de jour* for many high-end server manufacturers.

A next generation is already in the works. SLDRAM (*synchronous-link DRAM*) is under development by a nonprofit alliance of most of the world's memory manufacturers called, simply enough, SLDRAM Inc. The primary feature of SLDRAM will be dual instruction buses, which will essentially double throughput. You can keep up with the development of the technology at www.sldram.com.

DDR-RAM

DDR-RAM (double data-rate RAM, also called SDRAM II) is an upgrade of SDRAM that effectively doubles throughput by squeezing two read cycles into one shot of electricity. DDR-RAM has yet to make much of an appearance, and though it is cheaper than RDRAM it appears to be a short-lived project.

RDRAM

SLDRAM already has a competitor that just may win: RDRAM, or Rambus DRAM (sometimes called nDRAM) is a memory spec developed by Rambus Inc. While SDRAM tops out at 100MHz, RDRAM operates on system buses of up to 1,600MHz! RDRAM will also come only in special RIMM modules that are not compatible with SIMM or DIMM slots. Intel has licensed RDRAM for use on high-end motherboards and on video cards (discussion to come) and it should be showing up on servers by the end of 1999.

Watch for the fight with SLDRAM to be a bitter one that RDRAM ultimately wins. Rambus can be found online at www.rambus.com.

Error Correction

Contrary to a well-spread myth, computers do make mistakes. Just look at the original Pentium and its floating-point division problem.

Computers, being creatures of electricity, are prone to errors. While a magnetic disk drive may only make a mistake on one bit out of a billion, errors do occur. Because memory chips are prone to failure, and because a RAM chip's capacitors can discharge unexpectedly and result in the corruption of data in memory, error correction schemes were developed.

Parity

Parity is a well-established means of checking for data accuracy, and long-time modem users should be well familiar with parity settings. With parity error correction, an additional data bit, called the parity bit, is added onto each byte of data. If even parity is used, the parity bit that is added will make the total number of 1's in the byte an even number. If odd parity is selected, the parity bit will instead make the total number of 1's in the byte an odd number.

For example, using even parity to check the byte 1001 0010, the parity bit will be a 1, in order to make four 1's in the byte. Using the parity bit, you can reconstruct any of the other eight bits of data, if one of them is lost, because you know how many 1's and how many 0's are supposed to be in the byte. If more than one bit has been altered, however, the parity check will probably not detect an error. Because a double error in a single byte is so unlikely, though, parity is generally considered good enough for single-computer processing.

SIMMs and DIMMs are usually marketed as to whether they include parity support.

ECC

ECC (*error checking and correcting,* or sometimes spelled out as *error correction code*) works much like parity does, by taking a byte of data and generating a special code for the contents of that byte. With ECC, single- and double-bit errors can be detected and corrected.

In its standard implementation on a DIMM, ECC involves eight added check bits to cover a 64-bit data path. Note that this correction can occur on the DRAM chip, on the motherboard, or on both. For example, Intel has also built ECC into the L2 cache on the Pentium II processor. Compaq puts ECC operations on the logic board (enabling the use of cheaper RAM chips).

Data recovery with ECC is done much in the same way as parity checking. If a flaw is found, it is re-created from the ECC code. One bonus feature of ECC is that a log is typically kept of memory errors, so that conditions that may not be the result of chance data corruption can be troubleshot later.

ECC RAM is standard on most Pentium II and Pentium Pro systems.

Advanced ECC and Other Correction Schemes

Many server vendors offer their own version of ECC, like Compaq's Advanced ECC. These memory correction schemes are only slightly better than their standard counterparts

(Compaq's version will fix any single one-bit or four-bit wide error it finds). While these schemes are just as good as standard ECC, they certainly aren't worth paying extra for them.

Do You Need This?

Parity and ECC are cheap. Memory error correction accounts for about $50 of the cost of a server, and any server vendor who does not offer ECC on its memory is certainly a company of which you should be suspect. The bottom line is that accidents, while rare, do happen. By definition, a server should be resistant to those kinds of accidents, and ECC is certainly worth its extremely reasonable cost.

Video and Graphics RAM

With the growth of multimedia and desktop video, video performance quickly began to suffer under the strain of the requirements of multimedia applications. If you try to watch an AVI or MPEG file on your PC in full-screen mode, it will probably look jerky and skip frames. That's because the PC was really not intended for playing full-screen video, and the video RAM is insufficient for the task. To solve this problem, dedicated video RAM was introduced and has been continuously upgraded to provide better graphics performance.

VRAM

VRAM, simple *video RAM,* was introduced to boost graphics performance on video accelerator cards and on motherboards that have built-in video. It works by simply storing the current display pixel values and using that information as a starting point for updating the screen with each clock tick. VRAM decreases screen flicker and provides better performance, and it takes the onus of graphics processing off of the CPU. VRAM uses two access ports to boost performance further: one to refresh the display and one to update it.

VRAM is expensive and it doesn't scale well beyond 4MB. VRAM is also not optimized for Windows environments.

WRAM

WRAM, or *Windows RAM,* is, as its name implies, a Windows-only upgrading of VRAM. WRAM is also a dual-ported DRAM but is somewhat faster than VRAM, and because it can be built with fewer actual chips than VRAM, it is somewhat cheaper as well. For Windows environments, it is certainly a better choice than VRAM. WRAM is sold exclusively on accelerators offered by Matrox Graphics.

SGRAM

Synchronous graphics RAM (SGRAM) is the latest iteration of graphics-only RAM. Unlike VRAM and WRAM, SGRAM is a single-ported DRAM chip. However, speed is accelerated due to a dual-page operation feature (as in SDRAM), so performance is comparable to or better than WRAM. SGRAM is especially good at 3D graphics operations, making it highly sought after by CAD modelers and action game players. Prices are competitive with that of WRAM.

What Do I Need?

VRAM, WRAM, SGRAM: Which do you need for your server? In all practicality, none of the above. Unless you intend to start watching compressed films on your file server, any form of video RAM is overkill. Unfortunately, server vendors love to load up that system you're buying with video RAM, even though it will never be used. Be sure to look for this line item on your server price quotes. The savings for eliminating a graphics accelerator from the package can be several hundred dollars.

(Then again, many server vendors are beginning to put video RAM on the motherboard so you can't opt out of it. That's business.)

Further Reading

If there is information about RAM not contained in this section, then you don't need to know about it. Still, if you're convinced you don't have the whole story about the vagaries of RAM, you can start with the PC Webopaedia at www.pcwebopedia.com/RAM.htm and the RAM Guide at sysdoc.pair.com/ram.html. Both are excellent resources on computing in general.

INPUT/OUTPUT

Completing the unholy trinity of bottlenecks is input/output, the server's link to its storage and backup devices. Deconstructing I/O is no simple task, and it involves examining disk drive interfaces, partitioning standards, RAID levels, and other cryptic topics. It's no wonder that storage management is so poorly understood. Hopefully, this guide to what happens between the motherboard and the disk drive platter will help sort things out.

Hard Disk Drives

Imagine a small platter of metal (usually aluminum), spinning at up to 10,000 revolutions per minute. Picture another sliver of metal, hovering over this platter, about five microinches above the surface of the whirling platter. This sliver's job is to seek out magnetic information encoded on the platter by moving at a speed of about 60 miles per hour, and there are maybe 8 billion bits of data on this single platter. The sliver has to do this in all of 8 milliseconds.

This is your typical hard disk drive, circa 1998. The speed-to-size ratio is astounding and is the subject of dozens of analogies involving planes and flying skyscrapers. Hard disk drive technology has advanced rapidly in the past few years. Currently, 18GB disks with 8 millisecond seek times are the state of the art. 36GB disks are on the way.

While many texts could be written (and several have) outlining the inner workings of the hard disk drive, it is not the place of this book to deconstruct hard disk technology. Refer to any number of PC maintenance books for this kind of detailed information.

Partitioning and File Systems

Every disk drive must be formatted, and during this format procedure, a partition type or file system must be chosen. Because certain operating systems are compatible only with certain file systems, the decision is an important one.

Also, large drives are generally partitioned into small data spaces called volumes, in order to increase the storage efficiency of the drive by keeping the cluster size (the minimum unit of measurement on a disk) to a low number.

FAT (FILE ALLOCATION TABLE)   By far the most common file system is FAT, which limits volume size to 2GB or 4GB, depending on the implementation. FAT is used by DOS in a version called FAT12 and FAT16. Windows 3.x uses FAT16 with some of the features of a revision of FAT called virtual file allocation table (VFAT), to serve as an interface between applications and the disk. Windows 95 uses all of VFAT's features. In all FAT implementations, the actual file format is identical; for portability of data across multiple platforms, it is really the only choice. (Also note that NetWare uses a relatively sophisticated version of FAT as its default file system, as well.)

FAT32   Windows 95 OSR2 and Windows 98 both support 32-bit FAT, which offers much better data storage efficiency by reducing the size of each data cluster. With FAT32, you can actually squeeze more data onto a disk than you can with FAT, because the data is stored more compactly, with less wasted space. FAT32 also supports full 32-bit addressing, giving a volume the theoretical limit of 2TB (2 terabytes) in size. Because FAT32 is only compatible with late-version Windows 95 and Windows 98, drives formatted with the FAT32 file system cannot be accessed by other operating systems. While FAT32 is great for conserving space, it is also slower than standard FAT at large partition sizes.

HPFS (HIGH PERFORMANCE FILE SYSTEM)   HPFS is a file system used by OS/2 and could be used with Windows NT 3.51. You can also add support for HPFS manually to Windows NT 4.0, but it is discouraged. Volume size can be as large as 4GB or 8GB, depending on the implementation. In practical use, HPFS is almost never seen any more.

NTFS (NT FILE SYSTEM)   Often described as "UNIX-like," NTFS is a substantially advanced file system, including transaction logging, security settings, and volume spanning. Theoretical drive size can range up to 16 exabytes. NTFS is a little bulky, and it tends to be a bit slower than FAT. It is also only compatible with Windows NT, and NTFS partitions cannot be directly accessed by Windows 95 or DOS. Still, its features make it the file system of choice for Windows networks.

UNIX   UNIX has its own file systems—collectively called UNIX—which are largely incompatible with Windows systems. There are at least 16 different UNIX file systems, including the well-known UFS (UNIX File System) and NFS (Network File System). An excellent starting point for the gory details of UNIX file systems can be found at www-wks.uts.ohio-state.edu/sysadm_course/html/sysadm-65.html.

Hard Disk Drive Interfaces

Disks themselves are usually defined by their interface type, or how they connect with the hard drive controller. Interface technology has also advanced rapidly over the last five years or so, and interface advancements currently offer some of the most promising throughput enhancements in computing.

ESDI   After Seagate's ST-506/412 interface (typically used on massive and hefty drives with a capacity of 5MB) proved insufficient for moving large amounts of data, ESDI (Enhanced Small Device Interface) was established, in 1983. The ESDI operated at 3MB per second, although the drives attached to it could rarely keep up. After the introduction of IDE, the more expensive and lower-performance ESDI was quickly rendered obsolete. ESDI is effectively dead technology today.

IDE/ATA   These two terms go together and are synonymous. After the slow death of ESDI in the late 1980s, IDE (Integrated Drive Electronics or Intelligent Drive Electronics) took over as the standard and still remains popular as an inexpensive interface technology. ATA (AT Attachment) is the official name of IDE, as established by ANSI. Otherwise, the terms are identical. IDE/ATA is a 16-bit technology that has withstood many upgrades and enhancements (as you'll see in the next section).

IDE was revolutionary because it offered, as its name suggests, a disk drive with an integrated controller. Because hardware is simplified, installing an IDE device is simpler than installing an ESDI device. An IDE/ATA system can also be configured with two drives (the master and slave arrangement you're probably familiar with). Throughput of up to 8.3MB per second is possible with an IDE drive, although this is a theoretical limit.

Later versions of IDE were called Intelligent IDE drives, which offer better configurability and support additional ATA commands. Intelligent Zoned Recording IDE drives are even smarter, as they keep track of defective sector information in order to prevent data corruption.

EIDE/ATA-2   EIDE, or Enhanced IDE and its official name of ATA-2, are sometimes referred to by the following additional acronyms: Fast ATA, Fast ATA-2, ATA-3, and Ultra ATA, most of which are simply marketing terms. In a nutshell, all of these terms refer to the same technology, although ATA-3 and Ultra ATA introduced higher-speed transfer modes and a reliability feature called Self-Monitoring Analysis and Reporting Technology (SMART).

The main benefit of EIDE, et al. is to allow for the use of larger drives (IDE was limited to 504MB maximum). EIDE is also faster in theory, allowing for performance of up to 16.6MB per second throughput (33.3MB per second with Ultra ATA), thanks to block transfer technology (multiple read/write commands on a single interrupt), better addressing, and other advances. EIDE supports dual ATA host adapters and a total of up to four drives attached. The ATAPI (ATA Packet Interface) protocol for reading CD-ROMs and tape drives is also based on ATA-2. EIDE drives are available in many capacities, including sizes of up to 14GB.

SCSI   If you thought EIDE/ATA-2 acronyms were confusing, wait until you delve into SCSI. SCSI, or Small Computer System Interface, has evolved considerably from its roots (there's nothing "small" about SCSI anymore) and is the de facto standard for high-end disk and other storage device connectivity.

SCSI has been the standard way of connecting peripherals to the Macintosh since its inception, and SCSI started to appear on PCs in the late 1980s and early 1990s, after the technology had matured. Today, SCSI and IDE/EIDE compete at the desktop, but SCSI reigns in the server market.

The SCSI vs. EIDE debate rages fiercely, as SCSI devices are more expensive than EIDE devices, but they are also faster (in theory). You can add more devices to a SCSI chain (up to 15, or 45 to 60 with multiple channels) than EIDE as well, and SCSI has a much greater reach in the types of devices it can attach to. Because real-world transfer rates do not approach the theoretical maximums of disk drives, though, the performance question is often moot. The debate will probably not end anytime soon.

SCSI-1   The original SCSI was ratified by ANSI in 1986. It uses an 8-bit bus (often called "narrow") and could reach up to 5MB per second of throughput. SCSI-1 had trouble in the marketplace because manufacturers did not implement its features in the same way. It was much more successful in its second version.

SCSI-2   SCSI-2 was approved in 1990, and it substantially enhanced the state of the art of SCSI. (In fact, when you hear the term "SCSI" without modification, it usually refers to SCSI-2. SCSI-2 streamlined the use of cables and connectors that had caused confusion in SCSI-1 implementations, provided for active termination of the bus, improved diagnostics, and added support for many additional devices (including scanners and tape drives).

Basic, "Narrow," 8-bit SCSI-2 is often referred to as *Fast SCSI* or *Fast Narrow SCSI*. Performance tops out at 10MB per second, double the speed of SCSI-1.

One of the additional features of SCSI-2 was the option to use a wider cable and connector, with 68 pins instead of 50 pins. This type of connector is called a "wide" connector, and it uses a 16-bit bus, doubling bandwidth again. SCSI-2 devices connected using these connectors are typically called *Fast Wide SCSI* devices. Peak performance is 20MB per second, double the speed of Fast SCSI. Typically, SCSI devices are compatible from one version of SCSI to another, especially later revisions. However, narrow-to-wide converters may be required. It's always a good idea to keep them on hand for quick fixes.

(Note that there is also a 32-bit version of SCSI, but it has never been implemented in the real world.)

SCSI-3   Around 1994, a new revision of SCSI was put into the works under the broad header of SCSI-3, and it is still not finalized (and it probably never will be). SCSI-3's basic improvement was in better cabling and another doubling of speed to 20MB per second with a narrow bus. This is usually called *Ultra Narrow SCSI* or just *Ultra SCSI*. Rarely, SCSI-3 is referred to as Fast-20 SCSI.

A 16-bit version of Ultra SCSI is also available, called *Ultra Wide SCSI*, taking performance to 40MB per second. Just to make matters confusing, narrow implementations of SCSI-3 are relatively rare, so many people refer to Ultra Wide SCSI as Ultra SCSI also! If you hear reference to Ultra SCSI, the only way you'll know what it really means is by checking the connector: 68 pins means Ultra Wide SCSI; 50 means Ultra Narrow SCSI.

Note that with Ultra Wide SCSI devices, the total cable length of the bus is limited to 3 meters, and less as the number of devices increases.

ULTRA2 SCSI   Developers gave up on the SCSI numbering convention around 1997, and with the ink still wet on the SCSI-3 specs, work began on the next version, Ultra2 SCSI. One of the main problems with SCSI-3 is its painfully short cable length requirements. Connecting 15 drives with 1 meter of cable is not simple, and having that many drives in one space can get convoluted and tends to run hot—that is, if you can find a place to put 15 drives together. Rarely, Ultra2 SCSI is referred to as Fast-40 SCSI.

Ultra2 SCSI's companion technology, Low Voltage Differential (LVD) technology, enables faster data rates and longer cabling because it is less susceptible to noise. It also uses less power than traditional signaling technology (called HVD, or High Voltage Differential). LVD and Ultra2 SCSI allow cable lengths of up to 12 meters for 15 devices. You can also make a single board-to-drive cable of up to 25 meters.

Basic *Ultra2 Narrow SCSI* runs at 40MB per second; *Ultra2 Wide SCSI* runs at 80MB per second. Again, while Ultra2 SCSI "officially" refers to the Narrow flavor, it is commonly used to refer to both types.

Ultra2 SCSI will soon be offered with controller cards that use 64-bit PCI card slots. (We'll cover PCI and expansion slots in the following section.) This development will allow the use of two PCI channels by one controller; in other words, you can double bandwidth, giving a 64-bit PCI Ultra2 Wide SCSI card a maximum speed of 160MB per second.

ULTRA3 SCSI   Of course, a new version of SCSI is in the works, slated for release by storage vendors around the year 2000. Ultra3 SCSI will double performance again, to 80MB per second for narrow interfaces, and a whopping 160MB per second for wide interfaces. It will doubtless be just as confusing as its predecessors. With a 64-bit PCI card, throughput could theoretically reach a whopping 320MB per second!

FIBRE CHANNEL   Believe it or not, a new standard threatens to eliminate SCSI altogether, despite SCSI's enormous advances. That standard is Fibre Channel (often incorrectly written as Fiber Channel), a serial data transfer architecture that has been in the works for over five years without much in the way of tangible product introductions.

Fibre Channel is vastly different from SCSI, as can be seen in Figure 14-7. Fibre Channel works along the lines of a network, using serial connections of optical fiber instead of parallel cables to connect devices. The benefits of this are many. First, cable length restrictions are largely eliminated (up to 10 kilometers with optical fiber, 30 meters with copper). Also, up to 126 nodes can be placed on a Fibre Channel Arbitrated Loop (FC-AL), the lowest-cost design of a Fibre Channel network. Throughput is also enhanced, beginning at 100MB per second. The flexibility of Fibre Channel is endless; for building an enterprise data center, Fibre Channel will one day be the medium of choice.

If Fibre Channel is so great and so old, why doesn't anyone use it? After a long time in gestation, Fibre Channel drives are only now beginning to appear on the market. They are largely distinguished by the fact that you can't find a Fibre Channel controller to use them with and their ungodly prices.

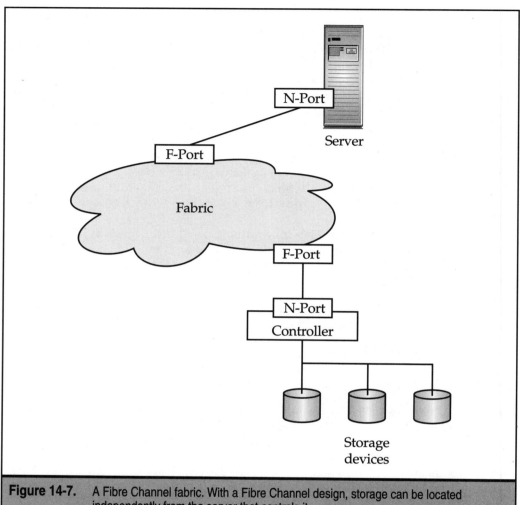

Figure 14-7. A Fibre Channel fabric. With a Fibre Channel design, storage can be located independently from the server that controls it.

Even when Fibre Channel controllers are introduced, building a Fibre Channel network is going to be very, very expensive. It's doubtful that SCSI will be replaced by Fibre Channel, for the same reason that optical network cable will never replace copper: it's too expensive to justify the benefits.

Still, Fibre Channel will inch its way into the enterprise over the next few years. While a detailed discussion of Fibre Channel is outside the scope of this book, the definitive place to look for further information is at the Fibre Channel Association's home page at www.fibrechannel.com.

Hot-Swap Drives and Spares

Before we leave the realm of disk drives for more esoteric matters, it's important to note that *any* server you consider purchasing should offer hot-swap drives, regardless of the interface type. Hot-swap drives are standard disk drives that come in special caddies called "trays." These trays are used to slide in and out of special slots in a server, specifically designed for hot-swap storage. Unfortunately, you can usually only buy these drive/tray combinations from the manufacturer of the server, and you will always pay much more for the drive with the tray than you would for the drive alone. There is really no way around this, unfortunately.

The main feature of hot-swap drives is that they can be replaced while the server is running, with no loss of data. This will be important when we begin our discussion of RAID and drive redundancy. Most controllers also support spare drives, drives that can be switched on automatically if one of the primary drives fails. Some controllers have "hot-add" features, which let you expand storage without powering down the system.

Again, it is highly recommended that any server you buy include hot-swap drives.

RAID

In the old days, RAID stood for redundant array of inexpensive disks. The modern definition is redundant array of independent disks. Presumably it was changed when people came to the realization that disk drives weren't really that cheap.

Regardless, the key word in the acronym is *redundant*. RAID is a very clever way to build fault tolerance into one of the least tolerant subsystems of a computer: the hard disks. Disks crash. In fact, they crash all the time, and when they crash, they're usually gone for good. While that 36GB drive we mentioned earlier sounds great in theory, imagine what would happen if 36GB of important data on the network you were charged with managing disappeared because the drive went south? Visualize your résumé being updated . . .

RAID was originally designed in 1987. It is simply a method of combining a number of disk drives so they appear as a single drive to the computer. Redundancy is built in to most RAID architectures, or levels, so that if any one drive fails (or more drives, in some cases), all of the data on the drive set can be reconstructed from the data remaining on the still operable drives.

Software RAID vs. Hardware RAID

RAID can be implemented in software or hardware. Any respectable drive controller can perform the back-end operations of RAID, but some software can as well. Most notable is Microsoft Windows NT, which has RAID built in to its Disk Administrator utility. With Windows NT, you can build and manage RAID arrays. Of course, virtually all of the sophistication and most of the speed of a hardware RAID solution will be lost. We encourage you to spend the extra money (usually under $1,200) and invest in a high-performance hardware solution.

RAID Levels

RAID arrays are defined by levels, each of which specifies a minimum number of disks and a certain level of redundancy. Your controller may support some or all of these RAID levels, but most controllers support all of the important ones.

RAID 0   RAID 0, also known as *striping* or *stripe set,* is not RAID at all, in that it provides no redundancy whatsoever. In a RAID 0 scheme, data is split equally, or "striped," among two or more drives on the bus.

RAID 0 has many advantages. For starters, it is extremely fast—with two drives, speed is roughly doubled over writing to a single drive; with three, it is tripled; and so on. RAID 0 is so fast because the controller can write data in parallel, instead of serially, one block at a time. RAID 0 arrays, unlike other RAID schemes, don't lose any of the drive space. Two 4GB drives can use RAID 0 to act like one 8GB drive. Five 4GB drives can emulate one very fast 20GB drive. The only limit is the number of devices on the bus.

Of course, what makes RAID 0 wholly inappropriate for the enterprise is its lack of fault-tolerance features. As mentioned above, RAID 0 has no redundancy, and if any drive in the array fails, *all data on all of the drives on the array* will be lost. In fact, as you add devices to a RAID 0 array, the risk of data loss increases with each device in proportion to the gain in speed. With 10 drives in an array, you are 10 times more likely to experience a crash, and thus, you put your data at 10 times the risk.

RAID 0, shown in Figure 14-8, is fine if you need very fast access to unimportant data that you don't mind losing. Of course, we haven't seen many networks that fit this description. (Also of note: Watch out for server vendors who tout high-speed disk performance; they are usually benchmarking their servers with RAID 0 arrays.)

RAID 1   RAID 1, or *mirroring*, is a very simple way to provide redundancy without sacrificing much speed. Drives in a RAID 1 array are "mirrored" so that they represent exact copies of one another. With any data that is written to or deleted from one drive, the same operation occurs on the other. You can also implement RAID 1 with three or more drives (although this is very uncommon), with every drive an identical copy of the others.

If a mirrored drive fails, the network doesn't skip a beat, because an up-to-the-millisecond copy is always on hand. The failed drive can be replaced, and all the data can be copied onto it without much trouble, thus restoring the RAID 1 array. RAID 1 is very logical and simple to do in software or hardware.

Another redundancy option similar to mirroring is called *duplexing*. Duplexing works the same way, but in addition to the two disk drives, the system has two drive controllers as well. This is to eliminate the single point of failure in all other RAID systems: the controller. In many cases, if a controller fails, all the data on drives attached to it will be lost, even if you replace the controller. Duplexing prevents this from simultaneously destroying both drives on an array.

RAID 1 is almost as fast as a single-drive system in most implementations, simply because a server rarely pushes the envelope on data transfer rates. Copying twice the

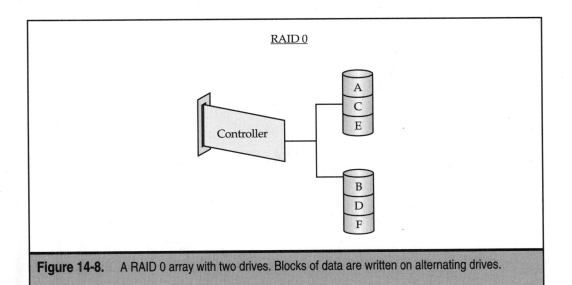

Figure 14-8.   A RAID 0 array with two drives. Blocks of data are written on alternating drives.

amount of data is usually possible within available bandwidth. The problem with RAID 1, as shown in Figure 14-9, is that you lose so much drive space. No matter how many drives are on the system, you can only utilize the amount of storage of the smallest drive. With two 4GB drives, your system only sees 4GB available, essentially wasting the other 4GB, except as backup. For many servers, the storage capacity of one drive, even a large one, is insufficient.

RAID 2   RAID 2 stripes data across multiple drives, much like RAID 0, but it also uses additional drives to store ECC information about the data on the striped drives. Because of the overhead required by the controller and the sheer number of drives (three drives needed to store ECC information on a four-drive stripe set), RAID 2 has never seen any practical implementations.

RAID 3   RAID 3 is similar to RAID 2, although only one drive is used to store redundancy information in the form of simple parity (called the "parity drive"). RAID 3 had minimal support for a long time until it was eventually canned in favor of RAID 5. The problem with RAID 3 is that performance suffers because, while the striped drives are speedy, the parity drive must be written to with every write operation. This slows down the entire subsystem.

Storage Computer Corp. has a trademarked operation called RAID 7 that mimics RAID 3, but at much higher speeds. It is very expensive, proprietary, and has virtually no installed base.

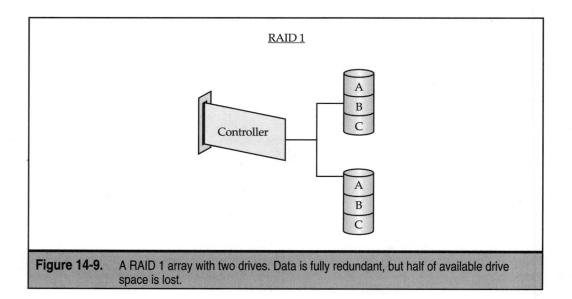

Figure 14-9.   A RAID 1 array with two drives. Data is fully redundant, but half of available drive space is lost.

RAID 4   RAID 4 is the same as RAID 3, only larger chunks of data are used. RAID 4 was implemented on several controllers but was soon abandoned due to the complexity of the controller and performance that was no better than RAID 3.

RAID 5   The current RAID system of choice, RAID 5, shown in Figure 14-10, is a fully redundant system that provides very fast read rates and better write throughput than RAID 2 through 4. Three drives are minimum with RAID 5, and like RAID 3, a parity calculation is made on each byte of data that is striped across the primary drives. The parity information is stored on a redundant drive.

Then, the operation shifts: Primary data is stored on the previously redundant drive and another drive, and parity information is stored on what was once a primary drive. The operation shifts again, and so on. This way, the parity drive bottleneck of RAID 3 and 4 is avoided by rotating the drive that receives the parity information. This way, all drives are written to in equal amounts, and each supports its own burden of parity information. If any drive fails, most controllers will automatically rebuild the data on a new drive once it is installed. In the meantime, the system will continue to run, just not as fast.

RAID 5 is popular because it provides reasonable performance in all metrics: Fault tolerance is provided for any single drive failure. The addressable space is equal to the sum of all but one of the drives. (Three 4GB drives net you 8GB of space; eight 4GB drives net you 28GB.) And performance, while considerably slower than RAID 1 and 0, is still much better than the other RAID levels. RAID 5 is probably the most popular RAID level today.

Note that a RAID 6 technology, which introduces additional fault tolerance to RAID 5 has been suggested, although no known implementations exist (RAID 6 would be extremely slow).

RAID 10   Also known as RAID 0/1, RAID 10 is sometimes (incorrectly) lumped in with RAID 1. RAID 10 combines RAID 0 and RAID 1 by allowing you to build a mirrored set of striped drives. With a minimum of four drives, two drives are used to stripe all data without parity information, and the two redundant drives simply hold copies of the two primary drives. This way, if any one of the drives fails, a copy exists that can be used in its place.

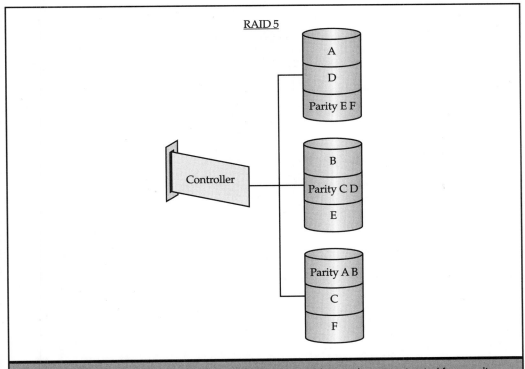

Figure 14-10.   A RAID 5 array. If any one drive fails, that drive can be reconstructed from parity information on the remaining drives.

Because no parity calculation has to be made, RAID 10 is very fast, almost as fast as RAID 1. However, you lose half your available drive space due to the required extra drives, and because of the 15-device limit on SCSI chains, scalability can be a problem with RAID 10. RAID 10, shown in Figure 14-11, enjoys a good amount of support by controller vendors, as the hardware is not substantially more complex than RAID 0 and RAID 1 hardware.

RAID 30   Aka RAID 0/3, RAID 30 involves mirrored copies of a RAID 3 array. There are very few RAID 30 implementations in the real world because it is limited by the problems of RAID 3.

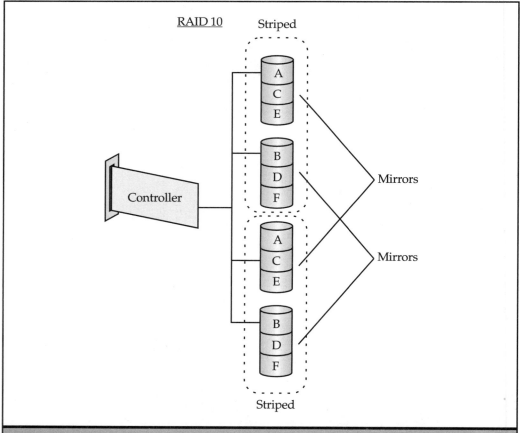

Figure 14-11.   High-speed redundancy with a RAID 10 array

RAID 50   Aka RAID 0/5, RAID 50 is a mirrored set of RAID 5 arrays. You need a minimum of six drives to implement RAID 50, and only two of those drives will represent the actual storage capacity of the array. (Six 4GB drives net you 8GB of space!) With a RAID 50 array, four of the six drives can fail and the system will still be able to be reconstructed. Since disk failures usually occur one at a time or all at once, however, RAID 50 is largely useless as a practical technology. Still, many controllers support it.

JBOD   JBOD, or *just a bunch of disks,* is the practice of simply adding multiple drives together so they can be addressed as one drive. Windows NT calls this a *volume set.* No striping occurs with JBOD. When one disk gets full, the controller simply moves on to the next disk without interruption. JBOD is cheap, unsophisticated, as fast as a single drive (since only one drive is accessed at a time), and provides no redundancy features. Recommended only for pennywise operations.

Controller Cards

When shopping for a storage controller card, you'll find low-end devices ranging from a few hundred dollars, to high-end cards that can cost $3,000 or even $5,000 apiece. Here's a brief guide to the standard features you'll find on the cards on the market.

Channels

Most modern controller cards fit in PCI slots and have SCSI interfaces of some sort. Ultra SCSI is the current standard, but it is quickly being replaced by Ultra2/LVD SCSI. SCSI cards are also distinguished by the number of channels they support. Low-end cards have one or two channels, each of which can host up to 15 SCSI devices. (Often, low-end SCSI cards will have one Ultra SCSI channel and one Ultra2 SCSI channel, but the variations are limitless.)

High-end cards typically have three channels, and four-channel cards are on the way (giving you access to 60 drives from one controller!). You'll also see these high-end cards beginning to be available in 64-bit PCI versions very soon.

I₂O

I_2O (Intelligent Input/Output) technology works at the motherboard and the controller. Put simply, I_2O takes the burden of I/O functions off the CPU altogether and places the burden of I/O in the hands of the controller. The concept of I_2O is actually quite old, dating back to mainframe servers.

I_2O simplifies device drivers and results in a modest improvement in speed. It also frees the CPU to do more math-intensive applications, which can help considerably in many computing environments. Still, don't expect a dramatic increase in the performance of I_2O-ready servers. While I/O functions are offloaded from the CPU, the actual burden of performing I/O functions is still present. It's just relocated to the controller.

Management Software

Most RAID cards come with added graphical management software tools. We've found these to be generally of good design, simplifying the often complex matter of managing your drive arrays. RAID management software can also be used to remotely manage drive arrays that are installed elsewhere on the network.

External Storage Systems

It's important to mention that all of your disk drive storage doesn't have to physically reside in your servers. External storage that either attaches to the external SCSI ports on your controller (*server attached storage*) or attaches directly to the network, as with a Fibre Channel system (*network attached storage*) is commonly available, although it generally comes at a premium price compared to internal storage.

External storage devices are becoming more intelligent; some even incorporate their own controllers. In fact, some external storage devices contain a full server implemented with minimal hardware (called a "thin server"), with the idea that you just plug them in to the network and, *voilà*, instant storage space.

Although a detailed discussion of external storage systems is outside the scope of this book, watch for this market to continue to emerge and for prices to continue to fall over the next few years.

Choosing an I/O Strategy

I/O presents many challenges and choices to consider when it comes time to expand your total storage space. While there's no "one right" solution, the following recommendation is a best-of-breed approach that will give you the best compromise of speed, total disk space, and fault tolerance.

If you're buying a new system, we recommend the following configuration. Use a separate boot drive to store system files. Install a PCI, I$_2$O-ready RAID card that supports RAID 5. Use five to eight hot-swap Ultra SCSI drives in your array (or Ultra2 if you can afford it), and configure one drive as a spare—again, if you can afford the cost. If you're running Windows NT, use the NTFS file system; otherwise, go with the default for the OS.

If you're adding storage to an existing server, consider replacing your old controller with a newer RAID card. Often, this simple change can double or triple performance, as newer RAID cards are much more efficient.

Additional Resources

Perhaps the best online guide to storage is The PC Guide's reference section on hard disk drives at www.pc.guide.com/ref/hdd/index.htm. Drive manufacturers like Quantum (www.quantum.com) and Seagate (www.seagate.com) and controller vendors like Adaptec (www.adaptec.com) typically have good storage resources as well.

SLOTS GALORE

Another consideration when purchasing a server is its expansion slots. Because servers and PCs are built with room to grow, you need a way to connect peripherals, RAID cards, NICs, video cards, and other expansion devices to the system. In the (very) old days, you needed an expansion card for everything: floppy drive, hard disk, and monitor. Even RAM went into a standard ISA slot. Today, most of these functions are built on to the motherboard; you only need an expansion card for new technologies.

Thus the expansion slot was born. Every device installed in an expansion slot communicates with RAM and the CPU through the I/O bus. Unfortunately, there are almost a dozen types of expansion slots in use now, and determining what's what inside your system can be confusing.

When buying a server, take stock of the expansion cards you want to use with it and make sure the server supports those cards. Many new servers have PCI slots only, and have tossed ISA and EISA support altogether. Other servers have only two or three slots to work with. Do your homework carefully, because the number of slots on a system cannot be altered short of replacing the motherboard (although, of course, an exception exists with very high-end servers that allow you to add slot modules).

ISA

Industry Standard Architecture (ISA) has been with us for almost 20 years, since the original IBM PC. It's amazing how common ISA slots are, even in new systems, and how pervasive the technology has become. While ISA finally appears to be on its way out, it's going to linger for another decade, at least, in existing systems.

Originally an 8-bit bus, ISA was expanded to 16 bits in 1984. The maximum bus speed of the 16-bit version (today's standard) is about 8MB per second. The 16-bit ISA slots usually support 8-bit ISA cards, as well. You simply plug the smaller card into the front part of the two-part 16-bit slot.

EISA

Extended ISA (EISA) was a revision of ISA completed in 1988, largely by Compaq. By giving the EISA technology away to all takers, EISA became a minor standard for even faster I/O on network file servers.

EISA is a 32-bit extension of ISA. It is compatible with the older technology (in fact, ISA and EISA cards look almost identical). If you look carefully at an EISA slot, you'll see that the connectors have two tiers: the upper tier connects to ISA cards; the lower tier connects to EISA cards. It's quite an innovative design. Because of its cost, though, it never really caught on.

The maximum throughput, in theory, of EISA is 33MB per second. EISA technology also includes automatic configuration of connected devices, making it easier to work with than ISA.

Microchannel

One of the classic failures of networking is IBM's Microchannel (also known as MCA) architecture. Microchannel was developed alongside EISA as another 32-bit expansion slot competitor, and IBM wanted to own the technology and collect royalties.

The closed nature of the standard plus the failure of MCA to be backwards-compatible with ISA doomed it from the start. Although it was fast and offered plug and play connectivity like EISA, you will be hard-pressed to find a Microchannel system today.

VESA

In 1992, a new variation of bus technology was introduced, called the "local bus." With local bus technology, expansion cards could access the CPU directly, through a high-speed connection to the CPU/memory bus. This gave I/O devices on the local bus an exponential leap in throughput, giving the Video Electronics Standards Association (VESA) bus a maximum speed of 133MB per second.

VESA, also called VESA Local Bus (VLB) or VL-Bus, looks like an ISA slot with two additional connectors on the end. While VESA was popular in the heyday of the 486 (in fact, VESA *only* works with the 486), it was quickly displaced within a couple of years by PCI. VESA is common on older 486 systems, but support for it has vanished along with the chip it required to run.

PCI

Peripheral component interconnect (PCI) is today's standard for expansion slot technology. PCI revolutionized the PC bus by building a new bus between the CPU and the old I/O bus. This avoided the problems of VESA, which relied on perfect timing with a specific CPU in order to work right. But like VESA, fast throughput of 133MB per second (or faster, in some implementations) is promised.

PCI connectors are small and thin. The one problem with PCI cards is that they are notorious for falling out of their slots. PCI devices are fully compatible with Intel's Plug and Play (PnP) standard for simpler device connectivity—in fact, PCI was the first standard to popularize PnP.

64-bit PCI

Just starting its commercial implementation is 64-bit PCI technology, an extension of 32-bit standard PCI. Thanks to clock upgrades and double the width of the bus, 64-bit PCI cards can reach up to 533MB per second. Of course, no device connected to the bus can go this fast, but at least you know the interface probably won't be the bottleneck.

64-bit PCI cards are starting to emerge in two applications: high-end RAID controllers and Gigabit Ethernet NICs. Both of these applications need all the bandwidth they can get, and 64-bit PCI is probably the least expensive way to provide it.

PCI Hot Plug

To enhance the redundancy and fault tolerance of a server, hot-swap technology is starting to come to PCI expansion cards as well. The theory is the same as with hard drives: If a card fails, you swap it out with a working one without turning the server off.

Right now, this takes special software to pull off, as hot-swap PCI is not built-in to any operating systems. Windows 2000 will have this capability built-in, and you can find several add-ons to NT 4.0 (like Micron's proprietary solution in its NetFRAME servers) on the market today.

Look for hot-swap PCI to become an important feature in the next generation of enterprise servers.

AGP

Accelerated graphics port (AGP) is another high-end expansion solution designed specifically for enhancing video performance. AGP is quite new (1997), and it provides video throughput ranging from 267MB per second up to 1GB per second and higher. Because high-end video support is usually not an issue with servers, you probably won't find an AGP port on most server systems.

PC Cards

PC cards (formerly PCMCIA cards), were popularized on laptops in the early 1990s as a quick and easy way to connect miniaturized peripherals the size of a credit card to your system. Everything from mini hard drives to modems to RAM upgrades to video capture cards to joystick input connectors has been implemented on the PC card platform.

PC cards work well for laptops, but because of the cost and limited throughput (most transfer data at 20MB per second, newer cards burst at 133MB per second) of PC cards, you'll rarely find them on desktops or servers, although they are usually supported if you want to add them.

USB

The universal serial bus (USB) has been a grandiose dream a long time in the making. At only 12MB per second, USB is not designed for ultrafast data transfer. Rather, its purpose is to make peripheral connectivity simpler than ever.

USB ports are tiny rectangular inputs on a system. No extra hardware or software is needed for USB devices. You simply plug the USB connector into the USB port, and that's it. USB even provides power to the device, so you don't even need to plug the device into the wall!

Despite its extreme ease of use, USB peripherals are still hard to find, but they are creeping onto the market very slowly. USB support is a great thing to look for on any new server you're considering purchasing, especially if you're tired of dealing with drivers and that tangle of cables.

1394

1394 is a technology that still hasn't found a name that's stuck. Called 1394 for its IEEE specification number, the technology also goes by the names FireWire, I-link, and Lynx.

1394 is all about speed. Implementations start at 100MB per second and can reach 400MB per second. Cabling is similar to USB, with data and power transmission over one link. Despite its high speed and easy connectivity, 1394's only real use right now is in connecting video cameras and VCRs to a PC for digital editing purposes.

1394 technology is quite expensive, too, so unless you want your server to do double duty as a multimedia editing bay, you don't need to buy a server that supports 1394.

SERVER MANAGEMENT

Most servers are sold with some form of management software, software that can be very helpful, of some use, or generally worthless. Most management software falls right in the middle: telling you if a disk has crashed or a RAM chip has gone bad—but you'll generally be able to tell all of that anyway without the software telling you. Most packages offer the primary benefit of allowing you to remotely monitor your server, so you don't have to be standing next to it to know that it crashed.

While you will find a few server vendors that offer proprietary management software bundled with their system (Compaq's is probably the best known), there are a few industry standards that you'll also see.

Intel LANDesk

If any server management package is an industry standard, it's Intel LANDesk Server Manager. LANDesk works with servers running NetWare 3.x and 4.x and Windows NT. Its primary function is sending you alerts when any number of parameter thresholds are exceeded—processor utilization is too high, disk space is running out, a NIC has failed, and so on. The warning message can be e-mailed to you, sent through an SNMP trap, or broadcast over the network. Complete log files are kept as well, so you can dig through the server's medical history if a problem does arise. LANDesk is bundled with about half of the servers we see; more details on LANDesk can be found at www.intel.com/network/server/index.htm.

Hewlett-Packard OpenView

HP's OpenView is a bit more sophisticated than LANDesk, and the package can actually be used (and is designed to) manage every device on your network from a central location through SNMP information. OpenView Network Node Manager is the standard server manager package shipped with Dell servers. You can get detailed specs at www.openview.hp.com/index.asp.

Server Management Hardware

Many servers and server management software packages can be extended in functionality by the addition of a hardware component. For example, Intel offers an add-on card for LANDesk that lets you monitor a server's temperature and perform remote shutdowns, among other duties. Dell offers a remote diagnostics card called Dell Remote Assistant Card (DRAC) that allows full server control through a modem connection to the card.

BACKUP

Sooner or later, it happens to even the best of us.

Your server is going to crash someday, and data will be lost. How simple and fast it is to recover from the crash is up to you. Whether it will happen is a foregone conclusion: it will. The only question is when.

It bears repeating: *Someday your server will crash.*

Take that to heart and repeat it as a mantra when your boss questions your purchase of a new tape drive or expensive backup software.

Disaster Planning

Now that we've established that servers crash, how do you prepare for the inevitable?

It's important to have a number of things on hand and be ready for the disaster when it happens.

For starters, make sure you use RAID in some form (covered earlier). This is by far the simplest and least expensive way to ensure 100 percent uptime. Next, it's critical to have good copy of your backups on tape. Every guide to computing will tell you this, and they're all right. Still, it's easy to ignore the advice altogether, or do a so-so job of managing backups, running them every other weekend, or only during "problem periods" on the network.

This is pure folly. Not only do servers crash unexpectedly, they also corrupt files accidentally, users write over important information, a new driver can cause a system conflict; in other words, it can get very messy without a second's advance notice.

Not only do you need backups, you need *good* backups. We can't count the number of times we've heard administrators claim they were doing regular backups, only to find out too late that important files were being skipped (usually because open files were not backed up). Tapes go bad too, usually after about three years. A tape backup does you no good if the tape distorts or altogether loses the data that's on it. It's cliched advice, but spot test your tapes on a monthly basis to make sure the data isn't garbage.

Spot checking also teaches you another important thing: *how* to run the restore application. Working with backup software is not always the simplest task. Doing a few restore runs with dummy files is good practice. Make sure you've built any required "emergency disks," too; when your system dies, there isn't going to be any simple GUI to run the restore operation from.

In case your emergency disks don't work, make sure you have a copy of the OS in hand in case you have to start from scratch. Also, make sure you keep your licensing information handy; this is especially critical with NetWare servers, which won't run at all without a valid license key.

With all this in hand, you can hope for the best but plan for the worst. It's going to happen, sooner or later.

Tape and Tape Drives

The central component of any backup system is usually the tape drive. As with all server technologies, tape drives have evolved considerably over the years, and the state of the market is, in all honesty, a mess. Once again, we'll try to sort out what's what.

QIC

QIC, or Quarter-Inch Cartridge, is the original standard for tape drives. Designed in 1983, QIC drives are still common today, as the technology has been continually updated.

Two types of QIC cartridges exist: DC, or data cartridge, is a large 4 by 6 by 5/8-inch cassette; MC, or mini cartridge, is a smaller 3 ¼ by 2 ½ by 3/5-inch cassette. The MC standard is far more common, because the DC-sized drives are difficult to fit into a server's drive bays.

QIC cartridges are specified by an alphanumeric code, and there are literally hundreds of them to choose from. Here is a small sampling of the important QIC standards. (Also, when shopping for backup devices, make sure you buy a drive that corresponds to the tape type you want to use!) You can find out anything you could possibly want to know about QIC at www.qic.org.

QIC-40-MC/QIC-80-MC   These two tape formats specify 40MB and 80MB (higher with compressed data) tape capacities; transfer speed is below 10MB per minute, and the connection is typically made through a standard floppy drive interface. These tapes and the drives that use them are very cheap, mainly because 40MB of storage is pretty useless these days.

QIC-30X0-MC   This series of tapes starts with the 255MB QIC-3010 and scales up to the QIC-3230, which holds 15GB of data. These drives can typically push about 9MB per minute to a tape, using a SCSI-2 or floppy interface. Many of these drives feature ECC features, also.

QIC-24-DC/QIC-120-DC/QIC-150-DC   The low-end of DC format drives, the QIC 24/120/150 can store 45MB to 150MB on a tape. Data transfer speed is about 12MB per minute, and the connector is a SCSI interface.

QIC-1000-DC/QIC-1350-DC   Storing 1GB and 1.35GB respectively, these tapes run at 18MB per minute and use a SCSI-2 connector. ECC is also included.

QIC-2GB-DC/QIC-5GB-DC/QIC-5010-DC/QIC-5210-DC   The biggest of the DC drives, the QIC-5010 can hold 13GB of data, and the QIC-5210 can hold 25GB; the other two drives have what should be an obvious capacity. They are otherwise feature-identical to the QIC-1000 drive.

DAT

The main problem with QIC is that, even on the newest of models, data transfer is painfully slow. At 18MB per minute, it would take almost four hours to do a 4GB backup. Even small companies have storage needs that far outweigh this, making QIC simply too slow to finish a backup in a timely manner (usually meaning overnight).

DAT (digital audio tape), also called DDS (digital data storage), changed that with its introduction. DAT uses a completely different encoding standard than QIC, called helical scanning, very similar to what a VCR uses, although video technology is not part of the DAT recording process. DAT drives connect to a SCSI port on your system and can cost up to $1,000 for high-end models.

Tapes and DAT drives currently come in three formats:

▼ **DDS-1**   Can store 2GB of uncompressed data, 4GB of compressed data.

■ **DDS-2**   Can store 4GB of uncompressed data, 8GB of compressed data.

▲ **DDS-3**   Can store 12GB of uncompressed data, 24GB of compressed data.

Compressed transfer speeds can reach 2MB per second, or 120MB per minute, about seven times faster than high-end QIC devices.

DAT drives are currently the standard for high performance at a reasonable cost. We recommend you start with DAT if you're new to backup.

8mm

Exabyte has marketed a drive that can record on 8mm tape—commonly known as videotape. 8mm drives offer storage of up to 40GB per tape with compression, and can write at a speed of 6MB per second—or 360MB per minute—making them very fast. These drives are very expensive, but they offer one of the best high-speed, high-capacity backup solutions currently available. Tapes are quite inexpensive, also.

DLT

DLT, or digital linear tape, was designed in 1991 and offers very fast performance (about 5MB per second) and high capacities (up to 70GB compressed). Like 8mm tape, it is designed for the high-end backup market, and is priced accordingly (drives can run up to $8,000). DLT drives can be very sophisticated, including tape changers and automatic tape rotation systems. DLT tapes themselves are also quite sophisticated and expensive as well.

Travan

In an attempt to revive the rapidly dying QIC format, 3M (now Imation) designed a new standard called Travan that is backwards-compatible with QIC mini cartridge tapes. Travan currently offers cartridges with about triple the capacity of comparable QIC tapes (400MB to 8GB of storage), but speed is still relatively slow at about 60MB per minute through a SCSI connection (floppy connectors are also an option). If you have many old QIC tapes you want to access, but want better performance, Travan is certainly worth a look.

Other Backup Devices

Outside the realm of tape, you'll find optical storage devices and other removable media storage devices, like the popular Iomega Zip drive.

A number of optical storage devices are on the market that can be used as backup devices. WORM drives (write-once, read-many), also called CD-R (compact disk-recordable) drives allow you to burn data on a blank optical disk, which is thereafter permanent and unerasable. Disks are very cheap (about $5) and data transfer rates reach 2MB per second or more on high-end SCSI devices. WORM drives are quite cheap these days, and capacity is around 650MB, the size of a CD-ROM. WORM makes a good solution for archiving data that you don't want to destroy.

The next step of CD technology is CD-RW (CD-rewritable), which works and performs like a WORM drive, but can be overwritten any time. CD-RW makes a good rewritable alternative to WORM, but currently, CD-RW disks cannot be read by CD-ROM or WORM drives, as the format is proprietary. (WORM-created disks can be shared with CD-ROM drives.) Recordable DVD will change this industry considerably in the next few years.

A number of inexpensive, cartridge-based devices are also available, providing high-speed storage. Iomega's Zip drive uses 100MB disks (a new model uses 250MB disks) and can write data at 1.4MB per second. Iomega's Jaz uses 1GB or 2GB disks and can write at 5.4MB per second.

Imation's LS-120, a drive that allows backward-compatibility with floppy drives, uses 120MB disks and writes data at 4MB per second. Other removable media storage devices are available from Sony and Castlewood, among others.

The problem with removable media drives like the Jaz is that the cartridges are very expensive. A 2GB Jaz disk costs about $150, about the cost of a 2GB hard disk drive. Using removable media drives for large-scale backups simply doesn't make a lot of sense.

OTHER SERVER CONSIDERATIONS

While CPU, memory, and I/O are the primary considerations when evaluating a server, there are a few other components that should at least cross your mind when you do your shopping.

Server NICs

Many server vendors are prone to simply sticking a $49 100Base-T NIC in your server and calling it an advanced server NIC. More often than not, if you want something that's truly advanced, you'll have to add it to your system after the fact.

Real server NICs, like the Intel EtherExpress PRO/100 Server Adapter, cost about $600 and include support for vLANs (virtual LANs), failover to a second card if the primary card fails, and load balancing and bandwidth aggregation for multiple NICs. Adaptec's Cogent Quartet NIC has four ports, so you can directly connect your server to multiple switches, thus avoiding a network failure should one of the switches crash.

Server NICs are expensive, but if you want the highest of fault tolerance and up-to-the-minute features, they can be invaluable.

Power Supplies

The server's power supply is something we normally don't consider, either. You want enough juice to run the server, and that's about it.

But power supplies, like any electrical component, can fail. Many power supplies are cheaply made, too, making them one of the least reliable parts of the system. If a power supply dies, it can be a real pain to replace it quickly, especially if you don't have a spare of the right form factor and wattage. (We've seen servers that require as little as 225 watts to run, and some that need as much as 900 watts and special, three-prong, "clothes dryer" wall sockets.) Make sure you know the power requirements of your server before you try to install it, or you may just be left holding the cord.

There are two power supply features to look for in today's servers. The first is redundant, load-balancing power supplies. In many servers, two or more power supplies can be installed in the case. Each plugs in to the wall with a separate cord, so you can plug the server into sockets that run off of different circuit breakers if you want a higher level of safety. The power supplies do two things. First, they perform load balancing, so neither supply will be overly taxed by the rising and falling power demands of the server. Second, if one fails, the other(s) can usually pick up the slack until the failed supply is replaced. These features vary from server to server, so check with your vendor to see exactly what is offered and how it works.

The second feature is hot-swap power supplies. Just like with disk drives, many servers can be configured with hot-swap power supply units. If a supply fails, you simply open a door on the back of the server, pull out the failed supply, and slide in a new one. Obviously, this is only of real value if the server has a redundant power supply and can keep running during this process; in this way, the server will experience no downtime at all.

Regardless of the power supply configuration of your server, make sure there are enough internal power connectors to feed the disk drives and other peripherals you install in the system. This is not normally a problem like it used to be in the early days of PCs, but it is still worth checking out in advance.

UPSes

All of that sophisticated power won't do you any good if the line to the building dies, so it's important to add an uninterruptible power supply (UPS) to any server you buy. You simply plug the server into the UPS and plug the UPS into the wall outlet.

UPSes work like standby batteries, waiting for the power to fail so they can take over until it is repaired. UPSes come in a variety of ratings, but basically, the bigger UPS you buy, the longer it will last during a power failure. Normally, this is only a matter of minutes, enough time for you to close any open files and perform a safe shutdown of the system.

UPSes also provide a second benefit: power filtering. We've yet to see a building that didn't have "dirty power," power that fluctuates substantially in voltage. Dirty power can be an elusive problem, and it has commonly been implicated in a number of data corruption problems that couldn't be traced to any other source. A good UPS eliminates this, as you'll get a steady 110 volts from the UPS, no matter what you get from the wall socket. This feature is invaluable, and because UPSes aren't too expensive, it's definitely worth it.

Most UPSes also come with management software so you can monitor the battery's condition as well as the voltage coming into and out of the UPS.

CD-ROM Drives

You need a CD-ROM drive on your server, obviously. However, you do not need the latest and greatest drive, which will only drive up the cost of the system; how often is it going to be used, anyway? Still, a nice drive is good to have; Compaq's tray- and caddy-less drives are especially handy. Some high-end servers are even equipped with two CD-ROM drives, in case you want to share CD-ROMs from a central location. Again, it's a handy addition, but you can certainly buy dedicated CD-ROM towers if you want this kind of functionality. The bottom line: Make sure the server has a CD-ROM drive, but don't sweat the specs.

CYA: Technical Support and Warranties

After you sign that check, server vendors are often reluctant to lend a hand in solving any problems in the system you've just bought. Warranties have been improving along with the hardware they cover, but in many cases, your basic warranty will not be sufficient, requiring the purchase of an extension.

For example, Compaq offers a three-year, on-site warranty on all server products, with second-business-day response. Unless you want to wait two days to get your server fixed, this warranty will probably not be sufficient. Dell offers one-year, on-site, next-business-day warranties on its server products, with second- and third-year parts delivery only. You also get a whopping five calls to technical support before you are charged for them. Again, this warranty strikes us as inadequate.

While upgrading warranties is inexpensive (usually under $200), the quality of technical support you get is wildly variant. If you can, give your chosen server vendor's tech support line a call before you buy. See how much of a hassle it is to get help when you really need it (you'd be amazed at the runaround you'll get from many big-name vendors). Do the same if you have to buy your system through a value added reseller (VAR), and see how much "value" it is really adding.

In the end, you'll probably feel your server warranty is a lot like your auto warranty: It's really not good enough, but you'll be glad to have it in case of a catastrophe.

NAME BRAND OR CLONE?

When it comes time to buy a server, there's always the question of whether to get a name brand server (Dell, Compaq, HP, and IBM), a second-tier system (Micron, NEC, and others), or a no-name server manufacturer (Polywell, Tangent, Omni Tech, and a cast of thousands).

Deciding whether to go first-class or to save a few bucks on a lesser-known server is only part of the issue. Performance varies from system to system, warranties are hardly comparable, but going with a name system gives you a little more assurance that the company will be around in a year to honor that warranty, anyway.

What's the verdict? Unfortunately, there is no easy answer. While a Dell server may run $5,000 more than a comparable Micron, it may also be twice as fast at I/O operations. A year ago, buying a server from the top-tier DEC might have sounded great; odds are, that product line has been discontinued since the merger with Compaq. What's the fastest server we've ever tested? It's not an IBM or an HP . . . it's a Polywell, and it costs a third of some enterprise systems.

So what advice can we give you? If you're a nervous type, definitely stick with a top-four system. If you are looking to save a few bucks and are willing to live on the edge, check out some of these lesser-known companies, especially if their systems are more feature-specific to what you're looking for. They might just surprise you.

HOW MUCH WILL IT COST?

We've done a lot of talking about servers in general, but what's it all really going to cost? Servers start at about $6,000 with reasonable configuration (don't believe an ad that quotes a lower price), and they go up from there.

Here's a rough guide to what different components should add to the price of a server, circa 1998. These prices are extremely volatile, so only use them as a general guideline.

A bare-bones system with a single-Pentium III motherboard, 4GB of storage, 64MB of RAM, and a case should run about $2,000, like a good PC. Functionally, you will not really be able to use this as a server. Adding CPUs starts at $500 to $1,000 for low-end processors and goes up to the thousands for Pentium III Xeon CPUs. Of course, just starting with Xeon processors will get you into five figures.

Adding a RAID card will be a minimum of $1,000, and could be up to $5,000, depending on the performance you want. Adding drives will run $300 to $1,000 each, depending on capacity or speed. Figure $550 for a 10,000rpm SCSI-3 drive with a 9GB capacity.

Adding RAM gets pricey at high capacities: $2,000 to add 512MB, $4,000 to add 1GB. For tape drives, figure $800 for an entry-level DDS-3 drive, all the way up to $7,000 for a high-end DLT system. A UPS will run about $650.

Building a solid midrange system, with dual 400MHz Pentium II processors, a good RAID card with three 9GB drives, 512MB of RAM, a DDS-3 tape drive, a warranty upgrade, and a UPS, will cost about $12,500 from a name-brand server vendor. This doesn't include a monitor or an operating system. Note, these prices may have come down about $1,000 in the last nine months.

Figure this price will be another $1,000 less from a no-name vendor, with the same components. Then again, it's largely impossible to find identical systems with the exact same components from two different vendors.

UPGRADING

The first rule of server upgrades is: If it ain't broke, don't fix it! Almost any IS manager can relate at least one sad tale of woe about how he or she thought an innocuous driver update or firmware patch would be simple and provide better performance . . . only to find out afterward that the server would no longer boot or had fallen victim to another dastardly fate.

If you must upgrade a server (and it is usually inevitable), make sure you back up everything, preferably more than once. Do it on a weekend, when you can take your time and make sure things are done right. Or better yet, have a consultant do it, so he or she will be responsible if it doesn't work right afterward.

WORKING WITH SERVERS

If you decide to open up your server yourself, make sure you take a few precautions.

ESD

First, electrostatic discharge (ESD) can fry any component with the touch of a finger. Merely shuffling your feet on the carpet can generate about 3,000 volts of static electricity or more. A typical component runs at about 5 volts, and if voltage exceeds that by much, the component will blow. The voltage you carry in your hand is enough to effectively wipe out a multimillion dollar server if you work on it without taking the proper steps to ground yourself.

ESD kits can be purchased that consist of a wrist strap and mat, which you connect to your server's chassis and yourself, effectively grounding yourself. If you don't want to buy an ESD kit, simply touch the chassis before you work on a server (and frequently, while you're working on it). This is most effective if the server is plugged in (but powered off!) because of the ground line from the power supply to the wall outlet.

Be sure to store components in static-proof bags (the same bags the components are shipped in).

Tools

The advent of the "tool-less server" has been a godsend. Most big-name server vendors ship servers that can be completely disassembled without a screwdriver. Thumbscrews hold the case together, and flip tabs hold drives and cards in their bays and slots. Amazingly, these servers are just as physically stable as their heavily encased counterparts.

Since you'll probably be dealing with older systems at some point, you should make sure you have a good selection of tools on-hand. These include the following:

▼ An assortment of flathead, Phillips, and Torx (the star-shaped head) screwdrivers

■ Needle-nose and standard pliers, and/or tweezers

■ A few wrenches of varying size

■ Chip inserters and extractors

■ Spare screws and jumpers (you'll be amazed at how fast these accumulate)

■ A flashlight (maybe the most useful of these tools)

■ A wire cutter, stripper, and crimper

▲ Compressed air

You can typically find kits that sell all of these tools and much more for well under $100, although you usually have to buy the flashlight separately. You can also invest in things like soldering irons, voltmeters, and logic probes, but shy away from tools like these unless you have the experience to use them.

Storage

As with most things, computer or otherwise, store your server in a cool, clean, and dry place. While keeping your server dry is usually not a problem, most IS managers aren't the tidiest people we know, and servers locked away in a closet tend to accumulate large quantities of dust.

It's important to keep your server as dust-free as possible. Dust and other grime is often a problem with bizarre errors, because the electrical contacts the dust is covering become unstable. Simply blowing the dust out of any computer with compressed air can give it new life. It should be one of the first steps you perform during troubleshooting and should be part of your regular maintenance program.

Heat is another big problem. At high temperatures, electrical connections again become less reliable. Get your server hot enough, and some components can actually melt or catch on fire. All the RAID and tape backup in the world won't help you recover if the building burns down.

Keep your server cool. Start with good air conditioning in the room. Make sure that the A/C isn't shut off at nights or on the weekends without your knowledge. Keep the cover on the server: most servers have a delicate air flow structure that is completely ruined if you operate the server without its cover. This also helps with the dust issue. Make sure all the fans are working, as well. A few server management software applications monitor fan speed and will tell you if one is about to die.

Finally, leave the server on, even if it isn't going to be used for awhile (like the weekend). Thermal expansion and contraction, as opposed to sheer heat, is what makes computer components fail. Keeping the system at a stable temperature is key.

FURTHER READING

If you're looking for a book specifically devoted to servers, good luck; we've never seen one. A good starting place for general server information is the Web site of any major server manufacturer, or try the PC Webopaedia (www.pcwebopedia.com), which offers a rich selection of technology definitions and links for further information. You can also check out the PC hardware reference section of your bookstore for basic questions about PC architecture and operation.

CHAPTER 15

The Glue

Now we have all these pieces of the network defined and identified in their proper place in the network framework. But how do you connect them and keep them? This is the function of layer 3 (the network layer) and layer 2 (the media access control layer) of the OSI model. In this chapter, we'll talk about wiring systems and the protocols that enable applications, systems software, and devices to communicate with each other over these wiring systems.

CONNECTIVITY 101

Back in the early days of networking, all networks were linear networks. This meant that a network consisted of a number of workstations connected by a single cable. At the time, this was fine because networks tended to be small, and so cable problems were fairly easy to isolate. On larger networks, however, locating a loose connection or cable break could be a difficult and time-consuming process, often requiring special—and expensive— equipment to determine the type and location of the cable problem.

To solve the problem caused by a single network cable, wiring centers, or hubs, were developed. The first hubs were nothing more than signal repeaters. They took a data signal from one cable segment and repeated it over another, extending the length of the network, as shown in Figure 15-1. However, these simple repeaters made it easy to divide networks into segments, meaning physical and/or logical groups of network users and resources. Dividing networks into segments enabled network managers to keep network users as close as possible to the network resources they used the most. This allowed the network administrator to control and isolate network traffic to a certain extent.

The potential usefulness of hubs went well beyond that of the first simple network repeaters. Soon after the appearance of the first basic hubs, a second generation of hubs appeared that offered management features. These hubs could collect management information from each network connection, then convert that information into a standardized format (for example, Simple Network Management Protocol), then export

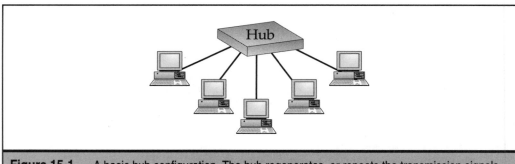

Figure 15-1.   A basic hub configuration. The hub regenerates, or repeats the transmission signals coming from the workstations.

that information to a number of management reporting systems. Often, these hubs also had buses that allowed them to support multiple transport protocols on the same high-performance backplane. Then, thanks to the high-performance backplane, hubs appeared that could support multiple logical network segments within the hub, meaning that a hub could now contain more than one segment, and that each of those segments could be managed separately. This enabled network managers to reconfigure network segments, making moves, adds, and changes on the fly and even from a remote console.

With these sophisticated new features came new roles for network hubs. Soon, network managers were using hubs to concentrate, or collapse, network nodes into increasingly complex hierarchies of networks, often within a single chassis. Simple, unmanaged wiring center hubs were used to connect end-user nodes to their login servers. These simple hubs were in turn connected to one another by more sophisticated hubs. These intermediate-level hubs were then connected by extremely feature-rich and highly manageable chassis-based hubs, some employing bridging or routing modules (see Figure 15-2).

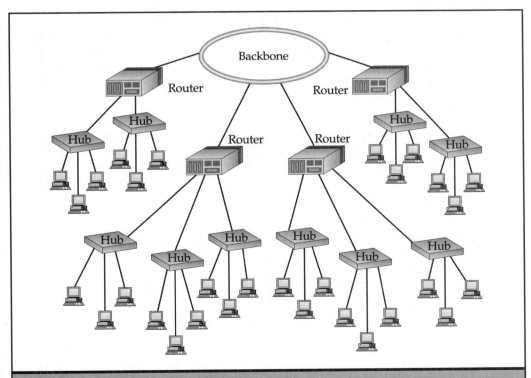

Figure 15-2.   A hierarchical network with hubs and routers concentrating network nodes at discrete levels

With this, the concept of structured wiring was born, and network managers began to realize its many benefits, including the following:

▼ Easier moves, adds, and changes

■ Centralized management

■ Improved scalability

■ Better monitoring of network events and statistics

■ Easier troubleshooting

■ Improved fault tolerance

■ Support for multiple transport protocols

▲ Support for multiple communications protocols

Types of Backbones

The term *backbone*, although it is tossed around rather loosely, really means a network that connects multiple local area network segments. In this sense, a backbone is a "network of networks" that handles internetwork traffic—that is, traffic that originates in one LAN segment and is transmitted to another. Network segments, on the other hand, handle local network traffic. Because the backbone provides both a physical and logical data path among all the nodes connected to it, the network segments and subnetworks must be connected to the backbone by devices capable of performing the necessary bridging and routing of data packets being transmitted. These devices may be switches (Figure 15-3), routers (Figure 15-4), and/or file servers (Figure 15-5) performing the bridging and routing functions among the network segments.

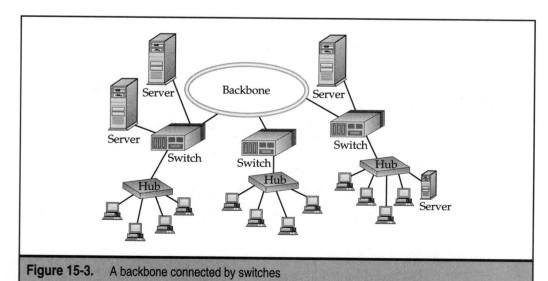

Figure 15-3.   A backbone connected by switches

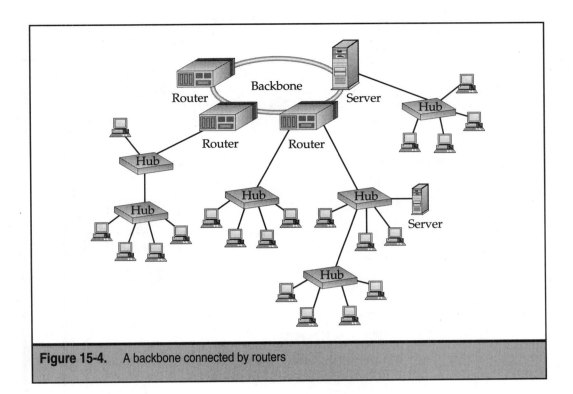

Figure 15-4. A backbone connected by routers

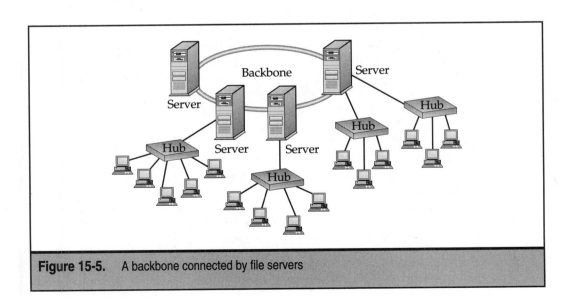

Figure 15-5. A backbone connected by file servers

Why Build a Backbone?

A well-designed backbone can bring order, ease of management, and the potential for improved performance to your network. Backbones enable network managers to centralize their network structures by providing a single point of monitoring, management, and control. Because all network servers are attached to a common cable, they can be moved to a central location. This centralization makes the network easier to configure, secure, and manage because:

▼   Repairs and maintenance are easier to schedule and perform.

■   All backups and archiving can be handled simultaneously.

▲   Telecommunications connections can be pulled to one central location.

What's more, network backbone designs have given rise to two related network designs that we touched on earlier: structured wiring and collapsed backbones. These two techniques further increase ease of network management.

Structured Wiring

Although any cable plant that involved a little forethought could be called a *structured wiring system*, the term is usually reserved for those standards-based wiring schemes that are hierarchically designed for easy management and expansion. Structured wiring systems generally incorporate a network design in which a central hub controls the flow of information between departments and also serves as a connection point for enterprise resources such as communications and applications servers (see Figure 15-6).

There are two keys to a good structured wiring system. The first is to keep network users as close as possible—both physically and logically—to the network resources they use the most. In Figure 15-6, for example, the users in Building A are directly attached to the server they use most frequently. This eliminates unnecessary internetwork traffic that can slow down the performance of the whole network. The second key is to design the system so that adding, moving, and changing users (which you will occasionally have to do to keep them as close as possible to their preferred network resources) are as easy as possible.

Collapsed Backbones

A *collapsed backbone* is essentially a "backbone in a box"—that is, an entire physical and logical data internetwork contained within a single device (see Figure 15-7).

Instead of running backbone media throughout the walls, ceilings, and floors of the building, each network segment is attached to a single hub or stack of hubs that connects all the segments and subnetworks to form the enterprise internetwork. The collapsed backbone design was a logical outgrowth of the centralized backbone network design. After all, if all the servers are in a central location for management purposes, the next step

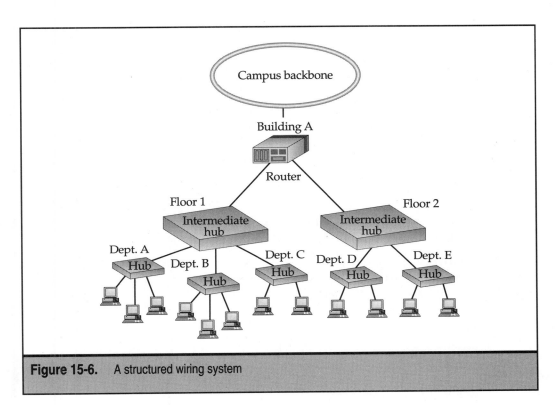

Figure 15-6. A structured wiring system

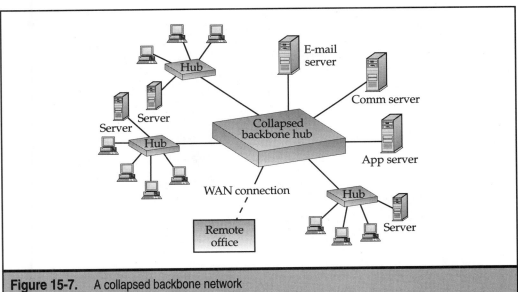

Figure 15-7. A collapsed backbone network

is to connect them to a single hub, replacing the backbone cable with the backplane of the hub. The advantages to this are many:

- ▼ Hubs are modular and easily scalable.
- ■ Hubs are built on a chassis with high-speed backplanes that provide a high-speed bus for expansion boards.
- ■ Most chassis-based hubs can simultaneously support multiple transport protocols, such as Ethernet, Token Ring, FDDI, and WAN.
- ▲ Most hubs offer optional integrated diagnostic and management tools.

Furthermore, a collapsed backbone extends the manageability of the centralized backbone by:

- ▼ Providing a central point for management of the entire network
- ▲ Providing better management of and security for network resources

A collapsed backbone design provides better management because it offers a single point of network monitoring and control, which also makes troubleshooting easier. It improves security because all servers are moved to a central management area. Most important of all, a collapsed backbone design makes it easy to implement a high-speed network.

How Do You Build a Backbone?

You can configure backbones physically to accommodate your segmenting scheme. For example, local area network segments on each floor of an office building are connected to a backbone that runs through the conduit from one floor to the next.

Regardless of the physical configuration of your backbone, the network segments and subnetworks must be connected to the backbone by devices capable of performing the necessary bridging and routing of data packets being transmitted.

Building a Backbone with Switches

This is one of the simplest and most straightforward ways to build a backbone, as shown in Figure 15-8. A switch is simply a specialized bridge that creates a virtual one-to-one

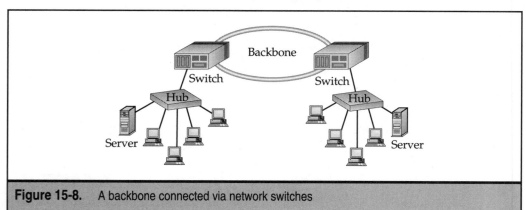

Figure 15-8.   A backbone connected via network switches

connection between a sending node and a receiving node. When a switch receives a packet, it sets up a connection between the sending node and the receiving node just long enough to transmit the packet. The switch then takes down that connection and waits for the next packet.

To build a backbone with switches, just connect the segments and/or individual nodes to switches, and the switches in turn are connected to one another on the backbone cable.

Building a Backbone with Routers

In a *router-based backbone*, a router or routers connect the segments to the backbone cable, as shown in Figure 15-9. A router functions as the connection point to the backbone for each segment. Using routers as the backbone can provide a level of fault tolerance that bridges can't. When the backbone is constructed of a dual-ring medium, such as fiber-optic cable, the ring will loop back on itself, the routers will adjust the paths, and the data will continue uninterrupted across the backbone.

Building a Backbone with Network File Servers

In a server-based backbone, like the one shown in Figure 15-10, each server forming the backbone contains two or more network adapters. One of the adapters connects the server to the backbone. This provides backbone access for the server and for all the network segments attached to the server. The other network adapter(s) provides the connection between the server and its network segment(s).

The backbone is by nature a high-traffic area, so it will be one of the first places to experience slow performance caused by high traffic. This is especially true in server-based backbones, in which the network file server (or servers) connects the network segments to the backbone cable. Most network operating systems have integrated bridging and routing functions that enable them to connect the segments, although requiring the server to perform these functions steals processing cycles from other vital server activities such as file management. Therefore, managers of large networks and/or networks with heavy traffic should dedicate file servers either to file management or

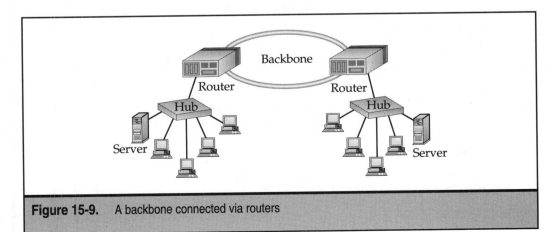

Figure 15-9. A backbone connected via routers

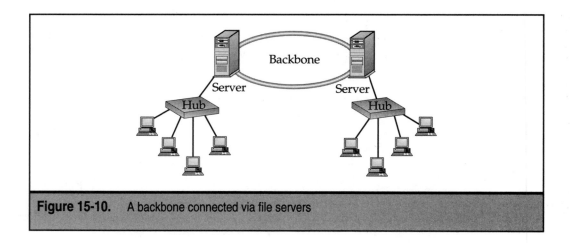

Figure 15-10. A backbone connected via file servers

bridging and routing functions, or consider building a backbone using bridges or routers. In small-to-medium-sized networks that have relatively low traffic, however, the servers may be able to provide backbone connectivity without seriously affecting server performance.

The Effects of Excessive Internetwork Traffic

As we mentioned earlier, the backbone is probably the area of your network where you will first feel the effects of excessive traffic. If you are experiencing slow network performance, therefore, the backbone is probably your first suspect. A fairly reliable indicator of a clogged backbone is slow network response when handling internetwork traffic (packets that originate on one network segment and are then transmitted to another), despite the fact that all the servers and workstations are not overworked.

Causes and Cures for a Clogged Backbone

To be sure that the problem is indeed excessive backbone traffic, however, you will need to conduct a few tests. First, check to make sure that the slow performance you experience is occurring only during internetwork transmissions. If slow performance is characteristic of all network transmissions, the problem may not be your backbone—or at least not the backbone alone. Determine the physical location of the network applications you are using when the network response slows. If these applications are on another network segment, you may indeed be suffering from excessive traffic on the network backbone.

Location of Applications

Before you conclude that more backbone bandwidth is what you need, however, ask yourself whether it's possible to move the applications onto the same segment as the user without slowing down performance for users on other segments. Be sure all users are as close as possible—both physically and logically—to the network resources they use most frequently. This eliminates unnecessary internetwork traffic. Of course, locating applications close to users is becoming increasingly difficult in this flat-architectured, Internet-driven world.

Inadequate Hardware

Next, check your workstations and servers. Ensure that your workstations have sufficient memory and processing power for the job. Also, check servers to make sure that they are not the bottleneck. If your servers are waiting on disk input/output, that's probably the cause of the network slowdown, and it can be alleviated by installing a faster disk subsystem. Likewise, insufficient memory (often indicated by memory swapping to disk), low throughput to and from the network adapter (resulting in dropped packets and retransmissions), and inadequate processors can all slow your servers and cause them to be a bottleneck on your backbone.

"Chatty" Communication Protocols

Another cause of congested backbones, especially on networks running very old versions of operating systems, is the communication protocol used by your network operating system. Among the functions of the communications protocol are creating service connections, getting network station addresses, and other tasks associated with transferring data from a station on one network to a station on another network. The communication protocol operates at the network layer as described on the International Standards Organization's Open Systems Interconnection model. Communications protocols include Internet Protocol (IP) and NetWare's Internetwork Packet Exchange protocol (IPX).

Some communications protocols generate a lot of traffic because for every request for service they send, they require a response from the station that is granting the services. Because of this constant "conversation" between the requester and grantor of services, these protocols are called "chatty" protocols. IPX, for example, is the classic example of a "chatty" protocol—request then response, request then response. Often these requests and responses are larger than one packet. Therefore, a chatty protocol significantly increases the number of packets being transmitted. Consequently, chatty protocols are not a good choice for backbone deployment.

Transmission Control Protocol/Internet Protocol (TCP/IP), on the other hand, is not a chatty protocol. Rather than sending a request for service, waiting for a reply, then sending the next request for service, TCP/IP sends all requests for service in a single burst, sometimes called a "packet burst." It then receives multiple responses from the grantor of those services. This makes it a better choice for a backbone protocol than IPX.

To ease the congestion that IPX can cause, in version 4 of it's NetWare operating system, Novell introduced PBURST NLM, a NetWare Loadable Module that enables the server and workstations to function in Packet Burst Mode, sending all service requests in a single burst. However, PBURST is not turned on by default. You will have to load PBURST manually or add the LOAD PBURST command to your startup.ncf file.

Small Packet Size

Also, bigger is better when it comes to packet size on the backbone. That's because one large packet obviously represents less traffic than a lot of little ones. This has a couple of indications. First, you should select a backbone protocol with the largest packet size available. Second, if you're running NetWare, you may have to make some adjustments.

Your NetWare servers could be needlessly creating more backbone traffic because they are limiting packet size to a 512KB maximum. By default, NetWare servers route a default packet size of 512KB. This is because 512KB used to be the largest packet that all routers could route. However, most routers these days will route at the maximum packet size for each protocol. Therefore, if you have a NetWare 4.X network, check to make sure your routers can handle a larger packet size. If they can, you may want to consider enabling the Large Internet Packet support.

The Final Analysis

Of course, the true and indisputable determination of where your backbone's bottleneck lies comes from in-depth analysis of your network traffic with a protocol analyzer. A protocol analyzer will help you determine whether packets are being dropped, resulting in retransmissions, and pinpoint where those packets are being dropped. It will also help you confirm whether your network has heavy internetwork traffic (data packets addressed to a node not on the same segment it originated). You can also use the protocol analyzer to determine bandwidth utilization, or the average percentage of bandwidth being used, on your network's backbone. If you are experiencing slow network performance and/or dropped packets, and if your network's bandwidth utilization over the backbone consistently averages over 50 percent, it's fairly safe to say that the problem is too much backbone traffic, and your network is a good candidate for implementing high-speed networking protocols.

What You Gain

Putting a high-speed protocol on the backbone will result in higher network throughput, and will eliminate any bottleneck caused by insufficient internetwork bandwidth. However, please be aware that a high-speed backbone usually gives subtle network improvements: faster internetwork transmissions and better server-to-server communication. The dramatic improvements in network response time—the kind that will make your boss call you to congratulate you and talk about your next raise—are not usually the kind realized through increasing bandwidth on the backbone. Those types of performance increases generally come from adding bandwidth within a local segment from the workstation to the local server.

Selecting a High-Speed Backbone Protocol

If you have conducted the necessary tests and have determined that you need to implement a high-speed protocol on your backbone, it's time to establish the selection criteria for this protocol. Overall, the most important features for a backbone protocol are

▼   Manageability
■   Fault tolerance
■   Scalability
■   Packet size
■   Packet overhead
▲   Maximum network span

Because manageability and fault tolerance are so important on the backbone, these two qualities must be paramount when you are selecting a high-speed protocol for this implementation. A protocol that currently supports only limited management systems is clearly a bad choice, as is a protocol that can't support a backup ring, spanning tree, or other disaster recovery system.

Easy and broad scalability is also another necessary feature of a backbone protocol because the protocol will need to be able to ensure low response times, even as you are adding servers. Important things to remember are the number of stations the protocol can support on a single LAN, as well as the packet size. Internetwork and server-to-server packets tend to be larger than local segment packets. Therefore, a protocol that can support large packet sizes tends to be more efficient on a backbone. As well, the amount of overhead (addressing and management information) per packet should be low to eliminate unnecessary traffic on the backbone.

Furthermore, consider maximum network extent. Backbones tend to be spread out over buildings or campuses, so be sure that the protocol you select can span your network without a lot of expensive repeating devices.

Finally, the backbone is not the place to pinch pennies. Losing a backbone link could cost you your job, so don't select backbone equipment on the basis of cost alone. Remember, the protocol that you select for your backbone doesn't have to be the same protocol you use throughout your network. Therefore, implementing a more expensive protocol on the backbone doesn't condemn you to overrunning your cabling budget on every segment.

LOCAL AREA PROTOCOLS

Now that you know how all these network applications and devices are connected, it's time you learned a bit more about the technologies used to connect them. These technologies function at layer 2 in the OSI/ISO Reference Model, and are widely used to connect networks within a relatively small geographic area, such as an enterprise campus.

Fiber Distributed Data Interface (FDDI)

Fiber Distributed Data Interface, or FDDI, was perhaps the first 100Mbps transport protocol available for local area networks. When it first appeared in the late 1980s, FDDI was expensive both to install and to manage. This was largely because the protocol ran only on fiber-optic cabling, which was scarce and difficult to install. Therefore, it was reserved almost exclusively for backbone use. Although most FDDI nodes are still mostly found on backbone segments, with the introduction of the protocol's copper wire implementation—twisted-pair physical media dependent (TP-PMD)—along with a drop in the cost of installing optical fiber, this protocol is finding its way to the desktops more often than ever before. Although, with the recent advent of other high-speed transport protocols that require less investment of time and money to implement, FDDI may have missed its chance for widespread deployment, it still may be the right choice for your network's backbone or power workgroup.

What Makes It the Same—and What Makes It Different

While there is nothing magic about FDDI as opposed to the other local area network transport protocols discussed in this book, FDDI is a significant departure from protocols we find defined in the IEEE 802 committee specifications. FDDI is a standard developed by the X3T9 committee of the American National Standards Institute (ANSI), and was originally conceived to transport data over fiber-optic cabling at 100Mbps. Since then, a copper cable implementation called TP-PMD has emerged, but has never enjoyed widespread popularity. Therefore, we will focus on the fiber-optic cabling implementation.

In its most basic form, an FDDI network is a group of computers, each with an FDDI network adapter installed, passing data packets around a ring. When operating in default mode, a computer receives a data packet from its neighbor on one side, then retransmits the packet to its neighbor on the other side.

In this scenario, each computer in the network is acting as a repeater, regenerating the data packet when it retransmits it. However, most FDDI adapters have a bypass mode, in which the device lets data packets pass by without retransmitting them. Bypass mode is used to keep the FDDI ring intact even when a computer is inactive. However, because a computer operating in bypass mode is not acting as a repeater (regenerating the data packets it receives), if too many computers placed next to each other in the ring are operating in bypass mode, the data signal may become very weak and limit the span of the network.

While a computer retransmits every data packet it receives, it sends a data packet of its own origination only when it receives the token. A token is a special data packet that serves the sole purpose of letting computers know that it has permission to originate a data packet on the ring. When a computer receives a data packet that it originated—after that packet has completely traversed the ring—the computer doesn't retransmit the packet again. If it did, packets would continue circling the ring ad infinitum, eventually overwhelming the network with unnecessary traffic. Instead, when the originating computer receives its data packet, it removes the data packet from the ring.

The network just described is a very basic FDDI ring. As we will see, the functions of an FDDI network quickly become more complex.

Framing the Data

FDDI uses a frame type different from that described in either the IEEE 802.3 (Ethernet) or IEEE 802.5 (Token Ring) standards. Although a comprehensive discussion of the types and contents of FDDI frames is beyond the scope of this book, it is important to understand that FDDI has its own frame structure. Figure 15-11 illustrates the composition of a frame.

FDDI carries much the same information in its Header field as do other protocols. The header contains information on originating station, frame classification, and unique frame identification.

The Class field identifies the frame as belonging to one of the eight (soon to be twelve) frame classes now defined in the FDDI protocol. Currently these are

▼ Neighbor information frames (NIF)

■ Extended service frames (ESF)

■ Parameter management frames (PMF)

■ Status report frames (SRF)

■ Status information frames (SIF)

■ Echo frames (ECF)

■ Resource allocation frames (RAF)

▲ Request denied frames (RDF)

The Type field identifies to which of the six frame types the frame belongs: token, void, media access control (MAC), station management (SMT), implementor, and logical link control (LLC). The Ver ID field shows the version of SMT protocol. The Transaction ID field is a unique identifier for each frame. The Station ID field gives the FDDI (not the MAC) address of the originating station. This is because some FDDI stations have multiple MAC addresses and therefore need identifiers for the protocol. This Station ID field also comes in handy if you are using hot-swappable FDDI devices, because it will maintain a constant ID for the station, even when the MAC addresses change.

Determining the Path

As mentioned earlier, FDDI is a protocol that employs a token-passing scheme to determine station access. Stations send and receive data packets when they receive the token—data transmission is not managed by a central controlling station as it is with 100VG-AnyLAN. This token-passing scheme guarantees each station on the network a certain amount of bandwidth. If you take the number of nodes on the network and

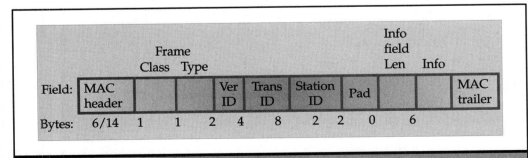

Figure 15-11.   Structure of a Fiber Distributed Data Interface frame

multiply it by the amount of time it takes each node to transmit a data packet, then you have the maximum amount of time it can take for any station to receive the token. This is what makes FDDI a deterministic network: each node will receive a minimum throughput that you can calculate.

While throughput on an FDDI network is fixed at any given time, it varies according to the number of nodes transmitting on the ring. Therefore, to join an FDDI segment, a station must follow a fairly strict set of procedures, which are part of FDDI's integrated management capabilities called station management protocols, or SMT (these are discussed later in the "Manageability" section of this chapter). These ring initiation protocols first initialize and test the link from the new station to the ring. Next, the station initiates its connection to the ring using a distributed algorithm called a claim token. The claim token process determines whether a token already exists, and if so, reconfigures the token's path to include the new station. However, if no token is detected, the claim token protocol requires that all stations attempting to join the FDDI segment transmit special packets, called claim frames. The stations use the claim frames to determine both

▼ An exact value for token rotation time

▲ Which station will initiate the new token

Once the token has been created and transmitted, it is used to arbitrate shared access for the stations using a timed token protocol. The first station to join the ring establishes and tests its link with the ring, then generates a token that is passed from station to station. When a station receives the token, it can then transmit a fixed amount of frames. To transmit information onto the ring, a station claims the token that is otherwise circling the ring.

FDDI has prioritization mechanisms implemented via bandwidth allocation. The first mechanism, called *synchronous bandwidth allocation* (SBA), enables managers to assign a fixed amount of bandwidth to a certain station or stations, thus giving them greater access to the token. In SBA, bandwidth is allocated to stations as a percentage of target token rotation time (TTRT), which is the preset time it takes the token to make one rotation of the ring. Obviously, the total bandwidth allocated via SBA should not exceed 100 percent of the available bandwidth (see Figure 15-12).

The second mechanism, referred to as the *asynchronous class of service*, takes the bandwidth that is not allocated via SBA and divides it equally among the stations on the ring. The asynchronous service works like this: each station keeps a token rotation timer that tells the station when next to expect the token. When the token next appears, the station compares the target rotation time (TRT), or expected time of arrival, to the TTRT, which is the preset time for the token to make one rotation. The TTRT is usually set at 8 milliseconds. If the TRT is less than the TTRT, the station can grab the token and send asynchronous data frames. If the TRT is greater than the TTRT, the token is late, so stations that have only asynchronous class of service must defer to stations with synchronous bandwidth allocation.

During times of heavy traffic, the TRT can get so long that stations sending data packets with low priorities can be completely restricted from access to the ring for a time.

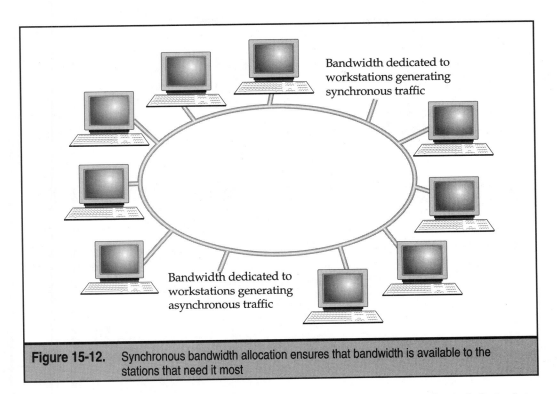

Bandwidth dedicated to
workstations generating
synchronous traffic

Bandwidth dedicated to
workstations generating
asynchronous traffic

Figure 15-12.   Synchronous bandwidth allocation ensures that bandwidth is available to the
stations that need it most

Eventually, however, all the stations with high-priority packets will send their data,
lowering the TRT and thereby letting stations with low-priority transmissions have a
chance to claim the token.

Cabling Considerations

FDDI networks are composed of a set of counterrotating dual rings and attached devices
and segments. The set of counterrotating dual rings is called the *trunk ring*. While devices
can be directly attached to the trunk ring, as described in our initial description of a basic
FDDI network, they can also be attached to the trunk ring via *concentrators*. Concentrators
are devices similar to multistation access units (MAUs) in the token ring world that
provide trunk connections to multiple stations. Devices that are directly attached to the
trunk must be dual-attachment stations (DASs); in other words, devices that are attached
to both of the counterrotating rings. Devices that are attached to the trunk ring via a
concentrator are single-attachment stations (SASs)—stations that attach to one ring only.

Making the Connection

In FDDI, network connections are made through a series of strictly defined protocols that
require that all FDDI ports have one of four identities: A, B, S, or M. Table 15-1 defines the
various port types.

Port Type	Function	Location
A	Exit point from station to secondary (backup) ring	All dual-attachment stations
B	Exit point from station to primary ring	All dual-attachment stations
S	Connects stations to one ring only	All single-attachment stations
M	Distribution ports that extend both primary and secondary rings	Concentrators

Table 15-1.   The Four Types of Network Connections Supported by FDDI

All stations on an FDDI network must have both an A and a B port. A tree connection occurs when an A, B, or S port connects to an M port. In this configuration, the node isn't attached directly to the trunk ring, but rather to a port on a concentrator attached to the trunk ring (see Figure 15-13).

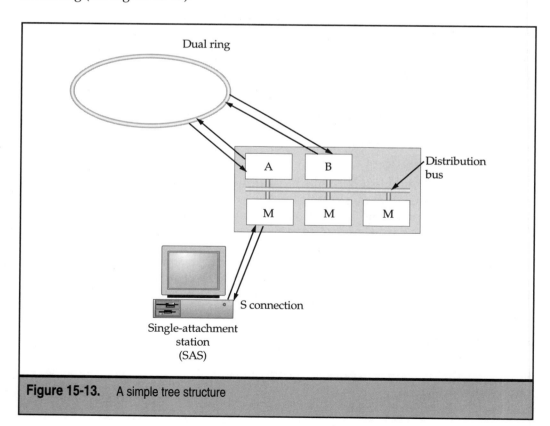

Figure 15-13.   A simple tree structure

Supported Media

FDDI can run on both multimode fiber (PMD) and single-mode fiber (SMF-PMD), as well as Category 5 unshielded twisted-pair cable and 150-ohm shielded twisted-pair cable (TP-PMD).

The Topology

The general topology used in FDDI networks is a dual ring with trees (see Figure 15-14), but there are variations:

▼   **Dual rings without trees**   This just means that all the stations are directly connected to the dual ring via DAS connections (see Figure 15-15).

■   **Wrapped ring with or without trees**   A wrapped ring is really a dual ring in which a cable fault or break has occurred. When the protocol senses a cable fault, it reroutes traffic from its direct path to the destination station to the roundabout secondary data path, essentially "wrapping" the data back around

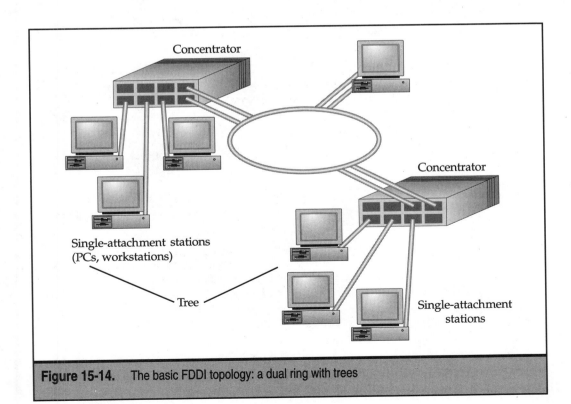

Figure 15-14.   The basic FDDI topology: a dual ring with trees

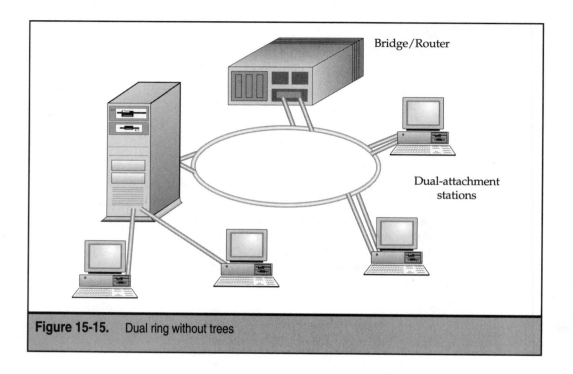

Figure 15-15.   Dual ring without trees

the ring until it reaches its destination. See Figure 15-16 for an example of a wrapped ring without trees. This type of topology is obviously inefficient, and should be used only as a disaster recovery measure in the event of a cable fault. Wrapped-ring configurations should be rectified as quickly as possible.

▲   **Single tree**   This is simply an FDDI network consisting of one tree (see Figure 15-17).

Whichever of these topologies you use, the cardinal rule remains the same: FDDI supports a maximum of two data paths—a primary data path and a secondary data path.

Cost of Ownership

Even after all these years, FDDI is an expensive protocol to implement. Hubs cost an average of about $750 per port, and network adapters for the desktop average a little over $300 each. What's more, if you use fiber-optic cable, you're going to encounter a major expense in training your staff to install and/or work with this medium. And then you're going to have to spend money to keep them, because there is a fairly strong demand for employees who are familiar with fiber-optic technology. Still, fiber-optic cabling has the

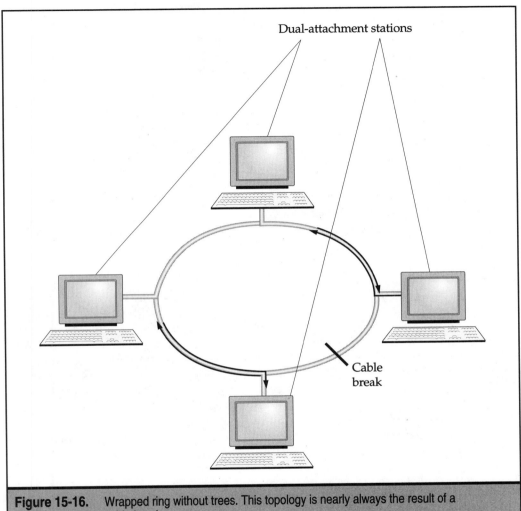

Dual-attachment stations

Cable break

Figure 15-16. Wrapped ring without trees. This topology is nearly always the result of a cable break.

capacity to support protocols that far exceed FDDI's current bandwidth, so depending upon your network strategy, it could be a good investment.

As we mentioned earlier, FDDI runs on either optical fiber or Category 5 UTP. However, the pinout for FDDI is different than that for Ethernet, so you'll need FDDI patch cables (it's a good a idea to color code these patch cables). Therefore, be prepared for some trouble calls resulting from Ethernet patch cables inadvertently being plugged into TP-PMD ports.

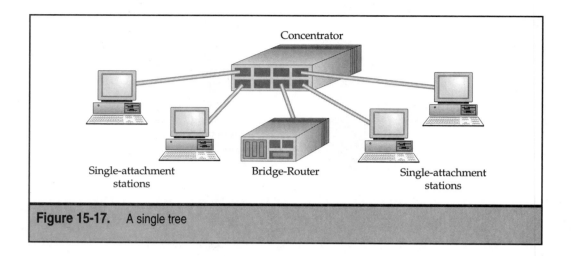

Figure 15-17.   A single tree

Scalability

FDDI is probably the most scalable of all the high-speed local area network protocols, with the exception of ATM. Its deterministic protocol, along with its synchronous and asynchronous bandwidth allocation mechanisms, make it easy to add stations while ensuring that response times meet the needs of the applications. What's more, FDDI supports up to 500 stations on a single LAN, and its maximum network extent is 200 kilometers when running over fiber-optic cabling.

FDDI's large packet size makes it a very efficient transport protocol for large packet sizes. However, for the current average packet size of between 256 bytes to 512 bytes, FDDI has extremely high overhead per packet.

If you are integrating FDDI into an existing 10Base-T network, there are many hubs available that support switching between the two protocols. Also, several vendors have recently announced the development of FDDI switches, which may enhance the performance of FDDI networks as they grow.

Setup and Configuration

As we mentioned earlier, installing FDDI is relatively difficult. However, because FDDI has been around for several years now, it should be fairly easy to find technical assistance. The initialization scheme required for stations wanting to enter the ring may cause some headaches during the initial configuration. However, once the FDDI network is up and running, it proves to be a solid and stable machine that needs very little maintenance.

Manageability

FDDI is both extremely fault tolerant and manageable. Because FDDI supports dual-homed, dual-attached backbones, each server on the ring can be connected to as many as two hubs on the same ring, so there is always an alternate path. Also, its support for counterrotating rings provides great fault isolation while simultaneously keeping the network running.

Unlike Ethernet, FDDI has a built-in network monitoring and management protocol called *station management* (SMT). Unlike the rest of the protocols in this comparison book, FDDI was designed with SMT as an integral part of it. SMT includes both network monitoring facilities at the link, node, and network levels, as well as remote network management capability via management information bases (MIBs).

It provides capabilities for fault isolation and recovery, statistics gathering, data error monitoring, and noise monitoring. In addition, it provides connection and configuration management. Even the previously described ring initiation procedures are a part of the station management protocol. However, providing these management and monitoring facilities also adds to the overhead of the protocol, and therefore can limit the efficiency and cost-effectiveness of the protocol, especially in desktop implementations.

Performance

FDDI has been a proven performer for some time. The elegance of the bandwidth allocation mechanisms really shows up in multimedia and video applications. As you run video applications, for example, you can add workstations to the FDDI ring without experiencing the slightest stall or shudder.

Furthermore, FDDI has a maximum data packet size of 4,500 bytes, which makes more efficient use of available bandwidth than 100Base-T with its 1,500-byte maximum. This larger packet size is especially helpful in applications with a large average packet size. In short, FDDI's performance gets very high marks.

Evolving to Survive

A related standard, FDDI-II, has emerged to transport data that cannot sustain delays. An example of this would be real-time, full-motion video. To accomplish the "zero-delay" standard, FDDI-II borrows from the circuit-switching technology of long-distance telephone carriers. FDDI-II multiplexes bandwidth into dedicated circuits that ensure packet delivery. These circuits can then provide isochronous, or circuit-based, services that offer a regular, fixed-length transmission slot that essentially provides a dedicated channel between stations. FDDI-II can support as many as 16 such circuits. Bandwidth on these circuits is allocated to stations on the basis of need, so maximum bandwidth varies from 6.144Mbps to 99.072Mbps. In turn, each of these channels may be subdivided into 64Kbps circuits. FDDI-II supports a maximum of 96 64Kbps channels.

FDDI-II has some drawbacks, however. First, all nodes on the network must be FDDI-II. If all nodes aren't, then the FDDI-II devices begin operating as FDDI devices. This lack of compatibility is not only inconvenient, it's extremely expensive because you will have the cost of replacing FDDI devices with FDDI-II devices as well as the cost of redesigning your network to make sure that all FDDI devices are on their own ring.

While FDDI has proven itself as a solid, fault-tolerant, high-performance vehicle for backbone deployment, there are several obstacles to implementing it at the desktop. Its high price, high overhead, and complete departure from the familiar 10Base-T cabling rules may prevent its widespread use at the desktop. You will probably have to spend a significant amount of time and money in finding, training, and then retaining people with expertise in fiber-optic cabling. Also, due to differences in pinout between Ethernet and FDDI, if you have both protocols at your site, there may be some confusion—and resulting troubleshooting—resulting from misplaced patch cables.

100VG-ANYLAN

In June 1995, the IEEE certified the 100VG-AnyLAN specification for the 802.12 standard. Long before that date, however, its proponents—led by Hewlett Packard Company, Inc.—heralded it as the ultimate trade-in opportunity for 10Base-T networks. Ethernet users have been told that the conversion from 10Base-T to 100VG-AnyLAN is so inexpensive and easy that there is no reason not to go with 100VG-AnyLAN. However, while 100VG-AnyLAN is a logical and cost-effective migration path for some applications, caveat emptor is the rule for the cautious network manager.

So Close, but So Far from 10Base-T

Although 100VG-AnyLAN has many similarities to the familiar 802.3 protocol, it employs data access and signaling methods that differ drastically from both Ethernet and Fast Ethernet. Rather than the familiar collision-based CSMA/CD protocol that the 802.3 and 802.3u standards use, the 802.12 data access method is known as *Demand Priority Access* (DPA), in which the workstation initiates data transfers and the hub acknowledges data and directs the transfer. This differs from CSMA/CD in two critical ways:

▼ Data transfer is controlled by the hub rather than the network adapter.

▲ Collisions are eliminated because each node is guaranteed a turn at sending data.

Theoretically, this deterministic protocol increases available bandwidth by eliminating collisions and retransmissions. However, being a complete departure from 802.3, it therefore will likely require some rethinking on the part of your technical staff and some redesign for your network.

Getting Framed

Although 100VG supports the frame formats of the existing 802.3 and 802.5 protocols (but not both simultaneously), the 802.12 transport protocol is nothing like either. The emerging IEEE 802.12 standard for transmitting 100Mbps over voice-grade unshielded twisted-pair wire represents a significant departure from the existing Ethernet standard in the area of data access.

SETTING PRIORITIES   One of the key differences between the 802.3 and 802.12 standards is also one of the prime advantages of the latter protocol: its ability to recognize two levels of priority in transmission requests. The 802.12 100VG-AnyLAN protocol recognizes normal-priority and high-priority transmission requests, with high-priority requests taking precedence. The priority level can be set either by the workstation or by the application, although as of this writing there were no generally available applications that took advantage of this ability to set priority. If a normal-priority request remains pending for more than 300ms, it is moved to the high-priority service queue.

DPA does more than simply allow you to set transmission priority. It also improves performance by removing the network overhead associated with the CSMA/CD access method. In CSMA/CD, all workstations contend for access to the channel. Collisions, which are fairly frequent, require detection and retransmission of the packet. Furthermore, the DPA scheme has a performance edge on CSMA/CD. This is because as collisions become more frequent as traffic increases on CSMA/CD networks, the resulting packet retransmissions slow performance. The DPA network, which has no contention for transmission and hence no packet collisions, is able to handle more traffic.

100VG-AnyLAN has something of a security advantage over the 802.3 standard as well. The 100VG-AnyLAN hub transmits packets only across ports attached to the destination address of the packet. This reduces the opportunity for unauthorized monitoring of transmissions.

The Architecture

The 100VG-AnyLAN topology must be in a physical star, with no loops or branches. The centerpiece of this topology, as specified by the DPA scheme, is a central hub, called the *root hub,* that controls the traffic. Each lower-level hub maintains its own per port address table that contains the addresses of the stations connected to each of its ports. If this sounds like the familiar polling architecture of yore—that's because that's exactly what it is.

HOW THE DEMAND PRIORITY ACCESS SCHEME WORKS   When a station sends a transmission request, the request is first received by the hub to which the station is directly attached. If the directly connected hub is the only hub in the network, it is the root hub and thus the central controller for network transmission. It will therefore service the transmission request in the station's turn in the polling and priority sequence. However, if the directly connected hub is not the root hub, it will send the station's transmission request on to the next-higher-level hub, which in turn will transfer the request on if it is not the root hub. Eventually, the transmission request reaches the root hub, which will then allow the local hub to service the transmission request in its turn. See Figure 15-18 for a bird's-eye view of the progress of a data packet across this topology.

HERE WE GO ROUND THE NETWORK   A 100VG-AnyLAN network functions something like a "round-robin," because each hub is polled in sequence, and each hub in turn polls each of its ports in sequence. Here's the process: Between packet transmissions, stations and hubs send a signal to each other indicating that the channel is available to make a transmission request. This signal is called an idle signal. When a station has a packet to transmit, it sends a transmission request signal to the hub. The transmission request signal includes the priority of the transmission request. The transmitting station then waits for a response, originating from the root hub, which grants it permission to transmit one packet onto the network.

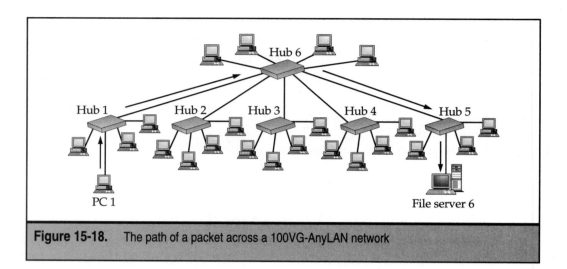

Figure 15-18.   The path of a packet across a 100VG-AnyLAN network

In 100VG-AnyLAN, the root hub controls all the data transmission. If the hub that receives the transmission request is the only hub in the network, it is the root hub, so it waits for any transmission in progress to complete, then services the port that is next in the polling sequence, giving that port permission to transmit one packet. However, if the hub is connected to a hub higher in the network, it waits for any network transmission in progress to complete, then signals a transmission request to the higher-level hub. In the same manner, the higher-level hub will pass the transmission request to the next higher level of hub—if any—until the transmission request eventually reaches the root hub.

The root hub determines which lower-level hub can then begin servicing transmission requests. When the right to service network requests passes to a hub, it services requests in port order (i.e., port 1, then 2, up to port *N*), and then passes control back to the higher-level hub. If a high-priority request is made anywhere on the network, however, the control passes immediately to the hub that has that request, and returns to the original hub after all high-priority requests have been serviced throughout the network. High-priority transmission requests occurring anywhere on the network always take precedence, and the root hub always allows the local hub that received the request to service the request, then return control to the hub whose turn it is. (See Figure 15-19.)

JOINING THE CLUB   Because of the deterministic nature of 100VG-AnyLAN, a station can't simply join the network and start transmitting. It must register itself with the root hub, which will assign the new station a place in the polling sequence. It works like this: When a station or hub wishes to join the network, it transmits and receives frames to and from the attached port. This is called a training sequence of frames. The training sequence helps the hub determine whether the new device is a station or another hub, which frame type it is using (either 802.3 or 802.5 frames), and whether the port will be allowed to operate as a promiscuous listener (a listener that looks at every packet). If the connecting

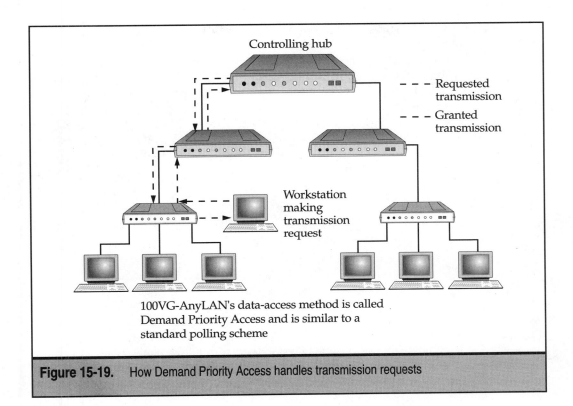

Figure 15-19.   How Demand Priority Access handles transmission requests

device is a station, the training sequence also determines the MAC address of the connecting station. While training is occurring, the network suspends its polling operations; fortunately, completing the training sequence takes about 5 microseconds. Based on the results of the training sequence, the hub either allows the new device to join the network or denies it access and transmits the reason why it will not be admitted.

Cable Design Considerations

The cabling rules for 100VG-AnyLAN are very similar to 10Base-T. In fact, of all the high-speed transport protocols, 100VG-AnyLAN has cabling rules closest to that for 10Base-T. However, there are some important differences.

WIRING ISSUES   In the 802.3 standard, one pair of wires is dedicated to transmitting data and another to receiving. Currently, in the 802.12 100VG-AnyLAN standard, all four pairs of wires both transmit or receive data (a two-pair implementation is planned), enabling each pair to operate at a signal rate of 25MHz. Because the deterministic protocol eliminates collisions, data throughput is theoretically at 100 percent, resulting in a 100Mbps network operating rate.

By sending out 25MHz signals, the protocol keeps radio frequencies within required standards. It also allows the use of voice-grade cable (Category 3). Using four-pair wiring, the 25MHz signal enables 100VG-AnyLAN to send and receive data simultaneously. 100VG-AnyLAN supports Categories 3, 4, or 5 UTP cable, Type-1 STP cable, and fiber-optic cable. Depending on the cable type, network span varies from 100 meters to 2,000 meters (see Figure 15-20).

Because 100VG-AnyLAN supports such a wide variety of cable types, you may be able to preserve your investment in your current network cable infrastructure. However, keep in mind that because 100VG-AnyLAN currently requires all four pairs of Category 3 UTP, you must be sure that all four pairs are terminated—and that may cost you some extra bucks.

TIP: Be sure that your twisted-pair cabling has twists all the way up to the pins of the cross-connect blocks. A section of untwisted pairs can cause crosstalk.

NOTE: 100VG-AnyLAN doesn't support flat cable in a twisted-pair topology.

HUB ISSUES   The maximum number of hub levels in a 100VG-AnyLAN network is five. However, your network will perform best if you keep it to three levels of hub cascading. Because three is the maximum number of hub levels allowed by 802.3, your network is probably already designed this way. However, each level of hubs shortens the maximum distance allowed between a root hub and an end node by 1km. Table 15-2 will help you determine the maximum distance between the root hub and an end node.

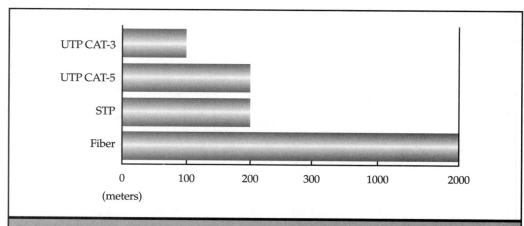

Figure 15-20.   In 100VG-AnyLAN, type of cabling determines the maximum network span

Type of Media	Number of Hubs Between Root Hub and End Node	Number of Levels in Network	Recommended Maximum Distances Between Root Hub and End Node
Category 3	1	2	100m
Category 3	2	3	75m
Category 3	3	4	50m
Category 3	4	5	25m
Category 5	1	2	200m
Category 5	2	3	150m
Category 5	3	4	100m
Category 5	4	5	50m
Fiber optic	1	2	4km
Fiber optic	2	3	3km
Fiber optic	3	4	2km

Table 15-2.   The Maximum Distances Allowed Between End Node and Root Hub

As a final cabling plant note, keep in mind that you shouldn't have more than seven bridges or switches between any two nodes in a network. This is a result of the IEEE 802.1d spanning tree protocol, not a limitation of 100VG-AnyLAN.

Preparing for 100VG-AnyLAN

One of the most unsettling things about plunging into 100VG-AnyLAN is its continued limited vendor support. Lack of competition in this market not only potentially limits the technical expertise available, but also may keep prices higher than for other better-established protocols. So, let the buyer beware.

You should scrutinize your cable plant before implementing 100VG-AnyLAN, carefully removing any 25-pair cables connected to devices operating in promiscuous mode (in which the device monitors all frames it receives), including the following:

▼ Cascaded (hub-to-hub) links, because the default configuration of an uplink port is promiscuous. The entire cable path from hub to device must be unbundled cable. Otherwise, the result will likely be severe crosstalk, retransmissions, and unreliable performance.

■ Links between routers and hubs.

■ Links between bridges and hubs.

▲ Links between a network analyzer and a hub. Network analyzers have to be configured as promiscuous so they can capture all network data.

You'll also have to check to make sure the distance between hubs does not exceed the specifications for 100VG-AnyLAN. Refer again to Table 15-2 for more information.

TIP: Spend a significant amount of time reviewing your cable plant to comply with 100VG-AnyLAN media and distance requirements. Also, if you are internetworking 100VG-AnyLAN with a 10Base-T network, be prepared to resegment your network to accommodate 100VG-AnyLAN bridging limitations.

Scalability

While the deterministic Demand Priority Access scheme makes 100VG-AnyLAN easily scalable with little drop in performance, growing a 100VG-AnyLAN network has its obstacles. Most of the scalability problems we noted are ones that you are most likely to encounter when migrating in phases from 10Base-T to 100VG-AnyLAN. For example, like all high-speed protocols, 100VG-AnyLAN requires a translational bridge between itself and 10Base-T. Furthermore, while there are no limitations on the number of nodes on a single shared 100VG-AnyLAN, it's a good idea to limit the number of nodes to 250 to maintain performance.

The rules governing network span in a 100VG-AnyLAN network depend not only on the type of cable used (see Figure 15-20), but also on the number of hub levels employed. Maximum network span for 100VG-AnyLAN networks varies from 100m to 2,000m, depending upon the media used. The maximum network length with Category 5 cabling is around 200m. Refer again to Figure 15-20 for information on maximum network span. Also, you can cascade up to five hubs (it supports four repeater hops per network segment, just like Ethernet). However, we recommend that you review your network design carefully and compare it to the 100VG-AnyLAN cable rules so you can be alerted to any potential problems. That's because each level of hubs shortens the maximum distance allowed between a root hub and an end node. For example, when using fiber-optic cabling, each level of hubs shortens the maximum distance from root hub to end node by 1km. Table 15-2 will help you determine the maximum distance between the root hub and an end node for fiber-optic cabling. Figure 15-21 illustrates the maximum distance between a root hub and an end node. In this example of a three-hub cascade using fiber-optic cabling, the maximum distance allowed is 3km.

TIP: Minimize the levels of cascading. Every level of cascading adds to arbitration overhead, which slows performance.

At this writing, there were only a few switches available for the 100VG- AnyLAN protocol. High speed notwithstanding, the ability to add switching—along with

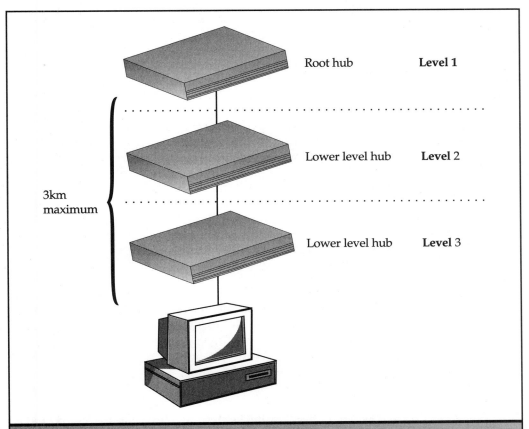

Root hub	**Level 1**	
Lower level hub	**Level** 2	
Lower level hub	**Level** 3	

3km maximum

Figure 15-21. The distance allowed between a root hub and an end node varies depending upon the number of cascaded hubs in between and type of media

management tools suitable to monitor simultaneous parallel paths—to a 100VG-AnyLAN network would enhance its scalability and make us feel more comfortable about its ability to support growth.

Manageability

Because 100VG-AnyLAN supports standard Ethernet packet types, interoperability problems are nonexistent. However, the protocol currently has no management tools that support bandwidth allocation and management.

Right now, the only security offered is the private-mode operation described earlier, which, when enabled, allows ports to receive only those packets addressed to the device attached to it. All ports not associated with the destination address receive an idle signal while the packet addressed to that destination is being transmitted. Although this level of security is sufficient for most installations, it may not be sufficient for extremely high security sites.

Performance

Performance is the strong suit of 100VG-AnyLAN. Because 100VG-AnyLAN can handle packet sizes of either 4,500 bytes or 1,500 bytes, it can support the current smaller average packet sizes and still maintain fast and efficient performance.

The real strength of 100VG-AnyLAN is highlighted when running multimedia applications. Even full-motion video runs under heavy network load with nary a flicker, thanks to the DPA scheme that assigned high priority to all the video frames. Furthermore, Hewlett Packard has stated that they have plans to add full-duplex capability 100VG-AnyLAN (which can be implemented only in two-pair environments such as two-pair shielded twisted-pair or two-pair fiber, support for which is currently unavailable), which will increase performance even more. All in all, however, the performance is extremely impressive right now.

Continuous Improvement

100VG-AnyLAN has improved since its introduction in 1994. When it was originally introduced, it didn't support redundant paths or the spanning tree protocol. Now, however, it supports redundant paths between any two hubs made via the spanning tree protocol, provided only one such path is active at any one time.

The Demand Priority Access scheme makes 100VG-AnyLAN a robust protocol that's especially well suited for multimedia and video applications. However, the protocol's lack of fault tolerance and dearth of management facilities make it less than ideal for backbone deployment. Its limited vendor support—it is still largely a Hewlett-Packard protocol—doesn't recommend it, either. Finally, because it almost but not quite complies with 10Base-T cabling rules, network managers should approach a broad-scale implementation with caution.

100BASE-T

From the beginning, the Fast Ethernet Alliance has heralded 100Base-T as the true and rightful heir of 10Base-T. With the IEEE's adoption of 100Base-T as the 802.3u standard in June 1995, the coronation is now complete. On its face, the succession seems logical, because in many ways 100Base-T appears to be just supercharged 10Base-T. For example, 100Base-T has retained the CSMA/CD media access method and most of the traditional cabling rules of 10Base-T.

Some argue, however, that 100Base-T is faster than most desktops require, yet slower than backbones demand. Moreover, the similarity but not strict conformity to 10Base-T cabling rules can cause confusion. This debate notwithstanding, it's probably the easiest high-speed protocol to merge into your existing 10Base-T environment—if you carefully choose the 100Base-T specification that's right for your network, familiarize yourself with and plan for the differences between 10Base-T and 100Base-T, and implement the protocol accordingly.

A Smorgasbord of Specs

The 802.3u specification adopted by the IEEE is defined in two parts. The first part defines the *data-link layer*, which is the layer in the OSI reference model that describes how the protocol handles sending and receiving data between nodes that are connected directly to one another. The second part of the IEEE 802.3u specification, and the part that is most significant to the network manager, is the *physical layer specification*. This is the part of the specification that defines the type of media over which you can run the 100Base-T protocol. The 100Base-T physical specification comes in four different flavors. Each is designed to accommodate 100Base-T on a different type of physical cable plant and is exacting in its requirements. Therefore, be sure to select the physical layer specification that suits your existing cable plant or be prepared to upgrade your cabling to meet the standard required by the specification.

Media-independent interface (MII) is the specification that provides MAC-layer connectivity to 100Base-T. This is similar to that of the attachment unit interface (AUI) connection in 10Base-T. The MII interface defines the way the 100Base-T protocol accesses the physical transmission media. In other words, the MII describes a generic 100Base-T interface that can connect to a transceiver that will connect in turn to 100Base-TX, 100Base-T4, or 100Base-FX (see Figure 15-22).

NOTE: The MII specifications allow only a 1-meter distance between the network adapter and the transceiver.

100Base-TX is the specification for running 100Mbps Ethernet over two-pair unshielded twisted-pair (UTP) cable and two-pair Type-1 shielded twisted-pair (STP) cable. This is probably the most familiar of the 100Base-T specifications. It provides for 125MHz signaling over each pair of cables, which can supply only 80 percent throughput due to its encoding scheme (called 4B5B). The 100Base-TX specification is described for both RJ-45 and DB-9 connectors. As you can see in the diagram in Figure 15-23, pinout for the 100Base-TX RJ-45 cabling is identical to that for 10Base-T, transmitting over wires 1 and 2 and receiving over wires 3 and 6.

CAUTION: Although you may be able to run 100Base-TX over Category 3 STP for short distances, don't try it. The errors caused by this implementation will outweigh the benefits of the increased bandwidth.

100Base-T4 is the specification for running 100Mbps Ethernet over four-pair Category 3, 4, or 5 UTP cabling. Until September 1995, there were no commercially available devices that supported this standard, but at the time of this writing there is increasing interest in and industry support for this specification. 100Base-T4 provides for 25MHz signaling over 3-pair, with 133 percent throughput as a result of its encoding scheme (called 8B6T). The 100Base-T4 specification allows only RJ-45 connectors. As you can see

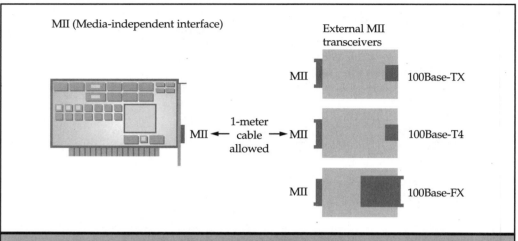

Figure 15-22. The MII describing MAC-layer connectivity to 100Base-T

◆ Cable: 2-pair Category 5 UTP, 2-pair Type-1 STP
◆ Connector: Category 5 certified RJ-45 or DB-9
◆ Signaling: 100Mbps = 1-pair × 125MHz × (80 percent for 4B5B encoding)
◆ RJ-45 pinout: same as 10Base-T

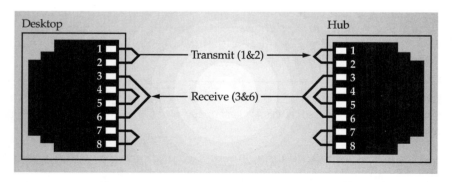

Figure 15-23. 100Base-TX is 100Mbps 802.3u running on two-pair twisted-pair cable

in Figure 15-24, the RJ-45 cabling is similar to 10Base-T, adding two bidirectional pairs that 10Base-T does not have. Choosing the 100Base-T4 specification may be an expensive proposition, however. Although the majority of network sites run either Category 3 or Category 5 UTP, most are running on 2-cable pairs. What's more, the additional 2-cable pairs required to meet the 100Base-T4 specification are often unavailable, having been appropriated for telephones, printers, or other uses.

100Base-FX is the 100Mbps Ethernet physical layer specification for 2-strand 62.5/125-micron fiber-optic cabling. It supports standard MIC, ST, or SC connectors. Signaling for 100Base-FX uses the 4B5B encoding scheme, which provides 80 percent of total output. Therefore, signaling is at 125MHz over a single strand. Currently, there isn't a great deal of interest in the industry or the network management community in running 100Base-T over fiber-optic cabling. This is probably because sites that currently have fiber-optic cabling are already running at 100Mbps using the FDDI protocol. Sites that don't currently have fiber can very likely implement 100Base-T more cost-effectively using copper.

It's important to pick the 100Base-T specification that is designed for the physical cable plant you have or are planning to build. That's because the various Fast Ethernet specifications are not interchangeable, and also because crafting the appropriate cable plant represents a significant portion of the cost of implementing 100Base-T. The decision

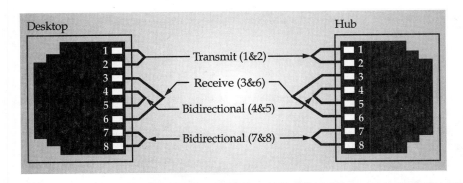

- ◆ Cable: 4-pair Category 3, 4, or 5 UTP
- ◆ Connector: Standard RJ-45
- ◆ Signaling: 100Mbps = 3-pair × 25MHz × (133 percent for 8B6T encoding)
- ◆ RJ-45 pinout: 10Base-T + 2 bidirectional pairs

Figure 15-24. 100Base-T4 is 100Mbps 802.3u over four-pair twisted-pair cable

table in Table 15-3 can help you select the appropriate physical layer interface for your 100Base-T network.

Understanding the Differences Between 100Base-T and 10Base-T

As we mentioned earlier, 100Base-T bears a lot of similarity to 10Base-T. Obviously, implementing 100Base-T will require that you replace your network adapters and hubs. Fortunately, the actual cost of the 100Base-T components is very low. Strong industry support indicates that competition may drive these costs even lower, currently ranging from $300 to $400 per managed port including network adapter. At the time of this writing, these prices were still dropping rapidly. However, there's much more to implementing the protocol than simply replacing equipment. Although it's also fairly easy to integrate 100Base-T into an existing 10Base-T network, there are some very important differences between how the two protocols work. The success of your high-speed network depends upon your knowing and preparing for these differences. These differences are discussed in the following sections.

If You Have	And You Are Using	Choose This Specification
Type-1 or Category 5 STP	2-cable pairs	100 Base-TX
Category 5	2-cable pairs	100 Base-TX
Category 5	4-cable pairs	100 Base-T4
Category 4	2-cable pairs	You must upgrade your cabling
Category 4	4-cable pairs	100 Base-T4
Category 3	2-cable pairs	You must upgrade your cabling
Category 3	4-cable pairs	100 Base-T4
Fiber-optic cabling		100Base-FX

Table 15-3. How to Choose the Correct 802.3u Specification for Your Cable Plant

Interoperability and Obstacles

To plan a successful implementation, you should be aware of certain technical character-istics of the 100Base-T protocol. Knowing these will help you determine whether 100Base-T is the appropriate protocol for the segment you have in mind, as well as alert you to any potential difficulties you may experience after implementing 100Base-T.

Narrowing the Window of Opportunity

One of the biggest obstacles in implementing a 100Mbps CSMA/CD protocol is the extremely short slot time available. Slot time is the window of time required for a network station to detect a collision. Figure 15-25 illustrates the effect of slot time on packet transmission. In 10Base-T, the slot time is 512 bits. A transmitting station "listens" to the network, waiting for an opening in the traffic so that it can send a packet. When an opening occurs, the station must transmit its packet before another packet comes hurtling down the network. This period of time that it has to transmit the packet and listen for a collision before another one comes is called the slot time. In 802.3, slot time is set at 5.12 microseconds (the time it takes to transmit 512 bits traveling at 10Mbps). This is the amount of time the station has to transmit a packet successfully, or "claim the channel" as it is called in 802.3 jargon. In fact, 5.12ms is all the time the transmitting station has to transmit the packet and receive a collision signal if the transmitted packet collides with another packet. That's because if the transmitted packet collides with another packet, the transmitting station must receive notification of the collision before the end of the slot time so that it can retransmit before another packet takes over the channel.

With the advent of 100Base-T, data throughput has been increased tenfold over 10Base-T, but the slot time of 512 bits has not been increased. A similar situation would be

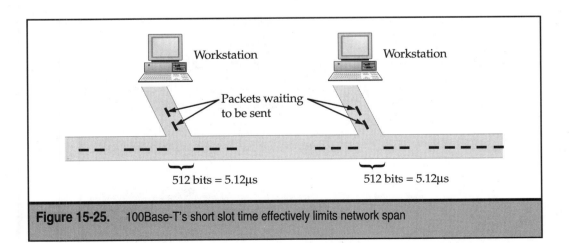

Figure 15-25.   100Base-T's short slot time effectively limits network span

if you ordinarily merged onto a highway traveling 30 miles per hour in your car. As long as all the rest of the traffic on the highway is traveling at 30mph, you need only wait for a gap of about three car lengths to safely merge into the traffic. Imagine then, if your car and all the rest of the traffic began traveling at 300mph, but you still attempted to merge onto the highway when there was only a three-car-length space available. Collisions would seem inevitable, wouldn't they? And so they are with 100Base-T. Therefore, to ensure that collision notifications are received by the transmitting station before the end of the slot time, the network span must be shrunk proportionately. For 100Base-T, this limits the maximum network span to approximately 210m.

The 100Base-T standard doesn't allow the latitude in configuring segments that 10Base-T does. It allows only two repeater hops per segment, unlike 10Base-T's three hops per segment. To observe the 210m maximum span, these repeater hops can be a maximum of only 10m apart. Obviously, this will affect how you design your cable plant (see Figure 15-26).

Scalability Considerations

Before you select 100Base-T, it's important to understand the limitations of the protocol. Most of the drawbacks of 100Base-T are due to its limited scalability. Because of its close kinship to 10Base-T, it suffers from some of the same problems (such as increased collisions and resulting slow performance) when subjected to heavy traffic. However, full-duplex Ethernet is a technology that has been implemented in 100Base-T protocols to help ease the same problem.

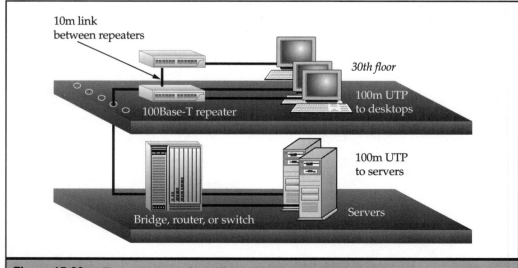

Figure 15-26.   The entire span of a 100Base network cannot exceed 210m

FULL-DUPLEX FAST ETHERNET: WHY AND HOW   The CSMA/CD access protocol itself may inhibit scalability. As you add more users and more bandwidth-intensive applications, the increased collisions may well prevent acceptable performance. However, 100Base-T switches, especially those that offer full duplex, may mitigate the collision problems of the CSMA/CD protocol. To explain how full duplex increases bandwidth, let's begin with an explanation of 100Base-T signaling.

There are two pairs of wires in star-wired 10Base-T and 100Base-T environments—one for transmitting and one for receiving. However, transmission and receipt cannot take place at the same time. Full-duplex Ethernet, on the other hand, allows transmission over one pair of wires and receipt over the other pair simultaneously, providing nearly full utilization of both pairs and thus sustainable high data rates. By installing MAC devices that support full-duplex Ethernet, you can double the effective bandwidth. Full-duplex Fast Ethernet can coexist with normal half-duplex Ethernet and make use of the existing 10Base-T wiring.

LIMITATIONS OF FULL-DUPLEX FAST ETHERNET   As attractive as it sounds, full-duplex fast Ethernet has a couple of serious drawbacks. The first is that it requires an investment in NICs, hubs, switches, firmware, and driver upgrades that support full-duplex operation. The second drawback is that it makes sense only in a few situations. Specifically, this protocol is effective only in point-to-point connections, and then only when there is traffic available to flow in both directions at the same time. Still, in backbone implementations where there is a great deal of traffic among servers, full-duplex Fast Ethernet is a technology that may be worth considering to make maximum use of the bandwidth available.

THE GOOD NEWS ABOUT SCALABILITY   The good news about 100Base-T scalability, as we mentioned earlier, is that it is fairly easy to integrate with existing 10Base-T networks. Despite the fact that it supports fewer hops than 10Base-T and thus may require some recabling, the 100Base-T protocol has a relatively small packet size for high-speed networks, and it handles smaller packet sizes well. Given the current 512-byte average packet size on networks, this gives 100Base-T an edge as a "transition-to-high-speed" protocol. Furthermore, many vendors offer hubs, switches, and network adapter cards that function both at 10Mbps and 100Mbps. These devices automatically sense whether they are attached to a 10Base-T or 100Base-T network and adjust their speed accordingly. This makes it relatively easy and cost-effective to convert from 10Base-T to 100Base-T in phases.

Manageability Issues

Because 100Base-T is so similar to 10Base-T, many of the familiar 10Base-T management tools are available for use with 100Base-T networks, such as protocol analyzers and hub management systems. This means that 100Base-T is not only very manageable, but very manageable at a reasonable price since very little new development effort is required. Nonetheless, at this writing, the industry has still not provided the wide selection of management tools for 100Base-T that it has for 10Base-T. We expect this situation to change quickly as 100Base-T deployment becomes more widespread.

Setup and Configuration Considerations

Because of its many similarities to familiar 10Base-T, installation and configuration of 100Base-T devices is extremely easy. Because there is no initialization routine required of stations wanting to enter the ring, it's very easy to add new stations. To make things even easier, it even uses the same pinouts as 10Base-T, as mentioned earlier.

CABLING CONSIDERATIONS Probably the biggest consideration in implementing 100Base-T is the cable plant. Differences in cabling rules between 100Base-T and 10Base-T are few but critical. For example, the maximum network span of 100Base-T is 210m. Therefore, you may have to recable portions of your network if you have made use of 10Base-T's 2,500m span. What's more, 100Base-T supports only two network hops, rather than three as with 10Base-T, and therefore you may have to reconfigure the segments that you are converting to 100Base-T to conform with this requirement.

CAUTION: 100Base-T doesn't adhere fully with 802.3 cabling specifications! A careful preimplementation review of your existing cable plant is critical.

SPECIAL CONCERNS FOR 100BASE-T4 There are also some issues unique to those few who select 100Base-T4. Because 100Base-T4 requires four cable pairs to operate over Category 3 cable, if all four pairs aren't terminated at your site, you'll have to upgrade the cable plant. If yours is a legacy cable plant, be sure to review it very carefully to be certain all four pairs are terminated. If not, you'll have to correct this situation before you can proceed with your 100Base-T4 implementation. This can be both costly and tedious, so factor that into your decision to use 100Base-T4.

100Base-T is probably best described as a high-performance economy model. It is probably the easiest of the high-speed network desktop protocols to implement. At $300 to $400 per managed port and falling, it nearly competes with 10Base-T in cost. It also saves you money as well as time by building on proven technology and expertise. It's easy to integrate into an existing 10Base-T network. However, because it is modeled so closely after 10Base-T, it has some of the slower protocol's inherent obstacles limiting its scalability.

TIP: As much as 100Base-T looks and acts like 10Base-T, it's not. The cabling rules are just different enough to cause you trouble, so be prepared to spend time locating and reconfiguring those portions of your cable plant that don't comply with 100Base-T specifications. However, more than any of the other protocols compared here, 100Base-T lets you lever your investment in staff training and expertise.

GIGABIT ETHERNET

As we mentioned in the last section, 100Base-T has become the high-speed networking technology of choice for most enterprises. For most networking applications, 100Mbps is more than sufficient bandwidth. However, there are some points on many networks that call for even greater bandwidth. For example, links connecting switches with multiple 100Base-T and/or 10Base-T ports, as shown in Figure 15-27, must be able to carry traffic from multiple 100Base-T ports.

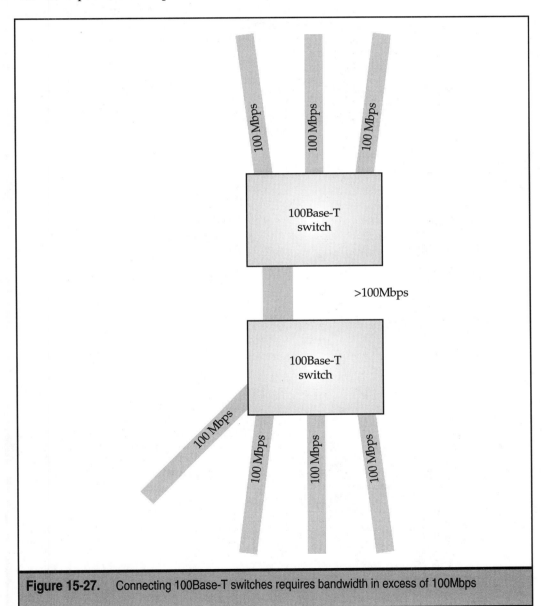

Figure 15-27. Connecting 100Base-T switches requires bandwidth in excess of 100Mbps

A year or so ago, the only choice network designers had in instances like this was to turn to a radically different type of high-speed link, such as Asynchronous Transfer Mode (ATM). This led to a variety of conversion difficulties—along with the accompanying expense of solving them—in what should have been a fairly simple design issue. For example, when aggregating 100Base-T switches using ATM, frames had to be converted to cells, virtual circuits set up and torn down, and other such conversion tasks performed. And all of this had to be done simply to aggregate several 100Base-T switches. Surely there had to be a better way. And now there is.

Gigabit Ethernet was developed to offer high-speed Ethernet transmission for campus networks. It maintains the same frame format, frame size, and access method of Ethernet, as shown in Figure 15-28, and allows high-speed switch aggregation at considerably lower cost and greater ease than ATM or many other technologies of similar speed.

The 802.3 Standard

The IEEE 802.3z standard for Gigabit Ethernet was ratified in June 1998. While Gigabit Ethernet tries to be simply a supercharged version of the familiar 10Mbps and 100Mbps Ethernet, its high speeds have required considerable deviation from the original 802.3 specifications. Despite attempts to keep Gigabit Ethernet MAC signaling as close as possible to the familiar 10Base-T specification, there are some differences that will affect how it is implemented.

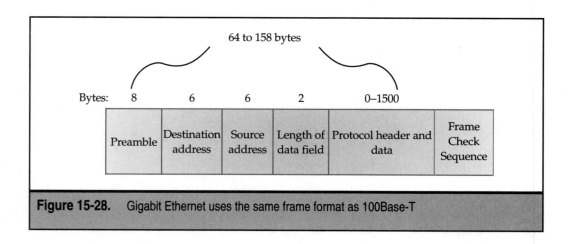

Figure 15-28.   Gigabit Ethernet uses the same frame format as 100Base-T

Most of the work involved in finalizing the 802.3z standard centered around the specifications for the physical layer. As the standard now exists, there are two specifications for fiber-optic cabling:

▼ 1000Base-SX

▲ 1000Base-LX

1000Base-SX

This is the physical layer specification for running Gigabit Ethernet over lower-cost multimode fiber in short-span backbones.

1000Base-LX

This is the physical layer specification for running Gigabit Ethernet over single-mode fiber campus backbones and long-span multimode fiber backbones.

There are also two specifications for running Gigabit Ethernet over copper cabling. At the time of this writing, neither of these has been finalized:

▼ 1000Base-CX

▲ 1000Base-T

1000Base-CX

This standard is for short-span copper runs used to support device clustering. Its total span is 25 meters and uses special data encoding, called 8B/10B, for high-performance data transmission. This scheme encodes each consecutive 8 bits of data (i.e., each byte) into a 10-bit transmission character. Transmitting these uniformly sized 10-bit characters enables the protocol to synchronize data transmission, thereby providing a recovery and retransmission mechanism when errors are detected. Furthermore, 8B/10B encoding uses a special character, called a comma character, to ensure byte and word alignment. The block diagram in Figure 15-29 shows the 8B/10B encoding scheme.

1000Base-T

This standard has not yet been finalized, but it describes Gigabit Ethernet operations over Category 5 cabling up to a distance of 100 meters or a total network span of 200 meters.

How Gigabit Ethernet Differs from 100Base-T

As a result, the configuration rules for Gigabit Ethernet differ from those for standard 10Base-T and 100Base-T. The biggest difference is probably in the maximum length of cable run. In the standard, single-mode fiber runs cannot exceed 3km, and multimode fiber runs should be under 550 meters. Right now, the majority of campus backbones use

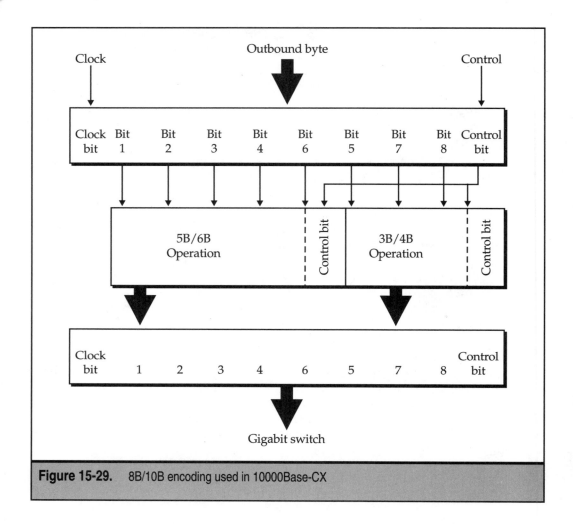

Figure 15-29. 8B/10B encoding used in 10000Base-CX

multimode fiber, and so can span up to the 2km limit of 10Base-T. Therefore, because many backbones are now multimode fiber spanning up to 2km, before implementing gigabit Ethernet, either the backbones will need to be shortened to under 550m, or they will need to be repulled with single-mode fiber.

The type of multimode fiber Gigabit Ethernet will support, as well as the kind of conditioning it will require to ensure its operation, is a substantial consideration. This is due to a signaling anomaly known as differential mode delay (DMD). DMD is a jitter that occurs when the beams of light traveling over multimode fiber don't travel straight through the fiber cable unimpeded. Instead, in instances of DMD, the light beams bounce off the sides of the cable, throwing off the timing of the data transmission and consequently causing errors when the data is received. The farther the data travels, the more pronounced the jitter and distortion. Therefore, without a workable solution, DMD might have limited the length of fiber that could be used for Gigabit Ethernet. The Gigabit Ethernet task force of the IEEE didn't want to shorten the maximum length allowed in the 802.3z specification, so they came up with a solution.

The solution the Gigabit Ethernet task force developed is called a *conditioned launch*. In a condition launch, the laser at the device originating the data stream first transmits a light pattern that deliberately and evenly distorts the light. This prevents any one individual mode from dominating amongst the jitter, so the data pattern is overwhelmed. This is the only way to ensure error-free transmission for up to 550 meters over multimode fiber. Therefore, network managers who are considering implementing Gigabit Ethernet over multimode fiber should be sure the equipment they select adheres strictly to the 802.3z standard.

Scalability Considerations

Before you choose Gigabit Ethernet, you should understand that for all its speed and ease of implementation, the protocol has limitations. Most of these limitations are due to its limited scalability. Just like 100Base-T, it has all the problems of a CSMA/CD-based access method when subject to heavy traffic. And because of its extremely high speed, it currently supports fairly limited network spans.

Gigabit Ethernet and Full-Duplex Support

Gigabit Ethernet supports full-duplex operation for both switch-to-switch and switch-to-node connections. As you will remember from the section on 100Base-T, full-duplex operation allows simultaneous transmission and receipt of data on the cable.

NOTE: Remember that full-duplex operation requires that all transmission devices support full duplex.

Cabling Considerations

As we mentioned, right now Gigabit Ethernet runs only over fiber. However, the 802.3ab specification, which is under development, provides for transmitting Gigabit Ethernet over Category 5 cabling. This specification only calls for a maximum network span of 25 meters. However, as usual, the market is outrunning the standards bodies. By the end of 1998, expect to see Gigabit Ethernet physical layer modules that will support 1,000Mbps over Category 5 cabling for distances of up to 100 meters.

Management

To pull off Gigabit Ethernet, you have to have the right management tools. Because Gigabit Ethernet supports the same frame format and size as 100Base-T, management tools for this technology aren't hard to find. In fact, they are most likely the very same tools that you are already using to manage your 10Base-T and 100Base-T networks.

NOTE: Be sure you can find and afford appropriate monitoring equipment that supports Gigabit Ethernet. As well, you may have to upgrade existing SNMP management information bases (MIBs) with Gigabit Ethernet extensions.

Of course, there are a few features no Gigabit Ethernet switch should be without. First and foremost is layer 3 functionality. The 1,000Mbps of traffic slamming through the pipes could choke a standard router, so Gigabit Ethernet switches not only need to be able to keep up at layer 2, but also handle layer 3 functions at wire speed. This will free routers from having to route core network protocols, preventing potentially serious traffic jams.

Cost

Gigabit Ethernet gear is decidedly expensive. At the time of this writing, Gigabit Ethernet switches range in price from nearly $15,000 to nearly $40,000. And there's no point in spending that kind of money unless people are going to notice the performance, right? Therein lies another problem.

Performance

When put to work, Gigabit Ethernet switches simply may not speed up networks appreciably. This isn't due to an inherent fault in Gigabit Ethernet, but rather in the design of network hosts and the operating environments running on them. With the notable exception of some flavors of UNIX, most network operating environments simply aren't prepared to process incoming traffic at rates of 1,000Mbps. Compounding matters, the flood of traffic overwhelms the I/O of even the fastest SCSI drive controllers. In other words, the server is the bottleneck, making all the bandwidth superfluous.

Even should server platforms speed up, one question will remain: How long will Gigabit Ethernet be a viable high-speed protocol? This is a serious question, due to the fact that network traffic is becoming an increasingly even mix of voice and data, but Gigabit Ethernet was designed for data only. Will it evolve to accommodate the demands of voice?

Support for Voice and Video

Voice and video traffic are notorious bandwidth gobblers, as well as extremely sensitive to delays. Will these types of traffic run well over Gigabit Ethernet? For although Gigabit Ethernet provides a wide pipe, it currently has no inherent mechanism for ensuring quality of bandwidth. However, you can use other technologies and quality of service protocols in conjunction with Gigabit Ethernet, although these present their own set of concerns:

▼ Resource Reservation Protocol (RSVP)

■ Virtual LANs (vLANs)

▲ Video compression

Resource Reservation Protocol (RSVP)

The Resource Reservation Protocol (RSVP), guarantees that a certain amount of bandwidth is set aside for a designated application. Applications use RSVP to request from the network a specific amount of bandwidth for a specific type of traffic. The job of RSVP is to set up bandwidth reservations over an established route. However, this protocol is still "emerging," i.e., there is no standard implementation. Which means that interoperability among different vendors' devices is not assured.

HOW IT WORKS When implementing RSVP, the receiving device determines how much bandwidth it will reserve for a given type of traffic. It can change this level as necessary. However, you can centralize this control of bandwidth reservations—at least somewhat—by requiring each receiving station to specify its bandwidth reservations to one central device. This central device then sets up the reservations for the entire network. However, there is a lot of overhead required in setting up and maintaining this centralized approach. For example, every time a node wanted to reserve bandwidth for a new sending node, the central node would have to send a notification to all senders. This would tie up a lot of bandwidth, defeating the whole purpose of RSVP.

RSVP sets up bandwidth reservations using *packet classifiers* and *packet schedulers*. These are routines installed on the receiving devices that make service decisions about each packet received. The receiving device determines whether the requested bandwidth reservation is possible, based on bandwidth resources available and policy restrictions, if any. If the resources are available, the device packet classifier and the packet scheduler reserve the specified bandwidth. The packet scheduler makes forwarding decisions based on the bandwidth reservations. The packet classifier routes the packet based on these forwarding decisions.

LET IT FLOW—BUT FILTER IT FIRST   How do receiving devices know how much bandwidth to reserve for a given application? They determine it by examining an application's *flow specification*, or *flowspec*. The flowspec is a pivotal part of the RSVP architecture. It specifies the bandwidth requirements of the application in question as well as identifying the application's data stream as coming from that application. The packet scheduler uses the bandwidth requirement specified in an application's flowspec to establish the bandwidth allocation for that application.

Not all packets will be able to take advantage of the bandwidth requested by the flowspec. That's because each receiving device also has *filter specs*. These are filters that designate which packets will receive priority treatment based on application or protocol header information. Packets that don't match the filter specs will not receive a guarantee of service. Instead, they will be transmitted on a best-effort basis only, even if they are addressed to the application's session.

The relationship of packet classifiers, packet schedules, flowspecs, and flow filters is illustrated in Figure 15-30.

Virtual LANs (vLANs)

Setting up filters or constraints between different groups of users is awkward and time-consuming with conventional bridges and routers. Network managers think in terms of workgroups, not the physical location of users. Therefore, they shouldn't have to

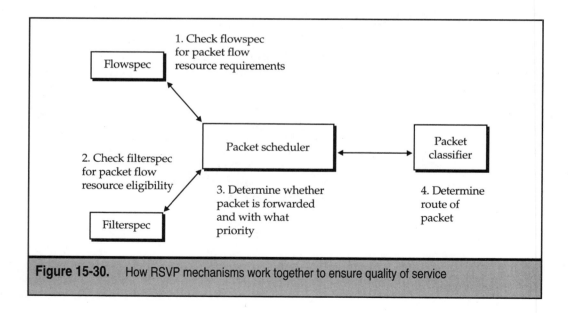

Figure 15-30.   How RSVP mechanisms work together to ensure quality of service

set up a series of filtering statements based on physical ports. The connectionless nature of Gigabit Ethernet posed some problems for setting vLANs. After all, the nature of the protocol's access method was based on broadcast. However, two emerging standards, 802.1Q and 802.1p, are enabling *virtual LAN* capability for packet-based networks.

SO WHAT IS A VLAN?   A virtual LAN is a list of device media access control (MAC) or network addresses that are independent of a physical port, much like an access list used by some router vendors. However, virtual LANs have network-wide significance. A device can access any other device on the same virtual LAN. Virtual LANs can define filters among themselves, just like routers can. Rather than configuring and reconfiguring routers every time end stations move, network managers can implement virtual LANs.

Devices on different media can be members of the same virtual LAN. Furthermore, users can move end stations onto any segment within the virtual subnet without requiring address reconfiguration.

Virtual LANs enable network managers to group devices logically regardless of physical location and provide dedicated bandwidth and services to each, as shown in Figure 15-31.

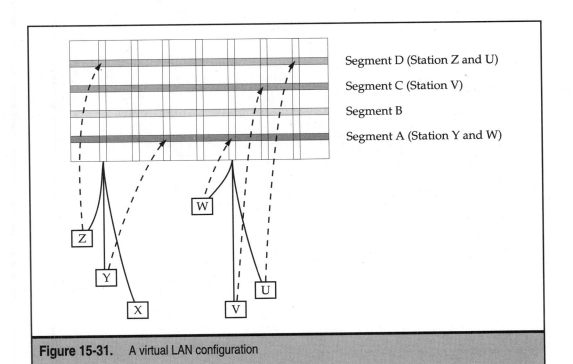

Segment D (Station Z and U)

Segment C (Station V)

Segment B

Segment A (Station Y and W)

Figure 15-31.   A virtual LAN configuration

In addition to address filtering and bandwidth allocation, virtual LANs also provide

▼ Simplified moves, adds, and changes

▲ Security features

SIMPLIFIED MOVES, ADDS, AND CHANGES   One of the major problems network managers have in large, routed networks is the big administrative effort required to perform moves, adds, and changes. This is particularly true of Internet Protocol (IP) networks, where each physical LAN is associated with a logical subnet, as shown in Figure 15-32. If a user needs to move from one floor of a building to another, the workstation typically has to be reconfigured with a valid IP address on the new subnet.

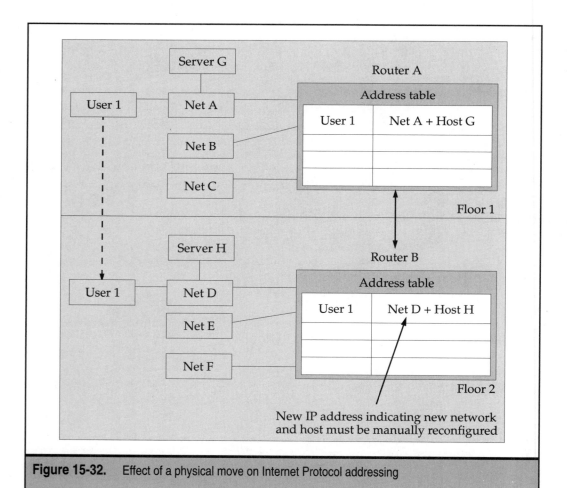

Figure 15-32.   Effect of a physical move on Internet Protocol addressing

To handle such moves, managers of legacy networks have to reconfigure routers manually. Virtual LANs, however, eliminate all of the manual address resolution and reconfiguration. Virtual LANs enable network managers to group devices logically regardless of physical location and provide dedicated bandwidth and services to each, as shown in Figure 15-33.

While networks obviously require routing capability, network managers would like to avoid having to manually reconfigure network address assignments every time users move from one network segment to another. Virtual networks let them do just that by identifying the physical address of a new device and associating it with a network layer address based on prior assignment without human intervention to the system or the end station. Users can plug into any port in the network, and the virtual LAN handles the rest.

SECURITY AND VIRTUAL LANS Virtual LANs can increase security on Gigabit Ethernet networks. Network managers can use virtual LANs to define filtering restrictions between groups of devices, providing tight security. Furthermore, Gigabit Ethernet switches that support vLANs offer port-level security by allowing administrators to restrict virtual subnets to specific physical ports.

Video Compression

The advent of high-quality standard video compression techniques makes it more feasible to use CSMA/CD access methods like Gigabit Ethernet for transmitting video data. The Moving Picture Experts Group (MPEG) working group of the ISO/IEC manages the development of international standards for compression and decompression, of moving

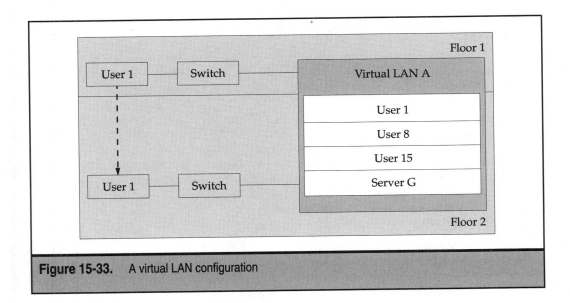

Figure 15-33. A virtual LAN configuration

picture images, and audio. MPEG has produced or is working on several standards for video compression:

▼ MPEG-1

■ MPEG-2

■ MPEG-4

▲ MPEG-7

MPEG-1   This is the standard for storage and retrieval of moving picture images and audio on storage media such as hard drives and optical disks. This standard specifies the following:

▼ Medium bandwidth (up to 1.5Mbps)

■ 1.25Mbps video 352 × 240 × 30Hz

■ 250Kbps audio (two channels)

■ Noninterlaced video

▲ Optimized for CDrom

MPEG-2   Finalized in 1994, this is the standard for digital television. Its initial goal was to develop a standard for digital encoding of television images at data rates under 10Mbps. In 1992, the goal changed to encompass coding of High Density TV (HDTV). This standard specifies:

▼ Higher bandwidth (up to 40Mbps)

■ Up to five audio channels (i.e., surround sound)

■ Wider range of frame sizes (including HDTV)

▲ Can deal with interlaced video

NOTE: MPEG-3 was originally the phase charged with developing the standard for HDTV. When MPEG-2 was broadened to include this standard, MPEG-3 became unnecessary.

MPEG-4   Begun in 1994, this standard is currently under development, although by the time you read this it will no doubt have been finalized. It is a standard for multimedia applications. The MPEG-4 group's charter is to standardize both the tools and the algorithms for coding multimedia applications. At the time of this writing, the draft standard specifies the following:

▼ Very low bandwidth (64Kbps)

■ 176 × 144 × 10Hz

▲ Optimized for videophones

MPEG-7   Also under development, this is a standard for content representation for information search.

Future of Gigabit Ethernet

Overall, we can't recommend Gigabit Ethernet for voice and video traffic. Even the Gigabit Ethernet Alliance says that Gigabit Ethernet handles multimedia, "But application needs substantial changes." (See "Gigabit Ethernet: Accelerating the Standard for Speed," Gigabit Ethernet Alliance, 1997.)

We can't really foretell how robust or long-lived Gigabit Ethernet will be. After all, it provides more bandwidth than any other technology available to us today. All we can say is that Gigabit Ethernet switches are fast, fairly manageable, very expensive, and—through no fault of their own—should make little impact on overall network performance.

FIBRE CHANNEL

Fibre Channel didn't begin life as a network transport protocol. In fact, the specification was not originally intended to work as a network protocol at all. It was first designed and developed to interconnect high-speed peripherals—for example, a cluster of high-performance computers—to a shared mass storage device. The result of this intent was a generic architecture that was a combination of both network and channel connection technology that concentrates on high-speed transmission and guaranteed delivery of data. This makes it suitable not only for connecting peripherals to hosts, but also for network connectivity over the short haul.

Going Through Channels

A channel connection provides either a direct or switched point-to-point connection between devices, such as a computer's processor and a peripheral device. The function of a channel isn't sophisticated in concept: it's supposed to transmit data as fast as possible from point A to point B. The destination address is not only predetermined, it is hard-wired—the data really can't go anywhere but its destination. Any error correction it performs is simple, and is done in hardware. Routing and address resolution aren't done because they aren't required. Therefore, there's no address and error-correction information that needs to be carried in the data packet, so the packet overhead is very low. Because of their point-to-point nature and consequently limited processing demands, channel connections are largely implemented in hardware.

Network connections, on the other hand, are multipoint connections that rely on addressing schemes to make sure that the data gets to the appropriate destination. Each data packet traveling along a network connection must contain an address, which each device on the network reads to determine whether the packet is intended for it. Furthermore, network connections routinely have relatively sophisticated error-detection and correction capabilities. Therefore, the packet must contain the address and error-correction information in its header, resulting in higher packet overhead than in a channel connection. However, network connections can support functions, such as routing, that a channel simply isn't designed to support.

Fibre Channel has features of both a channel and a network. It is a high-speed channel that connects devices to a network fabric. The network fabric describes the matrix of connections, from a single cable connecting two devices to a mesh created by a switch connecting many devices. The fabric can be pretty much any combination of devices, including hubs, loops, mainframes, and switches. A fabric can be created specifically to suit the application being supported. In any event, no matter how complex the network fabric is, as far as an individual Fibre Channel port is concerned, it manages a simple point-to-point connection between the workstation and the network fabric.

Fibre Channel's greatest asset is speed. Ethernet, at 10Mbps, transmits data far slower than computers can produce it. Therefore, the primary goal of Fibre Channel is to provide computing devices with a throughput mechanism that is closer to the speed of their processors. And speed it has—it delivers bandwidth from 133Mbps to 1.062Gbps over a wide variety of cable types, including multimode fiber, coaxial cable, and shielded twisted-pair wire, and can support a network span of up to 10km. In fact, Fibre Channel is so efficient and fast that it can deliver speeds of 100MBps (notice that is megabytes per second) in both directions simultaneously, which means it is effectively a 200MBps full-duplex channel.

Fibre Channel is extremely versatile because it is protocol independent. It is a generic transport mechanism, meaning that it can support command sets from several different other channel protocols, such as Small Computer System Interface (SCSI), Internet Protocol (IP), and High Performance Parallel Interface (HIPPI).

Its speed and guaranteed packet delivery make Fibre Channel a good protocol for connecting network devices in a relatively local environment, such as a workgroup or even a campus environment, as shown in Figure 15-34. But because of its high performance, wide network span, and support of various topologies such as point-to-point, arbitrated loop (which we will discuss in detail later in this chapter), and switched fabric, Fibre Channel has broader applications than as simply a networking protocol. It can connect LANs, midrange computers, mainframes, disk arrays, and server farms as part of one giant network.

The Standard and Its Supporting Groups

The American National Standards Institute (ANSI) ANSI X3T9.3 started work on the Fibre Channel standard in 1988. At that time, the main support for the protocol came from its supporting group, the Fibre Channel System Initiative (FCSI), headed by IBM, HP, and Sun Microsystems. The mission of the FCSI was to develop a high-speed open connection standard for Fibre Channel workstations and peripherals. This mission was accomplished early on. During its existence, the FCSI was a major influence in the design of the protocol, developing profiles and specifications that offered interoperability between existing architectures and Fibre Channel.

Since its ratification by ANSI in the early 90s, the Fibre Channel standard has been through many enhancements. For example, in 1991 the standard was modified to include support for copper and multidrop configurations. The greatest number of changes came in 1995, when the Fibre Channel Systems Initiative and Fibre Channel Association

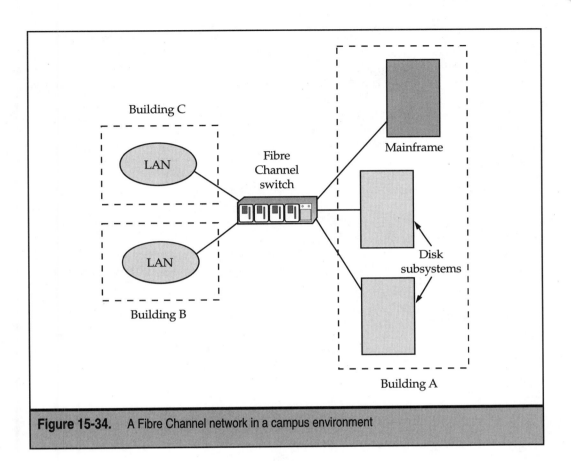

Figure 15-34. A Fibre Channel network in a campus environment

announced that the ANSI X3T11 committee overseeing the technology had adopted 2Gbps and 4Gbps data rates, a 400-percent increase over the previous 1Gbps ceiling. Shortly thereafter, the Fibre Channel System Initiative pronounced its job complete and passed its mantle as the standard bearer for Fibre Channel to the Fibre Channel Association, which has a little over 85 member companies. The Fibre Channel Association will pick up where FCSI left off. For information, contact the Fibre Channel Association, a 100-member consortium of Fibre Channel vendors, in Austin, Texas, at (800) 272-4618; e-mail FCA-info@amcc.com.

How Do They Do That?

Fibre Channel transports data in much the same way a router does. It reads the destination addresses of incoming packets, encapsulates the packets, and sends them across the fabric. Underlying data formats, packet structures, or frame types are not important to Fibre Channel devices.

As mentioned, Fibre Channel establishes point-to-point connections between devices. These connections are like switched circuits, and multiple circuits can exist simultaneously. The circuits are duplex connections that can provide 100MBps of transmission speed in both directions simultaneously. When a device wishes to transmit over a switching device or network, it simply requests a connection to that device. If the network is currently busy, the port tries to make the connection later.

The current Fibre Channel standard supports four transmission speeds: 133Mbps, 266Mbps, 530Mbps, and 1.062Gbps. Fibre Channel network equipment that supports 266Mbps and 1.062Gbps are now shipping from various vendors such as Ancor Communications, Inc., of Minnetonka, MN.

The Fibre Channel frame, as shown in Figure 15-35, supports a data payload of 70 to 2,112 bytes with a 24-byte frame header (preceded by a 4-byte Start of Frame delimiter). It is this relatively large payload supported by a very low overhead that allows such high end-to-end throughputs: 25MBps for 266Mbps Fibre Channel and 100MBps for 1.062Gbps Fibre Channel—speed close to that of the backplanes of some server systems.

The Fibre Channel architecture comprises five layers, designated FC-0 through FC-4, as shown in Figure 15-36.

Fibre Channel Layer 0 (FC-0): The Physical Interface

Layer FC-0 is the layer that defines the physical and media interfaces and the media. This is the layer that describes the electrical characteristics of the media, and includes the transmitters, receivers, connectors, and cables, upon which the Fibre Channel network runs.

The FC-0 layer also defines a system unique to Fibre Channel: the open fibre control system, which affects the Fibre Channel running over optical fiber. The open fibre control system is sort of a "back off and resend" fail-safe system that is required because the power of the optical laser used in Fibre Channel exceeds ANSI safety standards for optical lasers. You see, Fibre Channel connections often break due to this excessive laser power. When that happens, the open fibre control system in the receiving device detects

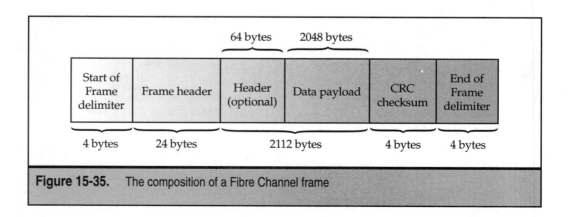

Figure 15-35.   The composition of a Fibre Channel frame

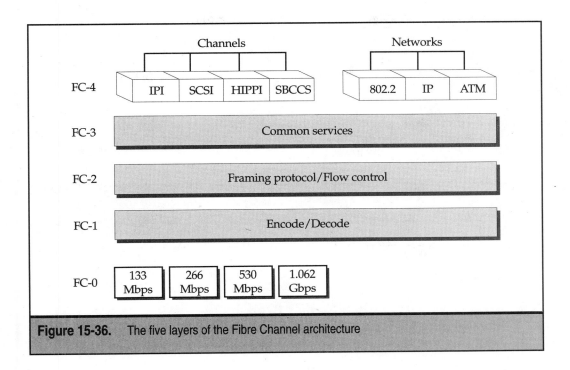

Figure 15-36. The five layers of the Fibre Channel architecture

the open link, then sends a lower-level laser pulse than that defined by the Fibre Channel standard. The lower-level laser pulse continues until both ends of the connection receive it. After the physical connection has been restored, the network connection resumes a few seconds later. Figure 15-37 shows a sample FC-0 link with open fibre control.

Fibre Channel Layer 1 (FC-1): The Transmission Protocol

FC-1 describes the transmission protocol layer; that is, the layer responsible for establishing the rules for transmitting each data packet. It defines the special data encoding scheme, called 8B/10B encoding, that Fibre Channel employs for high-performance data transmission. This scheme encodes each consecutive 8 bits of data (i.e., each byte) into a 10-bit transmission character. Transmitting these uniformly sized 10-bit characters enables the protocol to synchronize data transmission, thereby providing a recovery and retransmission mechanism when errors are detected. Furthermore, Fibre Channel uses a special character, called a *comma character*, to ensure byte and word alignment. The block diagram in Figure 15-38 shows the 8B/10B encoding scheme.

Fibre Channel Layer 2 (FC-2): Signaling Protocol

FC-2 is the signaling protocol layer. It defines the method of moving data between end devices on the network, called *node ports* or *N_ports*, through the Fibre Channel switching

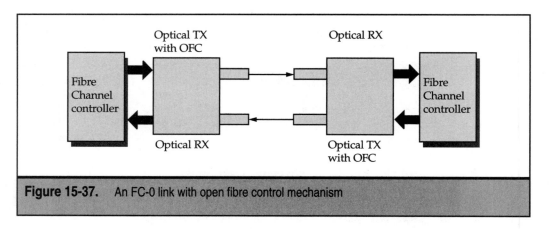

Figure 15-37. An FC-0 link with open fibre control mechanism

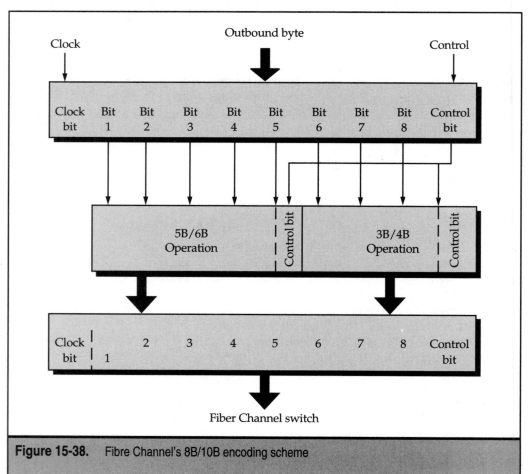

Figure 15-38. Fibre Channel's 8B/10B encoding scheme

device, called *fabric ports* or *F_ports*. The N_ports have a management system known as the Fibre Channel Link_Control_Facility that manages the physical and logical links between them. The FC-2 layer is concerned with defining the objects that will be managed by the Link_Control_Facility. These objects are called ordered set, frame, sequence, exchange, and protocol. Flow control, congestion management, and class of service designations are also handled at this layer.

ORDERED SET   An ordered set is a delimiter or "flag" used by Fibre Channel to signal events in low-level link functions. For example, the Start of Frame delimiter is an ordered set. The structure of an ordered set is a combination of four 10-bit characters, both data and special characters. This signaling helps Fibre Channel establish a network link when devices are first powered on. It also enables a few basic recovery actions.

FRAME   As we mentioned earlier, the Fibre Channel frame begins and ends with a 4-byte frame marker, followed by a 24-byte frame header containing addressing information. Next comes a large Data field that can contain up to 2,112 bytes (2,048-byte payload and an optional 64-byte header). The Data field is followed by 4 bytes for a cyclical redundancy error check and, finally, the 4-byte end of frame marker.

In classes of service that guarantee delivery, which we will define and discuss in detail shortly, each frame is acknowledged by the receiving N_port. These acknowledgments also provide notification of nondelivery of the frame to the transmitting N_port. The FC-2 layer also defines "Busy" and "Reject" signals that notify the transmitting N_port that a frame hasn't been delivered.

SEQUENCE   A sequence is the unit of data transfer in the Fibre Channel. It is a frame or group of related frames describing a single operation that has been put into packets for transmission over the Fibre Channel fabric. The FC-2 layer on the transmitting end is responsible for disassembling these sequences and packaging them in the frame size that has been set up by the transmitting and receiving ports—as well as all intervening ports on the fabric. On the receiving end, the FC-2 layer assembles these frames into the operation they describe, then passes them on to the higher layers of the Fibre Channel protocol. If an error occurs during the transmission of a sequence, the entire sequence is retransmitted.

Each sequence is assigned a Sequence Identifier, which appears in a field in the header of each frame sent over the fabric. In addition, each frame within the sequence is numbered with a Sequence Count identifier, which also appears in the frame header information.

This use of sequences allows Fibre Channel both to send large blocks of data without dividing it into smaller frames and to support other channel protocols, such as IP and HIPPI, transparently.

EXCHANGE   An *exchange* is a group of sequences that make up a single operation. An operation usually involves several tasks. For example, sending a packet of data can involve connection initiation, connection acknowledgment, packet transmission, and acknowledgment of packet receipt. Each of these tasks is a separate sequence, but together make up one exchange. Only one sequence at a time can be active in an exchange, although multiple exchanges can be active simultaneously.

The relationship among ordered sets, frames, sequences, and exchanges is illustrated in Figure 15-39.

CLASSES OF SERVICE   With Fibre Channel, flow control and delivery acknowledgment depend upon the class of service designated for the network traffic in question. Currently, three classes of service are defined within the FC-2 layer. These classes range from Class 1 service, which provides a dedicated connection with confirmed delivery of packets, to Class 3 service, which does not guarantee or confirm delivery of packets.

CLASS 1 SERVICE   In Class 1, data packets are delivered in the same order in which they are transmitted, and each frame's delivery is confirmed by an acknowledgment from the receiving device. If congestion causes a frame to be dropped, a busy frame is returned to the sender, which then resends the frame. This type of service is well suited to applications that require high-speed, guaranteed packet delivery such as full-motion video.

The Class 1 service also contains a service mode called *Intermix*. Intermix allows you to set priorities among data traffic. In Intermix, you can multiplex all classes of service over a single wire, but only Class 1 connections get guaranteed bandwidth. Frames sent within the other classes are only transmitted when bandwidth in excess of that needed for the Class 1 connection is available. This is similar to Fiber Distributed Data Interface's prioritization mechanism.

CLASS 2 SERVICE   In Class 2 service, no dedicated connection is established. Instead, bandwidth is shared rather than dedicated as it is in Class 1 service. The protocol uses multiplexing to send multiple frames over the wire simultaneously. The frames aren't necessarily received in the same order they are sent, and in fact may take different paths because Class 2 service allows packets to make use of the shortest path available at the time of transmission.

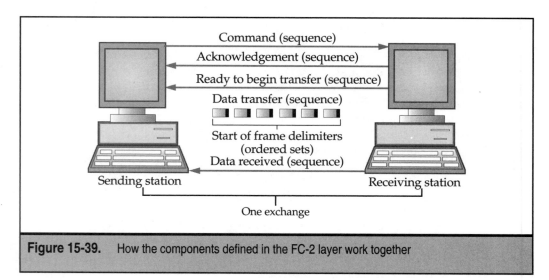

Figure 15-39.   How the components defined in the FC-2 layer work together

However, delivery of frames is guaranteed in Class 2. As well, just as in Class 1 service, in Class 2 service the sending device will get a "busy frames" signal if the receiving device can't process an incoming frame, so the sender knows to retransmit the frame. Class 2 service is therefore best suited for use in networks that aren't transmitting time-sensitive data.

CLASS 3 SERVICE   Class 3 is a connectionless packet-switched service like Class 2, but it does not provide guaranteed frame delivery. Thus, devices operating in Class 3 service require buffers on both the transmitting and receiving stations to avoid lost packets. Therefore, Class 3 is best suited for data that requires high-speed, time-sensitive transmission, but in which a dropped frame is useless if not received in time. Video-conferencing and teletraining are such applications.

FIBRE CHANNEL LAYER 3 (FC-3): COMMON SERVICES   The next layer of the Fibre Channel architecture, FC-3, defines common services such as support for multicasts and hunt groups. These functions are

- ▼ **Multicast**   Multicast delivers a single transmission to a group address that defines multiple destination ports.

- ■ **Hunt groups**   Hunt groups operate much like a telephone hunt group in which an incoming call can be answered by any one of a predefined group of phones. A hunt group is useful when connecting high-speed devices. It is a predefined group of ports attached to a single node, such as a set of ports belonging to a mass storage device. Frames addressed to a hunt group are delivered to any available port within the hunt group.

- ▲ **Striping**   Striping is a method of parallel transmission, similar to that of parallel printing. Fibre Channel can use multiple connections simultaneously to deliver a packet of data, striping the data across the connections to deliver it faster.

Fibre Channel Layer 4 (FC-4): Upper-Layer Protocol Mapping

The FC-4 layer is the top layer of the Fibre Channel architecture. This layer defines the upper-layer protocols (ULPs) that are interfaces to transport protocols, communications protocols, and other channel protocols. These ULPs allow Fibre Channel to support these other protocols transparently.

Cabling Considerations

Fibre Channel is in many ways a cable installer's dream, because:

- ▼ It is media independent. As we mentioned earlier, it supports single-mode fiber, multimode fiber, coaxial cable, and Type-1 shielded twisted-pair cable.

- ▲ Its huge maximum network spans on fiber media mean that it will operate on existing fiber runs.

However, the short supported distances on copper media—especially at high bandwidths—require that you review your cable plant carefully to make sure that existing cable runs don't exceed the maximum distances allowed by the Fibre Channel protocol.

Fibre Channel supports shared and switched connections just like most network protocols. However, one of the keys to Fibre Channel's versatility is its ability to support a topology that other protocols don't support well or can't support at all. That topology is a point-to-point connection with no intervening devices, which is called Fibre Channel Arbitrated Loop (FC-AL).

Fibre Channel Arbitrated Loop (FC-AL) has been receiving a lot of attention lately. This topology lets you connect multiple devices in a ring without using hubs or switches. This makes it a flexible and cost-effective solution for localized high-bandwidth applications. The loop can support up to 127 ports that share bandwidth. An example of FC-AL is shown in Figure 15-40.

In FC-AL, a port is granted access to the loop based on its port address, with the lowest port address getting access first. When this port completes its transmission, the device with the next lowest port address is given access to the loop, and so on. Only one pair of ports, a sending port and a receiving port, can be active in the loop at any one time. A loop can also be attached to a Fibre Channel fabric to enable ports on the loop to communicate with ports on the fabric.

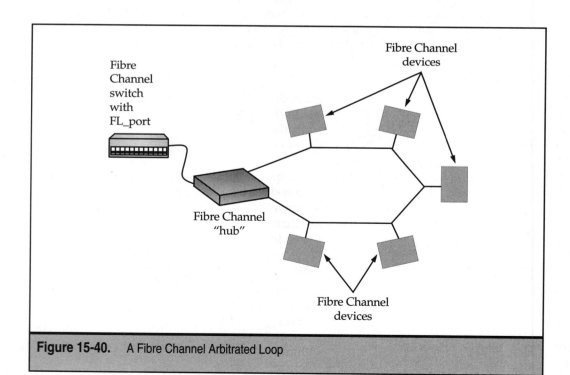

Figure 15-40.   A Fibre Channel Arbitrated Loop

Installation and Configuration

As we mentioned earlier, because of its large network span, Fibre Channel usually requires no physical changes to an existing user's Ethernet or token-ring-based network. As a result of its use of sequences and exchanges, Fibre Channel works with common channel protocols such as IP, SCSI, and HIPPI, so your applications will probably require no modifications, either.

I'd like to point out, however, that when you are dealing with an extremely high performance protocol like Fibre Channel, the computing power of the network devices could quickly become a bottleneck. For this reason, we recommend that all devices attached to the Fibre Channel loop and/or fabric have high-performance processors and high-throughput bus architectures.

Interoperability

At first glance, Fibre Channel appears ultrainteroperable. As we mentioned, Fibre Channel can support most channel protocols such as IP and HIPPI transparently. What's more, Ethernet, FDDI, and even ATM frames or cells can be transmitted over the Fibre Channel fabric thanks to the encapsulation techniques used to create sequences and exchanges.

Furthermore, Fibre Channel is a fairly mature ANSI standard, so its specifications are well defined and readily available. This may be one of Fibre Channel's greatest assets: it is an open, consistent interface. However, as of this writing, no vendors were shipping Fibre Channel adapters for routers. Without router support, Fibre Channel is a poor choice for backbones or other segments that have a wide variety of data paths and types of traffic.

Scalability

Fibre Channel is extremely scalable both in distance and number of networked devices. The Fibre Channel protocol supports up to 16 million nodes on a single fabric. Furthermore, because of its data prioritization and guaranteed delivery mechanisms, performance for critical applications will not drop significantly as devices are added to the network.

Also, Fibre Channel supports a network span of up to 10km. The maximum network span depends upon the type of media used and the transfer rate implemented. Table 15-4 shows the distances supported by the various media.

Taken together, this means that Fibre Channel is so scalable, aggregate data rates into the hundreds of gigabits per second or even terabits per second are feasible.

Manageability and Fault Tolerance

Fibre Channel supports a unique means of network management. Instead of having each node on the network perform its own management functions such as routing, configuration management, time synchronization, and fault management, Fibre Channel has assigned these functions to special management servers operating in the fabric. While this points to a single point of failure within the fabric, it does on the other hand free the nodes to concentrate on delivery of high-bandwidth transmission. For management

Types of Media	132.8Mbps	26.5Mbps	531.25Mbps	1.062Gbps
Single-mode fiber	10km	10km	10km	10km
50-micrometer multimode fiber	N/A	2km	1km	N/A
62.5-micrometer multimode fiber	500m	1km	N/A	N/A
Coaxial cable	40m	30m	20m	10m
Shielded twisted-pair	100m	50m	N/A	N/A

Table 15-4. The Maximum Network Span Supported by Each Type of Media Defined in the Fibre Channel Specification

reporting and monitoring, Fibre Channel supports Simple Network Management Protocol (SNMP), and most vendors implement SNMP management information base data with their network adapters and switches.

Performance

Fibre Channel is the highest performance protocol available right now in terms of raw bandwidth, throughput, and latency. As we mentioned, Fibre Channel can offer as much as 1.062Gbps bandwidth, with a real throughput (in full duplex) of 200MBps. Furthermore, switched Fibre Channel has extremely low latency. This is because Fibre Channel dedicates separate circuits to traffic, thereby minimizing buffering and consequently latency at the switch.

Advantages: Fibre Channel vs. ATM

Fibre Channel's only real rival in the area of performance is Asynchronous Transfer Mode (ATM), and much ink has been shed over the relative advantages of these two technologies. We will discuss ATM in detail later in this chapter, but I would like to highlight the main points of differentiation between them:

▼ Fibre Channel is better for migration and integration. As we have discussed, Fibre Channel supports most existing applications, communications protocols, and transport protocols transparently. On the other hand, ATM requires sophisticated LAN Emulation techniques to work with existing LANs, and these LAN Emulation technologies are currently proprietary.

■ Fibre Channel is a fairly mature ANSI standard. All of ATM's standards have not yet been finalized.

▲ Fibre Channel offers more raw throughput than ATM does.

However, before we take this comparison of the two protocols too far, I think we should consider that they are really designed to serve different segments of the high-speed networking market. Fibre Channel is really designed for a local environment comprised of high-speed devices needing access to other devices. It supports user nodes almost incidentally. ATM, as we will see, is fundamentally designed to integrate wide area and local connections seamlessly, and in many ways provides better support for user connections.

Disadvantages

Fibre Channel has two big drawbacks: it lacks good wide area integration capabilities, and there aren't a lot of people out there who know much about it. Therefore, it's best to implement Fibre Channel only for the local environment, and only if you already have or are willing to invest in the expertise to install and maintain it.

ASYNCHRONOUS TRANSFER MODE

Anyone who has read a network trade magazine or attended a technical conference in the last three years has heard about ATM. Asynchronous Transfer Mode seems to be the great networking hope of both the near and distant future; some vendors have even called ATM this decade's most significant networking technology. ATM promises to integrate LAN functions, WAN functions, voice, video, and data into a single uniform protocol and design. It also promises uniformity and scalability that will ultimately simplify network design and management. Therefore, nearly all complementary technologies are engineering "ATM readiness" into their own development.

All the hype notwithstanding, ATM offers some benefits that no other networking protocol has offered:

▼   **Speed**   ATM supports transmission rates of up to 622Mbps.

■   **Scalability**   ATM allows increased bandwidth and port density within existing architectures.

■   **Dedicated bandwidth**   This guarantees an application's consistency of service, which is not available in shared technologies.

▲   **Universal deployment**   ATM offers the potential of an end-to-end solution, meaning it can be used from desktop to local segment to backbone to WAN.

So, if ATM is so significant, what exactly is it? How will it improve your network? How much will it cost? When should you implement it? Because ATM will no doubt have an important role in your network before the end of the century, we will spend a great deal of time exploring exactly what ATM is, why it is so significant, where it is now in its development, where it is going, and the issues surrounding its implementation both in its current form and in the future.

How It Started

ATM began as part of the Broadband-Integrated Services Digital Network (B-ISDN) standard developed in 1988 by the Consultative Committee for International Telegraph and Telephone (CCITT). An extension of narrowband Integrated Services Digital Network (which defined public digital telecommunications networks), B-ISDN provides more bandwidth and enables more data throughput than narrowband ISDN. The B-ISDN reference model is shown in Figure 15-41.

As you can see, ATM lies directly on top of the physical layer of the B-ISDN reference model. However, it doesn't require the use of any specific physical layer protocol. Therefore, the physical layer could be FDDI, DS3, SONET, or others. We'll talk more about the reference model and its implications for ATM later in this chapter.

Who Started It

As mentioned earlier, Asynchronous Transfer Mode was originally defined by the Consultative Committee for International Telegraph and Telephone, a part of the United Nations charged with developing and recommending international standards for telecommunications technology and operations. This body is now more commonly known as the International Telecommunications Union, of which the CCITT is a committee. The ITU is currently formalizing standards for ATM.

In 1991, the ATM Forum, a consortium of vendors, carriers, and users, was formed to expedite industry agreement on ATM interfaces in North America. The ATM Forum is a driving force in the establishment of industry-wide ATM standards.

ATM: The Short Answer

In brief, ATM is a cell-switched, connection-oriented, full-duplex, point-to-point protocol that dedicates bandwidth to each station. It uses asynchronous time division multiplexing to control the flow of information over the network. ATM operates at bandwidths ranging from 25Mbps to 622Mbps, although most of the development time (and marketing fanfare) is going into 155Mbps ATM.

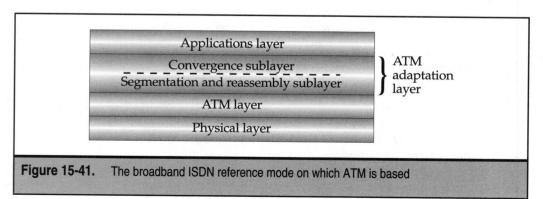

Figure 15-41.   The broadband ISDN reference mode on which ATM is based

Among the benefits offered by ATM are

▼ Excellent scalability

■ Legacy network integration

■ Bandwidth on demand

■ Ability to handle the entire range of network traffic—voice, data, image, video, graphics, and multimedia

▲ Adaptability to both LAN and WAN environments

If ATM Is the Answer, What Were the Questions?

Like all the high-speed protocols discussed in this book, ATM was developed as an alternative to existing transport protocols such as Ethernet and Token Ring that were obviously limited in bandwidth and scalability. However, ATM was also designed to handle multiple types of data simultaneously and with increased efficiency. Therefore, ATM had to be able to transmit a wide variety of bit rates and support bursty communications, since voice, data, and video traffic all exhibit bursty behavior.

NOTE: Most people don't think of circuit-switched voice traffic as bursty, but it is. In fact, a circuit-switched voice conversation utilizes far less than half of the available bandwidth.

What Is a Cell?

Packet switching, which utilizes bandwidth only when data traffic is present, was developed to handle bursty data traffic. However, packet-switching systems don't perform adequately for real-time, two-way traffic such as interactive video. ATM overcomes this limitation because it employs cells, which are fixed-length packets, rather than variable-length packets. Each ATM cell consists of a 48-byte payload and a 5-byte header, as shown in Figure 15-42.

Fixed-length ATM cells offer many advantages over variable-length packets:

▼ **Hardware switching capability** Because it is simple, predictable, and reliable to process fixed-length cells, ATM switching can be done at the hardware level, rather than requiring expensive and processing-intensive software to manage flow control, buffers, and other management schemes.

■ **Guaranteed levels of service** Networking and switching queuing delays are more predictable with fixed-length data cells. Therefore, switches can be designed to provide guaranteed levels of service for all types of traffic, even for delay-sensitive services such as voice and video.

■ **Parallel processing** Fixed-length cells allow cell-relay switches to process cells in parallel, for speeds that far exceed the limitations of bus-based switch architectures.

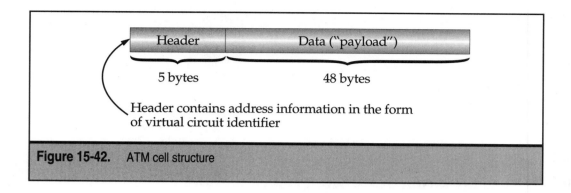

Figure 15-42.   ATM cell structure

▲ **Voice-processing capability**   Although ATM cells require bandwidth only
when traffic is present, they can still provide the equivalent of a time division
multiplexer time slot for continuous traffic. As a result, ATM can handle
real-time continuous traffic, such as digitized voice, and bursty traffic, such as
LAN transmissions, equally well.

The ATM cell is used to carry data transmitted between switches. A 48-byte segment
of the user data payload is placed in a cell along with a 5-byte header, forming the 53-byte
ATM cell. The cell header carries the information necessary for switch operation.

What Is Switched?

ATM does not employ shared bandwidth. Rather, each port on an ATM switch is dedicated
to one user. An ATM switch sets up a virtual connection between a transmitting node and a
receiving node. This connection is made on the basis of the destination address of each cell,
and it lasts only as long as it takes to transfer one cell. These data transfers can take place in
parallel and at full network speed. Because the cell is transmitted only to the port
associated with that specific destination address, no other port receives the cell, thereby
providing both low traffic and, as an extra bonus, high security.

ATM SWITCHING AND VIRTUAL CONNECTIONS   To communicate over the ATM network,
applications must first establish a *virtual connection* (VC) among switches. A VC is a
transmission path for an ATM data cell. The VC extends through one or more switches,
establishing an end-to-end connection for the transmission of application data via ATM
cells. VCs can be established in two ways. First, a permanent virtual circuit (PVC) can be
manually configured by a network manager. A PVC is dedicated bandwidth that
guarantees a level of service to a particular station. Network managers would configure
PVCs for mission-critical applications that must always receive high priority or for
permanent connections such as among routers and bridges. The second means of
establishing a VC is the switched virtual circuit (SVC). An SVC is a VC set up "on the fly"
as it is needed by the application.

VIRTUAL CIRCUIT IDENTIFIER   The cell header also contains two address fields, the *virtual path identifier* (VPI) and the *virtual channel identifier* (VCI) that together total 3.5 bytes and define the virtual circuit identifier, which is the route of the cell to a particular switch. These fields are updated by each switch in the path.

Virtual circuit identifiers tag the cells for a particular connection, then the switches transfer the data in a VC by hardware-based switching, triggering the VC connection tag in the cell header.

The problems of congestion and "VC routing" among multiple switches are still outstanding in the standards process. Congestion management is important because a small level of cell loss (e.g., 0.1 percent) gets magnified to a dramatically large frame loss (e.g., 20 percent). This is unacceptable, and several alternative congestion management policies are under active study and evaluation.

All ATM cells are the same size, unlike frame relay systems and local area networks, which have variable packet sizes. Using same-size cells allows the following:

▼   **Guaranteed bandwidth**   Variable-length packets can cause traffic delays at switches in the same way that cars must wait for long trucks to make turns at busy intersections.

■   **High performance**   Large volumes of data can flow concurrently over a single physical connection.

■   **Hardware switching**   In the short term, this yields higher throughput, and over time the technology can continue to exploit improved price/performance as processor power increases and incremental costs decrease.

▲   **Data prioritization**   ATM can deliver a deterministic response, which is essential to carry "latency-sensitive" communications, such as motion video and audio, or mission-critical, interactive data traffic.

What Is Connection-Oriented?

Connection-oriented means that a connection must be established between the transmitting and receiving computers before data is transferred. Each intermediate switching point must be identified and informed of the existence of the connection. Each packet is routed independently, and therefore each must carry a complete address of the ultimate destination.

What Is Full Duplex?

Full duplex allows transmission over one pair of wires and receipt over the other pair simultaneously, which provides nearly full utilization of both pairs and sustainable high data rates. By supporting full-duplex operation, ATM doubles the effective bandwidth of ordinary half-duplex transmission that is employed by most network protocols.

What Is Point to Point?

As mentioned earlier, ATM networks must establish a connection between the sending and receiving stations before transmitting a cell. This connection between two stations is the only concern of the ATM switch. Unlike a router, an ATM switch doesn't try to define this one-to-one connection in the context of all possible connections on the network. Instead, the ATM switch selects the route between the sending station and the receiving station, then informs the intermediate switches along this route to ensure that the resources for transmitting the cell are allocated through the network.

Once a cell's transmission route is established, the ATM switch then assigns a connection number to each point-to-point link along this route. Connection numbers are chosen independently for each of the point-to-point links in the transmission path. A path may be formed from a number of such links, with the links joined by switches. This means that a single cell carries a potentially different connection number on each different link of the connection path. A switch changes the connection numbers of each cell as it transfers the cell from one link to another. This change of connection numbers at the junction of two links means that the Connection Number fields only need to be big enough to distinguish the connections carried by a single link.

This point-to-point connection orientation of ATM and the changing of the connection numbers at each switch hop let ATM use small connection numbers rather than the large addresses required by most protocols. This makes ATM more efficient, because small connection numbers conserve space in cells and thus bandwidth, and also faster, because it makes for small lookup tables in switches.

What Is Dedicated Bandwidth?

Efficient bandwidth use is not the only issue addressed by ATM technology. In fact, different traffic types require different delay behavior, delay variation, and loss characteristics. ATM provides different qualities of services to accommodate these differences. ATM allocates bandwidth to each active station. The station requests the appropriate amount of bandwidth for each connection, and the network automatically assigns this bandwidth to the user. In reality, the bandwidth isn't actually dedicated per se. It is shared by other users, but the network ensures the requested level of service. The network can do this because it controls the number of simultaneous conversations on the network.

To access the network, a station requests a virtual circuit between the transmitting and receiving ends. During connection setup, the end station can request the quality of service it needs to suit transmission requirements, and ATM switches will grant the request if sufficient network resources are available. The guaranteed level of service of cell-based switched access is particularly useful for transporting real-time, interactive communication such as voice or video. ATM uses a protocol called User-to-Network Interface (UNI) to establish dedicated levels of bandwidth to stations and applications.

USER-TO-NETWORK INTERFACES (UNI)   ATM's UNI protocol provides multiple service classes and bandwidth reservation established during call setup of a switched virtual connection. The UNI defines the interoperability between the user equipment and the ATM switch port. A public UNI defines the interface between a public service ATM network, and usually supports a SONET or DS3 interface. A private UNI, on the other hand, defines an ATM interface between an end user and a private ATM switch, and would most likely have a copper or fiber-optic cable interface.

While the ATM Forum has successfully stabilized the UNI protocol, there are a couple of key issues that network managers should consider when choosing products. The UNI protocol in the products they select must coordinate the bandwidth allocated locally among other switches and internetworked LAN segments. It must also support a variety of network operating systems to guarantee multiple classes of service. Both of these issues affect the interoperability of the ATM network, and so the network managers should select products that support the network's current design and equipment.

How It All Works Together

The combination of cell switching and point-to-point connections with their resulting small connection numbers lets ATM break the core networking task into two separate components—*route determination* and *data forwarding* (better known as routing and switching)—and handle each with a different technology. To illustrate this separation of functions fully, let's first look at how a cell is transmitted across an ATM network.

Route Determination

Route determination is a computer-intensive function, typically software-based, that requires dynamic knowledge of the global network topology. Route determination in ATM is performed by establishing virtual connections, and the route determination occurs only once per data transfer session. ATM chooses a path for the cells of the connection (routes the connection) during establishment of the connection; all cells of the connection follow the same path. After connection establishment, only simple cell transfer operations are performed—operations that implement routing decisions made at connection establishment time. This keeps data transfer simple and efficient, but it requires a separate system for connection setup. The connection setup part of ATM is, and must be, based on connectionless protocols. The main difference between ATM and traditional networking solutions is that traditional networking must solve both components of the networking problem simultaneously. Thus, every packet in a traditional network carries the globally significant routing information, and every packet must be processed by routers before the data can be forwarded. This continual evocation of the route determination function is a very wasteful use of an expensive resource and becomes the network bottleneck due to the expense of wire-speed capable routers.

To illustrate the routing problem that the ATM architecture solves, let's consider a network backup. Suppose you must back up 2 gigabytes of data residing on a server on a routed network. The backup program will probably create ten million 200-byte packets, because 200 bytes is the most common transfer unit size permitted in routed networks. Each of these ten million packets will be assigned a network-wide routing address, and each router along the path processes these ten million packets separately—even though they are streaming continuously along the same route. This means that each router along the path must examine the network layer header of each packet, then compute the route again for each packet separately, despite the fact that the route is identical for all ten million packets. What a waste of processing power!

The scenario is very different with ATM. The ATM switch establishes the route only once with a virtual connection (VC). The switch then assigns a connection identifier to tag the route. Switches on the route are informed of the bandwidth requirements of the VC and are instructed to interpret the connection identifier appropriately. After that, all cells with that connection identifier are hardware-switched along the route, permitting the route determination function to service new requests rather than continually servicing the request of an established session. Thus, cells don't contain complex routing addresses. Instead, they are tagged with a small temporary connection identifier, which the ATM switches are instructed to map onto the route defined by the VC.

Data Forwarding

Data forwarding, on the other hand, is a hardware-intensive function requiring gigabits of switching capacity. ATM's cell-based switching allows simple switching which, like Ethernet switching, can be performed entirely in hardware. It is performed by ATM switches operating on ATM cells, and the ATM cell definition has been optimized for implementing a gigabit-capable, hardware-based switching capability. Therefore, cells are hardware-switched along the path previously established by the VC for the session.

ATM is primarily a format for use by switches and includes no access arbitration protocol. Each port on a switch behaves in many ways like a station. The cell header information in a received cell is used to look up forwarding information needed to route the cell within the switch. Error checking is performed in the cell header, and cells with errors are discarded. This cell header address information is changed at each switch to represent the route at the next switch. Addressing in the ATM cell is of local significance to a switch, in contrast to the MAC address, which identifies individual users either with locally or globally unique values.

ATM SWITCHES   *ATM switches* allow one desktop connection per port. Some ATM switches are nonblocking, meaning they have the capacity to support a backbone link equivalent to the sum of the input port speeds. In addition, a nonblocking switch transfers traffic directly from input to output without a store-and-forward process. Buffering is used only if multiple inputs attempt to access the same output simultaneously. In spite of occasional buffering, ATM is still superior to the slow, store-and-forward operation of traditional routers.

Scalable hardware-switching elements are the basis for the gigabit-speed backbone networks that can be built with ATM. Although gigabit switching seems far beyond the needs of today's 10Mbps desktops, nonblocking LANs are constrained to small numbers of ports without a gigabit switch in the backbone.

ATM SWITCH CONTROL POINT   The ATM switching function really consists of two parts: the switch hardware, which performs the actual switching, and the switch control point, which manages the switching fabric. The ATM switch control point maintains the switch fabric by:

▼ Managing requests for virtual connections (VCs)

■ Learning the ATM network topology

■ Maintaining the forwarding databases

▲ Enabling SNMP-based ATM network management

Cabling Considerations

ATM's topology is a mesh of switches. This means that any point in the network can be reached from any other point via multiple routes involving independent connections among switches. ATM doesn't require any specific physical layer protocols to accomplish this. ATM also has no distance limitations other than those imposed by the attenuation characteristics of the media used. This simplifies the building of the cable plant, because there really aren't any rules to constrain the design. However, it makes documentation all the more important, because with no rules as guidelines, it would be nearly impossible to decipher an undocumented cable plant.

ATM MEDIA SUPPORT   *Media independence* is a driving principle of ATM. Many physical layers are specified, starting at 25Mbps, including several for 100 to 155Mbps, and going all the way up to 622Mbps. ATM at 155Mbps will include support for Category 3, 4, 5 UTP, Type-1 STP, fiber-optic cable, multimode fiber, and single-mode fiber local area networks.

WIDE AREA NETWORK PHYSICAL INTERFACE   The 155Mbps WAN interface to the public network carriers will be based on the Synchronous Optical Network (SONET). As we mentioned earlier, SONET is an internationally supported physical layer transport scheme developed in the early 1980s.

Setup and Configuration

ATM is different from any LAN protocol you have ever managed. While its installation and configuration isn't physically difficult, it is complex. It requires a detailed level of knowledge about ATM as well as a great deal of careful planning. Therefore, be prepared to spend both money and time training, planning, and consulting before undertaking an ATM implementation.

Scalability

ATM can add scalability to legacy protocol networks. For example, in Figure 15-43, the network is connected by three 24-port Ethernet switches, each having two 100Base-TX uplinks connected to the other two switches to form a mesh. Such a network could provide nonblocking service for 60 Ethernet users—less than currently connected. Furthermore, as the number of users and switches grows, more switch capacity must be dedicated to backbone links than to desktop interfaces.

Using a 1.55Gbps ATM switch in the backbone adds ten ATM ports, each at 155Mbps, as shown in Figure 15-44. Only one ATM port is required from each Ethernet switch to provide connectivity among all ports. Whereas the network in Figure 15-43 could

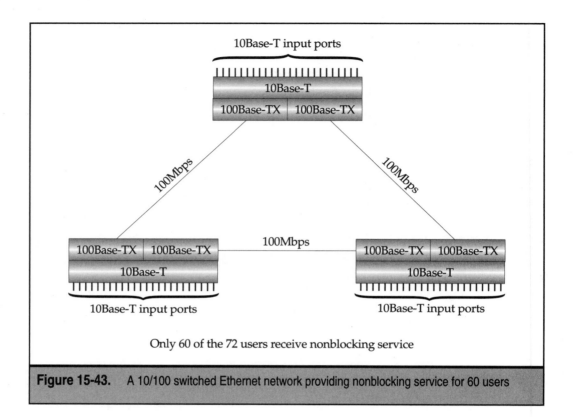

Figure 15-43. A 10/100 switched Ethernet network providing nonblocking service for 60 users

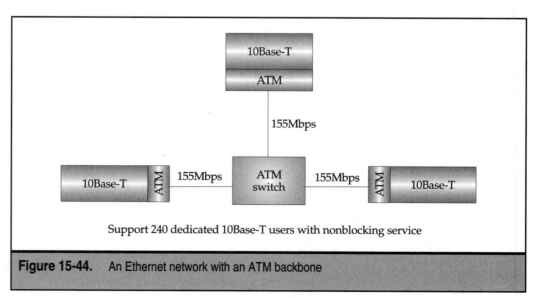

Figure 15-44. An Ethernet network with an ATM backbone

support only 60 users, the network in Figure 15-44 can provide nonblocking service for 240 dedicated Ethernet users, with room to grow.

Scalable ATM LAN switches on the market today can support as many as 100 155Mbps ports in nonblocking configuration. In conjunction with dedicated Ethernet access devices, these switches provide the foundation for a nonblocking network of 1,000 dedicated Ethernet users. As the ATM market matures, nonblocking networks with 1,000 155Mbps ports—or 10,000 Ethernet ports—will be achievable.

A need for nonblocking networks or high-speed desktop connections isn't necessary to justify ATM. Although ATM is most beneficial when used in a nonblocking LAN configuration, it can also be deployed in a blocking configuration to maximize bandwidth usage.

In a blocking configuration, the sum of the user port bandwidths exceeds the backbone link bandwidth, and contention for backbone links can occur. Constructing a network with potential blocking can be a cost-effective solution for customers in the early stages of migrating to ATM. For customers who are installing ATM to the desktop, current workstation processing loads may not yet require full use of the available bandwidth. In this case, more users can be added to the network than the backbone can support in a nonblocking configuration. When bandwidth-hungry workstation applications are deployed, bandwidth and switching capacity can be adjusted to produce a nonblocking configuration.

When combined with proper traffic management techniques, a blocking ATM network is capable of exceeding the performance of a shared-media LAN. Traffic management allows conventional LANs with relatively low-speed users to benefit from ATM with cost-effective blocking configurations.

Manageability

ATM backbones are easier to manage than those in most routed networks, because ATM eliminates a lot of the complexity required to configure large internetworks that have different addressing schemes and routing procedures. ATM hubs provide connections between any two ports on the hub, independent of the type of device attached to it. The addresses of these devices are premapped, making it easy to send a message, for example, from one node to another, regardless of the network type the nodes are connected to. In fact, simplified network management may be the primary reason for many users to migrate to an ATM-based solution, even prior to performance requirements dictating the transition.

Cost of Ownership

ATM is probably the most expensive technology discussed in this book. ATM products are likely to have a higher relative cost due to cell assembly and additional services. However, not only are ATM adapters and switches expensive, they are currently proprietary. This means that training and expertise will be vendor- and product-specific. If you change vendors, therefore, your costs will also likely include hefty training and integration expenses.

The ATM and the OSI Model

ATM reaches farther up the ISO-OSI model than most transport protocols, as shown in Figures 15-45 and 15-46. Therefore, to take full advantage of ATM, as well as to integrate it into existing legacy protocol networks, applications must be developed that support the higher-level implications of Asynchronous Transfer Mode.

The ATM Layer

What we have discussed up to this point are actions that take place at the ATM layer, which corresponds somewhat to the data-link and network layers of the ISO-OSI model. If ATM were like other protocols, these would be the only layers affected by ATM and we could end our discussion here. However, to ensure service levels by dedicating bandwidth to stations or applications, as well as to integrate networks of other transport protocols into an ATM network, we must explore the next higher level of the ATM reference model.

The ATM Adaptation Layer (AAL)

The *ATM adaptation layer* (AAL) sits above the ATM layer. This layer is where ATM translates user traffic from applications into ATM format. It is at this layer that ATM provides support for connection-oriented and connectionless applications, variable bit rate applications (like X.25 and local area network traffic, respectively), and constant bit rate applications (like video and multimedia).

Actually, the AAL is composed of two sublayers, the convergence sublayer (CS) and the segmentation and reassembly (SAR). Here's how they work.

CONVERGENCE SUBLAYER (CS)   The *convergence sublayer* permits the relaying of voice, video, and data traffic through the same switching fabric. It interprets the data coming in

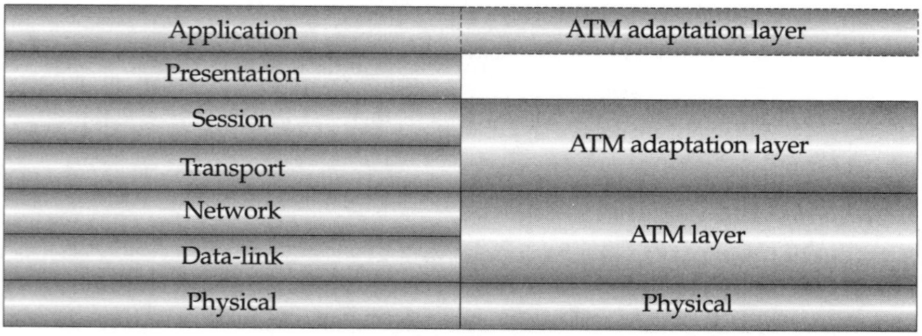

Figure 15-45.   The relationship among the ISO-OSI, B-ISDN, and ATM reference models

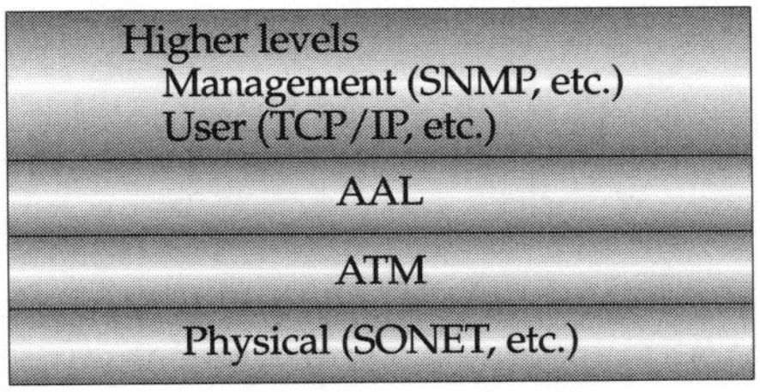

Figure 15-46. The Broadband-Integrated Services Digital Network reference model

from the higher-level application and prepares it for processing by the segmentation and reassembly sublayer. Obviously, the operations and functions performed by the convergence sublayer vary depending upon the type and format of incoming data.

THE SEGMENTATION AND REASSEMBLY SUBLAYER (SAR)   Before an application transmits data over an ATM network, the SAR sublayer segments data into 48-byte ATM data cells. Once the ATM cells reach their destination, the SAR sublayer reassembles them into higher-level data and transmits them to the appropriate local devices.

AAL-5   Because ATM can carry multiple traffic types, several adaptation protocols, each operating simultaneously, exist at the adaptation layer. For example, local area networks often employ the AAL-5 adaptation protocol, designed specifically to handle this type of variable rate data traffic. In the AAL-5 convergence sublayer, an 8-byte field, including data length and an error-detection checksum, is appended to a frame (or block) of user information (up to 64KB in length) coming from the higher-layer application. The AAL-5 frame is then separated into a stream of 48-byte data cells by the segmentation and reassembly sublayer, then sent along its way. At the receiving station, the SAR reassembles the cells into frames, and the CS processes, then removes the 8-byte Data Length and Error-Detection Checksum fields. The frame is then passed to the higher-level protocol.

AAL-5 is the foundation for LAN Emulation, a key technology in ATM integration and migration. We will discuss LAN Emulation in detail later in this chapter.

ATM Migration Issues

Installing ATM will probably require some dramatic changes in the design and equipment of your network. The concepts and rules of ATM are very different from those used in most local and wide area network protocols. For example, most LAN protocols are connectionless in nature, and therefore conflict on a very basic level with the connection-oriented ATM protocol. Another example is addressing. Because the ultimate goal of ATM is to be offered as a wide area public network, large addresses are going to be required to accommodate the millions of potential devices on a public ATM network. As a result, a scheme will have to be developed to resolve the smaller local area network addresses with the large ATM addresses. There is also a problem with standards and interoperability: ATM products from different vendors do not interoperate, and ATM LANs have only limited capability to interoperate with other LAN protocols. Connection setup and other issues stand in the way of internetworking between ATM and existing LANs. Knowing what issues to consider and what questions to ask will help ensure you make the right decisions both for the present and the future. Therefore, any integration and/or migration from legacy protocol networks to ATM's connection-oriented, dedicated, switched environment will require careful planning and execution.

Incomplete Interface Specifications

While the User-to-Network Interface (UNI) is a fairly well-established and stable specification, the ATM Forum has described and standardized several other interfaces to ensure interoperability of ATM networks. The Network-to-Network Interface for private networks, or P-NNI, is one such critical interface. The P-NNI handles

▼ Virtual connection arbitration

■ Congestion control

▲ Topology management

Without a stable P-NNI, vendors can't develop interoperable ATM equipment.

LAN Emulation

A major obstacle for the widespread acceptance of ATM in mainstream LANs is the integration of existing protocols such as Ethernet, Token Ring, and FDDI. As a point-to-point, connection-oriented protocol, ATM doesn't natively support the way legacy LAN protocols work.

The installed base of Ethernet isn't going to disappear soon. In fact, it will continue to grow for some time, particularly given its very low cost, standardization, new technology extensions such as switched Ethernet products, and huge installed base. Obviously, therefore, without providing an integration scheme for this large installed base, ATM will remain a niche technology for isolated pockets of high-end users.

NOTE: There are approximately 40 million Ethernet nodes installed today, and about 10 million new ones being shipped every year.

LAN Emulation for ATM is the migration technology that allows end stations running existing applications—even those that require features unique to the legacy protocol—to be adapted to ATM services. LAN Emulation is a program that emulates conventional local area network operation. It provides a sort of bridge between legacy

LAN protocols and ATM segments. LAN Emulation is tricky, because ATM is vastly different in many ways from the familiar LAN transport protocols of Ethernet and Token Ring. For example, as we mentioned, ATM is connection-oriented, while Ethernet and Token Ring are connectionless, meaning that packets go to all stations on the network and are acknowledged only by the station to which they are addressed. Also, ATM stations will have to provide support for broadcast and multicast operations that are so often used in Ethernet and Token Ring. Also, ATM uses a 20-byte addressing scheme, while Token Ring and Ethernet both use 48-bit MAC addresses. Therefore, LAN Emulation has to resolve the differing MAC and ATM addresses.

To review, LAN Emulation is a collection of services that translate between the higher-level protocols of connectionless protocol services and the lower-level, connection-oriented ATM protocols, as shown in Figure 15-47.

WHAT MAKES LAN EMULATION TRICKY   There are many issues that make LAN Emulation difficult to implement. Among these issues are

▼   **Address resolution**   Resolving Ethernet addresses to ATM addresses, then back again, is complex and time consuming.

■   **Broadcast and multicast support**   As a point-to-point transmission technology, ATM isn't suited to send a single packet stream to multiple recipients.

■   **Speed**   To provide the performance necessary for successful bridging between legacy and ATM networks, LAN Emulation devices have to have full wire-speed conversion and switching.

■   **Connection setup**   As we mentioned earlier in this chapter, ATM is a connection-oriented transport service. Legacy LAN protocols, on the other hand, are connectionless, meaning they send packets containing the full station address over the media without first establishing a connection with the

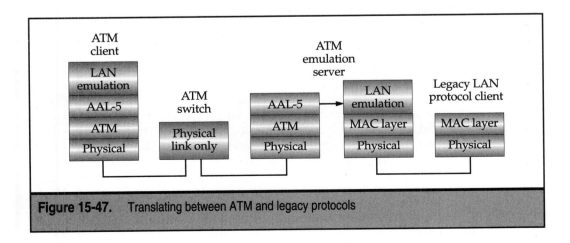

Figure 15-47.   Translating between ATM and legacy protocols

receiving station. The receiving station monitors all the packets on the media and accepts those that are addressed to it. With only 5 bytes of header, an ATM cell cannot carry the full destination address for each cell. Therefore, adapting existing network layer protocols that require the full destination address to ATM's connection-oriented cell-switching is a major challenge.

▲ **Lan Emulation User-to-Network Interface** One interface that has been developed to address this interoperability issue is the LAN Emulation User-to-Network Interface (LUNI). LUNI protocols allow the ATM network and its edge devices to control the virtual connections required for transmission and to emulate the connectionless nature of a LAN.

As we mentioned earlier, the ATM adaptation layer (AAL) sits above the ATM layer. The AAL formats data into the 48-byte ATM cell payload, a process known as segmentation. Once the ATM cells reach their destination, they are reconstructed into higher-level data and transmitted to the respective local devices in a process referred to as reassembly. Because ATM can carry multiple traffic types, several adaptation protocols, each operating simultaneously, exist at the adaptation layer. AAL-5 is the adaptation protocol on which LAN Emulation is based.

LAN Emulation sits above AAL-5 in the protocol hierarchy. In the ATM-to-LAN converter at the network edge, LAN Emulation solves data networking problems for all protocols—routable and nonroutable—by resolving LAN and ATM addresses at the MAC layer. LAN Emulation is completely independent of upper-layer protocols, services, and applications.

Because LAN Emulation occurs in edge devices and end systems, it is entirely transparent to the ATM network and to Ethernet and token ring host devices.

HOW LAN EMULATION WORKS Figure 15-48 shows how LAN Emulation works in a legacy LAN. Low-end PCs in an Ethernet environment access high-end servers with native ATM interfaces through a LAN/ATM switch. Because LAN Emulation makes ATM look like a classical LAN, standard bridging techniques allow the LAN/ATM switch to provide protocol-independent connectivity. No change is required in the legacy PCs, yet they experience improved performance because of the high input/output capacity of the server, made possible through the high-speed ATM interface. In addition, they benefit from the dedicated bandwidth provided by the switched LAN implementation.

MULTIPLE EMULATED LANS The ATM Forum LAN Emulation standard also supports the implementation of multiple emulated LANs within a single ATM network. LAN Emulation is implemented through a client/server model. It works like this: a LAN Emulation client, such as workstation software, resolves MAC addresses into ATM addresses. Each client connects to the server by a virtual connection. Only those clients connected to the same server can learn about each other and communicate directly. Logically segmenting the network across multiple server functions—which can be

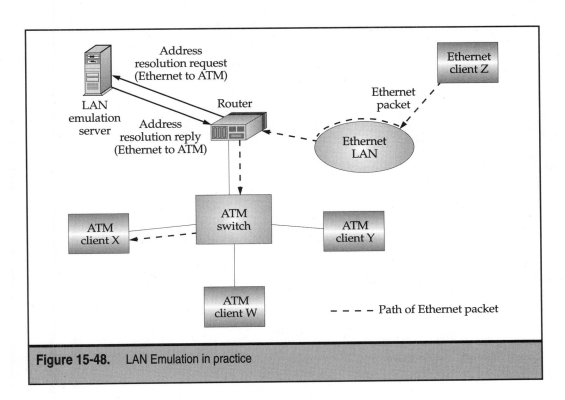

Figure 15-48. LAN Emulation in practice

stand-alone devices, software in end systems, or ATM switch modules—allows multiple emulated LANs to exist simultaneously on the same physical network.

Figure 15-49 shows the physical and logical view of multiple emulated LANs. In the physical view, the router runs two LAN Emulation clients—A2 for the accounting department and M2 for the manufacturing department. Each departmental server keeps track of its clients through a resident database. When accounting user A1 sends a packet to manufacturing user M1, the accounting server checks its database for a match. Finding none, it maps the MAC address to the router (A2/M2), which then forwards the packet to the manufacturing department server for delivery to M1.

The logical view looks like the physical layout of today's LANs and is consistent with the goal of LAN Emulation. Departmental clients communicate directly with each other, directly with servers, and indirectly with other departments through a network router.

LAN EMULATION AND SWITCHED VIRTUAL LANS There are now products available, such as 3Com's Transcend suite of network management applications, that allow network

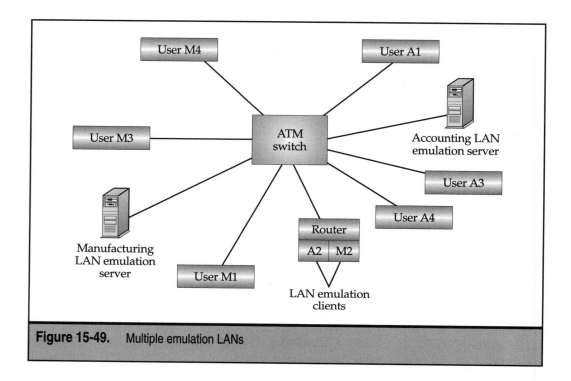

Figure 15-49. Multiple emulation LANs

managers to define multiple emulated LANs. When several different emulated local area networks communicate through one or more switches on an ATM network, the result is a switched virtual LAN, as shown in Figure 15-50. Managing virtual LANs can be difficult because managing physical connectivity isn't enough. You will have to be able to monitor and manage the logical interconnection across the LAN. With switched virtual LANs, routing is no longer a physical bottleneck, but a logical processing function that can be handled efficiently by the ATM switches.

Virtual switched emulated LANs offer the same benefits as garden-variety virtual LANs:

▼ Simplified moves, adds, and changes

■ Secure workgroups

■ Firewalls against broadcast storms

▲ Flow control to better utilize network bandwidth

It offers all of these benefits without requiring the purchase of new equipment or the recabling of network segments. Network administrators can manage segments just by

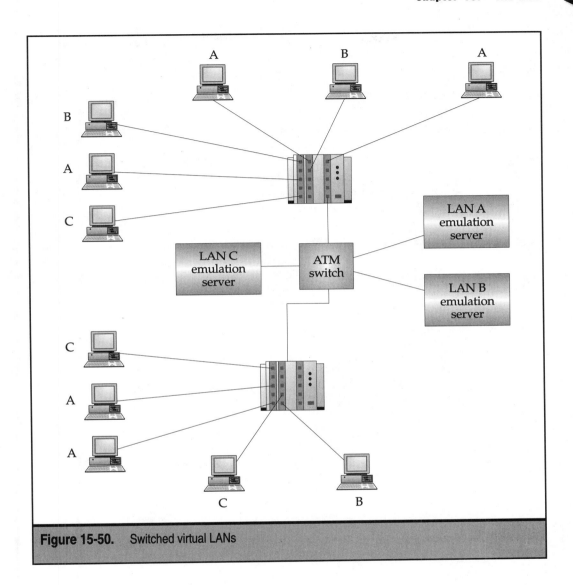

Figure 15-50. Switched virtual LANs

redefining groups in the network management system and/or reconfiguring software in the end device and/or ATM switch.

Routing Issues

Although ATM LAN Emulation greatly simplifies the creation of virtual workgroups, it doesn't change the role of routers on virtual LANs. Routers are still required to manage broadcasts and address resolution, as shown in Figure 15-51. As the network scales to higher-speed backbone links, the router must process traffic from these links at wire speeds in order to avoid creating a bottleneck.

ATM AND CONVENTIONAL ROUTERS Even though some high-end routers now have ATM interfaces designed to forward packets at ATM speeds of 155Mbps, conventional routers just aren't designed to take full advantage of ATM's performance capabilities. Today's routers are optimized for a balanced load of incoming and outgoing traffic across a number of interfaces, unlike the ATM edge routers that we described earlier.

A scalable ATM LAN architecture uses all of the functions of a router in a distributed manner. This enables the routing function to scale economically with the ATM network. A distributed router architecture separates the packet-forwarding functions from the

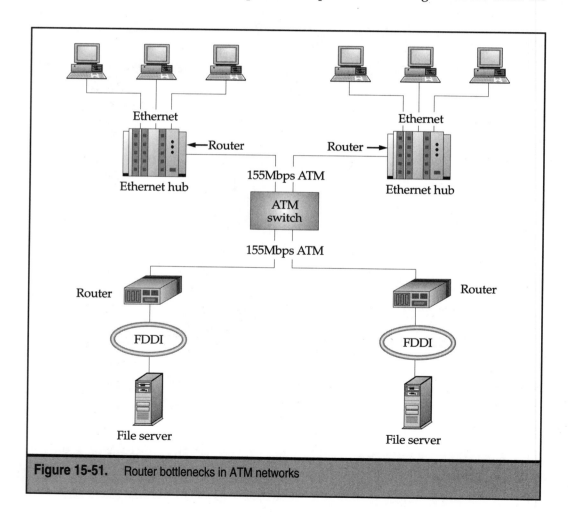

Figure 15-51. Router bottlenecks in ATM networks

routing functions. Routing functions are processor-intensive, but are performed on a relatively infrequent basis. Packet-forwarding functions, on the other hand, require little processing but high performance. In a distributed router, the packet-forwarding functions are performed by network access devices, as shown in Figure 15-52.

ATM switches are designed to perform many of the functions routers perform—to select an optimal network path, provide an efficient LAN and WAN interface, and provide internal security, flow control, and bandwidth management. As a result, routers are evolving into edge devices with the principal function of connecting multiple LANs to the ATM switch.

The easiest way for a router to use ATM is to use PVCs through the switched fabric. But this negates two of ATM's greatest strengths: dynamic connection and bandwidth allocation.

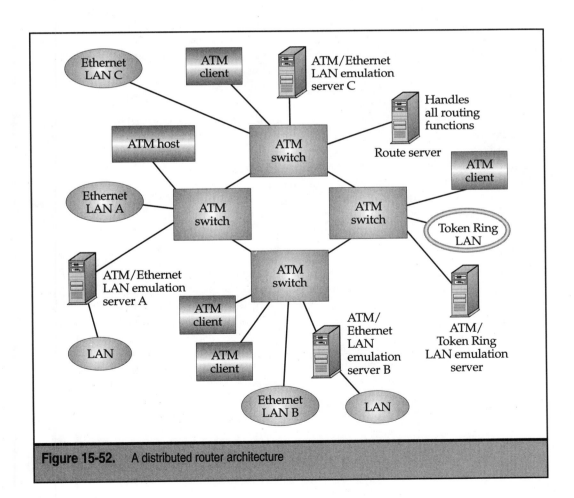

Figure 15-52.   A distributed router architecture

ATM VIRTUAL ROUTERS   Although edge routers are the router of choice among ATM vendors these days, much of the industry is buzzing with talk of a new kind of ATM router called a virtual router. A virtual router works very differently from an edge router. It combines a central route server and a number of multilayer switches—hardware-based devices that are nearly as fast as a conventional switch that work on the MAC layer, but much smarter—that link existing LANs. The thinking behind this virtual architecture recognizes that conventional routers are a bottleneck because, as we mentioned earlier, they calculate routes on a packet-by-packet basis. In a virtual router, on the other hand, LAN interconnection is achieved by the multilayer switch.

The multilayer switch forwards on the basis of MAC or network layer packet fields. But it doesn't handle the route discovery and topology updates. These functions are managed by the route server. Each port on the multilayer switch can be assigned its own subnet address, just as with a conventional router. As well, just as with an edge router, multiple ports can share the same subnet address. The route server runs the routing protocols and maintains a picture of the ATM and internetwork topologies. The route server can even act as a broadcast server and resolve address queries. As far as the end stations are concerned, the virtual router performs all the functions of a physical router: protocol processing, bridging, routing, and filtering.

Training Holes

Many vendors' ATM strategies are highly complex and require users to be experts in the product lines of multiple vendors. Because these products are proprietary, however, training in one vendor's ATM switch or LAN Emulation technology doesn't guarantee any knowledge applicable to another vendor's ATM products. Furthermore, the ATM Forum is still in the process of developing many of the specifications necessary to implement interoperable ATM networks, so solid training on these interfaces is not available because the information simply isn't available.

Expect to Phase It In

ATM is currently a very costly technology, so widespread deployment throughout your network is probably prohibitively expensive. As well, most of your segments don't require its 155Mbps to 622Mbps bandwidth. Therefore, migration to a switched network should be considered a process, a series of evolutionary steps as new technologies are phased in. So, plan to implement it in phases: first the backbones (especially campus backbones), video-intensive segments, and even trunked voice traffic from the PBX switches.

A transition to ATM will require consideration of the protocol suites at both specific sites and the overall enterprise. In some cases, ATM will initially be limited to a few directly connected workstations, while the rest take advantage of ATM in the backbone, enabling high-speed access to shared resources such as servers. This means that legacy network access to ATM will be important.

An incremental approach to ATM migration combines the best of the various technologies by enhancing existing network investments in three ways:

▼ ATM deployment extends the life of the installed base of network equipment by boosting performance.

■ Combined with such capabilities as LAN Emulation, ATM enhances network management and operations by allowing virtual network configurations.

▲ Incremental upgrades keep investment and technical risks low while ATM technology matures.

Figures 15-53 through 15-55 show one way to phase in ATM. It begins with implementing an ATM backbone.

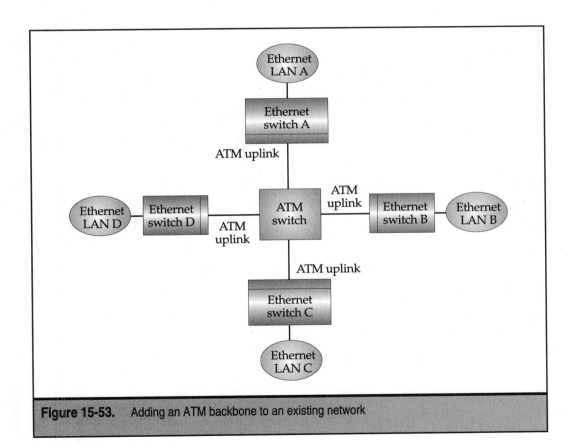

Figure 15-53.   Adding an ATM backbone to an existing network

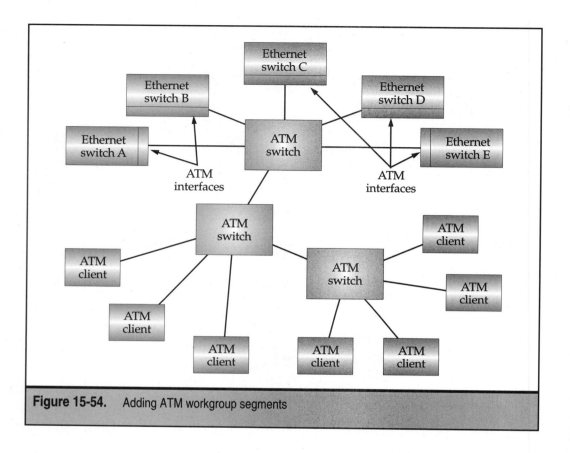

Figure 15-54.   Adding ATM workgroup segments

Next, the network plan progresses to add ATM workgroup segments, employing LAN Emulation to enable all network users to communicate with one another.

Finally, a collapsed router backbone—a single, high-performance router connects multiple segments into a logical network.

Desktop Migration Issues

Although ATM is usually considered primarily a backbone solution, most ATM networks are currently workgroups in which workstations and servers are connected directly to an ATM switch. Though ATM workgroups are usually small in size and centralized geographically, thus simplifying implementation, there are still several issues to consider.

MEDIA SUPPORT   Review your existing network infrastructure. Most ATM products currently run over multimode fiber and unshielded twisted-pair Category 5 copper at rates ranging from 25Mbps to 155Mbps. Due to the attenuation characteristics of copper,

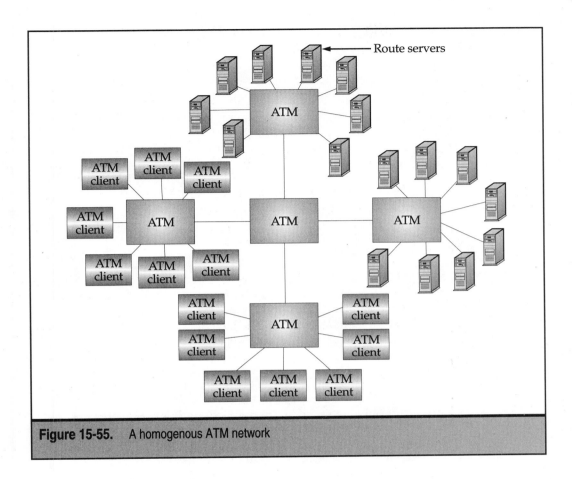

Figure 15-55.   A homogenous ATM network

the maximum distance for Category 5 cable runs is typically 100 meters. Multimode fiber, on the other hand, has a maximum cable length of 2,000 meters. Be sure your cable plan meets these requirements.

APPLICATION SUPPORT   Can your existing applications run over an ATM network? Because ATM is a lower-level protocol, this is usually not a problem. Most commonly, these applications are TCP/IP-based or based on PCs, Novell NetWare, or Microsoft Windows. However, are the applications you plan to use optimized to take advantage of ATM's dedicated bandwidth and data prioritization capabilities? To get the full benefit of ATM, whenever possible, choose applications that support these features.

COMPUTER COMPATIBILITY   In an ATM workgroup, each workstation must have an ATM network interface card (NIC). The NIC must be compatible with the bus type of the workstation, as well as with both the workstation and network operating systems. It is important that the NIC has been tested with both the type of workstation and the type of ATM switches you are using.

WAN Integration Issues

Although you can often integrate ATM into wide area networks without replacing any equipment, you will need some additional equipment, a thorough knowledge of applicable ATM interfaces, and a lot of careful planning.

There are four primary protocols required for successful internetworking over the wide area. They are

▼ Public User-to-Network Interface (UNI)

■ Public Network-to-Network Interface (NNI)

■ Intercarrier Interface (ICI)

▲ Data Exchange Interface (DXI)

PUBLIC USER-TO-NETWORK INTERFACE (UNI)   As we discussed earlier, ATM's UNI protocol provides multiple service classes and bandwidth reservation established during call setup of a switched virtual connection. The UNI defines the interoperability between the user equipment and the ATM switch port. A public UNI defines the interface between a public service ATM network, and usually supports a SONET or DS3 interface. It is the link between the ATM user and the ATM switch on the public ATM carrier's network.

PUBLIC NETWORK-TO-NETWORK INTERFACE (NNI)   As we also mentioned earlier, the NNI protocol provides virtual connection arbitration, congestion control, and topology management for private or public ATM network connections. It is the link between ATM switches within a public ATM carrier service.

INTERCARRIER INTERFACE (ICI)   The ICI defines internetworking mechanisms on wide area ATM networks. It lets you link between two ATM carriers' nets.

DATA EXCHANGE INTERFACE (DXI)   The DXI provides a standard ATM interface for legacy equipment. The DXI supports routing over ATM because it is based on packets rather than cells. It uses standard high-level data-link control (HDLC) framing, so unlike cell-based interfaces, it needs no additional hardware to transmit packet-based traffic. Therefore, it is the protocol that allows you to connect existing equipment to an ATM network.

To illustrate how each of these interfaces will affect the implementation of an ATM network, look at the network in Figure 15-56. This shows how a wide area ATM backbone might be integrated into an existing FDDI and 10Base-T network.

FDDI has an aggregate backbone bandwidth of 100Mbps, shared by all attached devices. The wide area ATM switch in this illustration has eight ports, each 155Mbps. Because those 155Mbps are dedicated to each attached device, the aggregate bandwidth is 8 multiplied by 155Mbps, or approximately 1.2Gbps.

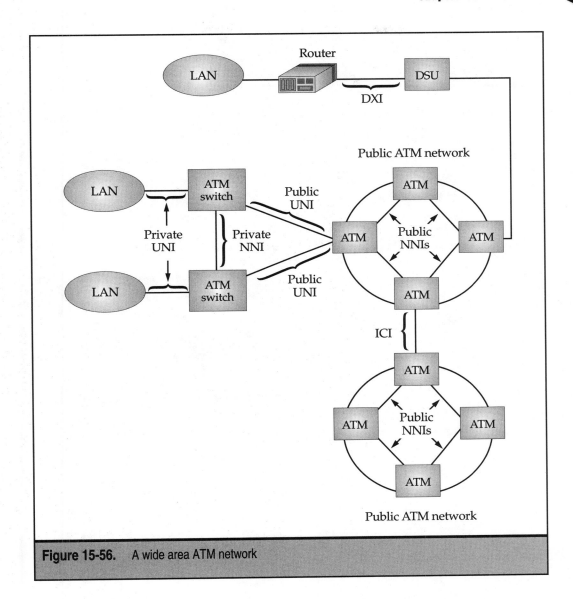

Figure 15-56.   A wide area ATM network

NOTE: The actual aggregate bandwidth of this example will fall somewhere between 155Mbps and 1.2Gbps, depending on the traffic patterns and usage.

An ATM UNI was installed in both the FDDI router and the 10Base-T switch so both devices could be connected to the ATM switch. The WAN connection to the ATM switch is through a Data Exchange Interface (DXI) to a service multiplexer, typically a special CSU/DSU. Thanks to its DXI, in addition to multiplexing traffic onto the wide area link, the service multiplexer performs AAL segmentation and reassembly, allowing non-ATM-capable devices to access the ATM network replacing hardware.

OTHER ISSUES TO CONSIDER Implementing a backbone with ATM involves many of the same issues and concerns as with any other protocol. Some of these are

- ▼ Security
- ■ Fault tolerance
- ■ Bandwidth requirements
- ▲ Management systems

AVAILABILITY OF ATM CARRIER SERVICES One of the big challenges you may face when implementing a wide area ATM network is finding a carrier service that both offers ATM and is reasonably priced. Although most digital service providers offer ATM, it isn't universally available yet because of lack of strong, widespread demand. Contracts may be available from service providers to ensure both availability and pricing, but obtaining one may require some persistence and negotiating skill.

Common carrier service providers acknowledge that ATM is definitely the future of wide area network communication. They understand that it erases the barriers between LANs and WANs, which are

- ▼ The drop in throughput between local area network protocols and public networks protocols
- ▲ Delays caused by store-and-forward WAN connection devices like routers

However, not all local exchange carriers (LECs) and interexchange carriers (IXCs) have installed integrated ATM/SONET digital networks to offer economical virtual private data network services. When they do, you can assume they will pass the heavy expense of installing these new networks on to the consumer. The good news is that ATM carries more traffic at reduced cost, which will eventually result in savings for the consumer. But that may be quite far off in the future, so be prepared for large ATM carrier service expenses for the wide area.

The Promised LAN

Overall, ATM holds excellent promise for nearly every network. It provides performance and functions never before available for the following:

- ▼ Electronic funds transfer
- ■ Voice annotation of memos

- Interactive training videos
- ▲ Design and manufacturing development in which collaborative efforts involve complex data objects residing on a variety of different, geographically dispersed processors

ATM probably is the future of transport protocols and networking in general. However, the future is not now. As we mentioned earlier, many vendors have been quick to announce plans for ATM products and systems, but as of this writing, there simply aren't any end-to-end open, viable, interoperable ATM systems available.

MOVING ON DOWN THE LINE

Now that you're thoroughly familiar with what goes on at layers 3 and 2, it's time to plunge into layer 1, the physical layer, and what that means in managing your network.

16

The Cabling

Here we are at the bottom of the networking food chain—the physical layer. This is the layer that defines the physical characteristics of the networking interface. This interface includes the connectors, electrical specifications such as voltage levels, and all mechanical components. In other words, the physical layer deals with the actual materials and signaling that ties the network together.

ALL THAT GLISTENS ISN'T COPPER

As you're no doubt aware, "cabling" doesn't mean "wiring" anymore. Network cable can be copper or fiber-optic cabling.

In the early days, of course, cabling was coaxial cable, which was the predominant type of cable used for constructing most mainframe computer networks and the early local area networks. Although you will still find a lot of coaxial cable around, especially in legacy mainframe networks, the predominant type of copper cabling being used is Category 5 unshielded twisted-pair (UTP) cabling.

CABLING PRIMER

For most readers, this will be pure review, but Table 16-1 gives the currently available types of cables and a little about their physical characteristics.

Media Type	No. Hubs from Root to End	No. Levels	Maximum Span
3	1	2	100m
3	2	3	75m
3	3	4	50m
3	4	5	25m
5	1	2	200m
5	2	3	150m
5	3	4	100m
5	4	5	50m
0.625 micron fiber	1	2	4km
0.625 micron fiber	2	3	3km
0.625 micron fiber	3	4	2km

Table 16-1. Physical Characteristics of Cable Types

THE TIA AND EIA CABLING STANDARDS

So, now you know the different types of cabling standards and how to identify them. You also know from the previous chapters that different network access methods have different specifications for length and network structure. But where do you get information on how to design the cable runs for your site?

The Telecommunications Industry Association (TIA) and the Electronic Industries Association (EIA) have created a set of international wiring standards that specify how to design and build a structured wiring system (see Chapter 15 for more on structured wiring). This series of standards is called TIA/EIA-568.

The standard for installing structured wiring for data and voice in commercial buildings is known as TIA/EIA-568-A. This standard specifies how to design and build six different portions of a cabling system in a commercial building:

▼   Work area wiring

■   Horizontal wiring

■   Telecommunications closets

■   Equipment rooms and cross-connects

■   Backbone, or vertical, wiring

▲   Entrance facilities

Work Area Wiring

Work area wiring is really just a term for junction boxes, faceplates, and connectors that connect the computers in an office area to the cabling system. For example, the TIA/EIA-568-A standard requires that each wall plate have both a data outlet and a voice outlet.

Horizontal Wiring

Horizontal wiring is the cabling that runs from the junction boxes. The TIA/EIA-568-A standard requires that each wall plate outlet be no more than 90 meters from the *telecommunications closet*. In the telecommunications closet, patch cables can be no longer than 10 meters. (This matches the 100-meter maximum segment distance for 10Base-T.)

Furthermore, the horizontal wiring for the voice network has to be 4-pair, 100-ohm unshielded twisted-pair cable of Category 3, 4, or 5. The data cabling, on the other hand, can be 4-pair 100 ohm UTP cabling, or 62.5/125mm fiber-optic cable, or 2-pair, 150-ohm shielded twisted-pair (STP) cabling, depending upon the access method the network will use.

Telecommunications Closets

The *telecommunications closet* used to be called the Intermediate Distribution Frame (IDF) in the olden days. It is the closet where all the hub and switches that connect nearby computers are located. It *cross-connects* these devices to a central server room.

Equipment Rooms and Cross-Connects

Equipment rooms are the server rooms. In other words, they are the central points of a distributed network. It is in the equipment room that the backbone cabling connecting the telecommunications closets terminates.

Backbone Wiring

As discussed in Chapter 15, backbone wiring runs among telecommunications closets—connecting them to the main network—and terminates in the equipment room. The maximum backbone spans are listed in Table 16-2.

Entrance Facilities

An *entrance facility* is the line of demarcation between a telecommunications service and the building's network. It is the point at which the service enters the building, and often is also the point where network connections that merely span a campus enter the building.

     For the most up-to-date information on TIA/EIA-568, check out their Web site at http://www.tiaonline.org.

REACHING UP FROM LAYER 1

And what connects to these cabling systems? As we mentioned in Chapter 15, layer 2 and 3 devices connect directly to the cabling system. We will now discuss the what, where, and how of connecting these devices in a bit more detail.

A Segment Defined

The definition of a network segment, or subnetwork, varies from network to network and protocol to protocol. In classic Ethernet networks, a segment is a cable that is terminated

Cable Types	Maximum Backbone	Passive Devices	Active to Passive Devices
62.5/125 fiber	2000m (6,560 ft.)	500m (1,640 ft.)	1500m (4,820 ft.)
Single-mode	3000m (9,840 ft.)	500m (1,640 ft.)	2500m (8,200 ft.)
UTP (voice)	800m (2,624 ft.)	500m (1,640 ft.)	300m (984 ft.)
UTP (data)	90m (295 ft.)	90m (295 ft.)	90m (295 ft.)

Table 16-2.   Maximum Backbone Spans

at both ends. In the 10Base-T realm, a segment is a hub or stack of hubs. In a Token Ring environment, a segment is one or more multistation access units (MAUs). The features that all of these configurations, shown in Figure 16-1, have in common is that:

▼   They all have the same network address.

■   They all share the same type of network protocol.

▲   All the stations connected to them "see" all traffic addressed to all the other connected stations.

This last feature means they must share access to the network with all other stations on the segment, either by waiting their turn (in Token Ring and other deterministic protocols) or by contending with all the other stations on the segment for access (in 10Base-T and similar contention-based protocols).

Whether you are using a deterministic protocol or a contention-based protocol, the more stations on the segment, the slower the response time. After all, network bandwidth is a finite resource, and the more stations that have to share it, the smaller the bandwidth available to each. One way to improve network performance, therefore, is to reduce the number of stations sharing the bandwidth—in other words, decrease the number of stations on a segment. This is called network segmentation.

Creating Internetworks

Clearly, you can't lower the number of stations on a segment simply by disconnecting them (okay, you could, but you'd better have your résumé ready). Therefore, the only way to limit the number of stations on each segment is to create more segments.

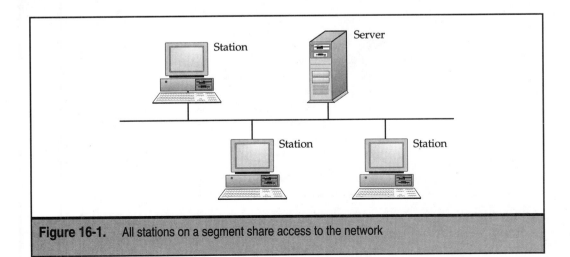

Figure 16-1.   All stations on a segment share access to the network

A group of segments that can communicate with one another is known as an internetwork. There are three ways to do this:

▼ Internal bridging

■ External bridging

▲ Routing

Internal Bridging

Internal bridging is a technique in which a server provides bridging between two or more network adapters installed in the server that is running an operating system that supports bridging, such as Novell NetWare or Banyan VINES. In an internal bridging configuration, the server provides all the bridging functionality. While this makes it easy and fairly inexpensive to implement, it also drains server resources that might be better utilized on critical processing tasks.

Internal bridging is a function that takes place in the MAC sublayer of the data-link layer in the OSI Reference Model, as shown in Figure 16-2. We will discuss this functionality in more detail later in this chapter.

External Bridging

Like internal bridging, external bridging is also a MAC sublayer function. It occurs when the bridging function is moved away from the server and is handled by another device. This device may be a PC running bridge software or a specialized bridge.

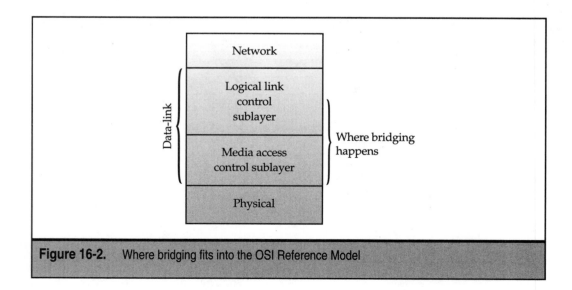

Figure 16-2. Where bridging fits into the OSI Reference Model

Routing

Routing is a function that takes place at the network layer of the OSI model, as shown in Figure 16-3. Because routers have access to higher-level information that bridges don't, they have more intelligence and can make decisions about when, where, and how data packets are to be routed through the network. This ultimately results in more reliable packet delivery.

In case you'd like a refresher course in bridging and routing—just to make sure you've done everything with them you can to relieve your network's congestion—I've included a primer on each of them.

The Bridging Primer

A bridge is an internetworking device that provides a way for a station on one network segment to send packets to stations on another segment. Bridging takes place at the data-link layer (DLL) of the OSI Reference Model, as shown in Figure 16-2. The DLL is divided into two sublayers: the logical link control (LLC) sublayer and the media access control (MAC) sublayer. Devices that support the IEEE 802 specification have a standard MAC sublayer that can receive data packets from multiple network transport protocols. Upon receiving a data packet, the MAC sublayer passes the data to the LLC sublayer, translates it to the destination segment's transport protocol, then places it on the destination segment. This process is illustrated in Figure 16-4.

Bridges serve many functions in an internetwork besides creating multiple segments to reduce congestion. Bridges can extend the network span by acting as repeaters, regenerating the transmission signal. However, bridges can also perform many functions that repeaters can't. Some of these functions are

▼ *Joining segments using different network protocols, like 10Base-T and Token Ring.* A bridge examines the addresses of packets and places them on the network segments where the addressee station or stations are located. Because bridging

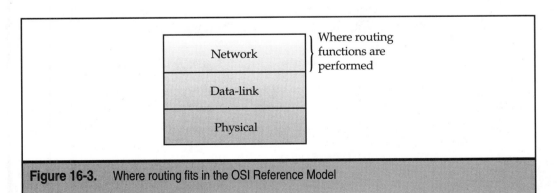

Figure 16-3. Where routing fits in the OSI Reference Model

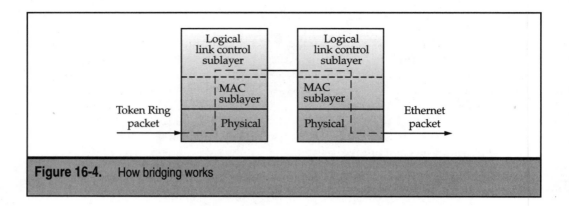

Figure 16-4.   How bridging works

takes place in the DLL, any device that conforms to the MAC specifications of the IEEE 802 standard—such as 10Base-T and Token Ring—can bridge to other IEEE MAC devices.

■ *Filtering packets rather than simply forwarding all of them.*   Without filtering, packets are sent everywhere on a network. When a packet arrives at a bridge, the bridge reads the destination address in the packets and determines whether it should forward the packet across the bridge. Bridges filter packets by reading the MAC layer address in the Ethernet or Token Ring frame, as shown in Figure 16-5, to determine on which segment the receiving station is located. They forward packets only to the segment or segments of the addressee stations.

■ *Resolving endless loops.*   Some bridged networks may inadvertently contain loops that could cause a packet to travel continuously, never reaching its destination address and being taken off the network. There are bridges that will detect such looping packets and remove them. This is done using the IEEE 802.1d Spanning Tree Protocol, which will be discussed later in this chapter.

■ *Learning the network and building address tables.*   This can be accomplished through source routing or transparent bridging, which are discussed later in this chapter.

▲ *Providing fault tolerance in the form of redundant paths for data packets to reach their destinations.*

Bridges Near and Far

Bridges can be either local or remote. A local bridge connects local area networks, which are by definition located within the same geographic area, as shown in Figure 16-6.

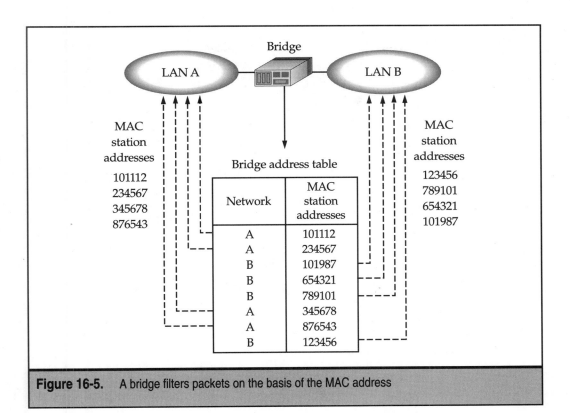

Figure 16-5. A bridge filters packets on the basis of the MAC address

Remote bridges, on the other hand, connect networks that are separated by greater distances. Therefore, remote bridges have interfaces to connect to wide area data carrier services such as ISDN or T1, as shown in Figure 16-7.

Net Learning

When bridges were first introduced, network managers had to configure them manually, typing in the addresses of every segment and station. Every time a station was added or dropped, the network manager had to edit the address table of all the bridges on the network to add or remove the station. As I mentioned earlier, however, bridges can now automatically learn the addresses of every station on the network. By doing this, they can filter traffic that isn't addressed to their segment and thus reduce network congestion. There are two methods a bridge device can use to learn its network: transparent bridging and source routing.

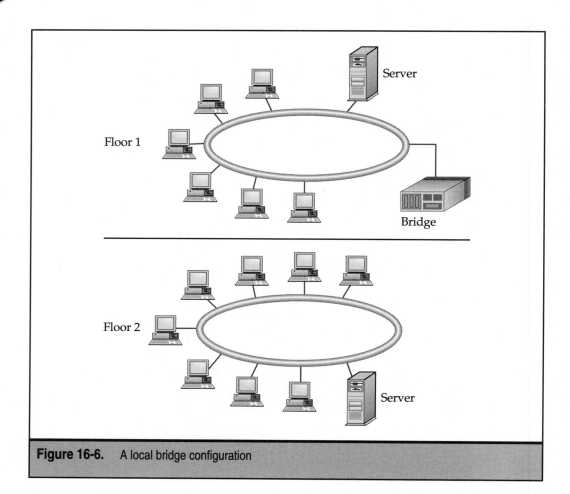

Figure 16-6.   A local bridge configuration

Looking Through a Transparent Bridge

Transparent bridging is a technique used on IEEE 802.3 (aka 10Base-T) networks. Transparent bridges start learning the network topology as soon as they are connected to the network. When a packet enters a port on a transparent bridge, the bridge notes the address of the network from which it received the packet, then examines the packet's source address and adds that address to a list of addresses of packets that the bridge has received from that network address. The bridge thus builds a table of source addresses located at each network address. As new stations are added or dropped from the network, the bridge updates this address table. The bridge's address table is held in the bridge's memory, and its size is limited by the amount of memory the bridge has allocated to table maintenance.

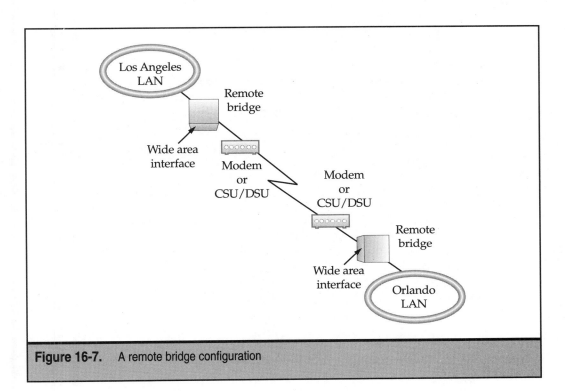

Figure 16-7.   A remote bridge configuration

Therefore, when a bridge hasn't received a packet from a particular address for some predefined amount of time, it clears that address from its address table to make room for new, more active source addresses. An example of such a table is shown in Figure 16-8.

Network	MAC station addresses
A	101112
A	234567
B	101987
B	654321
B	789101
A	345678

Figure 16-8.   Bridge address table

The bridge uses its table of addresses to determine whether to forward arriving packets onto another ring or send them on to the next device on the same network. It does this by examining the destination address of an arriving packet, then locating that address in the bridge's address table. If the packet is destined for a network segment attached to the bridge, the bridge channels the packet to that segment. If not, the bridge retransmits the packet to the next bridge on the ring. If a packet arrives with a destination address that isn't in the bridge's address table, the bridge tries to "discover" the unknown address. It sends a special frame to all network segments except the packet's source network. This frame contains a request for the destination address device to respond. If and when the destination responds, the bridge updates its address table with the new address. Through this process, the bridge eventually locates and learns the address of every station on the network.

Obviously, the larger the network, the longer it will take the bridge to learn it—and the more memory the bridge will need to maintain the address table. Therefore, if you are experiencing poor performance on a bridged network, you may want to check to make sure that the bridge has sufficient memory to hold all the addresses. If it doesn't, it will be constantly discovering, recording, and deleting addresses to make use of its limited memory, and it will therefore take more time to forward a packet than if the packet's address were readily at hand in the address table.

The Catch: Fault Tolerance and Endless Loops

As I mentioned, one of the things that bridges can do that repeaters can't is provide multiple paths for packets. This adds to the fault tolerance of networks, because if a segment of cable is cut or a bridge is down, these redundant paths offer an alternate route between the source station and the destination station, as shown in Figure 16-9.

However, this added fault tolerance is not without its price. On large interconnected networks, multiple bridge paths may form an endless loop, causing packets to circulate through the network and never reaching their destination, as shown in Figure 16-10. Not only do these circulating packets take up precious bandwidth, but the packets retransmitted to replace these "lost" packets add to the congestion, ultimately reducing performance and even causing the network to collapse altogether.

Spanning Tree to the Rescue

The Spanning Tree Protocol, developed by the IEEE 801 committee, solves the problem of endless loops created by multiple paths. It "tricks" the bridge into not seeing the redundant paths unless and until the primary path is not available. The Spanning Tree Protocol is a set of procedures implemented in firmware in the bridge itself. It works like this: The Spanning Tree Protocol gives each bridge a unique address—usually the MAC address of the bridge. Then, the algorithm assigns a unique address to each port on each bridge, as shown in Figure 16-11.

Next, the Spanning Tree Protocol calculates a "cost" for each port on each bridge. These costs are based on distance, cost of any carrier service to which they are attached, preferred path, and other factors that the network manager determines. Some bridging

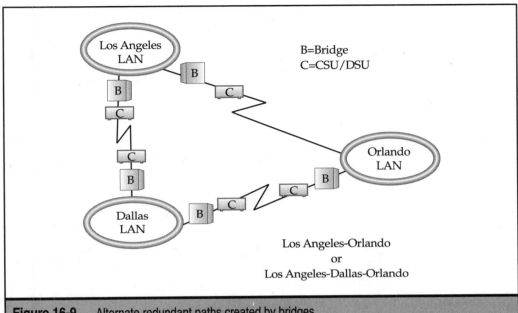

Figure 16-9. Alternate redundant paths created by bridges

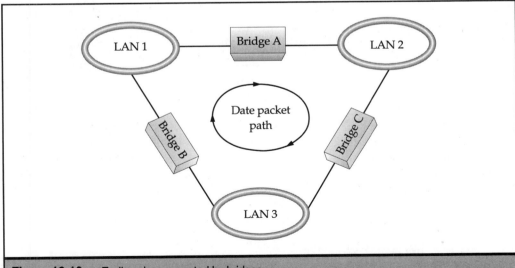

Figure 16-10. Endless loops created by bridges

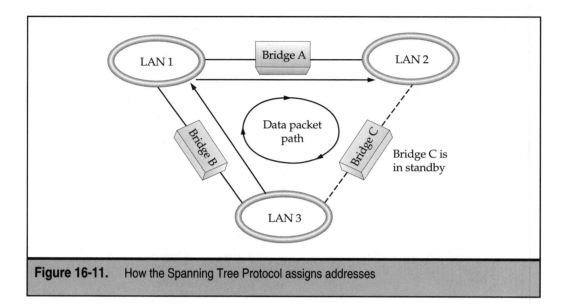

Figure 16-11.   How the Spanning Tree Protocol assigns addresses

software will automatically calculate a port cost based on vendor-defined criteria, allowing the network manager to change cost values as necessary. Other bridges require that the network manager manually enter all path cost information.

The next procedure for the Spanning Tree Protocol is the selection of a root bridge. The algorithm designates the bridge with the lowest address as the root bridge. Then, all other bridges calculate the cost of a path from each of their ports to the root bridge. The port with the least path cost to the root bridge is designated as the root port of the bridge.

NOTE: If more than one port on a bridge has the least-cost path to the root bridge, the port that has the fewest bridge-to-bridge hops is designated as the root port.

Finally, the Spanning Tree Protocol determines which paths will be the primary paths through the network to each destination contained in the bridge's address tables. All alternate paths are then put on standby, or temporarily disabled. Should a primary path become unavailable, the Spanning Tree Protocol will enable a standby path for the data being transmitted.

Source Route Bridging

Source route bridging is a routing technique used by Token Ring networks. Source routing is very different from transparent bridging because in source route bridging, the network adapter—as well as the bridge—maintains the address tables. The network adapter discovers all paths from the source station to the destination station using much the same means as a transparent bridge does. Furthermore, the network adapter is the device that makes the path decision. The bridge merely forwards the packet based on the routing information the network adapter has placed in the packet. Therefore, a bridge that supports source routing doesn't have to make route decisions for the packets it receives—the packets come with their routing information contained in them.

Source routing bridges build and maintain address tables just like transparent bridges. However, they don't have to determine the path the packet will take because that path has already been decided by the network adapter. Source routing bridges use their address tables to locate the device to which they should forward the packet. Therefore, source routing bridges don't have problems with endless loops, so building multiple redundant paths with source routing bridges doesn't require a procedure like the Spanning Tree Protocol.

Bridge Performance Issues

Segmenting your network with bridges isn't an automatic guarantee that your network's performance will improve. In fact, if the bridge you've selected isn't equal to the task, it might even slow things further. Therefore, it's important to evaluate the performance and features of the bridge itself before installing it. Here are the key criteria affecting bridge performance.

Forwarding Rate

Forwarding rate is the rate at which the bridge can transmit traffic from one port to another, expressed in packets per second. 10Base-T, for example, transmits a 64-byte packet at a maximum rate of 14,880 packets per second (pps). This rate is known as wire speed.

Memory

As we mentioned earlier, a bridge with insufficient memory will only be able to maintain small address tables. If your network is small as well, this might not be a problem. However, large networks require that bridges maintain large address tables. A bridge without enough memory to maintain a large address table will spend much of its processing power updating its address table with the addresses of the most recently transmitted packets. This can decrease your network's performance far more than the segmentation will increase it.

High-Speed Links

Sometimes a combination of segmentation and high-speed networking is what you need to speed up slow spots in your network, such as a backbone or server farm. Therefore, consider purchasing a bridge that has high-speed networking ports as well as 10Base-T or Token Ring ports. This way, you can implement a high-speed segment, then segment other portions of the legacy network.

The Router Primer

Routers, like bridges, provide a way for a station on one network segment to send packets to a station on another network segment. However, whereas bridges function at the DLL of the OSI Reference Model, routers function at a higher level, as shown in Figure 16-12.

Because routers function at the higher network layer, they have access to information contained in this layer about congested or collapsed network segments. As a result, routers can reroute packets around such failed segments and thus provide better network management, better fault tolerance, and more reliable packet delivery than bridges. Furthermore, routers can automatically route packets over specific paths selected on the basis of distance, cost, or traffic congestion. There are also special routers, called multiprotocol routers, that can join networks of many different communications protocols.

How Routers Work

Like a bridge, a router examines address information in a packet and sends the packet along a predefined route to its destination. Also like bridges, routers maintain address tables containing the location of other devices on the network. When a router receives a packet, it looks at these tables to see if it can send the packet directly to the destination. If not, it finds the closest router that can forward the packet to its destination and forwards the packet to this router.

And further like a bridge, a router doesn't have to be an external device. Some network operating systems such as Banyan VINES and Novell NetWare perform routing functions in the server. Just as with a bridge, you implement this by installing two or more network interface cards in the server, and the operating system handles the rest. However, again as in bridging, routing tasks can slow down a server, so many network managers install external routers to free the server's processors for file service functions.

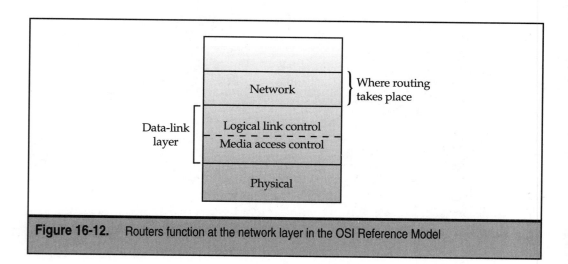

Figure 16-12.   Routers function at the network layer in the OSI Reference Model

MULTIPROTOCOL ROUTERS   A multiprotocol router can route multiple different protocols, such as TCP/IP, IPX, AppleTalk, DECnet, and others. If your network contains platforms running a variety of protocols, be sure to select a router that supports them all. A multiprotocol router has software that processes packets from each of the supported protocols.

Router Functions

As I've pointed out, the functions of a router seem, on the surface at least, very similar to the functions of a bridge. When a router receives a packet, it first error-checks the packet using a checksum value contained within the packet. The router then opens the packet and examines it to determine where the packet should be sent. It does this by examining the network layer protocol information that includes the destination address, and for some source-routing communications protocols, a predetermined path for the packet to take. If the packet's destination address is on the same network as the router, the router forwards the packet. If the destination address is not on the same network, the router locates the next router to which the packet should be delivered and sends the packet on to that router. Unlike a bridge, however, a router discards packets if it doesn't know or can't find the destination of a packet in its routing table. The router may also return an error message to the packet's source address. A router also discards packets that have exceeded the allowed number of router hops for its protocol type, assuming that the packet is in a loop. This is just the first of several differences that sometimes make routers a better choice for segmentation than bridges.

What Makes It Different Is What Makes It Special

Because routing takes place at the network layer, routers employ protocols that are capable not only of creating redundant data paths but also of managing them for the greatest efficiency of data delivery. Routing protocols select data paths based on cost, speed, distance, or network manager preference. These protocols can also reroute data paths around failed and congested network links. They can also prioritize traffic, making sure that high-priority packets go over the fastest network paths, for example, while low-priority packets are sent over the least costly packets. As the network manager, you can define high-priority and low-priority data paths, or even let the router define these for you based on your criteria.

An example of a wide area routed network is shown in Figure 16-13. If Houston wants to send a message to New York, the router can use either the 56Kbps direct-connect line or the T1 lines that connect through Chicago and Philadelphia. The router can determine the path based on the following:

▼   Packet priority

■   Speed

■   Cost

▲   Hop count

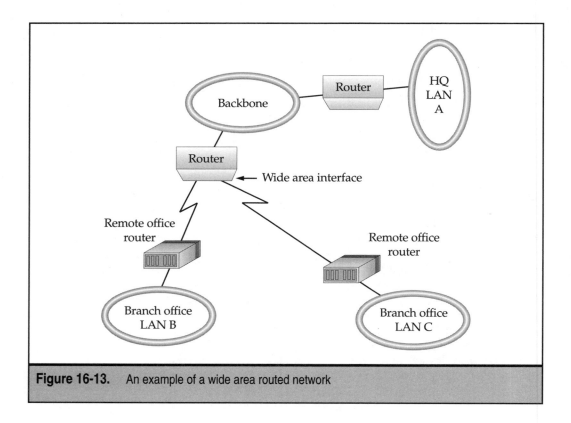

Figure 16-13.   An example of a wide area routed network

If these are high-priority packets, the router must determine the fastest route, which in turn will depend upon the amount of traffic already on each of these two routes. If cost is the criteria for route selection, then the router will probably choose the 56Kbps line. On the other hand, if hop count is the criteria, the direct 56Kbps line will be the best path.

Distant Routes

Like bridges, routers can be either local or remote. A local router has interfaces for local area network protocols such as Token Ring and 10Base-T. A remote router, on the other hand, has wide area network interfaces for services such as T1 and frame relay.

The Router Shopping Guide

Because routers are inherently more complex devices than bridges, there is a lot more to consider when evaluating and buying routers. Therefore, I've put together a list of criteria to help you make your router selection.

Compatibility and Interoperability

All the routers in your network should support the same protocols and routing methods. Small differences in implementation of routing protocols and compression methods can cause big interoperability problems. Therefore, you may even need to use the same brand and model of routers throughout your network.

Ease of Installation and Configuration

Router setup is not a job for the weak-spirited. Therefore, be sure to purchase a router that offers

▼ A streamlined installation program

■ Free training

■ Professional installation and configuration

▲ All of the above

Fault Tolerance

Your router is more than an internetworking device. It is also an integral part of your network management and cost control. Therefore, a failed router is a very expensive proposition. Be sure your router includes fault-tolerance features, such as redundant power supplies and "hot swappable" modules.

Planning Segmented Networks

Creating multiple segments with a small number of stations on each one will limit traffic, but it may not improve performance. If a user regularly has to access a server that is on another segment, it will take longer for the request to be transmitted to the other segment, and longer for the reply to be received, than if the server were on the same segment as the user.

Some additional tips on planning efficient network segments are

▼ Put users as close as possible to the resources they use the most.

■ Limit internetwork traffic.

▲ Make sure stations that need to can communicate with each other no matter what segment they are on.

When you create more segments, if the segment is interconnected to another segment with a bridge or router, it is possible to send packets between those segments. Network segments joined with bridges or routers form internetworks. Each segment has its own internetwork address.

Microsegmentation

Microsegmentation is exactly what it sounds like: creating many very small network segments. Limiting the traffic on a segment to that of only a handful of users can often increase performance dramatically by reducing collisions and dividing more bandwidth among fewer users. On a microsegment, stations don't often have to contend for access to the network, and they rarely have to wait for another station to finish transmitting before they begin their transmissions.

Microsegmentation can be done with common household objects—lots of hubs and patch cables. However, over the last three years a new, efficient, very manageable, and increasingly cost-effective way to microsegment your network has become available. This means of microsegmentation is known as LAN switching, and it has a lot to recommend it. Read on.

SWITCHING

When bridging doesn't quite cut it but routing is overkill, it's time to consider a switch. After all, a switch is really a specialized bridge that creates a segment of one. Here's how switches evolved from bridges. When your network first begins to slow down, you segment it. All the nodes on the segment still have to share the same 10Mbps bandwidth—with segmentation; however, there are fewer nodes to share that 10Mbps. Pretty soon, high-traffic users simply can't be segmented enough to keep response time acceptably low—unless, of course, there is only one user per segment.

Enter switching, which creates a virtual segment containing one node. Switches make a virtual connection between a transmitting node and a receiving node. This connection is made on the basis of the destination address of each packet, and it lasts only as long as it takes to transfer one packet—in essence creating a private segment for the user. Because the packet is transmitted only to the port associated with that specific destination address, no other port receives the packet, which provides both low traffic and, as an extra bonus, high security. In a switch, data transfers can take place in parallel and at full network speed.

Making the Switch

There are a couple of ways to implement switching, which we'll refer to as static and dynamic. Static switching, illustrated in Figure 16-14, can be accomplished through either module switching or port switching. In module switching, an entire hub module is assigned to a specific Ethernet segment so that all devices attached to the ports on that module are connected to the specified segment. Port switching, on the other hand, assigns devices to a segment on a port-by-port basis. Both module and port switching maintain segment assignments until they are manually changed by the network administrator, hence they are classified as static switching methods.

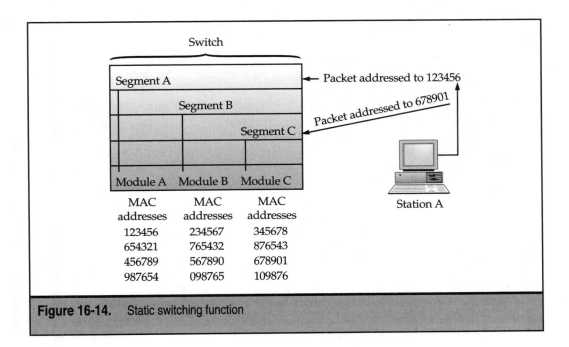

Figure 16-14. Static switching function

Dynamic switching, illustrated in Figure 16-15, is implemented by a switching method similar to that used in a telephone central office. Just as a telephone switch connects two callers only for the duration of their telephone call, the dynamic switch connects two ports long enough to transmit a single packet and then clears down the connection. For its

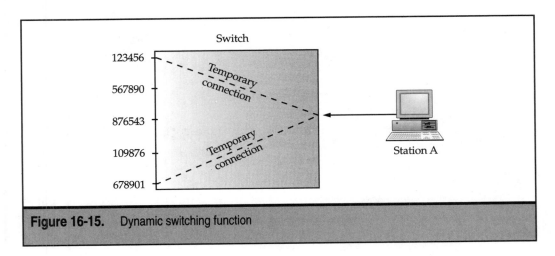

Figure 16-15. Dynamic switching function

duration, the connection has the full 10Mbps bandwidth rather than sharing the bandwidth with all of the devices on the segment. The switch can support several of these port-to-port connections simultaneously.

To illustrate dynamic switching, think of a packet traveling along a shared medium, shown in Figure 16-16, as something like an old-fashioned hotel bellboy meandering through the lobby with his message board. Not only is the message delivery painfully slow, but you've also got a security problem—anyone in the lobby can read the sign. A packet traveling along a switched network, shown in Figure 16-17, is like having a bellboy who knows you and knows where you're sitting in the lobby (you probably tipped him very well). Actually, a switched network is more like having one bellboy assigned to each guest in the lobby. Messages can be delivered to all guests simultaneously, and a switched network is therefore much faster.

There are two main types of switches: workgroup switches and network switches. The bellboy delivering a message to a single guest is an illustration of workgroup switching. A workgroup switch transfers data between pairs of end stations or nodes, as shown in Figure 16-18. A workgroup switch gives each node a dedicated 10Mbps connection. Each port on the switch is associated with one Ethernet address of the attached device.

A network switch, on the other hand, is better illustrated by a team of bellboys delivering messages between two conference rooms. They have to search from person to person to find the addressees. Although this takes more time than if they each knew the exact location of the addressees, it's still faster than having to go to each room in the hotel looking for the addressee. In much the same way, network switches support multiple Ethernet addresses per switch port, which provides wire-speed transfers between pairs of Ethernet segments attached to those ports, as shown in Figure 16-19.

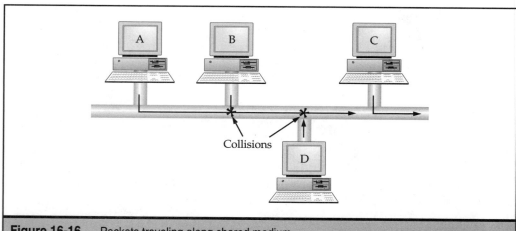

Figure 16-16.   Packets traveling along shared medium

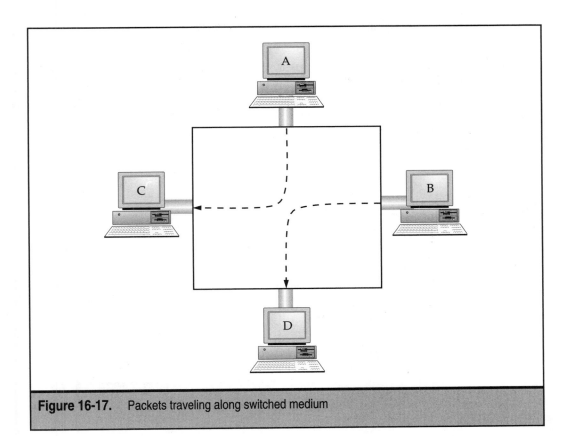

Figure 16-17. Packets traveling along switched medium

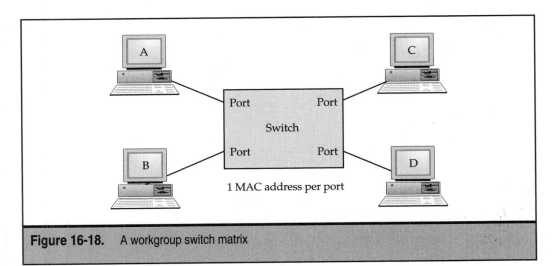

Figure 16-18. A workgroup switch matrix

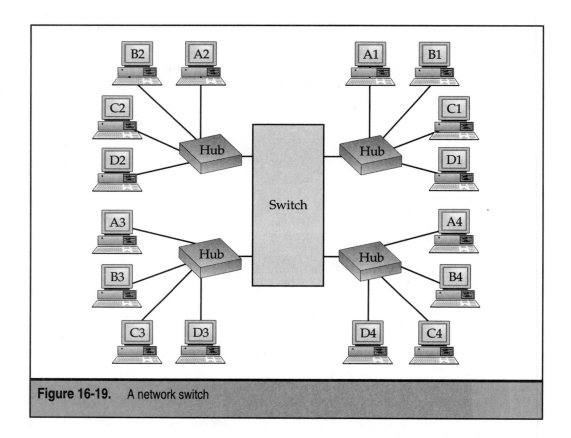

Figure 16-19. A network switch

Blocking vs. Nonblocking

An important aspect of how a switch operates is whether it is nonblocking. A nonblocking switch is one in which the number of output lines equals the number of input lines, so therefore data packets don't have to wait in the switch before being sent to their destination. A switch that isn't nonblocking can cause delays in packet transmission while the packet waits in a queue for access to one of the output ports.

Which Switch?

With at least 40 Ethernet and 15 Token Ring switches on the market—and more coming—selecting the right one for your network can be an arduous task. Obviously, you want the device that delivers the best cost of ownership/performance. But price lists, raw performance numbers, and features specifications reveal only half of the story. The other half—determining what it will take to configure, optimize, and manage the devices—is difficult to extract. It may seem as though you are doomed to evaluate every switch on the market. Fortunately, there's a much easier way.

Every LAN switch employs one of three basic architectures:

▼ Shared memory/CPU

■ Matrix

▲ Bus

The design you use generally determines the overall manageability, functionality, and scalability the device will provide. By understanding the benefits and limitations of each, you can get an idea which switch will meet the needs of your particular network and what it will cost to own it.

Hardware vs. Software

All switches manufactured to date are based on either software or hardware implementations. Hardware switching breaks down further into matrix and bus switching. The hardware switches generally offer faster performance; software switches usually offer greater manageability. Keep in mind, however, that this generalization doesn't hold true in every case.

Software switching, which is implemented in switches such as Alantec Corp.'s PowerHub and 3Com Corp.'s LANplex, works like this: A packet enters the software switch, where it is synchronized, converted from serial to parallel, and examined for address information. Once in parallel format, it is written cyclicly to fast memory. The switch searches its address table to find the destination address and establish the switched connection. Once the switched connection has been established, the packet is read from memory, reconverted from parallel to serial format, and transmitted via the switched connection, as shown in Figure 16-20.

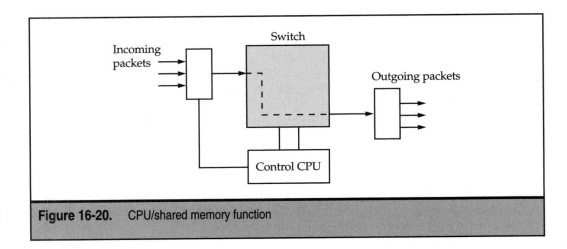

Figure 16-20.   CPU/shared memory function

If this sounds familiar, it should: Software switches are actually based on router technology (as we discussed earlier in this chapter) that has been optimized for frame switching.

One of the main benefits of this legacy is that software switches are founded on tried-and-true technology. One of the main drawbacks is that—just as with many routers—there may be considerable up-front configuration work. But if you and your staff are versed in router configuration, you'll probably find software switch setup a snap.

Because of its roots in routing, software switching is also a very flexible architecture; it can ease the integration of switching and routing for networks that need both functions. But software switching does have its caveats. Because all the switching is handled by the CPU and memory, software switching often doesn't scale well, and performance can drop significantly as you add stations and management features.

Buyer Beware

It's easy to understand why the CPU gets bogged down. It handles not only switching, but also all the garden-variety processor activities such as servicing interrupt requests and performing packet housekeeping tasks. In addition, every feature you add will pull CPU cycles, so the more you ask software-based switches to do, the more inconsistent their performance will be.

If you have a multiprotocol network or are interested in implementing virtual LANs, for example, software-based switching will get expensive in terms of performance, management, and help-desk calls. Both protocol translation and virtual networking weigh heavily on a software switch.

Software switching also tends to have difficulty handling broadcasts. This is because broadcast frames have to be placed in all output buffers, not just in one central location, which puts an additional strain on the CPU. And because a CPU can't multitask, broadcasts are not handled simultaneously.

Finally, the software-based switch offers a single point of failure in both the CPU and the shared memory.

The Hard Facts

Hardware-based switches, on the other hand, resemble bridges, operating primarily on the MAC layer. Unlike software switches, they receive, buffer, and transmit packets without involving the CPU. However, the two types of hardware switches—matrix and bus—accomplish this function by very different means.

Matrix switches, also called "crossbar" switches, are based on a point-to-point matrix. This straightforward, hardware-based switch fabric sets up connections between MAC addresses in very much the same way as old electromagnetic voice switches set up connections between telephones.

In essence, a frame enters the input port, travels down the matrix until it finds the "intersection" for the correct output address, then proceeds through that output port. Such switches, like Kalpana Inc.'s Etherswitch and NetWiz Ltd.'s TurboSwitch, are fast and easy to implement because the switching function requires no software configuration, as shown in Figure 16-21.

Matrix switching is implemented in one of three architectures:

▼ A concentrator, which has more input lines than output lines, so outgoing packets are queued

■ An expansion switch, which has more output lines than input lines, so incoming packets may be queued for access to output ports

▲ A nonblocking switch, in which the number of incoming lines equals the number of outgoing lines

The biggest drawback of a matrix switch is that its effective size is limited. It can only support a static configuration of the number of incoming ports multiplied by the number of outgoing ports, and nonblocking service is limited to the number of incoming ports squared.

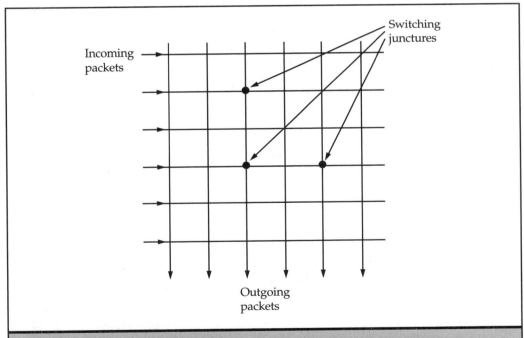

Figure 16-21. Matrix switch functionality

A variation of the matrix switch, known as the knockout switch, is shown in Figure 16-22. A knockout switch works just like any other matrix switch, with input ports being connected to output ports in standard crossbar fashion. However, a knockout switch also has a mechanism on each port for handling switch congestion. This mechanism places outgoing packets in a queue. Ordinarily, the packets leave the switch in the order in which they arrive. However, the knockout switch's congestion management mechanism can place high-priority packets at the beginning of the queue.

The performance of matrix switches is very consistent because they are not depending on a shared CPU to nail up and clear down the connections. Instead, each connection is made separately—and usually buffered separately—on the hardware matrix.

Matrix switches lend themselves to dynamic switching, whereby the switch connects two ports long enough to transmit a single packet and then clears down the connection. For its duration, the connection has the full 10Mbps bandwidth rather than having to share the bandwidth with the rest of the devices on the segment. The switch can support several such port-to-port connections simultaneously.

Matrix switches are also usually very fast because, if properly buffered, they tend to be nonblocking as a result of their one-to-one nature of input frames to output frames.

The difficulties with matrix switches, however, can also be attributed to their one-to-one design. Adding ports, for instance, can be complicated. Inputs must equal

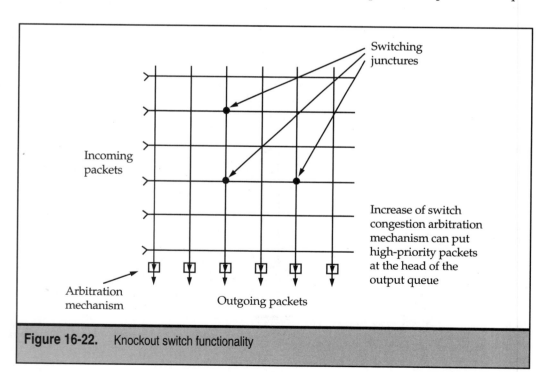

Figure 16-22. Knockout switch functionality

outputs, which makes it difficult—but not impossible—for vendors to integrate a "fat pipe," or higher bandwidth connection, into a matrix switch.

Management is also an issue with matrix switches—you can monitor only one connection at a time. So, monitoring everything that is happening in the switch is out of the question because there is no central point from which you can see all traffic.

Catching the Bus

Bus-architecture switches, such as LANNET Inc.'s MultiNet LET series and ONET Data Communication Technologies Inc.'s LANBooster series, employ a central bus on the backplane, over which all the traffic on the switch travels. (See Figure 16-23.)

By using time-division multiplexing, either statistical or static, the switch gives each port its own turn to send a packet on the bus. Because the time slot is fixed, known, and predictable, this design provides consistent performance under varying loads.

The bus architecture also makes bus switches a good choice for switching both asynchronous and isochronous protocols. The design handles one-to-many and many-to-one transmissions more elegantly than the matrix switch's inherent point-to-point orientation. And expanding the switch is relatively easy because inputs don't have to equal outputs. Finally, a central bus provides a somewhat more convenient vehicle for protocol translation than a matrix.

The bus architecture is also quite manageable. Having one central point over which all the traffic must flow lets you monitor all switch traffic simultaneously, and you can control

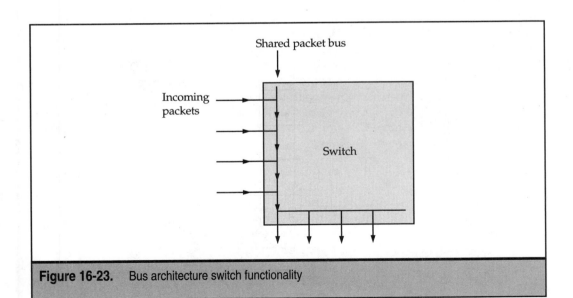

Figure 16-23. Bus architecture switch functionality

ports with signals on the central bus. So, if being able to see and manage all the traffic on the switch simultaneously is important, the bus architecture is the only way to go.

But bus switches also have a few drawbacks. They tend to be expensive, so brace yourself for sticker shock, especially when you purchase their management packages. And configuring and optimizing them can be overwhelming. By design, the bus architecture lends itself to static switching, in which ports maintain segment assignments until they are manually changed by the network administrator. Allocating the staff time to balancing and reassigning segment assignments can be expensive. On the other hand, it does let you fine-tune your network to peak performance—if you have the time.

Analysis Is Key

Armed with a working knowledge of software and bus and matrix hardware architectures, you can determine which design will be best suited to your network. Your network's unique traffic patterns and management needs, the expertise and size of your staff, along with your budget, will all play a significant role in your decision. The next thing to consider in evaluating switches is the specific measurements of their performance.

Measures of Switch Performance

Switches have their own criteria for measuring performance. To help you select the right switch for your network, we've included a description of the four major measures of switch performance.

FORWARDING RATE   As we mentioned, forwarding rate is the rate at which the switch can transmit traffic from one port to another, expressed in packets per second. Because 10Base-T transmits 64-byte packets at a maximum rate of 14,880 packets per second, this is known as wire speed for 10Base-T.

Switches have two different measurements for forwarding rate. The first, port-to-port forwarding rate, is the forwarding rate sustainable between two ports. The second is total forwarding rate, which is the maximum rate at which packets are transmitted through the network and received by destination ports. Total forwarding bandwidth, expressed in packets per second, is equal to or less than the number of virtual connections multiplied by the wire speed.

PACKET LOSS   Packet loss is the total number of packets transmitted at full wire speed minus the number of packets received by the destination station. Packet loss is an indication of how a switch handles excessive traffic at wire speeds. If the switch starts discarding packets when its buffers fill, it obviously isn't handling the heavy traffic very well. Therefore, high packet loss means the switch isn't adept at handling heavy traffic, whereas low packet loss means that the switch has implemented mechanisms for accommodating heavy traffic successfully.

Switches that have low packet loss generally have implemented one or a combination of two congestion management techniques. These switches either have huge packet buffers to hold incoming data packets until they can be processed, or they have a mechanism that, when the switch becomes overwhelmed, sends a jamming signal to transmitting ports preventing them from continuing packet transmission until the congestion has cleared.

LATENCY   This is the time it takes a packet to travel through the switch from the time it is received on the source port to the time it is transmitted on the destination port. Latency is affected by the forwarding operation of the switch itself.

In store-and-forward operation, the switch receives the whole frame before it forwards it to its destination. Once the whole frame has been received, the switch can perform error checking to ensure that it is not truncated or corrupted before sending it on.

In cut-through operation, the switch begins forwarding a packet after it receives the first 6 bytes of the packet—that is, just as soon as the destination address can be detected. This type of cut-through operation has no error checking, so some vendors—most notably Grand Junction (now a part of Cisco)—have implemented what they call FragmentFree operation. In FragmentFree mode, the switch begins forwarding a packet after the first 64 bytes have been received. Because most packet errors are resolved within the first 64 bytes—and because the 64 bytes is the smallest supported 10Base-T packet size—FragmentFree operation is a reasonable compromise between store-and-forward and cut-through operations.

Lack of error checking is not the only weakness of cut-through operation, though. Cut-through can only be used when you're switching data between two networks of the same speed. If you're switching from networks of different speeds, you cannot start transmitting a frame until you've got a complete frame ready to transmit. Therefore, any switch that is moving data between a low-speed interface and a high-speed interface must use store and forward. Also, cut-through may not necessarily provide a significant performance increase, because some protocols already handle small delays well enough to eliminate the advantage. For example, packet burst protocols are designed to allow for small delays, and therefore some latency within a switch will not decrease performance.

In the last year, many switch vendors have begun offering what they call adaptive cut-through operation as a compromise between store-and-forward and cut-through switch operations. In adaptive cut-through operation, the switch functions in cut-through mode, forwarding packets as soon as it receives the first 6 bytes of the packet. However, the switch monitors packet retransmissions, and if packet retransmissions exceed a certain threshold, the switch assumes this is due to packet errors and begins operating in store-and-forward mode. The switch will continue operating in store-and-forward mode, checking all incoming packets for errors before forwarding them, until the packet error rate has dropped below another predefined threshold. The switch then begins functioning in cut-through mode again.

Latency indicates how efficient the switch is handling traffic. The higher the latency, the more likely the switch may become a bottleneck. However, latency numbers are all so low—they're measured in microseconds—that the chances of the switch itself causing traffic jams are very unlikely.

THROUGHPUT　Throughput is the maximum number of packets generated and received with no packet loss. To test throughput, we sent Ethernet packets through the switching hubs at wire-speed, then we slowed the transmission rate until the hub forwarded all the data without dropping packets.

This measure will tell you what kind of performance you can expect when your switch is operating at full capacity. The higher the throughput number, the better the switch handles a full load, with fewer dropped packets resulting in retransmissions— and therefore, theoretically, lower response times.

10/100/1000 Switching

Sometimes switching alone isn't enough to speed up your network. Luckily, many switches available today offer a combination of high-speed network segments and switching, as shown in Figure 16-24.

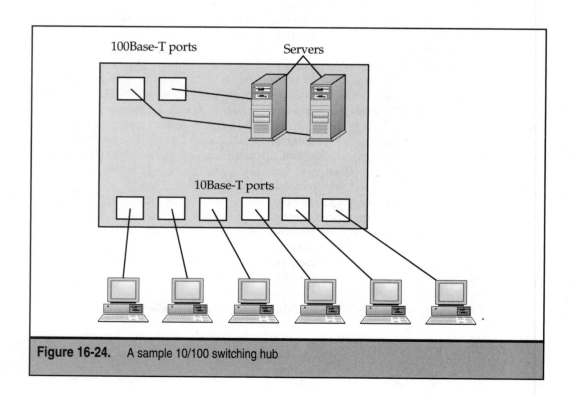

Figure 16-24.　A sample 10/100 switching hub

Candidates for 10/100/1000 Switching

So where are the places that will best benefit from combinations of high-speed switching? Here are a few places to consider:

▼ **Backbones and server farms** A single user might be happy with dedicated 10Mbps, but a server simply can't be. High-performance servers quickly saturate 10Mbps networks. Installing switched 10Mbps workgroup switches didn't really eliminate the performance bottleneck—all those users transmitting at the full 10Mbps have simply moved the bottleneck to the backbone.

▲ **Power workgroups** Even workstations are demanding a piece of the action. Those fast CPUs sitting on the desktop are processing more data and thus generating more traffic between desktop and server.

The essence of the 10/100 switching strategy is to increase bandwidth from the wiring closet to the server, leaving 10Mbps in place between the desktop and closet. The 10/100 "combination" switching approach has several advantages. Even if you aren't using Category 5 cable throughout your site, you can still take advantage of the 10/100 solution without having to pull new cable everywhere. You don't have to replace the Ethernet adapters in the workstations. You have an easy upgrade path to a total 100Mbps protocol. If you think that 10Mbps is all you will need at the desktop for the time being, 10/100 switching lets you get all the performance you need, where you need it, without having to pay for high bandwidth where you don't need it.

FULL-DUPLEX PROTOCOLS

Anyone who is tracking down high-speed network solutions should be aware of Full-Duplex Ethernet. To explain how it works, we first have to look at the architecture of 10Mbps Ethernet.

There are two pairs of wires in star-wired 10Base-T and 100Base-T environments—one for transmitting and one for receiving. However, transmission and receipt cannot take place at the same time. Full-Duplex Ethernet, on the other hand, allows transmission over one pair of wires and receipt over the other pair simultaneously, providing nearly full utilization of both pairs and thus sustainable high data rates. By installing MAC devices that support Full-Duplex Ethernet, you can double the effective bandwidth. Full-Duplex Ethernet can coexist with normal half-duplex Ethernet and make use of the existing 10Base-T wiring.

As attractive as it sounds, Full-Duplex Ethernet has a couple of serious drawbacks. The first is that it requires an investment in NICs, hubs, switches, and firmware and driver upgrades that support Full-Duplex operation. This can be very expensive. The second drawback is that it makes sense only in a few situations. Specifically, this protocol is effective only in point-to-point connections, and then only when there is traffic available to flow in both directions at the same time. Still, in backbone implementations where there is a great deal of traffic among servers, Full-Duplex Ethernet is a technology that may be worth considering to make maximum use of the bandwidth available.

A TIME FOR EVERYTHING

Each of these alternatives to high-speed networking has its place. The trick is knowing how to find that place. Here are a few rules of thumb to help you design your "alternative network."

Bridging

If your network is small and/or centrally located, segmentation with bridges is usually sufficient to improve performance.

Routing

Connecting more than a dozen segments with bridges can introduce excessive internetwork traffic, addressing complexity, and resulting endless looping problems—not to mention network management headaches. In such situations, you're well advised to consider using routers. As well, when your large internetwork includes wide area links—or multiple transport protocols such as 10Base-T, Token Ring, and perhaps even a high-speed backbone—routers are probably your best bet. Furthermore, when efficiency and economy of packet transmission are very important, such as when dealing with high-priority, high-security, and/or time-sensitive traffic, routers are definitely the choice.

Switching

Switching has become so inexpensive over the last few months that it now makes sense to weigh the relative cost of switching any time you are considering bridging. Switches offer more speed, more security, and often more manageability than bridges, so weigh these factors into your "to bridge or to switch" decision.

Switching may also be a reasonable alternative to routing, because switching offers high security and fast performance just like a router. However, if you must support multiple protocols and/or wide area traffic, routing is probably still the best choice—for now.

Virtual LANs

Virtual LANs can really be implemented as a complement to bridging, routing, and switching. While it promises "on the fly" resegmenting, remember that virtual LAN packages are often expensive and require a great deal of training for network managers to become comfortable with them. Therefore, currently, virtual LANs may be best deployed in large, widely dispersed networks, where their quick-response reconfiguration and remote access capabilities will offer a quick return on investment.

PART IV

The 'Nets

CHAPTER 17

Intranets and Extranets

Ｉf you listen to the buzz, you've probably heard that if you aren't running an intranet, you're not even in the networking game. And extranets are *the only way* to do business outside your enterprise. This may have many of you a little concerned. After all, what is this magical thing called an intranet that separates the players from the spectators in the networking arena?

INTRANETS DEMYSTIFIED

Despite all the hype and mystery surrounding the term, an *intranet* is just a network. It's the *type of traffic* that runs over it that makes it different. An intranet is a local network that runs TCP/IP and other Internet-related protocols. An intranet also features Web servers to publish content and allow access to back-end systems. The client interface for an intranet is a Web browser, and its mail system is Internet Mail. In other words, an intranet is a local network that supports Internet protocols and network, messaging, and application protocols.

What an intranet offers is a cross-platform, open architecture with great interoperability for UNIX, Macintosh, and Windows clients. It lets you develop new applications and systems quickly and at a relatively low cost. Properly designed, they can provide real-time multimedia, such as videoconferencing and live voice conversations. What it doesn't offer is magic.

Making New Rules

So, if an intranet is defined by the type of data traffic and the applications deployed on servers throughout the network, rather than the design of the network infrastructure, why all the fear and trepidation over the network design? Well, intranets have brought about two changes that have a big impact on physical network design:

▼   Increased internetwork traffic

▲   Increased bandwidth requirements

Increased Internetwork Traffic

The old 80/20 rule of networking has been turned inside out. When local area networks first emerged, 80 percent of all data traffic was local. In other words, almost all traffic was delivered to the same segment on which it was delivered. The advent of intranets has changed that, so that now at most 20 percent of data traffic is addressed to nodes on the same segment on which it originated.

Caution:
Network Architect At Work

How do you design a network? Literally from the ground up! A network architect takes a "layered" approach, based on the protocols established in the seven-layer International Standards Organization's Open Systems Interconnection model.

Over the next few pages, we'll show you how a network designer plans each layer of the network, starting with the physical layer and ending with the application layer. The result is a complete network diagram like the one shown on the next two pages.

Note that the network architect builds the network in the reverse order that the network is conceived. As outlined in Part I, the first thing a business must do is determine what it wants the network to do. That means selecting the appropriate applications. Then it works down the OSI model from the application layer to the physical layer. Once these conceptual decisions are made, the network architect builds the network, beginning with the physical layer and working up to the application layer.

We'll use the following diagram as the basis for illustrating the type of planning that takes place at each layer of the OSI model.

How do you design a network from the ground up? We'll use this diagram as the basis for illustrating the type of planning that takes place at each layer of the OSI model.

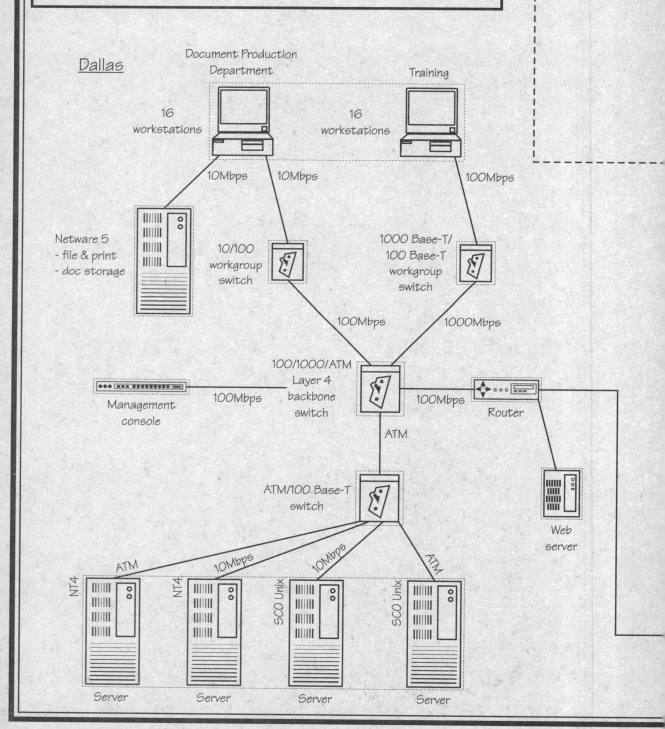

Dallas

Document Production Department

Training

16 workstations

16 workstations

10Mbps

10Mbps

100Mbps

Netware 5
- file & print
- doc storage

10/100 workgroup switch

1000 Base-T/ 100 Base-T workgroup switch

100Mbps

1000Mbps

100/1000/ATM Layer 4 backbone switch

Management console

100Mbps

100Mbps

Router

ATM

ATM/100 Base-T switch

Web server

NT4

ATM

NT4

10Mbps

SCO Unix

10Mbps

SCO Unix

ATM

Server

Server

Server

Server

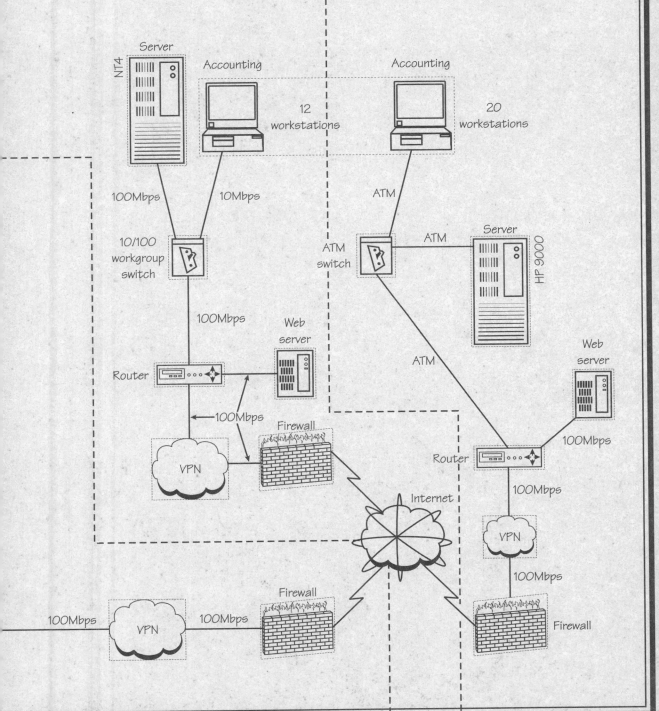

Chicago

New York

Server
NT4

Accounting

Accounting

12
workstations

20
workstations

100Mbps

10Mbps

ATM

10/100
workgroup
switch

ATM
switch

ATM

Server
HP 9000

100Mbps

Web
server

Router

Web
server

100Mbps

100Mbps

Firewall

Internet

Router

100Mbps

VPN

VPN

100Mbps

100Mbps

VPN

100Mbps

Firewall

Firewall

Layer One — The Physical Layer

Application
Presentation
Session
Transport
Network
Data Link
Physical

Specifies:
- Network span
- Cable type
- Segment Lengths
- Punchdown blocks
- Patch cables
- Electrical signaling
- Connectors
- Pinouts

Guidelines available:
- ANSI
- EIA/TIA

When planning the physical layer interface, the network architect specifies cable type, connectors, and maximum cable lengths. When wiring is planned, a site planning survey should be completed that considers wiring routes, communication closets, and telco demarcation points.

See Chapter 16 for detailed information.

 For fiber runs between buildings, you will need to consider available conduit and subduct space. A careful review of manholes, maps, and utility routes for overload or underground fiber runs should be made.

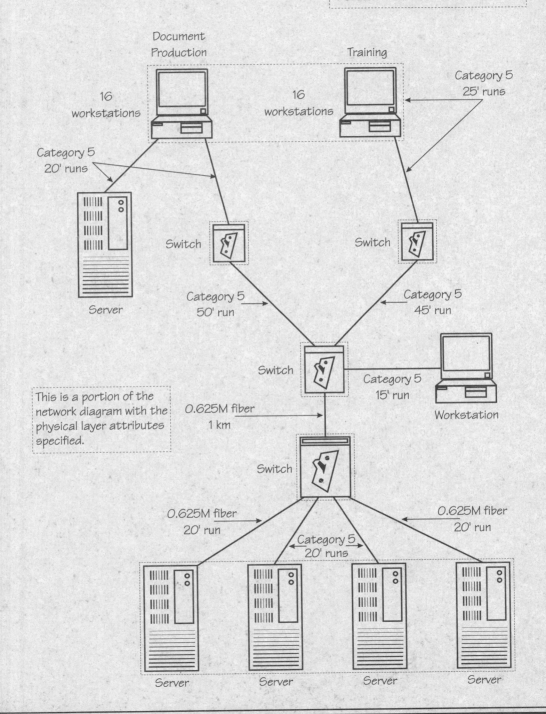

Notes:
- Category 5 four-pair terminated
- RJ-45 connectors and wall plates
- 0.625 micron SC connectors

Document
Production

Training

16
workstations

16
workstations

Category 5
25' runs

Category 5
20' runs

Server

Switch

Switch

Category 5
50' run

Category 5
45' run

Switch

Category 5
15' run

Workstation

This is a portion of the
network diagram with the
physical layer attributes
specified.

0.625M fiber
1 km

Switch

0.625M fiber
20' run

Category 5
20' runs

0.625M fiber
20' run

Server

Server

Server

Server

Layer Two — The Data-Link Layer

Application	
Presentation	**Specifies:**
Session	• Access method
Transport	-CSMA/CD
Network	-Token Ring
Data-Link	-Token bus
Physical	-Polling

Specifies:
- Access method
  - CSMA/CD
  - Token Ring
  - Token bus
  - Polling
- Media Access Control addresses
- Media Access Control devices
  - Hubs
  - Switches
  - Network interface cards

When planning data-link layer design, the network architect speicifies the access method (Carrier Sense Mulitple Access/ Collision Detection, Token Ring, etc.) and the Media Access Control addresses of the devices connected to the network. The network designer also determines which MAC layer devices — network interface cards, switches, and hubs — will be used in the network.

 Planning for MAN, FDDI, or Ethernet connectivity should also be completed at this layer.

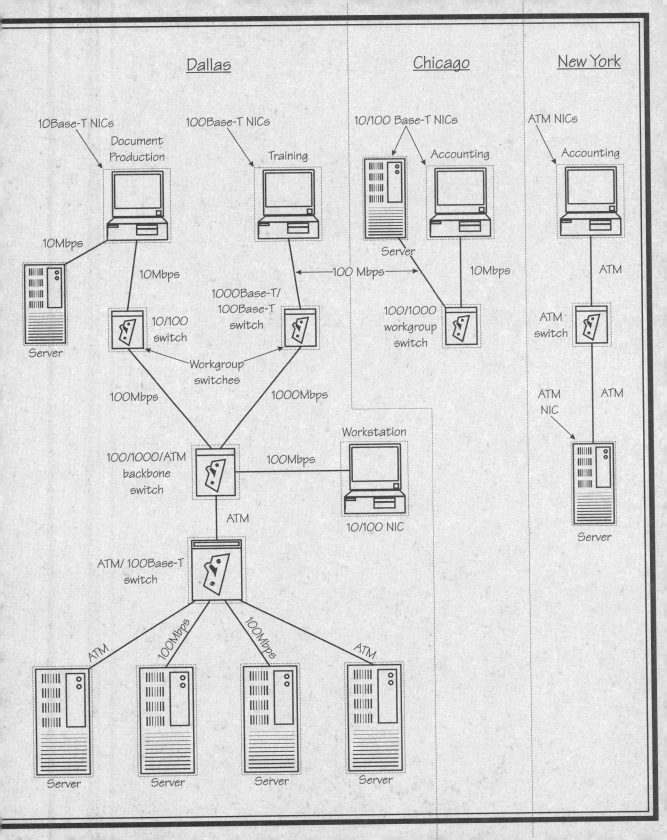

Layer Three — The Network Layer

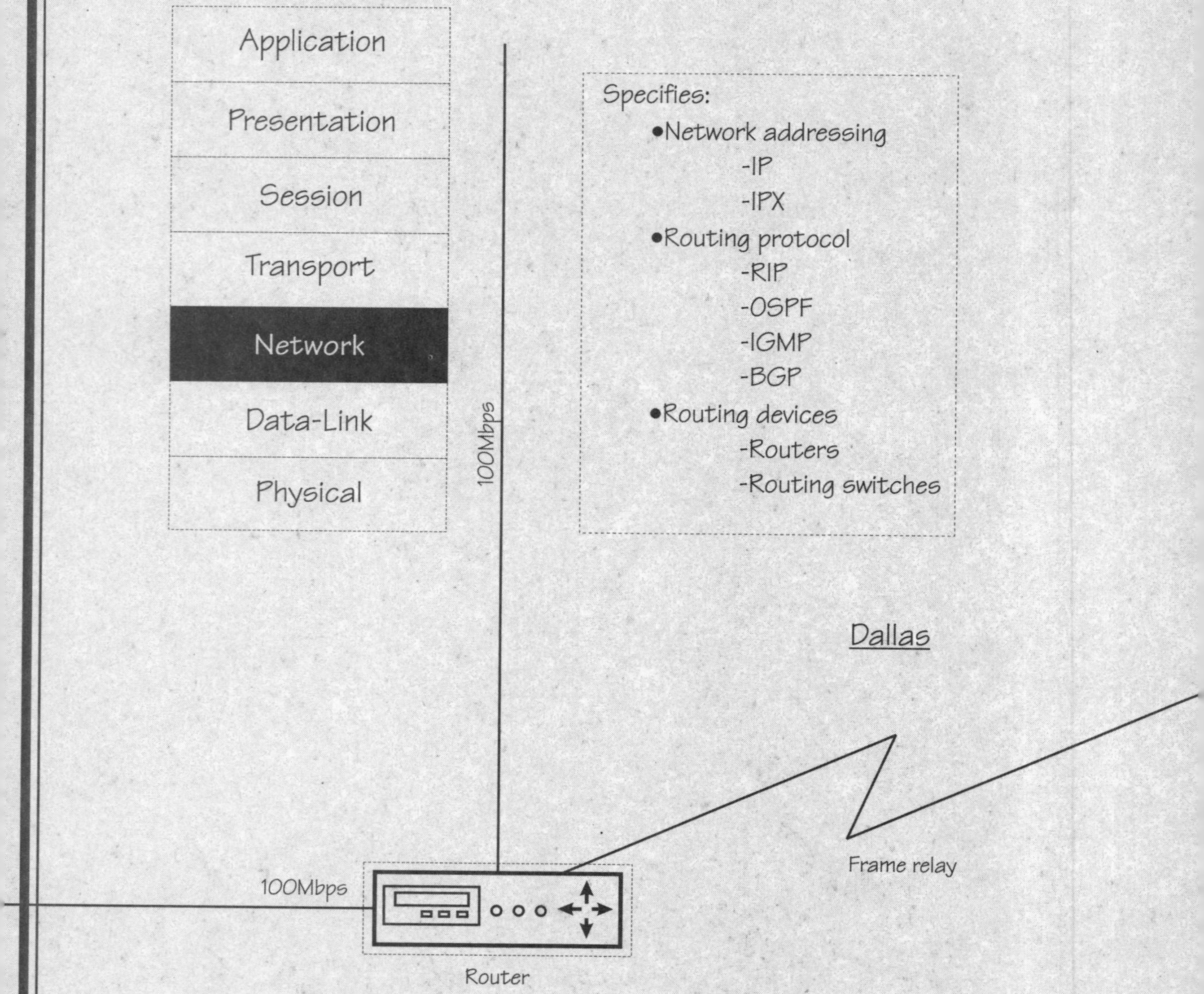

Application
Presentation
Session
Transport
Network
Data-Link
Physical

100Mbps

Specifies:
- Network addressing
  - IP
  - IPX
- Routing protocol
  - RIP
  - OSPF
  - IGMP
  - BGP
- Routing devices
  - Routers
  - Routing switches

<u>Dallas</u>

Frame relay

100Mbps

Router

At layer 3, the network architect designs the routing scheme. The architect develops a network addressing scheme — most commonly using Internet Protocol (IP) addressing — and specifies the types and locations of routers.

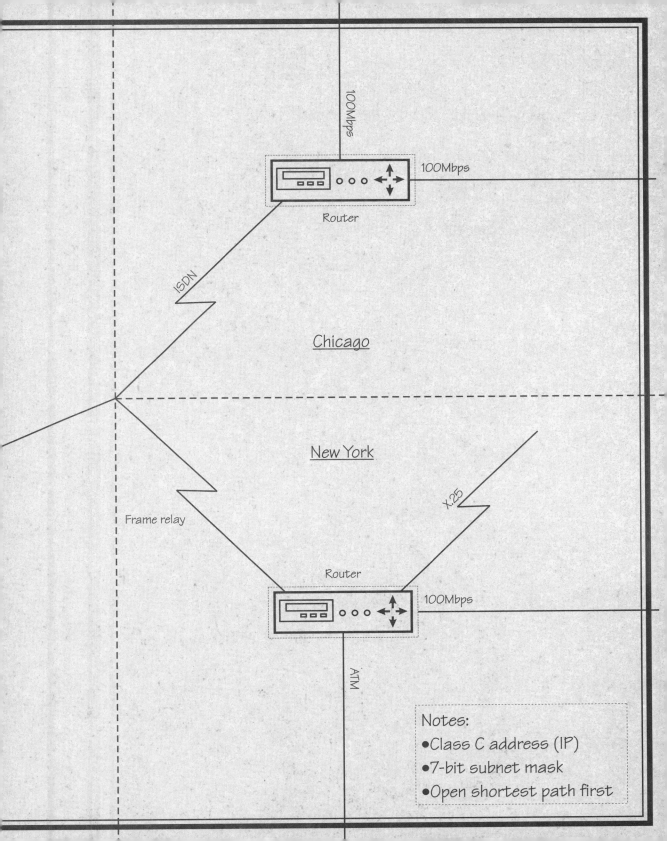

Layer Four — The Transport Layer

Application
Presentation
Session
Transport
Network
Data Link
Physical

Specifies:
- Transport protocol
  - TCP
  - UDP
- Application support for transport protocol
- Operating environment support for transport
- Device support for transport protocol
  - Layer 4 switch
  - routers

At the transport layer, the network designer plans for the requirements that different types of data transmission have for reliable delivery. The designer also specifies the network devices and platforms, such as layer 4 switches, that support the transport protocols used.

 See Chapters 11 and 17 for more on the transport layer.

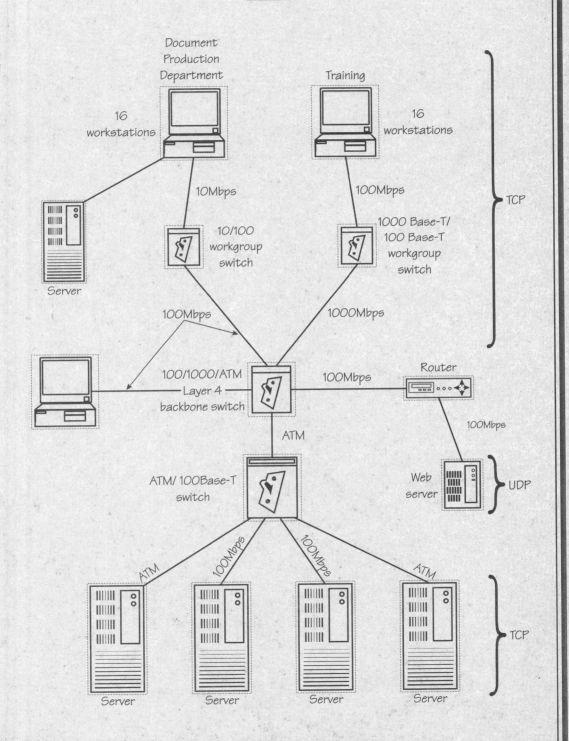

Dallas

Document
Production
Department

Training

16
workstations

16
workstations

TCP

10Mbps

100Mbps

10/100
workgroup
switch

1000 Base-T/
100 Base-T
workgroup
switch

Server

100Mbps

1000Mbps

100/1000/ATM
Layer 4
backbone switch

100Mbps

Router

ATM

100Mbps

ATM/ 100Base-T
switch

Web
server

UDP

ATM

100Mbps

100Mbps

ATM

Server

Server

Server

Server

TCP

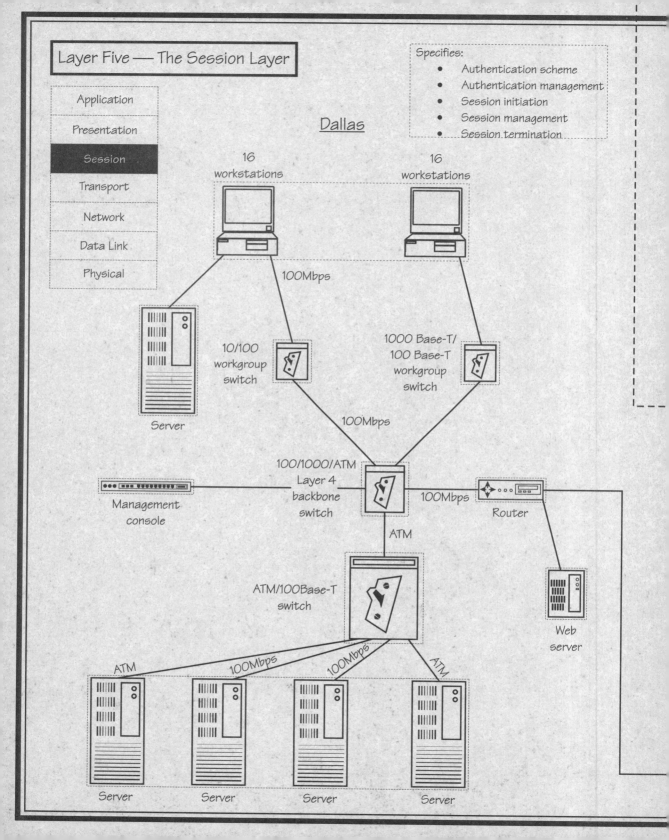

Layer Five — The Session Layer

Application
Presentation
Session
Transport
Network
Data Link
Physical

Specifies:
- Authentication scheme
- Authentication management
- Session initiation
- Session management
- Session termination

Dallas

16 workstations

16 workstations

100Mbps

Server

10/100 workgroup switch

1000 Base-T/ 100 Base-T workgroup switch

100Mbps

100/1000/ATM Layer 4 backbone switch

Management console

100Mbps

Router

ATM

ATM/100Base-T switch

Web server

ATM

100Mbps

100Mbps

ATM

Server

Server

Server

Server

In the session layer, the network designer specifies authentication routines run to ensure only authorized systems and users can access network resources. At the same time, it's important to plan and implement the security and management systems, including virtual private networks, firewalls, and security software.

See Chapters 12, 22, 23, and 24.

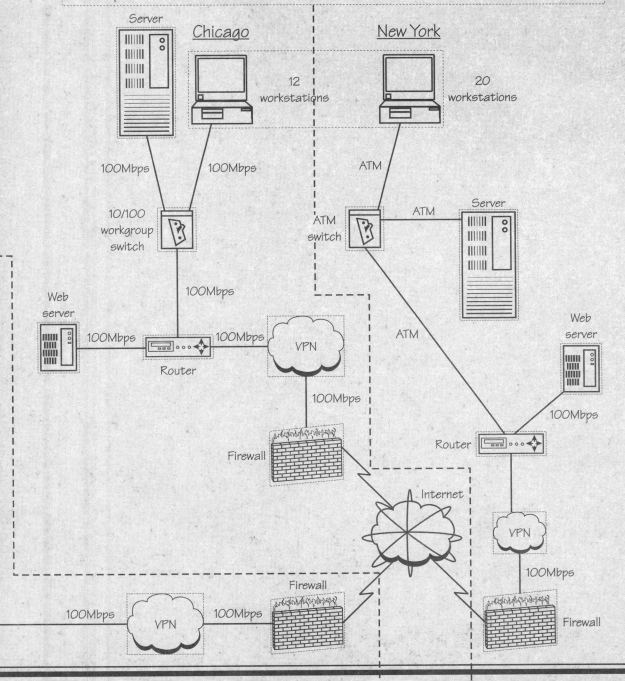

Layer Six — The Presentation Layer

Application
Presentation
Session
Transport
Network
Data-Link
Physical

Specifies:
- Transfer syntax
- Context
- Context management
- Data formatting
- Data translation

When designing the network at the presentation layer, the network manager determines the nodes that will need to communicate with each other and selects operating systems and gateway software that can interoperate.

See Chapter 10.

 This layer also provides for the representation of information that is communicated between or referred to by application processors.

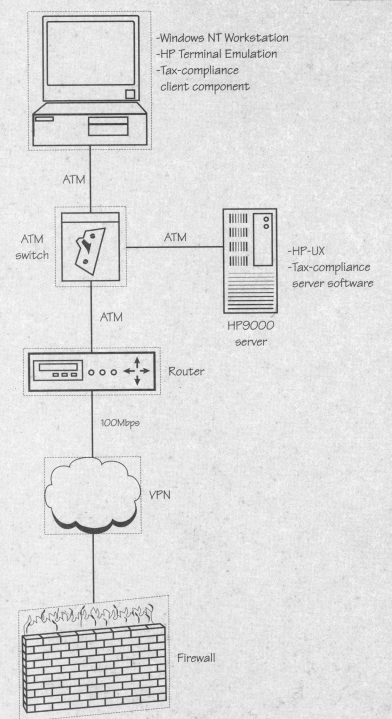

-Windows NT Workstation
-HP Terminal Emulation
-Tax-compliance
 client component

ATM

ATM
switch

ATM

-HP-UX
-Tax-compliance
 server software

HP9000
server

ATM

Router

100Mbps

VPN

Firewall

Layer Seven — The Application Layer

Application
Presentation
Session
Transport
Network
Data Link
Physical

Specifies:
- Applications
- Network file access for applications
- Network file transfer for applications
- Printer services for applications
- Application resource sharing
- User interface

When designing the application layer, the network architect selects the applications that meet the business needs of individual users and the enterprise as a whole.

Document
Production
Department
    Microsoft Excel
    WordPerfect
    Netscape Navigator

Accounting
    Microsoft Excel
    WordPerfect
    Netscape Navigator
    SAP

Training
IP/TV (Precept Software, Inc.)
QuickTime
Microsoft Excel
WordPerfect
Netscape Navigator

Accountants
IP/TV
Microsoft Excel
WordPerfect
Netscape Navigator
Tax Preparation & Compliance
    Software (Custom)

Increased Bandwidth Requirements

Not only has the destination of traffic changed, but also the nature of the traffic itself. The underlying application technologies in intranets and the Internet require much more bandwidth than the simple print and file services of LANs of yore. Intranets have made such things as videoconferencing and live newsfeeds a minute-to-minute possibility. And this has spurred demand for even more real-time, rich-graphic, multimedia information.

What enabled this technical revolution? More important, how do you design a network to support it?

INTRANETS: ENABLING TECHNOLOGIES

To understand how these applications have started gobbling bandwidth, let's take a look at the technologies that make intranets what they are. Essentially, there are four technologies that enable an intranet environment:

▼   HTML

■   HTTP

■   Component technology

▲   Push

Hypertext Markup Language (HTML)

Hypertext Markup Language (HTML) is the programming language used on the Internet to create Web pages. *Hypertext* is nonlinear text. This means that it lets you jump to a pointer or another source of information simply by clicking on it, rather than requiring you to scroll sequentially through a document until you arrive at the information you want.

Again, there is nothing magical about HTML. An HTML file is just a simple text file with embedded codes that are stored on Web servers. Upon initial access to a Web site, the Web server sends the client a default or *home* Web page in the HTML format. This page may have no links, or it may contain links to other pages at the same or other Web sites.

Coding HTML files is as easy as using word processor. In fact, you can create one using nothing more than a simple text editor and a few HTML codes. The codes largely consist of formatting instructions and pointers to other sources of information. When you open the source code of a Web page, you see HTML code. The next time you're on the World Wide Web, go to your favorite Web page. Click on Source from the View menu of your browser. For example, Figure 17-1 shows the Osborne/McGraw-Hill home page.

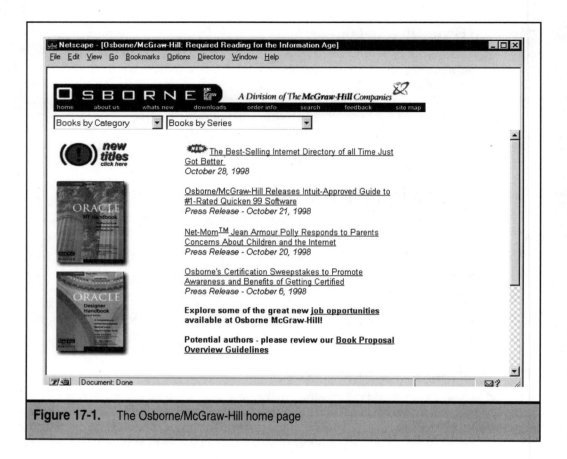

Figure 17-1.   The Osborne/McGraw-Hill home page

Figure 17-2 shows the source code for the same page.

The items enclosed in angle brackets are the embedded HTML codes, also known as *tags*. A tag marks the beginning of each format change. The end of a format change is indicated with a tag that contains a forward slash. For example, the title format of the page begins with <TITLE> and ends with </TITLE>.

Try this yourself. Type the following in a text editor or processor, then open it with any Web browser:

<HTML>

<HEAD>

<TITLE> *Your Name* **Home Page</TITLE>**

</HEAD>

```
<html>
<head>
<title>Osborne/McGraw-Hill: Required Reading for the Information Age</title>
</head>


<Frameset Rows="100, *" frameborder="no" border=0>


<FRAME SRC="topnav.html" name="topnav" scrolling="NO" NORESIZE border=0>

<Frame src="splash.htm" name="content" noresize border=0>

</Frameset>


<NOFRAME> This web site requires Netscape 2.0 or better or a similar frames
compatible browser. Please <A HREF="http://home.netscape.com">download the
newest version of Netscape</a>to view these documents.</Noframe>



</html>
```

Figure 17-2.   Source code for the Osborne/McGraw-Hill home page

<BODY>

<H1> Meet *Your Name*</H1>

You've probably always wanted to know someone like me, and now's your chance.

</BODY>

</HTML>

Of course, there are many development tools available for coding HTML documents. However, the principle is the same. Once you have created the text file with embedded codes and saved it, you can open it and view it with a Web browser.

HTML Access and Network Performance

So what's so dangerous about an HTML file? After all, text files with a few codes should pose no threat to a gigabit backbone! Well, HTML files, which have the filename extension HTML or HTM, can display far more than text. They can contain sound, images, and/or other multimedia objects. And to further stress network traffic, these objects are not stored in the document itself. Rather, the HTML document contains a pointer or reference to an image or sound clip or other multimedia object. These objects can reside in the same directory as the HTML document or in a different directory, or even on an entirely different server! When a user accesses the HTML document, the pointer also pulls up the file containing the multimedia object.

So, an HTML page is much more than just a text file with some embedded codes. It is comprised of the HTML file as well as any external files containing multimedia objects—provided, of course, that the servers containing these objects are all online and accessible. This mean that servers containing HTML documents—especially heavily accessed ones—should be connected with a switched mesh of high-bandwidth connections.

HTML Developments and Extensions

While many organizations are working to refine and develop HTML, Microsoft and Netscape—the two leading Web browser vendors—seem to lead the pack. Some recent improvements to HTML features are as follows:

▼ Scripts can automatically access related Web pages, thus taking strain off the Web server.

■ Dynamic HTML describes a combination of HTML, style sheets, and scripts that allow documents to be animated. The W3C is working to make sure vendor solutions are interoperable.

■ HTML Math displays complex mathematical and technical notations.

■ Web pages can be customized. With proper access, users can edit pages and save them on the original Web server.

▲ There is now support for international alphabets and multilingual Web pages.

Both companies have also developed their own proprietary "dynamic HTML." This extension of HTML combines scripts, style sheets, and *document animations*. The World Wide Web Consortium (also known as the W3C) is a standards body working to ensure that both companies' dynamic HTML are interoperable. To that end, the W3C has developed and put forth what it calls the Document Object Model platform. This allows scripts and routines to access and update the content and structure of documents automatically. It will also let these routines process information in the Web page and incorporate the results into the original page.

As you can see, these improvements will make HTML more functional, but may very well put more stress on your network as more and different types of multimedia objects are more easily available to Web pages. Therefore, it's important to stress that Web servers—especially popular ones—must be connected with the highest-capacity network links possible.

Hypertext Transfer Protocol (HTTP)

As we said earlier, intranets use Web technologies like the TCP/IP protocol to transport information between clients and servers. Intranet servers are repositories for HTML documents that can contain hyperlinks to other places in the same document, to other documents in the same directory, or to documents located on other servers. The protocol that lets a Web browser access a server to request HTML documents is known as *Hypertext Transfer Protocol* (HTTP). In short, HTML is the document formatting language for intranets, and HTTP is the command and control protocol that sets up communication between a client and a server and passes commands between the two.

To be more specific, HTTP processes hypermedia links among HTML documents and provides client/server communications on the intranet and on the Web. When a client points a Web browser to an IP address or server, the browser finds the address on the intranet and makes a connection to the designated Web server. First a lookup is performed at a Domain Name Server (DNS) that knows the server name and its IP address. This address is then returned to the browser, which then makes a connection to the server.

RFC 1945, which describes HTTP, sings its praises. " . . . the Hypertext Transfer Protocol (HTTP) is an application-level protocol with the . . . speed necessary for distributed, collaborative, hypermedia information systems. It is a generic, stateless, object-oriented protocol which can be used for many tasks, such as name servers and distributed object management system, through extension of its request methods (commands)."

Figure 17-3 shows how this works. When an intranet client requests information from a server, the server responds by sending HTML information to the client. When the information arrives at the client, its Web browser reads, formats, and displays the data. The connection between client and server is established by HTTP.

For heightened security, HTTP may establish the connection through Secure Sockets Layer (SSL), Secure HTTP (S-HTTP) protocol, or some other secure protocol. S-HTTP is a secure version of HTTP that provides more secure transactions between intranet clients and servers. For further security, the client and server can exchange encrypted information over a secure channel. We'll talk more about security, encryption, and secure channels later in this chapter.

The Evolution of HTTP

HTTP has evolved over the years. This is good news for intranet users, but can be bad news for network managers who have to keep response times low. We'll show you what we mean.

The original version of HTTP, first deployed in 1990, was called HTTP/0.9. It was a lean client/server protocol that provided basic data transfer functions. It was later replaced by version 1.0. Essentially, HTTP 1.0 supported MIME message formats, which could provide more information about the data being transferred between client and server. More data meant more traffic, and intranets started slowing down.

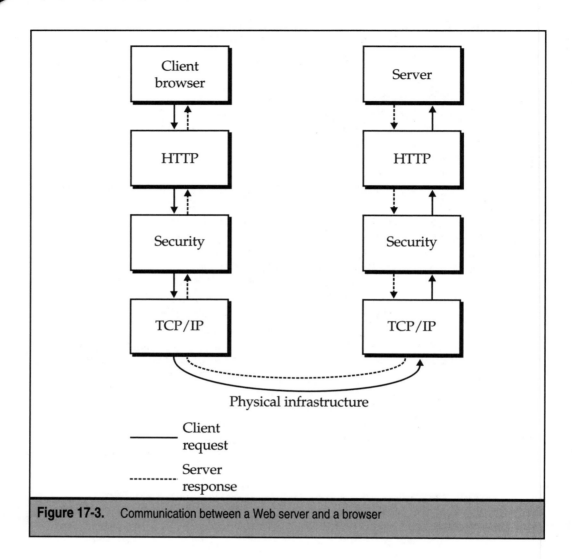

Figure 17-3. Communication between a Web server and a browser

HTTP1.1 AND S-HTTP (SECURE HTTP)   Web browsers and servers don't maintain persistent links during a session. This means that once the text of a page is transmitted from the server to the browser, the link is terminated. If the browser requests another object from the Web page, that object is downloaded as a separate transmission. In other words, each mouse click initiates a new, separate transmission. This means a lot of overhead in setting up and taking down links, which means a lot of traffic clogging up the intranet.

HTTP version 1.1 helps solve some of this by providing the capability for persistent connections and pipelining. This makes the connections between browsers and servers more streamlined and efficient. With HTTP 1.1, servers can transmit multiple objects to a client over a single TCP connection using larger packets. This reduces overhead. Furthermore, HTTP 1.1 allows a server to send more than one object in the course of a single connection.

This new version of HTTP also reduces network traffic by adding cache management to browsers. Under HTTP 1.0, when a browser refreshed a Web page, it downloaded the entire page. With HTTP 1.1, the browser compares the server page to the page it holds in cache. It identifies those items that have changed, and only downloads those items.

All these efficiency features reduce network traffic. In fact, HTTP 1.1 can improve network performance, in terms of number of packets and download times, by as much as 50 percent. Therefore, HTTP 1.1 is the choice for optimal intranet performance.

Component Technology

Component technology is *the* applications environment on intranets. In fact, a distributed computing environment such as an intranet is an ideal place to deploy component technology. In a component application environment, applications are split up into smaller components (also known as *objects* or *applets*), which are then distributed to users. These smaller components are easy to download and updated as needed. They also have an interface that allows programmers to combine them with one another to build complete applications. They are kept in sync with each other by *object request brokers* that coordinate the components throughout the network.

Component technology has a lot of advantages over traditional application development technology. For example:

▼ **Ease of enhancement**   You can add new components any time to enhance and expand application functions and features.

■ **Ease of updating**   Rather than updating an entire application, you can update only individual components.

■ **Shorter development cycles**   You can reuse existing code to build new applications, reducing development time.

▲ **Efficient use of resources**   Users don't have to install an entire application. They can install only the components they need. As well, by using standard languages like Java, you can combine components from different vendors to make new applications.

Component software has changed the face of most corporate intranets as well as the Internet. You can get components from Web sites to expand the functionality of enterprise applications and utilities, making it quick and easy to get the latest technology. More important, component technology makes it possible to design multitiered environments in which applications are broken up into different pieces that run on different computers and operating environments. For example, application services such as information retrieval, transaction monitoring, and application logic can run on different computing platforms, yet communicate across the network to present a unified application interface.

Component Development Languages

The two common development languages for component technology are Java, from Sun Microsystems, and ActiveX from Microsoft. The Web is chock full of components for both languages available for download. Some are simple components, such as three-dimensional spinning logo components. Others are more complex, such as financial or scientific calculation components. When you download a component to your Web browser, the component stays on your computer. It executes when you access the server containing the information it was designed to process. If the component ever needs to be updated, the new components are downloaded automatically the next time you access that server.

How the Pieces Fit Together

The component software development model consists of five pieces:

▼ Components
■ Containers
■ Scripts
■ Transaction monitors
▲ Object request brokers (ORBs)

COMPONENTS   Components are pieces of applications. More specifically, they are the programming code that makes up a piece of an application.

CONTAINERS   *Containers* are programming "shells" where components are assembled. The most popular containers are ActiveX for the ActiveX component development language and JavaBeans for the Java component development language. When a component is placed in a container, the component registers its interfaces so that other components within the same system know about it. Then, the component publishes its interfaces so that other objects know how to interact with it.

SCRIPTING LANGUAGES   Scripts are the languages in which component programmers write instructions that make components interact in a particular way. Again, the most popular scripting languages are ActiveX Script for the Active X component development environment and JavaScript for the Java component development environment.

TRANSACTION MONITORS   In transaction-based applications, such as financial applications, it's critical that the components are coordinated to ensure that the transaction is completed successfully. For example, transferring money from one account to another is a two-step transaction. First, funds are withdrawn from one account. Second, funds are deposited in the other account. Suppose that the first step is completed, but due to a network error the second is not. Unless the first step is "rolled back," there is no money in either account. Transaction monitoring systems keep track of such multipart transactions and ensure that failed transactions are returned to their original state.

An example of a transaction monitoring system is Microsoft's Transaction Server. It both processes and monitors transactions in a component application environment. Therefore, it operates as a transaction-based *object request broker*.

OBJECT REQUEST BROKERS (ORBS)   Components communicate with one another in object environments through *object request brokers* (ORBs). ORBs coordinate the registration, publishing, and execution of components, keeping them synchronized with one another across the network. An example of a common ORB is the one used in *Common Object Request Broker Architecture* (CORBA). CORBA is a cross platform architecture that allows components written for different operating environments to work together.

Push

Push technologies deliver information to network users without their specifically asking for it. This is a key technology for intranets, in which software must routinely be distributed to users' computers, or in which network users must regularly be informed of events.

NOTE: Traditional data transfer that takes place when a client requests information from another computer is called pull.

In the beginning, push was the means by which one computer sent information to a known network address even though no request for the information had come from that network address. Software distribution or regular data updates are examples of this original push technique. Now, however, push is best known as a Web technology that advertisers and news services use to provide information to their subscribers automatically without a specific request for that information.

Not All That Delivers Is Push

Here's how push technology works. Suppose a user, known as a *push client*, subscribes to a sports news service that employs push technology. This user wants an update every half-hour on the halftime and final scores of every basketball game being played in the United States. The sports news service will automatically send these scores to the user every 30 minutes.

But what appears to be push technology may not actually be so. Rather than having a push server initiate an update as server content changes and new information becomes available, these services have client software that actually initiates the communication by calling in unattended and requesting updated information in the users specified areas of interest.

Getting Pushy

Real push uses a technology called *IP multicast* to deliver information to subscribers. IP multicast assigns an IP Class D address, called a *multicast address*, to packets being sent out over the network. A Class D multicast address is 32 bits in length. The first 4 bits of the address identify it as a Class D address. The other 28 bits identify multicast groups.

Each multicast address defines a *channel* for broadcasting packets. A Class D address is something like a TV channel. When a host computer is assigned a Class D address, it is like selecting a particular channel on a TV set. The host computer receives packets being multicast by a particular source system or systems, just like a TV set receives signals from a particular TV station.

Host computers for subscribers that want to receive the information being broadcast are all assigned the same multicast address in conjunction with their regular, unique IP address. Once the multicast address is assigned to a computer, that computer has access to the multicast channel and can receive the information being sent over it. Host computers can be assigned more than one Class D multicast address, so they can therefore receive information from multiple channels. Host computers can join or leave multicast channels at any time. As well, any host computer can send to multicast channels by sending packets addressed to a multicast group.

Internet Group Management Protocol (IGMP)

Host computers subscribe to a multicast channel using the *Internet Group Management Protocol* (IGMP). This is a protocol that manages communication between subscribing host computers and their local multicast routers. Subscribing host computers use IGMP to tell local multicast routers that they want to subscribe to or leave a particular multicast group. If the subscribing host computer is the last device on that local network that is a member of the multicast group, it will remove itself from the multicast group, thus reducing network traffic.

Another traffic-reducing feature of IGMP is the *host membership report*. A multicast router periodically broadcasts a query to its local network asking if any nodes still want to receive multicast transmissions. Subscribing host computers respond to this query with a host membership report stating to which multicast groups they belong. If no subscribing host computers respond for a particular group, that group is dropped.

More Ways That Push Reduces Traffic

Note that multicast sends only one copy of the information being pushed, which all subscribing host computers receive. These packets only travel through routers that are connected to subscribers or to other routers that are designated to receive a particular multicast. Remember, routers must support *the* IGMP to transmit multicast packets. When a host computer transmits a multicast packet, the host computer's local router forwards the packet to multicast-enabled routers with attached networks that include members of the multicast group. This differs from broadcast technology, which sends a separate copy of the information to every host on the network. Clearly multicast reduces traffic over the intranet.

Push also reduces intranet traffic because the traffic resulting from requesting information is also eliminated. This is far more efficient than regular Web browsing, in which users cruise from Web site to Web site downloading pages. There is a flip side to this, however. As more users request frequent, regular delivery of information, network traffic will increase.

To avoid network resource crunches, you should carefully monitor how push technology uses your network's resources. Does everyone need to have football scores delivered every hour on the hour? How much of this pushed information is subsequently being stored on server hard drives? And is a steady flow of pushed information coming through the corporate firewall, choking out critical business traffic? Compression techniques can alleviate some of the traffic congestion. You can also configure push services to deliver only information that has changed, rather than entire Web pages. As well, whenever feasible, you may want to schedule push updates to take place during low-traffic periods.

EXTRANETS

Now that we've taken the mystery out of intranets and given you some pointers on how to keep their traffic running smoothly, let's move on to the next mysterious 'net: *extranets*.

An extranet is basically an intranet connected to the intranet of another organization. The two (or more) intranets may be connected via the Internet or a private network. That's it—again, there's no magic here.

But there *is* a lot work. Building an extranet requires a lot of planning coordination between the companies involved. Both partners must determine which data they will share, among which work groups, how they will share the data, and which applications they will use. Then, the companies must establish security to enforce these decisions.

There are two defining characteristics of extranets:

▼   Standard data exchange formats

▲   Security

Standard Data Exchange Formats

A *data exchange format* is simply a structured way of exchanging information. For example, companies that do business together need a standard means of exchanging order and billing information. To make sure that information flows smoothly between these companies, the format and structure of data such as purchase orders and invoices should adhere to mutually agreed upon standards. *Electronic data interchange* (EDI) is a widely used way of doing this, and it has been extended to work with Web technologies.

Another standard data exchange format is *Lightweight Directory Access Protocol* (LDAP). In practice, LDAP enables companies to exchange directory information in a standard manner. It is a directory service protocol designed on a client/server architecture that runs over Transport Control Protocol/Internet Protocol (TCP/IP). LDAP organizes information about a network object, called attributes, into records called entries. Attributes all have a type, which identifies what kind of object it is—such as an e-mail address or a compressed video file—and at least one value. In the example of an e-mail address, the value would be the actual e-mail address of the object. Each entry is identified by its *distinguished name* (DN).

All of this information is arranged in a hierarchical tree. The tree is built to represent geographical as well as organizational structure. For example, the object at the top of the LDAP tree is the country in which the object resides. Below that would be the state or enterprise in which the object resides. Below that might be the department or functional area. Below that would be the individual entry for the objects.

Because it is designed to run on a client/server model, the actual LDAP database can be located on one or more servers. When an LDAP client wants to find information on an object in the LDAP directory, it connects to an LDAP server and queries it. The server either replies by sending the client the requested information or sends the client a pointer to another server on which the requested data resides.

Security

After you have established the types of data you will share and the means by which you will share them, the workflow of your extranet is complete. But the extranet as a whole is far from being complete. Probably the most important, as well as the most complicated, task of building an extranet is designing and implementing its security. In effect, an extranet is a VPN, and a VPN is an extranet.

A VPN is simply a way to use the Internet instead of private, leased lines or POTS dial-up lines to extend network connectivity or remote access. While this has historically been done with standard ftp and telnet sessions, a VPN adds a few new and important elements to the mix: authentication, encryption, and tunneling (the encapsulation of data from any source or protocol within a TCP/IP data stream). This way, an e-mail transaction, data transfer, or remote session can be secure from prying eyes, something that isn't possible with standard ftp and telnet protocols.

Many firewall vendors, and all the major ones, were the first to jump on the VPN bandwagon, and with good reason. As the gatekeeper of your LAN, the firewall is the logical point on your network to perform encryption and authentication procedures, so insecure traffic never leaves the network. Firewall vendors also saw this as an excellent way to extend the functionality of what was then a rapidly maturing market with no place to go.

While this has forced the VPN market to mature rapidly, it has also confused the issue of when you need a firewall vs. when you need a VPN. To generate sales, vendors will automatically say you need both. While it's true that almost every VPN installation needs a firewall, the reverse is not always the case—even though your firewall may already have VPN features ready for you to activate.

To determine whether you need a VPN/extranet, and to familiarize yourself with the technologies that make up an extranet, it's a good idea to go back and reread that chapter.

THE LOCAL 'NETS

Hopefully we've dispelled the myths and mysteries of intranets and extranets. They are really just natural outgrowths of the technologies that have gone into the development of the father of all 'nets: the Internet. In the next chapter, we explore this phenomenon and how it does—or will—affect you local 'nets.

CHAPTER 18

The Internet

Get us on the 'net! This is probably one of the most frequent demands made of network managers today. But what does it really mean to "get on the 'net"? What exactly are your network users going to do once they get there? And what are the network design and management issues surrounding using the Internet? In other words, how will Internet usage affect your network?

A NETWORK IS A NETWORK

Despite the air of intimidation surrounding it, the Internet is just a network. Okay, it's the world's largest computer network, but it's still just a network. It consists of well over a million host nodes connecting tens of millions of users.

How It All Began

The Internet grew out of a project begun in the late 1960s by the Advanced Research Projects Agency (ARPA) of the Department of Defense. The goal of the project was to create a fault-tolerant computer network that could continue functioning even if one computer site were destroyed. Back then, this was quite a feat. After all, the old single-point-of-failure mainframe host-and-terminal model was just becoming widespread. Although computer sites could be fortified to withstand attack or calamity, all of the wires connecting the host computer to user terminals could not.

As well, the computers making up the network needed redundant connections. After all, a single wire was too easy a target, and made individual computers too vulnerable. Therefore, another goal of ARPA was a new computer network architecture that provided redundancy with relative economy.

The result was ARPAnet, as the first big network project was called, which explored new ways of creating a linked network. Stanford University, UCLA, UC Santa Barbara, and the University of Utah were selected as the four original ARPAnet nodes.

Decentralization is what made this early ARPAnet special. Instead of the network cables dictating the flow of information, each computer was assigned equal responsibility for receiving, interpreting, and transmitting network information. Also, ARPAnet marked the first implementation of the Internet Protocol (IP).

Internet Protocol (IP)

To understand IP, consider the scenario of sending a letter from Boston to Phoenix. You do not hand it to someone in the post office, who then gets in a truck and drives it to the proper address in downtown Phoenix. That kind of direct connection would cost a lot more than 33 cents for delivery, because it is terribly inefficient. A more realistic scenario might be that your letter is brought to the closest metropolitan post office, which sends your letter, along with a bunch of other mail headed for that ZIP code, to the airport to be flown to a regional post office in Arizona, which then sends your letter to the closest city post office, which routes it to a mail carrier, who delivers the letter to its destination.

Many intermediaries would be involved in the process, and a letter going from one point to another might take a different route from time to time. On its next trip, the plane leaving Boston might stop in Chicago to consolidate the Arizona mailbags into another plane headed for the Southwest.

IP works in a similar way in that it establishes connections from one point to another on a network via a route that is determined by the networked computers. The protocol part of IP is a set of rules for determining how a process should be carried out; in this case, the rules pertain to how information is sent efficiently and dynamically over a network. Messages, divided into small segments for easier handling, are put inside an IP packet, which is addressed and transmitted. Like the post office example, the message packets may make several "hops" from source to destination. The fewer the number of hops, the faster the message travels. Of course, other factors also play a part in the speed of transmission, which will be discussed shortly.

During the 1970s, ARPAnet grew as other universities and nonmilitary researchers were permitted to join. So many sites across the country joined that the original standards and communications protocols could no longer support the traffic—they needed to evolve. A new standard, called Transmission Control Protocol (TCP), was proposed in 1979 as a supplement to IP, and it was adopted in 1983 as TCP/IP.

The IP portion of the joint protocol takes care of routing the packets to their destination. The TCP part performs integrity checks on the data and enhances the reconstruction of the packets into the original message or file at the destination end. In this sense, using Internet communications is more reliable than sending mail through the post office, since packets can't get damaged, lost, or misrouted without the TCP/IP finding out and resending the necessary packets of information.

Today, TCP/IP is a foundation for over 100 different protocols for how data and messages should move among computers on a network. Part of the driving force behind this protocol's development was the desire to allow different kinds of computers to communicate with one another over a common network. If you are on a Sun workstation and want to send a file to a friend who is on a DEC Alpha workstation, you could do so over a TCP/IP network connection. Any computer that can use TCP/IP can communicate over the Internet.

Growth Factors

ARPAnet was still a few years of explosive growth and rebirth away from being called the Internet—a turning point in which TCP/IP played a key role. Many other organizations were sponsoring their own networks in the early 1980s and establishing connections to ARPAnet. CSNET established a network serving the engineering and computer science departments of various academic institutions. BITNET (Because It's Time Network) was created in 1981 to link instructors and researchers at colleges and universities using IBM mainframes. BITNET's European counterpart, EARN (European Academic Research Network), was formed shortly thereafter. Even though these networks were not strictly TCP/IP-based, they set up gateways to ARPAnet so that electronic mail messages could be exchanged. Other non-IP networks, such as the popular commercial services America Online and CompuServe, at one time simply had gateways to allow e-mail exchanges. Now that is changing for both the independent and commercial networks as they begin to offer full-service translators between their networks and what is known today as the Internet.

Industry terminology describes the act of connecting networks as internetworking, and uses the term "internetwork" for the network of networks that results. The term "Internet" was coined to refer to this global "network of networks" outgrowth of ARPAnet. Bridges, routers, and gateways are devices for linking networks to one another, as shown in Figure 18-1.

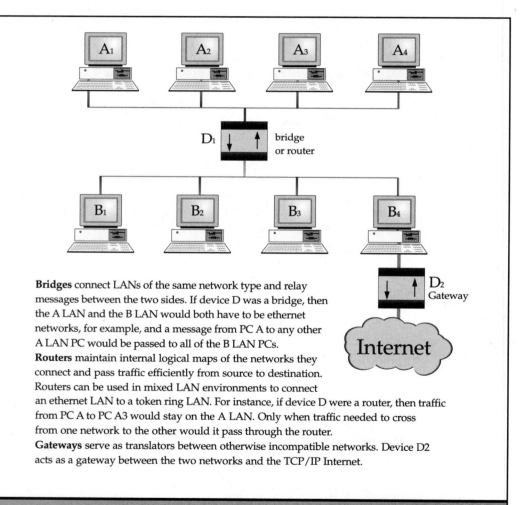

Bridges connect LANs of the same network type and relay messages between the two sides. If device D was a bridge, then the A LAN and the B LAN would both have to be ethernet networks, for example, and a message from PC A to any other A LAN PC would be passed to all of the B LAN PCs.

Routers maintain internal logical maps of the networks they connect and pass traffic efficiently from source to destination. Routers can be used in mixed LAN environments to connect an ethernet LAN to a token ring LAN. For instance, if device D were a router, then traffic from PC A to PC A3 would stay on the A LAN. Only when traffic needed to cross from one network to the other would it pass through the router.

Gateways serve as translators between otherwise incompatible networks. Device D2 acts as a gateway between the two networks and the TCP/IP Internet.

Figure 18-1.   Connecting networks with bridges, routers, and gateways

Computers that could be connected directly to the Internet were called host computers, or hosts. Typically, hosts were mainframes or minicomputers, which then had numerous users who connected to the Internet through VT100-type terminals. In the early 1980s, UNIX workstations proliferated and could support the same direct-to-the-Internet type of connections as the mainframe hosts, since the workstations had built-in IP. During this period, people were connecting Ethernet LANs, which could be comprised of many individual workstations, directly to the ARPAnet. Using routers, different kinds of networks could be connected together, so a token ring network could be linked to an Ethernet backbone, for instance. This capability led to an even greater acceleration in Internet growth.

In 1983, the Internet was formed when the military operations portion of ARPAnet split into its own network, MILnet, unburdening ARPAnet of some of its traffic load, yet allowing it to continue to serve as a research communications tool and information highway. Computers were assigned IP addresses, and gateways were set up to handle TCP/IP packet forwarding between ARPAnet and MILnet networks. As new networks and individual nodes were added to the Internet, they adhered to TCP/IP network conventions.

In 1987, the National Science Foundation (NSF) began a program to encourage the use of supercomputer resources. NSF funded a national high-speed backbone to connect its five supercomputer centers, thus forming NSFnet. Realizing that their purpose and structure were similar, NSFnet and ARPAnet began not only to interconnect but to merge their resources. ARPAnet's mission was declared complete and it ceased to exist as an active project in 1991. In November 1994, due to rapid commercial network expansion over the past three years, NSFnet started directing universities and government sites to find other network carriers, such as MCI, SprintLink, and ANS, to provide Internet services. By April 1995, NSFnet had withdrawn from its Internet role. The sponsorship resources that supported NSFnet are earmarked for future gigabit-bandwidth projects, which will be crucial for providing access over the Internet to services such as video.

An important consequence of the early government sponsorship was the restriction on commercial traffic. NSFnet's charter called for the support of "education and research" activities. The NSFnet's acceptable use policy (AUP) stated that commercial traffic or other for-profit information should not travel over its backbone. Although the Internet was dominated by academic and government networks, organizations offering access to the Internet to anyone willing to pay a fee also began to appear. The AUP prohibited commercial network traffic to travel over the NSFnet backbone, so these users could only communicate with other members of commercial Internet providers.

In 1991, an alternative backbone to NSFnet, called the Commercial Internet Exchange (CIX), was formed by three commercial access providers, AlterNet, CERFnet, and Performance Systems International (PSInet). Technically, CIX consisted of high-speed routers and high-bandwidth networks. In creating this alternative, CIX sidestepped the thorny issue of the NSF acceptable use policy while opening up the connectivity and opportunities to members of this commercial enterprise. Users who join the Internet today do not have to worry nearly as much about restrictions on the nature of the communications they send or who they may or may not be able to reach, because commercial access providers have established avenues that have a much wider latitude of acceptable use than the United States government-sponsored policies permitted.

The Internet continues to grow today, at a phenomenal rate of 10 to 15 percent more individual participants each month. North America, South America, Europe, Asia, Africa, and Australia are connected to the Internet; e-mail has been exchanged with Arctic researchers and NASA astronauts via TCP/IP satellite transmissions. Innovative applications of new technologies appear every day. The Internet is a rapidly changing domain—but far from perfect. But it continues to be a place of opportunity and challenge for those who participate.

The Business Side of the Internet

Aside from the cables, routers, and protocols, the Internet can best be characterized as a community. Estimates mark worldwide membership in mid-1998 at approximately 122 million users worldwide, 70 million in North America. Forecasts predict 1 billion Internet users by 2001.

In order to tap into the Internet for your own purposes, you should understand certain practical fundamentals. Since the Internet is composed of thousands of networks, there is no one central authority to contact and ask questions. To establish connectivity, you will need to find an Internet service provider (ISP), hook up your computer to the network, acquire the right set of tools, and develop your understanding of how you can travel safely and confidently on the Information Superhighway. See Figure 18-2 for an example of a typical individual connection.

Before connecting, you'll have to learn about and select an ISP.

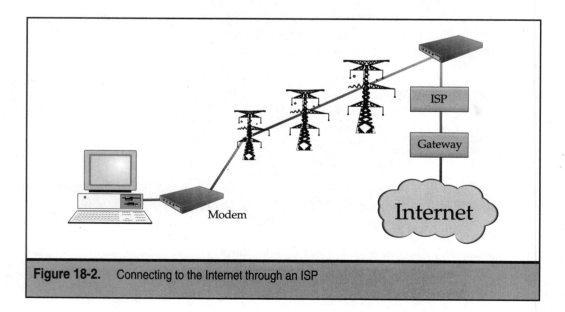

Figure 18-2.   Connecting to the Internet through an ISP

INTERNET SERVICE PROVIDERS

If you have ever driven through the countryside and seen the 200-foot towers that support high-voltage transmission used by utility companies to conduct power from station to station, you will readily understand the purpose of an Internet Service Provider (ISP). Before the power lines are connected to your home, the power is fed through a series of step-down transformers so that when you plug a toaster into the socket, it is connecting to 110 volts. You could not use, you do not need, and you would not want to pay for the higher level of power. In a similar way, an ISP provides the level of bandwidth that your personal or professional needs require. Bandwidth refers to the speed with which data travels, measured in bits per second (bps). Over a network connection, bandwidth makes an enormous difference in how much data you can send and receive in a given period of time, as Figure 18-3 shows. Bandwidth becomes increasingly significant as you learn to exchange not just text messages, but more space-demanding types of data, such as graphics, audio, and video. While a brief e-mail message takes up only 2.5KB, a typical scanned picture occupies 300KB, audio takes up about 475KB per minute, and one minute of video can require upwards of 1,800KB.

The goal of Level 3 access is to establish TCP/IP connectivity on the Internet through either of two methods: SLIP or PPP. It's important to understand how this portion of the connection works.

PPP and SLIP Connections

Point-to-Point Protocol (PPP) and Serial Line Internet Protocol (SLIP) are communication standards that allow a computer connected via a modem to act as a node on the Internet network. In addition to supporting TCP/IP, a modem connection from your PC to the Internet must support the underlying protocol for communicating over a serial line, such as is found with Plain Old Telephone Service (POTS). The serial line protocol is responsible for error control, packetizing the data, and other activities that allow TCP/IP programs to work together. PPP is the newer protocol, and it is considered to be more robust than SLIP. SLIP is virtually dead as a connection protocol today, and PPP is built in to most modern operating systems, including Windows 95, 98, and NT, MacOS, and Linux.

Selecting an Internet Service Provider

To get a list of local Internet service providers, check these commonsense sources first:

▼   If you know people who have a similar service, ask who is providing their service.

■   Call a local college or university computer center.

■   Simply check the phone book.

▲   Alternatively, consider a national ISP such as UUNet, Mindspring, Verio, or even (gasp!) America Online.

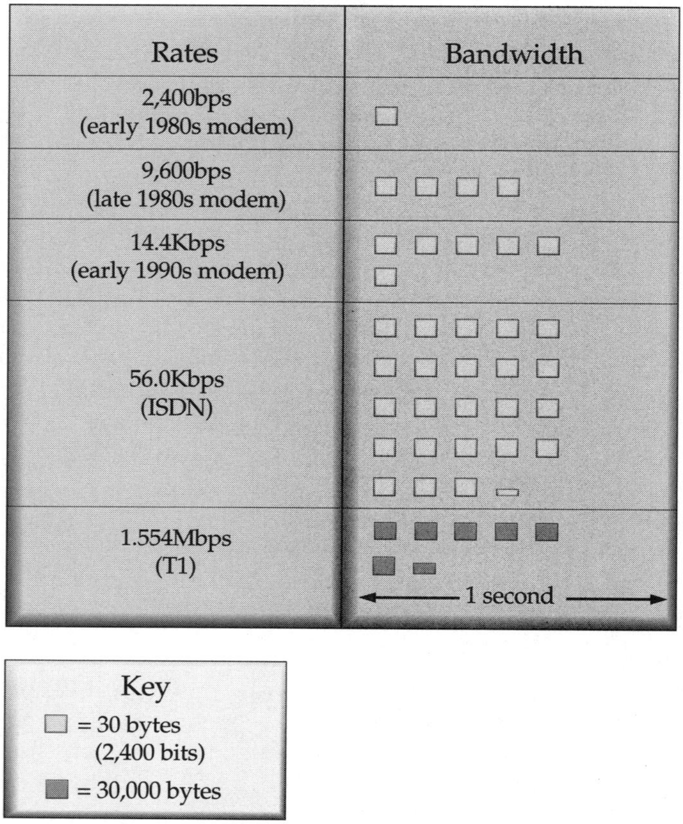

Rates	Bandwidth
2,400bps (early 1980s modem)	☐
9,600bps (late 1980s modem)	☐ ☐ ☐ ☐
14.4Kbps (early 1990s modem)	☐ ☐ ☐ ☐ ☐ ☐
56.0Kbps (ISDN)	☐ ▭
1.554Mbps (T1)	■ ■ ■ ■ ■ ■ ▪ ←— 1 second —→

Key

☐ = 30 bytes
    (2,400 bits)

■ = 30,000 bytes

Figure 18-3.   Transition bandwidth comparison

Below are several key questions to ask when comparison shopping for an ISP.

Does the ISP support the type of computer(s) that will be connected?   Whether you are connecting a UNIX, Windows, Mac, or other platform, you should make sure that your provider has experience with your type of computer so you can get good support. It is a good sign if they have a computer platform of your type that they use themselves at their location or that they at least have available for reproducing tricky problems. Many ISPs, for example, are reluctant to provide Mac support.

Does the provider have multiple points of presence?   ISPs have POPs just like long-distance carriers. To avoid paying long-distance charges to the phone company for your line connection (in addition to the service charge from your ISP), you will want to check whether you are making a local or long-distance call to your ISP at whatever point of presence you may need. Having multiple points also indicates that the provider has a regional presence and is a larger operation, which means greater resources to draw upon and also greater stability as a business. Find out whether they have been established for more than a couple of years and how many subscribers they now service. If your users will be doing a lot of travelling, a national ISP with far-flung POPs makes sense.

Does the provider place any restrictions on business uses of your account? Check their acceptable use policy in advance, and make sure the ISP is a member of the Commercial Internet Exchange (CIX, member list available at www.cix.org). Providers offering service to the public for a fee should understand that their users will have different needs for both personal and business matters. It is important to ask, though, because you would not want to invest your time setting up a system and find you have to move due to a policy violation.

What is the ISP's maintenance schedule? How often do they back up their system? If you are using this system to exchange business correspondence, you should be sure that daily backups are the norm. Recently, a system administrator's error wiped out over 150 pieces of mail to Star Communications Group one morning. Luckily, the messages were restored from a system backup that was only a few hours old. When disaster strikes, your system is only as good as its latest archive. Make sure your ISP is at least as vigilant in backing up data at their end as you are about safeguarding data at your end.

How will the ISP respond to service problems? Do they have a means of escalation for technical support questions? Do they have a direct number to call, or must you work your way through a phone tree? Are support technician phones staffed beyond 5:00 P.M.? Many telecommuters who work from home need support during evening and weekend hours. Do they respond to questions posed via e-mail or newsgroups as well? Is service guaranteed in writing, or are their support capabilities less structured and predictable than a written policy would indicate?

When you have a problem to report, ask if there is a help-desk tracking number system. The larger and better-organized support departments assign unresolved questions a log number and keep statistics on how quickly problems get fixed. When the frontline staff gets stumped, they have resources they can draw upon to get an answer. Often, an ISP tech support person will use the Internet to research questions. Sometimes, an ISP will maintain good relationships with outside consultants (who are often subscribers) to help answer questions. Find out what kinds of resources your potential ISP has available.

What will the startup and monthly costs be for using your Internet connection? Are there any additional costs or discount programs? You can expect a startup fee for setting up and activating your account (about $20), then a monthly maintenance fee ($15 to $25 for modem dialup access). Businesses should be particularly interested in applying for a custom domain name—your mailing address on the Internet (for more information, see the next section, "Internet Domain Names"). For a nominal fee ($30 to $100), your Internet Service Provider will discuss an appropriate domain name, fill out the forms, and make the application for you. (The application costs extra.)

Other services that may have fees associated with them are setting up mailing lists, making files available for downloading by anyone at any time, and setting up and maintaining World Wide Web pages. These services (and why they matter to you) will be described in greater detail in the "World Wide Web" section. Again, the best idea is to call a few ISPs and comparison shop to determine the going rates. Ask if they offer discounts for paying an annual fee instead of a monthly fee.

Can your ISP meet your future needs?   As your familiarity with the Internet grows, so will your use of it. Before you are ready to upgrade from dial-up to a dedicated connection, find out what options the ISP can offer. Can they assist you in setting up services such as FTP and World Wide Web servers? Will they provide wider-bandwidth dedicated lines at a competitive cost? Ask around at your local user group or chamber of commerce for others who have upgraded their capabilities through a particular ISP, and find out their experiences.

INTERNET DOMAIN NAMES

One of the first service matters you will conduct with your ISP is to get an Internet address so others can contact you. A fully qualified address includes the user ID and a complete domain description. For example, the address president@whitehouse.gov is a fully qualified address. The user ID, the part to the left of the "at" symbol (@), describes the account owner; the part of the address after the "at" symbol is the domain name.

Whether you opt for dial-up or dedicated line access, it is worthwhile to apply for a custom domain name for your business. Having your own domain name will make it easier for customers, contacts, suppliers, and others who want to reach you to remember your address and associate you with your organization. Individuals, on the other hand, may not wish to go through the trouble to apply for their own domain name, in which case they will be able to use the ISP's domain name. Consider the differences between the following two possible addresses for the same person (e.g., Dan Rather). On a custom system, dan_rather@news.cbs.com could be his address; on a system in which he used the ISP's domain, he might be cbs_rather@netcom.com.

A domain name has multiple parts, separated by a period. The rightmost portion of the name is used to indicate the highest level of the domain, known as the top level. Working backwards from that portion of the name, you get more and more specific information about the host. Take the address "dunxl.OCS.drexel.edu," for instance. Reading from the right, the .edu indicates an educational institution, Drexel University, within the department of OCS, and the specific machine name is dunxl, a Sun 670 UNDC host.

Also, country codes are being added to the list of top-level domains. There are over 300 country codes, and over half of those countries have Internet connectivity at present. Recent changes in the way domain names are assigned open up "geography" domains as opposed to "category" domains. For example, the domain name for a host at the School District of Philadelphia, sdp2.philsch.kl2.pa.us, has a country code as its top-level domain. If it had been assigned a couple of years ago, it most likely would have had an .edu suffix instead of the country code.

Associated with each domain name is a numeric address, known as the IP address. IP addresses are 32-bit numbers divided into four parts, sometimes called octets. Each octet, represented as a decimal number, can range from eight binary 0's to eight binary 1's—in other words, from 0 to 256. Sometimes these IP addresses are called "dot speak," since you pronounce the period as "dot." For instance, the IP address 128.182.62.99 would be read "128 dot 182 dot 62 dot 99."

By now, you may be wondering how these numbers and domains are assigned, especially given the unprecedented demand from new users. Though no central authority runs the Internet, various committees and sponsored organizations manage various aspects. Among those organizations is the Internet Network Information Center, or InterNIC for short. The InterNIC, started in 1993, is a five-year project (now in its sixth year of operation) funded by the National Science Foundation to provide network information services to the Internet community. The InterNIC is one of dozens of working groups and research groups guided by the largely volunteer Internet Activities Board. The InterNIC currently leases domain names at the price of $35 per year. You pay $70 up front for a two year claim to your domain name.

Previously, the names and IP addresses of machines could be kept in a single file maintained by the InterNIC, and that file was distributed to every host on the network. But as the size of the network grew, so too did the size of the file, not to mention the time to process domain name registrations. Now, the process is more decentralized. Instead of assigning individual names, the InterNIC assigns an Internet service provider a block of IP addresses, from which they assign a number to a unique domain name. These blocks of addresses are given out in three sizes. A Class C block is the smallest and most common. It would look similar to 192.3.44.*, and would allow a network administrator to assign up to 254 IP addresses. A small business or school district might be interested in obtaining one or more Class C addresses. A large organization or a regional ISP would be better off with a Class B address, which would give them the 128.3.*.* number space of 64,516 nodes. Very rarely are Class A blocks assigned, since they take the form of 0.*.*.* and hold the potential for over 16 million IP addresses. Class A addresses start with a number between 0 and 127, Class B addresses start with a number between 128 and 191, and Class C addresses start with a number between 192 and 255.

Generally, human beings are more comfortable with the domain names than the IP numbers. Computers, however, translate the name into an IP address so they can process it faster. This translation process takes place automatically when you send mail or request a service of a host computer via the Domain Name System. It is important to realize that sometimes you will request an Internet service such as a Web page or FTP directly and not be able to use it. Several reasons may account for this, including the following:

▼ The host providing the service is offline for maintenance or repair.

■ Too many other people are using the service at this time, and you will have to wait for an open port.

■ A network connection is having problems.

▲ Your specific IP number or domain name has been declined access because the administrators of the host no longer wish to offer public service due to resource abuse or excessive traffic loads.

Before you judge this capricious nature of Internet services to be unfair or poor customer service, consider the fact that the service is provided voluntarily in the first place. From a service provider's viewpoint, you might want or need to shut down a machine for system updates or to restrict users for security reasons. Or, if a service has become so popular that it begins to impact system performance, then it becomes necessary to restrict outside access to allow the organization's internal users to have priority access to information and resources.

CONNECTING TO THE INTERNET

The following is what you will need to connect to the Internet:

▼ Personal computer with a modem connection

■ Phone jack

▲ Communications software

One of the myths surrounding Internet connectivity is that you need the latest and most powerful CPU to take full advantage of these services. Almost any IBM-compatible computer that is capable of running at least DOS 6.0 or Windows 3.1 can be used; similarly, any Macintosh that can run MacOS 7.1 meets the minimum qualification for driving on the Information Superhighway (ISH). In other words, if your computer is running a current operating system and is meeting your other day-to-day needs, you should not have to upgrade your CPU just to get on the ISH. When cruising the ISH, CPU speed is usually not the limiting factor in your travels—modem speed is much more critical. The two areas you should consider first investing in are hard drive space and a fast modem. A modem is a device that translates the digital signals produced by your computer to analog signals, which can be handled by telephone lines.

Because of the vast number of files and programs available on the Internet, it makes sense that you have a sufficiently large hard drive to store downloaded information. The process by which a file is transferred from a host computer to your local computer is called downloading; uploading means sending a file from your local computer to the host. Although 100MB may seem like a large amount of free space, it really is not once you consider the size of the audio, graphic, and video files that are available for downloading.

A phone jack is necessary to connect to a dial-up or dedicated line network. The jack should be a standard RJ-11, and with standard twisted-pair wiring you can exchange information at reasonable speeds. For speeds higher than 56Kbps, you should use Integrated Service Digital Network (ISDN), Digital Subscriber Line (DSL), or a cable modem.

Larger organizations should consider dedicated lines such as a T1 line (1.54Mbps), or perhaps a T3 line (45Mbps). If you are looking to upgrade an existing connection, consider how fast the line must be, how frequently it will be used, and the capacity it will be required to handle in terms of the quantity of users and the type of data being transported.

You will need two kinds of software when using the Internet over a dial-in connection. First, you will need communications software to establish a PPP connection. Once that connection is established, your machine will be recognized as a node on the Internet and you will be able to run TCP/IP-based software (like a Web browser) for the particular Internet services you wish to use. Users with a dedicated connection will have a TCP/IP connection established already, and will be more concerned with providing client software and setting up Internet servers.

Internet Client Software

Once you have Internet access, you will want to become familiar with the tools that will enable you to make connections with people and resources. During your explorations, you will encounter the terms "client" and "server," used individually as well as together. "Client/server" describes the way a software tool is used. The client part of the software makes requests of the server side of the software. The server side performs the requested action, then returns the results of that action back to the client part.

When you use client/server tools, think of the two ends of a screwdriver. The handle is the front end you interface with as a user; the tip, which does the actual work, is the back end of the tool. In client/server terminology, the front end is the client and the back end is the server. For instance, when using e-mail you can command the client software on your computer to connect to the host machine and issue a request to the e-mail server to check for your mail. The mail server would then send the client any mail stored in the electronic mailbox.

The client software is generally responsible for providing the user with the interface, connection, and the translation. Client software is responsible for opening and maintaining a connection to the server, translating your commands into instructions suitable for the server, and interpreting the results of the server's work back into a useful format. Many current Internet programs employ a graphical user interface (GUI), complete with icons, pull-down menus, toolbars, scrolling windows, and mouse control. These functions are handled by the client application as they would be for any other applications you run on your Mac or PC.

E-Mail

By far, the application most widely used by Internet users is electronic mail, or e-mail.

E-mail can send more than text messages. One problem that developed as people started using GUI workstations and PCs is that they wanted to send diagrams, photographs, sounds, and movie clips to each other. A second problem that emerged from international connections is that ASCII is not equipped to handle many foreign character sets. MIME, or Multipurpose Internet Mail Extension, addresses both of these problems. MIME serves two main purposes:

▼ It provides a means for mail applications to communicate what type of data is in the mail.

▲   It provides a method for encoding non-ASCII data being sent through Internet mail systems.

The MIME standard, developed in 1992, supports text, binary files, graphic formats, PostScript, video, voice messages, and other message types.

You can find specialty client/server packages, such as Lotus Notes for Windows and Macintosh, or Slate for UNIX systems, that specialize in the exchange of multimedia e-mail if your needs require this capability on a regular basis. However, so long as your e-mail client software (as well as other software that might encounter multimedia data, such as World Wide Web clients) is MIME-compliant, your system should be able to handle these special cases.

When the post office sends mail, the mail can get lost, damaged, or be delivered late. Not only is e-mail cheaper and faster than using regular mail ("snail mail"), but it is also more reliable in many ways:

▼   Host systems, for instance, will verify that the domain name of the addressee on a piece of e-mail can be looked up in the Domain Name System before sending it.

■   If you have accidentally added a space or mistyped a character in the domain name, your mail will come back with a message telling you so right away.

■   If certain links along the way to your recipient's host are down, the path will be rerouted.

■   If the destination host machine is unavailable, your host will probably queue the mail and try to resend it for a period of days before giving up and letting you know it encountered a problem.

▲   If the recipient does not exist on the host machine, that host will return your message with an explanation.

NetNews

NetNews refers to the online conference discussions that are transmitted across the Internet. The term "Usenet" refers not only to the discussions but also to the special networks and protocols designed for this activity. Over 31,000 discussion groups on almost every topic imaginable can be found in NetNews groups. Participants can post questions, information, opinions, and even binary files for downloading. Where else can biophysicists find colleagues so easily? Fans of every U.S. sports team can find their buddies.

Different groups serve K-12, community college, and university educators. Using NetNews, you can discuss the latest business books, and you can even look through the help wanted ads posted by employers looking for both full-time and contract workers.

Browsing newsgroups can be a real education, given the variety of topics. Newsgroups have been around for a long time and have taken on many different formats, from text-only DEC Notes to fully GUI Lotus Notes. The majority of newsgroups are text-based. In general, newsgroups are meant to be participatory and open. However, universities and larger organizations often take advantage of the NetNews format and create restricted newsgroups that can only be read and posted to by their own members. Using secure wide area networks (WANs), organizations can develop valuable records while restricting access to project information from competitors. When a router is configured to act as a security device and filter out certain types of network traffic, it is called a firewall (see Figure 18-4). Organizations can allow their employees to read and post information to the Internet-wide discussion groups and prevent outsiders from viewing any proprietary information or accessing system security files, such as passwords, kept inside the firewall.

NetNews groups are structured in a hierarchy of categories to help readers identify relevant information. There are major categories, such as comp (computer hardware, software, and protocol discussions), news (topics related to Usenet announcements), and science (chemistry, physics, mathematics, and so on). There are also the controversial but popular categories such as the alt (alternative discussions about lifestyles, hobbies, and philosophies).

Newsgroups rely on NetNews Transfer Protocol (NNTP), which is usually supported by your TCP/IP connection. The way newsgroups work is that when a message gets posted,

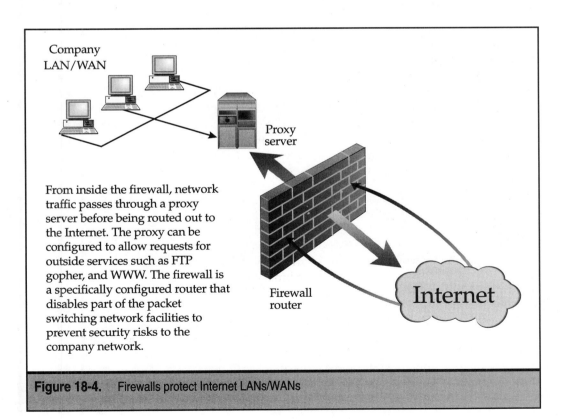

Figure 18-4.   Firewalls protect Internet LANs/WANs

it is passed from one NNTP server to another, making messages available worldwide in a very short period of time—from a matter of minutes to several hours. When you check a newsgroup from your workstation, the client software requests a list of the most current messages posted to the group. You can then browse or post to a potential audience of 100 million people.

With so many topics, it becomes a nontrivial matter for system administrators to maintain newsgroups. Accepting all NetNews groups, called a full feed, can require well over 500MB per day of bandwidth and storage.

Check with your ISP to find out if it provides a NetNews feed, since some providers do not; if so, find out if it is a full feed. If not, check out what groups are not available to determine if they are critical to your needs. Also of note are Web sites like DejaNews (www.dejanews.com) that archive NetNews feeds.

FTP

FTP stands for *File Transfer Protocol.* The abbreviation stands for both the network protocol as well as the service it provides. With FTP, you can search for and download public domain, shareware, and private files from all over the world. The ability to transfer both text and binary files across different computer platforms and networks makes a significant addition to your Internet toolkit.

To access an FTP site, you enter a full domain name. MIT sponsors an FTP site that has archives of NetNews discussions as well as current FAQs on a wide spectrum of topics arranged in seven major categories. A FAQ is a document of frequently asked questions (and answers) maintained by a volunteer who keeps the information up to date; enter the address ftp.rtfm.mit.edu to access this FAQ site. As with many public sites, this one allows anonymous login, which means that anyone can have access to this server as long as there is a free port to the host available. FTP servers can restrict access by requiring a nonpublic user ID and password. As a courtesy to the system administrator, enter "anonymous" as the user ID and your full e-mail address as the password on all public FTP servers.

World Wide Web

The World Wide Web (WWW) was created by physicists who were looking for a better way to cross-reference scientific research papers at the Swiss European Laboratory for Particle Physics (also known as CERN) in 1993. Since that time, it's become the fastest-growing Internet service. It is estimated that nearly 400 million Web pages exist, as of early 1999.

Web users crisscross information resources by following hyperlinks to different information resources and services. The most popular Web client is Netscape Communicator, which has versions available for PC, Mac, and UNIX platforms. Microsoft Internet Explorer is the only major competitor left on the market.

By entering a Web address, known as a Uniform Resource Locator (URL), a Web client can provide hypertext links to text, graphics, sounds, and movies. URLs are given in a format that lists the service first and then the host name and path. Services include http (for WWW), FTP, and mailto (for e-mail). Because the transition is subtle from one service to another in many cases, some users do not realize that Web documents can direct a Web browser to act as an e-mail client, browse gopher hierarchies, or download a file using FTP, as well as read and post to newsgroups. Beyond that, Web pages offer the ability to collect information from participating users through the use of forms.

Creating basic Web pages can be done on any platform using a simple text editor. The lingua franca of WWW is called HTML (Hypertext Markup Language), and it is characterized by simple tags bracketing text and giving it special properties when read by a WWW browser. For instance, to the "source," text might look like <B> Read This </B>; when read by a Web browser, it would look like this:

Read This

Of course, the syntax for creating these tags can be generated by various Web editors. Many editors for both the Mac and Windows PCs exist. You can even use your word processor as an HTML editor.

Creating your own Web page is the first step. The next step is creating a means for others to view your Web page and interact with it. When people speak of "publishing" their Web page, they are talking about putting it on a server so that others can access it via a URL. A whole host of software packages support this activity for direct IP-connected nodes. Netscape Enterprise Server and Microsoft Internet Information Server are big on the Windows platform. The free Apache Web server is the predominant UNIX Web server. You can also outsource your Web services to your ISP or a third party.

CONCLUSION

Prior to and during the 1970s, computers were regarded as centralized mainframes with which the select few would interact. In the 1980s, the personal computer led to a great decentralization of computing power and facilitated the rise of many an entrepreneur and small business. The 1990s is the decade in which the focus will become one of interdependent interconnections, and the Internet will continue to grow to support this demand as well as define its means.

With Internet access, you have the unprecedented opportunity to meet people and learn from them, access documents that will help you solve problems and answer questions, shop outlets on the Internet, and conduct business on a global scale. You can exchange messages, files, pictures, sounds, and video in addition to text. More and more organizations will find a Web server to be a key interface to their business community. E-mail and Web browsers will become popular alternatives for communicating and tracking down information at any time of day, from anywhere you can plug a laptop computer into a phone jack.

So, your wide area network link can connect you to a lot more than a remote office. When you use wide area networking technology to merge onto the Information Superhighway, you've begun to achieve that idealistic end of high-bandwidth, universal access to vast, well-organized information.

The Internet is very useful, but it is far from perfect. In the same way that automobile roadways are made up of a combination of dirt roads, paved streets, boulevards, and, yes, superhighways, so too will the information infrastructure be composed of a combination of copper wire, coax cable, fiber-optic cable, wireless communications, and other means.

Though it is challenging to keep up with the rapid changes that take place on the Internet, the early adopters of this technology who take the time to do so will have a clear edge in understanding this new environment and enjoying its advantages.

Organizations can use the Internet to inform the world about their products and services. Sophisticated Web pages can bring a whole new meaning to the concepts of marketing and customer service. Information exchange with other divisions of your organization, outside technical support, government agencies, and current and potential customers can be facilitated through the use of the Internet.

Remember that the Internet is not just about hooking up computers, but also about allowing people to make connections in new and interesting ways. The Internet is a network of networks for computers, people, and information. It is becoming as standard a part of business equipment as the telephone and fax machine. It is a new way of researching, learning, communicating, and working.

CHAPTER 19

Wide Area Connections

T here used to be a distinct division of responsibilities between "network management" and "telecommunications management." Network managers handled all aspects of the local area network up to the building walls or the campus gate. All data communications outside the local area network were administered by the telecommunication managers. This is still true in some organizations, but it is rapidly changing. Whether or not this is the case in your organization, you probably still need to read this chapter because the lines between local and wide area networking are blurring—rapidly.

If you're a network manager, you probably know that most wide area equipment vendors assume you know enough about data communications over the wide area to select and manage their wares. If you're a telecommunications manager, you know that the fastest growing part of your job is wide area data communications, and that requires an understanding of local area networking. In either case, you'll need an understanding of wide area networking and how it interoperates with local area networking.

One of the most compelling reasons to learn more about wide area networking, however, is that your users don't know the difference between local and wide area data communications—and they don't want to. Network operating systems and networked applications are becoming very "wide area aware," and are so good at hiding the location of data and programs that users mistake wide area performance problems for local performance problems.

For example, I know of a situation in which a user complained about how doggedly slow the network was because it had taken her almost a minute to retrieve a document. Upon investigation, I discovered that the document was on a server in another city, and she was accessing it over a 19.2Kbps dial-up line. The network operating system and the document management application she was using had done a great job of making the location and retrieval transparent to the user. It was so transparent, in fact, that I had a hard time explaining to the user that the problem wasn't an underpowered server or workstation or a slow LAN, but rather a wide area link that was many times slower than the local links—and couldn't be cost-justifiably upgraded.

This brings up another reason for studying the wide area. Whether you are in telecommunications or network management, because of the previously mentioned wide area transparency of applications and NOSes, you will have to troubleshoot wide area problems, as well as recommend and justify the cost of wide area solutions.

Chances are, however, that you need to learn about wide area networking because it is becoming your job. The neat lines between LAN administration and telecommunications management are disappearing in your company, and you want to be sure you are on top of things.

SO YOU THINK YOU'RE READY FOR THE LONG HAUL...

We'll begin with a brief sketch of what a wide area network is, how it functions, and who the players are. It's best just to read the rest of this chapter straight through, without worrying too much about looking up definitions or technical details. Each of the concepts introduced here will be discussed in detail in later chapters. The purpose of this chapter is to give you a broad overview of how the various components and players in a wide area network work together.

The Wide Area Defined

A wide area network (WAN) uses dedicated or switched connections to link computers in geographically remote locations that are too widely dispersed to be directly linked to the local area network media. These wide area connections can be made either through the public network or through a private network built by the organization it serves.

A typical WAN and the equipment required for WAN connections is shown in Figure 19-1. A router sends traffic addressed to a remote location from the local network over the wide area connection to the remote destination. The router is connected either to an analog line or a digital line. Routers are connected to analog lines via modems or to digital lines via channel service units/data service units (CSUs/DSUs). The type of carrier service determines the exact type of equipment the wide area will need to function.

Dedicated vs. Switched Lines

Wide area networks can include either dedicated or switched lines. A dedicated line is a permanent connection between two points that is usually leased on a monthly basis, as shown in Figure 19-2.

A switched line service doesn't require permanent connections between two fixed points. Instead, it lets users establish temporary connections among multiple points that last only for the duration of the data transmission, as shown in Figure 19-3.

There are two types of switched services available: circuit-switching services, which are similar to the services used to make garden-variety voice telephone calls; and packet-switching services, which are better suited to data transmission, as explained shortly.

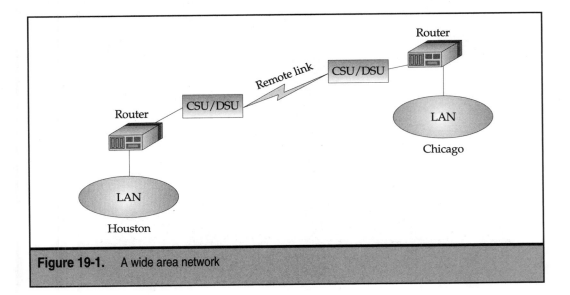

Figure 19-1. A wide area network

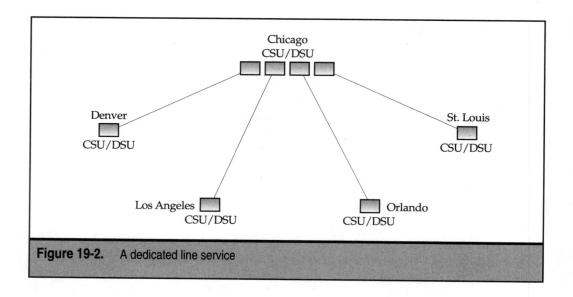

Figure 19-2. A dedicated line service

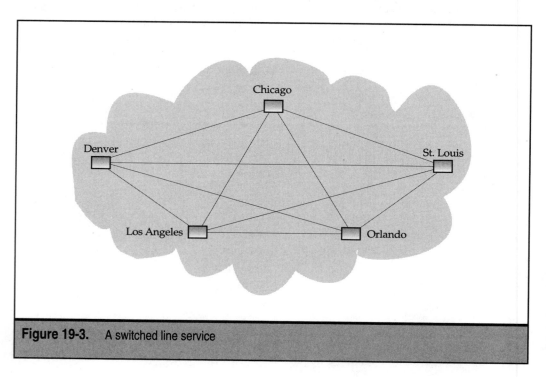

Figure 19-3. A switched line service

CIRCUIT-SWITCHING SERVICES In a circuit-switched connection, a dedicated channel, called a circuit, is set up between two points for the duration of the call. It provides a fixed amount of bandwidth during the call, and users pay for only that amount of bandwidth for the amount of time the call takes. Occasionally there is a delay at the beginning of these calls while the connection is being made, although new switching techniques and equipment have made this connection delay negligible in most cases.

Circuit-switching connections have a couple of serious drawbacks. First, because the bandwidth is fixed in these connections, they don't handle bursts of traffic well, requiring frequent retransmissions. Given that WAN connections are relatively slow anyway, retransmissions can make the performance crawl. The second drawback is that these virtual circuits have only one route, with no alternate paths determined. Therefore, when a line goes down, either the transmission stops or one of the users intervenes manually to reroute the traffic. Figure 19-4 illustrates a circuit-switched network.

PACKET-SWITCHING SERVICES Packet-switching services do away with the concept of the fixed virtual circuit. Data is transmitted one packet at a time through a network mesh, or cloud, with each packet having the ability to take a different route through the network cloud. This is illustrated in Figure 19-5. Because there is no predefined virtual circuit, packet switching can increase or decrease bandwidth as required, and therefore can handle bursts in packets elegantly. Taking advantage of the multiple paths of the network cloud, packet-switching services can route packets around failed or congested lines.

WHICH SWITCH? Whether to choose circuit-switching or packet-switching services depends upon two things:

▼ The type of traffic your network generates

▲ Your budget

If the traffic generated on your network is delay-sensitive, such as that generated by video applications, you'll need the fixed, guaranteed bandwidth of a circuit-switched service. Unfortunately, these services are very expensive. On the other hand, if your

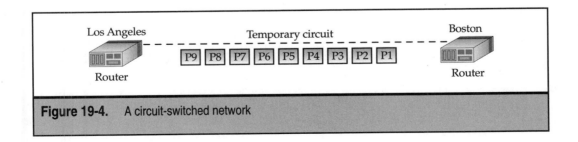

Figure 19-4. A circuit-switched network

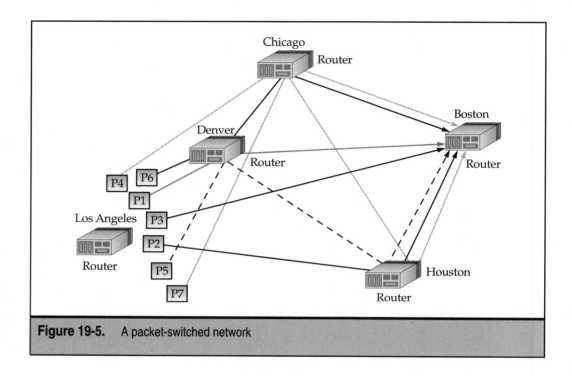

Figure 19-5.   A packet-switched network

traffic can stand delays, especially if it is "bursty" in nature, packet-switching services are reliable and also more economical than circuit-switched services.

Public Networks

Public networks are the wide area telecommunications facilities owned by common carriers and resold to users by subscription.

These common carriers include the following:

▼ Local exchange carriers

■ Interexchange carriers

▲ Value-added carriers

TIP: Each type of common carrier may offer wide area data services, and they often compete against one another in this market. Therefore, it's a good idea to check service availability and pricing with all of them.

LOCAL EXCHANGE CARRIERS (LECS)   Local exchange carriers include companies such as the Regional Bell Operating Companies (RBOCs), GTE, and other companies that handle local telephone and telecommunications connections. Until recently, these companies were restricted by federal law to handling local communications, providing point-of-presence (POP) facilities for long-distance carriers, and offering wide area communications services only within their local service areas, known as local access and transport areas (LATAs). However, recent legislation has permitted them to compete with long-distance carriers and eventually to discontinue providing POP facilities to their competitors.

INTEREXCHANGE CARRIERS (IXCS) An interexchange carrier (IXC) is a long-distance telecommunications carrier, such as AT&T, MCI, and US Sprint. Customers can choose the IXC of their choice. While many IXCs use the local POP facilities that local exchange carriers are required to provide, some IXCs built their own POPs, allowing customers to bypass the LEC and connect directly into the IXCs' long-distance services.

Just as the Telecommunications Act of 1996 has allowed LECs to go into the long-distance business, it has also allowed IXCs to compete in the local exchange carrier service market. Therefore, look for the lines between the LECs and the IXCs to disappear in the near future.

VALUE-ADDED CARRIERS (VACS) VACs, such as CompuServe Information Services and GE Information Services, often provide WAN services as a sideline to their core business. Typically, a VAC has a national private data network (PDN) it established for its own use, and resells the excess capacity of that PDN to its customers. Using a PDN saves you the trouble of acquiring the various carrier services and setting up your own switching equipment because the switching is done in the carrier's network. The VAC also handles the management and maintenance of the WAN services, and may even be able to do some protocol conversion for you.

Private Networks

A private network is just that—a private communications network built, maintained, and controlled by the organization it serves. At a minimum, a private network requires its own switching and communications equipment. It may also use its own carrier services, or it may lease them from public networks or other private networks that have built their own communication lines.

A private network is extremely expensive. The organization that builds one must be prepared to maintain and manage its own switching and communications equipment, as well as either build its own microwave or other long-haul carrier service, or negotiate to lease such service at a reasonable price. However, in companies where tight security and control over data traffic are paramount, private lines are the only guarantee of a high level of service. Furthermore, in situations where data traffic between two remote points exceeds six hours a day, employing a private network may actually be more cost-effective than using the public network.

Figure 19-6 shows a private network connecting three separate sites.

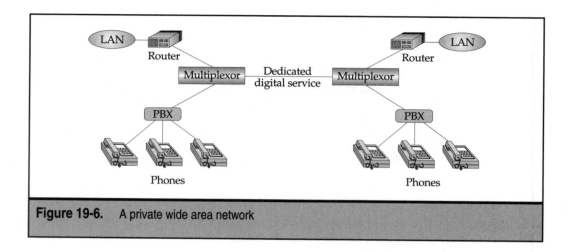

Figure 19-6.   A private wide area network

A Word About Routers and Routing

Routers play a crucial part in determining the efficiency of a WAN connection. Routers connect the local area network to the wide area network, learning the destination of devices on the internetwork and determining the best path for data traffic to reach its destination. For users of delay-sensitive applications, the router can make the wide area connection completely transparent or a frustrating swamp. For switched-services customers, who pay only for the bandwidth they use, an efficient router can save huge amounts of money in carrier service fees.

When selecting a router for your WAN, be sure to test how efficiently it uses the carrier service. Does the router terminate the connection when no traffic is being transmitted? Does it allow you to select the criteria for route determination—cost, shortest route, and so on? Does it correctly select the transmission route based on this criteria?

TIP: When purchasing wide area routers, try to get a substantial trial period or return period. This will enable to you to test the router thoroughly before making a final commitment.

Analog Lines

Analog lines are garden-variety voice lines that were originally developed to carry voice traffic. Analog lines are a part of Plain Old Telephone Service (POTS), and as such they are everywhere. Although digital data traffic isn't compatible with analog carrier signals, you can transmit digital traffic on analog lines by using a modem, which modulates digital signals onto analog carrier services. The maximum achievable transmission rate of digital traffic over analog lines is about 43,000 bits per second, although the international standard for this rate of transmission hasn't been completed. Currently, the fastest modems available transmit about 32,600bps, which is the transmission rate of the CCITT

ITU V.34bis standard. Even when modems are available that transmit at the higher rate, it will be significantly slower than the transmission rates achievable with digital lines.

Digital Lines

Digital lines are designed to carry data traffic, which is digital in nature. Therefore, your computer equipment won't need a modem to load data onto a digital carrier signal. Instead, it will use a channel service unit/digital service unit (CSU/DSU), which simply provides an interface to the digital line. Digital lines can transmit data traffic at speeds up to 45Mbps and are available as either dedicated or switched services.

Carrier Services

Different networks require different transmission rates, data prioritization, and levels of service. They also have different budgets available for wide area connections. Luckily, there are a variety of wide area carrier services available. We'll briefly describe the most popular.

Traditional Switched Analog Lines

As we mentioned earlier, traditional analog voice lines are the POTS we all know. They are widely available and inexpensive, and can theoretically support a data bandwidth of up to about 43,000 bits per second, although the current practical limit, as established in the V.34bis standard, is 32,600bps with compression. Analog lines come in two basic flavors:

▼ Dial-up lines

▲ Dedicated lines

DIAL-UP LINES   In dial-up access, a connection is made only when there is data to transmit. It is especially good for traffic that is not delay-sensitive, such as file transfers and electronic mail.

DEDICATED LINES   These analog lines provide the same data rates as dial-up lines, except that customers have a contract with the carrier that stipulates, in return for a flat fee, that the lines will always be available for the customer's immediate use.

Circuit-Switched Services

Circuit-switched services are switched carrier services that establish a virtual connection before transmitting data. Some of the most commonly used are as follows.

SWITCHED 56 SERVICE   This is a digital data service that transmits at 56Kbps. Because it is digital, it doesn't require a modem. Instead, it uses a CSU/DSU to provide an interface between the router and the carrier service. Switched 56 is most often used as a backup to higher-speed data services as well as for fax transmissions and file transfers.

INTEGRATED SERVICE DIGITAL NETWORK (ISDN)   ISDN is the first all-digital dial-up service. It will be discussed in detail in Chapter 20, so for now it is enough to note that it is a high-speed digital circuit-switched service that provides integrated voice and data services on which many other high-speed offerings are based, including Switched T1 services.

The basic ISDN service unit, called the Basic Rate Interface (BRI), has three channels (although some carriers don't offer all three in their packaging of the BRI): two provide 64Kbps data channels (called the "bearer channels" or "B channels") and a 16Kbps signaling channel (called the "D channel"). The ISDN Primary Rate Interface (PRI) provides 23 B channels and 1 D channel. In either interface, the D channel provides call setup and monitoring, keeping the B channels free to transmit data.

Packet-Switched Services

Packet-switched services, described in detail earlier in this chapter, do not function on the model of the virtual circuit. Connections don't need to be established before data transmission begins. Instead, each packet is transmitted separately, and each may take a separate path through the mesh of network paths that make up the packet-switched network. Although it is not as well suited for delay-sensitive traffic as circuit-switched services, packet-switched services do handle bursty traffic better. The most popular packet-switched services are as follows.

X.25   X.25 networks have been around since 1976, when it was mostly used to provide remote terminal connections to mainframes. They perform extensive error checking that ensures reliable delivery. However, X.25 networks are not suitable for most LAN-to-LAN traffic because of the time and bandwidth consumed by this extensive error checking. Still, X.25 operates at speeds up to 2Mbps, which is much higher than the previously described carrier services.

FRAME RELAY   Frame relay, which began life as a service of ISDN, provides services similar to X.25, but is faster and more efficient. Frame relay doesn't employ the extensive error checking of X.25. Frame relay is an excellent choice for organizations that need any-to-any connections on an as-needed basis. We will discuss frame relay in greater detail in Chapter 20.

Cell-Switched Services

In cell-switched services, the smallest unit of data switched is a fixed-size "cell," rather than a variable-size packet. This cell-based technology allows switching to be accomplished in hardware without complex and time-consuming frame-by-frame route calculation. This makes switching both faster and less expensive.

ASYNCHRONOUS TRANSFER MODE (ATM)   ATM, which will be discussed in detail later on, can currently transfer data at rates of 25Mbps to 622Mbps, and has the potential to transfer data at rates measured in gigabits per second. Many carriers already offer ATM services, with many more scheduled to do so in the near future.

SWITCHED MULTIMEGABIT DATA SERVICE (SMDS)   Like ATM, Switched Multimegabit Data Service is another cell-based service provided by the Regional Bell Operating Companies (RBOCs) in selected areas. SMDS uses cell switching and provides services such as usage-based billing and network management.

Dedicated Digital Services

Dedicated digital lines are often used to carry voice, video, and data. Digital circuits provide data transmission speeds up to 45Mbps. Currently, digital lines are made possible by "conditioning" normal lines with special equipment to handle higher data rates. The lines are usually leased from the local exchange carrier and installed between two points (point to point) to provide dedicated, full-time service.

T1   The standard—and most widely used—digital line service is the T1 channel. A T1 provides transmission rates of 1.544Mbps and can carry both voice and data. The 1.544Mbps bandwidth of a T1 is usually divided into 24 64Kbps channels. This is because a digitized conversation requires 64Kbps of bandwidth, so when T1s are divided into 64Kbps channels, voice and data can be carried over the same T1 service.

FRACTIONAL T1   Fractional T1 is for those who require channels at 64Kbps, but don't need a full T1. A customer can start with a number of fractional T1 lines and grow into a full T1 line when and as necessary. When a customer orders fractional T1 service, the carrier sets up a full T1 interface, but only makes the contracted bandwidth available until more is needed. The lines are fractional, meaning that they can be divided into channels for voice or data.

T3   A T3 line is equivalent to 45Mbps, or 28 T1 lines, or 672 64Kbps channels.

Performance Over the Wide Area

One of the reasons you are reading this chapter is probably because you are considering a new, high-speed wide area link. The press has been saturated lately with news of ATM and other fast wide area protocols, and you may be wondering if and how to go about implementing them. If you already have a high-speed link in place, but it seems slow, be sure to identify the performance problem positively before making any changes to your wide area network.

As we mentioned earlier, right now the wide area will always seem slower than the rest of your network. That's because currently most wide area carrier services simply aren't designed to carry the megabits-per-second bandwidths that local area protocols can sustain. This will change as ATM becomes more and more available—at higher bandwidths—over the wide area. However, until then, users who access programs and data over wide area connections will not receive anything near the performance they are accustomed to receiving over the local area.

If users complain of slow performance when accessing remote data and applications, you can almost be sure the problem is a slow remote link. However, to be thorough, check the following to make sure that the problem can't be solved locally:

▼ Inadequate hardware

■ Location of applications and data

■ Traffic patterns

■ Packet size

▲ Communications protocols

Inadequate Hardware

As always, check your workstations and servers. Ensure that they have sufficient memory and processing power for the job. Also, check servers to make sure that they are not the bottleneck. If your servers are waiting on disk input/output, that's probably the cause of the network slowdown; it can be alleviated by installing a faster disk subsystem. Likewise, insufficient memory (often indicated by memory swapping to disk), low throughput to and from the network adapter (resulting in dropped packets and retransmissions), and inadequate processors can all slow your servers and cause them to be a bottleneck.

Location of Applications

Before you conclude that more bandwidth in the workgroup is what you need, ask yourself whether it's possible to move all the data and applications, or at least the applications, onto the local area network. This goes back to ensuring that all users are as close as possible—both physically and logically—to the network resources they use most frequently. This eliminates unnecessary internetwork traffic, which is especially important when the internetwork link is over a wide area connection, with its generally much slower transmission speeds.

Traffic Patterns

Try to limit the data that travels over wide area connections to that which absolutely has to. That means making sure that, whenever possible, database and application maintenance, server backups, and software upgrades are done locally rather than over the wide area link.

Packet Size

Your NetWare servers could be needlessly creating more wide area traffic because they are limiting packet size to a 512KB maximum. By default, NetWare servers route a default packet size of 512KB. This is because 512KB used to be the largest packet that all routers could route. However, most routers these days will route at the maximum packet size for each protocol. Therefore, if you have a NetWare network, check to make sure your routers can handle a larger packet size. If they can, you may want to implement the Large Internet Packet parameter on your NetWare Server.

Communication Protocols

Just as with backbones, another cause of congested workgroup segments is the communication protocol used by your network operating system. Among the functions of the communications protocol are creating service connections, getting network station addresses, and other tasks associated with transferring data from a station on one network to a station on another network. The communication protocol operates at the network layer as described on the International Standards Organization's Open Systems Interconnection model. Communications protocols include Internet Protocol (IP) and NetWare's Internetwork Packet Exchange protocol (IPX).

Some communications protocols generate a lot of traffic because for every request for service they send, they require a response from the station that is granting the services. Because of this constant "conversation" between the requester and grantor of services, these protocols are called "chatty" protocols. IPX, for example, is the classic example of a "chatty" protocol—request then response, request then response. Often, these requests and responses are larger than one packet. Therefore, a chatty protocol significantly increases the number of packets being transmitted. Furthermore, if a route fails, the delay required to rebuild routing tables using this chatty protocol can delay the establishment of a new route. Consequently, chatty protocols can slow a wide area link tremendously.

Novell has solved many of these problems by replacing IPX with a new routing protocol, called NetWare Link Services Protocol (NLSP). NLSP doesn't use the request-reply routines that IPX does. Instead, it uses a link-state routing based on the Open Shortest Path First and Intermediate-System-to-Intermediate-System routing algorithms. This makes routes easier to manage and faster to recalculate should a path fail. It also lets network managers program preferred route selection based on cost, traffic congestion or priority, line speed, or other criteria.

Transmission Control Protocol/Internet Protocol (TCP/IP), on the other hand, is not a chatty protocol. Rather than sending a request for service, waiting for a reply, then sending the next request for service, TCP/IP sends all requests for service in a single burst, sometimes called a "packet burst." It then receives multiple responses from the grantor of those services. This makes it a better choice for a wide area link than IPX.

Tests to Confirm Insufficient WAN Bandwidth

Just as with the local area, the true and indisputable determination of where your wide area bottleneck lies comes from in-depth analysis of your network traffic. This analysis will reveal whether lack of bandwidth is the culprit, or whether there is some other problem on your wide area link that is causing the poor performance.

However, unlike the local area, for the wide area connection analysis you will probably have to rely on your carrier service provider to conduct these tests and report the results. In a later chapter, we will discuss in detail how to order and interpret these tests. From my experience, relying on these test results requires a leap of faith—don't be surprised if the report comes back with "nothing wrong." Even when you receive such a report, wait a couple of days to see if network performance improves anyway. On many occasions I've had a wide area link magically improve after I notified the carrier service we were having problems, even when the carrier service's investigation turned up "No Trouble Found."

TIP: When you first report a performance problem to your wide area carrier, just ask for a traffic analysis. Don't tell them you're considering upgrading to a faster wide area protocol.

Requirements for Wide Area Protocols

If you have conducted the necessary tests and have determined that you need to implement a high-speed protocol on your wide area connections, it's time to set the selection criteria for this protocol. Overall, the most important features for a wide area protocol are almost the same as for the backbone protocol:

▼ Performance

■ Manageability

■ Packet size and overhead

▲ Cost

Performance

Performance is paramount in a wide area connection, because with the exception of ATM, wide area protocols are much slower than local area network protocols. Therefore, to limit performance degradation as much as possible, select the fastest protocol you can manage.

Manageability

Manageability and fault tolerance are critical on the wide area, and yet they are largely out of your hands unless you have a private network. The majority of network and data communications managers will have to work with the public network providers to manage, troubleshoot, and repair their wide area links. Therefore, it's essential that you select both a protocol and a vendor you feel is capable of supporting that protocol.

Packet Size and Overhead

Packet size and overhead are more critical on wide area connections than on any of the other segments. This is because of the following:

▼ Wide area network protocols are often slow anyway, and unnecessary overhead and error checking, as well as smaller, less efficient packets, will simply slow them even more.

▲   Many carrier services charge their customers only for the bandwidth they use, so larger, more efficient data packets will save bandwidth and money.

Internetwork and server-to-server packets tend to be larger than local segment packets. Therefore, a protocol that can support large packet sizes tends to be more efficient on a backbone. As well, the amount of overhead (addressing and management information) per packet should be low to eliminate unnecessary—and potentially expensive—traffic over the wide area link.

Cost

Finally, the wide area is not the place to pinch pennies, and yet wide area protocols, with their frequent dependence on outside carrier services, can be wildly expensive to implement. The wide area is one place where it's very important to make sure that you have all the features your network requires, but no "extras" that you can live without.

TIP: Later chapters in this book discuss each protocol in detail, and make recommendations as to where they would be best implemented.

Ready to Roll?

Now that we've given you a brief look at the task before you, it's time to discuss some of the basic concepts of telecommunications and how they will affect your wide area network. Much of the terminology and practice of telecommunications is rooted in the public voice network, so understanding each requires learning more about the public telecommunications network and how it evolved. Therefore, the next few sections discuss the building blocks of telecommunications, then explain how they affect today's data communications services.

CODES AND SIGNALING

Let's start at the *very* beginning—how data gets from one place to another. These concepts hold true for both the local area and the wide area, so ensuring that we share a thorough understanding of them will make it easier for you LAN managers to make the transition to WAN administration.

Data gets from one place to another via codes that are transmitted on signals. This is true in all communications. You use sound codes, commonly known as words, that are transmitted by voice signals over airwaves to let people know what you're thinking. A sailor standing on a ship deck uses Morse code transmitted via visual signals over lightwaves to transmit information to another ship. Similarly, network data is sent from one computer to another using data codes, called frames, transmitted by electric signals over a medium such as copper cabling or microwaves. To make sure we're all coming from the same understanding of concepts and terminology, this chapter will start with the basics of data signaling and encoding, then talk about the issues they present in wide area networking communications. Veteran network managers who are comfortable with these concepts should feel free to skip this chapter.

Codes: Computer Words

As most of you know, the information created and stored by computers is in binary format. Information is encoded into patterns of 0's and 1's that computers can understand and process. Back in the dark ages of programming, this was done manually by very patient (and often obsessive) programmers who spent hours translating complex human thoughts into operational questions that could be answered either "yes" or "no." Nowadays, programmers have sophisticated programming languages and tools that allow them to write efficient code while still thinking (and usually living) more like human beings and less like machines. However, even these relatively easy to use languages are dedicated to one task: transforming information into binary digits, or bits.

To make sure that all computers read this encoded information the same way, standard translation codes have emerged. One of the most widely used such codes is the American Standard Code for Information Interchange (ASCII). Table 19-1 shows the entire standard ASCII set. ASCII assigns a unique pattern of 1's and 0's, or bits, to represent every letter and symbol commonly used in the English language. Each pattern is 8 bits in length. Each 8-bit pattern is called a byte. Seven of the bits represent the character or symbol, and one bit, called a parity bit, is used for error checking. The computer encoding the information establishes whether it will make use of even parity and thus make every byte even, or odd parity and thus make every byte odd. The encoding computer then sets the parity bit so that the byte is either an odd or even number. Any computer that subsequently reads the byte will know whether the data was encoded using even parity or odd parity, and will thus know that if it encounters an odd-numbered byte in even-parity information, the byte has been damaged and contains erroneous information.

Analog Signaling

An analog signal is one in which the amplitude (wave height) and frequency (number of waves per second) vary over a continuous range. In other words, an analog signal is a continuous signal that conveys information by variations in the height and width of its waveform. For example, Figure 19-7 shows an analog wave that starts out with short waveforms. Then, these waveforms become increasingly higher. Assuming these waveforms are signaling a voice conversation, you could imagine the first part of the conversation being quick whispers, gradually growing louder and more emphatic. The conversation might go something like this, "Please don't drum your fingers so loudly, because it's really irritating me. Please, please! I said STOP THAT!"

Also note that the waves in Figure 19-7 vary in width, forming irregular shapes. By this, we can deduct they are conveying many different sounds, such as those found in music or a voice conversation. If the waveforms were transmitting a single sound, like the same word or tone over and over again, all the waves would be of the same width.

D	H	O	M	D	H	O	M
0	00	00	nul	30	1E	36	rs
1	01	01	soh	31	1F	37	us
2	02	02	stx	32	20	40	space
3	03	03	etx	33	21	41	!
4	04	04	eot	34	22	42	"
5	05	05	enq	35	23	43	#
6	06	06	ack	36	24	44	$
7	07	07	bel	37	25	45	%
8	08	10	bs	38	26	46	&
9	09	11	ht	39	27	47	'
10	0A	12	lf	40	28	50	(
11	0B	13	vt	41	29	51	)
12	0C	14	ff	42	2A	52	*
13	0D	15	cr	43	2B	53	+
14	0E	16	so	44	2C	54	,
15	0F	17	si	45	2D	55	-
16	10	20	dle	46	2E	56	.
17	11	21	dc1	47	2F	57	/
18	12	22	dc2	48	30	60	0
19	13	23	dc3	49	31	61	1
20	14	24	dc4	50	32	62	2
21	15	25	nak	51	33	63	3
22	16	26	syn	52	34	64	4
23	17	27	etb	53	35	65	5
24	18	30	can	54	36	66	6
25	19	31	em	55	37	67	7
26	1A	32	sub	56	38	70	8
27	1B	33	esc	57	39	71	9
28	1C	34	fs	58	3A	72	:
29	1D	35	gs	59	3B	73	;

Table 19-1. The ASCII Character Set

D	H	O	M	D	H	O	M
60	3C	74	<	90	5A	132	Z
61	3D	75	=	91	5B	133	[
62	3E	76	>	92	5C	134	\
63	3F	77	?	93	5D	135	]
64	40	100	@	94	5E	136	^
65	41	101	A	95	5F	137	–
66	42	102	B	96	60	140	'
67	43	103	C	97	61	141	a
68	44	104	D	98	62	142	b
69	45	105	E	99	63	143	c
70	46	106	F	100	64	144	d
71	47	107	G	101	65	145	e
72	48	110	H	102	66	146	f
73	49	111	I	103	67	147	g
74	4A	112	J	104	68	150	h
75	4B	113	K	105	69	151	I
76	4C	114	L	106	6A	152	j
77	4D	115	M	107	6B	153	k
78	4E	116	N	108	6C	154	l
79	4F	117	O	109	6D	155	m
80	50	120	P	110	6E	156	n
81	51	121	Q	111	6F	157	o
82	52	122	R	112	70	160	p
83	53	123	S	113	71	161	q
84	54	124	T	114	72	162	r
85	55	125	U	115	73	163	s
86	56	126	V	116	74	164	t
87	57	127	W	117	75	165	u
88	58	130	X	118	76	166	v
89	59	131	Y	119	77	167	w

Table 19-1. The ASCII Character Set *(continued)*

D	H	O	M	D	H	O	M
120	78	170	x	124	7C	174	|
121	79	171	y	125	7D	175	}
122	7A	172	z	126	7E	176	~
123	7B	173	{	127	7F	177	del

Table 19-1. The ASCII Character Set *(continued)*

Sound is an analog waveform. The sounds that you hear with your ears are trans-mitted via air pressure. The changing frequency of the sound waves creates continuously changing air pressure on your eardrums, which your brain interprets as sounds. Most humans can't hear sound at frequencies below about 30 cycles per second, or hertz (hertz is just another way of saying "cycles per second"), or above about 20,000 hertz. That means that high-fidelity sound, such as in a recording of a symphony performance, consists of all sounds from 30 hertz to 20,000 hertz—and every frequency in between.

In telephony and telecommunications, sounds are transmitted via electric current. Most telephones today are analog communications devices. They use variations in electric voltage to transmit analog signals representing sounds. As the frequency of the sound waves varies, so does the electrical current being transmitted by the telephone. As the loudness varies, so does the amplitude of the waveforms in the electric signals.

Although it's technically possible, it would be extremely expensive to provide tele-phone transmission equipment capable of transmitting all sounds within the range of human hearing. Therefore, for reasons of efficiency and economy, telephone equipment only transmits a range of frequencies from 300 to 3,400 hertz. As we mentioned, most humans can hear sound in the 30 to 20,000 hertz range. Therefore, the telephone company's range of frequencies is well within the "safe zone" of audible sounds. It is also enough to make a person's voice recognizable and understandable (usually).

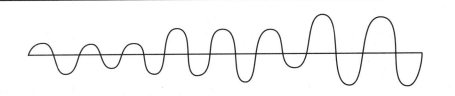

Figure 19-7. An analog waveform

"Okay," you say, "that's great for voice, but we're talking about connecting computers here. What does analog signaling have to do with that?" A lot, actually. You see, the majority of wide area telecommunications systems in use today were either originally designed to carry voice or were based on voice transmission technology. This introduces some technological challenges because, as we're about to see, computer signaling is very different from voice signaling.

Digital Signaling

Unlike sound and light waves, computer data is transmitted using digital signals. A digital signal doesn't use continuous waves to transmit information the way an analog signal does. Rather, a digital signal transmits information using two (or sometimes more) discrete signals. To illustrate, you can think of an analog signal as a violin, transmitting a wide variation of sounds. A digital signal, on the other hand, is like a drum. It has one sound, and you either hear it or you don't. Although this seems somewhat limited, anyone who's stayed up too late to watch an old jungle movie knows that elaborate systems of communication can be built around patterns of drumbeats.

Similarly, all computer data can be communicated through patterns of high- and low-voltage electrical pulses, or on and off states of electrical current. Figure 19-8 shows a representative digital waveform using two signals. Notice the square shape of the waveforms. This is the result of the digital signal's including only the two discrete states of "on" and "off"—it doesn't include all the values in between "on" and "off" the way an analog wave would. You can see how digital signaling lends itself to the transmission of binary data, with its on/off nature.

Digital signals offer more than an efficient way to transmit computer data. As we'll see later in this chapter, digital transmission facilities are generally less expensive to build and provide faster transmission than analog facilities.

The Importance of Being Well-Modulated

As you can see, digital and analog signals have very different natures. As a result of the elemental difference in waveforms, in their native forms digital and analog signals don't

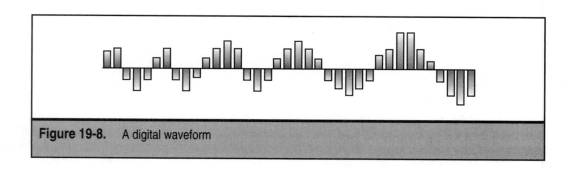

Figure 19-8.   A digital waveform

travel very well over each others' transmission systems. However, each can be converted to the other for transmission, then changed back into their original form when they reach their destination.

Modems and Modulation/Demodulation

Modem stands for modulator/demodulator. A modem is a device that modulates, or converts, digital signals to analog signals for transmission over analog communications channels. Anyone with a computer is very probably familiar with modems. Due to the fact that most of the telephone channels in the world today are analog, if you want your home computer to communicate with other computers and computer networks, you'll have to use a modem. A modem converts on/off digital signals into a continuous range of frequencies from 300 to 3,400 hertz so that these signals can be transmitted over standard voice telephone channels. Figure 19-9 illustrates how this works.

We'll talk more about modems later in this chapter. Right now, it's enough to understand what they do, why they do it, and that they are probably the most widely used data communications devices in the world.

CODECs and Coding/Decoding

A CODEC is a device that converts analog signals into digital signals for transmission over digital channels. Converting analog signals into digital signals involves taking samples of the analog waves, then quantizing the sample. This means that the CODEC takes frequent measures of the waveforms. In standard practice for voice conversion, the CODEC takes 8,000 8-bit samples every second. Next, the CODEC substitutes a digital value for the actual sampled value. This digital replacement is as close as possible to the sampled analog value—given the limited, discrete nature of digital signals.

For a very simple example, refer to Figure 19-10. Suppose the CODEC shown in the figure takes three samples of an analog wave. The sample analog frequencies are for 320

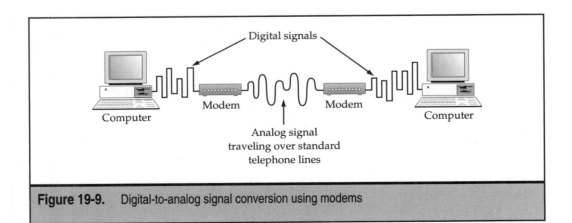

Figure 19-9. Digital-to-analog signal conversion using modems

hertz, 2,650 hertz, and 824 hertz. However, the digital signaling method employed by the CODEC supports only the following ten frequencies:

▼ 300 hertz   ■ 800 hertz

■ 400 hertz   ■ 900 hertz

■ 500 hertz   ■ 1,000 hertz

■ 600 hertz   ■ 1,100 hertz

■ 700 hertz   ▲ 1,200 hertz

The CODEC would quantize 300 hertz for the 320-hertz sample, 1,200 hertz for the 2,650-hertz sample, and 800 hertz for the 824-hertz sample. The CODEC would then digitize the quantized samples and transmit them over the telecommunications channel.

PULSE CODE MODULATION   The process of sampling, quantizing, and digitizing analog signals to transmit them over digital channels is called pulse code modulation, or PCM. Hidden in the sampling formula for PCM is an important number to remember. Recall that in normal PCM the analog signal is sampled 8,000 times every second, and each sample is 8 bits in length. This number, 8.8, yields the range of frequencies that defines the channel capacity, or bandwidth, necessary for a voice conversation over a digital channel—64,000 bits per second, or 64Kbps. You'll see this number—and multiples of it—over and over again when selecting telecommunications facilities and services. This is because, as we mentioned earlier, most telecommunications facilities were either designed for voice communications or based on technologies developed for voice communications.

It's Not Only How You Say It, but Also What You Say

Now that we have reviewed the structure of the codes that make up transmitted data, and we know how it is signaled over telecommunications facilities, it's time to take a look at why data is transmitted. Essentially, there are two kinds of information signals: signals for the data itself, and management signals that tell the data where to go and how to get there.

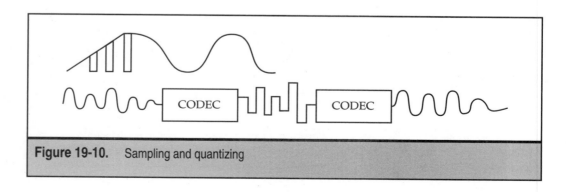

Figure 19-10.   Sampling and quantizing

Data Signals

Data signals are the signals that carry the data itself. These are the signals that carry a caller's voice to the callee's ear. They are also the signals that carry information from one computer to another. They are the signals that carry the "payload" data from its originating point to its destination. However, in some types of transmission systems, data signals alone would never get where they are going. They need another type of signal to guide them and ensure safe delivery.

Management Signals

Management signals are signals that tell data where to go and when. Some telecommunications systems rely on management signals to establish a connection between the calling and the called party, to control the flow of data between the parties, and then to clear the connection when the call is complete.

CONNECTION-ORIENTED COMMUNICATIONS "Connection-oriented" means that a connection must be established between the calling and the called parties before data is transferred. The voice telephone calls that you make every day are connection-oriented communications. When you dial a number, a connection is established between your telephone and the callee's telephone. This connection is unavailable to anyone else for the duration of your call. Furthermore, the information transmitted during this call—your conversation—isn't received by anyone but the two connected parties (except in certain illegal and/or unfortunate instances).

In connection-oriented communications, any and all intermediate points in the transmission path must be identified and informed of the existence of the connection. Different types of communications systems handle this in different ways. In later chapters, we will talk in depth about how connections are established, maintained, and cleared.

Because a connection is established in advance and monitored throughout the duration of the call, connection-oriented communications offer secure and reliable delivery of information. However, they also take time to set up and end, or tear down. They also generally don't make efficient use of the connection. Think about your voice calls—a lot of conversations consist of pauses and silences. By some measurements, the average voice call is over 60 percent "dead air." And yet, in connection-oriented communications, a connection is dedicated to a particular call until it is torn down. No other transmission can share the bandwidth dedicated to that call.

Connection-oriented communications obviously make full use of management signaling to set up, maintain, and tear down connections. However, there is a type of communications that doesn't require management signaling for connection management.

CONNECTIONLESS COMMUNICATIONS Connectionless communications are those in which no connection is established between the transmitting and receiving parties— which are always computers—before data is transferred. Packets are simply transmitted on the medium as soon as the computer's communications interface receives them. Therefore, there is no delay for call setup or teardown.

Local area networks use connectionless communications. LANs transmit data packets that are all of a uniform structure, containing origination and destination addresses in the header information that allow the network to route each packet to its destination. Since each packet already holds its address information, each knows where it is going, so it doesn't need to have a connection set up before being transmitted. This also means that packets from various origination addresses can travel together over the same cable. However, because bandwidth isn't dedicated to individual connections, all transmissions contend with one another for bandwidth, and therefore transmission delays are unpredictable when network traffic is heavy. This makes packet-based transmission undesirable for time-sensitive traffic like voice and data.

FLOW CONTROL   Even if a communications system doesn't use management signaling for managing connections, it may need it to control the flow of information on the medium. Flow-control signals tell devices when to start and stop sending data. They prevent receiving devices from being overrun by too much incoming data. When a computer receives data faster than it can process it, for example, it can send a signal to the sending device telling it to stop transmitting data. When the receiving computer "catches up" and is ready to receive more data, it sends a signal to the sending computer telling it to resume sending data. There are two methods for sending flow-control signals between computers: software flow control and hardware flow control.

In *software flow control,* the host computer receives control codes that tell it to start or stop sending data. These control codes are the ASCII codes DC1 and DC32, also known as XON/XOFF codes, and are sent from one computer to another in the transmitted data stream.

In *hardware flow control,* computers send electrical signals rather than control codes to one another to start and stop data transmission. By sending a level of electrical voltage defined as the Clear to Send (CTS) signal, the receiving computer tells the transmitting computer to start sending data. When the transmitting computer receives the CTS signal, it responds by sending another level of electrical voltage defined as the Ready to Send (RTS) signal, then begins sending data over the medium. By turning off the CTS signal, the receiving computer tells the transmitting computer to stop sending data.

ERROR CHECKING AND RETRANSMISSION   In some communications systems, when a receiving computer detects a transmission error, it requests that the damaged data be resent. This request for retransmission is made through management signaling as well.

Error checking is done through error-detection protocols such as the parity bit checking that we discussed earlier in this chapter. There are a variety of error-detection protocols used by communications systems. Some of these are MNP1, MNP2, MNP3, MNP4, V.22bis, LAPM, and V.42. Each uses a different methodology, or algorithm, for detecting misplaced bits in transmitted data. Some communications systems depend heavily upon such error-checking methods to detect problems in data transmission.

Other communications systems discard error-detection systems completely and depend upon either software applications to catch transmission errors or the grace of the transmission facility not to cause any errors.

So, now that we know why some transmission systems use management signaling, the next question is how? There are two different methods for transmitting management signals: in-band signaling and out-of-band signaling.

IN-BAND SIGNALING   On some telecommunications systems, management signals travel inside the same frequency bandwidth used for transmitting information, as illustrated here:

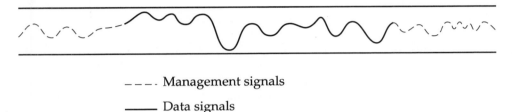

$- - - -$ Management signals

⸺ Data signals

This is called in-band management signaling.

Because they share the same bandwidth as the data being transmitted, in-band signals can't be transmitted at the same time that data is being sent. However, the signaling system must monitor data transmission so that it is ready to respond when data transmission ends. Therefore, there is some risk that the in-band signaling system might misinterpret data being transferred as a management signal. In-band signaling was originally developed to work with voice transmissions, and so the in-band signals are designed to avoid misinterpreting voice signals. However, when data is sent, the data might, unless precautions are taken, accidentally trigger the equipment that listens for control signals.

In-band signaling has several advantages over out-of-band signaling. Because they are the same frequency as data signals, in-band management signals can go anywhere their "payload" signals can go, over any transmission facility that can support transmission of the payload data. On the other hand, you can only use out-of-band signaling on transmission facilities especially designed for them.

Furthermore, in-band signaling is very efficient in detecting faulty media and transmission facilities. That's because you can't even establish an in-band connection over a transmission system that has problems in the portion of the bandwidth that transmits the payload data—it shares the same bandwidth as the data. In out-of-band signaling, however, the portions of the bandwidth transmitting the management signals could be just fine, even though the data transmission bandwidth is faulty. Therefore, the connection could be established, but no data could be transmitted.

Finally, in-band signaling can use several different frequencies, while out-of-band signaling is confined to a narrow signaling frequency, as we're about to see.

OUT-OF-BAND SIGNALING   Out-of-band signaling, illustrated here, is management signaling that uses a predefined frequency outside the bandwidth assigned to transmitting data:

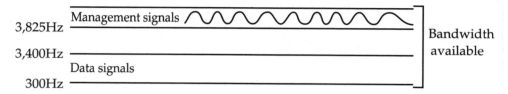

For example, 3,825 hertz is the frequency that the CCITT-ITU Signaling System No. R2 specifies for management signaling. This is well out of the bandwidth used for most voice and data transmission.

Out-of-band signaling does have a couple of advantages over in-band signaling. Because out-of-band management signals don't share the same bandwidth as data signals, there's no risk of misinterpreting or interfering with the data being transferred. As well, out-of-band signaling can take place during data transmission. However, in addition to the disadvantages pointed out earlier in this section, out-of-band signaling also needs extra bandwidth and extra facilities to support the signaling band. Furthermore, out-of-band signaling is also slower than in-band signaling, because all signals must be sent via a very narrow signaling bandwidth, whereas in-band signals can use the much wider data transmission bandwidth.

And What Does This Have to Do with My LAN?

Congratulations. Now you know how information is encoded, then signaled from one device to another over a wide area. You know how connections are made and managed to enable those signals to reach from the sender to the receiver. And you know a little bit about what happens when the data doesn't successfully reach its intended destination.

So what does this mean to you, the network manager? It means that to transmit data successfully from one point to another, it will have to be properly encoded. Luckily, computer data is digital in nature, so it comes properly encoded for transmission. At least that's one thing you don't have to worry about—for now.

Next, your network data must be loaded on to the transmission medium. If you are loading digital data on to a digital transmission medium, or analog data on to an analog trans- mission medium, this isn't a problem. However, if you're sending digital data over an analog transmission medium, you'll have to have modems to modulate the data on to and off of the transmission signal. If you're sending analog data over a digital transmission medium, you'll have to install CODECs to code the data on to the medium, then decode it when it arrives at its destination.

Finally, as we mentioned earlier, because your network data is connectionless in nature, and most wide area communications systems are connection-oriented, some method of routing connectionless data over a connection is required. Even if you choose a connectionless wide area system, you'll have to ensure that the addressing and routing schemes used by your LAN are properly interpreted by the wide area network. From experience, we can tell you that the equipment that enables this interface will be one of the most expensive—and most difficult to troubleshoot— in your wide area network.

The systems and equipment necessary to accomplish these tasks are the subject of Chapter 20 of this book. In them, we will discuss in detail the equipment, services, and protocol operations required for building wide area networks based on several different protocols. However, there is some vital ground to cover before we do that—namely, the nuts and bolts of telecommunications transmission and politics.

The next two sections will give you an inside look at the operations of wide area transmission facilities. They will explain the basics of trunking, switching, and transmission on which our current voice and data telecommunications systems are based. Then, we will discuss the rapidly changing regulatory environment that affects the services and equipment available to you for building your wide area network. Next, we will then introduce you to the cast of characters with whom you will need to work to build your WAN. Finally, we will walk you through the process of stating the requirements of your WAN. It will help you define your WAN in terms of what you want to be able to do, which will make choosing a protocol and/or service much easier.

BASIC TRUNKING

Let's continue our discussion of wide area networking basics by talking about the nuts and bolts of the public telecommunications carrier facilities. Why? Because most wide area networks begin with remote dial-up connections running over the public telecommunications network.

For offices with infrequent and/or light internetwork data traffic, dial-up lines are often the easiest and most economical solution for wide area networking. Learning more about the different types of dial-up connections will make you aware of the options you have in your dial-up service.

There are other reasons for learning about the public telecommunications network as well. As I said earlier, the majority of wide area telecommunications systems in use today were either originally designed to carry voice or were based on voice transmission technology. This is rapidly changing, but still the rule. This introduces some significant technological challenges when you are trying to transmit data traffic over voice facilities. Therefore, it will serve you well to take a close look at how public telecommunications networks work. You will then have a framework to help you identify potential problems and solutions for your wide area data network. Furthermore, you will be able to talk with telephone company employees using the terminology they understand, so you have a better chance of receiving the services you want.

Two Tin Cans and a String = a Loop

Let's start with the most basic connection available in the public telephone network, the line circuit. Line circuits, also called loops by veteran telephone technicians, are the individual circuits that are dedicated to a single device, such as a telephone or a modem. Figure 19-11 illustrates a line circuit.

Theoretically, it's possible to build an entire telecommunications network from line circuits. All you'd have to do is run a line circuit from your computer or telephone to every other computer or telephone with which you want to communicate. This would form a mesh network, like the one shown in Figure 19-12.

Are You Dedicated, or Are You Going to Switch?

A mesh network like the one shown in Figure 19-12 is an example of a network of dedicated circuits. Dedicated circuits have one function: they provide a data transmission path between two devices. Dedicated circuits, like those shown in Figure 19-12, have a lot of advantages. First, there is no need to dial a number. When Computer A wants to talk to Computer D, all it has to do is send a message over the loop to Computer D. There is no other device on that line circuit, so no one else could answer the call or receive transmitted data. Furthermore, when Computer D receives signals from the loop connected to Computer A, Computer D knows exactly who is calling. Because no other devices are using the line circuit, the data telecommunications would be very secure. As well, the two computers would never have to wait for an available line circuit between them, would never experience slow transmission because of heavy traffic on the loop, and would never get a busy signal when calling each other. You can see, therefore, why dedicated circuits are very widely used among devices that communicate frequently and/or carry sensitive data.

Of course, a mesh would also involve a lot of individual line circuits and a lot of cable. Practically speaking, you can't have a separate loop running from your telecommunications devices to every other telecommunications device with which you may want to communicate. That's why switches were developed.

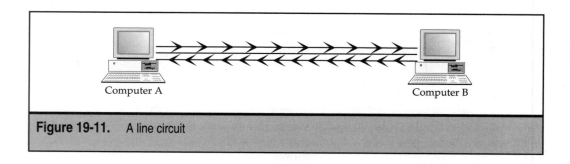

Computer A   Computer B

Figure 19-11.   A line circuit

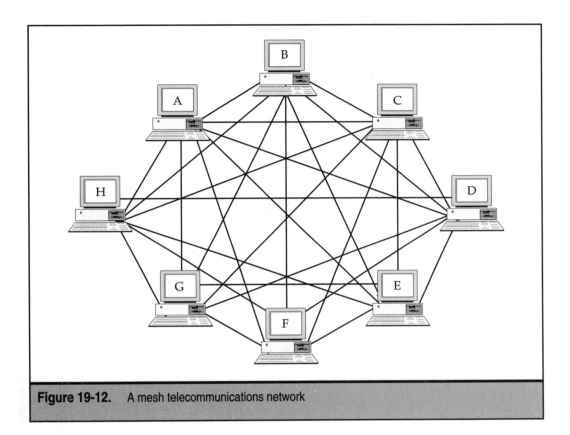

Figure 19-12.   A mesh telecommunications network

Figure 19-13 illustrates how a switch works. When Computer A wants to call Computer D, it sends a signal over its line circuit to the switch. The switch then makes a temporary connection between the line circuits of Computer A and Computer D. When Computer A finishes transmitting data to Computer D, the switch clears the temporary connection between the two line circuits.

Switches may be operated either by public telecommunications carriers or by private corporations that have built their own telecommunications networks. Switches that are owned by public telecommunications carriers are located in special facilities, called central offices (COs). Central offices are located in or near the geographical areas their switches serve. Switches that are privately owned are called private branch exchanges (PBXs), and they are located on the premises of the corporation that owns them.

The advantages of a switched telecommunications network over a mesh telecommunications network are obvious. The switched network requires a lot less cable, and is therefore much easier to manage. It is also a lot more efficient in design (you don't have all those line circuits sitting around unused most of the time).

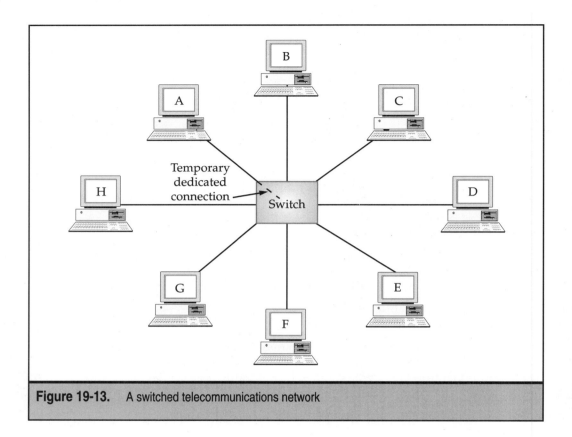

Figure 19-13. A switched telecommunications network

Of course, if anything happens to the switch, you will have a lot of telecommunications customers completely unable to communicate. That's why COs, the buildings where public telephone companies house their switching facilities, have well-protected power supplies and high security.

Pack Your Trunk

Okay, so it makes sense to have several computers or telephones communicate with one another over a switch. The switch enables every line circuit device (telephone, modem, or other telecommunications device connected to a loop) to talk to any other line circuit device on the switch. Because practically every line circuit device in the world can talk to any other line circuit device, does this mean that the whole global telecommunications network runs over one big switch? Although it would be great to have a switch with enough speed and capacity to handle all of the calls made in the world, the maximum number of calls that a switch on the public telecommunications network can handle is about 10,000.

Then how, you ask, do line circuit devices on one switch transmit data to line circuit devices on another? Over trunk circuits, which are two-way lines that connect two switches, as shown in Figure 19-14. Trunk circuits are also called tie lines.

Trunk circuits are another way in which a switched telecommunications network is more efficient than a mesh telecommunications network. Not only can a trunk circuit make outgoing calls as well as accept incoming calls (i.e., making it a two-way line), but it is also shared among all the line circuit devices connected to the switches. Therefore, the switch doesn't have to have a separate trunk for every line circuit device attached to it. In fact, in the public telecommunications network, the ratio of trunks to line circuit devices is usually about 1 to 15. Therefore, a switch serving 15,000 line circuits will have a trunk group of about 1,000. A trunk group is a setup of trunk circuits that all have the same basic function (e.g., connecting Switch 1 with Switch 2), as shown in Figure 19-15.

Routing to the Rescue

Line consolidation isn't the only benefit that switches offer the public telecommunications network. Alternate routing is an important feature, too. Look at the switched network illustrated in Figure 19-16. If Computer A wants to call Computer G, the call could take one of two paths. It could travel over the trunk group 1-2, or it could travel over the route formed by trunk groups 1-3 and 2-3. Having this option increases efficiency, because even when there are no circuits in trunk group 1-2, there may be circuits available in trunk groups 1-3 and 1-2. If the telecommunications network is designed to take advantage of these different paths for completing the call, you probably won't have to install additional trunks to accommodate heavy traffic between Switch 1 and Switch 2. This is called alternate routing, and it obviously allows you to build a far-reaching network more efficiently and economically.

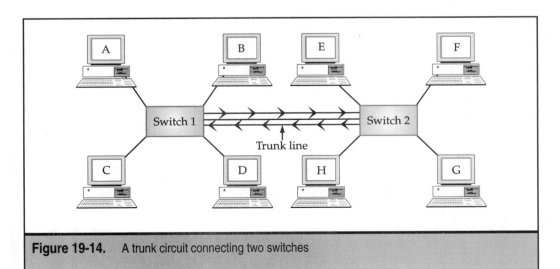

Figure 19-14.   A trunk circuit connecting two switches

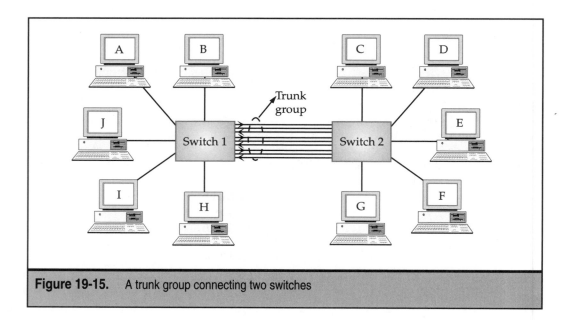

Figure 19-15. A trunk group connecting two switches

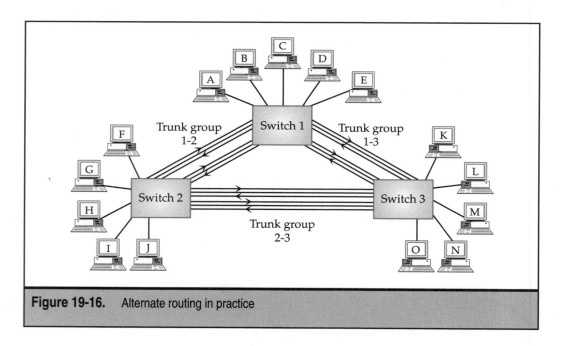

Figure 19-16. Alternate routing in practice

Types of Trunks

Now that you know what a trunk is, you need to know that there's more than one kind of trunk. Different types of trunks give you different ways to connect line circuit devices in remote locations. Here are the available types of trunks.

CENTRAL OFFICE (CO) TRUNKS   A CO trunk, shown in Figure 19-17, is a set of trunk circuits connecting a private branch exchange (PBX) to a central office that serves the PBX's local exchange. This is the type of trunk that connects your office's PBX to the public telecommunications network.

TIE LINES   A tie line, illustrated in Figure 19-18, is a trunk that connects two different locations. For example, I once worked for a company that had a tie line that connected its offices in Dallas and Houston. To call the Houston office, a caller in Dallas simply had to dial a code (in our case, it was "7"), then the device's 21-digit extension she was calling.

FOREIGN EXCHANGE (FX) TRUNKS   Foreign exchange trunks, shown in Figure 19-19, are something like tie lines. However, rather than connecting two offices, foreign exchange trunks directly connect a local line circuit device or PBX with a distant CO. This essentially makes a call from your office to the distant central office look like a local call. You might choose to use FX trunks to connect your office telephone system with a CO in

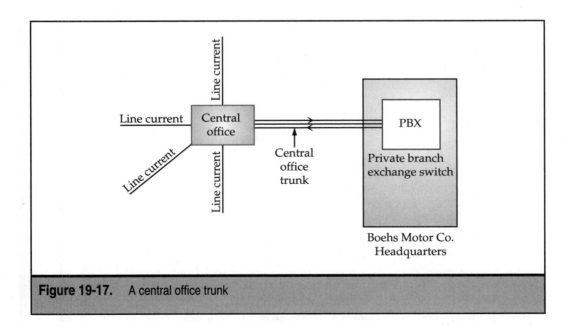

Figure 19-17.   A central office trunk

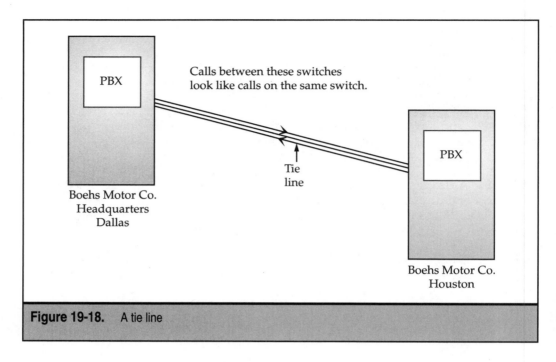

Figure 19-18.   A tie line

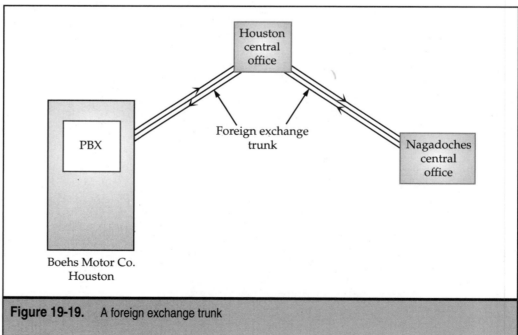

Figure 19-19.   A foreign exchange trunk

another city to which you make a lot of calls. For example, if your headquarters is in Nagadoches, but most of your clients are in downtown Houston, you might want to install a foreign exchange line to connect your PBX to a CO in Houston. This would provide a couple of advantages: 21-digit dialing (rather than 10-digit dialing) as well as service to a distant area at a fixed cost. Depending upon your calling volume, this fixed cost could be significantly lower than standard long-distance rates. However, if you don't have a high volume of calls to the distant location, a foreign exchange trunk could be ridiculously more expensive than regular long distance.

WIDE AREA TELECOMMUNICATIONS SERVICE (WATS) TRUNKS A WATS trunk, illustrated in Figure 19-20, enables callers to make or receive long-distance calls at bulk rate. WATS rates are calculated by total calling time rather than by time per call. There are two types of WATS trunks, inward and outward. Inward WATS gives you a means of letting line circuit devices call your site at no cost to the calling device. That's because inward WATS calls are billed to the called number.

WATS is available within a state (intrastate WATS) and between states (interstate WATS). You can customize your interstate WATS to include only certain areas. For purposes of tailoring WATS coverage, the continental United States is divided into five areas, called bands, beginning with the WATS subscriber's home state, Band 0, and extending outward. Hawaii and Alaska are in Band 6. WATS bands are illustrated in Figure 19-21. You can subscribe to all of the bands, or only to certain bands, for inward and/or outward WATS. When you select service to a particular band, you automatically get service to all of the bands between the distant band and your Band 0.

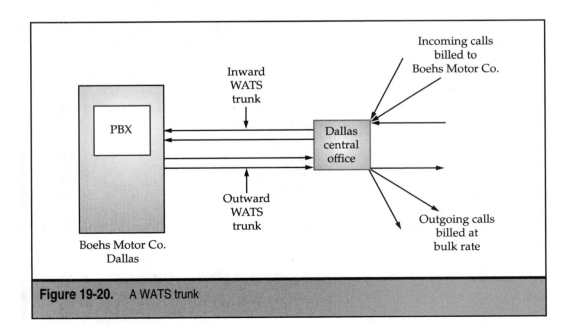

Figure 19-20. A WATS trunk

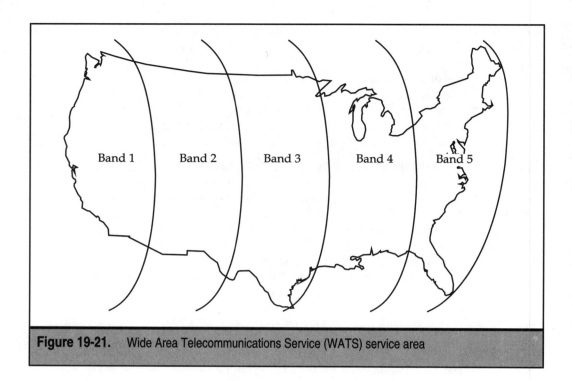

Figure 19-21.   Wide Area Telecommunications Service (WATS) service area

In the past, WATS rates were calculated quite strictly using a standard formula that included both total calling time and mileage. Now, however, most long-distance carriers are more than willing to negotiate WATS rates, so feel free to bargain for a good rate.

WATS can save you money, especially if your calling patterns are geographically scattered. Inward WATS is also a good choice if you have roaming remote access users. For example, if you have a lot of salespeople on the road who frequently dial in to the network from remote areas, WATS rates are much less than that of an equivalent amount of telephone credit card calls. It can even be much less expensive than an equivalent amount of standard long-distance calls if you have negotiated your WATS rate well.

DIRECT INWARD DIAL (DID) TRUNKS   Direct inward dial (DID) trunks, illustrated in Figure 19-22, let you dial a device on a PBX directly, without your call having to be answered and routed by an operator. This is because the extension address of the called device is included in the number and sent directly to the PBX by the connecting CO.

Obviously, DID trunks are vital to computers and computer networks that are connected by private branch exchanges. A modem dialing in to another modem on a PBX will not understand an answering human voice, and a human operator can't recognize

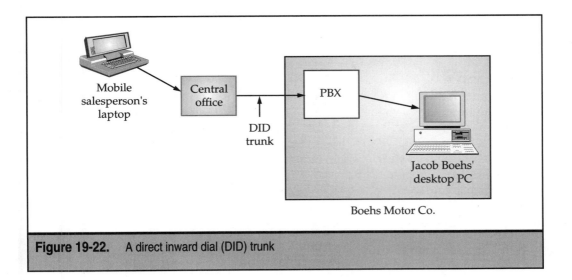

Figure 19-22.   A direct inward dial (DID) trunk

and route the call fast enough to prevent the calling computer from timing out because of no response by the called computer.

Off-premise extension (OPX) trunks, illustrated in Figure 19-23, are handy systems that I don't see as much as I used to. They connect an extension at a remote location to a PBX so that the remote extension appears to be on-site locally. Therefore, callers only

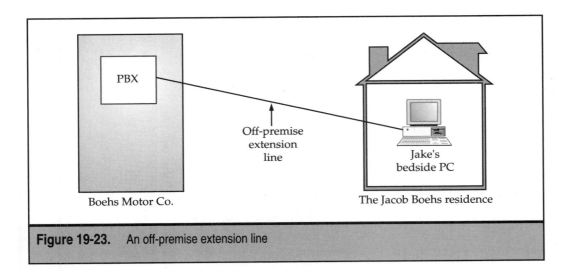

Figure 19-23.   An off-premise extension line

have to dial the four-digit extension to call the OPX line circuit device. This is very handy to connect a single off-site computer with a network located in a different part of the city.

Putting It Together

To help you put this all together, let's take a look at a typical switched data transmission session. Suppose, as shown in Figure 19-24, the calling computer is connected to Switch 1, and the called computer is connected to Switch 2 in another city. The computers are connected to their respective switches by line circuits. Switch 1 and Switch 2 are connected directly to one another by a trunk, and they also have indirect connections via Switch 3 and Switch 4.

Computer A places a call to Computer D by dialing the telephone number of Computer D. When Switch 1 receives the telephone number, it looks up Computer D's location in its routing table. This routing table includes the various trunk paths available to Computer D. The routing table will show the direct trunk as the best choice, so Switch 1 looks for an open circuit in the direct trunk group. If there is an open circuit in the direct

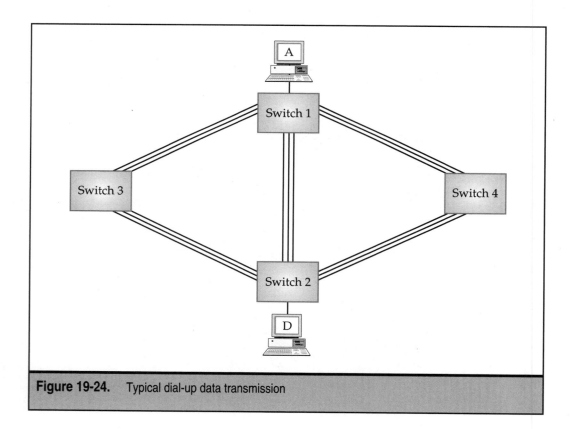

Figure 19-24. Typical dial-up data transmission

trunk group, Switch 1 will use that circuit to connect Computer A to Switch 2. However, if there is no available circuit in the direct trunk group, Switch 1 looks in the routing table for an alternate route.

In this example, there are two alternate routes: one route via Switch 3 and another route via Switch 4. From the illustration, it appears that both routes are of equal distance and include the same number of segments, so neither route is better than the other. In this case, Switch 1 would look for the first available circuit in either of the trunk groups and use it to complete the call. However, in reality, one path may actually be more efficient or cost-effective than another, and this information would be included in the routing table to help Switch 1 select the best alternate route.

When the call from Computer A reaches Switch 1—by whichever route—Switch 2 looks up the called party's number in its switch table. After finding that the called number is connected to Switch 2, the switch completes the connection to Computer D. Computer A can then transmit data to Computer D.

When the data transmission is complete and one or both computers hang up, all switches involved in routing the call restore the trunk circuits used in the call to their previous condition, making them available to other calls.

Now That Your Trunk Is Packed, We Can Move On

Now you've seen how telecommunications networks are put together with circuits, switches, and trunks. You've also seen that there are different types of trunks to enable different types of communications. You've also seen how a call is made and terminated. These aspects of trunking remain the same for all switched services, whether they are voice or data. Switched services, as we have just seen, establish a temporary dedicated circuit between the calling and called parties. All data is then transmitted over this temporary circuit, which remains in place for the duration of the transmission. When the transmission is completed, the circuit is cleared. There are two types of switched services, circuit-switched services and packet-switched services.

Circuit Switching and Packet Switching

The calls that we have been discussing up to this point have been circuit-switched calls. In circuit-switched calls, the temporary dedicated circuit established between caller and called party remains in place until all data is exchanged between these two parties and one or both of the parties terminate the call. During this data transmission, no other devices can use the circuit.

There is, however, another type of service, called packet-switched service, which doesn't set up a single circuit over which all data is transmitted in a continuous stream. Instead, the transmitted data is broken into small pieces and packaged into data packets, and each of these packets is transmitted separately over its own individual circuit. In fact, each packet could be sent over a different circuit! The temporary circuit remains in place for only as long as it takes to transmit the individual data packet. Then the circuit is cleared.

Because a packet-switching network consists of many individual circuits, most illustrations depict a packet-switched network as a "cloud" that encompasses all the switches over which individual data packets may be routed. This is illustrated in Figures 19-25 and 19-26.

When data is initially broken down into packets—before the data packets are transmitted—the sending equipment assigns each data packet a sequence number that designates the order in which the packets should be assembled. When the data packets arrive at their destination, the receiving equipment reassembles them in the proper order. At this point, the incoming information is ready for processing by the receiving computer.

Obviously, setting up these multiple circuits, ensuring delivery of all the packets, and reassembling them in the proper order requires different transmission procedures and equipment, and consequently different transmission facilities than standard circuit-switching transmission facilities. The type of transmission facilities available in your area, therefore, will have a strong impact on the type and cost of the wide area networking options available to you. In the next section, we will discuss the basics of data signaling procedures and the telecommunications facilities that enable data transmission.

BASIC TRANSMISSION

Transmission is the means by which your wide area network sends electrical signals. The transmission method and its quality determine whether the destination station receives data it can understand and process, or whether it receives "electronic garbage" and has to request a retransmission.

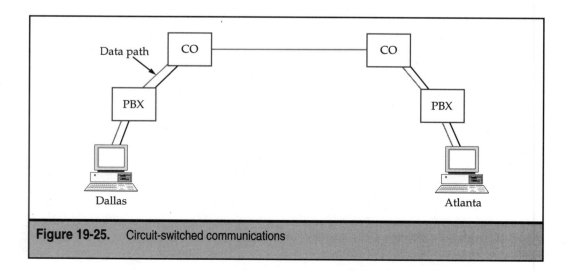

Figure 19-25. Circuit-switched communications

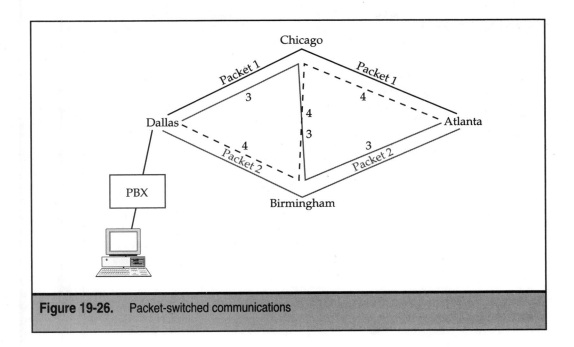

Figure 19-26.   Packet-switched communications

Many of the transmission methods widely used today were originally developed to transmit speech as part of the telephone network. As demand increased for wide area computer connections, these voice transmission facilities were adapted to transmit data—and they do a pretty good job with it. Transmission facilities were also developed especially for the transmission of digital information.

To help you select the appropriate services, you'll need to understand the transmission method they use. This will also help you understand the problems you may encounter with your transmission system. Therefore, this section begins with an overview of transmission facilities, discusses how they perform circuit and packet operations, and concludes with a discussion of transmission problems and how to recognize them.

Transmission Facilities: An Overview

Transmission facilities have several components. To understand what these components are and how they work together, let's walk through a transmission system. We'll start with the most basic component and work outward.

Transmission Media

The fundamental component of any transmission system is the transmission medium. This is the material over which the data signals travel. There are two general categories of transmission media, bounded (also called guided) and unbounded (also called unguided).

You are probably most familiar with using bounded media, which is just another way of saying "cable." Twisted-pair cable, coaxial cable, and fiber-optic cable are all bounded media—the signals travel within the bounds of the cable. Figure 19-27 shows an example of bounded, or guided, media.

On the other hand, you're probably no stranger to unbounded media, either. Microwave and satellite transmissions both travel through the air, which has no boundaries to speak of. The signals travel through the air—or any gas, for that matter— from transmitter to receiver. This is illustrated in Figure 19-28.

Unbounded transmission media are more commonly used for long-haul transmission between buildings. However, infrared transmission and other wireless transmission methods that employ unbounded transmission media (air) are becoming more common in short-haul transmission within buildings.

Copper transmission media, such as twisted-pair, are probably the most common transmission media inside buildings (although fiber-optic cabling is becoming more common). Furthermore, the interface between short-haul transmission media and long-haul transmission media is often copper. Because it is so common, and because improper copper wire (or metallic transmission facilities, as they are sometimes called) can cause problems, let's take a closer look at the different types of copper transmission media used for data communications.

METALLIC TRANSMISSION MEDIA   Basically, there are two different types of copper transmission media. The first is a two-wire facility and the second is a four-wire facility. The two-wire facility has one pair of wires. One wire is called the "Tip" and the other is called the "Ring." This four-wire facility, or cable, carries signals in both directions, as illustrated in Figure 19-29.

NOTE: The names "Tip" and "Ring" date back to the olden days of telephony, when manual switchboards used plugs that made the electric connection. The tip of the plug made the transmitting connection and a ring, farther back on the plug, made the receiving connection.

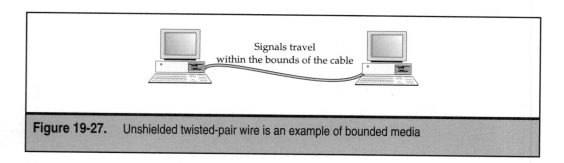

Signals travel within the bounds of the cable

Figure 19-27.   Unshielded twisted-pair wire is an example of bounded media

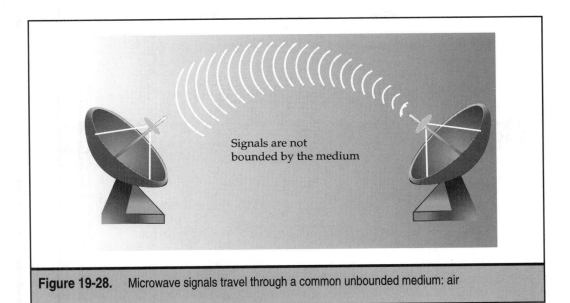

Figure 19-28. Microwave signals travel through a common unbounded medium: air

Two-wire cables are great for short-haul transmissions. They are also fairly inexpensive. Therefore, you usually see two-wire cables running between a modem and a PBX, or between a computer and a demarc, or between a PBX and a central office. Beware, however. If your cable installer reverses the tip and ring wires in the cable jack, you won't be able to transmit or receive data over that facility.

For long-haul transmission over copper, however, a four-wire facility is better. A four-wire facility, or cable, has two pairs of wires. The pairs are designated Tip and Ring,

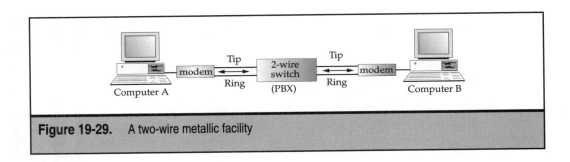

Figure 19-29. A two-wire metallic facility

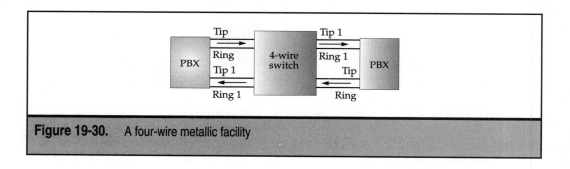

Figure 19-30. A four-wire metallic facility

and Tip 1 and Ring 1. Each pair of wires carries information in only one direction: Tip and Ring transmit and Tip 1 and Ring 1 receive. This is illustrated in Figure 19-30.

Four-wire cables are better for long-haul transmission because they can carry signals farther without any loss or distortion. They are more expensive than two-wire cables, so you usually don't see them used inside buildings. However, despite the increased expense, it sometimes makes sense to use four-wire cables inside buildings because you can connect them directly to long-distance metallic transmission facilities, which are all four-wire cables.

HOW TO MAKE 2 = 4   As we mentioned, long-distance transmission facilities are all four-wire cables. Since so many internal transmission facilities are two-wire cables, how do you interconnect the two? Through the use of a four-wire termination set (called a 4WTS in the trade), that's how. A four-wire termination set matches both the signal paths and the impedance between the two-wire facilities and the four-wire facilities, as shown in Figure 19-31.

Transmission Facilities

Of course, a transmission system is much more than media. The media must be connected to transmitting and receiving devices—and often to many devices in between.

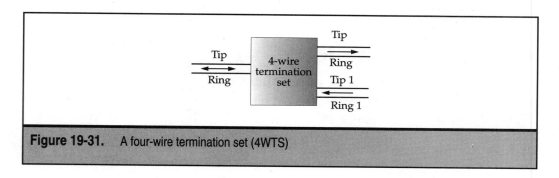

Figure 19-31.   A four-wire termination set (4WTS)

Some devices enable multiple signal transmissions to share the same communications channel. These devices are called *multiplexors*. Other devices monitor the signals traveling over the media.

There are still other devices that periodically strengthen signals should they become too weak. These devices either amplify or completely regenerate the signal, depending upon the type of carrier system involved, as you are about to see.

Carrier Systems

The entire collection of transmission devices connected by the media is called the carrier system. A generic carrier system is show in Figure 19-32. Carrier systems usually transmit several channels of signals simultaneously, and they come in one of two types: analog and digital.

ANALOG CARRIER SYSTEMS   Analog carrier systems were designed to transmit voice signals. Although they can carry data signals, they are really best for voice signals. Over the

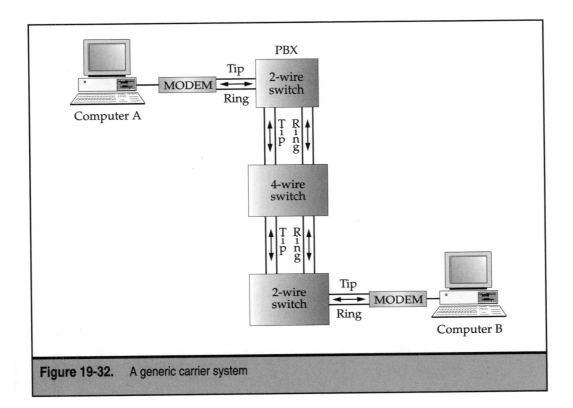

Figure 19-32.   A generic carrier system

past several years, we've seen telecommunications carriers rapidly replacing their analog carrier systems with digital carrier systems. The function of a typical analog carrier system is illustrated in Figure 19-33.

To send data over an analog carrier system, the data must first be loaded on to an analog signal by a modem. The digital service unit (DSU) then sends the signal over the transmission medium to a frequency division mutiplexor (FDM). The FDM packs the signals together so that it can send multiple signals over one transmission channel simultaneously. It does this by "stacking" transmission signals in different frequency ranges within the same transmission channel. To do this, the FDM adjusts the frequency of the signals it carries, temporarily raising or lowering them for the duration of transmission, then returning the signals to their original frequencies when they arrive at their destinations. For example, Transmission 1 might have been raised in frequency from 300 to 3,100 hertz (remember, the range of frequencies carried by a standard analog telephone line) to 60,000 to 63,100 hertz. Transmission 2 might have been raised from 64,300 to 67,100. By adjusting the frequency of the signals temporarily, several transmissions can share the same channel without colliding with one another. This process, called frequency division multiplexing, is illustrated in Figure 19-34.

When a signal on an analog carrier system becomes too faint, the system uses devices called linear repeaters to amplify the analog signal.

DIGITAL CARRIER SYSTEMS   Digital carrier systems were specially designed to transmit data. These carrier systems are becoming more and more common. A typical digital carrier system is illustrated in Figure 19-35.

A digital carrier system carries digital signals—the same kind of signals produced by a computer. Therefore, we don't need a modem to convert the computer's digital signals to analog signals as we do with an analog carrier system. However, we will need a digital service unit. The DSU doesn't convert the signal. Yet it does provide transmission

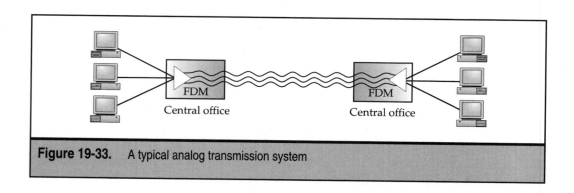

Figure 19-33.   A typical analog transmission system

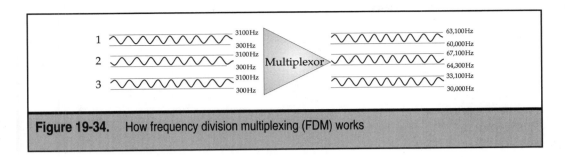

Figure 19-34.   How frequency division multiplexing (FDM) works

control, timing synchronization, and frame synchronization for the digital signal. Furthermore, for higher-speed transmission systems such as T1 (which we will discuss in Chapter 20), it converts regular digital signals to a special format that enables the signals to be transmitted at the T1 rate of 1.544Mbps.

The DSU then sends signal over the transmission medium to a time division multiplexor (TDM). The TDM packs the signals together just like an FDM. However, it accomplishes this in a different way. Rather than allocating a portion of the frequencies to the various transmission signals, the TDM allocates time slots to the various transmission signals. To do this, the multiplexor divides the transmission channel into time slots, then allocates time slots to the various transmission signals. For example, Transmission 3 might have every third time slot, Transmission 2 might have every fourth time slot, and so on. This is another way several transmissions can share the same channel without colliding with one another. This is called time division multiplexing, and it is illustrated in Figure 19-36.

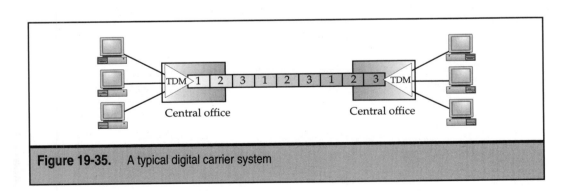

Figure 19-35.   A typical digital carrier system

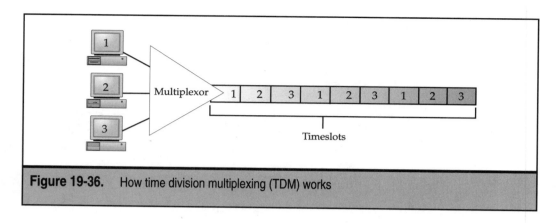

Figure 19-36. How time division multiplexing (TDM) works

When a signal on a digital carrier systems becomes too faint, the system uses devices called regenerative repeaters to regenerate the digital signal.

How It Works in Practice

Okay, we've seen how transmission systems are put together, so let's see how they work in operation. As we discussed earlier in this chapter, there are two basic types of telecommunications services: circuit services and packet services.

Circuit-Switching Services

In a circuit-switched connection, a dedicated channel, called a circuit, is set up between two points for the duration of the call. It provides a fixed amount of bandwidth during the call, and users pay for only that amount of bandwidth for the amount of time of the call. Occasionally there is a delay at the beginning of these calls while the connection is being made, although new switching techniques and equipment have made this connection delay negligible in most cases.

Circuit-switching connections have a couple of serious drawbacks. First, because the bandwidth is fixed in these connections, they don't handle bursts of traffic well, requiring frequent retransmissions. Given that WAN connections are relatively slow anyway, retransmissions can make the performance crawl. The second drawback is that these virtual circuits have only one route, with no alternative paths determined. Therefore, when a line goes down, either the transmission stops or one of the users intervenes manually to reroute the traffic. Figure 19-37 illustrates a circuit-switched network.

Packet-Switching Services

Packet-switching services do away with the concept of the fixed virtual circuit. Data is transmitted one packet at a time through a network mesh (or cloud), with each packet

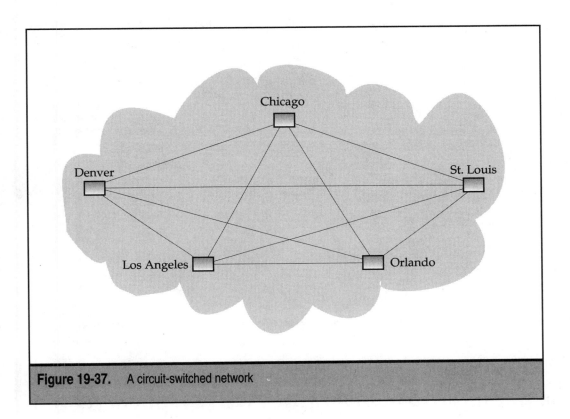

Figure 19-37.   A circuit-switched network

having the ability to take a different route through the network cloud. This is shown in Figure 19-38. Because there is no predefined virtual circuit, packet switching can increase or decrease bandwidth as required, and therefore handles bursts in packets elegantly. Taking advantage of the multiple paths of the network cloud, packet-switching services can route packets around failed or congested lines.

You can see why packet-based services are so well suited to the bursty, binary, packet-based signals generated by the computers on a local area network. You can also see why the traditional circuit-oriented services of the public telecommunications, emphasizing continuous signals in a continuous range of frequencies, is not ideally suited to connecting local area networks. Nonetheless, many wide area networks are connected by these traditional services, so you would probably benefit from some knowledge of the common problems that occur with them. Chapter 23 deals with some of the more common aspects of troubleshooting these facilities.

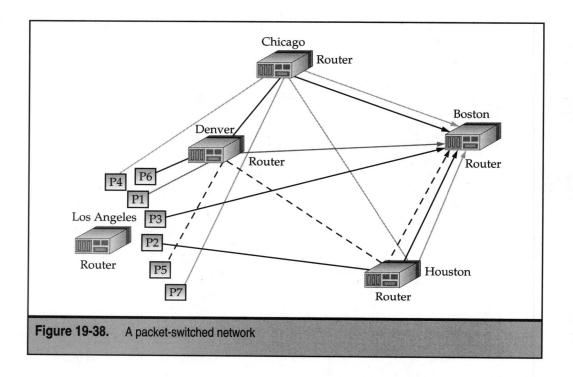

Figure 19-38. A packet-switched network

THE REGULATORY ENVIRONMENT: PAST, PRESENT, AND FUTURE

You have to read this section . If you don't, you will be utterly confused every time you try to purchase wide area networking products and services. Actually, you will be confused anyway, but it will be worse if you don't read this chapter. That's because the telecommunications industry is in the throes of a deregulation plan that may dwarf even that of the airline industry deregulation of a couple of decades ago. Deregulation means change. Change means confusion. However, "In confusion there is profit," as Tony Curtis' character said in *Operation Petticoat*.

So, read this section.

First Is the Deed

Or in this case, the Act. The Communications Act of 1934, to be precise. The first comprehensive approach to regulating telecommunications—which in those days was pretty much telegraph and telephone—was the Communications Act of 1934. Its stated purpose was, generally, "to protect the public interest, convenience, and necessity." The 1934 Act is the bedrock on which all telecommunications philosophy, discussion, and regulation has been based.

The Federal Communications Commission

One of the basic assumptions of the Communications Act of 1934 was that local monopolies of communications services were a necessary evil. Therefore, since monopolies are by nature fairly immune to market pressures, this piece of legislation created a federal agency to make sure none of these monopolies got out of hand and stopped acting in the public interest. That agency, the Federal Communications Commission (FCC), is still regulating the telecommunications industry today. It still has the same jurisdiction granted it by the 1934 Act: interstate and foreign telecommunications, but not intrastate telecommunications.

The State Public Utilities Commissions

While telecommunications oversight, policy, and regulation at the federal level is the province of the FCC, at the state level these functions are performed by each state's regulatory agencies. These agencies are usually called public utilities commissions (PUCs). As we will see later in this chapter, this can add different levels of complexity, confusion, and cost to administering an interstate network.

The 1956 Consent Decree

The FCC took its job of overseeing monopolies seriously, and often engaged monopoly holders when the agency thought the telecommunications providers had overstepped their bounds. The result was antitrust lawsuits. One of the most famous antitrust suits was settled by a 1956 Consent Decree in which AT&T was in essence granted a virtual monopoly over public interstate long-distance telephone services in return for submitting to more rigorous regulation and oversight.

The Carterphone Decision (1968)

One of the privileges of the monopoly granted to AT&T was the restriction that only equipment manufactured by AT&T's Western Electric division could be connected to the public telephone network. However, in 1968, Carter Electronic Corporation, which wanted to be able to sell telephones it manufactured to the public, won a lengthy legal battle that ended with what is known as "The Carterphone Decision." The FCC ruled that "a customer desiring to use an interconnecting device [a telephone] . . . should be able to do so."

Thus a new industry was born. The industry of manufacturing telephones, and eventually answering machines, modems, and other such devices that "interconnect" to the public telephone network, took off with the Carterphone Decision.

The U.S. District Court's Modification of Final Judgment

Between January 1, 1984, and February 8, 1996, however, the most powerful influence in national telecommunications was not the 1934 Act, the FCC, or the state PUCs. It was, rather, a Modification of Final Judgment approved by U.S. District Court Judge Harold Greene. The MFJ, as it is known, settled yet another antitrust lawsuit by the U.S. Justice Department against AT&T. The MFJ made significant changes to the 1956 Consent Decree, and the effects of these changes are still being felt.

The premise of the MFJ is that providers of telecommunications services no longer needed to be monopolies. Okay, well, they still needed to be monopolies, but not to the degree they had earlier thought. So, the court went about the task of trying to define and oversee the creation of various limited monopolies. This task was even more complicated than it sounds, as you are about to see.

[Some] Competition at Last

The MFJ finally legitimized competition in long-distance telecommunications. Before the MFJ, companies like MCI and the forerunners of Sprint were allowed to offer competitive long-distance services only by jumping through a variety of regulatory hoops that would grant them the status of "specialized carriers." With the MFJ, long-distance service became an openly competitive industry.

Breaking Up Is Hard to Do

One of the most significant changes mandated by the MFJ was the redefining of the nation's local exchange carrier (LEC) and interexchange carrier (IXC) system. A local exchange carrier is any company that provides local telephone service—the kind of service that connects your telephone on 6th street to the telephone in the bakery shop on 44th street. An interexchange carrier is, generally speaking, a long-distance service provider. These are overly broad definitions, but they'll work for our purposes now. We'll expand and refine these definitions later in this chapter when we talk more about LECs and IXCs.

The MFJ required that AT&T divest itself of (that is, give up) its local telephone companies. These 24 telephone companies, known collectively as the Bell System, had been wholly owned by AT&T. Together, AT&T and the Bell System served over 140 million individual telephones, had over $150 billion in assets, and employed over a million people. The rest of the nation's telephones—about 40 million at the time—received local telephone service from about 1,400 small independent telephone companies. Considering this, you would be hard-pressed to argue that AT&T didn't have a monopoly on all types of telecommunications services commonly available at the time.

The MFJ required that the Bell companies be broken up into 22 Bell Operating Companies (BOCs) that reported—depending on where they were located geographically—to one of seven holding companies, called Regional Bell Operating Companies (RBOCs). See Figure 19-39. Today, these RBOCs receive nearly 80 percent of all revenues from local telephone service nationwide.

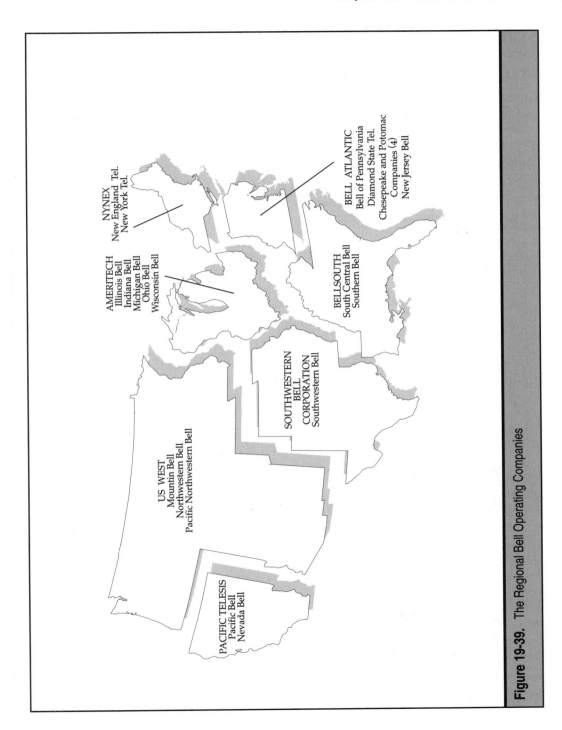

Figure 19-39. The Regional Bell Operating Companies

NYNEX
New England Tel.
New York Tel.

AMERITECH
Illinois Bell
Indiana Bell
Michigan Bell
Ohio Bell
Wisconsin Bell

BELL ATLANTIC
Bell of Pennsylvania
Diamond State Tel.
Chesepeake and Potomac
Companies (4)
New Jersey Bell

BELLSOUTH
South Central Bell
Southern Bell

SOUTHWESTERN
BELL
CORPORATION
Southwestern Bell

US WEST
Mountin Bell
Northwestern Bell
Pacific Northwestern Bell

PACIFIC TELESIS
Pacific Bell
Nevada Bell

AVERTING THE BELL PERIL   When AT&T was divested of the RBOCs, many restrictions were placed upon the latter. This is because the various industries were afraid that the RBOCs could use their huge capital bases with guaranteed rates of return to also enter into and easily dominate other related areas of business, creating de facto monopolies in those areas. Therefore, equipment makers successfully inserted language into the MFJ that restricted AT&T and the Bell Operating Companies from making common carrier switches and other telco equipment. Cable television companies successfully lobbied for a restriction to prevent LECs from delivering video services for ten years after the effective date of the MFJ. Newspaper publishers and long-distance telecommunications carriers had their concerns addressed as well. In summary, the MFJ allowed the RBOCs to provide the following:

▼ Intra-LATA local exchange service

■ Cellular mobile telephone service

■ Electronic mail service

■ Voice storage and retrieval service

■ Voice messaging service

■ Yellow Pages directories

▲ Customer premise telecommunications equipment sales and distribution, but not manufacturing

Under the MFJ, the RBOCs could not provide the following:

▼ Inter-LATA services

■ Information services such as online databases and Internet access services

■ Untariffed and/or unregulated products and services

▲ Manufacturing of customer premises equipment

What This Country Needs Is More Acronyms

In addition to breaking up the Bell System, the MFJ mandated that telecommunications service areas, called local access and transport areas (LATAs), be created to determine which calls were local and which were long-distance. A LATA is one of approximately 200 (and growing) geographic areas within the local telephone service providers' territories. I can tell by your glazed look that this requires a little explanation.

A local telecommunications service provider has to divide its territory into LATAs. Under the MFJ, offering service within a LATA was the sole privilege of the local telecommunications service provider. Between LATAs, long-distance companies such as MCI and AT&T competed to offer service. But inside the LATA, the local provider had no competition. As you might have guessed, intra-LATA calls became some of the most expensive telephone calls you could make because there was only one provider.

Equal Access for All

Now is a good time to point out a critical technical issue in making a long-distance call. A long-distance carrier can't take a call from a central office in one LATA to a central office in another. Also, it can't bring the call from the caller's building to the central office, nor from the central office to the callee's building. Only a local exchange carrier is allowed to traverse this "last mile," as it is called. Therefore, all interexchange carriers are wholly dependent upon local exchange carriers.

The MFJ, no doubt recognizing that the BOCs might feel a certain partiality toward their former owner (AT&T), stipulated that all local exchange carriers had to provide equal access to all interexchange carriers. Of course, that left the LECs to charge everyone hefty access fees for local access services. In fact, some IXCs have reported that nearly half their revenues go to pay local access fees.

Thus, under the MFJ, a local exchange carrier was defined as a company that provided telecommunications services within a single LATA. Conversely, an interexchange carrier was a company that provided telecommunications services that spanned one or more LATAs. Interexchange carriers couldn't compete with local exchange carriers. Local exchange carriers had to offer equal access to their facilities to all interexchange carriers. Complicated, but neat.

What About the Independents?

The MFJ concentrated on limiting the enormous economic clout wielded by AT&T and the former Bell System. Therefore, it largely ignored the independent telephone companies, probably thinking that for the most part they simply were in no position to threaten free-market forces. As a result, the MFJ doesn't limit or restrict the independent telephone companies in terms of product and service offerings.

NOTE: There is one notable exception to the preceding paragraph. GTE was bound by its own Consent Decree with the U.S. Department of Justice. This Consent Decree contained many provisions that were similar to the MFJ.

Never Quite Finished

The MFJ and its many complex provisions were constantly under scrutiny. There were many revisions. For example, in 1991 the FCC ruled that the BOCs could offer video programming services. This was called video dial tone, and would have allowed the Bell Operating Companies to prepare and deliver actual programs over their network. This turned out to be currently unfeasible, but it was nonetheless a major departure from the original language and intent of the MFJ, which prevented the BOCs from controlling any of the content that they transmitted over their network.

And Now It's Done

All this changed in January 1995, when the FCC decided that intra-LATA traffic should no longer be a monopoly. This meant that long-distance carriers could compete with local exchange carriers for intra-LATA service. And this greased the wheels for the next sweeping change in telecommunications regulation and policy, the Telecommunications Act of 1996.

The Telecommunications Act of 1996 (February 8, 1996)

The whole intent of this sweeping new legislation is to provide telecommunications users with more choices of:

▼ Vendors

■ Service offerings

▲ Pricing options

Furthermore, as with every effort to limit regulation and stimulate free market forces, the crafters of the Telecommunications Act of 1996 hope it will encourage creativity and enterprise, resulting in more and better emerging technology with lower prices and broader accessibility. Of course, telecommunications service providers also hope it will enable them to move into lucrative new markets from which they had previously been banned.

The Madness

The 1996 Act lets IXCs offer intra-LATA service, thus allowing them to compete directly with the LECs to provide local service. This makes the IXCs very happy, because they have been paying exorbitant access charges to the LECs for years. As we mentioned earlier, about half of an IXC's revenues go to pay LEC access charges. Now the IXCs have a chance to keep that money in-house.

The 1996 Act isn't just a boon for interexchange carriers. Being the fair and reasonable piece of legislation that it is, the 1996 Act also lets local exchange carriers go into the long-distance business. A LEC can start offering long-distance services outside its region right now. Furthermore, a LEC can offer intra-LATA (long-distance) services within its region if and when it can prove that it has competition in its local exchange business. Finally, the 1996 Act allows LECs to enter the video services business much more easily and with fewer restrictions than the MFJ did.

This has resulted in a kind of telecommunications services free-for-all, with LECs doing all sorts of things that would have been unthinkable (and quite illegal) under the MFJ. Besides taking the fairly predictable step of offering long-distance services to their cellular phone customers, LECs—particularly the RBOCs—began making some far-reaching (and some might say bizarre) strategic moves. For example, US West's Media Group began merging with a cable company (Continental Cablevision) as the ink was drying on the Telecommunications Act of 1996. Pacific Telesis bought into a wireless services company (Personal Communications Services) with the plan of providing wireless video services. Pacific Telesis was then purchased by SB Communications.

The Method

Okay, so the plan is to fling markets wide open in this high-cost-of-entry industry. And just exactly how will newcomers be able to compete with the vast assets and expertise of companies that have been operating for decades as near monopolies in the tele-communications industry? Here are a couple of methods outlined in the 1996 Act.

WHOLESALING   Wholesaling is based on the requirement that existing carriers allow anyone and everyone to resell their services on a "nondiscriminatory basis." This means that anyone who wants to get into the telecommunications business can select which services of, say, Nynex they want to resell. And Nynex has to sell them the services without restricting them from reselling those services. This means that a lot more companies you never heard of will be cold-calling you to offer discounts and special telecommunications services. More important, as we mentioned earlier, it enables interexchange carriers like AT&T, MCI, and Sprint to almost immediately offer local exchange services (that infamous "last mile" service) as part of their long-distance services. And expect them to do so in droves. By some estimates, providing local exchange services is almost twice as profitable as providing interexchange services.

Of course, wholesaling also means that until all the various competitors get around to building their own networks of transmission facilities, all they will be doing is reselling your same providers' services under new names. But this is nothing new. It's pretty much what happened in the aftermath of the MFJ, when everyone and his cousin went into the long-distance reselling business.

INTERCONNECT   The interconnection provisions of the Telecommunications Act of 1996 prevent any LEC from charging other carriers "unreasonable rates" for terminating calls on its network. That means that not only do they have to provide access, they have to charge a fair and reasonable rate for it. This is the provision that gives competitors a shot in the local exchange carrier market. It breaks the monopoly of the LEC, and also makes the LEC share its infrastructure.

The interconnection agreements are reached through negotiating sometimes very complex and incredibly specific agreements with the LECs. If a LEC wants to make competition painful, they certainly have the leverage to do so.

Cable Controversy

The 1996 Act calls for the deregulation of the cable television industry within three years. The cable television companies grew up under a completely different set of regulations than the telephone companies, so deregulation affects them differently, although almost as dramatically. You see, telephone companies developed under the auspices of the 1934 Act, which assumed telephone networks were a monopoly to be run in the public interest. Therefore, telephone companies have had little choice about what signals they carried. For example, everyone with a telephone could plug into the old Bell System. By contrast, cable television networks were developed much later, as private companies that could pick and choose which signals they broadcast. In short, cable television companies could control—and profit from—the content of their signals, whereas telephone companies could not.

Under the 1996 Act, telephone companies can choose whether to continue functioning as public entities with no control over content, or as private networks that can both control and make money from the content of the signals they carry. They may further choose whether they want to become a third type of carrier that handles only video services. This means that you may see companies that you formerly thought of as interexchange carriers or local exchange carriers become information distribution and retrieval services. The very nature of heretofore familiar companies could change dramatically.

FUTURE DIRECTIONS OF CABLE   Cable television companies may further get a boost out of the Telecommunications Act of 1996. The 1996 Act opens the way for them to enter a variety of information delivery markets. This leads to a lot of interesting possibilities, because cable has the potential of delivering very high bandwidth (higher than T1 speeds), and because cable television companies already have most of the nation's residential areas wired. The emergence of asymmetric digital subscriber line technology (see Chapter 20) shows that interest in this area is growing.

There are, however, mitigating factors. Most applications, business or otherwise, don't yet need the extraordinary bandwidth that cable can provide. Furthermore, right now most of the cable infrastructure is designed to carry only one-way (broadcast) traffic. It would have to undergo massive updating to be able to handle two-way, high-bandwidth interactive communications. But letting cable television companies get into the "alternative telephone business" gives them a means to pay for these upgrades and overhauls of their transmission and distribution facilities, so you're probably wise to keep an eye on service offerings from cable television companies.

"And ISDN for All"

In addition to all the changes we've discussed so far, I need to point out that the 1996 Act requires that public telecommunications service providers must offer access "to both basic and advanced services." However, the Act doesn't go on to define what that means. I suppose we could all agree that an analog dial tone is the minimum basic requirement for telephone service (although in this day of touch-tone investment banking, I might be inclined to argue). But what is the maximum service that telecommunications companies are required to provide? A chicken in every pot and ISDN in every jack?

Think about the implications of this. The 1996 Act requires that all public telecommunications providers (as we have always defined telephone companies) must provide "basic and advanced services" to everyone, but private providers (like cable TV companies) have no such mandate. Further, the 1996 Act allows nearly all tele-communications providers to reclassify themselves as public or private. When faced with the additional burden of this "universal access," not to mention increasing competition and hence lower profits, which would you choose? How will this shape the telecommuni-cations industry if public carriers begin to dwindle in number?

Make Your Mark

Luckily, I don't have to construct the implementation procedures for the 1996 Act. The FCC does. And is. It continues to interpret and design how and under what competitive circumstances to open local exchange markets as well as what constitutes universal service and how to provide it. And it has been doing this on a very tight schedule, with its deadlines having ranged from 6 to 18 months from the signing of the 1996 Act. But these things take time, and it's still not entirely finished. Of course, we can all keep abreast of what's happening and offer our comments by contacting the agency:

FCC
1919 M Street, N.W.6
Washington, DC 20544
(202) 418-0260
http://www.fcc.gov/

State Impact

However, as we stated early in this chapter, the individual states have the responsibility of interpreting the rules for competition within their jurisdictions. To assist state regulatory agencies in interpreting the requirements of the 1996 Act, the legislation outlines a 121-point "competitive checklist" that includes the following:

▼ Interconnection

■ Access to 911 service, directory assistance, and other core services

■ Local loop transmission from central offices to customer premises

■ Local transport from the trunk side switches

■ Access to network elements

■ Use of switches unbundled from any other transport or services

■ Access to poles, conduits, and rights-of-way

■ White Pages directory listings for customers of competitive carriers

■ Nondiscriminatory access to databases and signaling necessary for call routing

■ Interim number portability

■ Access to resources necessary for local dialing parity

■ Reciprocal compensation

■ Resale of telecommunications services

▲ Nondiscriminatory access to telephone numbers

Even using the same checklist, the states are undoubtedly going to interpret things differently. But as we said earlier in this chapter, there's nothing new about that. State public utilities commissions have always had the prerogative of interpreting federal telecommunications legislation and regulations.

What Does All This Mean to You?

From the preceding discussion, it is pretty clear that it's going to be awhile before anyone really knows what all the provisions and consequences of the Telecommunications Act of 1996 are ultimately going to mean. However, let me present you with my interpretation of the best-case and worst-case scenarios.

First, the Bad News

The manic mergers will probably result in more buyouts, consolidations, confusion, and rising prices in the short term. There will be a befuddling assortment of new players, some not all that financially or operationally stable. And of course, no one has had time to learn the new rules of engagement mandated by the 1996 Act, so although you know what services you want, it may often be unclear who is offering them and/or how to get them.

Furthermore, the increased ability of telecommunications to bundle services will work against you for awhile. That's because if you don't see an itemized price list, you'll never know how much you're paying for each component service or product. Nonetheless, you have more negotiating leverage than you had in the past, so just demand an itemized bid—and go bargain hunting for each item on the bid.

And Now, the Good News

In the best of all possible worlds, the 1996 Act could mean that your telecommunications service providers, rather than relying on their monopolies to make money, actually start trying to woo you. They listen, they negotiate, they create new products and services and bundle them in ways that suit your needs. They deliver on time. They give you what they promise. They fix problems rather than point fingers. They give you good prices. You can take advantage of all the confusion and negotiate a better deal than you ever thought possible for all your contract services.

First, you can do "one-stop shopping" for an end-to-end WAN link. The same provider can potentially sell you the long-distance service as well as the access to the long-distance carrier's point of presence (POP). Your long-distance carrier may be able to provide local access to the long-distance POP, sell you routers, FRADs, and multiplexors, as well as configure, manage, and maintain the whole system from end to end. And this could in turn make complex carrier technology, such as ATM, available to you on your site as part of your service from your vendor.

Second, it can let you bundle all of your company's telecommunications services—from cellular phones to long-distance credit cards to ISDN links—in one account with one provider. This can give you substantially more bargaining power when negotiating contracts.

Third, the Telecommunications Act of 1996 offers the potential of new services and products heretofore unimagined, like electronic data vaulting and high-speed, two-way interactive video services between offices.

Fourth, tariffs will probably disappear eventually, being replaced by freely negotiated contracts. A tariff is a published price that sets the allowed rate for telecommunications services and equipment. The FCC requires that tariffs be established only for specific services and facilities. Tariffs are set by a formal procedure involving carriers filing proposed prices, which are then reviewed, amended, and ultimately either approved or rejected by the FCC. Tariffs, therefore, contain the most complete and precise descriptions of carrier offerings. Further, tariff offerings cannot be dropped or changed without government approval. LEC tariffs are under the jurisdiction of state authorities. Once established, a tariff constitutes a public contract between the user of the product or service and the telecommunications carrier, and it can't be changed except by the express permission of the FCC. Therefore, a tariffed service is a service for which the carrier must publish its pricing and file it with the FCC. Up to now, carriers have been responding to their competitors' tariffs rather than their customers' needs. Now they will most likely start responding to their markets—which means you.

Overall, the Telecommunications Act of 1996 is your friend. Like most friendships, this one will require work and commitment, but the potential payoff is great.

THE PLAYERS

Building a WAN, especially a high-speed one, is not a one-person job. It's not even a one-company job. In fact, you're going to require the services of a whole team of manufacturers, resellers, and distributors of several goods and services. You can easily become confused in the tangle of equipment and service providers, each having their own very specific area of responsibility. To further complicate things, the deregulation imposed by the Telecommunications Act of 1996 is going to allow—but not require—some vendors to enter new areas. In short, you are going to need the proverbial scorecard to keep the players straight. In this chapter, we provide you with that scorecard.

The Roster

Here in brief is the roster of players in the high-speed WAN game. To help you learn which position each plays, refer to Table 19-2.

If you're wondering why there are so many different participants, each with their own specialized area of expertise, you must have skipped the preceding section. That is

Local exchange carriers	Intra-LATA
Interexchange carriers	Inter-LATA
Value-added carriers	Inter-LATA
Resellers	Inter-LATA
Bypass carriers	Intra-LATA

Table 19-2.   Types of Telecommunications Vendors and What They Do

where we explain the regulatory environment in which wide area telecommunications exists, and therefore why there is a bewildering number of vendors with whom you must deal.

The Lineup

Here is a brief summary of the entities that will affect the cost and availability of telecommunications services for your wide area network. We have grouped them according to the positions they play on the team: Governmental and Regulatory, Service Providers, Equipment Vendors, and Management.

Government and Regulatory

As discussed earlier, there are a variety of governmental and regulatory bodies responsible for making sure our nation's telecommunications services are reliable, dependable, and accessible. We'll start with the federal agencies and work our way to the states.

All telecommunications regulations begin with legislation, from the Communications Act of 1934 to the Telecommunications Act of 1996. Therefore, if you're concerned about how government regulations and policies are affecting your choices as a WAN manager or just a private citizen who likes to surf the Internet, you need to keep up with what the following legislative bodies are doing.

THE U.S. HOUSE OF REPRESENTATIVES   The House of Representatives Telecommunications and Finance Subcommittee of the Commerce Committee is where most of the action starts on telecommunications matters.

THE SENATE   The Communications Subcommittee of the Senate Committee for Commerce, Science, and Transportation is the Senate's counterpart to the House Telecommunications and Finance Subcommittee.

THE FEDERAL COMMUNICATIONS COMMISSION   As we said earlier in this chapter, one of the basic assumptions of the Communications Act of 1934 was that local monopolies of communications services were a necessary evil. Therefore, since monopolies are by nature fairly immune to market pressures, this piece of legislation created a federal agency to make sure none of these monopolies got out of hand and stopped acting in the public interest. That agency, the Federal Communications Commission (FCC), is still regulating the telecommunications industry today. It has the same jurisdiction granted it by the 1934 Act: interstate and foreign telecommunications, but not intrastate telecommunications.

THE U.S. DISTRICT COURT   Legal challenges to federal laws and regulations, as well as antitrust suits by the U.S. Department of Justice, are filed in a U.S. District Court. Charged with the job of interpreting the spirit and the letter of telecommunications laws, U.S. District Court judges can be the most powerful makers of telecommunications policy in the world. Just look at Judge Harold Greene and the Modification of Final. Therefore, when a telecommunications law or regulation is being challenged, keep an eye on the deliberations and decisions of the presiding court.

THE STATE REGULATORY AGENCIES   This is where much of the telecommunications policy that affects you is made. While the Federal Communications Commission has jurisdiction over interstate and foreign telecommunications, your state's regulatory agency, usually its public utilities commission, determines how the telecommunications business is conducted within the state borders. The result is a wide disparity of telecommunications laws. For example, my beloved Texas enjoyed intrastate long-distance competition long before most other states. This was because the Texas Public Utilities Commission chose not to prohibit competition for intrastate long-distance, while the public utilities commissions of most other states chose otherwise.

Service Providers

Now we leave the heady realm of public telecommunications lawmakers and regulators and turn to the people who actually deliver the services available.

LOCAL EXCHANGE CARRIERS   A local exchange carrier (LEC) is any company that provides intra-LATA telecommunications services. That is, they handle telecommunications services that originate and terminate within the same local access and transport area. LECs include companies such as Regional Bell Operating Companies (RBOCs), GTE, and other companies that handle local telephone and telecommunications connections. Until recently, these companies were restricted by federal law to handling local communications, providing point-of-presence (POP) facilities for long-distance carriers, and offering wide area communications services only within their LATAs. However, as you know, the Tele- communications Act of 1996 allows them to enter other areas of endeavor, such as providing long-distance (inter-LATA) service if they can prove they are facing competition in their local (intra-LATA) market.

LECs are regulated by the public utilities commissions of the states in which they operate. Therefore, Pacific Telesis, for example, must have separate operations for both California and Nevada, because the operations in the two states are subject to the separate regulations imposed by the public utilities commission of the state in which the operation takes place. Therefore, if you were a Pacific Telesis customer with sites in both California and Nevada, you might find that the rules and regulations governing the types and costs of local (intra-LATA) services vary greatly between the two sites, even though you were using the same provider.

INTEREXCHANGE CARRIERS   An interexchange carrier (IXC) is a long-distance telecommunications carrier. That is, an IXC is an inter-LATA service provider, offering telecommunications services that originate in one local access and transport area and terminate in another.

The major IXCs are AT&T, MCI, and Sprint—among many others. Customers can generally select the IXC of their choice, provided of course that the IXC offers service in their area. While many IXCs use the local POP facilities that local exchange carriers are required to provide, some IXCs have now built their own POPs, allowing customers to bypass the LEC and connect directly into the IXCs' long-distance services. This could only occur in those states, such as my own dear Texas, whose public utilities commissions allow such competition in the local area.

> **NOTE:**   The Federal Communications Commission refers to IXCs other than AT&T as other common carriers (OCCs).

Just as the Telecommunications Act of 1996 has allowed LECs to go into the long-distance business (under certain circumstances described above), it has also allowed IXCs to compete in the local exchange carrier service market. Therefore, look for the lines between the LECs and the IXCs to blur very quickly—at least in certain markets—and eventually disappear entirely.

THE PLAYBOOK   About the only way to define current telecommunications service functions and responsibilities is to trace a long-distance (that is, inter-LATA) call from its origination to its termination. Figure 19-40 illustrates the path of this call. You'll want to refer to this diagram frequently as we discuss "Who's on First."

For this example, suppose I, sitting here in El Granada, CA, decide to place a call to my mother in Fairview, OK. The dial tone I get when I pick up the receiver is provided by

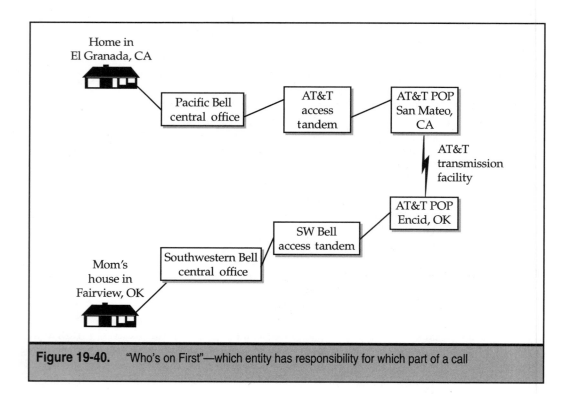

Figure 19-40.   "Who's on First"—which entity has responsibility for which part of a call

US West, my local exchange carrier (LEC). Of course, I'm going to get that same dial tone from my local exchange carrier (Pacific Bell) whether I want to call across town (although in El Granada, you could shout across town, so no dial tone would be involved) or across the planet. As I dial my mother's number, the central office owned by the local exchange carrier (Pacific Bell) receives the dialing signal and routes the call.

My long-distance carrier is AT&T (this is not a reflection of an endorsement, just a habit). When I signed up with AT&T, the long-distance carrier made the necessary arrangements with my local exchange carrier (Pacific Bell) to have all my long-distance (inter-LATA) calls routed to the point of presence (POP) in the local exchange carrier's (Pacific Bell) central office. Therefore, when I begin to dial the "1+" number of my mother's house, the local exchange carrier's (Pacific Bell's) switch also receives a routing code that tells it to route the call to the access tandem for AT&T (my interexchange carrier), which is located in nearby San Mateo.

NOTE: An access tandem is a special switch that a local exchange carrier (LEC) uses to concentrate all trunks leading from a central office to a particular interexchange carrier's (IXC's) point of presence (POP). Each interexchange carrier (IXC) that provides services to a central office has an access tandem connection at that central office. Therefore, depending upon the caller's choice of interexchange carrier (IXC), a call might be routed to AT&T's access tandem, or MCI's access tandem, etc.

POP FLY   As I mentioned earlier in this book, a point of presence (POP) is a location within a local access and transport area where an interexchange carrier connects to the local exchange carrier's facilities. Remember that the local exchange carrier (LEC) is required by law to provide the interexchange carriers (IXC) with access services to the intra-LATA networks.

NOTE: An interexchange carrier (IXC) may have more than one point of presence (POP) within a LATA. Furthermore, the point of presence may be multiuse, meaning that it may handle both public and private network calls.

Once my call goes from the local exchange carrier's central office access tandem and on to AT&T's point of presence, my call is now the responsibility of AT&T, my IXC. Therefore, AT&T must route the call and make sure it gets through to the AT&T POP for the local access and transport area (LATA) in which Fairview, OK, is located. Not surprisingly, AT&T's point of presence serving the LATA for Fairview, OK, isn't located in Fairview, OK. Instead, AT&T's point of presence for my mother's local access and transport area is in Enid, OK (at least it was the last time I checked).

So how does the call get from Enid, OK, to the central office serving Fairview? AT&T has cleverly thought of that, and has contracted intra-LATA services from Southwestern Bell or Pioneer Telephone Company or some other local exchange carrier authorized to provide intra-LATA services within that particular local access and transport area. For purposes of this call, let's say that Pioneer Telephone Company has agreed to carry my call from the AT&T point of presence in Enid, OK, to the central office serving Fairview,

OK. During this phase of its journey, my call is now the responsibility of Pioneer Telephone Company.

HOME RUN   My call is now within spitting distance (sorry, Mom) of its destination. Pioneer Telephone Company has made sure the call has reached the central office serving Fairview, OK, and now it's time to bring it on home to Mom. This is the infamous "last mile" of a telephone call—the part of the call that until now has been the sole province of the local exchange carrier serving that area. In this case, the LEC providing local telephone service to my mother's house is Southwestern Bell. So, when the call comes from AT&T's POP to Pioneer Telephone Company's transmission system to Pioneer's point of presence in the Southwestern Bell central office serving Fairview, OK, Southwestern Bell switches the call to the cable pair leading to my mother's home. The phone rings. Mom picks it up. I say hello.

And then I get a lecture about how I work too hard.

You can see how coordinating all these different service providers involves a lot of planning and negotiating—especially on the part of the interexchange carriers who have (until a few years ago) been at the mercy of the local exchange carriers to provide local access connection services. It also is expensive: every one of the providers involved in our example call needs to charge for its services and make a separate profit. Add to this the fact that until recently the local exchange carriers had no competition for their services, and therefore could charge pretty much what they wanted (subject to state regulatory agency approval, of course), and you can see why telecommunications services can get very expensive very quickly.

VALUE-ADDED CARRIERS (VACS)   Value-added carriers (VACs), such as CompuServe Information Services, often provide wide area network services as a sideline to their core business. Typically, a VAC has a national private data network (PDN) it established for its own use, and resells the excess capacity of that PDN to its customers. Using a PDN saves you the trouble of acquiring various carrier services and setting up your own switching equipment, because the switching is done in the carrier's network. The VAC also handles the management and maintenance of the WAN services, and may even be able to do some protocol conversion for you.

RESELLERS   A reseller is anyone who buys telecommunications services from a provider of those services and resells them. Under the provisions of the 1996 Telecommunications Act, this could be anyone. Your Great Aunt Edna in Poughkeepsie could talk AT&T into leasing her an end-to-end T3 loop between her LEC and your office, then resell those services to all your clients in upstate New York. This means that a lot more people you never heard of will be calling you offering telecommunications services. Some will be very knowledgeable, using reselling as a means to start out in this high-barrier-to-entry industry. Others may know about as much about telecommunications as your Great Aunt Edna. So ask a lot of questions.

BYPASS CARRIERS   Bypass carriers are carriers that sell access to their own local private telecommunications network as a gateway to an interexchange service. They will provide connections from your site to their local point of presence. From there, the bypass carrier may transmit your call on its private interexchange network, or send your call over an access tandem to the POP of another interexchange carrier.

Equipment Vendors

Until recently, Bell Operating Companies weren't allowed to manufacture equipment, although they were allowed to sell, lease, and distribute it. Because, as with any product or service, you can often get better deals straight from the manufacturer, this means that equipment vendors are a part of a WAN manager's life.

If you were just the Telephony Manager, you would probably have to deal with purchasing station sets (aka telephones) and private branch exchange or PBX (aka customer premises switches). This means you would deal with the major switch vendors such as Northern Telecom and ROLM, and/or their distributors and resellers. You might even purchase some equipment on the secondary (i.e., used) market. There would still be a lot of features and options to compare and evaluate, but your choices of manufacturer would be relatively limited.

But you're the Wide Area Network Manager, so in addition to having an intimate knowledge of the PBX, you must also purchase the modems, DSU/CSU units, PADs, multiplexors, FRADs, and routers required by the specific protocol you are implementing over the wide area. Furthermore, you must be familiar with any and all interface devices and software that may be required to connect your WAN to your PBX—if that's the plan.

To complicate matters, there's no one-stop shopping in the WAN equipment arena. FRAD manufacturers don't usually make multiplexors. Modem manufacturers don't offer a line of routers. Therefore, you are going to have to sort through equipment component by component and vendor by vendor. There's no shortcut to this.

I can offer one piece of advice, however: start with your service vendor. Ask them exactly what components are necessary and what makes and models they support. Then talk to the manufacturers of those components. Have them educate you on each. Ask them to supply you with a list of resellers and distributors of their equipment. Then shop for your best deal.

INTERCONNECT COMPANIES   One of the privileges of the monopoly granted to AT&T was the restriction that only equipment manufactured by AT&T's Western Electric division could be connected to the public telephone network. However, in 1968, Carter Electronic Corporation, which wanted to be able to sell telephones it manufactured to the public, won a lengthy legal battle that ended with what is known as "The Carterphone Decision." The FCC ruled that "a customer desiring to use an interconnecting device [a telephone] . . . should be able to do so."

Thus a new industry was born. The industry of manufacturing telephones and eventually answering machines, modems, and other such devices that "interconnect" to the public telephone network took off with the Carterphone Decision.

Management

There are a couple of types of management that will affect your life as a Wide Area Network Manager. These are your building management and telemanagement.

Your Building Management

These guys hold the keys to the kingdom and can either make your life simple or a living nightmare. You see, whether you lease your office space or are an "internal customer" of your company's Facilities Management Department, typically your building management owns the right of way between your switch (or PBX) and the demarc (point of connection to the LEC and/or IXC service provider). Therefore, if your building management is organized, efficient, and knowledgeable, you will have no problem getting suitable cabling between your data communications equipment and the demarc. If, however, they are *not* organized, efficient, and knowledgeable, you will have the equivalent of a 21-foot-thick-lead wall between your network and your WAN service provider.

My best advice is to make nice with the facilities group. Take them donuts, admire their children's pictures, and ask them to show you the intermediate distribution frames and main distribution frame of your building. Memorize it. Then volunteer to do your own wiring—just to save the facilities folks some time and aggravation.

Telemanagement

Somebody somewhere is watching your network, monitoring the equipment, and tracking the calls. Somewhere reports are being compiled about how many calls are being made to where for how long. And you are going to have to account for every detail of those reports.

Therefore, every time you change vendors, upgrade your equipment, expand your telecommunications services, or negotiate a new interexchange carrier service rate, be sure your telemanagement service is updated to reflect those changes. The most convenient way to do this is with interfaces between your WAN equipment and the telemanagement service your company is using, but that's not always possible. However you can accomplish this—just do it. It will make your life a lot easier in the long run.

Now We're Ready to Play

You've got the team roster, you've got the playbook, and you've got the scorecard. It seems like now we're ready to pick a protocol and install our WAN. Read on.

DETERMINING THE REQUIREMENTS FOR WIDE AREA CONNECTIONS

Now that you know what a wide area link is, where it came from, and a little of what you might expect from wide area communications in the future, it's time to get down to the business of planning your wide area network. The first step in this is to determine your network's WAN requirements. What kind of speed, security, and flexibility do you need in your wide area communications?

The Bandwidth Question: How Much Speed?

Before you do anything, you'll have to get some idea of how much your wide area network connection is going to be used. Obviously, the more traffic that will be traveling over the network, the more bandwidth you will need on the WAN to provide acceptable performance.

NOTE: Remember that currently wide area network links simply don't support the high-bandwidth protocols that local area networks do.

How Much?

The best way to estimate the traffic that will be running over your wide area link is to take a sample of your current wide area network traffic. Your current telecommunications carrier should be able to do a traffic study of your wide area link to see exactly how much bandwidth or how many minutes of wide area telecommunications service you use during which times of the day. Be sure the report includes at least one full month's worth of traffic. An analysis of a single day or even a single week of wide area network traffic simply isn't enough to reveal usage patterns.

Analyzing your telephone bill is another way to calculate usage, but this is only valid if you are currently using a usage-based service. A usage-based service charges you for only the amount of service you use, measured either in minutes or bandwidth. If you are currently paying a flat fee for your telecommunications service, your telephone bills really won't give you accurate information on actual telecommunications service usage.

Of course, a traffic sample and analysis is a viable option only for those of you who already have one or more wide area links. If you are trying to build your first wide area link, you'll need to estimate the telecommunications traffic. One of the best ways to do this is by conducting a survey of your network users. Ask all the network users that will have access to the wide area link just how often they will be communicating with people and resources at the remote location. Then ask them what they will be doing during that communication—file transfers? videoconferencing? electronic mail?

Finally, be sure that you measure traffic patterns and calculate estimated wide area usage for both sides of the wide area link. This will severely affect your bandwidth requirements.

And When?

Don't forget to ask the users the times of day and days of the week or month that they will be using the wide area link. This will not only help you determine how much bandwidth the link needs, it may help you save money. That's because, just like airlines and hotels, telecommunications companies price their services cheaper during off-peak periods. Therefore, you may be able to arrange for the heaviest usage to occur during off-peak rate periods.

You'll find a sample traffic survey form at the end of this chapter that you may want to adapt for use in your own traffic survey.

Turning Survey Data into Traffic Figures

Suppose the traffic survey you conduct reveals the usage detailed in Figure 19-41. Notice how easily you can identify weekends and holidays, because there's hardly any WAN traffic on those days. You can also guess which days are month-end from the heavy telecommunications traffic. The Accounting Department must be pulling billing information from the remote office.

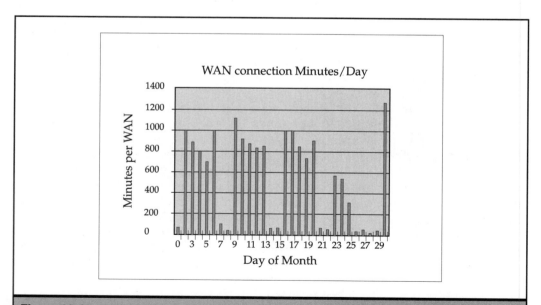

Figure 19-41.   The first step in bandwidth planning on the WAN: measuring call minutes/day

DON'T DESIGN FOR THE AVERAGE DAY   You may look at the traffic analysis and assume that all you have to do is divide the total amount of traffic captured for the month by the number of days in that month. You might think that if you simply take an average of the heavy traffic days and the light traffic days, throwing out the weekends and holidays, you'll hit a happy medium bandwidth figure that will meet the needs of your company's average business. *Wrong*. If you design a WAN link to carry only the average bandwidth required throughout the month, during the heavy traffic periods, fully half of the users are going to be unable to access the remote office via the WAN. However, you don't want to build the network to handle all the traffic on your busiest days with top performance, because that means most of the time you would have idle WAN bandwidth. The trade-off between performance and cost wouldn't be satisfactory. Therefore, you're going to have to design your wide area link to accommodate all traffic on all but the busiest days. To figure out how to do this, you'll have to identify and quantify your WAN's busy days and busy hours.

For most businesses, some days of the week are regularly much busier than others. For example, airline reservations centers are much busier on weekdays than on weekends. This means you can't simply use the average business day traffic as your WAN's minimum daily requirement of bandwidth. Instead, you should calculate your network's busy day average, which is the average traffic of the five highest traffic days of a typical month.

Next, it's time to look at how your WAN bandwidth requirements will vary throughout a typical day. Suppose again that the results of your traffic survey look like the usage in Figure 19-41. Just as you can easily spot holidays and weekends in Figure 19-41, in Figure 19-42 you can see when people arrive at the office, when they go to lunch, and when they leave for the day.

If you analyze your wide area traffic over a month or more, you'll probably find that there are two busy periods per day—one in the morning and one in the afternoon—that are just about equal in both length and traffic density. Take the average traffic of these two busy periods and divide it by the total number of hours included in the busy period. For example, for the traffic shown in Figure 19-42, you would calculate the average busy hour traffic like this as described next.

TIP: Professional traffic engineers have found that a single busy hour represents between 12 percent and 16 percent of the total traffic for the day. Therefore, if you can't get detailed hourly call information for your wide area network, you'll probably be safe assuming that one busy hour of traffic equals about 14 percent of the total traffic for the day.

PROTOCOL ANALYZERS   Next, it's time to translate these minutes and hours of traffic into actual packets sent and received. This means you will need to calculate the average packet size of your local area network. Currently, the average packet size for the LAN is 512 bytes. However, using a protocol analyzer, you can determine the average size of data packets traveling across your particular network. A protocol analyzer can be configured to monitor packets for the specific topology and protocol of the segment, letting you monitor the traffic on the segment to which it's connected. A protocol analyzer will help you determine not

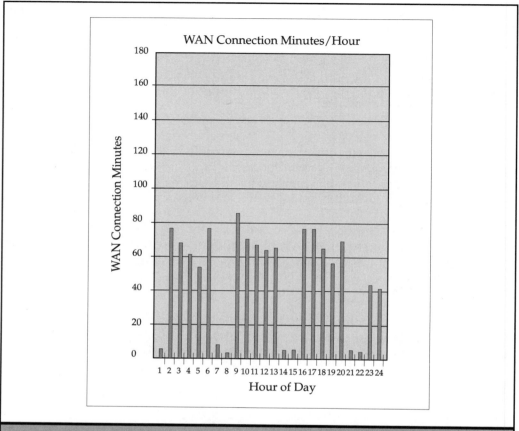

Figure 19-42.   A typical distribution of call minutes/day

only the average bandwidth utilization on the segment, but also the average packet size and composition. As well, a protocol analyzer can assist in spotting trends in traffic, peak traffic periods, and devices that are generating bad packets or acting as network bottle-necks.

If you don't have your own protocol analyzer, you can rent one or even hire someone to bring in a protocol analyzer and do the traffic monitoring and protocol analysis for you. Most network integration firms offer protocol analysis services. In any event, don't proceed with plans for implementing a wide area network until you have monitored your network with a protocol analyzer and are familiar with packet sizes and traffic patterns on the LAN.

TIP: When you calculate your bandwidth needs, you need to consider the packet size of the wide area protocol you'll be using. This will vary from protocol to protocol, as you will discover in the next section. Therefore, when you narrow your selection of protocols to two or three choices, you may want to recalculate your bandwidth needs for each individual protocol using the packet size of each.

What This Means in Bandwidth

Now that you have all the measurements, it's time to see how they add up. I had originally planned to launch you into an exhaustive methodology of calculating erlangs and performing regressions until you found the perfect bandwidth amount to meet your wide area networking needs cost-effectively. Then I realized this couldn't be done without also launching into a crazed dissertation on queuing and probability theories, and giving pages of recursive equations with their attendant "do loops."

As you can see, I'm babbling already. And you're already starting to doze off.

Besides, none of this is really necessary for you, the Wide Area Network Manager. After you have calculated the busy day and busy hour loads, you have a general idea of the bandwidth you will need to accommodate your wide area network traffic comfortably. This will let you know whether you should be shopping for high-speed wide area protocols or more pedestrian services.

Once you have selected a wide area networking service or protocol, however, it's wise to ask your telecommunications service provider to perform some traffic engineering analysis to determine the ideal amount of resources (whether they be measured in circuits or committed information rates) to support your wide area networking needs cost-effectively. Telecommunications service providers have entire departments dedicated to this type of traffic engineering, and you should take advantage of their services to ensure the best, most economical bandwidth for your WAN.

For your clarification, the following section contains an extremely brief definition of the terms and equations used in traffic engineering. Don't worry, there won't be a quiz.

NOTE: Everything I know about traffic engineering I learned from *Reference Manual for Telecommunications Engineering* by Roger L. Freeman, now in its third edition (New York: John Wiley & Sons, 1989). I don't recommend undertaking serious traffic engineering work without it.

What's an Erlang?

An erlang is a measure of telecommunications traffic. One erlang equals one transmitting station using 100 percent of a single transport resource 100 percent of the time. The erlang was developed as a measure of traffic wait probability in 1917 by Danish mathematician A. K. Erlang, and has been the standard measure ever since. The formula for calculating the erlang load on a data telecommunications link is

(no. of packets/sec.) × (no. of bytes/packet) × (no. of bits/byte)/(bits/sec)

This equation yields a measure of load on a single transport circuit of a given bandwidth. The key is that the number of circuits provided must be equal to or greater than traffic erlangs. Otherwise, packets will start queuing for transport at a far greater rate than the transport circuits can carry them, and consequently they will be lost.

CALCULATING THE PROBABILITY OF CIRCUIT BLOCKING   The equation for determining the probability of blocking is called the erlang-B equation, and without launching into the aforementioned crazed dissertation on queuing and probability theories, let's just say that this is the recursive form of the equation:

$$B(a, k) = (a \times B(a, k - 1))/k + a \times B(a, k - 1)$$

where

a = erlangs
b = number of resources (circuits)
$B(a, k)$ = probability of circuit blocking

CALCULATING THE PROBABILITY OF A PACKET'S BEING LOST BECAUSE A CIRCUIT IS BLOCKED   The equation for determining the probability of a packet's being lost due to its circuit's being blocked is called the erlang-C equation:

$$C(a, n) = (B(a, n))/(1 - a/n \times (1 - B(a, n))$$

where

a = erlangs
n = number of resources (circuits)
$B(a, n)$ = erlang-B equation
$C(a, n)$ = probability of losing packets due to circuit blocking

FINDING THE AVERAGE DELAY TIME   With the two preceding calculations, you can determine a packet's average delay time under any given traffic load this way:

$$T = L/C + (C(a, n) \times L)/((1 - a/n)) \times n \times C)$$

where

a = erlangs
L = packet length (in bits)
n = number of resources (circuits)
C = line speed (in bits/second)
$C(a, n)$ = Probability of blocking
T = average message delay time

FINDING THE AVERAGE QUEUE LENGTH   Finally, you can find the average amount of time a packet will spend waiting in a queue under any given traffic load by using this equation:

$$q = (C(a, n) \times a/n)/(1 - a/n)$$

where

a = erlangs
n = number of resources (circuits)
$C(a, n)$ = erlang-C equation
q = average number of packets in a queue

ERLANGS IN HAND, WE CONTINUE   Therefore, to find the most cost-effective type of service for a given traffic scenario for each type of protocol or service you are considering:

1. Calculate the erlang.

2. Round the erlang to the next integer and use this number as the number of resources.

3. Run the equations for average delay time and average queue length, varying the number of resources (circuits) until the average delay time/queue length is less than the transmission time of a single packet (in bits per second) and the average queue length is less than a single packet in length (in bits).

4. Multiply the number of resources (circuits) times the cost per circuit.

Voilà! You have the most cost-effective amount of bandwidth to meet the traffic needs of your wide area network. See why I recommended that you let your telecommunications service provider do this?

Get Out Your Pencil—There Are Lots of Variables

If you choose to run the preceding calculation yourself, you may find that you'll have to run it several times, because there are a plentiful variety of wide area networking services and protocols from which to choose. In the United States, the most popular tariffed telecommunications services are the following circuit-switched offerings:

▼   56Kbps circuit

■   Multiple 56Kbps circuits

▲   One DS1 (1.544Mbps) circuit

Furthermore, as we are about to see, there are a variety of wide area network protocols available through negotiated contracts with telecommunications carriers that are even better suited to high-speed wide area packet-based traffic such as LAN traffic. These services include the following:

▼   Switched Multimegabit Data Service

■   X.25

■   Frame relay

■   Integrated Services Digital Network

- isoEthernet with Integrated Services Digital Network
- Asynchronous Transfer Mode
- ▲ Asymmetric digital subscriber line

Flexibility

If your wide area network traffic varies widely from day to day or hour to hour, you'll need to investigate the flexibility of the service or protocol you're considering. Many services and protocols are designed to let you pay for only the traffic you use, while others accommodate traffic bursts in excess of the bandwidth for which you have subscribed. Frame relay, for example, lets you commit to an average bandwidth, called the committed information rate, while allowing your WAN traffic to burst above this rate when total traffic over the resource allows.

Recommendations

After all this discussion of determining your particular requirements for a wide area network protocol or service, I think I owe you a few pointers. The following are my personal recommendations—based on my own experience as well as research—for the appropriate protocols and services for each type of wide area function.

File Transfer

If you're just doing a batch transfer of files from one office to another, my recommendation is to use a traditional circuit service, which we will discuss in Chapter 21. If the file transfers are light and/or intermittent, a switched-circuit service will suit you just fine. If the file transfers are constant and/or lengthy, a dedicated-circuit service may prove more cost-effective.

Multimedia and Videoconferencing

Those of you who are contemplating using multiuser multimedia and videoconferencing over the wide area network might want to look into using a combination of Integrated Service Digital Network.

Wide Area Workgroup

For workgroup applications, such as Lotus Notes, over the wide area, my favorite is traditional circuit services. They're solid, stable, relatively inexpensive, and easy to install and maintain.

Internet Access

Frame relay is rapidly becoming one of my favorite technologies for Internet access. This is because it is flexible, inexpensive, and easy to install and maintain. Chapter 21 gives you the details.

WAN Usage Survey

We are preparing to install a wide area network link to connect our local area network with the local area network in our   [Fill in location]   office. To ensure proper performance, we need to know approximately how often you will be sending and/or receiving information from the   [Fill in location]   network. To help us estimate this, please take a moment to answer the questions below.

Please return this form to the Director of Information Services, M/S [Fill in mail stop] by [Fill in Date].

How many of the following types of information will you be sending to the remote office each day? At what time of day (if you can predict)?

	No.	Time of Day	Size of Document
Spreadsheets	_____	_____	_____
Word processing documents	_____	_____	_____
Databases	_____	_____	_____
Facsimile documents	_____	_____	_____

What will be your primary means of communication with the remote office after the WAN link is in place?

	No.	Time of Day	Size of Document
Electronic mail	_____	_____	_____
Telephone	_____	_____	_____
Overnight document delivery	_____	_____	_____

Do you foresee using the following means of communication with the remote office? If so, what time of day and how frequently?

	No.	Time of Day	Size of Document
Electronic mail	_____	_____	_____
Groupware/group discussion databases	_____	_____	_____
Videoconferencing	_____	_____	_____
	_____	_____	_____

CHAPTER 20

Wide Area Protocols and Devices

W hen it comes to building wide area links, you have a wide variety of choices. Sometimes, it may seem as though there are too many choices. In this chapter, we will describe the following various wide area communications protocols and services available to your network, and explain the following:

▼   Where and how they are best used in a data network

▲   The types of equipment necessary to implement each

T1 SERVICES

Introduced in 1962 as part of the Bell System's transmission facilities, T1 services are the mother of all telecommunications services. They are the most widely used telecommunication services in the world, with well over a million miles of T1 facilities in North America alone. As well, T1 services are among the most reliable and cost-effective wide area communications services available today. At the time of this writing, T1 will be the standard against which you compare all other wide area networking protocols.

T1 Defined

T1 services were an important part of the evolution and transition from analog to digital telecommunications services. T1 is both the largest and one of the fastest growing components of both local exchange carrier and interexchange carrier transmission facilities, as well as the most common transmission service in large private networks. But what exactly are T1 services?

T1 is the name for both the transmission service and the transmission facilities for a communications service that uses time division multiplexing (TDM) to concentrate up to 24 64Kbps digital channels into one 4-wire full-duplex circuit. This means that a full T1 service has a total bandwidth of 1.544Mbps.

As we have discussed in the preceding chapters, 64Kbps is the bandwidth of a standard voice channel running over a digital service. Therefore, as you can guess, T1 has its roots in voice transmission technology. However, it is an extraordinarily adaptable service, and has come to serve data communications well. Here's how.

NOTE: In analog-to-digital conversion, the sampling rate for the analog voice frequency is 8,000 times per second. These samples are encoded into 8-bit bytes. So, 8,000 samples/sec × 8 bits = 64,000 bits per second, or 64Kbps bandwidth.

Time Division Multiplexing

The time division multiplexor packs the signals together by allocating time slots to the various transmission signals. To do this, the multiplexor divides the transmission channel into time slots, then allocates time slots to the various transmission signals. For example, transmission 3 might have every third time slot, transmission 2 might have every fourth time slot, and so on. This is another way several transmissions can share the same channel without colliding with one another. This is called time division multiplexing (TDM), as illustrated in Figure 20-1, which is the basis of T1 frame operations.

In T1 service, the TDM simultaneously sends and receives 24 different signals—one for each channel.

Frame Operations in T1

In T1 service, devices called channel banks (a special type of digital multiplexor that is illustrated in Figure 20-2) convert analog signals into digital frames. A frame contains a 1-byte sample from each of the 24 64Kbps channels being transmitted over the T1, plus a single framing bit for timing and delineation purposes.

Besides the analog-to-digital conversion functions, the channel banks provide signaling interfaces for the central office trunk or the local exchange loop. This means that the conversion and multiplexing are not apparent to the user.

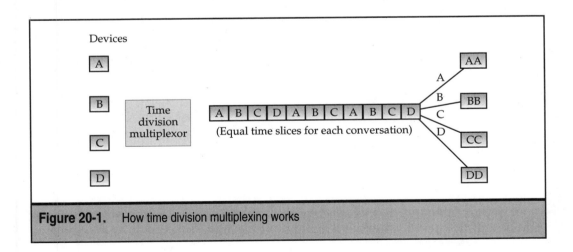

Figure 20-1. How time division multiplexing works

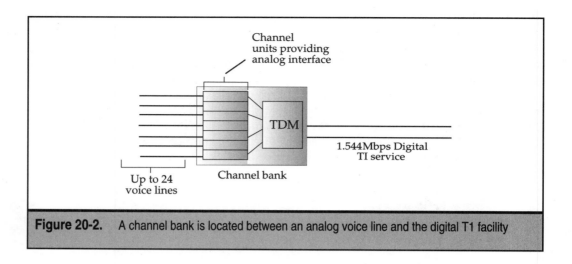

Figure 20-2.   A channel bank is located between an analog voice line and the digital T1 facility

The Framing Bit

The T1 framing bit provides a synchronization mechanism that the service uses to set signal rates and duration, as well as sampling intervals. In a completely synchronous TDM network, all participating nodes must use timing provided by a single master network clock. As we will see in a moment, the framing bit also provides the means for transmitting management and control information. (See Figure 20-3.)

The T1 transmission service then combines the frames in groups of 12, which are called *superframes*, as shown in Figure 20-4.

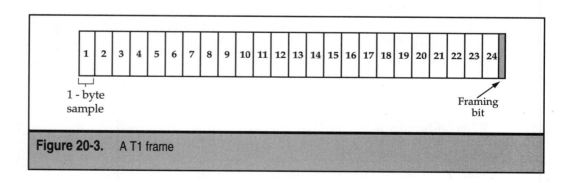

Figure 20-3.   A T1 frame

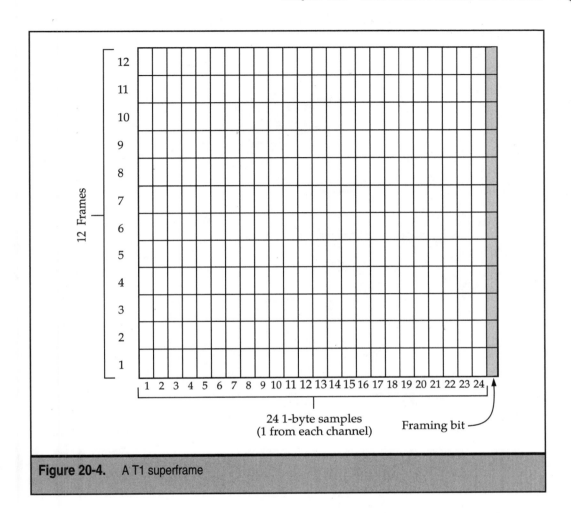

Figure 20-4. A T1 superframe

Next, the superframes are combined into groups of two (for a total of 24 frames), which are called *extended superframes,* as shown in Figure 20-5.

Over the years, T1 service engineers and developers have created signaling and control codes for T1. And where, you might ask, do they put these codes, considering that the only frame overhead is the single framing bit? They do this in a couple of ways. First, they create patterns by changing the framing bit after each frame. Therefore, it's not

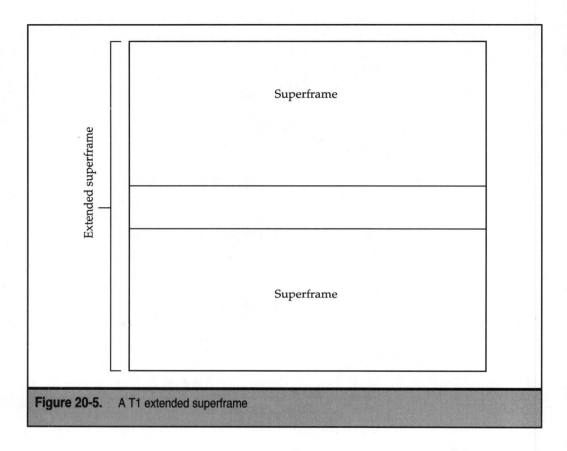

Figure 20-5. A T1 extended superframe

actually the state of the framing bit, but rather the *pattern* of states of a *sequence* of framing bits that transmits the signaling information. Another way T1 services transmit management and control information is by using the middle frames of either a superframe or an extended superframe (i.e., frames 6 and 12, respectively) to transmit this information.

T1 Signaling

As we mentioned, a T1 signal contains 24 64Kbps channels. This 24-channel signal is called a DS1, and has a total bandwidth of 1.544Mbps. Each individual 64Kbps channel is called a DS0. When two DS1 signals are multiplexed, the resulting 48-channel signal is called a DS1 C. In fact, there is a whole hierarchy of T1 signaling from which you can order, as shown in Table 20-1.

DS	No. of 64Kbps Channels	Total Bandwidth
0	1	64Kbps
1	24	1.544Mbps
1C	48	3.152Mbps
2	96	6.312Mbps
3B	672	44.736Mbps
3C	1,344	91.053Mbps
4B	4,032	274.176Mbps

Table 20-1. The T1 Signaling Hierarchy

As you can see from the table, the higher the DS signal designation, the higher the bandwidth the T1 transmission facility must support. For example, a DS1C requires a T1 transmission facility that can support bandwidth of 3.152Mbps. A DS2-level signal, consisting of four DS1 signals (96 DS0 channels), requires a 6.312Mbps transmission facility.

NOTE: You may notice that in Table 20-1 the total bandwidths for each T1 signal level are higher than the sum of the voice channels. For example, a DS1 has a total bandwidth of 1.544Mbps, and yet if you do the math (24 channels × 64Kbps/channel), you get a grand total of 1.536Mbps. The difference is the framing bit.

T1 Transmission Facilities

As we said earlier in this chapter, T1 signals are sent over a 4-wire facility. A 4-wire facility, or cable, has two pairs of wires. The pairs are designated Tip and Ring, Tip 1 and Ring 1. Each pair of wires carries information in only one direction: Tip and Ring transmit, and Tip 1 and Ring 1 receive. This is illustrated in Figure 20-6.

Four-wire cables are better for long-haul transmission because they can carry signals farther without any loss or distortion. They are more expensive than two-wire cables, so you usually don't see them used inside buildings. However, despite the increased expense, it sometimes makes sense to use four-wire cables inside buildings because you can connect them directly to long-distance metallic transmission facilities, which are all four-wire cables.

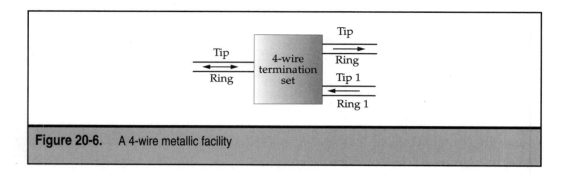

Figure 20-6.   A 4-wire metallic facility

In T1 transmission, all 24 channels are transmitted over a single 4-wire facility. One pair transmits data while the other pair receives data. As you can see, this makes T1 a very economical transmission service.

T1 Transmission Outside Your Facility

For years, T1 transmission service required a repeater every mile. This repeater completely regenerated the signal and sent it along its way. Now, however, repeaterless T1 is becoming the T1 transmission facility of choice. It uses a redesigned repeater that needs regeneration only every 5 miles, thus saving on equipment costs. Therefore, if you're thinking of building a new private T1 facility, you should probably insist on repeaterless T1.

Carrier Systems

Figure 20-7 illustrates how all the components of a typical T1 carrier system work together. This particular system consists of a DS1 (24 channels) over a long-distance (interexchange carrier) network. Channel banks connect the local area network to channel service units/data service units (CSUs/DSUs), which transmit the data signal to a TDM located at the LEC's central office. The multiplexed signal is then sent to the IXC's POP via its local access tandem, then transmitted across the IXC's inter-LATA trans- mission facility.

In addition to providing an interface to the central office facility, CSUs/DSUs perform line-conditioning, error-correction, signal management, synchronization, and circuit-testing functions.

NOTE: You'll remember that line conditioning is really just the art of placing repeaters at the correct intervals to compensate for signal loss.

Preparing for T1

Keep in mind that your local access loop may not be ready for T1. That's because your local cable pair may have connections running off it. These connections are called bridge

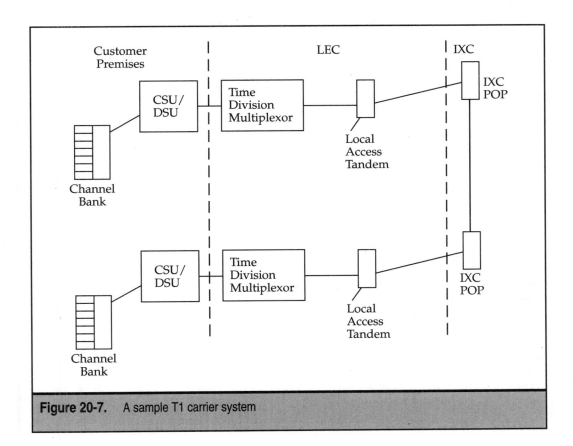

Figure 20-7. A sample T1 carrier system

taps, and they aren't supposed to be there. But sometimes when the telephone company is installing a new customer, they run a line from the new customer's premises and join, or tap, into an existing, unused local loop left behind by a former customer, as shown in Figure 20-8. The former customer's tap is disconnected at the former customer's site, but still joined to what is now your local loop. Such taps can cause signal distortion that doesn't affect analog signals but wreaks havoc with T1. Therefore, any bridge taps must be removed.

Next, the LEC will have to check your line to remove any devices that were installed to condition analog lines. As mentioned earlier in this chapter, conditioning means adjusting lines to reduce signal distortion. Unfortunately, some devices, called loading coils, that reduce signal distortion for analog signals can actually cause distortion in digital signals. Therefore, loading coils will have to be removed before you can use the loop for T1 services.

Finally, your LEC will test your line to see if it meets T1 specifications. If it does, you're good to go. If it doesn't, the phone company will have to install another line.

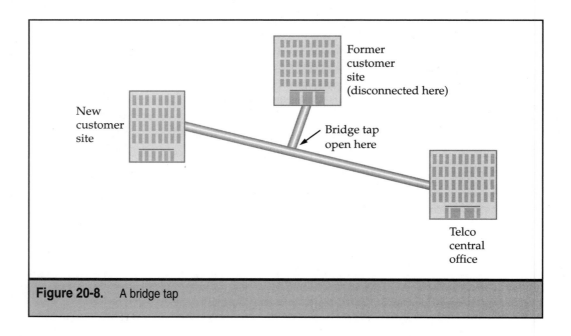

Figure 20-8.   A bridge tap

DS1 Bipolar Signal Formats

Signals are sent over a T1 transmission facility in the familiar binary format known as bipolar. In bipolar format, alternating positive and negative pulses represent one binary signal state; in other words, every time the signal changes from positive to negative or negative to positive—a change of signal state known as a pulse—a binary 1 is transmitted. When the signal doesn't change state, or pulse, a binary 0 is transmitted.

NOTE: The scenario described above is actually true only in alternate mark inversion (AMI) signaling. Alternate mark inversion is an older signal type, which is currently being replaced by another type of signaling, known as alternate space inversion (ASI), in which pulses transmit binary 1's and the absence of pulses transmits a binary 0. However, much of the T1 facility throughout North American is AMI-compliant. Therefore, in this chapter we will assume AMI signaling.

With such long strings of 0's and 1's being transmitted, there is an everpresent danger of frames losing synchronization. That's because in voice transmission, a frame consisting only of 0's is sent to indicate that a voice signal is being transmitted. This means that if the timing on both the receiving and transmitting ends isn't precise, the receiving end could be interpreting a frame as part of Channel 1, for example, when it was really part of the data for Channel 2. While in voice transmission this isn't such a big deal—you could easily understand a voice conversation even if a few samples were missing—in data it is deadly. Computers can't fill in the blanks of missing or misinterpreted bit streams. Remember that

T1 was originally developed for voice transmission, so it didn't contain a mechanism for detecting and correcting such slight synchronization errors.

A BIT OF A SOLUTION AND A BIT OF A PROBLEM   To prevent the frames consisting of nothing but 0's, which play such havoc with synchronization on the T1 channel, T1 developers and engineers began taking advantage of a difference in coding between voice and digital technology. Voice-encoding techniques require only 7 bits per 8-bit byte. Therefore, in voice encoding, the eighth bit was used for call status signaling.

In digital signaling, the eighth bit is always a 0, thus indicating a digital signal. When no data is being transmitted, instead of sending a frame of 0's, as with voice signaling, the channel sends a series of frames that look like Figure 20-9, with a 0 in the eighth position and 1's in the second through seventh positions. This prevents a series of eight consecutive 0's, the "nothing to transmit" signal in voice transmission.

This solves the problem of synchronization, but introduces another problem: inefficient coding. When only seven bits of the 8-bit frame are available for data, a 64Kbps T1 channel can carry only 56Kbps of actual data. This inefficiency was undesirable, but tolerable until the advent of using T1 as an interface to Integrated Digital Services Network services, which requires a full 64Kbps data channel.

Luckily, the ever-resourceful T1 engineers developed two alternate signaling formats to provide a full, well-synchronized 64Kbps T1 channel: B8ZS and ZBTSI.

BIPOLAR WITH 8-BIT ZERO SUBSTITUTION (B8ZS)   Bipolar 8-bit zero substitution (B8ZS) replaces the analog "nothing to transmit" signal consisting of a block of eight consecutive 0's with a bit-stuffing code, illustrated in Figure 20-10. While this encoding technique frees all 8 bits for data transmission, it unfortunately also violates the encoding rules of the previously mentioned AMI coding technique. In AMI, every other binary 1 signal must be encoded as the opposite polarity of the preceding binary 1 signal. As you can see in Figure 20-10, bit 5 and bit 7 are both 0's, thus breaking the AMI coding protocol. Therefore, any equipment on the T1 network that supports AMI coding would have to be replaced before implementing B8ZS signaling. This could be a very expensive proposition indeed!

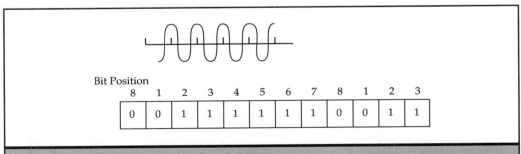

Figure 20-9.   A T1 digital "nothing to transmit" frame

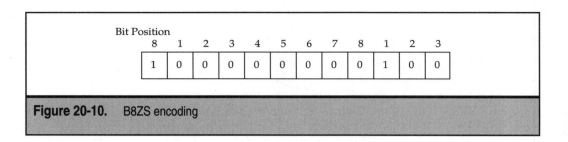

Figure 20-10.   B8ZS encoding

ZBTSI: A SOLUTION IN THE EXTENDED SUPERFRAME   Fortunately, there is an alternative to B8ZS encoding to get a full 64Kbps per T1 channel. Another method, called zero byte time slot interface (ZBTSI), was developed. Rather than using a bit out of every byte to identify and synchronize data frames, ZBTSI encodes all such information for an entire extended superframe (24 frames) into a single frame—the sixth frame—within each extended superframe. This is illustrated in Figure 20-11.

ZBTSI works like this: After examining all of the data bits in the extended superframe, the transmitting CSU/DSU then generates a cyclical redundancy check (CRC) checksum. This CRC checksum is encoded in a single frame of the extended superframe. The receiving CSU/DSU uses this CRC code to check for data errors.

T1 Equipment

As you can gather from the preceding discussion, T1 service requires a variety of equipment in addition to the routers and bridges you will need for any wide area networking service or protocol. Just to be sure you'll know what you need when it comes time to put together a purchase order, here's a checklist of the equipment you may need.

CSU/DSU

As we mentioned before, a channel service unit/digital service unit connects a digital service like T1 to a channel bank or other type of multiplexor. It serves several functions, including signal regeneration, line-conditioning, error-correction, signal management, synchronization, and circuit-testing functions.

Digital Multiplexor

As we have discussed, digital multiplexors are devices that convert analog frames to digital frames. Channel banks, illustrated earlier in Figure 20-2, are simple digital multiplexors. There are also very sophisticated multiplexors that can support many different levels of input—from a fraction of a DS0 to multiple DS0 channels—converting them all to digital transmission. Some are even self-reconfiguring so that transmission service continues even if a portion of the T1 network goes down.

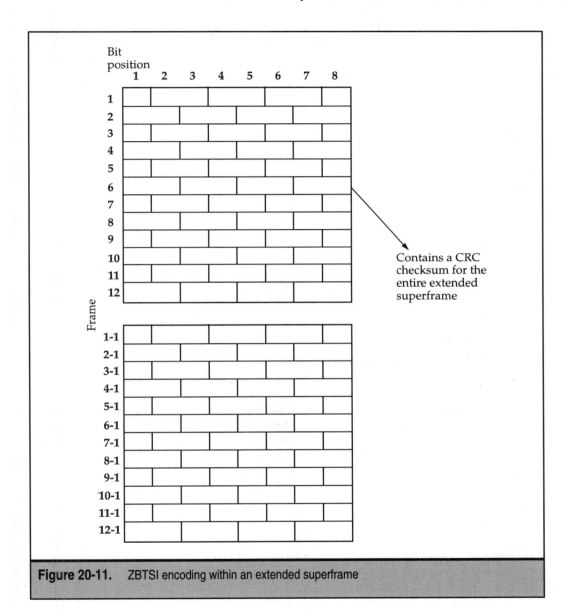

Figure 20-11.   ZBTSI encoding within an extended superframe

Digital Cross-Connect System (DCS)

The digital cross-connect system (DCS), shown in Figure 20-12, is a new type of multiplexor that transmits separate 64Kbps channels from one T1 transmission facility to another without having to pass through additional interfaces.

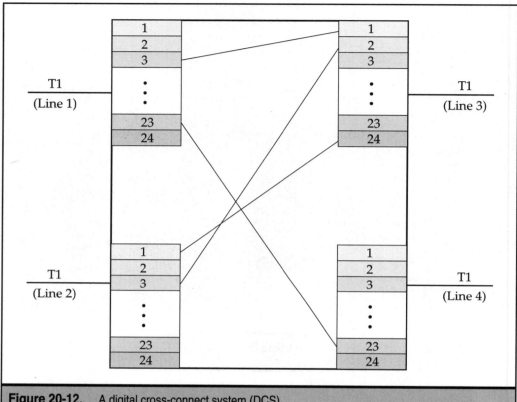

Figure 20-12. A digital cross-connect system (DCS)

Before the advent of digital cross-connect systems, T1 signal transmission could get complicated and ugly very fast. As illustrated in Figure 20-13, if you had to transmit data signals from a channel in one T1 facility to another T1 facility, you had to demultiplex all the signals, patch the channel that had to be connected to the next T1 into a channel bank, run through a switch, then run to another channel bank to be remultiplexed into the signal that the next T1 would then carry.

Obviously, this required a lot of equipment and a lot of time. Therefore, as you can imagine, digital cross-connect units were warmly received. Using a DCS let the network manager send traffic from any of the 24 64Kbps channels in a T1 to any other T1 connected to the same DCS, as shown in the lower right portion of Figure 20-14.

Digital cross-connect system devices make T1 service more cost-effective because they let you separate channels to carry different kinds of data without requiring a lot of

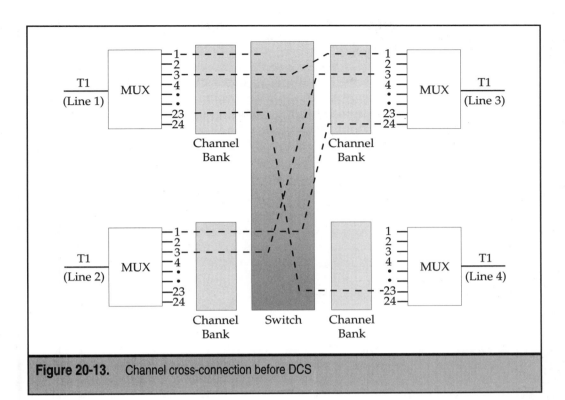

Figure 20-13.   Channel cross-connection before DCS

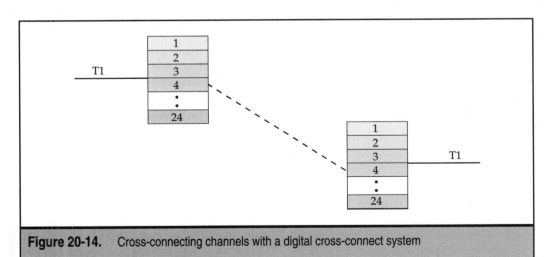

Figure 20-14.   Cross-connecting channels with a digital cross-connect system

extra equipment. They also come in a wide range of sizes, from as few as four or eight DS0 channels to over 100 DS0 channels.

Digital cross-connect system devices also have the ability to reconfigure your T1 network "on the fly." This means that the device can reroute signals from an inoperative T1 service to one that is properly functioning. This offers you a better probability that your T1 service will continue even in the event of the failure of a T1 service.

However, one of the most important things the digital cross-connect system has brought to T1 service is the ability to sell 64Kbps channels separately as fractional T1, which we will discuss later in this chapter.

Flexibility

One of the predominant reasons for the popularity of T1 is its extreme flexibility. As we discussed earlier in this chapter, you can purchase T1 service in an extremely wide variety of bandwidths, ranging from 1.544Mbps to 274.176Mbps. One of the most popular denominations of T1 is called T3 service, which consists of 672 64Kbps channels. You can also purchase less than full T1 as well. T1 service that's purchased in bandwidths less than 1.544Mbps is called fractional T1.

Fractional T1

One of the lovely things about T1 is that you can subdivide it and purchase it by the channel. Therefore, even if you don't need a whole T1 for your local access, you can take advantage of the speed, economy, and flexibility of your IXC's T1 service.

CAUTION: Your local exchange carrier (LEC) may not offer fractional T1 service. Therefore, you may have to pay for a complicated and very expensive substitute service from your LEC to transmit your data the "last mile" between your site and your interexchange carrier's point of presence. Before committing to T1 services from your IXC, be sure your LEC supports a fractional T1 interface.

Fractional T1 isn't really a fraction of 1.544Mbps. As illustrated in Figure 20-15, it's the whole enchilada. That's because fractional T1 is really just a pricing scheme for T1 service. It is the name telecommunications carriers have given usage-based T1 service.

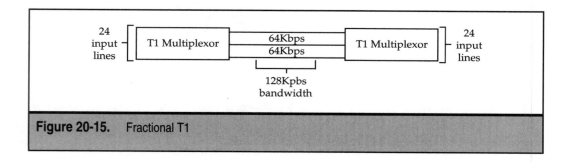

Figure 20-15.   Fractional T1

With fractional T1, you get a whole T1 interface, with at least 1.544Mbps of bandwidth. It's just that you only pay for the number of bandwidth channels you order.

A SMORGASBORD OF SERVICES Furthermore, 24 separate 64Kbps channels give you the option of using T1 interfaces to carry other kinds of services, such as local access to a long-distance carrier's (i.e., interexchange carrier, or IXC) point of presence. As well, T1 supports these services in either dedicated or switched facilities.

NOTE: Remember that dedicated service is a local access service that a LEC dedicates to a single user for its exclusive, full-time use. These rates are generally flat, fixed monthly rates that don't vary with usage. A shared service is local access that a LEC makes available to many customers who share it. Users pay for only the access service and facilities they use.

Availability

You can find T1 service practically everywhere. Even if you live in a radio hut in Greenland, your telecommunications interface is probably T1. However, as shown in Table 20-2, other countries have established different names and standard bandwidth offerings for their T1 services. That means that interoperability isn't necessarily automatic. Therefore, if your wide area network extends beyond North America, make sure you know exactly what needs to be done to make your T1 service interoperable with the equivalent service of the host country.

Cost

T1 is probably the lowest-cost wide area telecommunications service available anywhere.

T1: A Telecommunications Basic

As you can see by now, T1 is the workhorse of the telecommunications industry. It is reliable, easy to manage and install, relatively inexpensive, and very familiar throughout the telecommunications industry. T1 service comes in a variety of bandwidths, and T1 facilities can carry a variety of signals. Don't let your data signals leave home without it.

SWITCHED MULTIMEGABIT DATA SERVICE

Switched Multimegabit Data Service (SMDS) is not actually a protocol, but rather a "metropolitan area service." In essence, it is a method of transmitting Asynchronous Transfer Mode (ATM) cells over a shared bus. First deployed in 1992, SMDS gained momentum when the Regional Bell Operating Companies (RBOCs) and other local exchange carriers began feeling the heat of competition from interexchange carriers (IXCs) in local markets, and felt the best defense against that competition was a high-speed data transmission facility. As a relatively low-cost and definitely high-speed switched data service, SMDS seemed the perfect

DS	No. of 64Kbps Channels	Total Bandwidth	
		Japan	Europe
0	1	64Kbps	64Kbps
1	24	1.544Mbps	
1B	30		2.048Mbps
1C	48	3.152Mbps	
2	96	6.312Mbps	
2B	120		8.45Mbps
3	480	32.06Mbps	34.64Mbps
3D	1,440	97.73Mbps	
4A	1,920		139.26Mbps
4C	5,760	397.2Mbps	
5	7,680		565.15Mbps

Table 20-2.   Sample T1 Service in Japan and Europe

solution, and many local exchange carriers (LECs) in large metropolitan areas began offering the service.

Today, SMDS is currently offered only by local exchange carriers (although whether and how the Telecommunications Act of 1996 affects this remains to be seen). SMDS provides transmission rates in the T1 to T3 range on demand, so customers pay only for the bandwidth they use. Obviously, this can be more efficient and cost-effective than leasing dedicated, point-to-point lines if those lines are not fully utilized.

What Is . . .?

Switched Multimegabit Data Service is a marriage of the features of a shared-medium LAN and ATM. It is based on the IEEE 802.6 protocol, which defines the transmission of ATM cells over a shared bus. However, SMDS cells aren't identical to ATM cells: they use an 8-bit Access Control field while ATM uses a 4-bit generic Flow Control field. This is due to the fact that SMDS is a shared-medium, connectionless service, and therefore requires a more detailed address than the switched, connection-oriented ATM (which we will discuss in detail in a later chapter).

SMDS was developed by Bellcore and is based on the IEEE 802.6 metropolitan area network standard. It is a cell-based, connectionless, packet-switched network that focuses on transmitting data—and data only. SMDS cells are switched from source to destination through one or more SMDS switches. These switches are connected by high-speed trunks, such as DS1 or SONET transmission systems, as shown in Figure 20-16.

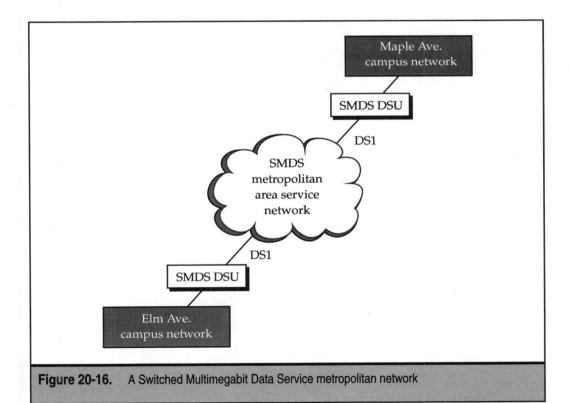

Figure 20-16.   A Switched Multimegabit Data Service metropolitan network

NOTE: Although SMDS supports shared media, Bellcore's adaptation concentrated on point-to-point implementation. You can understand this when you consider that nearly all of the transmission facilities handled by the LECs to that time were exclusively point to point in nature, not shared media or rings.

Cell-Based?

"Cell-based" means that the basic unit of data transfer is a fixed-length cell rather than a variable-length packet. Packet switching, which utilizes bandwidth only when data traffic is present, was developed to handle bursty data traffic. However, packet-switching systems don't perform adequately for real-time, two-way traffic such as interactive video. Cell switching overcomes this limitation because it employs cells, which are fixed-length packets rather than variable-length packets. Each SMDS cell consists of a 48-byte payload and a 5-byte header, as shown in Figure 20-17. Because these packets are identical to ATM packets (in fact, they are ATM packets), SMDS is considered by many to be a stepping-stone to ATM connectivity.

Switched?

SMDS does not employ shared bandwidth. Rather, each port on an SMDS switch is dedicated to one user. An SMDS switch sets up a virtual connection between a transmitting node and a receiving node. This connection is made on the basis of the destination address of each cell, and it lasts only as long as it takes to transfer one cell. These data transfers can take place in parallel and at full network speed. Because the cell is transmitted only to the port associated with that specific destination address, no other port receives the cell, which provides both low traffic and (as an extra bonus) high security.

Connectionless?

Like ATM, SMDS defines a service at the user-network interface. But, unlike ATM, which is a connection-oriented service, SMDS is a connectionless service. "Connectionless" means that no connection is established between the transmitting and receiving computers before data is transferred. Packets are simply transmitted on the medium as soon as the SMDS interface receives them. Therefore, there is no delay for call setup or teardown.

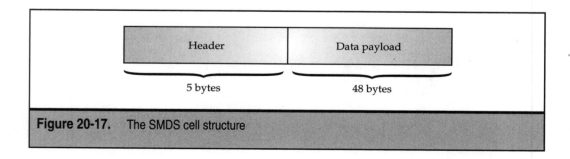

Figure 20-17.   The SMDS cell structure

In SMDS, the switch takes essentially connectionless data cells and maps them into a virtual circuit for transit through the network. The station's network adapter substitutes an 8-byte SMDS address for the 6-byte address used by legacy LAN protocols. The transfer may be in cells or in packets, as we will see shortly, but it always appears connectionless to the end user.

The Architecture

As we mentioned, SMDS is based on the IEEE 802.6 metropolitan area network (MAN) standard. This standard specifies a high-speed network protocol that runs on a shared dual fiber-optic bus. The SMDS network is a dual-bus design that forms an open ring, as shown in Figure 20-18. Physically, it looks like a star, and in this respect it is somewhat similar to token ring, which is a logical ring topology that forms a physical star because all cables are connected at a central hub. If the SMDS bus is cut, the open portion is automatically closed to "heal" the ring.

Standards Compliance

SMDS is not only compatible with the IEEE 802.6 metropolitan area network (MAN) standard on which it is based, but also with the Broadband ISDN (B-ISDN) model, illustrated in Figure 20-19. As a result, SMDS supports a fixed-length cell size of 53 bytes, as well as the ATM adaptation layer (AAL) protocols 3 and 4. SMDS also provides some services that aren't described in the MAN standard, such as management and billing, which we will discuss later in this chapter.

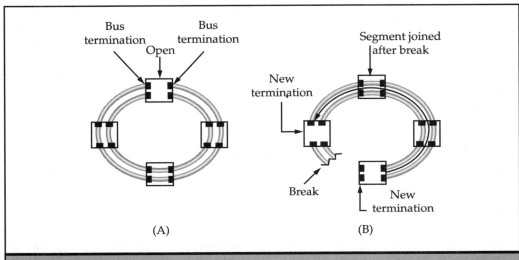

Figure 20-18.   The SMDS dual fiber-optic bus architecture

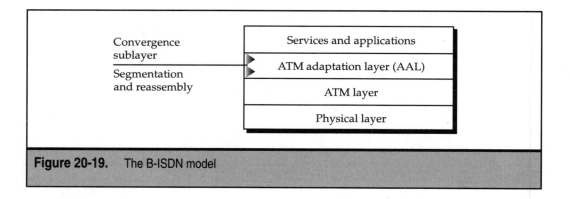

Figure 20-19.   The B-ISDN model

Data Exchange Interface

Because SMDS supports the transmission of data only, most of the data sent on the SMDS network is received from legacy local area networks in the form of packets. To avoid having to convert these packets into cells on every segment, the SMDS data exchange interface (SMDS-DXI) was developed. SMDS-DXI supports routing over SMDS services. SMDS-DXI is based on packets rather than cells. It uses standard High-level Data Link Control (HDLC) framing, so (unlike cell-based interfaces) it needs no additional hardware to transmit packet-based traffic.

SMDS-DXI makes implementing SMDS easy and inexpensive, because the HDLC hardware necessary to support SMDS-DXI is easy to obtain, relatively inexpensive, and time tested. SMDS-DXI also supports the low-speed access of legacy protocols, giving network managers more flexibility over bandwidth choices, and thus more control over costs (remember, in SMDS, users pay only for the bandwidth they use).

Where . . . ?

Switched Multimegabit Data Service is a metropolitan area service. Therefore, it is currently available only from LECs. As discussed earlier in this book, local exchange carriers are companies such as the RBOCs, GTE, and others that handle local telephone and telecommunications connections. Until recently, these companies were restricted by federal law to handling local communications, providing point-of-presence (POP) facilities for long-distance carriers, and offering wide area communications services only within their local service areas, known as local access and transport areas (LATAs). However, recent legislation has permitted them to compete with long-distance carriers and eventually to discontinue providing POP facilities to their competitors.

As carriers prepare for ATM, some are installing SMDS as a stepping-stone to ATM. MCI and GTE, for example, are offering SMDS. AT&T, on the other hand, seems to be a proponent of the "pure" ATM network. Because SMDS uses the same cell-switching technology as ATM, carriers can offer SMDS service running on ATM switches. In fact, many carriers are installing ATM switches that implement all of the fast-packet technologies, including not only SMDS but also frame relay and X.25 interfaces.

How . . .?

SMDS is a fast-packet technology, meaning that the protocol leaves error checking and flow-control procedures up to the end nodes. The belief is that current telecommunications transmission technologies and facilities transmit data with very few errors, so the complex and sophisticated error-checking mechanisms of earlier protocols are no longer necessary. If a packet is missing, the receiving node requests a retransmission. The network protocol itself is not burdened with this type of error checking. Asynchronous Transfer Mode and frame relay are also fast-packet protocols that do not include error checking as a network function.

Figure 20-20 shows the basic configuration of a customer connection to the telephone company's SMDS network.

Access Method

The IEEE 802.6 metropolitan area network standard specifies access to the shared-media dual fiber-optic bus via the distributed queue dual bus (DQDB). DQDB divides the bus into vacant time slots, which any connected station can fill with data cells for transmission. All attached stations can access the bus at any time until the bus is saturated. Theoretically, the DQDB access method supports up to 512 nodes and operates at 150Mbps on a network that can span up to 160km. The DQDB transmitting node can transmit packets of up to 9,188 bytes. These packets are disassembled into smaller 53-byte cells (48-byte data payload with 5-byte header) to fit into the SMDS slots. After transmission, they are reassembled at the receiving end.

Why . . .?

As a switching technology, SMDS has advantages over building private networks with dedicated digital lines such as T1 or even with ATM. These advantages include ease of

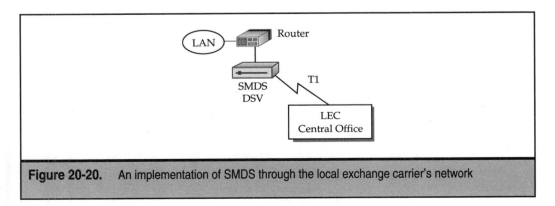

Figure 20-20.   An implementation of SMDS through the local exchange carrier's network

installation and configuration, manageability, scalability, interoperability, performance, and cost.

Installation and Configuration

As shown in Figure 20-21, customers installing an SMDS network need only set up one line into the LEC's SMDS network. In a T1 environment, users would have to set up lines between all the sites that need interconnection. Its connectionless nature provides any-to-any connections between a variety of sites without the delays involved in call setup and teardown procedures. Therefore, SMDS offers LAN-type communication over metropolitan areas. Once information reaches the SMDS network, it can be switched to any site or to multiple sites.

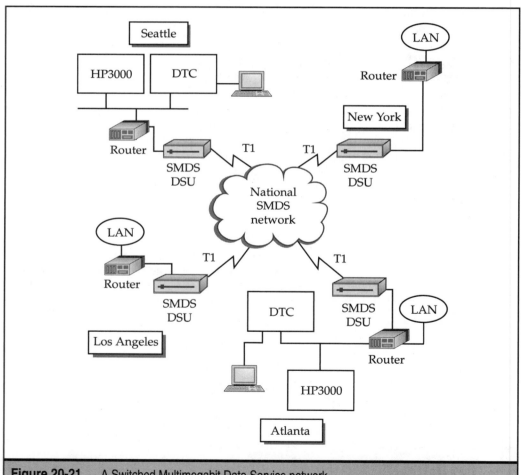

Figure 20-21.   A Switched Multimegabit Data Service network

Furthermore, the connectionless nature of SMDS makes it easy to add and drop sites in just minutes. Adding or dropping sites in an ATM network, with its connection-oriented protocol, would require reconfiguring the entire network.

Manageability

SMDS offers some nice management features that many other protocols, such as ATM, don't. For example, SMDS provides usage-based billing as well as a feature that controls network access to prevent nodes from monopolizing the network. It also has an address screening facility that heightens security by limiting communication to a group of addresses, and lets you build a private logical network over the public SMDS network. SMDS also provides usage statistics and other network management data directly to the end users. Finally, SMDS lets you construct data packets on top of the basic ATM cell structure, letting you take advantage of both packet features and fast cell switching.

Scalability

Switched Multimegabit Data Service is widely and easily scalable. Because it is easy to add and drop connections—and because you only pay for the bandwidth you use—SMDS can provide flexibility and connection options to accommodate quickly changing needs.

Furthermore, SMDS isn't just a MAN service. Despite its emphasis on the metropolitan area, SMDS is also a WAN service that can span long distances. This means that, theoretically, it's easy to expand an SMDS network to span the city or the nation. However, MCI is currently the only long-distance carrier offering SMDS, and the availability varies among local exchange carriers.

SMDS also has a wide range of access speeds, from 56Kbps to 45Mbps, which gives you many options for building high-speed segments. For example, you could build a 45Mbps backbone, then link lower traffic sites to the backbone at 56Kbps. And remember—you're only paying for the bandwidth you use.

Interoperability

Switched Multimegabit Data Service provides a fairly high level of interoperability with existing network infrastructures. It supports most existing network environments, including TCP/IP, Novell's IPX, AppleTalk, DECnet, SNA, and OSI. Furthermore, as we mentioned in our discussion of the DQDB access method, it allows a data unit of up to 9,188 octets. Thus, SMDS can encapsulate entire packets from most LANs.

Perhaps most significantly, the SMDS Interest Group and the ATM Forum have collaboratively developed specifications for SMDS and ATM service internetworking. However, if you are considering using SMDS as a means to migrate to ATM, you should note that SMDS supports the ATM adaptation layer 3/4. As you saw in Chapter 15, most LAN Emulation is based on ATM adapter layer 5. This means that when it comes time to integrate your existing local area networks into your high-speed backbone, you may have to convert to ATM to take advantage of LAN emulation. Later in this chapter, in the discussion of Asynchronous Transfer Mode, there is a complete discussion of LAN emulation and the issues surrounding it.

Performance

As we mentioned, SMDS supports a wide range of network and access speeds. It currently provides for user access at DS1 (1.544Mbps) and DS3 (45Mbps) rates. Network access requires a dedicated line running at a DS1 or DS3 rate.

Cost

Over the metropolitan and wide area—in which transmission media are relatively expensive to purchase, install, and maintain—the economics of shared media, which SMDS offers, are compelling. The cost of the service is usually a flat monthly fee based on the bandwidth of the links. Furthermore, SMDS offers easy expansion abilities. You simply pay for another port connection charge and the related usage fees.

However, the buyer should beware. Because the local exchange carriers are the primary providers of SMDS, there is usually no competition for the service in any given area. Therefore, you may want to weigh the cost of SMDS against other services.

TIP: It's hard to predict network usage. Therefore, to keep SMDS usage fees from playing havoc with your budget, try to find a carrier that offers a flat monthly usage fee or a monthly cap on SMDS usage charges.

Support Group

The SMDS Interest Group (SIG) is the biggest promoter of Switched Multimegabit Data Service. It is an association of SMDS product vendors, service providers, carriers, and end users. The SIG has not only user groups, but also working groups that promote SMDS and work on specifications. The technical working group works on improvements to the IEEE 802.6 standard, while the intercarrier working group suggests enhancements to the standards that dictate the interconnection and management of intercarrier SMDS. They also sponsor a user group and, of course, have a public relations group that organizes seminars and disseminates information about SMDS availability.

For additional information, contact SMDS Interest Group Incorporated, 303 Vintage Park Drive, Foster City, CA 94404-1138, Telephone (415) 578-6979, Fax (415) 525-0182, http://www.sbexpos.com.

Disadvantages

While SMDS seems like an easy-care, cost-effective solution, it does have some significant disadvantages. Weigh these carefully before taking the plunge.

Limited Multimedia Support

As we mentioned at the beginning of this chapter, the local exchange carriers began implementing SMDS to help them compete in the long-haul data transmission market. Therefore, they didn't spend much time developing voice and video support for the service. As a result, SMDS can only transfer data. It doesn't offer deterministic transmission (like frame relay) or guaranteed, sequenced-packet delivery (like ATM).

Limited Usage

Currently, there are just a couple hundred or so companies in the United States that are actively deploying SMDS. Even though SMDS is expanding rapidly, such a small market may not be able to guarantee sufficient revenue to keep many vendors in the market, which ultimately limits your choices in SMDS equipment and services as well as increasing your costs. Although many SMDS vendors and industry analysts are predicting that this number will grow substantially, there are just as many naysayers who believe that SMDS has missed its opportunity as ATM products become cheaper and more plentiful.

Limited Vendor Support

As we mentioned, SMDS is far from universally available. It isn't offered by some local exchange carriers, and MCI is currently the only long-distance carrier offering SMDS.

The Future

To be perfectly candid, SMDS has an uncertain future. While it is a relatively cost-effective method for transmitting data at high rates, its relatively restricted availability and data-only orientation have limited its usefulness. There is also some confusion over which direction it should develop. Some users would like to enhance DXI, making it more of a complementary service to connection-oriented protocols. Others would like to see vendors and carriers put more energy into developing multimedia support, making SMDS a service choice in its own right that competes with connection-oriented services. However, in both areas, SMDS has more than enough well-grounded competition to prevent its widespread adoption.

X.25

Poor old X.25. It is probably the most misunderstood wide area data transport protocol, and yet it's also the most venerable. Although it is indeed the granddaddy of all wide area data transport protocols, it is nowhere near drawing its last breath. Yet the industry press and pundits seem to have already buried it. Let's take a look at the history and functions of this pioneering protocol.

An Early Packet-Switching Protocol

X.25 first emerged in 1976. In that year, the Consultative Committee for International Telegraph and Telephone (CCITT) of the International Telecommunications Union (ITU) put forth its recommended specifications for connecting data terminal equipment to packet-switched data networks. That recommendation, X.25, had been developed mostly as a protocol for connecting remote dumb terminals to mainframe computers. However, its flexibility and reliability made it a perfect platform on which to base an entire generation of data communication standards.

In brief, X.25 is a connection-oriented interface to a packet-switched wide area network that uses virtual circuits to deliver individual data packets to their proper destination on the network. The X.25 protocol is not at all concerned with operations on the local area network. The X.25 protocol routes packets to the boundary of the WAN closest to their destination address. At that point, the X.25 protocol delivers the packets into the routing domain of the LAN protocols.

X.25 and the ISO/OSI

X.25 appeared well before the International Standards Organization (ISO) finalized its Open Systems Interconnection (OSI) protocol model, so it wasn't defined in exactly the same terms as the seven-layer model. Instead, the specification for X.25 describes three layers, as shown in Figure 20-22, which more or less correspond to the bottom three layers of the OSI model. These layers are the physical layer, the link access layer, and the packet layer.

The Physical Layer

In X.25 terminology, the physical layer is called the X.21 interface. This interface specifies the electrical and physical interface between the data terminal equipment (DTE) and the X.25 network. Although X.25 has its own specialized physical interface in X.21, in the early days you would often find the old standby RS222-C or V.35 substituted for the X.21 interface.

The Link Access Layer

The link access layer of the X.25 model corresponds to the media access layer of the OSI model. The link access layer describes the type of data transmission and frame composition

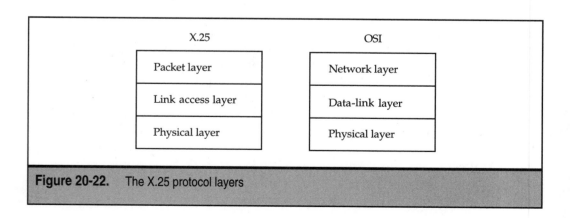

Figure 20-22. The X.25 protocol layers

X.25 supports, as well as the Link Access Procedure-Balanced (LAP-B) protocol used for establishing virtual connections, handling flow control in a balanced asynchronous session, and tearing down circuits when the transmission is complete. It is in this layer that the frame composition, flow-control procedures, and error-checking mechanisms are defined. LAP-B includes a means of acknowledging receipt of each packet at the destination station.

The Packet Layer

In the packet layer, X.25 sets up reliable virtual connections throughout the packet-switched network, which we will discuss in detail shortly. These virtual connections enable X.25 to provide the point-to-point—or connection-oriented—delivery of data packets, rather than the connectionless, or point-to-multipoint, delivery of packets that takes place in other transport protocols such as 10Base-T.

WHAT ARE PACKETS?   Think of a data packet as a letter sealed in an envelope and ready to mail. Like a letter, a data packet is a unit of information that can travel independently from its source to its destination. It's packaged and addressed so that no additional material or information is necessary to deliver it. Where a letter travels between persons via a postal system, a data packet travels between devices via a network. A data packet can convey many different kinds of information, such as application commands and messages, management commands and messages, or plain old garden-variety data.

Packets have two main parts. First is the data itself, often called the payload. Second is the address information, usually called the header. Figure 20-23 illustrates this. In addition to source and destination addresses, headers can also include routing, error-checking, and control information. Each packet is a discrete envelope of information that has its own addresses and routing information. The transport protocol, such as 10Base-T or X.25, defines the specific fields of which the frame is composed.

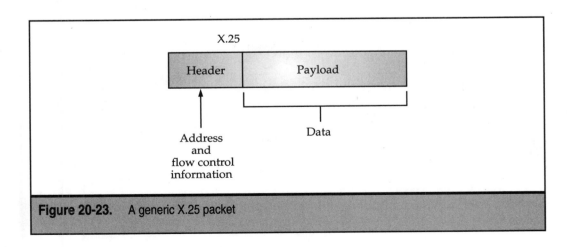

Figure 20-23.   A generic X.25 packet

In packet communications, a single chunk of information is broken down into many small, individually addressed packets of data. The transmitting station then sends these packets out over the communications network to the destination station. At the destination station, the packets are reassembled into the original large chunk of information, then processed by the destination station. The equipment that breaks down, addresses, and then later reassembles the packets is called a packet assembler/disassembler (for obvious reasons), or PAD. The PAD has multiple ports, as shown in Figure 20-24. Two computers in Poughkeepsie use their local PAD to access different computers. PC 1 calls the PAD and requests a virtual circuit to America Online in Pennsylvania. PC2 calls the same PAD, but requests a virtual circuit to a company mainframe in Waco, Texas. The PAD takes data from both computers, packetizes the data, and forwards it out over a single high-speed line to the X.25 network. The network switching devices route the packets to their destinations.

The inner workings of a PAD are governed by three additional protocols:

▼ X.3, which specifies how the PAD actually assembles and disassembles the data packets

■ X.28, which defines the interface between data terminal equipment and the PAD

▲ X.29, which defines the interface between data communications equipment and the PAD

WHY PACKETS? So why go to all this trouble to chop one nice, long stream of information into a bunch of little packets? Because packets are very efficient and foolproof, that's why. For example, suppose a communication link breaks down in the middle of a data transmission, as shown in Figure 20-25.

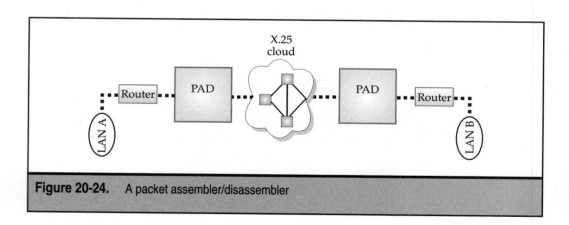

Figure 20-24.   A packet assembler/disassembler

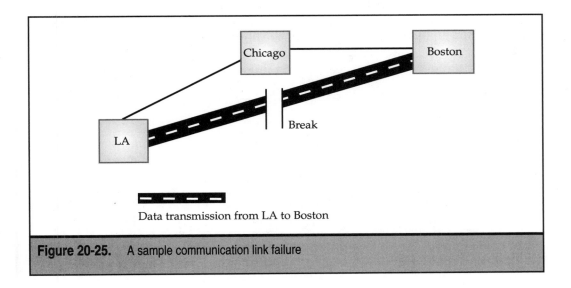

Figure 20-25. A sample communication link failure

If this were a circuit communication, the transmission would be halted and the sending station would have to reinitiate the communication over another route, then retransmit all the data, as shown in Figure 20-26.

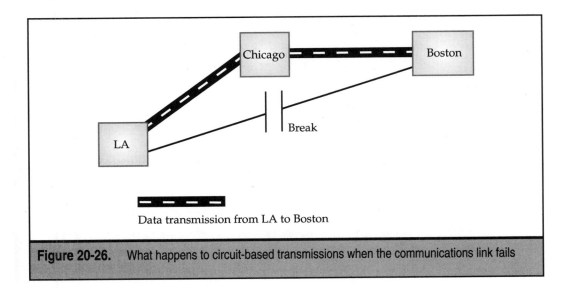

Figure 20-26. What happens to circuit-based transmissions when the communications link fails

However, if this were a packet-based transmission, as shown in Figure 20-27, as soon as the receiving station (or any other station on the route) sensed that the route was inoperative, the packets would be immediately rerouted over another transmission path. As well, only those packets that were actually lost would have to be retransmitted.

So, where do packets come from? I'll give you a brief tour of the packetizing process within the framework of the International Standards Organization's OSI model, shown in Figure 20-28.

A PACKET'S PROGRESS   A packet begins in the application layer. Let's say an application running in Computer 1 wants to send some data to Computer 2. The information goes from the application layer in Computer 1 all the way down to the physical layer protocols, which send the data—called a protocol data unit (PDU)—over the network to Computer 2. Each protocol layer tags the PDU with information that the corresponding protocol layer on Computer 2 will need to process the PDU. Think of it as each layer having its own bulletin board space on the PDU, and each layer pinning a note on its bulletin board addressed to its Computer 2 counterpart. (See Figure 20-29.)

Once the data reaches Computer 2, it goes back up the OSI protocol stack in Computer 2 until it reaches the application layer, where the application that needs the data can process it. As the PDU goes up through the layers, each protocol layer peels off the information put there by its corresponding layer on Computer 1. The protocol layers on Computer 2 use the information provided by the protocol layers in Computer 1 to process the PDU correctly. For example, packets are assigned sequence numbers by the transport layer. This sequence number tells the receiving station the order in which the packets should be processed. Therefore, as shown in Figure 20-30, the transport layer on

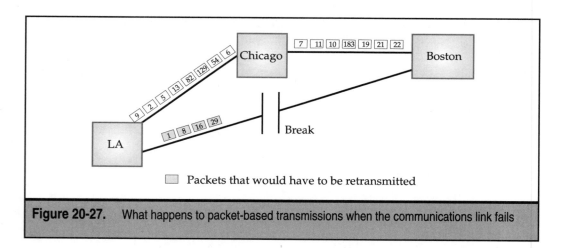

Figure 20-27.   What happens to packet-based transmissions when the communications link fails

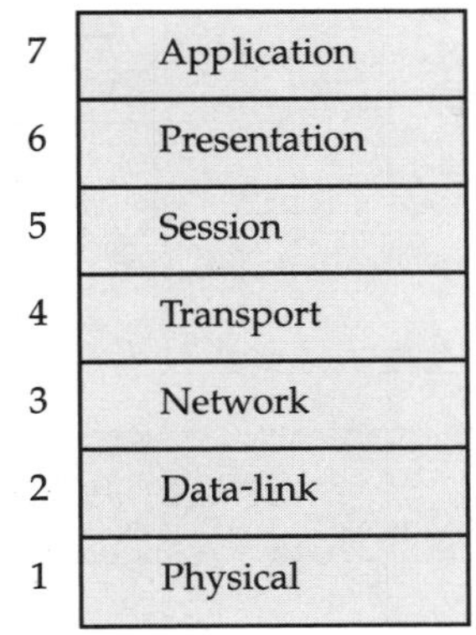

7 Application
6 Presentation
5 Session
4 Transport
3 Network
2 Data-link
1 Physical

Figure 20-28. The International Standards Organization's OSI model

Computer 2 will read the sequence number assigned to the packet by the transport layer on Computer 1 and process the packets in that order.

Computer 1
Application
Presentation
Session
Transport
Network
Data-link
Physical
Computer 2
Application
Presentation
Session
Transport
Network
Data-link
Physical

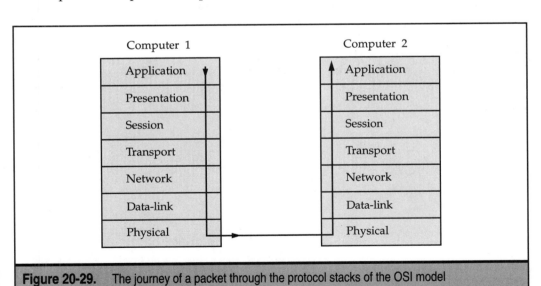

Figure 20-29. The journey of a packet through the protocol stacks of the OSI model

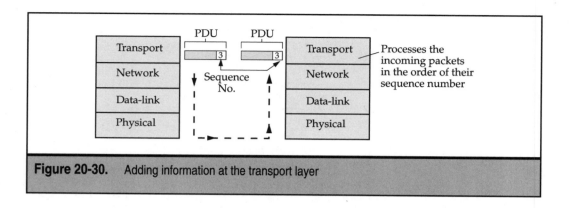

Figure 20-30.   Adding information at the transport layer

THE MAIL CARRIERS OF PACKET NETWORKS   Okay, you now know that a data packet contains its destination address. But who—or what—reads that address and makes sure the packet gets there? This job is done by bridges, routers, and switches, which look at either the MAC address (bridges and switches) or the network address (routers) to which the packets are being sent, and determine through which port the packets should be forwarded.

Bridges and switches forward packets on to the next appropriate bridge or router and/or filter packets so they aren't transmitted onto the wrong segment. As shown in Figure 20-31, they check the media access control (MAC) layer address of the packet against a table of such addresses. If the destination address is contained in the table, they forward the packet to the segment that contains that address. If the destination address isn't on the table, they just forward the packet on to the next node in the network in hopes that the destination address is contained in that device's address table.

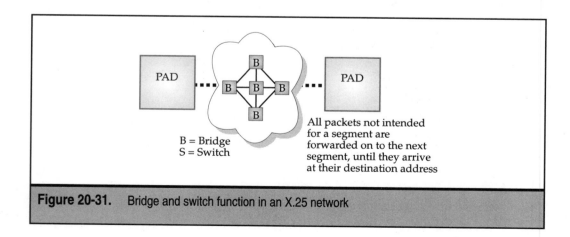

Figure 20-31.   Bridge and switch function in an X.25 network

Routers, as shown in Figure 20-32, send packets over predefined routes to the destination address. Routers use various criteria such as least cost and shortest path to map the best path through the network for each data packet. Administrators can either configure routers manually or allow the routers to use their own algorithms to calculate the best routes. In either case, routers determine data transmission paths using either connectionless or connection-oriented communications methods, which we will discuss next.

Packet Connections

Packet-switched networks seem to lend themselves to connectionless service, meaning that no connection is established between the transmitting and receiving computers before data is transferred. Packets are simply transmitted on the medium as soon as the network interface receives them. Therefore, there is no delay for call setup or teardown. However, these services aren't always reliable, because they have no means of guaranteeing packet delivery or of determining when packets have been lost.

Connection-oriented means that a connection must be established between the sending and the receiving stations before data is transferred. The voice telephone calls that you make every day are connection-oriented communications. When you dial a number, a connection is established between your telephone and the callee's telephone. This connection is unavailable to anyone else for the duration of your call. Furthermore, the information transmitted during this call—your conversation—isn't received by anyone but the two connected parties.

In connection-oriented communications, any and all intermediate points in the transmission path must be identified and informed of the existence of the connection. Different types of communications systems handle this in different ways.

Because a connection is established in advance and monitored throughout the duration of the call, connection-oriented communications offer secure and reliable delivery of

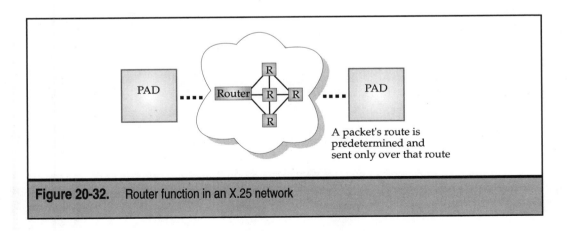

Figure 20-32.   Router function in an X.25 network

information. However, they also take time to set up and tear down. They also generally don't make efficient use of the connection. Think about your voice calls—a lot of conversations consist in large part of pauses and silences. This is somewhat true in data transmissions as well. And yet, in connection-oriented communications, a connection is dedicated to a particular transmission until it is torn down. No other transmission can share the bandwidth dedicated to that call.

X.25 is a connection-oriented protocol. It establishes a connection between sending and receiving stations before data is transmitted. However, for each connection made, only one packet of data is transmitted. This overcomes one of the major problems of connection-oriented communications: tying up a channel until all data has been transmitted. This is because, in the case of X.25, "all the data" means one packet. Figure 20-33 illustrates this point. At the same time, X.25 retains the reliability of connection-oriented communications.

Obviously, if data is transmitted at the rate of only one packet per connection, it generally takes many thousands of connections to complete a single packet-based data transmission. These many connections and the devices that make them are called a packet-switched network.

What Is a Packet-Switched Network?

A packet-switched network is really a dense mesh of point-to-point connections, like the one shown in Figure 20-34. At first, a packet-switched network looks like a circuit-switched network—and at a very high level, it works the same way. A virtual connection is established between the sending station and the receiving station, and then the sending station transmits data to the receiving station. When the transmission is complete, the virtual connection is cleared away. However, this is where the similarity ends.

In a circuit-switched network, all the data is transmitted in a single session. In the case of a packet-switched network, however, only a single packet of data is transmitted over a

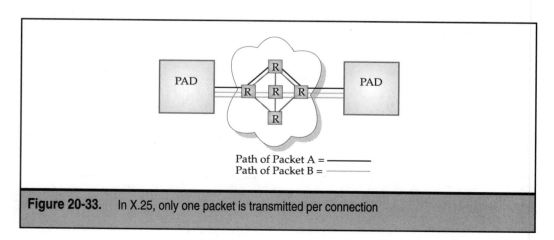

Path of Packet A = ————
Path of Packet B = ————

Figure 20-33.   In X.25, only one packet is transmitted per connection

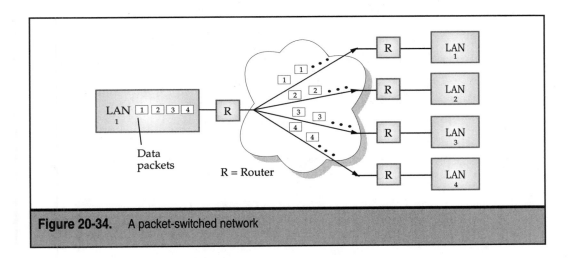

Figure 20-34.   A packet-switched network

virtual connection. That's right, in a packet-switched network, data transmission takes place one packet at a time, with each packet being transmitted separately, possibly each taking a different path between sending and receiving stations.

By definition, a packet-switched network provides "any to any" connectivity. This means that any station in the network can transmit data to any other station in the network over a wide variety of possible transmission paths. This is somewhat different than the point-to-point type of connectivity that defines a circuit-switched network. It's because of this pervasive connectivity that packet-switched networks are depicted as clouds, as in Figure 20-34.

Making Connections in a Connectionless World

Although, as we mentioned just a bit earlier, packet-switched networks can offer connection-less service, they can also support connection-oriented services that establish virtual circuits through the switches. Data travels over these virtual circuits one packet at a time, as shown in Figure 20-35.

Virtual Circuits

A virtual circuit (VC) is a transmission path for a datagram. A datagram is a discrete data unit that can move through the network independently. A VC is a predetermined path through a network over which datagrams travel. Keep in mind that a datagram can have several alternate paths over any given packet-switched network. Therefore, establishing

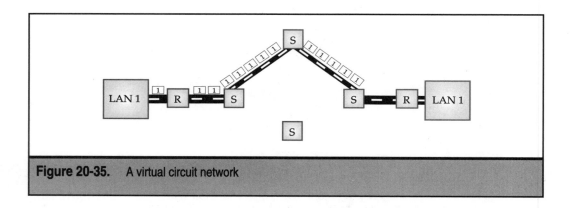

Figure 20-35.   A virtual circuit network

a path before transmitting a datagram will both improve performance by shortening delivery time and increase throughput by reducing datagram overhead. This is because the datagram header won't have to include routing information—it will only have to have source and destination addresses.

Because on a packet-switched network data travels one datagram at a time, and because the connections established are virtual connections rather than hard-wired connections, the packet-switching protocol can and does occasionally change the path between the sending station and the receiving station. The path may change because of

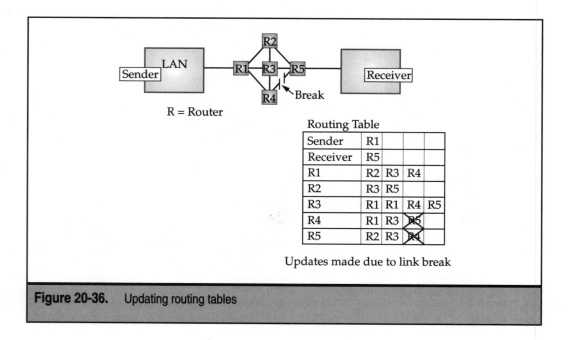

Figure 20-36.   Updating routing tables

inoperative circuits or excessively heavy traffic. Whatever the reason, and however the datagrams' paths may change, the transmitting and receiving stations must maintain the virtual connection and update the routing information periodically, as shown in Figure 20-36. In this example, the virtual circuit encompasses the local area network interface, the multiplexed connection between the routers, and the links through the network.

PERMANENT AND SWITCHED VIRTUAL CIRCUITS The VC extends through one or more switches, establishing an end-to-end connection for the transmission of data via datagrams. VCs can be established in two ways. First, a permanent virtual circuit (PVC) can be manually configured by a network manager. A PVC connects transmitting and receiving stations and is defined in advance. Therefore, at the time the datagram is transmitted, establishing this type of connection requires no setup time. A PVC is dedicated bandwidth that guarantees a level of service to a particular station. Think of a PVC as something like a dedicated telephone circuit. In public X.25 carrier services, customers select the end points of the PVCs they want to establish, then the carrier establishes and maintains those connections. If the desired end points change, the customer must contact the packet-switching service carrier to arrange for the PVCs to be reconfigured. Generally, network managers reserve PVCs for those highly vital connections, such as connections among routers, that must take priority over all other network connections.

The second means of establishing a VC is the switched virtual circuit (SVC). An SVC is a temporary VC set up on the fly between transmitting and receiving stations as it is needed by the application. A switched virtual circuit lasts only as long as necessary to complete the data transmission. It is torn down, or disconnected and cleared away, when the data transmission session has been completed. Think of an SVC as something like dial-up telephone lines. Either the network manager or the transmitting application has to configure and establish a switched virtual circuit immediately before data transfer. This isn't necessarily as daunting as it might seem: some public packet-switching carrier services offer a dynamically configured SVC that does not require customer intervention to establish.

X.25 AND VIRTUAL CIRCUITS X.25 supports both switched and permanent virtual circuits. This makes it more flexible than many other packet-switched protocols. For example, frame relay supports only permanent virtual circuits, although discussions are currently underway in standards committees to specify a switched virtual circuit mode for frame relay.

VIRTUAL CIRCUIT IDENTIFIERS In connection-oriented services, the network switches add a circuit identifier to each packet to identify the destination circuit. Virtual circuit identifiers tag the packets for a particular connection, then the switches transfer the data in a VC by hardware-based switching, triggering the VC connection tag in the packet header.

Benefits of Connection-Oriented Service

Connection-oriented services via virtual circuits in a packet-switched network combine the benefits of a circuit-switched network with a packet-switched network. Packets are transmitted in an orderly fashion from sending to receiving station, but they can be rerouted to avoid network failures and congestion. Because the route has been predefined, delays associated with route determination are minimized or eliminated altogether. The receiving station can reassemble the packets with minimal delay.

Other Concerns in a Packet-Switched Network

It's a good idea to keep the size of packets small. There are a lot of reasons for this. One is that if a packet (or packets) is corrupted, only those packets containing errors need to be retransmitted. Therefore, the smaller the packets, the less time that needs to be spent in retransmission. Furthermore, large packets are resource hogs, tying up transmission

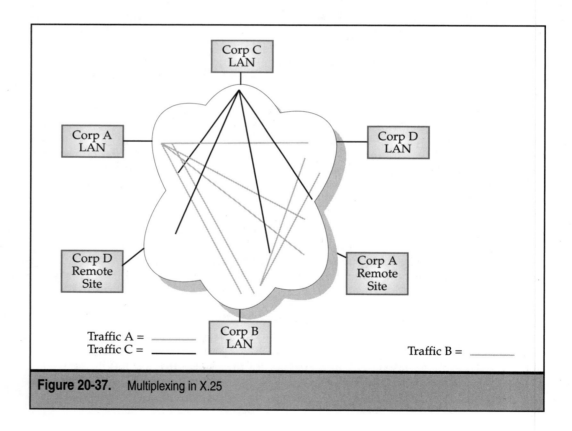

Figure 20-37.   Multiplexing in X.25

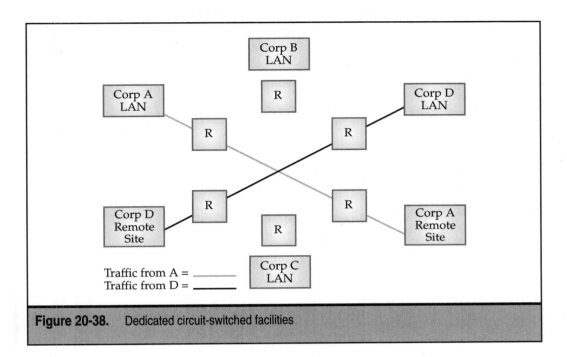

Figure 20-38. Dedicated circuit-switched facilities

resources longer than is necessary. In general, the smaller the packet size, the more efficient the data transmission.

Flexibility

Through multiplexing, X.25 lets multiple users communicate with many other users simultaneously over the same packet-switched network, as shown in Figure 20-37.

This means that any facility with an access point to the X.25 cloud can send packets to any other facility with an access point to the X.25 cloud. This is very different than dedicated circuit facilities, which provide dedicated bandwidth between two points and two points only, as shown in Figure 20-38.

Performance

In 1976, the X.25 standard supported a maximum transmission speed of 64Kbps. Unfortunately, most of this bandwidth was devoured by the protocol's extensive error-checking overhead. In 1992, the ITU issued a revised X.25 standard that, among other enhancements, increased the maximum supported speed to 2.048Mbps. In fact, France Telecom has been offering 2.048Mbps X.25 service for years.

The narrow bandwidth of its early incarnations has given X.25 a bad—and un-deserved—rap as a low-speed protocol. Actually, X.25 has the potential to have a throughput as high as frame relay—and even higher!

Of course, the packet-based nature of X.25 can have a bad effect on performance. For example, because packets share router ports, when traffic is extremely heavy, delivery delays are nearly inevitable. Even though the routers can direct packets around the most congested parts of the network, users may still experience slow performance.

On the other hand, its packet-switching nature gives X.25 the ability to accommodate bursts of traffic over and above the average bandwidth. Circuit-switched networks, on the other hand, can offer only a finite and inflexible amount of bandwidth between the sending and receiving stations. Because this bandwidth is fixed, it can't handle bursts in traffic in excess of the specified bandwidth.

HEAVY OVERHEAD   The overhead in X.25 is extensive compared to most other packet-switched protocols. This is due to the protocols extensive error-checking and reliable-transmission mechanisms. In X.25, every router and switch along a data path must completely receive each packet, check its destination address, and then perform error-detection routines before sending it on the next leg of its journey. As a result, each node in an X.25 network maintains a table containing management, flow-control, and error-checking information against which each packet is checked. In addition, destination stations in an X.25 network are responsible for detecting lost or damaged packets and requesting a retransmission.

Reliability

The X.25 has ironclad reliability and data integrity. It accomplishes this through an intricate process of data packet acknowledgment and error checking. Every time a sending station transmits a packet, the receiving station must send a response packet in reply. Usually, although the internals of X.25 packet switches are undefined by standards and therefore proprietary, most X.25 networks require a data-link layer acknowledgment from every node through which the packet passes and a network layer acknowledgment from the receiving station, as shown in Figure 20-39.

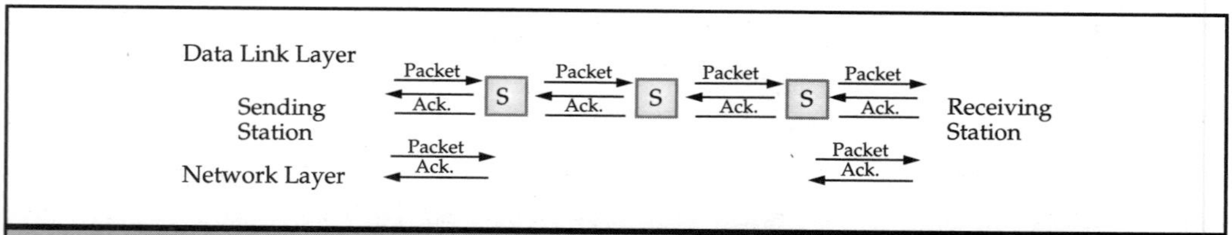

Figure 20-39.   Packet acknowledgments required by the X.25 protocol

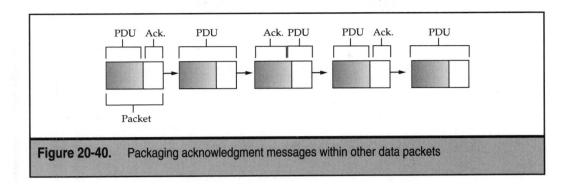

Figure 20-40.   Packaging acknowledgment messages within other data packets

Goin' My Way?

At first, this seems like an awful lot of chitchat across the network. Not necessarily true. You see, the acknowledgments don't have to be contained in discrete, separate packets. Instead, acknowledgments can be tucked into data packets that are traveling in the opposite direction (toward the sending station), as shown in Figure 20-40. This variation of full-duplex operation makes efficient use of network resources—and puts the "delay" caused by the acknowledgments in their proper perspective. A properly designed X.25 packet switch can even postpone packet acknowledgment messages until they can be drop-shipped with data traveling in another packet, thus improving the throughput of the switch and the network as a whole. Of course, if within a reasonable time period there are no data packets traveling in the opposite direction, the switch will have to send a separate acknowledgment packet, thus appearing to increase the latency (the time between the arrival of a packet at a switch port and the packet's departure out another port) of the switch.

Ordering X.25

X.25 networks are fairly easy to install and maintain. In fact, if you're so inclined, you can avoid the public carriers altogether and build your own private X.25 packet-switching network. All you have to do is install packet assemblers/disassemblers on your LANs, attach them to X.25 routers on each local site, then connect the local site with dedicated leased lines, as shown in Figure 20-41.

Of course, it's usually easier and more cost-effective to go the public carrier route. In the United States, X.25 is widely available from many different carrier services and value-added carrier services. Among X.25 providers are AT&T, CompuServe, and Pacific Bell. X.25 is a contract service rather than a tariffed one, so charges vary from carrier to carrier. Pricing is based on the number of packets transmitted and/or connection time.

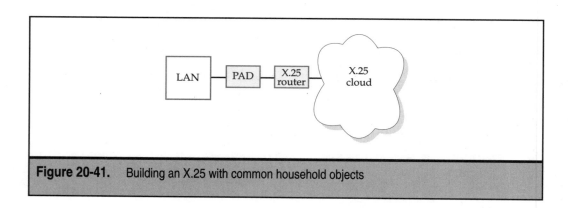

Figure 20-41. Building an X.25 with common household objects

TIP: Before you sign up, you should analyze whether X.25 is actually the best service for your wide area data network. Unless you have an extremely large number of nodes to connect, X.25 is probably not a cost-effective choice. Other services, such as plain old dedicated switched lines or even frame relay, will give you higher-speed service at a lower cost. That's why in the United States, X.25 is used mainly as a supplement to or backup for leased lines.

However, outside the United States, you may find that X.25 is the only game in town for wide area data transmission. In many companies, leased lines are nearly impossible to get through public carriers and/or they take months—and even years—of lead time to procure. Furthermore, in other countries, telecommunications customers aren't allowed to use modems on a public carrier's network.

X.25 and Frame Relay

You probably have heard a lot of talk comparing X.25 to frame relay. You have probably even heard some idle prattle about how frame relay is just a faster version of X.25, and how frame relay will ultimately replace its older cousin. Most of this is just silliness.

While frame relay is more streamlined than X.25, the older protocol offers much that simply isn't available from frame relay. The most obvious benefit is error handling. Granted, transmission facilities are much more reliable than they used to be, and lost data packets and their resulting retransmissions aren't the continual problem they were in the past. Nonetheless, when reliability is everything, frame relay cannot rival X.25's guaranteed packet delivery and error-checking mechanisms. Furthermore, X.25 offers the ability for carriers to add a lot of value to the X.25 transmission service, including features such as:

▼ Virtual private wide area data networks.

■ Packet forwarding—Receiving stations can designate a backup station to receive packets when the primary receiving station is busy or inoperative.

■ "Collect calls"—Sending stations can designate (with the receiving station's authorization) that the destination address pay for the transmission.

▲ Hunt groups—A group of stations can be jointly designated as a single destination so that traffic directed to one station can be received by any station in the hunt group (this is related to packet forwarding).

When You Need the Full Arsenal

Frame relay doesn't—and isn't designed to—provide the optional services that X.25 was conceived to offer. Where X.25 is a full-service Hum-Vee, frame relay is a dune buggy. They both scramble over the sand with sure-footed grace. What's more, the dune buggy can outpace the Hum-Vee in nearly every situation. But I know which one I'd take into heavy action.

FRAME RELAY

Frame relay is a spawn of Integrated Services Digital Network (ISDN). It is the packet-switching data service portion of ISDN, which has been unbundled and offered as a separate service. While relatively low-speed, frame relay's improved packet-switching architecture offers some features that may appeal to the network manager seeking to speed up a wide area data connection.

Son of ISDN

Before frame relay emerged as a protocol in 1989, it was actually part of the ISDN standards. As the packet-switching component of ISDN, frame relay was designed to provide a very high speed packet-switching data transmission service to provide connectivity between devices such as routers, which required high throughput for short durations. Then the developers of frame relay realized that the principles behind the protocol could be applied outside the realm of ISDN. As a result, frame relay was developed as an independent protocol for stand-alone use.

What It Is

Much like X.25, frame relay is a packet-switching protocol that connects two local area networks (LANs) over a public packet-switched network. In essence, a frame from one LAN is placed in, or encapsulated in, a frame relay frame. It is then transmitted through the frame relay network to the destination LAN. Frame relay uses statistical multiplexing techniques to load data from multiple sources at the customer site on a single line to the frame relay network. Statistical multiplexing essentially provides the LAN with bandwidth on demand, meaning that the network can get the bandwidth it needs when it needs it without having to reserve the bandwidth in advance and hold it unused until it is needed.

Each frame relay packet contains addressing information that the network uses to route through the telephone carrier's switches. Frame relay can be implemented using either private networks or a public carrier service. By placing responsibility for managing the network infrastructure in the hands of the frame relay service provider, using a public data network lets frame relay subscribers minimize service and equipment costs.

Frame relay offers improved performance over X.25 because it has very limited error-detection and correction routines, which we will describe in detail later in this chapter. The result of the streamlined packet delivery mechanism is data transmission speeds of up to 45Mbps.

How It Works

Like the X.25 protocol, frame relay divides the user data stream into packets that are transmitted over the carrier network and reassembled at their destination. However, frame relay does it much faster than X.25. What follows can be thought of as the nuts and bolts of how frame relay transmits data—and transmits it so quickly.

Frame Relay vs. Packet Switching

Like X.25, frame relay is based upon the principle of packet switching, which makes it well suited to data applications. In frame relay, data is divided into variable-length frames that contain destination addresses. These frames are then forwarded into the

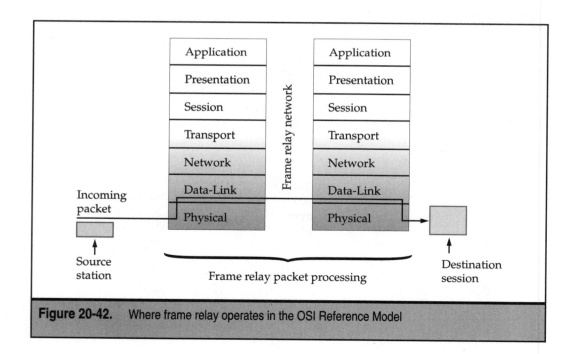

Figure 20-42.   Where frame relay operates in the OSI Reference Model

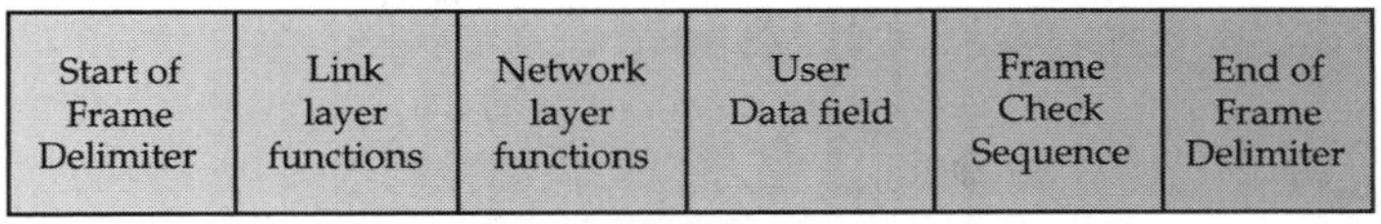

Figure 20-43.   A sample data packet

frame relay network, which delivers them. On its surface, this looks exactly like packet switching. In fact, the real difference between frame relay and packet switching lies under the hood: packet switching operates at layer 3 of the OSI Reference Model, shown in Figure 20-42, while frame relay operates at layer 2—and even then it doesn't implement all of the layer 2 functions. This means that frame relay is a simpler protocol than X.25 and other packet-switching protocols, implementing less error checking and correction but offering more speed.

To understand frame relay's advantages and how it achieves them, let's take a look at how X.25 and other layer 3 packet-switching protocols work, then compare this to frame relay's simpler operation.

PACKET SWITCHING AND HOW LITTLE IT MEANS TO YOU   Figure 20-43 shows a sample X.25 packet. As you can see, the packet includes a field containing network layer information. A packet contains six major components:

▼   **Start and End of Frame Delimiters**   This is an 8-bit sequence that signals the beginning of a packet. The Start of Frame Delimiter and End of Frame Delimiter are crucial to determining when a packet begins and ends, because X.25 packets are not fixed in length.

■   **Link Layer field**   This field contains information to handle packet errors and flow control. The link layer functions manage error correction and recovery as well as detecting whether there are sufficient buffers in the destination packet switch to receive the packet.

■   **Network Layer field**   This field contains the information necessary for the packet to establish an end-to-end connection between the transmitting and receiving stations. The network layer is responsible for setting up and tearing down a connection for each packet transmitted, as well as providing some flow-control procedures.

■   **User Data field**   This is the data "payload" of the packet. It's usually 4K or smaller in size.

▲   **Frame Check Sequence**   This is a 2-byte field containing a checksum to determine whether the packet has been damaged or corrupted during transmission. A checksum is calculated on an arriving frame and compared with the FCS field, which was calculated by the sender. The packet is discarded if there is a mismatch and the end-stations must resolve the missing packet.

As you can see from reviewing the packet structure of an X.25 network, this protocol involves a lot of packet processing. Not only is an end-to-end connection established for each and every packet sent, but the packet is checked for errors by both the link layer protocols and the Frame Check Sequence. As well, both the link layer and the network layer provide extensive flow control, which controls the rate at which devices transmit packets into the X.25 switch. If the receiving switch is unable to accept any packets from the transmitting station because it's congested, the receiving switch won't acknowledge receipt of the packets. Furthermore, it issues a "send no more packets" message to the transmitting device. When the congestion within the receiving switch clears, it will send the relevant "OK to send again" message to the originating device. This guarantees that the receiving switch will never have to discard data for reasons of lack of buffer capacity and offers one more level of data transmission reliability. The protocol's developers considered this level of packet processing necessary because of the relatively unreliable transmission links available at the time.

These extensive error-checking and flow-control mechanisms do indeed ensure packet delivery. However, they also slow the transmission of packets and therefore reduce the performance of the network as a whole. Luckily, two things happened that have helped make these mechanisms less important. The first was the advent of much more reliable high-speed transmission systems that delivered packets with much fewer errors and corruption. The second was the development of applications within the end-user stations that were designed to detect and recover packet errors. As a result of these two innovations, network designers were eager and able to do away with these cumbersome— and now unnecessary—error-checking procedures.

FRAME RELAY TO THE RESCUE   Frame relay was developed on the assumption that the transmission media is reliable and relatively error-free and that the end-user applications can detect and recover from packet errors. Therefore, frame relay discards packets that contain errors. Also, if a frame relay switch's input buffers are full, it discards incoming

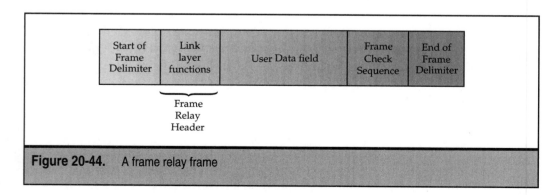

Figure 20-44.   A frame relay frame

frames until the congestion clears up. In short, frame relay makes little attempt to detect errors and congestion, and no attempt whatsoever to correct them.

So what does it do? A frame relay switch has three core functions:

▼ Routes incoming frames to the correct outgoing port.

■ Checks the Frame Check Sequence field to determine whether the frame contains an error. If so, it discards the frame.

▲ Checks to determine if its buffers are full. If so, it discards incoming frames until the congestion clears up.

That's it. No connections are established, no flow control is maintained—no Level 3 functions are performed at all. If you look at the frame relay frame structure shown in Figure 20-44, you can see that the frame doesn't even contain fields for the information necessary for the switch to perform these functions.

Frame Format

The frame structure for the frame relay packet is pictured in Figure 20-44. Very similar to the X.25 packet, the frame relay packet has the following components:

▼ **Start of Frame Delimiter** This is an 8-bit sequence that signals the beginning of a packet.

■ **Link Layer field, also called the Frame Relay Header** This field contains addressing information and what little flow-control management frame relay does. The Link Layer field also detects whether there are sufficient buffers in the destination packet switch to receive the packet. This field has two subfields:

  ■ **Data Link Connection Identifier (DLCI)** This is the address of the logical connection that is multiplexed into the channel.

  ■ **Discard Eligibility (DE)** This indicates whether the frame can be discarded in the event of network congestion. We'll discuss the use of the DE subfield later in this chapter.

■ **User Data field** This is the data "payload" of the packet. It's usually 4K or smaller in size.

▲ **Frame Check Sequence** This is a 2-byte field containing a checksum to determine whether the packet has been damaged or corrupted during transmission.

Frame Relay Network Devices

So how do these almost-but-not-quite-X.25 frames travel over the frame relay network? A station sends a data packet to a router, which sends the packets across the port connections composed of either permanent virtual circuits (PVCs) or switched virtual circuits (SVCs) to a frame relay switch or router, which reads the destination address contained in the DLCI subfield of the Frame Relay Header. The network device then routes the frame to the proper destination over the frame relay network. At the other end of the network, the frame relay information is stripped off and the data is reassembled in its native packet format, which can then be processed by the receiving station.

Frame Relay Connections

Frame relay supports several different types of connections, all of which work together to form the frame relay network mesh.

PORT CONNECTIONS   A port connection is a physical access point on the frame relay network that defines the maximum amount of data sent on to the network across all PVCs at any time. A single network interface can support multiple ports. The port connection is the interface to the public or private frame relay network, and at the time of this writing is generally available at 56/64Kbps, 128Kbps, 256Kbps, 384Kbps, 512Kbps, 768Kbps, 1.024Mbps, and 1.536Mbps. The port connection dynamically allocates data across the permanent virtual circuits.

Frame relay uses a multiplexing technique (which we will discuss later) that allows a large central site to be connected to a public frame relay network with a single router port and a single high-speed connection to the network. Because the circuits are not dedicated to a specific site the way point-to-point services are, multiple transmissions to many different sites can take place simultaneously.

PERMANENT VIRTUAL CIRCUITS   A PVC is a path through the frame relay network that connects two points. A PVC is dedicated bandwidth that guarantees a level of service, called a committed information rate (which we will discuss later in this chapter), to a particular station. The network manager orders PVCs from a frame relay service provider, which configures them according to the network manager's specifications. Permanent virtual circuits remain active and available to the subscribing network at all times.

SWITCHED VIRTUAL CIRCUITS   Switched virtual circuits (SVCs) were added to the frame relay standard in 1993. A switched virtual circuit is a virtual circuit established "on the fly" as needed by the transmitting application, adding to the flexibility of the bandwidth for the circuit. However, while SVCs are now a part of the frame relay standard, no carriers are currently offering them—and some carriers don't plan to.

Relief for a Stuffy Network

As we mentioned, the frame relay protocol has no flow-control mechanism. Therefore, frame relay networks have no procedure for slowing or stopping data transmission when the network is congested. There is a means of notifying stations when the network becomes overburdened, but if the station's application isn't designed to respond to the notification by suspending transmission, the station will keep sending data on to an already jammed network. Therefore, when a frame relay network gets congested, it starts discarding frames.

The network can select frames to discard in one of two ways:

▼ Arbitrary selection
▲ Discard eligibility

In arbitrary selection, the frame relay network simply starts discarding packets when it gets congested. This is certainly effective, but it doesn't distinguish between packets that were sent under the auspices of the customer's committed information rate (CIR) and packets that were sent as part of a burst over and above the CIR. What's worse, though, is that it doesn't distinguish between vital data transmissions and transmissions that contain idle chitchat. That's why many frame relay users prefer the discard eligibility method of removing frames.

End users designate the discard eligibility of frames within transmissions by configuring their routers or switches to set flags within the frame relay data frames. For example, a customer may configure its router to flag all administrative traffic DE ("discard eligible"), but not flag all manufacturing-related transmissions. Then, should the network become congested, frames from the administrative traffic would be discarded—to be retransmitted by the application later when the network is not so busy—while all manufacturing traffic would continue. Using the DE flag lets you determine which information is most important to you and ensure that it receives a higher transmission priority than less important data.

Getting What You Pay For

As we mentioned, frame relay has no flow-control mechanism. Therefore, users can theoretically send as much data as they want over the frame relay network. This means that the protocol has no means of preventing a single bandwidth-hungry station from monopolizing the entire bandwidth for the same flat fee. This is why frame relay carrier services have developed the CIR.

When you order frame relay service and its attendant virtual circuits from a frame relay provider, you will be asked to specify a committed information rate. The CIR is the minimum bandwidth that your carrier will guarantee to be available to your PVC 24 hours a day, 7 days a week. The committed information rate is not tied in any way to the speed of your physical connection. Therefore, you could have a 1.544Mbps physical connection but only a 64Kbps CIR. You determine what your CIR should be by estimating your normal network traffic (or your budget—the higher the CIR, the higher the cost of the frame relay PVC).

AND GETTING MORE... If your network traffic exceeds your committed information rate, you're not necessarily out of luck. Frame relay can theoretically accommodate bursts in excess of the allocated bandwidth. Therefore, if the frame relay network receives a transmission from your network that bursts beyond your committed information rate, the frame relay network will attempt to open additional circuits to complete the transmission. When the network is not congested, sometimes you can send data bursts as large as twice your CIR.

Don't count on being able to exceed your CIR on a regular basis, however. Bursting above the CIR can occur only when the network isn't congested. We'll explain why later, in the section on statistical multiplexing. Still, you should be able to plan on sending some traffic bursts, which means that frame relay network designers must build networks with sufficient capacity to handle the CIR plus a reasonable amount of bursts in excess of the CIR.

To provide some guidelines to frame relay network designers, most frame relay carrier services have adopted two additional guaranteed rates. These are the committed burst rate (CBR) and the excess burst rate (EBR). The CBR is the maximum amount of data rate that the network provider agrees to transfer under normal network conditions. The EBR is the maximum data rate over and above the CBR that the carrier's network will try to sustain. EBR data is automatically flagged DE.

Management and How Little There Is of It

The frame relay protocol really has no integrated management. Therefore, what little management information the network devices require to control the connections between end stations and the network mesh is provided out of band, meaning this information travels over a separate virtual circuit. The management system that provides this information is known as the local management interface (LMI).

The LMI is very much a "bare bones" management system, providing only four basic functions:

▼   Establishing a link between the end user and the network interface

■   Monitoring the availability of frame relay circuits

■   Notifying network stations of new PVCs

▲   Notifying network stations of deleted or missing PVCs

Statistical Multiplexing and Bandwidth on Demand

As we mentioned, frame relay was designed to handle bursty traffic efficiently and even elegantly. Therefore, much of the traffic you see on frame relay networks is bursty in nature, which means that much of the time these devices are transmitting little, if any, data at all. Rather than waste money on idle bandwidth for a large number of bursty connections, frame relay gives network managers the ability to connect multiple bursty connections to the same segment. The strategy is that on only a very few occasions will two or more connections send a burst of traffic at the same time, and when some of them do, there is enough buffer capacity in the frame relay switch to capture the frames and transmit them as bandwidth frees up.

Statistical multiplexing is the technique for the interleaving of data from several devices onto a single transmission line. Figure 20-45 is a simplified illustration of how7 statistical multiplexing works. Each device with data to transmit is allowed a transmission slot on the network. If the device has nothing to transmit, however, its slice of bandwidth is

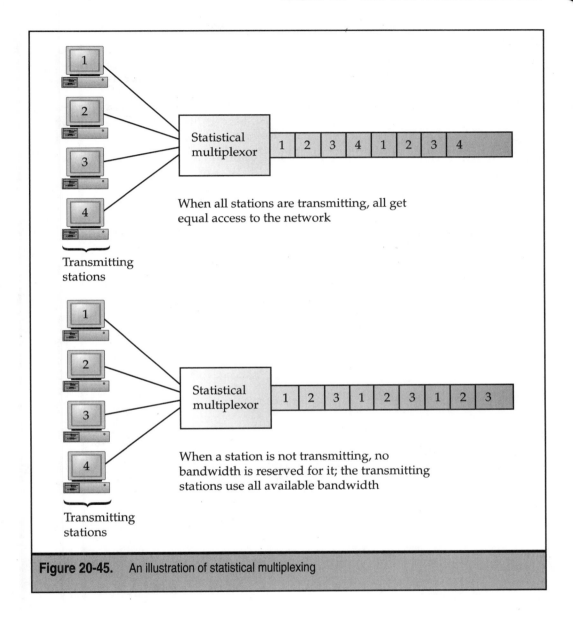

Figure 20-45. An illustration of statistical multiplexing

allocated to a station that does have data to transmit. This is how frame relay accommodates bursting in excess of a subscriber's committed information rate—it makes use of bandwidth currently unused by other stations on the network.

Installation and Configuration

When you are preparing your order for frame relay service, there are a few issues you need to work out before placing the call to the carrier service. These are as follows:

▼ **Access method** This is the speed of the connection between your site and the carrier's frame relay network. You have several options, and the speed you select will determine the type of access line required:

- 56/64Kbps over switched 56 or ISDN lines
- 128Kbps over ISDN lines
- 384Kbps to 1.544Mbps over fractional T1 or T1 lines

■ **Physical location of the frame relay devices at your site** As we mentioned earlier, you'll need a router with a frame relay WAN port. Furthermore, your carrier will need to install a frame relay assembler/disassembler on your premises, as shown in Figure 20-46.

▲ **Committed information rate, committed burst rate, and excess burst rate** You will need to determine your network's traffic requirements—or your budget limitations—before you begin ordering the service.

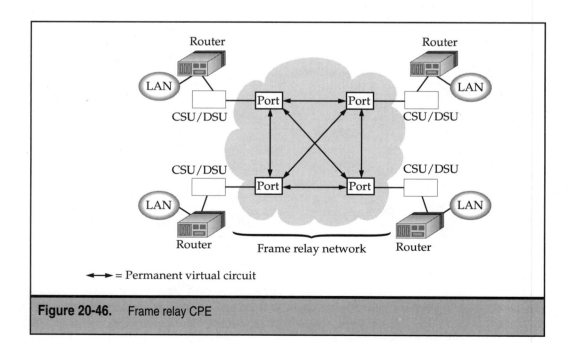

Figure 20-46. Frame relay CPE

To configure your router for frame relay, all you have to do is enter the data-link connection identifier (DLCI) information furnished by the frame relay service provider in your router's configuration tables. While you will be responsible for the LAN-to-router connection and router-to-FRAD connections, your local telephone company will be responsible for the FRAD-to-central-office connection. Furthermore, your local telephone company and your frame relay carrier together will be responsible for the central office-to-frame-relay network connection. Clearly, this leaves a lot of room for finger-pointing, so be sure you're comfortable with the expertise of the carriers—and be patient.

Availability and Pricing

Most wide area carriers in major metropolitan areas offer some flavor of frame relay service. However, destination cities and pricing vary a great deal, so make sure you verify that the carrier you are considering indeed offers frame relay services to all the locations you want to connect.

As we mentioned, frame relay can be very cost-effective, especially when compared with leasing multiple point-to-point connections. Generally, frame relay is very cost-effective for companies that have multiple sites in multiple geographically distant locations. Most leased-line connectivity is priced through federally regulated tariffing, which provides a fixed monthly fee plus an additional mileage fee. Frame relay, on the other hand, is usually priced on a flat fee, based on the port access speed and committed information rate. The monthly rates for frame relay service are in the neighborhood of $125 for 56Kbps service up to around $650 for 1.544Mbps service. However, you should be aware that these services come with a fairly hefty one-time installation fee of around $1,500 per port. If these rates are significantly lower than the costs involved in establishing a point-to-point dedicated line network to connect the same locations, then you should definitely consider implementing frame relay.

Management and Fault Tolerance

One of the beauties of using frame relay is that, if you are using the services of a public frame relay carrier, your physical management responsibilities are very limited. Adds and changes to your services require nothing more from you than a call to your carrier. Fault tolerance is also the responsibility of the carrier, and frame relay offers automatic rerouting of PVCs when a connection fails.

On the other hand, as we have already mentioned, frame relay as a protocol isn't known for its manageability. There are only a few management features offered with frame relay, and those are implemented via out-of-band signaling. However, here are a few optional services available that may make your life easier:

▼ Simple flow control provides XON/XOFF flow control for those network devices that require flow control.

■ Multicasting so stations can send frames to multiple destinations.

▲ Global addressing that lets applications emulate LAN addressing.

Frame relay also offers the security benefit of having only private lines access the frame relay mesh. There are also some optional security features you can implement from your carrier, such as password protection and a feature that logs stations off the network after a predefined period of inactivity.

Interoperability

Frame relay offers good interoperability now, and also holds the promise of quicker and easier interoperability when SVCs are supported by the public carriers. SVCs could connect ISDN to frame relay networks, and they may eventually give users the ability to dial up frame relay connections.

You may want to consider routing nonlocal area network protocols over frame relay as well. It may seem a bit strange at first, but frame relay is often much more cost-effective than other wide area transmission protocols, so it's worth a look. To route non-LAN protocols over the wide area, you'll need a device called a frame relay assembler/ disassembler (FRAD). A FRAD takes data packets from other protocols—such as SNA, asynchronous, and even X.25—and breaks them into pieces, encapsulates the packet pieces in a frame relay frame, and sends them over the frame relay WAN to its destination. At the other end, the frame relay headers are stripped off the packets, and they are reassembled as packets in their original protocol, where they can be processed by the receiving stations. Figure 20-47 illustrates this.

A FUNI WAY OF INTERCONNECTING Most ATM switch manufacturers have announced support—or at least an intention to support—for frame relay and ATM connectivity. The ATM Forum has offered a proposal, known as Frame-to-User Network Interface (FUNI),

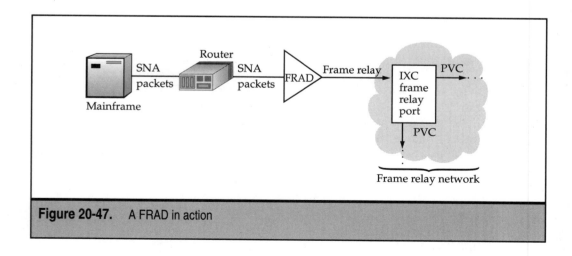

Figure 20-47. A FRAD in action

designed to set standards for connecting 56Kbps to 1.544Mbps circuits to ATM networks using a frame structure much like frame relay's. However, we've yet to see any actual FUNI installations, so the success of this proposal is yet to be seen.

INTERCONNECTING THE CARRIERS   Different frame relay carriers implement the service in different ways, and as a result many of them are unable to interoperate. Not only do they often use different switches, but they also may implement different congestion control and signaling methods. The Frame Relay Forum has set about to resolve some of these interoperability issues by developing a set of interconnection specifications called the Network-to-Network Interface (NNI) standards. Theoretically, if all carriers use frame relay equipment that adheres to these standards, the interoperability problems will cease to exist.

Performance

Frame relay is generally available at CIRs from 56Kbps to 1.544Mbps. As well, it supports much higher burst rates—up to 45Mbps. Furthermore, frame relay has low network latency of about 20ms.

Scalability

Scalability is the hallmark of frame relay. The ease of adding more bandwidth via the CIR, along with the ability to send bursts of traffic well over the CIR, make frame relay one of the most flexible wide area protocols around. At the same time, thanks to frame relay's use of statistical multiplexing, providing this flexibility doesn't result in wasted idle bandwidth.

Can Your Vendor Do This?

Whether you're selecting a vendor to implement a frame relay WAN from scratch or to provide a specific device for your existing frame relay WAN, there are certain questions to answer fully. Although every frame relay network is different, and every expansion and upgrade within each network is unique, there are basic questions that are relevant to every frame relay project. To help you get started with the vendor selection process, we've provided a sample list of four questions to put to each prospective vendor. We've divided these questions into issues of experience, interoperability, performance, and management. Please note: for those of you implementing a frame relay network for the first time, we've assumed you have done your homework and are certain that frame relay is the correct protocol choice given the traffic, type of data, speed, transmission reliability, and internetworking characteristics of your vendor.

THE EXPERIENCE QUESTION   Has your vendor ever done this before? Are the technicians who have done it still on staff? This may seem silly, but it could be the most important question of all. You don't want to subsidize on-the-job training for your vendor's technical staff. Get references and check them thoroughly. Ask for the names of the technicians who performed the work. Make sure that those technicians are still employed by the vendor. Ask to interview them. Consider writing the name(s) of the experienced technician(s) into your bid acceptance.

THE INTEROPERABILITY QUESTION   Are you a member of the Frame Relay Forum? If not, does your equipment meet the frame relay standards? This is particularly relevant to equipment vendors. Ask them to provide examples—complete with references—of other vendors' equipment with which they have successfully internetworked. Be sure to check the references thoroughly. The last thing you need is to be bound to a single vendor because their frame relay implementation is "almost" in compliance with the standards set by the Frame Relay Forum.

THE PERFORMANCE QUESTION   What is the maximum line speed supported now—and 12 months from now? Obviously, 2.048Mbps should be the minimum. And for now it can be the maximum. Your vendor should have—or at least have plans for—support for speeds up to 45Mbps. And it wouldn't hurt to check the cost of upgrading to these higher speeds.

What are the switching speeds, expressed in frames per second, between a) trunk ports, b) access ports, c) access and trunk ports. Get speeds for frame sizes varying from 128 bytes to 2,048 bytes. This question helps you ensure that the equipment can switch frames as quickly as it can receive them. For example, connected to a 2.048Mbps line, your router will receive about 2,000 128-byte frames per second. So if you have a device that can be configured to support more than one 2.048 line, yet can switch at a maximum of 2,000 frames per second, the router is actually a bottleneck.

TIP: You can expect the best performance on the trunk-to-trunk ports, so have your vendor quote the access port-to-trunk port switching speed, too.

THE MANAGEMENT QUESTIONS   How does the router handle congestion management? How does it handle recovery?

Congestion and overflow compose the number one management issue for frame relay, so this is a key question. Ask whether the equipment complies with the CCITT and/or ANSI standards for congestion management, and if so, how. Explore whether the vendor's implementation uses the discard eligibility bit to let the equipment or the user set the discard priority of frames. What management facilities do they offer? Frame relay is not famous for its inherent manageability. Therefore, it pays to spend some quality time learning the management facilities offered by the proposed system or equipment. The number one feature you should require is congestion notification, since—as we noted above—congestion management will be your overriding concern with frame relay.

Another critical management issue is routing. The system should provide both manual and automatic routing, because although you will prefer manual routing for priority traffic, it would be silly to try to manually define routes for every frame of every priority. And, as with most systems, your frame relay system should provide useful troubleshooting and diagnostics utilities. You should also expect the system to provide comprehensive statistics on traffic levels, speeds, and discarded frames. You can use this information not only for network administration purposes, but also for billing information if your network has a chargeback system. Finally, if security is an issue, have the vendor describe security features in detail to see whether they meet your needs.

Searching for a frame relay vendor can be like a treasure hunt without clues. It can be frustrating and tedious. However, the stakes are high, so it's well worth the effort it requires. Although this list is by no means comprehensive, these questions will give you a map to follow while hunting for the right vendor for the job.

The Good News

Frame relay services require less hardware than dedicated circuits. With dedicated circuits like 56Kbps and T1, because of their point-to-point orientation, you need two channel service units (CSUs) and two routers for each circuit—one per connection. So, for a configuration like the one shown in Figure 20-48, you will need five CSUs and five routers at each site.

With frame relay, on the other hand, you will need only one router and one CSU at each site, as shown in Figure 20-49.

Frame relay services typically cost less, yet give you more bandwidth. A dedicated circuit gives you the stated amount of bandwidth and no more. However, a frame relay circuit can support bursts of bandwidth well above your committed information rate (CIR).

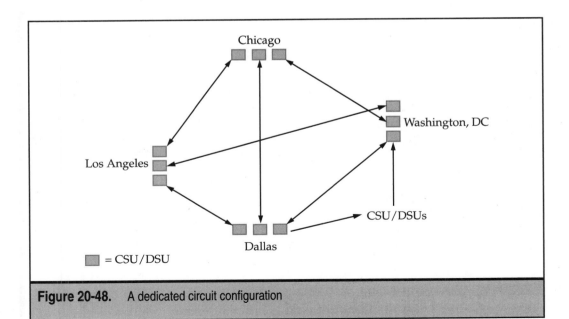

Figure 20-48.   A dedicated circuit configuration

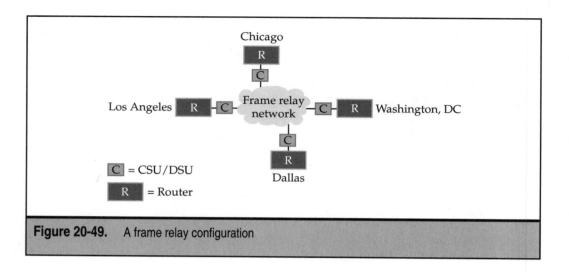

Figure 20-49.   A frame relay configuration

It's faster and easier to reconfigure a frame relay network than a dedicated circuit network. Adding a new location to a dedicated circuit network requires that the end user purchase new equipment and order new lines, which can take anywhere from a few days to a few weeks to organize. Adding a new location to a frame relay network is simply a matter of adding an access port and configuring new PVCs, both of which are done by the carrier and can often be completed in a couple of days.

The Bad News

When frame relay was proposed to the standards committees in 1988, it was quickly defined and approved. It was subsequently implemented and supported by many local and interexchange communications carriers. By late 1991, frame relay was both widely available and widely implemented by users. At the time, the Federal Communications Commission didn't consider frame relay a basic service, and therefore it wasn't tariffed—that is, the FCC didn't require carriers to publish and abide by a set rate for frame relay service. Instead, the price of frame relay services was negotiated privately and separately between the carrier and each frame relay customer. This negotiated price was then written in to a contract between the two parties. Shrewd customers were sometimes able to negotiate very favorable pricing through this procedure.

In October of 1995, however, the FCC changed its mind. It now considers that frame relay is so widely used that it constitutes a basic service. As such, the FCC requires frame relay carriers to tariff the service. Although this may be more equitable, it also eliminates the possibility of getting a bargain, because prices of tariffed services are much less flexible than those of untariffed services.

Voice and Frame Relay

Originally, people didn't think voice (or video) could run over frame relay due to the protocol's variable-length frames. However, many vendors, including Micom Communications, are now offering multiplexors that put both voice and data on frame relay bandwidth with very acceptable performance.

Frame Relay Forum

The Frame Relay Forum is an association of frame relay users, vendors, and service providers based in Mountain View, California (415/962-2579). The organization is made up of committees that create implementation specifications and agreements for the purpose of developing frame relay standards.

INTEGRATED SERVICES DIGITAL NETWORK

The evolution of the ISDN species has been a long and difficult process. You have no doubt been hearing about Integrated Services Digital Network (ISDN) for nearly a decade or more. From its conception, it was proclaimed by the telecommunications pundits as the public telephone and telecommunications interface of the future. But for years no practical, productive, cost-effective implementations materialized. As a result, both users and providers began attributing new definitions to the acronym ISDN, the kindest of which was probably "I Still Don't [K]Now."

Today, however, ISDN is finally booming. It is available in most large metropolitan areas now, where the service providers report a backlog of installations—mostly to residences. Because ISDN integrates data, voice, and video signals into a digital (as opposed to analog) telephone line, it can provide an efficient and cost-effective way to connect office LANs with high-bandwidth digital services, and to provide home "telecommuters" with the same digital services they are accustomed to having at their offices. Furthermore, ISDN has developed international standards for providing many digital services, making it easier for data networks to span countries and continents.

The Primordial Mire

The origin of the ISDN species is the narrowband ISDN standard. The first ISDN standards defining end-to-end digital interfaces appeared in 1984, handed down by the Consultative Committee for International Telegraph and Telephone (CCITT). The CCITT issued additional defining standards in 1988. ISDN was considered a major advance for a couple of reasons. First, it specified digital network services that would be delivered over the existing integrated digital telephone networks. Second, it offered a top performance of 2Mbps in the local link, and either 64Kbps or 128Kbps over the wide area. At the time narrowband ISDN began to emerge, analog modem speeds topped out at 9,600bps.

While ISDN never became the wide area high-bandwidth digital service of choice for local area network connectivity, it is certainly no dinosaur. It's now considered a cost-effective way to provide

▼ Remote access to users who dial into their companies' LANs

■ A suitable link for some LAN-to-LAN connections

■ High-bandwidth interoffice fax traffic

▲ High-speed access to the Internet

ISDN is a flexible service that automatically switches among different devices attached to it. For example, it will provide digital services to a phone, a fax machine, or a PC, all of which can be attached to the same ISDN interface. ISDN can also be used as a local access link into frame relay and X.25 networks.

Anatomy of the ISDN Species

ISDN is a service composed of two types of channels: bearer channels and signaling channels. ISDN providers have combined these two channel types to construct two different types of ISDN service offerings: the Basic Rate Interface and the Primary Rate Interface. We will define each of these channel types and rate interfaces, then discuss the signaling techniques that they use to make integrated voice and data transmission possible.

Channel Types

As we mentioned, ISDN uses two types of channels, one type for transmitting data and the other for handling the management signaling and call control. These two types of channels are called bearer channels and signaling channels, respectively.

BEARER CHANNELS   Bearer channels do one thing: they carry data. Hence the name "bearer." These channels "bear" user information across the ISDN network. The B channels are 64Kbps circuit-switched channels of the same type used to handle a regular voice telephone call, although the ISDN B channels are digital channels rather than analog channels like Plain Old Telephone Service (POTS) uses. The B channels are set up, then taken down when the call is complete. They can connect any two ISDN sites.

SIGNALING CHANNELS   ISDN also specifies a second type of channel, called a signaling channel or D channel. The D channel is separate from the B channels, providing out-of-band signaling to set up, control, and tear down calls. Because all this call control signaling is done on a separate channel, the calls are set up much faster than if the signaling information had to share bandwidth with the actual data. For example, the D channel provides the network with the number of the party to call while the data is waiting on the B channels to be transmitted. Therefore, as soon as the call is set up, data transmission can

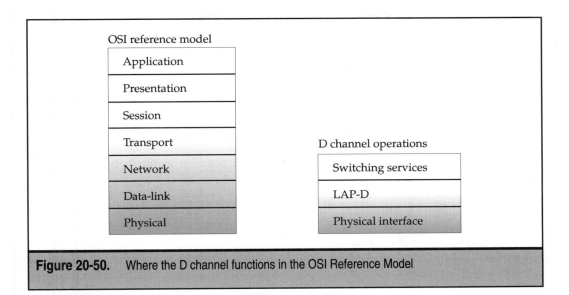

Figure 20-50.   Where the D channel functions in the OSI Reference Model

begin. The D channel signaling is a function of the physical, data-link, and network layers relative to the OSI protocol model, as shown in Figure 20-50.

Different operations are performed at each layer of the OSI Reference Model. Here's a brief description of how D channel signaling protocols work within the OSI Reference Model.

Physical Layer Functions

ISDN's physical layer protocol sets up a 64Kbps, circuit-switched connection. It also supports the physical interface for the network terminal adapter (we will discuss this a little later in this chapter), which supports the connection of multiple devices simultaneously. Finally, this protocol manages circuit testing and monitoring functions.

Data-Link Layer Functions

ISDN's data-link layer protocol sets up the virtual paths through the networks for data frames. This protocol also manages call control and signaling functions via the Link Access Procedure for D Channel (LAP-D), which is the procedure that works across the signaling (or "D") channel.

Network Layer Functions

ISDN's network layer protocol handles all circuit-switching and packet-switching services. The network layer creates the addressing and route-determination information that the data-link layer uses to set up virtual paths.

It's All in the Packaging

As we mentioned, ISDN carriers have developed two standard service offerings, called rate interfaces, that combine the bearer channels and the signaling channel in different densities. These are called the basic rate interface (BRI) and the primary rate interface (PRI).

Basic Rate Interface ISDN

The basic rate interface (BRI) usually consists of the two 64Kbps B channels for data transmission, plus one 16Kbps D channel that provides signaling for the B channels. With the proper equipment, you can bond the two B channels of the BRI together to get a maximum bandwidth of 128Kbps. Therefore, the BRI is appropriate for use in connecting small offices, small to medium-sized local area networks, or for telecommuters working from home who want to connect to their company's LAN.

Notice that I said the BRI usually consists of two 64Kbps B channels. Some ISDN providers offer BRIs with only one B channel and one D channel, or with only one D channel. In fact, the smallest unit of ISDN that can still be called ISDN is the D channel. The D channel provides the out-of-band signaling that really defines ISDN and makes the service what it is.

Primary Rate Interface ISDN

The primary rate interface (PRI) channels are available to ISDN subscribers who need more bandwidth than a BRI can provide. They are based on the DS1 rate of 1.544Mbps and include 22 B channels and one 64Kbps D channel to do the signaling. The B channels can be bundled in one of the following configurations, referred to in local exchange carrier terminology as H services:

▼ H0 channel: 384Kbps (6 B channels)

■ H10 channel: 1.472Mbps (24 56Kbps B channels)

■ H11 channel: 1.536Mbps (24 B channels)

▲ H12 channel: 1.92Mbps (30 B channels)

The lines can be used as a high-speed trunk for transferring large files and other continuous data streams or be subdivided with a multiplexor to provide channels for multiple devices. By providing a range of service options, the PRI can be configured to handle compressed video, video telephones, and teleservices.

ISDN's Function in the Wide Area Food Chain

ISDN is a significant departure from the other wide area data services discussed in this book. ISDN and its attendant equipment actually perform much of the processing and data signaling that used to be the exclusive responsibility of the carrier's central office (CO) equipment. Transferring these functions from the CO to your PC is one of the causes of much of the difficulty and confusion in ordering, configuring, and troubleshooting ISDN. Therefore, we should probably spend some time talking about the functions in question: what they are, where they have traditionally been done, and how ISDN changes all of that.

A Plain Old Telephone Service (POTS) call, the kind of analog call that we have placed and received nearly every day of our lives since we were able to dial, doesn't require much from the equipment at our houses. As Figure 20-51 shows, all of the processing of voice and data takes place at the local exchange carrier's central office switch. Our analog phones simply contact the telephone company's switch and tell it whom we want to call. The telco's switch does all the rest. In essence, our analog phones are not much more than amplifiers with dials.

An ISDN call, on the other hand, requires that the equipment on the customers' premises be much more sophisticated. ISDN telephones and PC adapters must be able to process information and determine what kind of signal—voice, data, fax, etc.—is being received, and respond by routing the data to the appropriate device.

Figure 20-52 shows the route of an ISDN call from your premises through the public switched network and to its destination. Your call is first set up when your equipment sets up a connection with the central office switch using Digital Subscriber Signaling System 1 (DSS1).

Once the call is set up between your site and the central office via DSS1, it's time to set up the next leg of its journey. For better or for worse, the signaling needed to route the call within the public switched network is not DSS1. Instead, the public telcos use a system called Signaling System 7 (SS7), which can handle both digital and analog calls, to route calls between central offices. Therefore, at the telco your DSS1 instructions are converted to SS7 signals. SS7 manages call control, including call setup and teardown.

When your call reaches the last central office on its route, it is then converted back to DSS1 format for transmission from the last central office to its final destination—the party with whom you wanted to communicate in the first place.

Your ISDN equipment is required to interact with both DSS1 and SS7—something your POTS telephone was never required nor designed to do. It is this interaction with two large and complex external signaling systems that brings about many of the configuration nightmares associated with ordering, installing, and using ISDN.

Great Moments in Evolution: SPID-ing in the Ocean

Although you can probably have a long, happy, and productive career as an ISDN user without knowing the details of DSS1 and SS7, there is one requirement of DSS1 that will affect you immediately and continue to do so for as long as you use ISDN. This requirement is a Service Profile Identifier (SPID). SPIDs are identifying numbers assigned to your ISDN line at the time it is set up by the local exchange provider. Be sure to write this number down and keep it in a safe place, because configuring your equipment will undoubtedly require entering a SPID. You see, the SPID identifies individual logical processes connected to the ISDN interface and prevents contention among different processes on the ISDN bus in the event that incoming calls are received

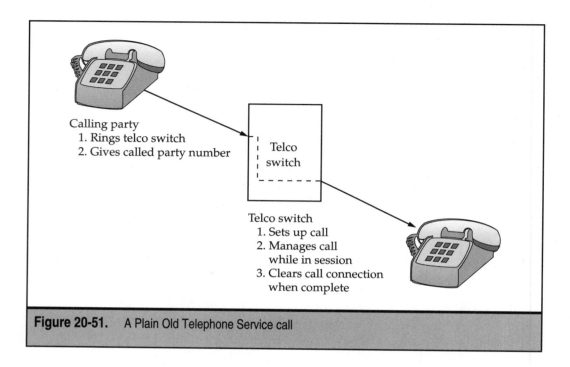

Figure 20-51. A Plain Old Telephone Service call

while a device is actively using the B channel. This is the procedure in DSS1 that lets you connect several devices to one ISDN line. Furthermore, the SPID, together with another parameter required by DSS1, the Terminal Identifier (TEI), identifies the ISDN equipment connected to the ISDN interface. A single TEI might have multiple SPIDs

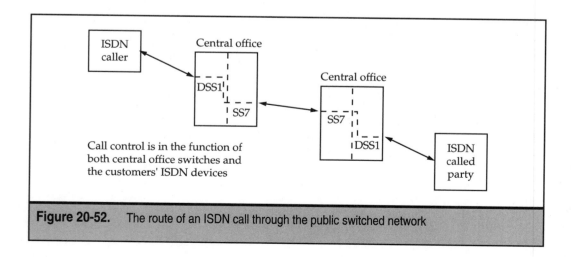

Figure 20-52. The route of an ISDN call through the public switched network

associated with it. Negotiating among the SPIDs is complex—so much so that some ISDN providers have found it easier to support bus contention, and thus allow you only one SPID per bearer channel.

The Goal of Evolution: What These Services Can Provide

Services provided by ISDN operate at higher protocol levels than simple phone connections. After all that negotiating among your computer's ISDN adapter, DSS1, and SS7, they should. These services use the B channels for transmission and the D channel for signaling. We describe them briefly here:

▼ Bearer services

■ Supplementary services

▲ Teleservices

Bearer Services

In the most basic sense, ISDN bearer services don't really do anything that other protocols don't do. These are the services that carry data from end to end. They come in two types:

▼ Circuit mode

▲ Packet mode

CIRCUIT MODE VS. PACKET MODE *Circuit mode* is pretty much the same as the circuit switching we have discussed in various chapters throughout this book. In circuit mode, a connection is established between the caller and the called party, and the circuit remains dedicated to that conversation until one of the parties disconnects. The two parties are the only ones who can use the connection for as long as they maintain the call. Even if no data is being transmitted, while the call is in session, all the bandwidth associated with that circuit is dedicated to that call. This can be very wasteful, since many conversations are largely "dead air." See Figure 20-53.

Packet mode solves the problem of unused, dedicated bandwidth. Packet mode breaks up a single conversation into small pieces, gives each of these pieces an address and a sequence number, and sends them on their way over the wire—along with packets from many other conversations. Because each packet has its own address, it can share bandwidth with other packets without scrambling data transmissions. Furthermore, each packet could take a different route to the called party, as shown in Figure 20-54.

Packet-mode transmission isn't nearly as wasteful as circuit-mode transmission, because several conversations are using the same connection. Therefore, when one conversation isn't transmitting anything, the other conversations sharing the connection can use that idle bandwidth to transmit more of their data. Ultimately, this means that the

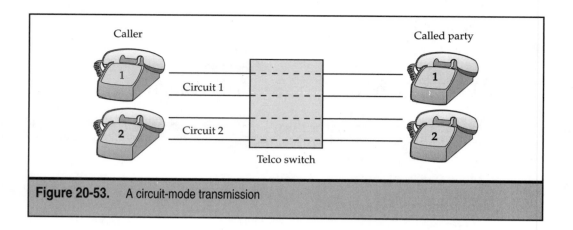

Figure 20-53. A circuit-mode transmission

carrier needs less packet-switching equipment than circuit-switching equipment to support the same number of conversations.

ISDN bearer services offer both circuit-mode and packet-mode services. Circuit mode uses B channels to transmit data and the D channel to control the call. Packet mode can use both the B and the D channels to transmit data.

Generally, circuit-mode services are best for voice traffic and packet-mode services are best for data traffic, but this isn't always the case. ISDN packet-mode bearer services offer a virtual circuit service that can handle analog traffic, such as voice, quite well.

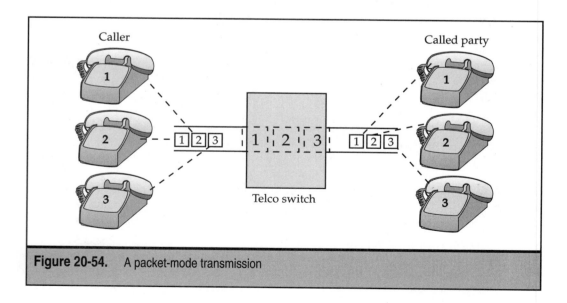

Figure 20-54. A packet-mode transmission

Supplementary Services

These supplementary services are exactly that: services in addition to the bearer services that provide added functionality. Supplementary services vary from ISDN provider to ISDN provider, so this is just a representative list of the types of services you may find available.

CALLING LINE IDENTIFICATION PRESENTATION　This is similar to Caller ID, which is becoming widely available for incoming calls on most public telephone systems. It identifies the number of the incoming caller.

MULTIPLE SUBSCRIBER NUMBER　This service assigns a different telephone number to each device attached to your ISDN interface. For example, suppose you have a telephone, a modem, and a fax device all on one ISDN interface. With Multiple Subscriber Number service, each of these would have its own telephone number. Then, when a call comes in for the telephone, the telephone will ring. When a call comes in for the fax, the fax will answer—you get the idea.

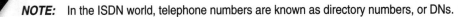

> **NOTE:**　In the ISDN world, telephone numbers are known as directory numbers, or DNs.

CALL OFFERING　These are services such as Call Transfer and Call Forwarding that let you control where the call goes after it rings your number.

▼　**Call Transfer**　Anyone who has worked in an office with a PBX is familiar with this one. When you answer a call, then find the call needs to be sent to someone else, you can transfer it to the right person.

■　**Call Forwarding Busy**　This service lets your calls be directed to another number if they come in while you are on your phone.

▲　**Line Hunting**　Known in the PBX world as a hunt group, call hunting defines a group of telephones that can answer any call coming in to any telephone in the group. This enables an incoming call to ring—one phone at a time—at each telephone in the group until it is answered.

CALL WAITING AND CALL HOLD　Thanks to the out-of-band signaling of the D channel, ISDN adds a new dimension to these familiar services.

▼　**Call Waiting**　Unlike the familiar POTS, when a call comes in on your ISDN line, your conversation isn't interrupted. This is because signaling is done on the separate D channel ("so that's why the D channel is so cool"). This is especially handy when you're using your modem—incoming calls won't break your data connection. That's right—you can keep Call Waiting on while using your modem.

▲ **Call Hold**   ISDN lets you put multiple calls on hold simultaneously without tying up a separate connection for each call. That means you'll have a tough time "busying out" your phones.

MULTIPARTY SERVICES   ISDN also offers a variety of multiparty services such as conference calling.

Teleservices

Teleservices are sophisticated services that ISDN can provide because it operates at higher levels in the OSI reference model than POTS. Although currently not widely used in this country, they are often considered the future direction—and the real value—of ISDN. Some of these teleservices are

▼ **Telefax**   Group 4 fax capability that uses digital information at 64Kbps.

■ **Teletex**   Provides end-to-end messaging between two devices using standard character sets.

■ **Videotext**   Enhances Teletex services by adding a text and graphics mailbox.

▲ **Videotelephony**   Provides television transmission service over ISDN.

Making ISDN Happen

Now that you know what ISDN is and what it can provide, how do you get it? Acquiring and configuring the equipment and services for ISDN is far from simple. Here's a roadmap and checklist for making sure you and your local exchange carrier have all the right stuff for ISDN.

The Local Exchange Carrier's Part

The first, most critical, and least controllable issue in getting ISDN service is whether your local exchange carrier (LEC) is able and willing to provide it. Here's what you need to find out.

THE LEC'S ISDN SWITCH   Does your carrier offer ISDN? If your carrier doesn't have an ISDN-ready switch in your area, it doesn't offer ISDN. If it does offer ISDN, you'll need to find out how ISDN is implemented on the switch so you can configure your devices to communicate with it. The key to how ISDN is implemented on the LEC's switch is contained in two pieces of information you must get from your LEC:

▼ Which ISDN protocol (NI-1 or NI-2) they use

▲ What type of ISDN switch they have

When you configure your ISDN equipment, you will need to enter either or both of these pieces of information.

NATIONAL ISDN-1 (NI-1) AND NATIONAL ISDN-2 (NI-2) PROTOCOLS   The NI-1 protocol is the BRI protocol used by the Regional Bell Operating Companies (RBOCs). It is the first step in establishing a consistent ISDN definition for the United States. As such, it enables all NI-1 compliant devices to connect to any switch that supports the NI-1 protocol. A newer version of the protocol, NI-2, is emerging.

If your ISDN device and your provider's switch support either the NI-1 or NI-2 protocols, then that's all the compatibility information you'll need. However, it usually isn't that simple. Note that NI-1 is used mostly by the RBOCs. Other LECs may not use this protocol, and therefore to configure your ISDN device to communicate with their switch, you'll need to know the manufacturer of the switch.

Media

The next issue is the wiring from the LEC's ISDN switch to your premises. If you're lucky, your local access is fiber-optic cable, and you can skip to the next section. However, more than likely your local access loop is copper. In this case, your twisted-pair local access wire must be no more than 18 kilofeet (a little under 3.5 miles) in length. If it exceeds this length, your telephone company may be able to install a midspan repeater between the central office and your premises. A midspan repeater regenerates the ISDN signal and doubles the distance allowed between the central office and your premises.

Even though your local access loop meets these specifications, it may not be ready for ISDN. That's because your local cable pair may have connections running off it. These connections are called bridge taps and they aren't supposed to be there, but sometimes when the telephone company is installing a new customer, they run a line from the new customer's premises and join, or tap, into an existing, unused local loop left behind by a former customer, as shown in Figure 20-55. The former customer's tap is disconnected at the former customer's site, but still joined to what is now your local loop. Such taps can cause signal distortion that doesn't affect analog signals, but wreaks havoc with ISDN. Therefore, any bridge taps must be removed.

Next, the LEC will have to check your line to remove any loading coils, which are devices that were installed to condition analog lines. Conditioning means adjusting lines to reduce signal distortion. Unfortunately, techniques that reduce signal distortion for analog signals can actually cause distortion in digital signals.

Finally, your LEC will test your line to see if it meets ISDN specifications. If it does, you're good to go. If it doesn't, the phone company will have to install another line.

The Home Front

Assuming your LEC is able to provide ISDN service to your premises, the next step is to select the proper equipment to use that service. There are two major pieces of equipment you will require: a network terminal adapter and either an ISDN adapter or bridge.

NETWORK TERMINAL ADAPTER   A network terminal adapter (NTA) is a device that connects your data or telephone equipment to the local exchange carrier's ISDN line. In

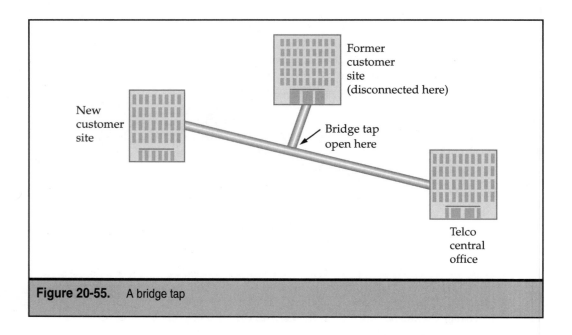

Figure 20-55.   A bridge tap

the United States, the customer purchases and installs the NTA, while in other countries the local exchange carrier owns and maintains it.

The NTA connects both terminal equipment (TE) and terminal adapter (TA) devices to the local loop. TE devices are equipment; telephones and computers that are ISDN compliant. TAs are interfaces; adapters that connect non-ISDN equipment to the ISDN service.

In the United States, the NTA is connected to the local exchange carrier's ISDN service via the U interface that is described next. The customer's equipment is connected to the NTA via an S/T interface, also described later in this section, that allows up to eight devices to connect with and be addressed by the NT device.

Figure 20-56 illustrates the NT device and the eight possible connection points for TE and TA devices. Note that not all NT devices are the same. Some may have only two connectors, one for data equipment and one for a phone. Additional devices are then daisy-chained together.

INTERFACES   Your NTA equipment provides three different types of interfaces to support connected devices. These are described here:

▼   **U interface**   This interface transmits full-duplex information on a single wire pair. This means information travels in both directions simultaneously. The U interface supports only one device.

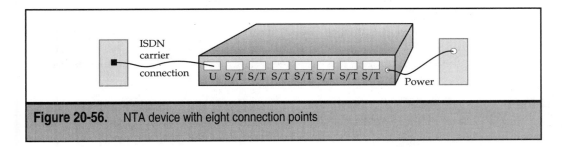

Figure 20-56.   NTA device with eight connection points

- ■ **S/T interface**   This interface breaks the ISDN signal into two paths: transmit and receive. Each signal is now carried on a separate pair, and you are allowed to connect multiple devices.

- ▲ **R interface**   This interface allows you to connect a POTS telephone to your ISDN service. The telephone will function, but it won't provide all the features that an ISDN telephone connected to an S/T interface would.

ISDN ADAPTERS   ISDN terminal adapters, also commonly known as ISDN modems, come in internal and external models, just as analog modems do. And these two models have the same benefits and liabilities as their analog cousins: internal modems support higher internal data transfer rates, while external modems provide more diagnostic information and control.

SERIAL PORT CONNECTIVITY   If you select an ISDN terminal adapter that connects to your computer through a serial port, you'll need to be sure to install a serial port driver that supports ISDN's higher bandwidth. Otherwise, the serial port will become a serious bottleneck, and all that extra bandwidth for which you are paying will be useless. For example, the highest serial port data rate supported by Microsoft Windows for Workgroups 3.11 is 19,200bps—considerably below ISDN's common 64Kbps. There are several high-speed drivers for serial ports available both as freeware and on the commercial market, including TurboCom/2 from Pacific CommWare.

INTEGRATED NETWORK TERMINAL ADAPTERS   Some ISDN terminal adapters have integrated NTA devices. This may save you a little expense as well as time and trouble when configuring your ISDN devices for the first time. However, it can also limit the number of devices you can connect to your ISDN line to the number of S/T ports the adapter vendor supplies—usually much fewer than provided by external NTAs.

MULTIPLE B CHANNELS   Not all ISDN terminal adapters support more than one B channel. If you plan to pay for more than one B channel, be sure your network terminal adapter supports it. As well, be sure the equipment you select can bond multiple B channels if you hope to take advantage of the 128Kbps or higher bandwidth possible by combining bearer channels.

ISDN AND TELEPHONES   Your ISDN service will require ISDN telephones unless your terminal adapter has an R interface. The R interface supports analog equipment like standard telephones. You can also buy separate adapters that will convert existing analog telephones to ISDN telephones. However, keep in mind that standard analog telephones can't take advantage of some special ISDN services such as Caller ID.

ISDN EQUIPMENT FOR LANS   Installing ISDN equipment for LANs requires a bridge or router with an ISDN interface, as shown in Figure 20-57. Cisco and Ascend are among the router vendors currently offering ISDN interfaces. The ISDN router is connected directly to the ISDN wire, so it must be configured not only to route traffic to the appropriate segments but also to interoperate with the ISDN network. This involves many of the same tasks as configuring a stand-alone PC, including entering the correct SPIDs and DNs.

Configuration and Installation

Now that ISDN connectivity is becoming cheap and readily available, organizations of all sizes are flocking to install it for the increased bandwidth and therefore increased functionality it offers over garden-variety 56Kbps lines. However, as you have probably surmised from reading this chapter, implementing ISDN isn't nearly as simple as installing those 56Kbps lines. It takes a lot more than a mere telephone call to the local exchange carrier. In fact, it's fairly safe to say that right now, to be a sane, successful ISDN user, you must also be an ISDN expert.

You'll have to understand what's involved in implementing ISDN before you commit to a full-scale installation. To help you do this, I've put together a cheat sheet of issues that you must address before, during, and after the installation of ISDN.

FIRST: ORDERING WHAT YOU WANT   Ordering ISDN from your local exchange carrier (LEC) is like walking into Baskin-Robbins and ordering gelato. Even if somebody behind

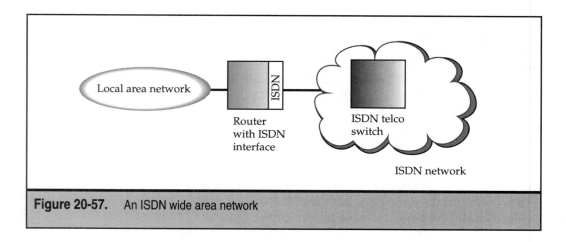

Figure 20-57.   An ISDN wide area network

the counter understands what you said, they may never have heard of it before. And even if the clerk has heard of gelato, he or she may not really know what it is, much less that he or she can provide what you want. Even if you find a clerk who understands that gelato is ice cream, and that he or she can sell it to you, you may still not be any closer to getting the flavor you want than when you walked in the door.

Not every LEC offers ISDN, and not every company that does can offer the type of ISDN that you need. Different switches are provisioned, or configured, to provide different types of ISDN service. Therefore, the first thing you have to determine is which ISDN features you want, then ensure that your LEC can provide them.

WHAT ARE YOU HUNGRY FOR?   What is the real reason you need more bandwidth? Do you want to do videoconferencing? Do you want to send more faxes faster? Or do you simply want to speed up file transfers? Do you want to use ISDN to transmit voice? Data? Both? What's the maximum bandwidth you anticipate needing: 64Kbps? 128Kbps? More?

Make a list of all the bandwidth-gobbling applications you may want to implement over the next year or so. This will be absolutely vital to selecting the ISDN service you need.

WHAT'S ON THE MENU?   As we mentioned, ISDN comes in two packages, or rate interfaces. The BRI provides two 64Kbps bearer channels (B channels) that carry transmission signals and one 16Kbps D channel that carries signals that control the calls on the B channels. The PRI provides 22 64Kbps B channels and one 64Kbps D channel. The rate interface you choose entirely depends upon the number of connections and amount of bandwidth you need.

HOW MANY CHANNELS?   Many veteran ISDN users think that the smallest ISDN component that still retains the properties of ISDN is the BRI. This isn't true. The real molecule of ISDN is a single D channel. So, for a BRI, you could have two B channels and one D channel, or one D channel and one B channel, or simply one D channel. This gives you some ability to scale your ISDN connection to meet your needs. As well, the PRI comes in several different bandwidths as well, as shown below:

▼   384Kbps (6 B channels)

▥   1.472Mbps (24 56Kbps B channels)

▥   1.536Mbps (24 B channels)

▲   1.92Mbps (30 B channels)

ISDN À LA MODE   Once you have decided how many channels you want to order, you need to find out which mode of data transmission you will be using on each channel. As we described earlier in this chapter, ISDN services are either circuit mode or packet mode. At the time of this writing, ISDN offered ten different circuit-mode services and three different packet-mode services (and counting), each designed for transmitting a different type of data. Generally, circuit-mode services are preferred for voice and other analog transmissions, while packet-mode services are better suited for data.

> *TIP:* New services are being added to ISDN all the time, so ask your LEC representative to explain in detail each type of bearer service they offer so you can select the most appropriate for each channel.

IF THERE'S ROOM FOR DESSERT . . .   Additional services are available for ISDN, just as they are for regular telephone services. As we described earlier in this chapter, some of the additional services available are videotext, teleconference, Caller ID, Call Waiting, and Call Forwarding.

> *TIP:* Don't forget your long-distance carrier and Internet access provider. If you can't find a long-distance carrier in your area that can handle ISDN, there's really no point in implementing it for long distance, now is there? Ditto for your Internet access provider, if you were planning to use ISDN primarily as a high-speed access service.

CONFUSION SETS IN   Now—and only now—it is time to call your LEC to order ISDN. If you are told that ISDN is not available, be sure to ask them:

▼   Why

▲   When it will be available

The reason for asking "why?" is because LEC order takers have been known to tell callers that ISDN isn't available rather than admit they have no idea what ISDN is. So, if you get an answer like, "it's a proprietary technology," or "the standards haven't been finalized," or even "ISDN is another company—you'll have to contact them," you'll know you haven't found the right person. Believe me, this has happened.

When you finally find the right person, and when that person tells you that ISDN is available in your area, you can start describing the type of ISDN service you need.

56/64KBPS?   Your LEC representative may tell you that the ISDN service available is 56Kbps. While this isn't really ISDN, it isn't necessarily bad. This 56Kbps service is ISDN that has been adapted to work on an LEC's existing T1 systems. It's frequently offered in places where full 64Kbps ISDN isn't yet available. The popular ISDN protocols can accommodate 56Kbps service until full 64Kbps ISDN service is available, so there's no need to avoid it simply because it's not "the real thing."

LINE SETS   Furthermore, while you're talking to your LEC representative, he or she may use terms such as line sets. A line set is a term used by the National ISDN Users' Forum (NIUF) to describe the different combinations of B channels (from 0 to 2) with the D channel and the kinds of information (circuit-mode data, packet-mode data, and/or voice) that you want to transmit on these channels. For example, Line Set 1 has no B channels and one D channel on which you can transmit packet-mode data. Line Set 6 has one B channel on which you can transmit voice and one D channel on which you can transmit packet-mode data. The various combinations of channels and call types are identified by number, currently Line Set 1 through Line Set 29. To avoid having to memorize all the line set numbers and their corresponding descriptions, just tell the representative how many B and D channels you want and what kind of information you want to transmit on them. Then, the representative can find the correct line set number that describes this configuration.

The representative should also ask you about feature sets. As we mentioned earlier, a feature set is another NIUF term that describes a combination of either circuit-mode or packet-mode data services and/or call management services. There are at least ten different feature sets, detailing everything from data throughput rate to Call Forwarding options. Have your representative provide you with the latest information on available feature sets, then make your selection after you've had a chance to study them.

Finally, after you have selected the number of channels, call type(s) supported on those channels, and the features and interfaces you want, you will have completed the ordering process. Your LEC should send you a letter or form confirming your order and specifying the services contained in it. This letter should also include the telephone number(s) of your new ISDN connection(s) (which are known as directory numbers or DNs in the ISDN world), as well as your Service Profile Identification number, or SPID. Write both of these down and keep them in a safe place! You will need them when configuring your ISDN equipment.

Cabling Considerations

ISDN cabling uses eight pins, as shown in Figure 20-58, and therefore requires RJ-45 connectors. Furthermore, ISDN cabling is straight-through, not crossed the way standard

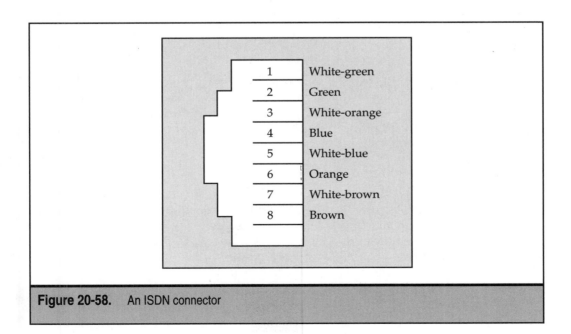

1	White-green
2	Green
3	White-orange
4	Blue
5	White-blue
6	Orange
7	White-brown
8	Brown

Figure 20-58. An ISDN connector

POTS cabling is. Therefore, you will require special ISDN cables to connect your ISDN adapters and/or bridges to the ISDN jack.

Performance

ISDN isn't really such a high-speed performer. The maximum bandwidth available from an ISDN BRI is 128Kbps, and that is only providing that your BRI includes two B channels and that your equipment and service providers all support bonding the two channels together. The maximum bandwidth available through a BRI is 1.92Mbps, through what is called an H12 channel that consists of 30 B channels and one 64Kbps D channel. Again, the equipment and all the parties—the local exchange carrier, the access software provider, and the called party—must support the bonding of the B channels.

The Broadband ISDN standard, an emerging standard that we will discuss later, will support data transmission rates of up to 622Mbps. However, this standard is not yet finalized, so the cap on ISDN remains at the narrowband ISDN rate of 1.92Mbps

Management and Fault Tolerance

While ISDN inherently provides you with many different call management and control services, some of which were described earlier in this chapter in the section entitled, "The Goal of Evolution: What These Services Can Provide," management of the ISDN service is wholly in the hands of LEC. Optimizing and troubleshooting ISDN service is therefore a tedious—and often fruitless—exercise involving multiple telephone calls to a service provider and long waits for repair people to respond.

As for fault tolerance, remember that your ISDN provider may have only one ISDN-ready switch per area. If so, when something goes wrong with that switch, you're out of service until it is repaired.

Scalability

ISDN is probably the most scalable wide area high-speed protocol available. With the proper equipment and services, it can be scaled from a simple 14.4Kbps modem connection to 1.92Mbps. However, as we've described earlier in this chapter, configuring your equipment and services to support this scalability is no simple matter, and sometimes it's simply not possible to get the needed cooperation among vendors to make it a reality.

Availability and Pricing

As we mentioned, ISDN is currently available in most major metropolitan areas, and it's availability is spreading rapidly. As ISDN becomes more readily available, prices for ISDN PC cards are falling sharply. You can now buy an ISDN modem with a built-in NT-1 for around $200.

Pricing for ISDN services varies widely. In certain areas, during special promotions conducted by the LEC, ISDN installation rates are free. In other areas during peak pricing

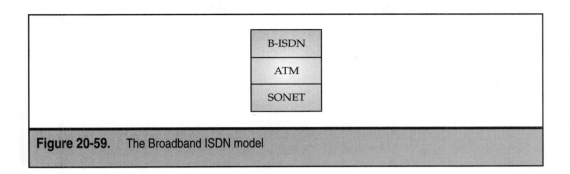

Figure 20-59. The Broadband ISDN model

times, ISDN installation can be as much as $400 per line. Monthly rates vary just as much, ranging from $30 to over $100 per line per month.

> **TIP:** In the past few months, several LECs across the country have begun to raise their ISDN rates from the bargain basement to the outlandishly expensive. The reason given is that the demand for ISDN far exceeded initial projections, and that the market isn't nearly as price sensitive as they had first thought.

The Future: Broadband ISDN

The ITU-T is currently working on specifications for the Broadband ISDN model, shown in Figure 20-59, which will deliver up to 622.08Mbps full-duplex data transmission. These high data rates will support sophisticated two-way interactive transmissions, store-and-forward multimedia broadcasts, and multimedia messaging and retrieval services.

The B-ISDN standard is also the basis for Asynchronous Transfer Mode, which we'll discuss later. ATM and B-ISDN appear to be the direction in which the whole voice and data networking is going.

Advantages

ISDN is an affordable, scalable high-speed protocol. In areas where it is available, it can be fairly inexpensive to implement and expand.

Disadvantages

ISDN has some major disadvantages to overcome. As we described in painful detail in the "Configuration and Installation" section earlier, simply ordering ISDN services requires a level of expertise most busy network managers don't have time to develop. Becoming an expert on the installation and configuration of ISDN devices, especially in different LEC areas, is usually out of the question for most network managers. That means hiring integrators and consultants, and that means a lot of extra expense.

Furthermore, gaining the cooperation of the various vendors and providers can be difficult. For all its fairly long history, ISDN is still unfamiliar to the technical staffs of many providers. It may be some time before the LECs can train their employees to provide the level of service with ordering, selection, installation, and troubleshooting that most network managers require.

Narrowband ISDN's maximum bandwidth is also limited well below that of other promising high-speed wide area protocols, so it may only be a stopgap measure on the way to protocols such as ATM.

ASYNCHRONOUS TRANSFER MODE

Anyone who has read a network trade magazine or attended a technical conference in the last three years has heard about ATM. We cover ATM at length in Chapter 15.

DIGITAL SUBSCRIBER LINE SERVICES AND CABLE MODEMS

As we mentioned in Chapter 19, the new regulatory environment brought about by the Telecommunications Act of 1996 offers new business opportunities for telecommunications companies. Among these new opportunities is the ability for telephone companies and cable television companies to offer interactive information services over their existing networks—most notably for Internet access. This is already happening in some areas. The technologies that are making this happen are digital subscriber line (DSL) and cable modems.

While digital subscriber line services and cable modems are targeted mostly for home use in both technology and pricing, they may also be an important high-speed wide area networking service for telecommuters, small businesses, and businesses located in suburban areas. Of course, it's hard to determine from all the babble about these technologies whether, when, and how cost-effective these services will ultimately be. Therefore, I think it's in your best interests to read on.

Digital Subscriber Line (DSL)

Digital subscriber line services are a recent product offering (generally under trial circumstances) from local exchange carriers that show a great deal of promise as high-speed Internet access services.

DSL services provide simplex (one-way) digital transmission over two pairs of wire—the same twisted-pair cable found in millions of telephone subscribers' homes today. DSL is an end-to-end technology, meaning the signal doesn't require conversion from analog to digital. Instead, DSLs use intelligent adapters at each of the circuits to split the existing twisted-pair cabling into two channels: upstream and downstream. The upstream channel transmits data from the subscriber's premises to the telephone company's network facility. The downstream channel transmits data from the telephone company's network to the subscriber's premises. All the while, the telephone service in the subscriber's premises remains virtually the same.

Besides using existing cable plant and networks, DSL has the benefit of bringing tremendous bandwidth to the subscriber's premises. Downstream traffic can be delivered at speeds of up to 60Mbps (using very-high-bit-rate DSL, described later) and upstream traffic can be transmitted at speeds ranging between 576Kbps and 1Mbps.

Furthermore, DSLs are simple to configure. This will come as a relief to anyone who has struggled with configuring and using Integrated Services Digital Network. A DSL is far easier to configure and use than ISDN.

Finally, because of all the advantages we've listed so far—using existing infrastructure and ease of deployment—DSL services should be fairly inexpensive, especially in terms of bandwidth for the buck. Some industry analysts expect DSL service prices to settle at about $40/month—for unlimited access—within a year or two after they are widely available.

However, therein lies the biggest drawback for DSL services. They aren't widely available yet. While GTE and other big players in the telecommunications industry have begun consumer trials of DSL services, at the time of this writing the trials were still underway and no resulting conclusions or projections about broad commercial DSL service offerings had been reported.

One of the other main drawbacks of DSL services is that they are distance-sensitive. This means that it is really good only for providing service over short distances. However, the signal can maintain its strength for up to 18,000 feet (with asymmetric digital subscriber line, depending upon the bandwidth it's supporting) from the central office without amplification or conditioning. However, this 18,000-feet maximum distance still allows telephone companies to reach over 85 percent of their service areas.

DSL Equipment

DSL signal transmission requires a new device on both the user and the phone company ends of the line. This device functions more like a network adapter than a modem (because the DSL signal is digital from end to end), and right now is fairly expensive and scarce.

For example, ADSL adapters currently cost anywhere from $900 to $1,500 each, and are available from only a handful of manufacturers, including Westell Technologies and Amati Communications Corporation. However, many reports from the press and industry analysts predict that in 1999 we will be able to buy ADSL adapters for under $300.

DSL Service Offerings

Because it is a digital signal, DSL services can divvy the composite two-way bandwidth pretty much any way the designers want to. This helps explain why digital subscriber line services come in a variety of different types:

▼ Asymmetric digital subscriber line (ADSL)

■ High-bit-rate digital subscriber line (HDSL)

■ Very-high-bit-rate digital subscriber line (VDSL)

■ Symmetric digital subscriber line (SDSL)

▲ Rate-adaptive digital subscriber line (RADSL)

Asymmetric Digital Subscriber Line (ADSL)

Asymmetric digital subscriber line is probably the DSL about which you've heard the most. It's been fairly popular with the press and industry analysts, and is currently the subject of a six-month trial in Irving, Texas, by telecommunications service giant GTE. In this trial, GTE is monitoring the success its 30 subscriber participants are having in getting the new, high-speed service to work over GTE's existing cable plant.

ADSL was originally developed to deliver full-motion video from telephone companies to their subscribers' homes. Therefore, ADSL employs what is known as forward error correction. Digital video transmission applications currently can't employ error-control procedures on the network layer. Forward error correction ensures that the line is free of noise and errors before the data is transmitted. However, forward error correction also makes ADSL very attractive for all data transmission, because it reduces data errors caused by line noise.

ADSL is called "asymmetric" because it doesn't provide equal bandwidth on both upstream and downstream channels. Taking into account that—for now, at least—most network users download more information than they upload, the original version of ADSL provides downstream bandwidth of 1.544Mbps (the same rate as a T1) and upstream bandwidth in the range of 64Kbps (the same rate as ISDN). However, current versions deliver downstream bandwidth of 6Mbps and upstream bandwidth in a range between 576Kbps and 640Kbps. What's more, ADSL network data transmission can take place simultaneously with voice telephone calls—over the same telephone pair. It does this via a multiplexing technique that reserves a third channel—4kHz of the bandwidth—for a voice telephone conversation.

Because ADSL is deployed over an existing network infrastructure, it's simple and inexpensive. Therefore, once commercially available, you should be able to implement it quickly just by installing an ADSL adapter and connecting to your telephone company's network (they'll have installed an ADSL at their POP).

ADSL SIGNALING STANDARDS   Currently, there are two wholly incompatible ADSL signaling standards competing for dominance: carrierless amplitude modulation (CAP) and discrete multitone (DMT).

CARRIERLESS AMPLITUDE MODULATION (CAP) CAP is the modulation technique used by cable TV companies. It employs phase and amplitude modulation (FM) methods, as shown in Figure 20-60, that transmit a lone signal down the cable at speeds of up to 1.5Mbps. The major proponent of CAP is AT&T, which gives it quite a bit of clout, indeed.

DISCRETE MULTITONE (DMT) DMT is the modulation technique endorsed by the American National Standards Institute (ANSI). It was developed more recently than CAP, so DMT product has just started appearing on the market. DMT signaling divides the total bandwidth into 4kHz channels—into 256 of these channels, as shown in Figure 20-61. These smaller channels each carry a portion of the transmitted data. All of the data carried by each of these small channels is reassembled at the receiving end of the channel.

ADSL using DMT lends itself to supporting 32-bit multitasking, multithreaded operating systems. Because all its channels are multiplexed on the fly into slower 4kHz channels, you should be able to perform multiple simultaneous real-time, online operations.

No doubt all these "standards wars" are a little scary. The last thing you need is a proprietary wide area network link, especially one upon which all your users rely (such as for Internet access). However, don't worry. To help bring about a lasting peace in the standards uprising, in 1994 the ADSL Forum was formed. Its charter is to promote ADSL standards and generally spread the ADSL gospel, and it now has 60 or more members from throughout the telecommunications industry.

Among the ADSL Forum's current priority projects is a bit interface for connecting ADSL directly to ATM. In fact, the dynamic bandwidth allocation of DMT will probably also enable ADSL to promote widespread use of ATM, easily allocating as much or as little bandwidth as necessary to accommodate switched streams of 53-byte cells. In fact, the ATM Forum has recognized ADSL as one of the supported physical layer transmission protocols to run ATM over unshielded twisted-pair media.

High-Bit-Rate Digital Subscriber Line (HDSL)

HDSL is probably the best known DSL service. As it was originally designed, HDSL employed two pairs of copper wire to transmit 1.544Mbps bandwidth in each direction. It

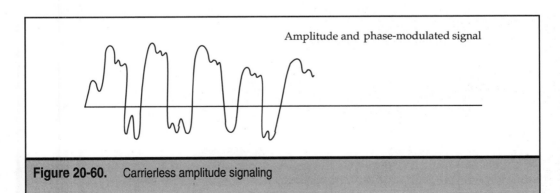

Amplitude and phase-modulated signal

Figure 20-60. Carrierless amplitude signaling

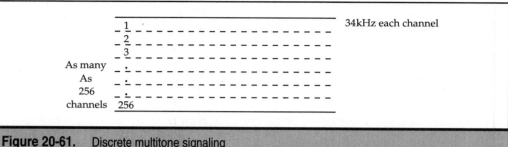

Figure 20-61.   Discrete multitone signaling

could support these two-way T1-speed transmissions for a distance of up to 12,000 feet, and yet at a fraction of the cost of conventional T1 service. As such, HDSL shows some of its greatest potential in carrying cost-effective telephone service to hard to reach areas.

HDSL isn't without its problems, however. In addition to supporting only 2/3 the distance of ADSL, it also requires two pairs of cable.

NOTE: There is a version of HDSL that uses only one pair of copper wire, but it only supports two-way transmissions of up to 768Kbps. This is still sufficient for most data transfer needs, including most videoconferencing.

Another problem with HDSL is that it can't support voice traffic nearly as easily as ADSL does. To conduct a regular voice conversation over HDSL would require special converters and modems that ADSL just doesn't require.

Very-High-Bit-Rate Digital Subscriber Line (VDSL)

Originally conceived as a replacement technology for protocols that required fiber-optic cable and coaxial cable, VDSL offers downstream bandwidth in the range of 51Mbps to 55Mbps. It is very much like ADSL in that it divides the transmitted signal among multiple channels that dynamically allocate bandwidth, which can transmit ISDN or voice conversations.

Its upstream channel supports throughput of 1.6Mbps to 2.3Mbps to the network. However, VDSL can only carry these high bandwidth signals for a short distance—only for a range of about 1,000 feet to 6,000 feet—which means that there may be a very limited number of places where its deployment makes sense.

VDSL SIGNALING STANDARDS   VDSL is experiencing the same struggle between CAP and DMT signaling that plagues ADSL. However, VDSL is nowhere close to being a standards-based technology. Right now, VDSL is far from being commercially available, standard or not. One reason is that currently the silicon circuitry for VDSL adapters is extremely expensive. There isn't yet a specification for mass producing VDSL silicon. However, the most promising entry in the race to develop low-cost VDSL chips is Amati Communications Corporation, which has a strategic relationship with NEC Corporation to develop a VDSL transceiver on one silicon chip.

Symmetric Digital Subscriber Line (SDSL)

This is the version of ADSL that supports equal bandwidth in both upstream and downstream channels. Right now, SDLS supports a symmetric bandwidth of 384Kbps per channel. While this is much slower than the other varieties of digital subscriber line service, it's still more than sufficient for videoconferencing. As of this writing, however, no commercial trials of SDLS had yet begun.

VDSL SIGNALING STANDARDS   Just as with ADSL, VDSL has competing, incompatible signaling standards vying for dominance. Originally, there were two additional signaling schemes besides carrierless amplitude signaling (CAP) and discrete multitone signaling (DMT), but recently the battle seems to have come down to these two signaling standards.

NOTE: Multiple contending signaling schemes are really more a problem for equipment vendors than for end users. Your telephone company will tell you which signaling type it supports, and you'll just go purchase equipment that supports that type of signaling. Still, multiple signaling schemes add to the complexity and confusion of implementing DSLs, as well as limiting the interoperability of DSL systems.

Rate-Adaptive Digital Subscriber Line (RADSL)

Rate-adaptive digital subscriber line is a type of ADSL service that adapts itself to the network over which it transmits data. This means that RADSL adjusts its speed based on the quality of the signal and the distance over which that signal must be transmitted. RADSL supports a wide variety of fallback digital rates on one line, and it can adapt to any of those rates on the fly. Therefore, no matter how far you have to transmit a complex signal, RADSL will make sure it arrives intact.

Telephone companies originally developed RADSL to deliver movies to subscribers' homes. The downstream channel of RADSL can support transmissions of up to 7Mbps, while its downstream channel can transmit from the users' premises to the network at bandwidths up to 1Mbps.

RADSL SIGNALING STANDARDS   Oddly enough, RADSL also suffers from the CAP vs. DMT struggle. It would seem on the surface that the adaptive nature of RADSL would lend itself almost exclusively to the multiple 4kHz channels of DMT. However, currently the only vendor offering commercial RADSL is Paradyne, a wholly owned subsidiary of AT&T, which is the major proponent of CAP encoding. Again, I'm confident that the capable offices of the ADSL Forum can help resolve these signaling standards conflicts and let RADSL vendors and subscribers get down to business.

Cable Modems

Cable modems are just that: modems that connect your computer or local area network to the community antenna television (CATV) cable network. Cable modems promise throughput rates of 40Mbps downstream and 2.5Mbps and higher upstream. Unfortunately, most CATV cable plants aren't two-way active. That means they can't support both upstream and downstream data traffic. After all, they were designed as a data delivery system, not as an interactive wide area link. In fact, to work around this one-way infrastructure, some cable modems such as the Surfboard from General Instruments use the coaxial cable infrastructure combined with a traditional telephone modem. The cable provides the downstream path, as it was designed to do, while the upstream data transfer is handled by the modem.

Form and Function

A cable modem by its very nature works differently from a digital subscriber line service. DSL services provide each user with a dedicated connection. Cable modem subscribers, on the other hand, will share an Internet feed (see Chapter 18 on the WAN and the Internet) with all other subscribers in their region. This Internet feed has bandwidth equal to one cable television channel, with data packets addressed to all subscribers traveling over the same channel. Each data packet contains a user ID in its header, and your cable modem will pick out only those packets addressed to you.

If you think this sounds like a local area network, you're right. In fact, a lot of the proposed cable modem and CATV Internet access systems use a transport protocol that is similar to 10Base-T in function.

Of course, this means that cable modems are going to have the same usage-based traffic problems that collision-based LAN transport protocols have. The more users on the network, the less bandwidth is going to be available to you. Therefore, even though your cable company may tell you that you have a 10Mbps wide area connection, you're only going to get a piece of that connection. And the more users that are connected to your channel and actively using it, the smaller the slice of the channel's bandwidth that is going to be available to you.

Furthermore, there is currently no standard cable modem format. And there probably won't be one for a while, because so many cable companies are going to have to upgrade their plants to support two-way connections that no one knows what the cable system of the future is going to look like.

DSL vs. Cable Modems

So which is the better option, a DSL service or a cable modem?

For those of you who are occupying buildings in a central business district, it seems pretty clear that you'll have DSL service available before cable modems are a real option. After all, CATV cable networks were developed and designed primarily to serve residential areas, so chances are your cable companies aren't concentrating on upgrading their networks in the business districts. Furthermore, don't forget that telephone companies won't have to upgrade their networks the way cable companies will.

However, both CATV operators and telephone companies will have to upgrade their facilities to become regular Internet service providers (ISPs). This means that they'll need routers and high-speed service facilities at all of their central offices.

Furthermore, DSL service, because it depends on only a standard cable pair, will let you pick and choose among DSL providers the same way you can now pick and choose among long-distance providers. The CATV cable modem service, however, is provided only by your local CATV operator—and only according to the transmission techniques they choose to offer.

On the other hand, if you are located in a suburban area where DSL and cable modem service are equal possibilities, remember that DSL service is several months, or even years (depending upon where you live), from widespread commercial availability. Cable modem service is being offered now—provided your CATV operator's infrastructure can handle two-way transmission. In that case, remember that upgrades to CATV plants will be expensive, and that expense will be recaptured from you, the users.

On the other hand, remember also that there are a lot more cable modem vendors than DSL adapter vendors, and more competition will likely keep prices lower.

Of course, chances are that wherever you are, either of these services is a long way off. They both have significant benefits, while they both have real and present delays and pitfalls. My rule of thumb is that DSLs will probably become a very viable and popular high-speed wide area service for businesses, while cable modems will be the darling of telecommuters and home businesses—until increased usage clogs the networks and makes performance unacceptably slow. Both, however, have the potential to speed up wide area network access—especially Internet access—so both bear watching.

Are You Ready to Order?

Okay, now that you have seen your options, which wide area service or services would you like to order? And how do you do it? We'll discuss this in the next chapter, so read on!

CHAPTER 21

Purchasing and Managing Wide Area Services

This chapter covers topics related to purchasing and managing wide area services. The areas covered include:

▼ Tariffed services

■ Contract services

■ Value-added carriers

■ Requests for proposals

■ Bills for services

▲ Things that can go wrong

We begin with a discussion of what tariffed services are and how they may affect your budget.

TARIFFED SERVICES

When you're choosing a wide area networking service or protocol, you should find out early on whether the service you want is a tariffed service or a contract service. This determines how much flexibility you're going to have when negotiating the price of this service with your chosen vendor.

What Is a Tariff?

As we mentioned early in this book, a *tariff* is essentially a published price list for telecommunications services or facilities. This price list becomes a public contract between the user of the telecommunications service and/or facility and the supplier.

Which Services Are Tariffed?

As we hinted in the first paragraph, not all telecommunications services and facilities require tariffs. The regulatory bodies governing tariffs typically require that all basic telecommunications services—in most definitions, those that are widely available and widely used by the general public—be tariffed. This means that telecommunications companies must file tariffs for services like Plain Old Telephone Service (POTS), as well as T1 and T3.

However, the criteria for requiring a tariff get fuzzy when new services, such as frame relay and Integrated Services Digital Network (ISDN), cross the line from being specialty services used by a few large entities to a widely used, commonly available service. At the time of this writing, in fact, there was a debate raging over whether frame relay should be classified as a tariffed service.

How Do Price Lists Become Tariffs?

And just how does a price list become a public contract? Through government regulatory action, of course. This means that not just any old price list put together by a telecommunications common carrier or equipment supplier can be called a tariff. Far from it.

The tariff procedure begins by a telecommunications service and/or facility provider preparing a complete price list of the service they plan to offer. These are excruciatingly detailed documents, and are confusing and exhausting to peruse. However, they generally contain the best, fullest, and most reliable descriptions of what telecommunications services are supposed to provide, so they're worth studying.

After telecommunications service and facility providers prepare their price lists, they submit them as filings for government regulatory review—generally by the state public utilities commission (although, as we will see, the regulatory body with jurisdiction varies with the type of service or facility being offered). The presiding government regulatory body studies the tariff, and often holds public hearings, called "rate hearings," to gather public opinion about the proposed rates. This is almost always the case when the proposed rates are higher than previous rates.

After reviewing the proposed rates and holding hearings, the regulatory body may amend the price list. Then the price list is either rejected, sending it back to the telecommunications provider to start over again, or approved, thus becoming a tariff. Once the price list becomes a tariff, the services detailed in the tariff can't be altered or discontinued without approval of the regulatory body that sanctioned it.

Who Has Jurisdiction?

The Federal Communications Commission (FCC) regulates the interexchange carriers (IXCs). While AT&T, as the 800-pound gorilla of the IXC industry, is required to file tariffs, in an action called the Competitive Carrier Proceeding, the FCC decided it didn't need to regulate that breed of telecommunications service provider called an other common carrier (OCC) (the non-AT&T common carriers), which meant the OCCs didn't have to file tariffs anymore. However, believe it or not, most of them do so voluntarily, although they call their filings rate structures instead of tariffs.

The local exchange carriers (LECs), on the other hand, are regulated for the most part by the state public utilities commissions (or their equivalents). Therefore, they must file tariffs with their state public utilities commissions for nearly all of the services they provide. There is one notable exception to this, however, and that is the local access service they provide inter-LATA carriers.

NOTE: You remember local access service from earlier chapters. It's the "last mile" service from a telecommunications user's building to the point of presence of the user's chosen interexchange carrier.

This local access is regulated by the Federal Communications Commission, and therefore the LECs must file tariffs for this particular type of service with the FCC. As though having to file tariffs with two different regulatory bodies wasn't demanding enough, LECs must file a different type of tariff with the FCC depending upon whether they provide dedicated access or shared access to an IXC. A dedicated access service is local access that a LEC dedicates to one IXC for its exclusive, full-time use. These rates are generally flat, fixed monthly rates that don't vary with usage. A shared access service is local access that a LEC makes available to many customers who share it. IXCs pay for only the access service and facilities they use.

Table 21-1 provides a cheat sheet of the various (and multitude of) different kinds of tariffs. It also shows which government regulatory agency has jurisdiction over each type of tariff. In short, interstate traffic is the responsibility of the Federal Communications Commission. Intrastate traffic, whether intra-LATA or inter-LATA, is subject to the jurisdiction of the public utilities commission of the state in question.

Why File Tariffs?

The regulatory structure that approves tariffs is actually the reason that tariffs exist. In a heavily regulated industry, normal market pressures of supply and demand don't work to keep costs and services offerings in line. Therefore, the whole point of tariffs is to ensure that the public gets the telecommunications services they need at prices that aren't predatory, but lets the suppliers recover their costs and make a decent profit.

Back in the days before the Modification of Final Judgment and the Telecommunications Act of 1996, telecommunications services were provided by a monopoly in the form of AT&T. Because all telecommunications services came from one supplier, the supplier could use the proceeds of a high-profit service to underwrite some of the costs of a lower-profit service. A case in point is the high-profit local exchange carrier service and the more competitive and hence lower-profit long-distance service. Of course, with the current competition, such transfer of profits from one service to another is not only

	Intra-LATA		Inter-LATA	
	Dedicated	Shared	Dedicated	Shared
Access	PUC	PUC	FCC	FCC
Transport	PUC	PUC	FCC	FCC

Table 21-1.   Who Administers Which Tariffs?

uneconomical, it's illegal. So the aim of tariffs now is to recover costs, distributing this burden as equitably as possible among those who use the services. It's still a little socialistic, but that's the price of regulation.

What Do Tariffs Mean to Your Budget?

So, what does this mean in terms of pricing? Are there any bargains to be found among the fixed, published rates? On the local level, as you can imagine, the big differential in price comes between shared services, like the shared access service we discussed earlier, and dedicated services, like the dedicated access service. Users who opt for dedicated services will generally pay more than those who choose shared services.

Unlike that of local exchange services, interexchange services pricing has three components: local access on the originating end, the actual long-distance service, and local access at the call destination. To further complicate matters, each component can be obtained as either a dedicated or shared service, and therefore a separate tariff must be filed for each of the six different service types:

▼ Shared originating local access

■ Dedicated originating local access

■ Shared long-distance service

■ Dedicated long-distance service

■ Shared destination local access

▲ Dedicated destination local access

As a rule of thumb, if you are a high-volume user, you can get a better deal by selecting dedicated services. That's because you pay a flat fee no matter how much you use the service. Of course, you'll have to compare the flat fee for the dedicated service against the cost of usage-based charges for a similar amount of use of a shared service.

WHO PAYS FOR WHAT?   When you're weighing the cost of dedicated local access services against shared local access services, you need to know who pays for which of the three components. No, it's not the same for both dedicated and shared services. If you choose dedicated services, you'll generally also pay the entire cost of the local access yourself. In fact, you will most likely be billed directly by the LEC that provides the dedicated local access services. However, if you choose shared local access services, your interexchange carrier (IXC) usually picks up the tab for the local access components. Of course, there's no free lunch: the IXC recovers the cost of the local access in the long-distance rates that it charges you. Figure 21-1 gives two sample IXC price structures and illustrates who pays for which charges in each.

Bedtime Stories: How to Read a Tariff

It's inevitable. To make sure you understand the pricing of the services you're selecting, you will no doubt at some time have to resort to actually reading the silly things. To

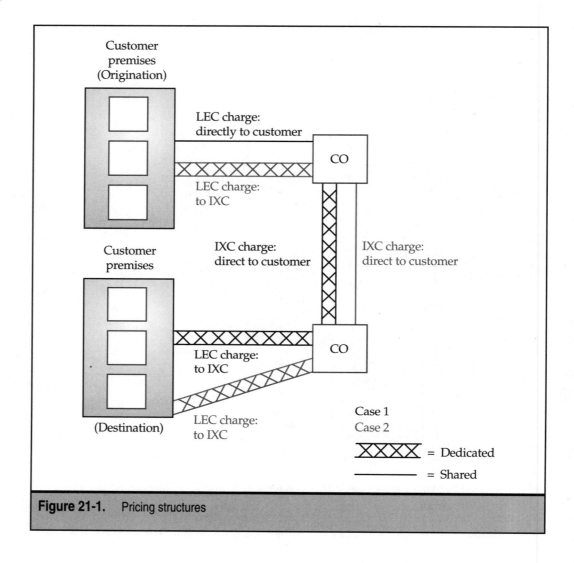

Figure 21-1.   Pricing structures

render aid and comfort as you undertake this grim task, I'm providing a quick guide to tariffs. Hopefully it will lessen your pain.

Tariff Components

Luckily, tariffs all contain the same basic components. These are

▼ Fixed charges

■ Distance-sensitive charges

▲ Unit price

FIXED CHARGES   Fixed charges are a figment of dedicated services. Fixed charges cover the costs of interface facilities for telecommunications services dedicated to a single user. Because the facilities are used by only one customer, the full charge for these facilities is paid by that customer.

DISTANCE-SENSITIVE CHARGES   The distance-sensitive component of a tariff is fixed unit cost per mile of transmission. This may be a flat rate per mile, or it may be volume-sensitive, meaning that as the number of miles increases, the cost per unit decreases.

Does this mean that telecommunications services providers employ people to measure the distance origination to termination of every possible call made in the United States? Of course not (although it would be a fun job). For tariff purposes, telecommunications services providers calculate the distance between the LEC central office (CO) and the IXC point of presence (POP), as illustrated in Figure 21-2.

Actually, this is just the concept behind measuring distances. Nothing so heavily regulated as the telecommunications industry could operate on such a simple principle. Therefore, the concept of distance measured between physical facilities was enhanced and expanded into the concept of wire centers.

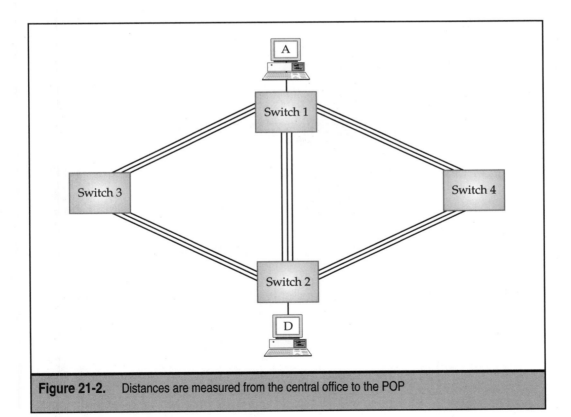

Figure 21-2.   Distances are measured from the central office to the POP

WIRE CENTERS   Wire centers are switching centers. This is the place where all the local loops to the customers' premises connect to a LEC switch. A switching center is also the place where the interexchange carriers' points of presence connect to the LEC switch. In short, wire centers are where the physical facilities of all the different components come together.

To keep track of all these wire centers, all the players in the North American telecommunications industry worked together to develop the Coordinate System, shown in Figure 21-3. The Coordinate System is really a grid that lets telecommunications service providers, their customers, and their regulatory authorities calculate call mileage (somewhat) accurately.

As we mentioned earlier, LEC distance-sensitive components are calculated from between the originating customer's premises and the wire center. Interexchange carrier distance-sensitive tariff components are calculated between wire center coordinates, which are identified (according to a spellbinding piece of work called AT&T Tariff #10) by the first six digits of North American telephone numbers.

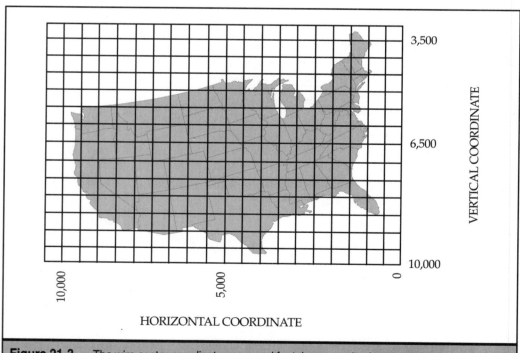

Figure 21-3.   The wire center coordinate map used for telecommunications pricing structures

NOTE: All public telephone numbers in North America are coordinated under an agreement called the North American Numbering Plan (NANP). The NANP identifies individual telephones with a 10-digit number. The first three digits indicate the number plan area (NPA). Digits four through six indicate the local exchange. Together, these first six digits give enough information—for tariff purposes—to calculate the distance-sensitive component of a tariff. Bellcore and other private companies have developed electronic databases that link the first six digits of every telephone number in North America with their corresponding wire center coordinates. These databases are commercially available, so you may want to use them to double check tariffed rates.

UNIT PRICE   The unit price component is similar to the distance-sensitive component. It is a fixed cost per unit of time that a telecommunications service or facility is used. Again, it may be a flat rate per unit or it may be volume-sensitive. Furthermore, a unit price may vary with the time of day or day of the week. For example, the fact that most long-distance service is cheaper between the hours of 5 P.M. and 8 A.M. weekdays than it is between the hours of 8 A.M. and 5 P.M. is a function of unit pricing that varies with the time of day. Usually, telecommunications service providers charge less during low-traffic periods, just as airlines and hotels charge less for their services during low-traffic periods.

Putting It All Together

So, how are these components assembled to give you a true and correct picture of the tariffed rates for the services you want?

SHARED SERVICES   Shared services have both a fixed-charge component and a unit component, as well as a distance-sensitive component for long-distance services. However, most of the price of a shared service is the unit component.

DEDICATED SERVICES   Dedicated services generally have a fixed-charge component as well as a distance-sensitive component for long-distance services.

Figure 21-4 illustrates two hypothetical services offerings and the tariff components that make up the price of these offerings. The first offering is dedicated access to a dedicated inter-LATA service. The other offering is a bit more complicated: dedicated local access at origination to shared inter-LATA service, then shared local access at termination.

It's pretty easy to see from our examples what a meticulous and painstaking job calculating tariffs can be. Luckily, your service provider is largely charged with this. However, the wise wide area network manager takes the time to double check tariffs occasionally.

What Types of WAN Services Are Tariffed?

I believe tariffs will disappear, being replaced by freely negotiated contracts. A tariff is a published price that sets the allowed rate for telecommunications services and equipment. Tariffs are set by a formal procedure involving carriers' filing proposed prices, which are then reviewed, amended, and ultimately either approved or rejected by the FCC. Tariffs, therefore, contain the most complete and precise descriptions of carrier

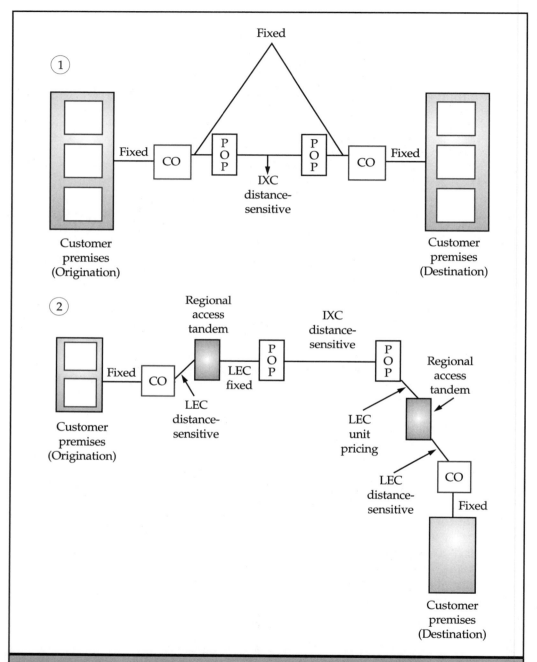

Figure 21-4. Two different types of service and their tariff elements

offerings. Further, tariff offerings cannot be dropped or changed without government approval. LEC tariffs are under the jurisdiction of state authorities. Once established, a tariff constitutes a public contract between the user of the product or service and the telecommunications carrier, and it can't be changed except by the express permission of the Federal Communications Commission. Therefore, a tariffed service is a service for which the carrier must publish its pricing and file it with the FCC. Up to now, carriers have been responding to their competitors' tariffs rather than their customers' needs. Now they will most likely start responding to their markets—which means you.

CONTRACT SERVICES

Now you know about the intricate, involved world of tariffed services. But what if the wide area networking service you've chosen isn't tariffed? How do you define a level of service and establish a price? This chapter is designed to help you answer these questions.

All telecommunications services that aren't tariffed services fall under the category of contract services. Contract services are generally those telecommunications services that aren't considered a widely used, basic necessity to public telecommunications, such as Integrated Services Digital Network and frame relay. The bad news is that because these services aren't tariffed, you can't be sure you're getting the best price around—you can't even be sure you're getting a standard level of service. The good news is that, also because these services aren't tariffed, there's a great deal of room for negotiating and bargaining, enabling you potentially to get a much better deal than if these services were bought off a standard price list.

Think of It As Buying a Car

As I said, negotiating a contract for telecommunications services gives you the opportunity to cut a better deal than the next person. This makes purchasing a contract service something like buying a car, whereas purchasing a tariffed service is more like buying the gasoline. Providers of tariffed telecommunications services, like gas station owners, are selling a very interchangeable service. All gasoline has the same chemical makeup, and except for octane levels (of which all gas stations offer a variety) and the odd cleaning agent, it's all pretty much the same stuff. Furthermore, all competing gasoline providers by now have pretty much the same discovery, refining, and distribution methods, so gas station owners are making about the same level of profit for each gallon of gas sold. Therefore, all that service station owner has to do to set prices is to keep track of the prices of their competitors' products—which is pretty easy since these prices are posted on big billboards over every gas station—and price their gasoline accordingly. As the consumer of these services, it's very easy for you to get the going price for, say 93 octane gasoline, but it makes it nearly impossible for you to negotiate a bargain for it. After all, when was the last time you were able to convince your local gas station owner to give you an extra 10 cents a gallon off the price of unleaded in return for your promise to fill your car at his station every Saturday for the next two years?

Similarly, tariffed telecommunications services are all configured and priced the same by the state regulatory agencies. And since these basic services have been around for some time, most of the providers of these services have essentially the same technology in their transmission and distribution systems. While this makes it really easy for you as the consumer to get the going price, it also makes it impossible for you to get a lower price or more features for those services.

Size Matters

When negotiating a contract for wide area networking service, remember that in telecommunications—just as in any other industry—the big customer has more clout. Those customers with the potential of spending hundreds of thousands of dollars annually or even monthly on services are going to have a lot more room to negotiate than shops that will spend only a few hundred dollars a month. Therefore, many of the negotiating tactics discussed next will prove successful only for large customers. However, the overall strategies will be helpful to all those negotiating for contract services, no matter what their size.

Negotiation Strategies

Your strategy will set the overall tone for your negotiations. It should summarize your goals and your approach to achieving those goals. With that in mind, let me suggest that your strategy should consist of two principles: something for nothing and just ask.

Something for Nothing

Let's be honest. Your goal is to get the service for free. Of course, that's not possible, but that should be your starting point. You want to get as much service and support as you can for as little money, time, and grief as possible. One way to approach this is to begin negotiations by thinking, "How much is the service provider going to pay me for installing, managing, and just generally dealing with their service and staff?"

Just Ask

With the ultimate goal of something for nothing in mind, enter negotiations always remembering this: *It can't hurt to ask.*

Ask for free installation. Ask for free training for your staff on the protocol, its implementation, and troubleshooting. Ask for a full-time representative from the telecommunications service provider to be assigned onsite at your location—for free. Ask the service provider to pay for all local access charges. Ask for the world. All they can say is no.

Negotiation Tactics

Tactics are the things you do to realize your strategic goals. While everyone's negotiation style (and therefore their tactics) varies, these are a few techniques that I have found very useful.

Know Your Limits

The key to negotiating any contract successfully is to know the maximum you are willing to pay for a service before you begin negotiations. Put a value on the wide area service by determining how much it will increase productivity and how much it will cost you in staff time for support and maintenance. If you can't get the wide area service for this amount or less, walk away.

When calculating your bottom line, be sure to include all vendor-provided services that you absolutely must have: training, technical support, management reports, etc.

Get a "Most Favored Nation" Clause in Your Contract

If at all possible, include language in your contract that guarantees that you will get pricing at least as favorable as any other client of the telecommunications service provider. Of course, you may not be able to find out how much the provider's other clients are paying, because their contracts are generally not publicly available. However, should you discover that another client of the vendor is getting a better deal than you are, a "most favored nation" clause in your contract will require the telecommunications service provider to give you the same pricing.

Beware of Long-Term Contracts

Don't sign a contract for more than two years. Of course, there are exceptions to this, but beware. If your telecommunications service vendor is willing to offer you extravagant incentives in return for a long contract, you've got to figure they expect the market prices of those services to drop fairly dramatically over the term of the contract.

Don't Forget Nondisclosure and Confidentiality Agreements

When you install a new WAN service, the telecommunications service provider may very likely have staff hanging around your office for extended periods of time—during which they may have access to confidential corporate information. Therefore, be sure that you require the telecommunications service provider to have all of their employees working on your account sign nondisclosure and confidentiality agreements. These agreements state that the telecommunications service provider's employees will not divulge any information they may discover about your business and your network.

The Cop Shows Have a Point

Everyone who's watched a police drama on television knows the old "good cop, bad cop" routine: When questioning a suspect, a police officer enters the interrogation room and, acting nasty and threatening, demands the suspect tell all. Then the officer leaves the room. A second officer enters the room and, acting friendly and reasonable, informs the suspect that if he or she will just make a deal with the "good" officer, the suspect won't have to endure any more invective from the "bad" officer. After switching off like this a few times, the suspect eventually gets tired of the verbal abuse and cuts a deal.

The same tactic can work in negotiating for a telecommunications service—or anything else for that matter. The "bad guy" (or gal) has to be of higher rank than the "good guy" (or gal). First the "bad guy" hurls invective at the telecommunications service provider about how little the service means to him or her, and how little he or she is willing to allocate for it—then leaves. Next, the "good guy" explains to the vendor how much he or she wants the service, but of course, can't have it unless the price is REALLY reasonable ("I mean, you can see what I'm up against."). The provider wants to make a sale, doesn't want to deal with the "bad guy" any more, and wants to help out the "good guy" who will be the main point of contact once the sale is made. It can work.

Know Your Provider

Be sure that your telecommunications service provider is big enough, well established enough, and technically advanced enough to provide you with the level of service you need. Especially in the current environment of mass deregulation, you will find small providers and resellers that just aren't up to meeting the challenge of supporting large, mission-critical wide area links.

Training and Education Make Great Bargaining Points

If you're introducing a new wide area technology into your network, you'll probably want to learn as much about how it works and how to manage it as you possibly can. The better trained you and your staff are, the better able you will be to support your own network and ultimately advance in your careers. So, training and education in the service or protocol you want to purchase should be very attractive to you.

As well, it's attractive to the telecommunications service provider. After all, when the provider is unable to reduce the price of the service any further, it may still be able to offer training at no additional cost. You may even be able to arrange for you and your staff to attend training sessions designed for the provider's own employees. It never hurts to ask.

Write a "Tariff Elimination Clause" into Your Contract

You can expect the FCC and PUCs to eliminate many tariffs over the next few months and years. Given the regulatory environment we described in Chapter 19, it's inevitable. If your contract also includes tariffed services, this means you may be obligated to continue paying the tariffed rate even after the tariff is abolished. Therefore, be sure to include language in your contract that lets you negotiate prices for services that were tariffed at the time of execution but become "untariffed" during the term of the contract.

Look for Wide Area Networking Services from LECs

As the Telecommunications Act of 1996 takes effect, don't overlook the wide area service offerings of the local exchange carriers. They are relatively new in the long-distance market, and therefore hungry for market share. As a result, they may be willing to offer deals that more established wide area service providers aren't.

Access Fees Could Be a Big Source of Savings

In past negotiations, I have had a lot of luck in asking wide area service providers to pay at least part of the cost of local access fees. In some cases, I've received an annual lump sum payment equal to the cost of all access fees paid. You can imagine how good that made my budget look. Keep this in mind when negotiating your service contracts.

CHANGES TO EXPECT Now that the Telecommunications Act of 1996 is going into effect, look for more competitive pricing in local access fees. As the long-distance carriers enter the local access market, more competition means lower prices—and the telecommunications service providers know it. Therefore, pay close attention to the pricing of local access services in your contract. You may even want to include language that requires your wide area service provider to pass all of its local access savings on to you! It's been done. And it doesn't hurt to ask.

Make Quality of Service Part of the Contract

A sound strategy is to link service outages to a refund on your service bill. This is particularly important in the current deregulatory environment, in which many small resellers are buying and repackaging service from larger vendors. When a resold service goes down, the reseller may just point a finger at the provider with one hand and hold the other out for a check from you. Be sure that your contract states that no service means no payment.

Everyone Wants to Win

The old "win-win" platitude has some validity. Although ultimately you'd like to get the service for free, you also know that a vendor that feels it got a bad deal isn't going to be as responsive and helpful as a vendor that feels it got a fair deal. And chances are you are going to need your vendor's help throughout the term of the contract. Therefore, keep in mind that you want your vendor to be sufficiently satisfied with the terms of the contract to give you prompt, attentive, and helpful support after the sale.

VALUE-ADDED CARRIERS

When you're building your wide area network, you don't necessarily have to build your own private network. In fact, most wide area networks aren't private networks. Instead, the WAN designers use telecommunications services provided by value-added carriers (VAC), sometimes also called public data networks.

Private Wide Area Networks

A private network is a network built with public transmission facilities and privately owned switching equipment, as shown in Figure 21-5. Even though the telecommunications transmission facilities are owned by a public service provider—usually a local exchange carrier—they are leased by the individual corporation for its exclusive use. In other words, the corporation doesn't share the portion of the transmission bandwidth that it leases with any other customers of the telecommunications service provider.

A private wide area network is fairly secure because no one else has access to your bandwidth. It also has very reliable performance because you aren't sharing the telecommunications transmission facilities with anyone else. However, it is also an expensive proposition, both because you have to purchase all of your own switching equipment and you have to pay for the full cost (plus profit) of the transmission facility.

Public Wide Area Networks

You can build a wide area network without going to the trouble and expense of building a private network. You can use wide area and metropolitan area network services owned by providers other than a LEC. These other providers are known as public data networks, or value-added carriers. In fact, the majority of corporate wide area networks use value-added carriers to provide some or all of their wide area networking services. While value-added carriers offer circuit-switching services such as switched 56 and Integrated Services Digital Network, the most popular WAN services they provide are packet-switching services such as frame relay, Switched Multimegabit Data Service (SMDS), X.25, and, more recently, Asynchronous Transfer Mode (ATM).

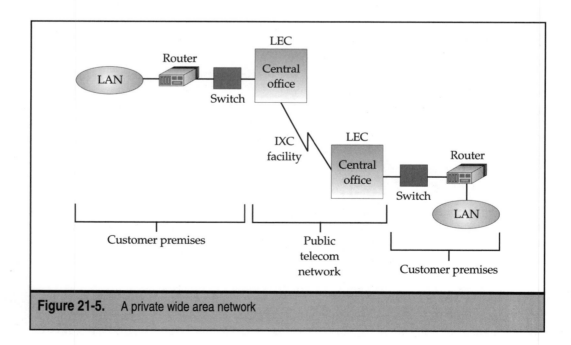

Figure 21-5.   A private wide area network

Value-Added Carriers

A value-added carrier provides packet-switching or circuit-switching services to corporate clients. Generally, a value-added carrier has a global network connecting its switching equipment to end users all over the world, comprised of the value-added carrier's own private lines as well as lines leased from other carriers. Value-added carriers can be either local exchange carriers, such as the Regional Bell Operating Companies, or interexchange carriers such as AT&T, MCI, and Sprint. As well, a value-added carrier may be a company that has constructed large wide area networks for its own use, then resold excess transmission capacity to corporate clients.

An example of the latter type of value-added carrier is CompuServe, which has constructed a massive packet-switched data network to allow its clients to access its information service. Some years back, CompuServe realized that most of its WAN was used most heavily at night, with much of its bandwidth lying idle during the day. CompuServe realized that it could resell this bandwidth to corporate customers who experience the heaviest network usage during the day, and began leasing access to its X.25 and frame relay networks.

Like local exchange carriers and interexchange carriers, value-added carriers offer their wide area networking services either a flat-rate monthly charge for a fixed amount of bandwidth, or usage-based charges.

In a value-added carrier's network, intra-LATA access to telecommunications transmission services is provided via local exchange carriers (LECs), as pictured in Figure 21-6. Usually, the value-added carrier installs a dedicated leased line between its customer's facility and the local exchange carrier's central office. The value-added carrier has an access tandem at the local exchange carrier's central office, which provides the customer with access to the value-added carrier's point of presence. From the point of presence on, the customer is using the value-added carrier's network.

Why Use a Value-Added Carrier?

Using a value-added carrier can save you blood, sweat, and tears. It can also save you money over building a private network, because it's very expensive for an individual corporation to lease dedicated telecommunications services over long distances. Furthermore, a value-added carrier provides one-stop shopping for the telecommunications transmission facilities, switching equipment, and service. This is because the value-added carrier is responsible for maintaining equipment, providing switching services, and dealing with troubleshooting and maintaining the transmission service.

Using a value-added carrier also has administrative advantages. In addition to eliminating the possibility of fingerpointing among the various service providers required to deliver wide area networking services, a value-added carrier may also be able to provide you with billing services, such as cost center allocation and departmental chargebacks. And the value-added carrier can consolidate all of this into a single itemized bill, which is much easier to analyze and monitor than the two or three bills you would

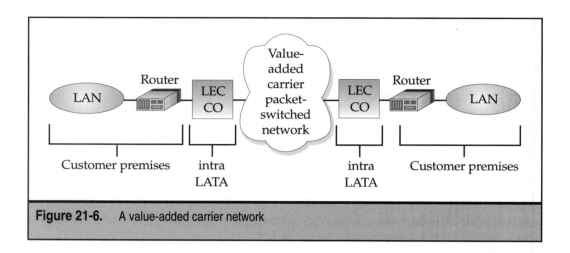

Figure 21-6.   A value-added carrier network

otherwise get from your local exchange carrier, your interexchange carrier, and your telecommunications resellers.

Furthermore, with their vast networks, value-added carriers have more redundancy available to provide backup delivery paths for your data should a link fail. As well, your value-added carrier may even offer such services as protocol conversion and bill processing.

Give Us Names!

If using a value-added carrier appeals to you, you'll probably want to start contacting them now to investigate the services they offer. Listed below are some of the major value-added carriers:

- ▼ Infonet Service Corporation
- ■ Tymenet Global Network
- ■ CompuServe Information Services
- ■ GE Information Services
- ■ AT&T Network Services
- ■ networkMCI
- ▲ Sprint

TIP: Not all value-added carriers are created equal. The services, protocols, and access locations vary from VAC to VAC. Be sure to study the product offerings carefully before selecting a value-added carrier.

Value-added carriers can prevent a lot of headaches for the wide area networking manager. Certainly they are not a panacea to all wide area networking issues; however, they are a resource you can't afford to overlook.

PREPARING A REQUEST FOR PROPOSALS FOR WAN SERVICE

So far, we have discussed the basic technological concepts on which wide area networking is based. We've explained who provides and who regulates the transmission of these services. We've also talked about how to define the criteria for selecting a wide area networking service or protocol. We then went on to discuss a variety of wide area networking services and protocols. By this time, you should have a pretty good idea of what type of WAN service you want, who your prospective vendors are, and under what terms you will probably have to deal with them.

Now it's time to talk about how to get what you want.

Talking Turkey

In this section, we'll show you how to prepare a Request for Proposals (RFP). A Request for Proposals is a document in which you state which telecommunications services and/or protocols you want and the terms under which you want them. After you prepare an RFP, you can send it to all prospective vendors. The vendors can then prepare proposals for providing the requested telecommunications services. From these proposals, you can select the vendor that most closely meets your technical, support, and budgetary requirements.

The steps in RFP preparation and vendor selection are as follows:

1. Define WAN requirements.
2. Prepare an outline for the RFP.
3. Write a draft RFP.
4. Submit draft RFP to coworkers for review and comment.
5. Prepare final draft of RFP.
6. Send RFP to vendors.
7. Evaluate vendor responses.
8. Prepare and submit questions to vendors.
9. Select vendor.

Step One: Define Your Wide Area Network Requirements

The first step in writing a successful Request for Proposals is defining what you want in fairly intricate detail. This means that you have to work through the thought process described in Chapter 19 to determine the requirements for your wide area network.

> **TIP:** Don't make the RFP so specific that vendors don't have any leeway in their product offerings. Oftentimes vendors will know of new or emerging technologies and methods that may be perfect for your environment. If the RFP is too specific, the vendors won't feel they can even suggest an alternative.

After you have carefully defined your requirements and selection criteria, you're ready to start outlining your Request for Proposals.

Step Two: Preparing the Outline

Before you begin writing a Request for Proposals, take some time to jot down all the points you want to cover in the RFP. Figure 21-7 contains an example of an outline for a Request for Proposals.

The principal components of a Request for Proposals are

▼ Technical goals

■ Technical requirements

■ Administrative requirements

■ Price

▲ Vendor qualifications

Technical Goals

The Technical Goals section of your RFP is an explanation of why you need a wide area network and the results you expect from it. You should include a description—complete with layout and cable plant diagrams—of the local area networks you want to connect over the WAN. Give details on the LAN transport protocol, the number of users, and the number, location, and supported protocols of any and all of your routers.

EXAMPLE Kali Hai Corporation would like to connect the local area network in its remote office in Milwaukee, Wisconsin, with its local area network at the company's headquarters in Big Sky, Montana. Our goal is to enable 521 users in both offices to collaborate interactively on multimedia development projects. We will be using videoconferencing and groupware to facilitate the collaboration. At the same time, we plan to improve interoffice communication via electronic mail. Our goal is to eliminate overnight mail deliveries between these two offices.

I. Technical Goals

    A. Issues and problems

    B. Expectations of proposed solution

    C. Current LAN environment

        1. Size of LAN

        2. Description and layout of LAN equipment

        3. Cable plant diagram

II. Technical Requirements

    A. Bandwidth requirements

    B. Management requirements

    C. Standards compliance

    D. Evaluation criteria

    E. Due date for project completion

    F. Maintenance and support

III. Administrative Requirements

    A. Staff training

    B. Nondisclosure agreements

    C. Documentation

    D. Format of response

    E. Work plan

    F. Implementation Schedule

IV. Price

    A. Format of pricing elements

    B. Permitted price fluctuations

    C. Payment terms

V. Vendor Qualifications

    A. Number of employees

    B. Number of years in business

    C. Gross revenues

    D. References

Figure 21-7. A sample outline of a Request for Proposals

Kali Hai Corporation's headquarters has a 2,500-node, 1,800-user 10Base-T network running Novell NetWare 4.1. Copies of the network diagram are attached in Exhibit A. As well, schematic diagrams of the cable plant in both the headquarters and remote offices appear in Exhibits B and C, respectively.

Technical Requirements

This is the section of the RFP in which you describe the amount of bandwidth, the hours of availability, and the acceptable level of performance. You should also include your expectations regarding compliance with standards, as well as management and maintenance of your wide area telecommunications service.

Finally, the Technical Requirements section is the appropriate place to include evaluation criteria. These should be described in a somewhat broad manner, leaving the door open for the vendor to present new ideas.

EXAMPLE   Kali Hai Corporation has conducted a survey to determine how much traffic will be passing over our local area network. We have determined that we have a busy-hour load of 3.8 erlangs and a busy-day load of 15 erlangs. We need to accommodate those loads between 8:30 A.M. and 5:00 P.M. with no lost traffic.

Security and fault tolerance are of utmost necessity to Kali Hai Corporation. Therefore, Kali Hai Corporation requires proof of a high-security transmission facility. The corporation also demands that sufficient backup service is available to ensure no less than .5 percent WAN link downtime per year.

Kali Hai Corporation has no full-time wide area networking staff. Therefore, the vendor should be prepared with the proper test equipment, tools, and trained staff to undertake the responsibility of all maintenance, reconfiguration, troubleshooting, repair, and upgrades. The vendor must respond to requests for support services within 2 hours of notification by Kali Hai Corporation.

The vendor will be required to keep a duplicate of all wide area networking equipment on-site at Kali Hai Corporation so that repairs can be made quickly. KHC also requires that telephone support be available 24 hours a day, 7 days a week via a toll-free number.

The products of the participating vendors will be evaluated on the basis of bandwidth, management, and price.

Administrative Requirements

Believe it or not, ensuring that all your bases are covered administratively is probably the most difficult and tedious part of preparing your RFP. There are a lot of administrative details involved in preparing a good RFP, including the following:

▼ Ensuring nondisclosure of proprietary company information

■ Detailing the due date of the response to the RFP

■ Required format for the responses to the RFP

- Means of submitting proposals (electronically? Certified mail?)
- Work plan and implementation schedules
- Documentation of wide area network
▲ Staff training requirements

Price

When preparing the pricing portion of your RFP, you should specify how you want the prices presented. Be sure to specify all the components you want the vendor to include in the RFP. For example, if you don't have appropriate cabling for the WAN link, be sure to tell the vendors that their proposals should include bringing your cabling up to specification.

Most likely, you'll want separate pricing elements for service, equipment, installation, maintenance, and repair. This way you can compare vendors' prices more easily. You will also want to direct vendors to present optional services and equipment as a separate element. This way, you can fairly compare the basic services offered by each vendor.

This is also the section of the RFP in which you'll want to address payment terms. Will you make progress payments, meaning you will pay predesignated portions of the expenses after the vendor reaches certain predesignated milestones in the WAN project? Or will you withhold all payment until the WAN installation is done to your satisfaction?

NOTE: If you find a telecommunications service vendor that will let you withhold all payment until you're satisfied, let me know!

Finally, what happens if prices increase or decrease dramatically after you accept the vendor's proposal, but before the work is complete? You may want to include some language in the RFP that states the maximum allowable price fluctuations.

Vendor Qualifications

This is very important. This is a long-term commitment you're contemplating, and you want to be sure your vendor will be around. Require that all vendors submitting proposals include a description of their companies, including date founded, number of employees, and gross revenues. Request references to see how well their customers regard them. Have them send proof of any technical certifications their staff has. Ask for any information you can think of that indicates the vendors' stability and level of service.

Step Three: Write Draft Request for Proposals

Now that you have an outline, the RFP should almost write itself. Prepare a draft copy, read it through, make your changes, then let others take a stab at it.

Step Four: Submit Draft RFP for Review and Comment

Always gather as many ideas as possible about the requirements of your wide area network. Let everyone in your department have a chance to make improvements to your RFP. This may take more time than you'd like, but it is well worth it.

Step Five: Prepare Final Draft of RFP

Once you have everyone's comments, it's time to prepare the final RFP. By now, you should practically have the whole thing memorized, so this step will likely be very easy.

Step Six: Send RFP to Vendors

Send your RFP to all vendors that you think might be qualified to support it. Get vendor referrals from as many places as possible, so you'll have a large pool of vendors from which to choose.

Step Seven: Evaluate Vendor Responses

Again, do this in a group. After the due date for vendor response, distribute copies of the proposals to everyone in your department. It's good for you to get everyone's perspectives, and it's good for your staff to be included in the selection process. After all, they're the ones who are going to have to live with the WAN link.

Get everyone's opinion on each of the proposals. Go over each element of the proposals carefully, comparing them on each element. Also, make a list of any questions that arise. It's very important to quiz the vendor closely about every concern that you and your staff have.

Step Eight: Prepare and Submit Questions to Vendors

These are the questions that arose during the evaluation session. Put the questions in writing and submit them to the vendors. Request that the vendors respond in writing. This way, there will be little room for misunderstanding the vendors' product and service offerings. For a sample list of questions that you should submit to every vendor on your short list, turn to the next section.

Step Nine: Select Vendor

By now, you should have a very warm and cozy feeling about one of the telecommunications vendors. Inform that vendor, by letter, that it has received the contract to build your WAN link.

With the RFP written and the bid awarded, you are ready to start building your wide area network. While it's being built, it's a good idea to set up your maintenance procedures.

QUESTIONS FOR THE FINALISTS

So you've written your RFP, and you've received several interesting responses. How do you determine which telecommunications service provider will give you the best deal? Here is a list of questions designed to help you find the best provider for your network.

Vendor Background Questions

1. How long have you been in business? This will obviously give you some idea of the stability of the company.

2. How many people do you employ? In support? In sales? In engineering and design? Beware of small companies, especially those that seem to have an inadequate number of technical installation and support staff.

3. Do you own your own transmission facilities? Companies that don't own their own transmission facilities may be unable to help you during service outages. They are essentially at the mercy of the owner of the transmission plants.

4. If you don't own your own transmission facilities, from whom do you lease them? If the company you are dealing with doesn't own its own transmission facilities, find out who does and question them on their support capabilities and service record.

5. Who provides troubleshooting, support, and repair for your services (or equipment or protocols)? If the company doesn't use its own employees to provide these key services, be wary. Find out who does provide these services and question them closely on their capabilities.

6. How many times have you installed this equipment (or service, or protocol)? Let your service provider practice on someone else. Hire a company that has installed this service many times before.

7. Can you provide references from a company of the same size? Be sure that the provider can support a company of your size and requirements. There's a big difference between being able to support a small company with an infrequently used wide area link and a big, demanding company that depends upon its wide area link every minute.

8. How many similar wide area systems have you installed in this area? A successful frame relay installation in Chicago doesn't automatically translate into a similarly successful installation in Dallas. This is because the local exchange carriers (LECs), public utilities commissions (PUCs), regulations, and equipment vendors are all different in each locality. Make sure your prospective telecommunications service provider knows the ropes in your area.

9. Where is your nearest support location? Make sure it's close enough for prompt support and "home town" attention.

10. Who will be our account executive? A savvy telecommunications service provider will have your account representative selected before they even go in to make the sales pitch. This is an indication of the level of organization of the provider and hence the quality of service it can provide.

11. What is your federal tax identification number? An established carrier will have one and won't hesitate to give it to you. You'll need this for your records, anyway.

12. Can you provide an annual report or an audited financial statement? It's an important guide to the financial stability of the telecommunications service provider.

13. If you are a subsidiary, what is the name of the parent organization? Know who you're dealing with.

Installation Questions

1. Will installation be done by your employees? If not, by whom? Be wary of the provider that hires third parties to install their service. This is an indication of a small, poorly established provider.

2. What must we do to prepare our site for installation? This will prevent any unpleasant surprises and consequent delays.

3. How soon can installation begin? An experienced, well-established telecommunications service provider will be able to tell you immediately when the installation process can begin and all the steps involved. If they seem to flounder with this question, beware: they may never have done it before. Worse, they may never have done it successfully.

4. Will there be a preinstallation survey to ensure that all is in order before the installation begins? An organized telecommunications service provider will do this as a matter of course. It saves them time and trouble, makes their operation more efficient, and prevents a disappointed customer.

Equipment Support Questions

1. Will we need to purchase any equipment before installing the wide area networking service or protocol? Believe it or not, some telecommunications service providers may not make this clear. Be sure you understand exactly what you'll need to have on hand before the service can be installed.

2. Is equipment owned by the provider or the end user?

3. Who maintains the equipment? This could be the manufacturer of the equipment, the reseller, the telecommunications provider, or the end user. Make sure you know and are comfortable with the answer to this question.

4. Do you provide on-site service and maintenance?

5. How much will on-site service calls cost?

6. What environmental conditions does the equipment require? Who is responsible for ensuring that those conditions exist? There's nothing more frustrating than having to postpone an installation because there were certain environmental requirements—of which the telecommunications service provider failed to make you aware—that had to be met before the installation could begin. Question the telecommunications service and/or equipment provider about requirements for the following:

    A. Air conditioning

    B. Space

    C. Static control

    D. Power

    E. Location

7. What is the turnaround time for equipment support calls? Don't wait until it's too late to discover that your contract only provides for "next day" response. Make sure your vendor can provide a response time you can live with.

8. Is there remote troubleshooting and support available? This can save you both time and expense. A vendor that can offer remote troubleshooting may offer a very strong advantage.

9. What is the expected service life of the equipment?

10. What is the mean time between failures of the equipment? Make sure the telecommunications equipment isn't going to be a constant source of pain and problems. My rule of thumb is that if I find out that the MTBF is less than three years, I don't go near it.

11. How often does the equipment need servicing?

12. Is there a toll-free number available for equipment support?

13. During what hours of the day and days of the week is equipment support available?

14. How long is the warranty? What does it cover?

15. Are hot spares available? When you can't wait for a new part to be delivered, can your telecommunications equipment vendor provide you with a spare?

16. Who manufactures the equipment?

Software Support Questions

1. Does the system in question include a software component? For what? Management? Troubleshooting? Some telecommunications service providers offer management and support software that can save you time. These

software applications could be anything from diagnostic software to applications that help you analyze your wide area networking service bills. Find out about all your options.

2. Is software support included in the contract price?

3. Are software upgrades included in the contract price?

4. How long is the initial software support period?

5. During what days of the week and hours of the day is software support provided?

6. Is there a toll-free number for software support? It may not seem like much, but a toll-free number is handy and money-saving.

7. How often is the software upgraded? Frequent upgrades indicate unstable software. They are also a drain of time and resources. Therefore, beware the frequently upgraded software.

8. Who owns the software? Is the vendor reselling it? If the telecommunications service provider is simply reselling the software, they may not be able to support it properly. In that event, it may not be worth much to you.

9. Who supports the software for the vendor? A third party? Or a regular employee of the vendor?

10. What is the turnaround time for software support calls? Don't wait until it's too late to discover that your contract only provides for "next day" response. Make sure your vendor can provide a response time you can live with.

11. Is there remote troubleshooting and support available? This can save you both time and expense. A vendor that can offer remote troubleshooting may offer a very strong advantage.

Training Questions

1. How much training will be required for our staff to use and maintain the service (or equipment or protocol)? Be sure that you aren't biting off more than you can chew. If you don't have the staff hours to devote to learning how to work with the new service, it may not be the right service. Or it may be that your vendor doesn't have the staff to support the service properly, and is relying on the end users to do their job for them.

2. Will you provide the necessary training?

3. Is the cost of training included in the price of the contract?

4. Where will training take place? Ideally, any training should take place on-site, or at least in the same city. No doubt you will have neither the budget nor the staff hours to send your employees to a remote city for training. Be sure the vendor can provide a satisfactory level of training locally.

5. When can the training begin? Be sure the vendor can schedule to have your staff trained before the service is installed and running. On the other hand, make sure they don't train your staff so long before the installation date that your staff has forgotten everything by the time the service is implemented.

6. Who will conduct the training? Insist on meeting and approving the trainer before any contracts are signed, especially if your telecommunications service provider is going to employee a third-party trainer to work with your staff.

GETTING WHAT YOU PAY FOR: REVIEWING THE BILLS

Reviewing the bills from your telecommunications service provider is a little like balancing your checkbook. Both jobs are tedious and painstaking, but they result in information that you can use to guide future actions. Furthermore, while under ideal circumstances you could live a long and happy life without ever balancing your checkbook or reconciling vendor charges against services provided, you know that in reality mistakes are all too common. Therefore, I've written this section to offer some assistance in performing this grim task. Hopefully it will make it, if not more pleasant, at least more worthwhile.

The Importance of Itemization

The most important thing you can do to prepare for bill reconciliation is to require that your telecommunications service provider send you an itemized statement. This is the only way you can see exactly what services you are (supposed to be) receiving and exactly what you are being charged for those services. This is the first step in any sane bill reconciliation procedure.

Bill Reconciliation

Reconciling your telecommunications service provider bills is the process of validating the amounts that your telecommunications vendors are charging you. Let me tell you right now that without a telemanagement system this process is truly overwhelming.

Telco vendors realize that they make errors in billing, almost always in their favor, but they do not have a way to fix the discrepancies unless you, the consumer, point out the errors.

Bill reconciliation is performed by downloading some form of electronic media that contains your local and long-distance telephone bills onto a telemanagement system, spreadsheet, or specialized application that will allow you to analyze and interpret the information. If you're using a telemanagement system (TMS), you'll need a conversion utility to convert the telco call records to the same format as the TMS call record. Every vendor supplies their billing information in different formats and on different media. A common media must be selected between the two systems.

How It Works

Once the telco detail is downloaded and converted, the spreadsheet, reconciliation application, or TMS sorts the telco's call detail records (and in the case of the TMS, the TMS system's call detail records) in a chronological order.

Bill Reconciliation with a Spreadsheet or Specialized Application

Reconciling your telecommunications service provider's bills without the help of a call detail report is going to be tough. That's because you have nothing against which to compare the vendor's itemization of services provided. However, there are a few things you can look for on your bill:

- ▼ Lease charges for equipment that you own
- ■ Itemized charges for fees that have been waived
- ■ Longest call detail
- ■ International call detail
- ▲ Calls to the 809 area code

LEASE CHARGES FOR EQUIPMENT YOU OWN   One of the most common mistakes I've found in wide area networking service bills is a rental charge for a piece of equipment that is owned by the end user. This frequently happens in large organizations in which the end user has chosen to purchase a piece of WAN equipment that is more commonly rented from the service provider. Therefore, be sure you understand and approve every charge on your statement.

ITEMIZED CHARGES FOR FEES THAT HAVE BEEN WAIVED   This is especially important for wide area networks using contract services. Be sure that you are not being charged for any fees or services that should have been waived under the terms of your contract.

LONGEST CALL DETAIL   For those of you with dial-up service, take a look at the ten longest calls itemized on the statement. Oftentimes, when a hacker breaks into your telecommunications system, he or she will make a few very long (and very expensive) telephone calls, then go away. Therefore, checking to make sure that the longest calls on your statement are actually legitimate is often a good indication that your system is hacker-free that month. While this is far from a foolproof test, it is a good rule of thumb.

INTERNATIONAL CALL DETAIL   Check the itemized international calls. This is a common source of incorrect billing as well as toll fraud. As well, it's often the easiest kind of billing discrepancy to spot, since most corporations make far fewer international calls than domestic calls.

If your corporation is involved in a lot of dial-up international WAN access, however, you may want to verify only the longest international calls. This is similar to the verification of the ten longest calls discussed earlier.

VERIFY DIAL-UP CALLS TO THE 809 AREA CODE AND TO CHINA   For reasons not wholly understood, most fraudulent calls—both voice and data—are made to the 809 area code and to China. Therefore, a good "quick cut" of bill reconciliation is to make sure that all dial-up access to the 809 area code and to China is legitimate.

MANAGING WIDE AREA SERVICES

When things go wrong in the world of wide area networking, there's often not a lot that the ordinary WAN manager can do to fix or even diagnose the problem. That's because problems with transmission facilities can usually only be confirmed by the telecommunications service provider, who—quite frankly—has a vested interest in reporting "No Trouble Found." Of course, shortly after you, the WAN manager, receive that report from your telecommunications service provider, you're likely to discover that the problem with the WAN link mysteriously disappears. You'll never know what, if anything, was wrong with the WAN link, nor how it was fixed.

This section is designed to give you a little help in troubleshooting WAN link problems. It won't prepare you to make precise diagnoses, but it will help you spot possible causes of WAN link trouble. It will also enable you to talk intelligently with your telecommunications technicians and make sure they are doing a thorough job of troubleshooting and repair.

Things That Go Wrong

Although, as we all know, there seems to be an endless variety of problems that can strike our networks at any time, most of the problems experienced on wide area networks are due to one of two culprits:

▼   Traffic congestion

▲   Transmission problems

Traffic Congestion

Managing your wide area network traffic is different from managing traffic on your local area network. You'll find that the SNMP-based management systems that have given you such wonderfully detailed information on your local area network don't work over the WAN. Although, as mentioned in Chapter 19, at the time of this writing we are beginning to see a few wide area network management applications, most notably Network Probe from Network Communications Corporation of Bloomington, MN, for the most part they simply don't provide the in-depth statistics that we've come to expect from LAN management applications. Furthermore, these applications aren't—at least yet—tightly integrated with the local area network devices, so they can't give you a comprehensive view of what's happening on your network.

For the time being, you will have to rely almost completely on your telecommunications service provider for wide area network traffic analysis and service usage information. Currently, most management and diagnostic systems for wide area services and protocols are geared for use by service providers.

This doesn't mean you will be left entirely out in the cold. You can and should periodically request traffic analyses from your telecommunications service provider to find out how much traffic is going over your wide area link, how frequently the line is unavailable due to excessive traffic, and whether the link is experiencing drops and retransmits. This will let both you and your provider know whether the wide area link is functioning properly, as well as whether you need more bandwidth.

Transmission Problems

Everyone has experienced bad transmission quality at some time or other. Faint signals, loud static, and distracting echoes are all the result of a problem in the signal transmission system. In this section, we will discuss the main culprits: loss, distortion, and noise.

TRANSMISSION LOSS   Loss is simply that: a loss of signal power. When the transmitted signal loses too much power, it becomes too faint to interpret. This causes the receiving computer to request a retransmission, slowing transmission time.

Loss is a normal and expected phenomenon. The farther a signal travels, the more power it loses. This is similar to the difference in volume you notice when you are standing right next to a screaming baby and when you are standing three blocks from it (although it's annoying wherever you are). Most transmission systems are designed to compensate for loss by using repeaters—either linear or regenerative—to strengthen the transmission signal when it becomes too weak.

SIGNAL DISTORTION   As we have seen, a data transmission is composed of a number of frequency components that form a complex signal (see Figure 21-8). All of the various components of this signal are in a precise relationship to one another in both the timing and the magnitude of the waveforms. If for any reason the signal components were to shift in relationship to one another, the signal would be distorted and the information being transmitted would be incorrect and/or unintelligible. There are three major types of distortion that commonly occur in transmission systems: frequency shift distortion, attenuation distortion, and delay distortion.

If, in the course of transmission, a signal's *frequency* is shifted either higher or lower, the signal is distorted. This is called *frequency shift distortion*, and it is a major menace in analog transmission. This is because many analog carrier systems haven't been designed to minimize and correct frequency shift distortion, due to the fact that it isn't a major problem in voice transmission. After all, people can generally interpret words even if they are delivered in a pitch higher or lower than expected. Computers, however, can't make this adjustment.

Therefore, if your wide area network is using an analog carrier system, and receiving computers keep requesting retransmissions, you may want to ask your telecommunications service provider to put a frequency counter on the circuit in question. The frequency counter sends a signal of a known frequency from one end of the circuit, then measures the signal at the receiving end of the circuit. If the frequency of the received

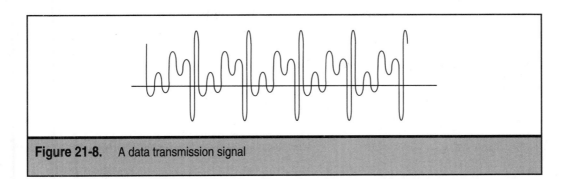

Figure 21-8.   A data transmission signal

signal is the same, the circuit isn't experiencing frequency shift distortion. However, if the signal arrives at a different frequency from that at which it was sent, your provider will need to take corrective measures.

Attenuation distortion is related to transmission loss. Sometimes transmission loss doesn't occur uniformly over all frequencies. For example, sometimes higher frequencies experience more loss than lower frequencies, as illustrated in Figures 22-9 and 22-10.

You can generally fix attenuation distortion by placing inductors, called loading coils, on the transmission cable at precise intervals.

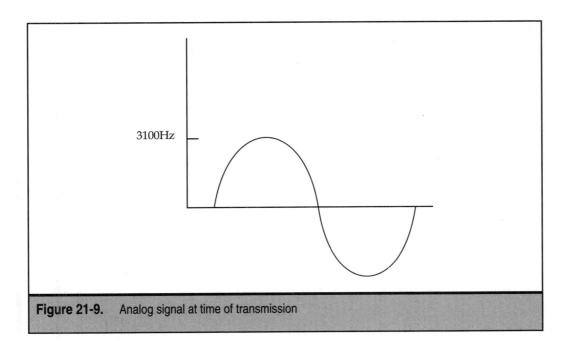

Figure 21-9.   Analog signal at time of transmission

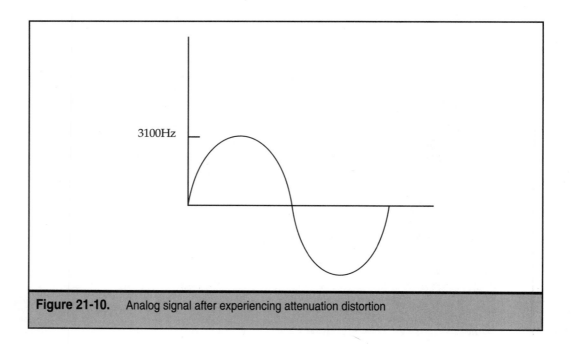

Figure 21-10.   Analog signal after experiencing attenuation distortion

CAUTION: The introduction of loading coils can cause problems should the transmission facility ever be used for transmitting digital signals. We'll talk more about that in later chapters.

Delay distortion is caused by timing differences among waves within a signal. As though things weren't complicated enough, signals travel at different speeds over a transmission medium. The speed of a signal depends upon its frequency: higher frequencies travel faster than lower frequencies. Therefore, a complex signal waveform that is made up of several different frequencies may end up being scrambled because the high-frequency parts of the signal arrive at the destination well before the low-frequency parts of the waveform.

Just like frequency shift distortion, delay distortion isn't a big problem in voice transmission. However, it can wreak havoc on data signals. To make things worse, delay distortion isn't easy to detect or measure. However, it can be fixed by adding delay equalizers to the transmission facility.

NOISE   Noise is extraneous energy that meddles with signal transmission. There are a couple of different types of noise: background noise and signal-dependent noise.

Background noise comes with the territory. It comes from a variety of sources that create a constant noise whether or not a signal is being transmitted.

A big part of background noise is caused by heat. Electrons everywhere are always colliding, causing heat. The heat feeds on itself—heat makes molecules move faster, causing electrons to collide more, thus generating more heat. To make things worse, electrons are not only clumsy, but they're noisy, too—electrons make noise when they collide. So one electron bumps into another, and pretty soon you have a low roar buzzing on your transmission medium. This is called *thermal noise*.

Another source of background noise is electromagnetic coupling. Because transmission media is run all together, cables are usually lying right next to other cables. And all of these cables are carrying currents of varying levels. Currents create electromagnetic fields that are often strong enough to disrupt transmission. Electromagnetic coupling can also occur any time transmission media are run too close to a power line, fluorescent light, or other source of electric current.

As we mentioned, *background noise* comes with the territory. Although it is unavoidable, it also has much less effect on data transmission than on voice signals. Successfully transmitting intelligible data signals requires a fairly narrow range of frequencies and power levels. Understanding human speech, on the other hand, relies on slight nuances in very complex waveforms. What's more, computers aren't nearly as sensitive to low-level noise as people are.

Just for your information, the test for background noise is called the circuit-message noise test (C-message test for short). The test involves sending a test signal over a circuit on which a special filter has been placed. The filter blocks out the frequencies that don't interfere with voice transmission, sending only the noise to the receiving end. At the receiving end, the noise levels can be measured and analyzed.

The second type of noise is *signal-dependent noise,* which is generated by circuit components as a result of an actual signal being transmitted. Sometimes the signal and the devices that transmit it generate noise, especially when repeaters and equalizers are present.

Impulse noise occurs when the signal receives a large injection of energy. This extra energy "spikes" the signal, distorting it beyond recognition. An example of impulse noise might be lightning.

While impulse noise is no big deal for voice signals (if it gets too bad, you'll just wait until the spike passes, then start talking again), it is another big problem for data transmission. Impulse noise can easily destroy individual bits or even entire frames of data.

Whenever telephone circuits follow adjacent paths, they are susceptible to *crosstalk*. Crosstalk occurs when one channel picks up part of a signal traveling on another channel. It may also be the result of frequency division multiplexing, in which some transmission signals may slightly overlap each others' frequencies, as shown in Figure 21-11. In any case, it produces unwanted signals in the distributed circuit.

ECHO   A transmission echo is pretty much the same as any other kind of echo. It is the reflection of energy back to its source. When your voice echoes, the energy of your voice bounces off a wall, a mountain, or a building, and is reflected back to you. When a transmission signal echoes, the energy bounces off an interface to a multiplexor, a repeater, or a transmission facility and is reflected back to the transmitting station.

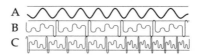

Figure 21-11. Overlapping of multiplexed frequencies

Echoes wreak havoc on both voice and data transmission. There are basically three types of echoes: transmitter echo, receiver echo, and singing echo. As we mentioned above, these echoes may be reflected by interfaces to a number of different devices. However, most frequently the culprit is a 4-wire termination set (4WTS), which we discussed earlier in this chapter. As you no doubt remember, a 4WTS is the interface between a 2-wire facility and a 4-wire facility.

Transmitter echo occurs when the transmitter "hears" its own transmission returned. Transmitter echo is illustrated in Figure 23-12. It's especially disruptive in voice transmission, but it also causes problems in data transmission.

Receiver echo is much more disruptive for data transmission than transmitter echo. As illustrated in Figure 23-13, receiver echo occurs when the signal is reflected back to the transmitter by the 4WTS at the receiving end, then bounced again off the 4WTS at the transmitting end of the circuit and sent back toward the receiver.

Singing echo is feedback, pure and simple. The signal goes into an endless loop of being bounced between the two 4WTSs, as shown in Figure 23-14, and is distorted beyond all recognition.

The longer the distance of the transmission, the worse echoes distort the signal. Over short distances, the echo doesn't have time to confuse the receiver. That's because the

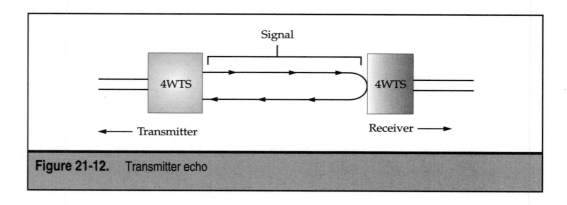

Figure 21-12. Transmitter echo

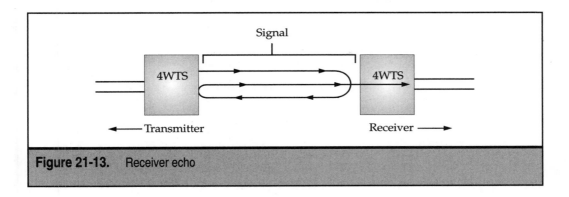

Figure 21-13.   Receiver echo

echoed signal arrives and dissipates before the receiver has interpreted the original signal, so the receiver might not notice the echo at all. At longer distances, though, the echo arrives well after the receiver has started processing the original signal. Therefore, the receiver may interpret the echo as a new signal, which the receiver may not be able to process quickly enough. This can cause corruption and retransmission of transmitted data.

Luckily, there is help for echoes. They can be fixed by balancing the impedance of the 4WTS with the impedance of the 2-wire facility, as shown in Figure 23-15.

Now That We Know What's Broken, Who's Going to Fix It?

In this section, we've seen what can go wrong with WAN links, as well as a little about how to diagnose and even fix them. Right now, you're probably wondering whose responsibility it is to fix them.

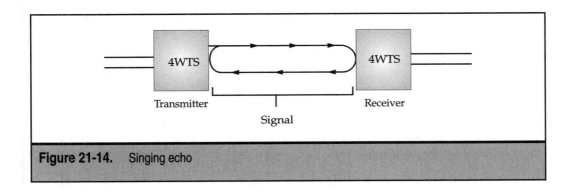

Figure 21-14.   Singing echo

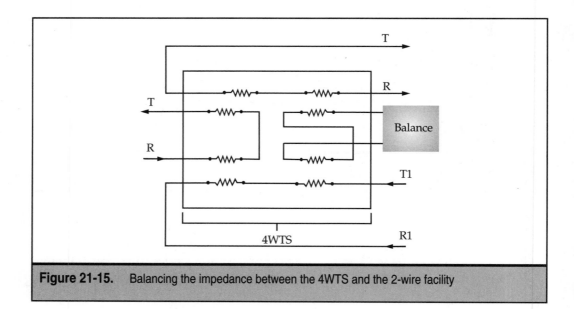

Figure 21-15.   Balancing the impedance between the 4WTS and the 2-wire facility

Clearly, there are a lot of things that can go wrong in a lot of different places. Who fixes them depends entirely upon where the problem occurs. Different portions of the transmission system belong to different entities, and all of the ownership is determined by federal laws and regulations. To make matters more confusing, the laws and regulations seem to be in a constant state of flux.

Unfortunately, the best advice I can offer right now is to monitor the situation closely. As the effects of the Telecommunications Act of 1996 unfold, we'll no doubt see the role of the various telecommunications service providers change. Perhaps eventually telecommunications service providers will all function a little like the value-added carriers we mentioned earlier in this chapter, who take end-to-end responsibility for wide area links. Who knows, maybe, just maybe it will soon be easy to find the right person to handle the problems on the WAN links, wherever they occur.

CHAPTER 22

Encryption

Authentication, which will be covered in detail in Chapter 23, is an obvious requirement for most computer users and definitely for any business. The need for encryption is a bit different, and as such, encryption tools have a slightly different audience.

The key distinction is this: with authentication, the goal is to simply prove that people communicating across electronic links are who they claim to be. With encryption, you have to assume that that electronic link is vulnerable to tampering or compromise by malicious outsiders. Encryption is designed solely to foil that tampering.

THE ORIGINS OF ENCRYPTION

The first well-known implementation of encryption dates back to Julius Caesar, who reportedly used a simple substitution cipher to communicate with his friends and generals on the battlefield.

You're probably already familiar with the Caesar cipher, where the alphabet is rotated some arbitrary number of letters in one direction in order to scramble a message. One simple example involves rotating one letter to the right, thus:

Plaintext: **A   B   C   D   E . . .**

Ciphertext: B   C   D   E   F . . .

A message encoded with a Caesar cipher would look like this:

Plaintext: **The monkey flies at midnight.**

Ciphertext: Uif npolfz gmjft bu njeojhiu.

While the "security" that a Caesar cipher gives you is largely nonexistent, Caesar ciphers are still around today. Their major implementation is known as "ROT13," a cryptosystem in which the alphabet is rotated 13 places either way such that A = N, B = O, C = P, and so on. As a bonus, with ROT13, the same algorithm can encrypt and decrypt the plaintext.

ROT13 is used in many situations where the recipient will want to avoid seeing the plaintext until later: mainly, puzzle answers and movie or video game "spoilers." Most newsreaders and many e-mail clients have ROT13 built in (in Netscape Messenger, this feature is under View | Unscramble).

ENCRYPTION TODAY

Not to do any disservice to the ancient Romans, but ROT13 as a secure encryption algorithm is simply not going to cut it today. Today's encryption environment is a high-stakes, mission-critical market.

The search for a secure cryptosystem began in earnest in the 1800s, and became more and more involved with the two World Wars. The successful Polish/British cryptanalysis of the Enigma, a German encryption device used during World War II, is legendary in the crypto community.

Today, the search is not so much on a secure cryptosystem (there are dozens that have never been broken), but rather on how to keep these cryptosystems out of the hands of terrorists and other nefarious sorts. An answer has not exactly been forthcoming.

ENCRYPTION IN PRACTICE

The same issues surround encryption that surround authentication. Early implementations of encryption solutions were built upon secret keys. With the advent of public key cryptography, public-key-based encryption applications are now the preferred method of secure electronic communications.

As with authentication, secure messaging is the primary use for encryption tools. Client-based applications like Netscape Messenger, WorldTalk WorldSecure Client, and Entrust/Express extend the functionality of an individual's e-mail reader by allowing the use of digital signatures and encrypted messages. You can also obtain personal encryption tools like Symantec Norton Your Eyes Only, SecureWin Technologies SecureWin, Entrust/ICE, and WinMagic SecureDoc, each of which allow you to encrypt files stored on your hard drive. Then there's secure Web browsing: protocols like SSL and S-HTTP, which are used on Web servers (and are built in to your Web browser) to provide secure communications over the Internet. We'll discuss each of these applications in turn.

You'll find that authentication and encryption products are almost always one and the same. Your e-mail application plug-in can authenticate a message through a digital signature, encrypt it with a secure algorithm, or do both. In fact, it's very rare for a user to send an encrypted message without also authenticating it. The added benefits of verifying the sender's identity and the integrity of the message are considerable. And, since the bulk of the processing burden is consumed by the much more involved encryption algorithm, the addition of a small hash-and-sign operation after encryption is finished is usually insignificant when compared to the speed of the encryption operation.

Building the Encrypted Message

Let's assume you have successfully obtained a digital certificate from your certificate authority (local or off-site), and your public and private keys have been successfully installed on your local machine. The full details of certificates and CAs can be found in Chapter 23, which we'll assume you are familiar with.

Your next step, as with authentication, is to compose a message and include any attachments you'd like. With encryption, the use of attachments is commonplace, as messages that need encrypting are much more likely to be composed of large, ongoing document projects like strategic business plans, corporate financials, or project development specs.

Regardless of the message content, you simply instruct your messaging system to encrypt the message, and digitally sign it if you'd like, as shown in Figure 22-1.

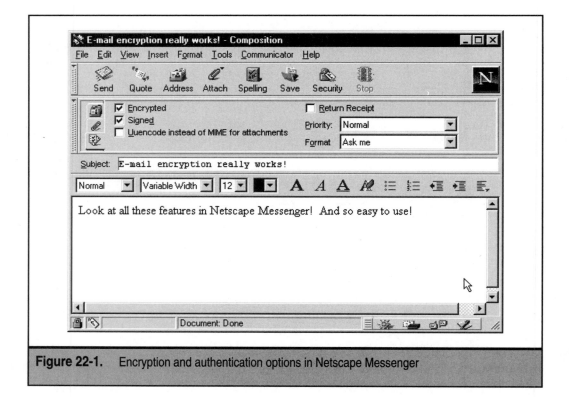

Figure 22-1.   Encryption and authentication options in Netscape Messenger

The Encryption Process

After you choose to send the message, your client will encrypt it for you using your recipient's public key. You can obtain your recipient's public key through a common CA that you are both a member of, or your recipient can directly mail his or her key to you (though this is less secure).

If you have elected to digitally sign your message, it will be hashed, and then the hash value will also be encrypted with your private key. This differs from the encryption algorithm, where the recipient's public key is used to encrypt the message. Figure 22-2 outlines how these two functions work together in one transaction.

Without delving too deeply into the theoretical arcana of encryption, the idea is to apply a one-way algorithm against the digital contents of your message and convert that message into garbage that can only be decoded by the intended recipient.

In order to do that, you will likely have to choose an algorithm to perform the encryption, and as with everything in computing, there is substantial debate as to which algorithm is best. Here is my take on the messy state of today's encryption algorithms and which one you should use.

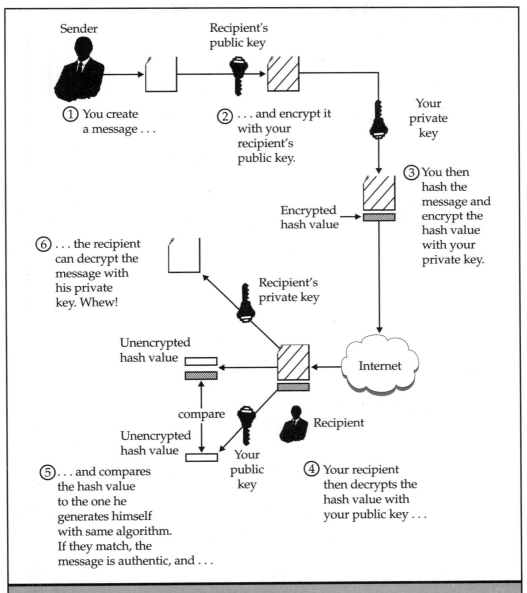

Figure 22-2.   Encrypting and digitally signing a message

Encryption Algorithms

Encryption algorithms is a complicated topic with RSA, DES, and DSA the best known (although each has a different application). Be advised that both public and secret key algorithms are discussed below.

RSA

RSA is the grandfather of cryptographic algorithms, and it is widely regarded as the most secure encryption algorithm on the market in wide use. It is also the only real choice for a public key cryptography algorithm (most of the algorithms below are secret key algorithms). Invented by (and named for) Ron Rivest (of MD5 fame), Adi Shamir, and Leonard Adleman in 1977, RSA uses two large prime numbers and some essentially one-way mathematics to generate a public and private key pair. To encrypt, the plaintext is subjected to an exponential function involving the recipient's public key. It can only be decrypted with the corresponding private key. RSA is widely implemented today, and is, in fact, in wider use than any other public key cryptosystem.

Recently, RSA sponsored a challenge to break a 56-bit private key, and the attack was successful in 39 days of brute force number crunching. On the whole, RSA has stood up extremely well to attacks and is regarded as secure. The algorithm is patented (and subject to licensing) and expires in the year 2000.

DSA

DSA (Digital Signature Algorithm) is part of the NIST's DSS (Digital Signature Standard), proposed for use in 1991. For all intents and purposes, when you hear about DSA and DSS, they are both part of the same thing: a standardized algorithm for performing digital signature calculations. DSA's introduction sent shock waves through the crypto community, with many of its members assuming a conspiracy was afoot to do away with RSA in favor of a government-developed standard.

Unlike RSA, DSA is only good for digital signature functions. It is not designed for encryption at all. As such, it is more limited in its application (in fact, the NIST has no public key cryptography standard at all, although DES is certified as a secret key standard). Much of DSA's criticism focuses on its functionality (limited), its speed (slightly slower than RSA; although with RSA the signature takes longer, with DSA, the verification takes longer), and its origins (the NSA, which many feared had embedded a trap door into the code). After complaints that the key length was too short and the security of DSA was called into question, the length was doubled.

We're getting up on a decade later, and the battle between DSA and RSA still rages on. Lawsuits are pending, patent infringements have been alleged, and DSA is slowly starting to show up in some applications. With the force of the government behind it, it's only a matter of time before the field becomes interminably muddied.

DES

Originally developed by IBM, DES (Defense Encryption Standard)—also known as DEA and DEA-1—is another much-maligned cousin of RSA. Contrary to common belief, DES is *not* part of a public key cryptosystem at all. Rather, it is a simple and not entirely secure secret key cryptosystem based on an algorithm called a block cipher. DES is the officially certified cryptosystem of the U. S. government, much to the chagrin of cryptographers everywhere.

DES keys have been quickly broken through brute force and through an attack called linear cryptanalysis, although these attacks are not altogether feasible. Of greater concern is the problem of secure key exchange, which we discuss in Chapter 23. So, with all these drawbacks, why is DES accepted as a standard? It is 100 to 10,000 times faster than RSA because of its simplicity. It's also just as secure as any other secret key algorithm on the market.

Triple-DES

To mitigate some of the problems with DES, Triple-DES (often abbreviated as 3DES) was developed. Triple-DES, in its widest implementation, uses two keys to strengthen the security of DES-encrypted plaintext. In standard Triple-DES, the plaintext is encrypted with key #1, decrypted with key #2, and reencrypted with key #1. This makes cryptanalysis much more difficult than standard DES. Triple-DES is a widely implemented standard for secret key cryptosystems, although it is not approved as a government standard.

Key Exchange with Diffie-Hellman

Diffie-Hellman (invented in 1976) was the first public key algorithm ever devised, although it cannot be used for encryption. Instead, Diffie-Hellman is used to solve the key exchange problem of secret key algorithms like DES. Diffie-Hellman uses a simple formula to take two random numbers generated by the sender and receiver and use them to generate a secret key that only the two of them can know, even if the entire transmission between the two parties has been overheard. Diffie-Hellman can also be extended to work with more than two parties.

If you choose to employ DES, you'll need some way of exchanging the secret key. This can be done with a key exchange algorithm like Diffie-Hellman, or you can simply generate a secret key, then use a public key algorithm like RSA to encrypt the secret key, and then send that encrypted message to the recipient. Using Diffie-Hellman instead of RSA in this situation allows you to avoid two problems: first, using RSA means setting up some form of PKI, which can be a pain; second, Diffie-Hellman's patent has expired, so it's free—unlike RSA.

Then again, if you opt to use RSA to encrypt DES keys, you're going to have to set up a public key infrastructure anyway, so why not just use the more secure RSA algorithm for all your cryptography needs, instead of having RSA and DES together? That's a question no one will be able to answer for you (although there are thousands who would like to try)!

The Endless List of Other Secret Key Block Ciphers

Most cryptographic algorithms you'll hear about are block ciphers like DES. They are designed for use with secret key cryptosystems, and you'll have to come up with another way of exchanging keys (like Diffie-Hellman or RSA for encrypting the key, as described above). Block ciphers are called this because they work on fixed-size chunks, or blocks, of plaintext data at a time. Typically, this is 64 bits. A block cipher will encrypt the first 64 bits of your message, then move on to the next 64 bits, and so on, until the end is reached. Each block is treated separately and independently. This often causes block ciphers to be slow in comparison to stream ciphers, which we'll cover in a moment.

RC2—RIVEST CIPHER 2 RC2 (also known as "Ron's Code 2") is another Ron Rivest job, a proprietary block cipher built for RSA Data Security as a secret key alternative to DES. The code remains a secret and is not patented. It's also two or three times faster than DES and can be made as secure or as weak as you'd like through longer or shorter key lengths. RC2 has another thing going for it in that software manufacturers can gain speedy export approval if their security products use 40-bit keys and RC2 algorithms; DES is rarely approved for export at all regardless of key length. RC2 is no more vulnerable to attack than DES and is an excellent (and free) alternative.

RC5—RIVEST CIPHER 5 RC5 is a fast block cipher with multiple routines (like Triple-DES) designed to heighten security. Keys can be up to 2,048 bits in length. RSA is patenting RC5, which means it will require a license to use. There is currently minimal support for RC5 in the real world.

IDEA—INTERNATIONAL DATA ENCRYPTION ALGORITHM IDEA is a 128-bit secret key algorithm that has considerable popularity as an alternative to DES. Its speed is also comparable to DES, and even though 2^{51} of the 2^{128} possible keys are regarded as weak, IDEA is considered fairly strong. (It sounds like a lot at first, but those weak keys are extremely unlikely to be chosen, statistically speaking.) IDEA is patented, and is the algorithm behind the encryption functions of PGP (see Chapter 12; RSA is used for key management and digital signatures). Otherwise, IDEA has found only moderate acceptance.

SKIPJACK Skipjack (completed in 1990) is the algorithm behind the highly controversial Clipper chip, the NSA's hardware solution for providing encryption services with a catch: the secret key is escrowed and can be used by the government for "backdoor" access to otherwise secret communications. Skipjack itself uses 80-bit keys and its details are classified, but small groups of cryptographers with limited access to the algorithm have found it to be secure. The key escrow issues behind Clipper, however, are the main concerns that Skipjack has found itself embroiled in. Skipjack can only be implemented in government-authorized hardware, not in software.

CAST   CAST is a 64-bit algorithm designed by Canadians Carlisle Adams and Stafford Tavares. CAST was named for its inventors and in homage to its strength (as in "cast iron") and its randomness (as in "cast dice"). The inventors were right: CAST has stood up remarkably well to all sorts of attacks, and it is widely implemented in software today. It may also become a standard for the Canadian government, and it is patent pending.

BLOWFISH   Blowfish is crypto expert Bruce Schneier's take on a block cipher. It was designed to be fast, simple, and to use keys up to 448 bits long for extra security. Schneier's experiment was a grand success. The algorithm is in the public domain, and it has found wide acceptance in real-world applications.

SAFER—SECURE AND FAST ENCRYPTION ROUTINE   SAFER is a block cipher developed in 1993 by James Massey for Cylink Corp. It has implementations with 64-bit keys and 128-bit keys and is freely available. It is considered to be secure, but has not found wide implementation in the real world, although support for it appears to be growing.

GOST   GOST is a Soviet bloc algorithm used for unclear purposes during the Cold War. GOST uses 256-bit keys and is extremely secure. There is also a GOST digital signature algorithm like DSA. As a Russian algorithm, you are unlikely to run into it in any commercial application.

LUCIFER   Lucifer is a 128-bit block cipher dating back to the early 1970s. It has been broken by several different cryptanalytic attacks and is essentially a dead algorithm.

FEAL   FEAL is a Japanese block cipher with 64-bit keys. It was intended to be a faster alternative to DES, but turned out to be ridiculously simple to break, and is now one of the laughingstocks of the cryptography community and has virtually no support outside of theoretical applications.

Secret Key Stream Ciphers

These algorithms belong to a different family of secret key ciphers than the above algorithms, called stream ciphers. Stream ciphers are designed to work on small units of data (usually one bit at a time), rather than large blocks as block ciphers do. Thus, a stream cipher is generally much faster than any block cipher. Much of the research into stream ciphers is still theoretical, though, and real-world applications are currently limited to a handful of algorithms, outlined below.

RC4—RIVEST CIPHER 4   RC4 is the leading stream cipher, and it is officially a trade secret of RSA Data Security, although the code has been leaked through the Internet. Still, it is subject to license from RSA. RC4 has been shown to be quite secure, and if key length is kept at 40 bits, developers can quickly gain export approval. RC4 can be found in many cryptographic software applications and is part of the Cellular Digital Packet Data specification.

SEAL—SOFTWARE-OPTIMIZED ENCRYPTION ALGORITHM   SEAL is a pseudo stream cipher completed in 1993 and optimized for 32-bit processors. SEAL is very fast, but it is also very new and has not been subjected to many cryptanalytic attacks. A patent is pending.

PKZIP   Roger Schlafly's compression algorithm also includes encryption if you choose it. An early stream cipher, PKZIP encryption can be hacked in a matter of a few hours on any PC. If you want security on your compressed files, you should not use PKZIP's built-in encryption.

WAKE—WORD AUTO KEY ENCRYPTION   WAKE is another stream cipher that is very fast, although this algorithm has been found susceptible to some attacks. It has waning support in the industry, but can still be found in a few applications.

Other Public Key Ciphers

The preceding are the most widely used public key ciphers. However, there are other public key encryption technologies available, which we will discuss briefly.

POHLIG-HELLMAN   Pohlig-Hellman is a simple, proprietary public key cryptography algorithm that is surprisingly similar to RSA. It is rarely implemented in the real world, but it is available for license.

ELGAMAL   ElGamal is currently the only public key cryptography algorithm (there are literally thousands of versions) that can be implemented without obtaining licenses and paying royalties. It is similar in design to the Diffie-Hellman algorithm, is comparable in security to RSA, and is only slightly slower than RSA. Has there been a mad rush to ElGamal? No. Will you find it supported in any software application? Perhaps, but RSA currently remains infinitely more popular in use.

ELLIPTIC CURVE CRYPTOGRAPHY   Expect to hear a lot more about elliptic curve cryptography in the coming years. Elliptic curves are geometric and mathematical constructs that can be used in place of the modular multiplication operations in traditional public key cryptosystems. Elliptic curve mathematics was originally touted to be superior in its ability to hold up against cryptanalytic attacks, but that claim has been debated and is questionable. Outside of one implementation by NeXT Computer, elliptic curve cryptography has yet to really find any wide implementation. However, it has become something of a buzzword in the cryptography field, so expect to see implementations popping up over time, along with a more official word about its security.

So Which One Do I Use?

Choosing from this mess is no simple task, although there are some guidelines you can follow:

▼   If you want a genuine public key cryptography solution for internal use, RSA will serve all your needs admirably.

■   If you are developing software for a government entity or need to communicate with government employees, you may be stuck with a secret key encryption scheme (DES) and DSA for digital signatures. Key exchange can be done through RSA or Diffie-Hellman.

▲   If you need simple secret key cryptography (for personal or limited use), Triple-DES, RC2, CAST, and Blowfish are all excellent choices and will provide plenty of speed.

OTHER FUNCTIONS OF ENCRYPTION

As we will do with authentication in Chapter 24, we've focused our discussion of encryption on secure messaging, as that is its most prevalent implementation. Of course, encryption has many additional functions outside of sending secure e-mail.

Personal Encryption Tools

The most obvious use for encryption is for protecting sensitive data on your computer, whether or not you intend to share this data with anyone else. If physical access to your computer is a possibility (and really, where isn't it?), then a personal encryption tool is a great way to protect your data.

Do a Web search for these types of systems and you'll find hundreds. That's because while designing a full-fledged PKI system is extremely difficult, building a one-shot, stand-alone personal encryption application is pretty simple. In fact, any decent programmer can put together an encryption tool in a manner of minutes, and source code for most of the common algorithms is freely available.

Still, it's probably best to leave cryptography to the experts, and encryption software is very affordable; it could easily earn back its value by discouraging data theft attempts. Look at packages like Network Associates' PGP for Personal Privacy or Symantec's Norton Your Eyes Only for a couple of mainstream encryption tools, both of which are bristling with advanced features, as shown in Figure 22-3.

With personal encryption tools, the algorithm is not as important as it is in secure messaging. For example, if you encrypt a file on your hard drive, you can implement DES without fear that your private key is going to be compromised, because you never transmit the key to anyone else.

You can protect your key any way you see fit—on a floppy disk, on a cryptographic token, or just leave it on the hard drive. The other side to this coin is that you absolutely need a stellar password to protect access to your key. Remember: If someone can gain physical access to your system, your private key will be easily obtainable. Only a very strong password will be able to prevent them from making your encryption scheme completely transparent.

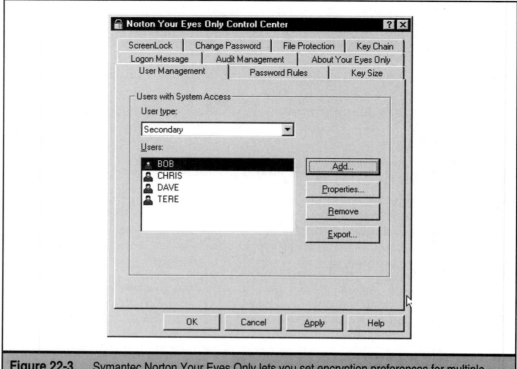

Figure 22-3. Symantec Norton Your Eyes Only lets you set encryption preferences for multiple users

File- or Disk-Based Encryption?

There is some debate over which is better—applications like Norton Your Eyes Only, which encrypt on a file-by-file (or directory-by-directory) basis; or programs like WinMagic SecureDoc, which encrypt at the block level of your disk drive, generally encrypting the entire contents of the drive. While file-based encryption tools let you have more control over the encryption process, disk-based tools are faster and more secure because they encrypt everything on the drive—including temporary and swap files that may unwittingly hold remnants of confidential information.

The jury is still out, and both kinds of personal encryption tools have their uses. If your cryptography needs are limited, with only a few files needing protection, a file-based tool will probably suit you just fine. For mission-critical security or heavy encryption usage, a disk-based tool with the private key stored on a floppy disk or cryptographic token is your best bet.

Encrypted Web Browsing

Secure Internet services will become more and more important over the coming years, and secure browsing protocols are already in wide use.

S-HTTP

S-HTTP is the Secure Hypertext Transfer Protocol, and it is also known as HTTPS or https. S-HTTP is an application-layer extension to the standard HTTP Web protocol, designed to support encryption during an HTTP session. Because it is application dependent, S-HTTP is limited in its deployability. It can also be implemented without the use of public key cryptography.

SSL

SSL, or Secure Sockets Layer Handshake Protocol, was developed by Netscape and is the current public key cryptography standard for secure Web browsing and transaction processing. SSL is built-in to Netscape and Microsoft browsers and most Web servers, and it operates on TCP port 443. Unlike S-HTTP, SSL is a transport-layer service and is therefore application independent, so whether you are using HTTP, ftp, Telnet, or even gopher during your Internet session, the encryption process will occur transparently on the client system. This makes it preferable to S-HTTP for the major encryption need on the Internet: e-commerce.

As a Web site designer, you simply configure SSL on the server and then specify which pages require an SSL connection for access. CGI and other API routines can also be written to work with SSL.

When a client tries to access an SSL-enabled page, as shown in Figure 22-4, the server sends the client its certificate and algorithm preferences to the client. The client then generates a secret key, which it encrypts with the server's public key and sends back to the server. The server decrypts the secret key and authenticates it by sending an acknowledgement back to the client, encrypted with the secret key. The client then verifies that everything is kosher by returning the acknowledgement with the client's digital signature. The secure Web session is now enabled.

SSL supports a number of cryptographic algorithms. RSA is used during the initial handshaking steps. For the secret-key-encrypted acknowledgement, RC2, RC4, IDEA, DES, and Triple-DES are all used, based on configured preferences. MD5 is used as a message-hashing algorithm.

SET

SET, or Secure Electronic Transaction, is an emerging protocol for e-commerce, developed by Visa and MasterCard. It works much like SSL does, only it adds a bank or credit card company to the loop. Eventually, it should displace SSL for e-commerce transactions, as Internet purchasing continues to grow in popularity.

For more details, refer to Chapter 3, where we outlined the history and intricacies of the SET protocol.

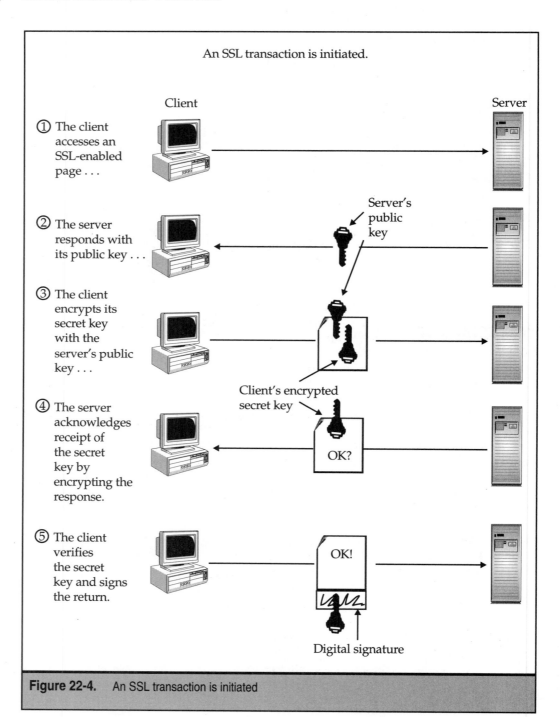

Figure 22-4.   An SSL transaction is initiated

SPEED CONSIDERATIONS

Let's face it. Cryptographic security comes at the expense of speed.

As key lengths get longer, so does the time it takes to encrypt a file. In fact, encrypting 2MB worth of files on a 400MHz dual Pentium II system takes over three minutes with Triple-DES and a 2,048-bit key. That's on a fast system; imagine how long it takes on an average PC.

As data storage formats and the e-mail that contains them grow larger and larger, this problem isn't going to get any better. Also, because necessary key lengths continue to grow, the problem of slow cryptography will continue to worsen.

Keep in mind that for a stand-alone e-mail client, where encryption tools are used on an occasional case-by-case basis, the few extra seconds an encryption routine adds to the task of sending a message is of little consequence. Because encrypted files are only slightly larger than their nonencrypted counterparts, network performance should not be affected by implementing cryptography on your network.

On the other hand, if you are running a Web server that serves up a substantial number of SSL-enabled pages for e-commerce or another secure application, the toll of performing numerous encryption tasks might become a difficulty.

Cryptographic Accelerators

In order to combat this problem, vendors are starting to enter the market with cryptographic acceleration hardware, PCI cards, or SCSI devices that have dedicated cryptographic processing chips for increasing the throughput of encryption and digital signatures operations. Rainbow Technologies' CryptoSwift series and nCipher's nFast products are among the market leaders.

Of course, there's a catch. Cryptographic accelerators like the ones mentioned are very specialized devices. Currently, CryptoSwift only supports SSL transactions for Netscape and Microsoft Web servers. nFast only supports SSL on Netscape. If you use S-HTTP, you're out of luck. And if SSL is displaced by SET or another emerging e-commerce protocol (which is very likely), these devices will suddenly be useless.

And they aren't cheap. nCipher's high-end accelerator costs over $10,000. That might be more than the server you connect it to costs. Before you invest in a crypto accelerator, make absolutely sure you need it. Make sure you aren't using SSL on pages where encryption isn't needed, and make sure the cryptographic processes are the bottleneck. Even busy e-commerce sites rarely perform more than one or two transactions per second. The top nFast box can crunch out 300 RSA signings per second, which may be much more than you'll ever need.

PROBLEMS IN PUBLIC KEY CRYPTOGRAPHY

Problems? In an emerging field like public key cryptography? It's probably stating the obvious, but public key cryptography is littered with problems that are going to take at least a decade to solve. Speed, which we touched on above, is a big one. Here are several more to get you thinking.

Cryptanalysis

Whenever a new algorithm or cryptographic implementation is introduced, cryptanalysis is sure to follow, and that's a good thing. Cryptanalysis is the science of discovering the original plaintext of an encrypted message, or recovering the private or secret key without prior knowledge.

Cryptanalysis ensures that algorithms are safe and that key lengths are long enough. RSA Data Security is perpetually sponsoring challenges (with prize money) to break its codes and recover private keys, and every few years an attack is successful. We've discussed weak algorithms and vulnerable key lengths in the section on algorithms above.

Cryptanalysis can be accomplished in a number of ways:

▼ **Ciphertext-only attacks**   Given the encrypted text of several messages, the attacker attempts to deduce the plaintext and/or the encryption key.

■ **Known-plaintext attacks**   Given the encrypted text and plaintext of several messages (obtainable through any number of ways), the attacker attempts to deduce the key. Obviously, this makes the attack easier than a ciphertext-only attack.

■ **Chosen-plaintext attacks**   Given the encrypted text and plaintext of several messages, the attacker also gets to choose the plaintext that gets run through the algorithm. This is more powerful than both previous attacks, because certain blocks of plaintext may reveal weaknesses in the key used to encrypt it.

▲ **Adaptive-chosen-plaintext attacks**   The same scenario as a chosen-plaintext attack, but the attacker can alter the plaintext for encryption at will. This is the most powerful form of attack that's widely known.

Several other less widely used attacks exist as well. Other forms of attack, like the so-called "rubber hose attack" that involves extortion, bribery, or torture, are not classified among cryptanalytic attacks, even though they are probably the most effective!

The problem with cryptanalysis arises with algorithms and key lengths that have not been widely studied and tested, yet are held up as secure. It's conceivable that a way to successfully reverse any algorithm has been discovered and not publicized. This is a common fear over government-sanctioned algorithms like Skipjack, but it's equally possible for any given encryption algorithm.

Over time, as computers becomes faster and cheaper, cryptanalytic attacks will become easier and easier to accomplish. In the minds of many, this is not a big concern, as key lengths can always be extended. In the minds of a few, a successful cryptanalytic attack is just a matter of time, no matter how secure you believe your algorithm and private key to be.

Poor Password Selection

This problem goes hand in hand with poor physical security. If your computer is stolen or someone breaks into the building, the key is in an attacker's hands and is protected only by a password of your choosing. Many of us have bad password selection habits: using a spouse's name, a phone number, or a simple word that we believe only to have meaning to us—or so we think.

Password crackers have become extremely sophisticated pieces of software that can often make short work of your key protection in a matter of hours. Forget advanced cryptanalysis—it's much easier to determine someone's private key by simply hacking the password that's used to encrypt it.

Therefore, it's critical that you and your users utilize well thought out passwords that are long enough to defy brute force character-based attacks and are not composed of a single, simple word. It's also important to change your password often: Every 60 to 90 days is a good figure that shouldn't cause too many headaches.

While this is undoubtedly good advice (you'll find more in Chapter 12), we are creatures of habit. Even worse, we're lazy when it comes to typing in passwords, and the shorter it is, the easier it is to remember. Instilling good password habits into your users isn't simple, but it can certainly pay off in the long run.

Attacks on Certificate Authorities

Let's assume your public key algorithms are secure, your key lengths are long enough, and your passwords are steel-reinforced. Your building is secure, you use cryptographic tokens and smartcards where necessary. You've basically done everything you can to build a secure environment. You're safe, right?

A potential weak link in the chain is the certificate authority, which you wouldn't normally think of as a place to attack. Of course, it makes perfect sense: Attack the PKI at its central nervous system and gain access to the entire chain.

Masquerading

The simplest attack is one where an outsider simply presents himself or herself as a trusted member of the organization and applies for a digital certificate. This will only work if the trusted member he or she is masquerading as does not already have a digital certificate; this may be quite common in implementations where the system is not used very often or where some less technical users rarely use e-mail at all.

In any case, when the attacker receives the certificate of the trusted member, he or she simply presents himself or herself as that person, and can then work his or her way into receiving sensitive communications. If your initial authentication process is secure, this kind of attack shouldn't be a problem. However, it is something you'll need to watch for if you outsource your CA operations.

Certificate Theft

A more sophisticated attack involves actually stealing the digital certificate of an exiting user. The attacker absconds with the certificate of a legitimate user on the system, then presents himself or herself as that user. The certificate can be stolen in any number of ways—through a request for a lost ID or copied directly from a user's computer, either in person or through a remote attack. Proper configuration of the CA and management of the key reissuance process is key to avoiding certificate theft, as is physical security and network firewalling.

Certificate Authority Private Key Compromise

The CA has its own private key, the master key that is used to issue, validate, and revoke all the certificates in the PKI. If a hacker obtains the private key of the CA, he or she can begin to perform these functions himself or herself, a frightening thought. It is therefore critical to ensure that the private key of the CA is exceptionally well protected. It should be as long as possible and should usually involve some form of cryptographic token or smart card security to protect it. The CA's private key should also be changed regularly, at least once a month.

Nefarious Deeds

Then there's bribery and other nefarious deeds, intended to get coerce a legitimate ID out of one of your security officers. There's not much you can do to prevent this outside of careful employee screening and random auditing.

Key Revocation

People quit. People get fired. Keys and passwords are compromised. These are the realities of business. What do you do if any of these things happens?

Revoked digital certificates are placed on what's known a Certificate Revocation List (CRL). This is simply a list of certificates that have been revoked before their scheduled expiration.

In a perfect world, every time a signature is checked, the CRL should be consulted. Unfortunately, key revocation was not heavy on the minds of the original PKI designers, and CRL implementations are currently iffy at best. The problem is that, in order to be thorough, the CRL must be nearly endless. New entries can be added, but old ones can not be removed until they would normally have expired (this can be a matter of years). This means that a CRL will typically begin to stretch into hundreds, thousands, or tens of thousands of entries for large organizations, and if complete authenticity is desired, this CRL must be checked every time a digitally signed message is received. This can take a very long time.

In order to mitigate the speed issue, many authentication clients simply don't check CRLs during signature authentication, leaving a gaping hole in the overall security of the process. Furthermore, many CRLs are only updated once a day or even once a week, leaving a time lag when the CRL's work is most critical—immediately after a firing or the discovery of the theft of a certificate.

Even worse is the interaction between multiple CAs and the distribution of these increasingly lengthy CRLs. How do you securely manage multiple CRLs for multiple organizations? No one has really figured out a method that works well, and there should be substantial research into improving the CRL process, probably through the implementation of a tree-based CRL standard, over the next few years.

Cross-Certification

Cross-certification is the process wherein two Certificate Authorities exchange key information and generate a trust relationship between each other. Cross-certification is particularly important if, for example, your company and your top customer want to build a web of trust, but each of you has your own in-house PKI.

It sounds simple, but this is certainly not a trivial task. First you'll have to be absolutely comfortable with the security policies of the other company. How are IDs issued? How is the CA protected from attack? What algorithms does the company use? If you're satisfied with the answers, then you have achieved an important first step.

Even then, the secure transmission of key information between two CAs is difficult enough, but as both organizations grow larger, the trust relationship becomes progressively more difficult to manage. The key revocation issues we discussed in the previous section are compounded when multiple CAs must be updated.

Take all of these concerns and add a third company to the mix. And a fourth. And a tenth. As the number of CAs in the web of trust grows linearly, the complexity of managing the web grows geometrically. With 10 companies, there are 45 trust relationships that may be required. And all of these companies may not trust each other. In fact, if two of them are your customers, some will likely be competitors who specifically do *not* trust each other. As you can see, the trust problems get complicated, quickly.

This is one of the major arguments for outsourcing your CA: Let someone else deal with this mess. Still, it's a difficult problem that is going to remain difficult for some time. While some PKI solutions do address cross-certification agreements, there is considerable confusion and skepticism over their security. This is an area that will have to be watched over the next few years, as the procedure for cross-certifying CAs is streamlined and secured.

Multinational Issues

If you want to use encryption products in a foreign office, build a web of trust with a foreign company, or export a software product with encryption features built in, you're staring at a huge mess.

Thanks to Cold War treaties, cryptography products are covered under U.S. munitions laws, alongside guns and tanks. This means that if you sell an encryption product overseas without a license, you can be convicted for foreign arms dealing!

The government takes this very seriously, and numerous inventors (even cryptography hobbyists) of encryption products who post their applications on the Internet have found themselves visited by men in black who abscond with all the computer equipment in the house. Even presenting material *about* cryptography in public has been subject to government scrutiny, although, thankfully, this has lessened considerably.

Still, if you want to implement encryption off of American soil, you'll need to make sure the product you purchase is approved for overseas use. Typically, 40-bit cryptographic products are allowed anywhere, since these keys can be cracked through brute force in a matter of hours or days. Some 56-bit products have been allowed to be exported, although the government typically requires the purchaser to present proof that some kind of key escrow plan is in the works.

Subsidiaries of U.S. companies and their foreign offices can typically obtain 128-bit encryption products. However, 255-bit products are not allowed for export. Also, if you are a bank or another financial company, you'll typically find it easier to get better encryption products for e-commerce usage (meaning, you won't necessarily be able to also use the system for secure e-mail).

On the other hand, the United States has no import restrictions on foreign cryptography products, so you can implement, for example, a full-blown 255-bit encryption system between a U.S. office and an Irish subsidiary using a PKI from Baltimore Technologies, an Irish company. Of course, if you have offices in other countries, you'll be subject to their import restrictions as well, and this can get complicated pretty fast.

Managing a multinational encryption network is currently a mess, but this should get better over the next few years, as post–Cold War hysteria continues to lessen, as Europe unites to become the ECC, and as cryptography products continue to gain popularity domestically.

Key Escrow

Key escrow is simply the practice of backing up private keys. It is a vehemently controversial topic.

Key escrow, as a technology, is not necessarily a bad idea. If you are the security officer of a company and one of your users forgets his or her password or crashes his or her hard disk, key escrow saves you the trouble of revoking the old digital certificate and creating a new one. Instead, you can simply restore his or her private key from a secure backup, and the user will be up and running as if nothing had happened. Provided there is no possible way for an outsider to obtain these key backups, key escrow can be a great thing.

Key escrow, as a government initiative, scares the pants off of most people. As part of the NSA's Capstone project, the government has been trying to mandate that encryption products contain key escrow features, ostensibly so that if cryptography products fall into the hands of drug dealers and arms traders, the government can read their e-mail.

With the exception of the Clipper chip, the government's key escrow initiatives have failed. To most, the idea reeks of Big Brother. There is also the issue of the security of the key escrow agent. Would any sane person trust the government to safely store all the private keys in the world without fear of the database being compromised? Government computers are subject to more hacking attempts than any others, and many of these attempts are successful. What about a third party to store the escrowed keys? Wouldn't that be an inviting target to hackers? And how are all of these keys going to be transmitted to the escrow agent without fear of compromise along the way?

These serious questions and others have stalled the key escrow initiative, perhaps permanently. Still, the idea is constantly kicking around, but unless businesses are required to implement escrow services, don't expect to see off-site key escrow services implemented any time soon.

Limitations of Public Key Cryptography

There are also some built-in problems with public key cryptography that make it difficult to implement. One of the major issues is how do you encrypt files for numerous recipients? Because encryption is done with the recipient's public key, only one person can be the recipient of an encrypted transmission. To anyone else on the CC: list, the file will be unreadable. If 100 people need the file, do you encrypt the file 100 different times? In truth, a secret key encryption system works much better in this situation.

What if keys are corrupted or lost, and there's no quick way to authenticate that the request for key reissuance is genuine? During initial setup of a digital identity, this is usually not a problem. But if a key is corrupted in the middle of a busy workweek, how do you take care of the situation without disrupting business?

Entrust and its brethren have been working toward on hybrid public/secret key cryptography systems to address issues like these, but with each change made to a cryptosystem, the more potential it has to be broken open. While public key cryptography is still in its infancy, it's issues like these that are slowing its deployment.

User Training

If you've made it this far, you've done better than most. While we've done our best to keep the text at a real-world level, the concepts contained in this chapter and the next are still exceptionally heavy on theory.

Introducing something with the complexity of a PKI into your organization is going to leave you wondering how you teach the foundations of cryptography to your user base.

The sobering realization is that you can't.

The average manager simply wants the e-mail to work, be fast, and be secure. That's it. He or she isn't interested in the opposing merits of DES and RSA. And they're not concerned with key escrow debates. To him or her, hashing means something completely different.

How do you train a user like this about the importance of verifying the certificates of users outside the company, using a long enough key, or protecting his or her key with an appropriate password? It isn't easy.

In user training, stay away from heavy technical details and work on real-world applications of the technology. This goes for any new technology, but it's especially appropriate for encryption and authentication. Explain the benefits of proper use of the tools, how they are properly used so as not to defy company policy, walk them through the signing and encryption procedures, and warn them of the consequences of improper use. And keep your door open for questions. There will be many.

ADDITIONAL RESOURCES

It's hard to squeeze everything you need to know about cryptography into two chapters. If you want in-depth details about algorithms, cryptographic theory, large number factoring, cryptanalysis, and government initiatives, we can recommend two excellent references.

First is Bruce Schneier's book, *Applied Cryptography*, the avowed bible of the cryptographic industry, which contains just about everything you could possibly want to know about encryption and authentication. It's very heavy on mathematical theory, but it's an invaluable reference, even including C source code for implementing cryptographic algorithms yourself.

Another good reference is RSA Data Security's "Answers to Frequently Asked Questions About Today's Cryptography." This reference is currently in version 3.0 and has the added benefit of being free for download from RSA's Web site at http://www.rsa.com/rsalabs/newfaq. You will probably notice that, because the FAQ is kept up by RSA itself, it is heavily slanted in support of its own products and proprietary algorithms. As RSA is the undisputed industry leader in cryptographic services, this isn't as bad as it sounds, but it is important to keep in mind while you're browsing its pages.

CHAPTER 23

Authentication

If you walk into a grocery store to buy a nice bottle of Cabernet, any number of authentication processes occur, maybe without your knowledge. If you pay with an ATM or debit card, you'll enter your PIN code at the terminal. The PIN and card information is then wired to the bank, where the PIN's accuracy is verified and your available balance is checked.

Pay by a credit card, and the cashier may check your signature on the receipt against the one on the back of the card. The credit card processing company will also be contacted to ensure the card hasn't been reported stolen and that your credit line hasn't been exceeded.

If you write a check, the cashier will probably ask to see your driver's license to verify it matches the address printed on it. The cashier will likely record your license number as a safeguard, too, and may use a computerized check verification service to ensure you aren't committing fraud.

If you're fortunate enough to appear under 21 years of age, the cashier will want proof of age as well. The authentication process doesn't stop there—you can also authenticate the merchant, checking its various business licenses. You can even authenticate the bottle of wine, by making sure it hasn't been tampered with, and later that night, by making sure the vineyard and/or year printed on the cork corresponds to that on the bottle.

In a nutshell, unless you're gray on the head and carrying a lot of cash, you'll go through four or five simple authentication transactions in the space of a minute's time.

Authentication is something we do every day. Whether through a policeman's badge, a credit card number, a secret handshake, your business card, or the password you use to access your computer at work, authentication is a vital part of every business, and even daily life.

THE EVOLUTION OF COMPUTER AUTHENTICATION

Even in the early days of computing, authentication was basic and commonplace in commerce and government, particularly after the two World Wars and the dawn of the Red Menace. It thus remains a bit of a puzzle as to why authentication was never of real concern during the advent of computers.

Obviously, networked computers, and especially a beast like the Internet, had not been conceived of. If a computer was purchased, it was only going to be usable by a highly skilled individual with keys to the building and a specific purpose. Computers of the day weren't particularly useful, anyway. Perhaps they performed calculations too tough for the slide rule, or they calibrated a telescope. Either way, it was nothing anyone was going to go out of his or her way to *steal*.

Those days are long since gone, of course, but only in the last five to ten years have computer security and user authentication reached any semblance of being modern. Even now, authentication is a substantially advanced computing concept, and understanding the vagaries of digital certificates, hashing algorithms, certificate revocation, and hardware tokens can be daunting.

Still, we'll try our best within.

Passwords

Beyond locking a computer behind a thick door, passwords were the first real manifestation of computer security. And while a password is better than nothing, in most cases, it's not better by much. Still, many people place full faith in the ability of a password like "Julie" to protect their most sensitive personal and business information.

Cracking passwords is one of the simplest tools in the hacker's toolkit, and it's often the first avenue any hacker will try in attempting to break in to a system.

If simple guessing doesn't do the trick, or if accounts without passwords are not found, "brute force" (going letter by letter through the alphabet) often does the trick, and could crack a simple password like "Julie" in a few minutes. Even long and apparently obscure passwords like "persimmon" can be cracked quickly using a "dictionary attack," where a list of commonly used password text files is used to expedite the cracking process. (As it turns out, "persimmon" is often on that list.)

Many modern operating systems can be configured to store dictionary files like these locally, and prevent users from ever using the passwords contained in them in the first place. Many administrators also enforce minimum password lengths, as well, but many more system admins are not so strict, and on most networks, anything goes.

Even if an administrator is perfect in his or her job of preventing obvious passwords and requiring a sufficient minimum length and frequent changes, problems still remain. The more complex a password gets, the more help a user needs to remember it. How many times have you seen a password scribbled on a note and taped to a computer monitor? Or how often does one user share his or her password with another, not having time to go through the tedious logout-and-login procedure just to switch computers? As well, passwords can be easily coerced from unsuspecting users over the phone.

While the password problem will never be resolved, remember this: A good password is a long password. It also includes numbers, spaces, and nonalphanumeric characters. And of course, you should be able to remember it without having to write it down. Some good examples:

▼ 4score&7YEARS

■ BornOnThe18th!

▲ CalLicense295/XJG

It's not likely that a brute-force or dictionary attack will ever come close to cracking these passwords. (Then again, you may still be stymied because older systems will not accept many passwords like these!)

For protecting user information in public key cryptography and digital certificate applications, which we will cover shortly, passwords should be even more complex than those listed above. For these applications, a random line from a book is commonly used—for example, "He blooped across the used car lot now."—the first line on page 96 of Kurt Vonnegut's *Breakfast of Champions*.

Just don't underline the passage.

IP Address Authentication

While they are not altogether secure, passwords are generally sufficient security on closed networks.

When you connect your LAN to the Internet, that's a different story altogether.

We covered the basics of IP-based authentication in our discussion of firewalls in Chapter 12, but the topic bears repeating here. In a simple firewall configuration, you allow and deny access to your network based, in part, on the IP address of the computer requesting access.

If your network consists of the IP range 220.220.220.0 to 220.220.220.255, your authentication policy is simple: allow anyone in the 220.220.220.* range in, and keep everyone else out. You can further add remote, trusted users to the allowed range, thus building an access policy that can be applied both inside your organization and outside it.

IP Spoofing

"IP spoofing" is a commonly talked-about hack that involves a hostile computer masquerading as a trusted machine on your network, as shown in Figure 23-1. It essentially involves forging the address of the target machine (which is generally crashed or busied out with a DoS attack) and behaving as the target would in its stead. The result is bypassing a firewall and gaining full access.

While this attack has been known about since at least 1985, it is still a very difficult hack to pull off, and it is extremely rare in its occurrence. Most firewalls can now be configured to thwart spoofing attacks, but it often requires a savvy network administrator to do it (or at least a helpful manual).

Secret Key Cryptography

A major problem exists with IP-based authentication that often makes it inappropriate. First, any address-based security is only useful if you are attempting to authenticate the use of a shared resource. If you are trying to verify the identity of the sender of an e-mail message or ensure that message is complete, IP-based solutions are useless. For messaging purposes and file content validation, only a key system will work.

Key-based cryptography was designed to mitigate some of the weaknesses of password security and provide a new level of protection for secure messaging. Secret key cryptography was the first manifestation of a key-based cryptosystem.

Secret key cryptography is very simple in its application. The sender and receiver of a message or file simply agree on a key beforehand. A key is an alphanumeric expression that an encryption or decryption algorithm uses as the variable in scrambling or signing the message or file.

The size and content of the key is irrelevant. The important thing is that it is *secret*, and is known only by the two parties who desire secure communication. A message is signed or encrypted using a secret key, it is transmitted to the recipient, and is then verified or decrypted, also using the same key, as shown in Figure 23-2.

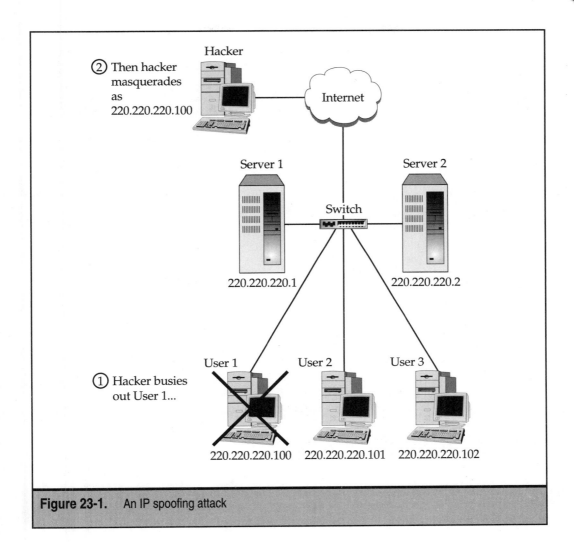

Figure 23-1. An IP spoofing attack

There's nothing inherently wrong with this procedure. In fact, if you can guarantee that the secret key is known only by the two parties and the key is used once and only once, this is one of the most perfect cryptosystems known, similar to the use of a "one-time pad."

The problem arises in exchanging that secret key. You can't very well send it in plain text e-mail, read it over the phone, or even drop it in the mailbox. The problem is further compounded when you involve more than two people who want to communicate. If you consider, for example, a company of 50 people who want secure communications, and

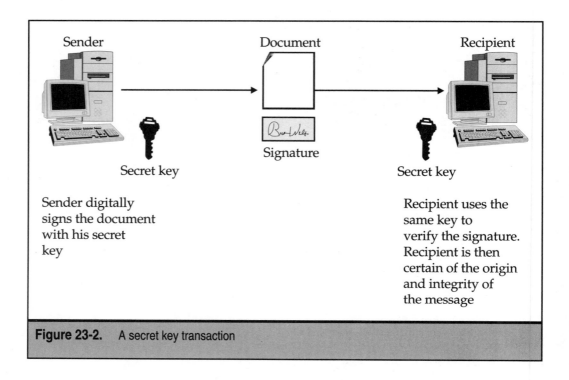

Figure 23-2. A secret key transaction

one is fired, a new key must be generated quickly and transmitted to the remaining employees. Managing this kind of system quickly becomes messy.

Authentication (as opposed to encryption) poses its own problems for secret key cryptography. Part of the point of authentication is to be able to prove, not only to your intended recipient but also to an independent third party that a message is genuinely yours. A message signed with a secret key can only be verified by the intended recipient. And conversely, how do you authenticate a message sent to you from someone outside the organization?

Public Key Cryptography

These limitations led to the advent of public key cryptography in 1976, when Whitfield Diffie and Martin Hellman (of Diffie-Hellman fame) described the concept. It's a very clever idea.

The critical difference between public key cryptography and secret key cryptography is that it uses two different keys for encryption and decryption. In public key cryptography, keys are paired up as "public" and "private"—a matched set that are usable only as a pair. The public key, which is made freely available to the world, can be used to encrypt a message. Only the bearer of the corresponding private key can decrypt the message. This private key is kept by its owner on a machine to which only he or she has access. This way, a secure e-mail can be sent from one person to another, without the two ever having corresponded before, simply by the former looking up the latter's public key.

Authentication works along a similar line. Using your private key, you use a "hashing algorithm" to generate a unique digital signature for an electronic message. Using your public key, the recipient can verify that the message is intact and that you indeed are the authentic author of the message.

The critical point to remember is that, in both an encryption and an authentication scenario, the transaction is one-way and cannot be reversed. Because the nature of the underlying cryptographic algorithms makes them unidirectional, a public key cannot be used to derive the private key upon which it is based. Once the private key is generated through a suitably random procedure, the public key is of minimal value in trying to determine the private key through brute force. But at the same time, the public key can absolutely prove the authenticity of a user or a message!

Public key cryptography solves many of the key management issues associated with the distribution of keys under a secret key infrastructure. Still, despite over 20 years in the making, public key cryptography is far from mature, and it has a number of remaining challenges before it becomes a fully proven and stable technology. Regardless, for the time being, public key cryptography presents the best option for authentication and encryption in any environment.

PUBLIC KEY CRYPTOGRAPHY AND AUTHENTICATION

What are the real functions of authentication?

Sure, it's important to be able to verify that Steve is the true sender of the message, but what else is authentication good for? Actually, more than you might think. Here's a rundown:

▼ **Verification of identity** Robert (the receiver) can verify that Steve (the sender) indeed sent the message.

■ **Ensuring the integrity of the message** Steve's message was not altered in transit (intentionally or accidentally). Robert cannot subsequently alter it after receipt, either.

▲ **Nonrepudiation of the message** Steve cannot later claim he did not send Robert the message.

E-mail is notorious as having none of these three traits, so how do you go about adding these features to something as insecure as electronic messaging? It starts with obtaining a digital certificate.

Digital Certificates

In order to generate keys, whether secret or public/private, a user needs a digital identity. This is established through obtaining a digital certificate (VeriSign calls it a digital ID). In full standards-compliant public key cryptography, these certificates are called X.509 public key certificates.

The analogy to a passport is commonly made with such a certificate. Like a passport, a digital certificate proves your identity and is issued and verified by a recognized authority. In cryptography, this authority is known as a certificate authority (CA), which we'll discuss in depth later in this chapter.

Digital Certificate Structure

Every time you digitally sign a message, you attach a copy of your digital certificate to it. Your digital certificate contains all the information a recipient would need to verify the authenticity of the message. A VeriSign digital ID is described below. (You can get more information about VeriSign, a leader in cryptography that we will use as a reference repeatedly in this chapter, at its Web site at http://www.verisign.com.)

Essentially, Figure 23-3 summarizes the X.509 certificate structure, a standardized way of organizing certificates.

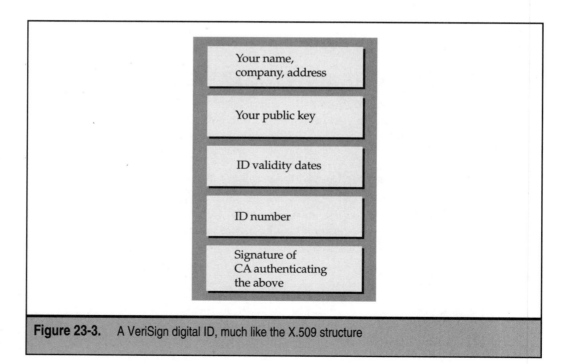

Figure 23-3.   A VeriSign digital ID, much like the X.509 structure

Note that the digital certificate not only contains information about you, but it is also certified as genuine by a third party, usually the MIS or security manager of your company, or an outside security solution provider like VeriSign or Entrust.

Where Do You Get a Digital Certificate?

Again, digital certificates are issued by certificate authorities. If you're looking for a digital certificate for personal use, you can obtain an ID through a company like VeriSign or Entrust. The cost is about $10 a year. If your company is rolling out digital certificates to many or all of its users, you may want to build your own CA on company grounds.

The CA simply provides a way for other users to verify your identity, and you can also use the CA to verify the authenticity of those who send messages to you. More on the intricacies of CAs follows later in this chapter.

So now we get down to the nitty-gritty details on public key cryptography. To fully explain the process of authentication, we'll follow the creation of a digital identity and an authenticated message from start to finish. We'll start with the backbone of public key cryptography: the certificate authority.

CERTIFICATE AUTHORITIES

A certificate authority (CA) is the central authority that issues digital certificates to a defined body of users, systems, or other components of a computer network. By digitally signing each of the certificates it issues, the CA implicitly connects the identity of the certificate's owner to a public key inside the certificate. This way, the authenticity of the digital certificate cannot be questioned. Figure 23-3 illustrates this concept.

The CA doesn't just issue certificates; it verifies them as well. Users on the network can use the CA's own public key certificate (sometimes called the root key) to authenticate the certificates of other users on the network. This way, users can be assured that the credentials other users present are legitimate, because the CA vouches for their authenticity.

Without a CA in the mix, public key cryptography would be prohibitively difficult. This is the very problem that PGP (see Chapter 12) faces today. Because a user's—and a company's—web of trust can grow infinitely large and complex, mainly due to the Internet, it would be unfeasible for each user to try to manage the additions, deletions, and changes of all of his or her contacts' digital certificates. A third party is required to centrally manage these services and, as discussed in Chapter 22, the services in question quickly become more complex than you may realize.

The Roles of the CA

A certificate authority performs a number of services for its "CA domain," the population of users and systems over which it has responsibility. The major responsibilities of the CA are as follows:

▼ **Issuing digital certificates**   The CA is responsible for creating certificates according to the specifications of the security officer. The CA can generate keys, or the user can generate his or her own keys and present them to the CA. We'll discuss certificate issuance in depth in the following section.

■ **Publishing digital certificates**   The CA has to allow access to the public keys of users in its CA domain for use in verifying messages and providing encryption services. Typically, these keys are stored in an LDAP directory.

■ **Revoking digital certificates**   If an employee is fired or a private key is compromised, that digital certificate must be invalidated. The management of this information requires a certificate revocation list (CRL), and will be discussed later as one of the problems of public key cryptography.

■ **Updating digital certificates**   Certificates expire after a predetermined time in order to prevent a brute-force factoring attack against a public key from being successful. A new certificate must be subsequently issued, and the CA must be updated accordingly.

▲ **Digital certificate backup**   If a private key is lost, a good CA must have some means of recovering that key. Keeping copies of private keys is also part of a key escrow scheme, a controversial requirement for some exported cryptography products.

Digital Certificate Issuance ·

As we've outlined above, digital certificates are issued by a certificate authority, be it centralized within your company, provided as a service by your school, or outsourced to a third-party provider like VeriSign.

If you intend to use your digital certificate outside the user base of the company or school that issued it to you (and who wouldn't want to?), then your CA must in turn have an authenticated identity. This is done by giving the CA a digital certificate of its own, and that digital certificate must be publicly verifiable. Usually, the CA simply obtains its digital certificate from one of the above well-known and reliable certificate providers, thus ensuring its public key is a matter of public record.

If you build your own CA in-house, you can set up restrictions and regulations over obtaining a digital certificate. You can require users to meet you in person, provide proof of identity in the form of a driver's license or a passport, obtain fingerprints and photographs, and even run a background check. The point is that the underlying technology doesn't really matter: you can be as stringent or as lax as you'd like, because you are a *person* actually issuing the certificate. (Yes, a computer performs all the technology behind it, but you are the one in control.)

If you obtain a personal digital certificate from VeriSign, you can obtain an ID in two classes. A Class 1 ID authenticates your e-mail address only and is placed in the publicly available VeriSign directory so it can be easily looked up by anyone on the Internet. For better authentication services, you can obtain a Class 2 ID, which authenticates your name and personal identity as well. A Class 2 ID is not really any harder to obtain (and because the transaction is not face to face, it's impossible to be sure who is really requesting the ID in the first place). The cost is $9.95 a year for a Class 1 ID, $19.95 a year for Class 2. Entrust offers a certificate similar to a VeriSign Class 1 ID for free.

What this all means is that your decision over whether to develop your own CA or outsource CA functions will depend, in part, on how much control you want over the certificate issuance procedure. We'll further discuss the in-house/outsource debate later in this chapter.

Key Management

Although securely issuing digital certificates is a certificate authority's most visible task, the management of those certificates and the keys they maintain is of paramount importance. Key management services are essential for building and maintaining a web of trust, because unless the CA has some means of identifying trusted and untrusted certificates, not to mention revoking trusted certificates that have gone sour, its services are useless. Once a public key has been issued, tracking and monitoring that key is essential.

Key management entails a number of services, outlined below:

▼   Specifying and tracking of untrusted certificates

■   Generation of random public key pairs

■   Secure storage and backup of private keys

■   Revocation and reissuance of new key pairs as they expire

■   Distribution of the CA's public key to publicly available directories

▲   Cross-certification with other CAs

But key management isn't just the job of the CA. Try as we might to entirely unload the burden of managing security from the user, it is still the user's job to keep his or her private key secure on his or her local machine. The user must also be able to securely obtain his or her key pair to start with, as well as transfer public keys with users outside the organization. This is especially true if CA activities are outsourced, or if cryptography services are limited to a handful of users who need it.

If a user's key is lost, corrupted, or compromised by an outsider, it is the user's responsibility to inform the rest of the world before any damage occurs. Again, this burden must be placed on the shoulders of the user alone.

As you can likely imagine, this is all a substantial amount of work, not only for the user, but especially for the CA. A CA has to be managed perfectly; there is no room for error, or else the entire infrastructure could crumble. And managing all of this is no small feat, especially considering the newness of the technology and its underlying theories to most network administrators.

These issues and others are the primary forces that drive the decision of implementing a public key infrastructure inside the organization our outsourcing it altogether.

Internal vs. External CAs

If authentication services will be a fringe feature for many of your users, if only a few actually need the services that advanced cryptography provides, or if your company's e-mail traffic doesn't consist of much financial or trade secret information, the decision about whether or not to outsource your CA is a simple one. If this describes your company, without a doubt, you should outsource your CA.

Cryptography is undoubtedly one of the most abstract and difficult-to-grasp concepts in modern computing. Furthermore, setting up and managing a certificate authority within your own walls is the most abstract and difficult part of cryptography, and it's not a task that you should embark upon lightly.

Still, for many companies, especially those heavily invested in e-commerce, providing in-house CA services is a critical part of establishing themselves as a legitimate purveyor of goods and services on the Internet. If you can fully manage you company's cryptography needs on your own—and provide related services to your employees, customers, and suppliers—you'll go a long way toward building the elusive web of trust that we so often talk about.

The Internal CA

There are some substantial advantages to having your CA on the premises. They revolve around the issue of control.

An in-house CA gives you, as the security officer, control over who has access to anything and everything. You set the standards for who can and who cannot obtain a digital certificate. You can require potential users stand before you as proof of who they say they are, submit proper identification, undergo drug and polygraph testing—whatever you desire! The point isn't *what* you do, it's that *you* are the one doing it.

This type of due diligence will give you (as well as your customers, suppliers, and boss) enormous faith that the users who are signing documents with their digital certificate are genuine, and haven't somehow subverted the issuance authentication process (not an altogether difficult feat in many cases). Therefore, if you need or want absolute control over the issuance of certificates (for example, if you allow customers Web-based access to your intranet to directly place their own orders into production), an in-house CA is really your only option.

Sounds great, huh? Well, building your own CA isn't exactly a picnic.

The problem is that the underlying technology of CAs is so new and immature, and not many people have much experience in this area, so the possibilities for making a mistake somewhere during the process are literally endless, despite the vehement claims of the vendors of CA software. And making a mistake on your CA is not like making a typo on the corporate home page: If you do it wrong, you may let the entire world have complete access to your most sensitive documents.

Then there are cost considerations. If you build your own CA, you won't have to pay per-user charges for each digital certificate you issue, like you will with most outsourced CAs. On the other hand, you *will* have to pay a small fortune for the hardware, software, staff, and added physical security you will need just to get the CA up and running. CA software generally requires some big iron to run, and the CA application itself doesn't come cheap. You'll also need someone, perhaps full-time, to manage your PKI, and while you may be able to find someone with limited experience in this area, they aren't exactly going to work for minimum wage.

Finally, electronic security, as we discussed in Chapter 12, hinges on physical security. You can't exactly let everyone have physical access to the CA itself, lest you risk a brilliant and accidental DoS attack by someone turning the CA off. At the same time, the CA must be fully available for your users and outsiders to verify a digital signature's authenticity or obtain a public key for one of your employees. This is not an altogether simple thing to do.

The External CA

Is the prospect of the in-house CA driving you to insanity? You're not alone. Many large and well-known companies have opted out of the "build it here" strategy and, instead, have chosen to let a seasoned company like VeriSign perform CA services for them.

The benefits of the external CA can be significant. A major benefit is that, by outsourcing your CA services, you virtually eliminate the headache of managing it internally. Instead, that management is done by an admitted—and verifiable—expert in the field of public key cryptography. What if your CA crashes? What if your CA is the target of a DoS attack? What if a user has a problem at 3 A.M. on a Sunday morning? Have you thought about these issues and how to resolve them? Probably not, but you can be sure that your CA provider has. Or at least you can check.

Outsourcing the CA also lets you implement a PKI much more quickly and at a substantially lower cost. Because the software is already installed, debugged, and managed by experts, adding your company to the already existing PKI is a matter of adding a few users. Outside of some setup fees, monthly or per-user charges are the only real costs involved, and in the short run these will invariably be far less than building your own CA from square one. These issues are typically what drive companies to outsource their CAs during a PKI pilot program. Often, they are so happy with the service, they never build their own CA in-house.

Another major benefit to outsourcing your CA is that your customers and suppliers may already have a relationship with the same company to which you outsource your

CA operations. In this instance, setting up a cross-certification relationship is a snap; just tell your CA provider what other companies you trust, and you're finished. We'll see why this is not so simple for in-house CAs in the following chapter.

Of course, there's a drawback to all of these cost savings and manageability boons, and it's the same thing that makes the in-house CA so appealing: control. By outsourcing your CA, you are, in essence, outsourcing an important security function for your company.

Why is this a problem? It's like asking a stranger off the street to watch a pile of cash for you—permanently. You don't know a thing about the stranger, but perhaps he or she claims to be a well-known security authority. Should you trust that person?

It's not as bad as it sounds. You probably outsource the physical security to your building, in the form of an alarm system or a security guard. You trust your bank not to lose or steal your deposits, too. What's the big deal about another link in the security chain? Well, companies like VeriSign are quite new, and they don't have the complete faith of the industry just yet. While VeriSign certainly has a regal lineage, coming from RSA Data Security, one of the pioneers of cryptography, it isn't exactly AT&T. You don't know who VeriSign hires, and you don't know what its physical security is like. But by outsourcing your CA, you still have to hand over your security policies to the company and indirectly give it access to all of your trade secrets.

Is this a problem for you? If you are a military defense contractor, you bet it is. If you're a gas station, it probably isn't. If you're somewhere in between, well, you'll have to decide for yourself.

A potentially bigger concern is the issuance on digital certificates. If a company 2,000 miles away is issuing certificates on your behalf, how do you know they aren't giving the certificates to charlatans, competitors, or criminals? In a nutshell, you don't. You are once again at the mercy of your provider to do the right thing.

One final concern is that of legal liability. If you perform all cryptographic functions in-house, you are responsible for any security breaches—for example, if a supplier's financial information is compromised on your system, the company can sue you over it. Giving control of your CA to an outside source complicates this situation by making the CA provider liable as well. The full legal ramifications of outsourcing a CA is beyond the scope of this book, but it may be a consideration of yours and merits further research. Be aware that companies like VeriSign are working toward mitigating these risks by providing "insurance" in the event of security breaches.

Hybrid Solutions

If neither of these options is perfect for you, you can also consider a hybrid solution like VeriSign OnSite, where administration and key issuance is performed within your company, but back-end processing, disaster recovery, and support are done outside the organization by the provider. This solution can also be much cheaper than building a full-blown PKI in-house, as it involves a much lower up-front commitment.

Many companies are finding hybrid solutions like these to provide the right mix of security, ease of administration, and cost. They are certainly worth examining if you're investigating a PKI solution.

PUBLIC AND PRIVATE KEYS

Now that you understand public key cryptography in the abstract as well as the form and function of certificate authorities, it's time to turn to a more in-depth analysis of public key cryptosystems and how they work.

As we've said earlier, the central idea behind public key cryptography is that a different key is used for each side of an encryption or authentication transaction. Public key cryptography begins, at the user level, by obtaining a key pair.

Obtaining a Key Pair

So where do you get a pair of keys? It starts by simply setting up your digital certificate. Your certificate authority will generally be responsible for generating your private key and its corresponding public key. When your certificate is generated, a private key of the appropriate length is transmitted to you, and your public key is stored on the CA's publicly available directories.

Some PKI implementations generate key pairs at the client level, so the private key is never transmitted over the network. Obviously, in some security-intensive environments, this option is quite appealing and necessary. Of course, this creates a problem by eliminating the ability for the CA to properly manage and back up key pairs. This is a much greater problem for outsourced CA environments, where a private key may have to be transmitted over the Web.

Either way, once your certificate is generated, your public key is embedded within it, and your private key is stored on your local hard drive. Your private key is then protected by a password of your choosing.

Public Key Derivation

Your private key and public key are irrevocably linked. Without delving too deeply into number theory, the idea is as follows.

Your private key is a randomly generated number: Generally, it is a binary number between 40 and 255 bits in length. (We'll discuss key lengths in the following section.) A one-way mathematical translation involving what is called a "superincreasing knapsack sequence" is then performed (the underlying algorithms vary depending on the implementation), and the resulting answer is your new public key. The public key size will likely be between 512 and 2,048 bits.

Again, your public key is placed on the CA and your private key is stored locally.

Key Length

Much ado has been made about key lengths in the trade press of late, with good reason. As the length of your private key grows, the difficulty of breaking it through a brute-force attack also grows, exponentially. The longer your private key, the far more difficult it is to hack. Because of U.S. government trade restrictions (more on this in Chapter 24), only cryptographic products with shorter keys are permitted for export outside the United States.

Table 23-1 outlines the comparative strengths of commonly used key pair lengths. Note that 56-bit keys are rapidly entering the "minimal strength" category.

When you choose a key length, either for yourself or for your organization, it's important to remember that the added security of longer keys comes at the price of much slower performance. Hashing and encryption algorithms are notoriously slow, and while even a slow server can keep up with the demands of numerous 40-bit digital signature operations, a flurry of 255-bit signatures is a different story. This level of security requires more advanced hardware and probably some form of cryptographic acceleration product.

Currently, 128 bits is the generally accepted key length for "unbreakable" security. For smaller organizations, 128-bit keys should not put too great a strain on server operations, either, so it is a good compromise. Cryptographic speed concerns are covered in Chapter 22.

Personal Key Management

If you tape your network login password to your monitor, you're not engaging in good security practices. If you opt not to protect your private key with a good password, or if physical security is lax in your organization, you run the same risks with a public key cryptosystem, no matter how good the underlying technology, the infrastructure, and the algorithms are.

Keeping your private key secure and out of the hands of outsiders is what makes public key cryptography work, and, as with any security scheme, it's the human element that is the weakest link in the chain.

Strength	Public Key Length	Private Key Length
Minimal	512	40
Moderate	768	56
Strong	1,024	128
Military	2,048	255

Table 23-1.   Comparative Strengths of Key Pairs

Coming up with unique and unguessable passphrases that you can still remember is a painful, arduous task. It's so much easier to use your spouse's name, your birthday, or your phone number instead of taking the time to come up with a better passphrase.

Your private key is stored on your computer's hard drive. If you use multiple computers, you'll have to store a copy on each of those systems. If an intruder gains access to one of those machines, what's to stop him or her from simply copying your private key to a floppy disk, taking it home, and using it as his or her own?

Only a password.

We covered good password practices at the beginning of this chapter, but it bears repeating. If someone is going to attack your PKI, it is not likely the attacker will try to figure out your private key through brute force. Much more likely is that he or she will try to steal your private key and attack the much easier password that safeguards it through a dictionary attack.

No matter how good your password is, this method will always be much simpler for a hacker to do. The best you can do is stymie the process by making that task much more difficult.

So, what do you do if your password is compromised, or if you find evidence of a physical break-in? Notify your security officer immediately. A crack security administrator can invalidate your digital certificate in seconds and quickly issue you a new one. Your old certificate will find itself on the certificate revocation list, and that information will have to also be replicated to any CAs that trust your organization's CA.

Key pairs also expire, in order to further foil the brute-force attack we said would never happen. When your key expires, it is your responsibility to securely obtain a new one, much as you did when you obtained your original digital certificate.

Good personal habits in managing your private key are crucial to the success of any public key infrastructure.

Public Key Authentication in Practice

Now you know everything that leads up to the actual use of a key pair in an authentication transaction. We'll now walk through the authentication procedure from start to finish.

Once your digital certificate is in place on your computer, you are ready to compose your message. Your message can consist of anything, and it can include attachments as well. Once it is complete, it is treated as an unalterable work until it is received at its destination. If the attachment is stripped or garbled along the way, the signature will not confirm the integrity of the message.

Regardless, you're now ready to hit that Send button to get the message on its way.

Hashing

The next step is hashing the message.

Rather than computing a digital signature for the entire message, a shortcut is typically used to boil the message down to its essential parts. This is especially valuable for large messages, which would take a considerably long time to sign. This shortcut is called hashing (or digesting).

A hash function is a one-way mathematical computation that takes an input of any size and returns a fixed-size string, called the "hash value." These functions are called one-way because they are very difficult to reverse. That is, it's simple to get a hash value for a given string, but it's almost impossible to reconstruct the string given only the hash value. For a good hash function, it is also infeasible to find two different messages to hash to the same value—although, statistically speaking, they must exist. This is known as the algorithm being "collision-free."

Most secure messaging systems will let you choose the algorithm you want to use to hash messages with. Without guidance, this can be an exercise in picking a random cryptic acronym from a list. Here's a guide to what's what:

▼ **MD2 – Message-Digest 2** Ron Rivest developed MD2 in 1989, and it is suitable for older (8-bit) computers. Note that because it is an 8-bit operation, MD2 is very slow. MD2 produces a 128-bit hash value, as do MD4 and MD5.

■ **MD4 – Message-Digest 4** A next-generation hashing algorithm, developed by Rivest in 1990. MD4 uses iterative hashing operations and was architected for 32-bit machines, so it is very fast. It was soon found that MD4 had certain cryptanalytic weaknesses, and is commonly regarded as a broken cryptosystem among the cryptographic community. It should really not be used at all, but it is nonetheless still supported by many PKI systems, mainly due to its impressive speed. (Note that MD3 never made it out of the lab due to flaws.)

■ **MD5 – Message-Digest 5** Rivest fixed MD4 in 1991 with MD5. It is quite similar to its predecessor, but is much more secure. This security comes at the expense of about 25 percent of the speed of MD4, unfortunately. Still, MD5 is one of the leading hashing algorithms for 32-bit machines. It is an excellent choice if you are choosing your own hashing algorithm within a security application.

■ **SHA – Secure Hash Algorithm** SHA was developed by NIST and NSA in 1991 as part of their Digital Signature Standard (DSS)—developed to be the authentication standard for the U.S. government. SHA produces a 160-bit hash, using a system similar to MD4. Messages must be less than 2^{64} bits in length. It is considerably slower than MD5 (about half MD5's speed—what did you expect from a government project?) because of its longer hash length. It is regarded as fully secure. It is commonly supported by most crypto software packages.

■ **SHA-1** SHA was tinkered with in 1994 to correct an unpublished flaw with SHA. Otherwise, SHA-1 is essentially identical to its predecessor.

■ **RIPE-MD** RIPE-MD is a European-developed algorithm similar to MD4. It has not been implemented in the United States in any widespread applications that we've seen.

■ **HAVAL** HAVAL is a hardened version of MD5 that lets you produce hash values of 128, 160, 192, 224, or 256 bits. It is, by its nature, even more secure than MD5, and much slower as well (but faster than SHA). There is very little support for HAVAL in today's cryptographic software.

▲ **Davies-Meyer and many other symmetric block algorithms** Many lesser-known hash functions use modified encryption algorithms to perform hash functions as well, the idea being that if the encryption function is secure, then the hashing version of it will be secure, too. There are dozens of these hash functions, and most are painfully slow (MD5 is 20 times faster than Davies-Meyer). Some are secure and some are not, and none are widely supported. Avoid, if for no other reason than compatibility.

The bottom line on which function to choose? MD5 or SHA-1 gives the best combination of speed and security.

Encrypting the Hash Value

Regardless of which hashing function you choose, after the message has been hashed, the hash value and your private key are used to create a digital signature. This is done by encrypting the hash value with your private key. The resulting signature is appended to the message and sent on its way.

We examined the process of encryption along with the various encryption algorithms in detail in the preceding chapter.

Examining the Signature

Once the recipient has the message in hand, it's time to take it apart.

First, he or she takes the reputedly intact message, and uses the same hash function that you did to get a hash value.

Second, the recipient obtains your public key from a central certificate authority, and then decrypts the digital signature appended to the e-mail he or she has just received. If this is successful, the signature will decrypt to reveal the hash value that you received when you hashed the message in the first place. If this value (the value you sent) matches the value that the recipient obtained by hashing the message, then the message has come through intact.

As you can see in Figure 23-4 if any information—either the message itself or the signature—has been altered in transmission (intentionally or not), the signature will not decrypt to the proper hash value and the message will not be authenticated. Further, if your public key has somehow been altered, the digital signature will not decrypt to the proper hash value. Thus, if any link along the chain is compromised, the operation will fail, ensuring authenticity.

Key Expiration

Now that you know how to use your key pairs, there will come a time when, inevitably, they expire. Again, this is done to protect the keys against a long-term brute-force attack, just like passwords should frequently be changed to thwart dictionary attacks.

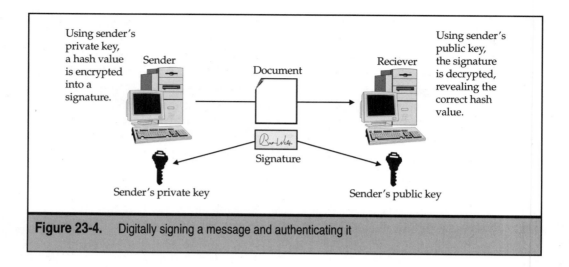

Using sender's private key, a hash value is encrypted into a signature.

Sender

Document

Reciever

Using sender's public key, the signature is decrypted, revealing the correct hash value.

Signature

Sender's private key

Sender's public key

Figure 23-4.   Digitally signing a message and authenticating it

The time until expiration is set by the CA. Six months to a year is typical before renewal is required. The idea is to make the time to expiration much shorter than the time it would take to derive the private key for a given public key through a brute-force factoring attack. For 128-bit keys, this time can be on the order of centuries, given the state of today's hardware.

When your key does expire, you simply apply for a new one, the same way you did when you initially obtained your digital certificate. Then, you're ready to start the process again.

ADVANCED AUTHENTICATION TOOLS

Public key cryptography not good enough for you? Perhaps you traffic in military intelligence, or are the chief developer of Microsoft's next operating system. If you have extreme cryptography needs, there are devices out there to help you obtain the security you need.

Cryptographic Tokens

Despite its confusing name, a cryptographic token is simply any hardware device that stores your private key, in lieu of your hard drive. The idea behind a cryptographic token is to let you separate your computer and your private key, in the event the former is stolen or compromised. Since cryptographic tokens are generally small, they can be locked in safes or carried on your person.

Cryptographic tokens can be as simple as a floppy disk: just insert your floppy into your system when you need access to the key. While this is a very cheap method of building a physical layer of security, it is certainly not recommended. The general instability of floppy disks and the ease with which anyone else would be able to use it if it was stolen make storing your key on a floppy a bad idea. Still, it's a simple example of a token.

More advanced are PC Card tokens like the Luna from Chrysalis-ITS. These tokens are PCMCIA card-based devices that store your key for you in flash memory. The Luna also has a built-in cryptographic accelerator to speed up crypto algorithms. Just like a floppy, you can remove the Luna altogether when you aren't using your system, and because it's based on a PC Card instead of a standard like a disk, it is considerably more difficult for a thief to read its contents. These cards cost about $200 to $300 each.

Other cryptographic token implementations get even more interesting. Datakey has designed a token embedded within a plastic key that you put on your key chain. When you need cryptographic services, you insert the key into a base unit that connects to your machine. It's a clever way to instill good security habits into your users, as they won't likely go home without their keys . . . for cryptography or their car!

Smartcards

Note that the unfortunately similar terms "smartcards" and "smart cards" are often used interchangeably but are completely different concepts. *Smart cards* are chip-enabled cards like credit cards that work as electronic cash; we discussed smart cards in Chapter 3. *Smartcards* are simply magnetic cards that contain user information: in most cases, a digital certificate and private key. Although this usage is nowhere near standardized, and you'll usually have to figure out which is which by context, we'll try to keep the two terms straight within the confines of this book.

Smartcards work exactly like other tokens, although their low cost often makes them much more attractive to implement. Smartcards are finding acceptance in a number of implementations, although they are still relatively new on the scene. Smartcards are especially popular for use in containing the root key for certificate authorities—a critical private key that, if compromised, can create much more trouble than any one user's key.

Biometrics

Now we get into the James Bond stuff: thumbprint scanners, radio badges, voiceprint identifiers, retinal scanners, and their ilk. Commenting on biometric devices like these is difficult without sounding alternately paranoid and condescending. The problem with most biometric devices is that they are limited to enhancing physical security. Most thumbprint readers simply allow and deny access to a computer as a whole. If a crook can bypass the device, he or she can often gain complete access to the compromised system. Even though they seem high tech and very secure, many biometric devices may lull you into a false sense of security.

Regardless, if your organization needs something like a retinal scanner, *you already know it*, and you don't need us telling you otherwise. In situations where security is critical and money is no object, these devices can be indispensable. For everyone else, try investing in some user training as a first step toward advanced security.

CHAPTER 24

Virtual Private Networking

Virtual private networks (VPNs) sneaked quietly onto the networking scene a few years back, apparently while no one was looking. Since their inception, VPNs have become the Next Big Thing in remote access, but figuring out if you need one, which one to use, and how to go about implementing your own VPN has largely remained a poorly understood exercise in confusion.

So what is a VPN? A VPN is simply a way to use the Internet instead of private, leased lines or POTS dial-up lines to extend network connectivity or remote access. While this has historically been done with standard ftp and Telnet sessions, a VPN adds a few new and important elements to the mix: authentication, encryption, and tunneling (the encapsulation of data from any source or protocol within a TCP/IP data stream). This way, an e-mail transaction, data transfer, or remote session can be secure from prying eyes, something that isn't possible with standard ftp and Telnet protocols. E-commerce applications, particularly EDI applications that need regular or perpetual connections, are also a driving force for VPN technology.

Many firewall vendors, and all the major ones, were the first to jump on the VPN bandwagon, and with good reason. As the gatekeeper of your LAN, the firewall is the logical point on your network to perform encryption and authentication procedures so insecure traffic never leaves the network. Firewall vendors also saw this as an excellent way to extend the functionality of what was then a rapidly maturing market with no place to go.

While this has forced the VPN market to mature rapidly, it has also confused the issue of when you need a firewall vs. when you need a VPN. To generate sales, vendors will automatically say you need both. While it's true that almost every VPN installation needs a firewall, the reverse is not always the case—even though your firewall may already have VPN features ready for you to activate.

Do You Need a VPN?

It's not as simple a question as it sounds. Deciding whether you need a VPN is a function of several things, which we'll address in turn.

Security Requirements

VPN security is a double-edged sword. As opposed to a typical leased line, which is part of your private network, any Internet-based traffic will, by necessity, be less secure, no matter how good the encryption and authentication schemes you put into place are. Compared to POP3 e-mail over the Internet or a modem-to-modem dial-up connection that can be easily tampered with, though, a VPN will be much more secure due to the VPN's encryption.

It's safe to say that a defense contractor is unlikely to use a VPN to transfer highly classified military secrets, because the security drawbacks, however minor, are still there. In fact, that defense contractor will probably use VPN-class encryption to secure documents at all times, even on a private network with leased lines. Clearly, for some applications, there is no such thing as a "reasonable security risk."

At the other extreme is a casual user who uses the company network to jot off a few quick e-mails to colleagues and friends, doesn't access confidential files, and isn't privy to company secrets. In this case, a VPN is too much. Any nonsecured Internet service, like using a POP3-enabled e-mail server or a local dial-up connection, will do. The following drawback may also make VPNs downright unappealing.

Speed Requirements

If you read the previous two chapters, you know that the added security of authentication and encryption services comes at the expense of your network's speed. With a VPN, *everything* is authenticated and encrypted, and if your traffic doesn't start out as IP-based, it's encapsulated and tunneled, to boot. All of this stuff will be responsible for making your network quickly slow down, with typical performance degradation in the general range of 50 percent, based on our personal experiences. A 128Kbps ISDN connection becomes 64Kbps. A 28.8Kbps modem connection becomes 14.4Kbps. Is substantially better security worth dropping half your available bandwidth? In many cases, it's not.

Network Protocols

Running an all-NetWare 4 network and want to use the Internet as a transaction medium? If so, you've got little choice but to install some kind of VPN that can translate NetWare's IPX-based traffic into TCP/IP traffic and then undo it at the other end. Your other choice, of course, is probably what you're already doing: use leased lines to connect sites and let remote users dial in to centrally managed modem banks.

Existing Infrastructure

Take the previous example a step further. Suppose your company has 300 users in five sites around the country, each of which is connected with a frame-relay T1 connection to the local RBOC (Regional Bell Operating Center). Routers and carrier service unit/data service units (CSU/DSUs) are installed at each site, and you also have three dial-up modem banks for remote access users, all of which are scattered across the country.

This is a fairly small network, but ripping out this existing, and probably quite stable, infrastructure to replace it with a virtual private network is going to be a nightmare, involving the wholesale gutting of your network. It will all have to be done at once, too, and it will likely involve a long period of adaptation and frustration for your users.

With VPNs nowhere close to maturity, jumping headfirst into a network redesign in order to use them may not make sense. Then again, if you've got an investment in the aforementioned equipment and services that's probably running in the five figures-per-month range, the final benefit of VPNs may be the deciding factor:

Money

When you get down to brass tacks, the VPN exists for one real reason: It's cheap. If it wasn't, people would be content with the fully secure, full-speed leased lines they've had for decades. While installing a VPN can be a pain, and it may entail some hefty up-front charges, once you've got the system running there are no recurring expenses aside from your connection to the Internet—an expense you're probably already paying. This way, all those permanent virtual circuit (PVC) charges can go out the window, and you can use the cash for something else (like doubling your bandwidth!).

While VPNs certainly vary in their cost, and you may run into costs you hadn't considered in advance—including router maintenance fees and the cost of hiring staff that can manage the VPN—you'll usually find a properly implemented VPN solution cheaper than its leased-line counterpart.

VPN Paradigms

Site to Site

The VPN makes a lot of sense, and causes the fewest headaches when applied in a site-to-site implementation.

In a site-to-site implementation, you install two or more gateways that serve as VPN way stations. Often, as mentioned earlier, this is the same device as your firewall, although it does not have to be. A typical network diagram is shown in Figure 24-1.

This diagram works best in situations where both offices are relatively large and have substantial traffic flowing between each site. For example, San Francisco may house the corporate accounting database, and the Austin site uses it for generating invoices. Or, Austin houses the corporate quality documentation and procedural manuals, which need to be accessed by all users at both locations.

If the WAN is used less intensively—for example, if users are only checking e-mail at a centrally located server, or if just a few users in Austin need access to files in San Francisco—a version of the site-to-user implementation (described and outlined below) can be used and will be less costly.

Site to User

Replacing modem concentrators and other remote access devices, along with getting rid of long-distance charges, is another benefit of using VPNs, this time, in a remote user-to-central LAN implementation.

In this implementation, the firewall usually is not responsible for encrypting and tunneling. Instead, a dedicated server running some kind of tunneling service (we'll cover the various flavors in a moment) sits on your LAN and does that for you. A typical network topology is shown in Figure 24-2.

A VPN installation like this is generally much easier to implement because it minimizes disruption to your existing network. The only real change involved is switching off your remote access devices and setting up the new tunnel server properly. Client-side changes involve simply installing a few new protocols, services, and/or small applications and

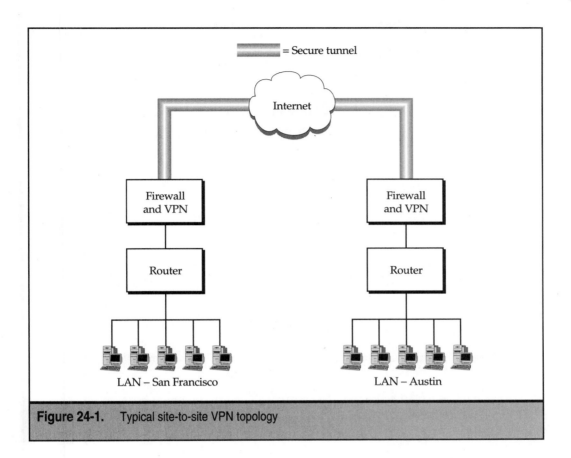

Figure 24-1.   Typical site-to-site VPN topology

configuring them properly. In many cases, it may not be quite this simple, but you get the basic idea.

Multifunction VPNs

With multiple sites and remote users, you may need some combination of the above two topologies. As the number of sites and users grows, and the reach of your network spreads, this can get substantially more complex, and may involve multiple and varied VPNs for different classes of users and remote sites. Obviously, as networks grow and change, adding more layers of hardware and software, maintenance becomes more difficult.

One of the benefits of a VPN is that, even though a 20-site network in four countries with 500 remote users sounds difficult to manage, it's far easier to set up with a VPN than

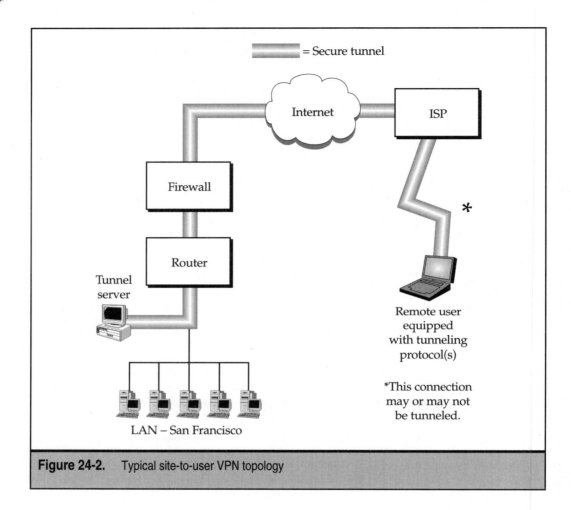

Figure 24-2. Typical site-to-user VPN topology

with a traditional WAN-and-modem combination. Adding a site involves obtaining an IP address—or range of IP addresses, depending on the number of network devices in the LAN—your new location and updating your routing tables—no waiting three months for the phone company to set up a leased line and straighten out the billing. It may not be Plug and Play, but it does beat the alternative.

Proper VPN Deployment

It is critical to keep in mind that you should only employ a VPN—or a WAN, for that matter—where you absolutely need it.

Do your sites maintain their own servers, sharing nothing but e-mail among them? If so, you don't really need a VPN. You can use a simple Internet connection to swap e-mail messages and save the headache of maintaining a VPN. If you have a few users at remote sites that report to a central location, you can set these people up with a site-to-user VPN connection and minimize your investment in additional equipment.

The same rules apply to remote or work-at-home users. For each user, ask yourself, does this person *need* all of his or her transactions with the office encrypted? If your CFO works at home, maybe he or she needs this, but does a technical writer working on help documentation? How about a graphic designer? Probably not.

Also, if the VPN is going to be used solely for e-mail, consider installing a simple, Post Office Protocol 3 (POP3)–enabled mail server that can be accessed through the Internet regardless of location. If encryption is needed, you can implement a PKI for S/MIME secure messaging on a user-by-user basis like we outlined in the previous two chapters.

The bottom line is that VPN may be a hot buzzword, but it doesn't mean you need one on every PC and laptop in the office.

Introducing Tunneling

In VPN brochures, you'll often read of tunneling as a glorious feature of VPNs. If you think about it, tunneling is actually a required component to make the Internet-based VPNs work. It's not a feature at all; it's a necessity that no VPN will work without, and the bottom line is that it slows you down.

Tunneling is simply the encapsulation of any form of data stream encoded with any protocol (IP, IPX, AppleTalk, SNA, or NetBEUI . . . it doesn't matter, in theory, at least) into IP-based traffic that can be routed over the strictly IP Internet. Figure 24-3 briefly outlines how this works.

Historically, there have been three widely used tunneling protocols in VPN installations: PPTP, AltaVista Tunnel, and L2F. We'll cover each in turn, along with the emerging tunneling protocols.

VPNs and Tunneling Protocols in Practice

The defining characteristic of any VPN is the protocol that underlies it. Whether it's a free and open protocol like Microsoft's PPTP or a proprietary one like AltaVista Tunnel, the tunneling protocol defines what you can and cannot do, and what your network design will look like when you get finished.

Microsoft PPTP

One of the earliest and most pervasive VPN implementations, Microsoft's Point-to-Point Tunneling Protocol (PPTP) was designed to be an extension to the PPP protocol, the standard service used for remote access on Windows machines.

PPTP was designed and is best suited for site-to-user implementations, and as you can probably guess, the Windows NT platform is the best one to work with. PPTP is built

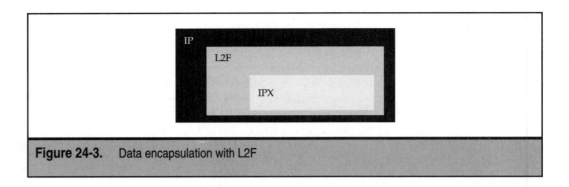

Figure 24-3. Data encapsulation with L2F

in to Remote Access Services (RAS) on Windows NT Server 4.0. It is also enabled on the Windows NT Workstation and Windows 98 clients and can be obtained for Windows 95 with the Dial-Up Networking (DUN) 1.2 upgrade, freely available at http://www.microsoft.com/windows/downloads/contents/updates/w95dial-upnetw/default.asp. The upgraded Windows 95 Dial-Up Networking client is shown in Figure 24-4.

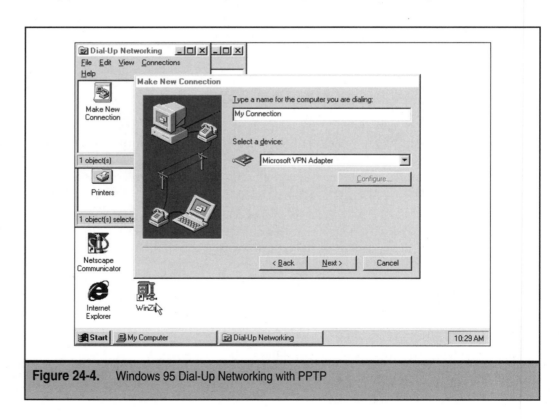

Figure 24-4. Windows 95 Dial-Up Networking with PPTP

To enable a VPN on a Windows NT network, you simply configure the server and client components, connect both to the Internet, and you're through. The connection is encrypted with 40-bit RC4 or DES in most implementations. (A 128-bit version can be enabled with the latest Windows NT Service Pack if you are only using the VPN domestically.) Authentication is performed with Challenge Handshake Authentication Protocol (CHAP), MS-CHAP (Microsoft's version of CHAP), or Password Authentication Protocol (PAP), a clear-text password transmission. Each of these will be discussed in a later section.

You can also obtain third-party remote access servers that support PPTP if you don't want to use Windows NT's RAS to do it. Ascend, Extended Systems, and 3Com/U.S. Robotics all offer PPTP-enabled remote access products.

While PPTP is an excellent and extremely cheap solution for providing secure remote access, there are some limitations you should keep in mind. First, if you aren't running a Windows NT network, PPTP is not for you. PPTP also supports only the major client/server protocols of IP, IPX, and NetBEUI. If you have AppleTalk clients or need mainframe connectivity, PPTP will not do the job.

AltaVista Tunnel

Digital Equipment Corp.'s AltaVista Tunnel 98 is the latest in a line of proprietary VPN products from this security leader. AltaVista Tunnel has been around for a few years, and it has proven to be a stable and relatively inexpensive solution, although it is a proprietary one that will have to adapt or be displaced by emerging standards-based solutions. This is an important point to remember if you're looking to invest in VPNs for the long term.

AltaVista Tunnel runs on Windows NT, BSD UNIX, or Digital UNIX. Its distinguishing feature is that it uses user-based authentication, as opposed to IP-based authentication, to initialize secure connections. This means that a user can roam from place to place and ISP to ISP without changing his or her dial-up settings. AltaVista Tunnel can also be used to build site-to-site tunnels, because each server component can also be used to connect to another server component (unlike Windows NT RAS).

AltaVista Tunnel uses 40- to 128-bit RC4 for encryption, and uses MD5 to hash data for verification that it has not been corrupted or tampered with. Unfortunately, because AltaVista Tunnel uses user-based authentication to verify its connections and open tunnels, it is regarded as somewhat less secure than other VPN solutions. Because security is the prime objective of a VPN in the first place, it certainly bears consideration.

L2F

L2F, or Layer 2 Forwarding, was pioneered by router king Cisco Systems, which should tip you off to its defining feature: It's ghastly expensive to implement.

Cisco has L2F built into its Internetwork Operating System (IOS), so a VPN can be built largely using an existing Cisco environment—so you don't actually have to invest in a lot of additional equipment, provided you already have a Cisco infrastructure. Of course, if you haven't, it's going to cost you—a lot. The Cisco PIX firewall/router costs about $20,000. If you are building a secure network from scratch and don't have routers, firewalls, or VPNs, this isn't that extreme. On the other hand, if you are simply looking for a VPN solution to add to an existing, non-Cisco network, you'll probably want to look elsewhere.

While Cisco is the leader in L2F technology, it is also in use by other companies in remote access products, most notably Nortel and Shiva.

L2F works for site-to-site and site-to-user implementations. It is also one of the more robust encapsulation protocols, tunneling IP, IPX, AppleTalk, SNA, and more. For multi-protocol networks, an encompassing tunneling protocol like L2F may be your only choice.

In addition to CHAP and PAP authentication, L2F supports Terminal Access Controller Access Control System Plus (TACACS+) and Remote Access Dial-In User Service (RADIUS). Encryption is handled with IPSec (to be discussed below). L2F also works with dynamic or static IP addresses, making its flexibility in deployment virtually limitless. Of course, you'd expect that for the price you'll pay.

L2TP

When both PPTP and L2F were submitted as standards to the Internet Engineering Task Force (IETF), what arose from the ashes was the Layer 2 Tunneling Protocol (L2TP), a new specification that would support both prior standards. L2TP is supported by Cisco, Microsoft, Ascend, and 3Com/U.S. Robotics, and it provides the best of both worlds: full multiprotocol support that does not require preregistered IP addresses. It is, however, geared toward dial-up connectivity, not site-to-site implementations. L2TP will be included with Windows 2000 and may replace PPTP altogether. The standard should be finalized by the time you read this.

Encryption and authentication are handled at the PPP level, before tunneling takes place. However, IPSec has been proposed as a means of providing end-to-end authentication and encryption to L2TP tunnels.

Expect to see a massive shift to L2TP as the standard underlying tunneling protocol over the coming months and years. Even without the final standard, implementations are already beginning to show up.

IPSec

IPSec, or IP Security, is an ambitious set of standards emerging alongside L2TP, and it is particularly well suited toward site-to-site VPN implementations.

Besides being a tunneling protocol (sometimes called Layer 3 tunneling), IPSec includes an authentication, encryption, and key management scheme as well. IPSec will work with current IPv4 networks or with the upcoming IPv6 networks, as well. Even more important, IPSec authentication and encryption will work with L2TP if you want to use L2TP for remote access purposes, and IPSec will be deployed along with that protocol in Windows 2000. Within the next 12 to 24 months, expect to see IPSec become the standard for secure wide area communications.

IPSec's final barrier is using multiple certificate authorities for key management schemes. Currently, IPSec only works if both sender and receiver have been issued certificates by the same CA, although the protocol is fully X.509-compliant. This should be resolved before IPSec is widely released, when the Public Key Infrastructure Exchange (PKIX) protocol is finalized.

IPSec uses MD5 or SHA-1 to hash messages and ensure their validity. The encryption scheme is done using Encapsulating Security Payload (ESP), a protocol that allows for the session to be encrypted in tunnel mode (where the entire IP packet is encrypted and encapsulated within a second IP packet) or transport mode (where only the payload of the packet is encrypted). The encryption algorithm can be set by the user or security administrator and includes most major algorithms.

IPSec is already showing up in VPN products currently available on the market, including VPNs from AXENT, Check Point, Network Associates, Secure Computing, and RADGUARD. It seems to be working remarkably well, and should find even greater acceptance in the marketplace once Windows NT 5.0 is released.

SSL and SOCKSv5

SSL has also been used with SOCKSv5 (short for "Sockets") authentication to build proprietary VPN solutions like the one offered by Aventail. This scheme works much like any SSL Web session and can include things like virus scanning and content screening because it works at the session layer. Implementations like this are really only appropriate for remote users, not site-to-site implementations, mainly because of performance problems with SSL. It seems unlikely that proprietary VPN implementations like this will gain popularity in the face of emerging solutions like L2TP and IPSec.

Authentication with VPNs

When we talk about VPN authentication, we're discussing something different than messaging authentication, which we covered in depth in Chapter 23. Authentication on VPNs deals with the issue of how you determine who to open a tunnel to (and who not to). Because users or other sites are remote and not connected to your LAN, this is typically more problematic than a simple password prompt.

Then again, sometimes it isn't. A few VPNs, like those offered by Novell and Aventail, allow you to use your NetWare directory or Windows NT domain information to validate users, thus sparing you from having to set up special accounts just to access the VPN. Using a Windows 95 client with PPTP to connect to a Windows NT 4.0 remote access server works along the same lines. The real trick comes when you need to securely transmit user and password information without fear of interception.

PAP

PAP, or Password Authentication Protocol, has a very misleading name. It's one of the most widely supported authentication protocols, but it is rarely used. That's because PAP authentication consists of sending password information in clear text, which really provides no security at all. It should certainly be avoided.

CHAP and MS-CHAP

Challenge Handshake Authentication Protocol comes in two flavors: CHAP and MS-CHAP, Microsoft's version of the protocol. CHAP is one of the most common authentication protocols and is built in to most VPN products, including Windows NT. CHAP works by performing an MD4 hash on the password and using that as part of the authentication and encryption session key. Because CHAP and MS-CHAP rely on passwords to authenticate a user, they are not as secure as key-based authentication schemes.

SKIP

SKIP is Simple Key Management for IP and has typically been used with IPSec to perform key management functions. SKIP was quickly displaced by other key management schemes, although you'll still find lingering support for it in current VPN products. Because it is certainly nearing its imminent death, you should look to other key management authentication protocols.

ISAKMP/IKE/IKMP

These three key management protocols, Internet Security Association Key Management Protocol (ISAKMP), Internet Key Exchange (IKE), and Internet Key Management Protocol (IKMP) are all intertwined, and are now hopelessly indistinguishable unless you really dig into the protocol specifications. Essentially, when you hear about any of these, you can assume they are referring to the same thing. IKMP is the latest version of the protocol, and we'll refer to it thusly.

IKMP is a framework for key exchange. It is used during the establishment of a secure tunnel to determine which authentication, hashing, and encryption algorithms are used, key length, time until key expiration, and the actual keys to be used during the communication. IKMP is a solid protocol, and is the preferred method of key management for IPSec interoperation.

Currently, vendors offering IKMP support with their VPNs include the software of the preferred CA provider with the product or simply build their own CA right into the VPN. When PKIX is finalized, this should become a much more elegant solution, allowing full CA interoperability.

You should find wide and growing support for IKMP as IPSec and PKIX continue to take hold.

RADIUS

Remote Access Dial-In User Services (RADIUS) is a very well-established and well-supported standard protocol, especially useful for tracking accounting information on a per-session basis. RADIUS is supported by virtually all site-to-user VPN implementations due to its excellent abilities at providing reports with which scaling decisions can be made. You'll find a RADIUS server used to authenticate most users who dial in to an ISP.

RADIUS support is generally only important if you are considering using your users' ISP to authenticate that user back to your own corporate server for added security. This type of arrangement can get messy, quickly, due to interoperability issues between RADIUS servers from different vendors. If you want to implement some kind of authentication scheme involving RADIUS, you'll likely need to seek the aid of a professional.

TACACS+

Terminal Access Controller Access Control System Plus (TACAS+) is an old standby of Cisco. The protocol is built in to Cisco's IOS and can be used much like RADIUS to authenticate users during the establishment of a VPN tunnel. TACAS+ is integrated with L2F in Cisco routers and remote access servers, and it has fairly wide support among other VPN vendors. The protocol is mainly distinguished by maintaining its own internal access list for use after a user is authenticated, so the remote access server can assign rights to network resources appropriately. The future of TACACS+ is unclear with the rise of IPSec.

SOCKS

SOCKS (the latest version is called SOCKSv5), a cute contraction of "Sockets," is a session layer protocol typically used for authentication services. Typically, it is implemented with firewall products that are integrating authentication into a proxy server, but it has also been used with SSL, as described above, to build VPNs.

Support for SOCKS had been largely nonexistent until the version 5 release, when a flurry of promotion by its originator, NEC, led to its adoption by several companies. Its proponents now include Aventail (SOCKS' original licensee), Attachmate, Bay Networks, IBM, Netscape, Oracle, and Intel, all of whom aim to implement SOCKSv5 in upcoming security and WAN products.

Because SOCKS operates at a higher level in the OSI model, it is easier to manage. This necessarily affects performance, however, and higher-level protocols are generally less likely to be secure due to the many layers that lie beneath them.

Whether SOCKS will mature into a companion to IPSec alongside L2TP remains to be seen, but it's a developing segment of the security market that bears keeping an eye on.

Encryption with VPNs

As with most security products and implementations, VPN encryption is nowhere close to standardized. Virtually all of the major algorithms we discussed in Chapter 22 are supported by one VPN product or another, although Triple-DES is the most prevalent algorithm you'll find in use today.

IPSec/ESP

Even emerging security standards like IPSec's ESP do not specify what algorithm to be used during encryption routines. ESP can support any secret key cryptography algorithm, including DES, Triple-DES, IDEA, Blowfish, RC5, and CAST. ESP's default algorithm is 56-bit DES, due to potential export restrictions.

MPPE

Microsoft Point-to-Point Encryption (MPPE) is the encryption standard for PPTP. MPPE uses 40-bit RC4 (again, due to export restrictions) and works slightly different than normal RC4 encryption (hence the new name for the process), but the routine is essentially the same. Expect to see MPPE evolve to provide better performance and support for cryptographic accelerators with the release of Windows 2000.

Another Option: Outsourcing Your VPN

Like a PKI and certificate authority implementation, a VPN can be outsourced to one of any number of telecommunications providers looking to profit by aiding network managers who may not have the time, inclination, experience, or funds to set up their own VPNs within the organization. The thinking is, apparently, if you aren't going to lease a line from them, you might as well pay them for something.

Here's a simple and brief guide to the major VPN service providers.

AT&T WorldNet

AT&T WorldNet offers one of the farthest-reaching VPN services around, including 300 points of presence, toll-free dial-ups, and 56Kbps, ISDN, and high-speed access options available. Another great feature of the AT&T WorldNet VPN is its end-to-end service level agreement (SLA) that provides a refund of 5 percent of the monthly service charges if the VPN is down for ten minutes or more during any single day. The maximum value of the refund is 25 percent per month and one month of service per year.

WorldNet supports RADIUS for authentication and has packet filter firewalls installed at all edges of its network. Pricing is based largely on speed and option services. A 16Kbps connection runs about $100 per month, and a 1Mbps connection runs over $2,000. Local dial-up charges are billed at about $3 per hour, and flat-rate plans are available. You can get more information at AT&T's Web site at www.att.com.

networkMCI Internet VPN

MCI's VPN service combines the company's Internet presence in 50 countries with managed security services by Check Point Secure Remote software. Remote access clients contain a directory of all MCI dial-up numbers locally, and the directory is dynamically updated to allow full utilization of MCI POPs.

To use the system, VPN customers must also use MCI's managed firewall service. All billing is consolidated, and there is a fixed component. Pricing ranges from $2 to $6 per hour for remote user dial-up connections. International rates are two to three times that. Prices include 24x7 customer support.

MCI's SLA is even more aggressive than AT&T's, including a full day of free service for each ten-minute outage, and three days of service for any outage of three hours or longer. Performance statistics are also available in near real time. Full details are available online at www.mci.com.

Sprint

Sprint, the perpetual laggard in cutting-edge data services, is still not quite ready with its VPN service, and details of exactly what that will be are difficult to come by. You can watch Sprint's Web site at www.sprint.com to keep track of developments.

Infonet Virtual Enterprise

Infonet Services Corp., a data networking vendor, offers toll-free ISDN VPNs through 46 countries, supporting simultaneous connections to multiple destinations, token-based password authentication with Security Dynamics SecurID, monthly call detail reporting, and an upgrade path from ISDN to dedicated lines. Full details are available at the company's Web site at www.infonet.com.

IBM Global Services Managed Data Network Services

IBM Global Services Managed Data Network Services has a long name and a slew of features to match it. 56Kbps and ISDN dial-ups are supported, and the company offers line bundling/channel aggregation features to achieve analog speeds of 224Kbps and digital speeds of 256Kbps. IBM's 1,300-plus POPs are globally located in 50 countries, and SLAs are negotiable and offer "progressive credits."

Since it's IBM, SNA tunneling is naturally supported, which makes it a prime candidate for remote mainframe connectivity. SecurID authentication is also supported, and a Web content filtering option is available to boot. IBM's Managed Data Network Services support up to four simultaneous connections to remote hosts, and, finally, IBM will even order your ISDN lines for you. If you have historically dealt with IBM and enjoy the customer service it provides, this service is comprehensive and certainly worth looking in to. Complete details are available at http://domino.www.ibm.com/globalnetwork/mdnsvc.htm.

TCG CERFnet

TCG CERFnet is a large ISP that was one of the first to roll out VPN solutions. TCG offers turnkey VPN solutions that have the primary benefit of your never having to call a telco or other notoriously unresponsive big company to get your system set up. TCG offers access speeds from 28.8Kbps to 155Mbps. Currently, service is limited to the cities of San Diego, San Jose, Los Angeles, Chicago, New York City, Princeton, Philadelphia, and Boston. Check www.cerf.net for details.

Other ISPs

Most large and many small ISPs have VPN offerings of some sort available. Whether you need local VPN services for home users or large-scale, nationwide connectivity for traveling salespeople, check with your current ISP and see what it has to offer. It probably won't be as comprehensive as what AT&T or IBM offer, but it may be all you need.

Service Level Agreements

As with most other wide area networking services, VPNs are typically covered by service level agreements (SLAs). Most national service providers guarantee about 99.6 percent availability (under six minutes downtime per day) before refunds or credits are offered. The AT&T and MCI SLAs are outlined in the previous section.

Unfortunately, what SLAs do not currently guarantee is performance, or quality of service (QoS). While the network may be up, and may still be very slow due to the vagaries of Internet-based communications. Performance is rarely, if ever, guaranteed, because there's nothing that can feasibly be done about the problem. Bandwidth is limited, encryption slows things down, and network congestion enters too many variables; all of this is responsible for general uncertainty that makes quality of service SLAs a distant reality, at best.

The Future of Remote Access

So where does all of this leave us?

As digital convergence takes hold, high-speed dial-up access will become increasingly prevalent, making remote access less of the pain it currently is. The same goes for operating system sophistication; Windows 98 and 2000 are much more sophisticated in the way remote access is handled. As L2TP and IPSec continue to spread through industry, standards-based remote networking will make it easier for everyone to communicate.

It's not a bed of roses, though. The road to seamless remote connectivity is filled with potholes, and remote access, specifically remote access *security*, has not been traditionally at the top of anyone's development list. Still, an increasingly roaming and telecommuting workforce will demand this kind of progress. As such, the next few years should be extremely interesting ones on the VPN front.

Other VPN Resources

If you're considering investing in a VPN, a good place to start is with the ICSA (www.icsa.net). The ICSA certifies VPN software and hardware after doing its own independent testing, and the organization is a good general source about all security topics (it also certifies firewalls).

For more reading material on VPNs, you'll find the field a bit narrow. The only moderately helpful book we're currently familiar with is Charlie Scott, Paul Wolfe, and Mike Erwin's *Virtual Private Networks*. This slim volume (177 pages) focuses mainly on the practical aspects of implementing VPN solutions on Microsoft PPTP, AltaVista Tunnel, and Cisco PIX. It does not cover much in the way of VPN theory and emerging standards like IPSec, but the publisher says a second version is in the works.

You may also find IBM's "Redbook" on virtual private networks to be helpful in understanding more about the underlying technology of VPNs. It is, as is to be expected, extremely biased toward IBM remote access and security products, but it does contain a substantial amount of more general information. It can be ordered from IBM or viewed online at http://www.redbooks.ibm.com/SG245201/sg245201.html.

Online, you'll find other good VPN references and starting points at VPNet (http://www.vpnet.com) and Tom Dunigan's VPN page (http://www.epm.ornl.gov/~dunigan/vpn.html).

CHAPTER 25

Unified Messaging

The next big test for computer networking is going to be the integration of computer data networks, telephone/voice/fax networks, and video/cable networks. It's called "digital convergence," and it's going to change the very fabric of networking as we know it.

Someday, anyway.

The promise of a unified network of networks has been rumbling for a long time. And while the day is approaching (you *can* make a telephone call over the Internet, but you won't enjoy it), there are still many hurdles to be overcome before its arrival.

In the meantime, unified messaging seems to be the current digital convergence application of choice: the idea that you can access a central location to retrieve your voice mail, e-mail, and incoming faxes—whether you are at your computer or at a pay phone. The implementation is a powerful concept. In reality, it's still a bit elusive.

Why Has Unified Messaging Taken So Long?

In the old days, no self-respecting telephone technician would touch a computer network. At the same time, network administrators fought tooth and nail to avoid having the PBX placed under their control. Voice and data traffic didn't mix. Ever.

The modem was probably the device that started the trend toward digital convergence, the idea being that if you could send data over telephone lines, why not send voice over data lines, too? Voice over frame relay, once considered impossible because of the way frame relay works, is now commonly used to connect satellite office telephones to headquarters, using the same routers that run the data network. This way, expensive midday long-distance charges are avoided in favor of much cheaper frame relay charges.

ISDN enables simultaneous voice and data traffic over a single line and is perfect for work-at-home users who often need both transmitting at the same time.

And now there's voice over IP, which promises to end, or greatly reduce, long-distance charges by putting calls through the publicly available Internet circuits. The lure of international calls at no charge is quite seductive. Too bad the technology has been so slow in coming, and pilot projects are only now starting to be rolled out to the enterprise as a whole.

It makes sense to look to disparate messaging systems to attempt to consolidate systems. Today's road warrior may need to check two or three voice mail systems, the company's e-mail system, personal e-mail account (or more than one), and he or she may have to call a live person to see if any urgent faxes have been received. Then there are pagers, cellular phones, and PDAs. The typical "checking messages" routine in the hotel room at night drags out for hours. It also entails dragging around a lot of heavy equipment and remembering a dozen account names, access numbers, and passwords.

The burden is a heavy one, but consolidating all of the above is not so simple.

From the beginning, data and voice networks were never intended to work together. In fact, it's almost as if they were intended *not* to work together. Voice mail and e-mail systems are built with completely different standards and use different hardware, and even different cabling. Directory structures between the two are incompatible. The underlying infrastructure is completely incompatible (phone wiring vs. network wiring). And it requires a completely separate skill set to learn to manage, for example, a PBX vs. a file server.

Building a single place to store and manage all message types, centralized with a global directory system that can be accessed via phone or computer, is not that easy.

But it's on its way.

Unified Messaging Architectures

If unified messaging sounds good to you, you need to start your research by determining what type of messaging architecture will work best for you. This will drive the amount of new hardware and software you'll have to purchase, how much of your existing infrastructure you'll be able to use, and most important, how much it's going to cost.

Traditional Messaging Architecture

Traditionally speaking, the PBX, fax machines, and e-mail server have been completely separate devices (see Figure 25-1). If faxes are accessible in nonpaper versions through client PCs, it generally requires special hardware and software to do so. Otherwise, voice mail is accessed only through the telephone, and e-mail is accessed only through computer.

The costs associated with this type of setup are probably familiar to you, because it's likely what you're working with already. A PBX system, fax machines, and an e-mail server must all be purchased and managed separately. These expenses vary widely, depending on the sophistication of the hardware and software you buy.

Integrated Client Architecture

This unified messaging architecture, shown in Figure 25-2, involves the same three services as a segregated architecture, but uses special client software to allow users to access all types of messages from one PC. Sometimes, the same access can be obtained through a telephone connection to the voice mail server.

The key to this architecture is that, as with a segregated architecture, three separate systems must still be maintained and managed. The only changes are the substantial added complexity of the interconnectivity wiring (see Figure 25-2) and the cost of special software on the client to access all three systems.

A good example of this in action is UniTel's add-on to the Microsoft Outlook e-mail client. (See www.unitel-inc.com for details.) Northern Telecom's Symposium Messenger is another multiple-server solution that provides users with a single client to access all messages, or you can access them through a Web browser.

While this solution is more expensive than others (at about $125 per seat), it still requires separate administration of multiple servers. Some solutions, like UniTel's, give

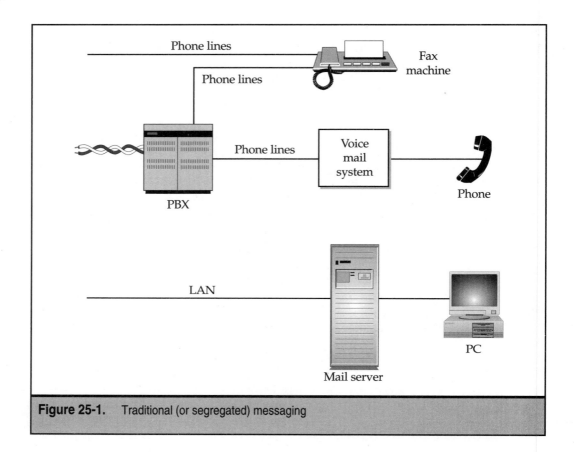

Figure 25-1.   Traditional (or segregated) messaging

you access to all message types through a single application, other solutions require two or three different clients to access all of your messages. This isn't overly efficient, and is really not very good at solving the problems that unified messaging was designed to address in the first place.

Note that there are endless variations of this architecture, but basically they all work like this.

Integrated Server Architecture

Integrating messages at the e-mail server is one way to partially eliminate the decentralized management problem. Server integration also allows the user to use one e-mail client to access all types of messages. It also greatly simplifies the complexity of wiring of your infrastructure, as you can see in Figure 25-3.

With this architecture, all messages reside on one server—the e-mail server—where they are all managed. The voice mail server doesn't normally store messages with this

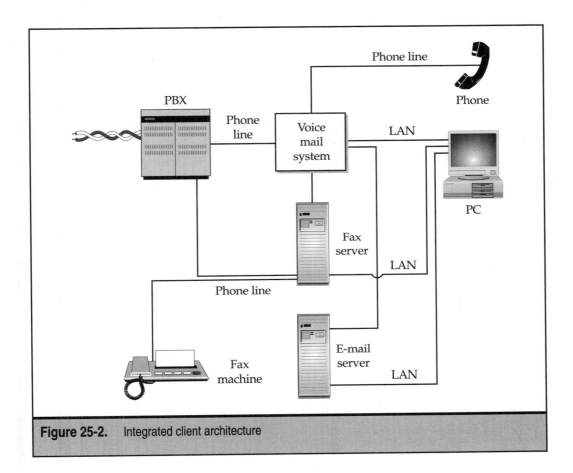

Figure 25-2.   Integrated client architecture

architecture; it simply forwards them to the e-mail server for retrieval. The voice mail system, however, will still be responsible for storing and playing the user's personal "out of the office" messages. Additional hardware includes a text-to-speech card in your e-mail server, and a dedicated expansion card in your PBX to provide connectivity to the LAN.

Note that if your e-mail server crashes, your users will lose all connectivity to e-mail, voice mail, and faxes. This is the predominant point of contention between server- and client-based messaging integration vendors. While integrated client vendors claim this single point of failure is unacceptable for such a critical function as messaging, the integrated server camp downplays the risk as less serious, saying that the ease of centralized system management outweighs the risks. It's really up to you to decide.

With a server integration architecture, telecom and IT are officially combined. Centralized management and access through a single e-mail client (or through the

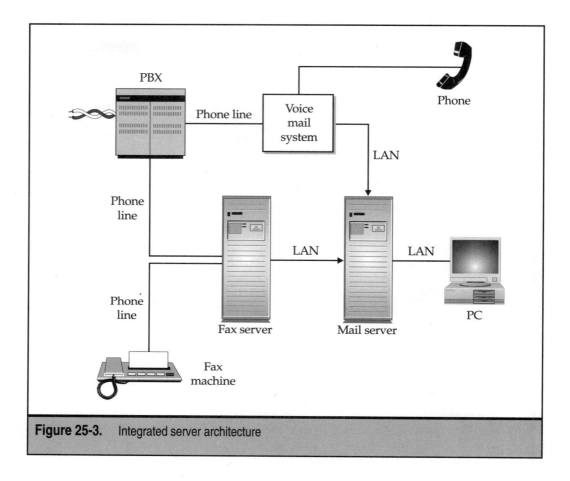

Figure 25-3.   Integrated server architecture

telephone) are possible. However, such systems are expensive. Lucent's Octel Unified Messenger, probably the best-known unified messaging system, starts at $200 per seat for very large installations. This isn't something you can buy off the shelf and set up over the weekend, either; it's a long-term proposition that requires expert systems integrator consultation (essentially, from Lucent). You can read more about Octel Unified Messenger at www.octel.com.

Hybrid Architectures

At least one system combines the features of client- and server-based messaging integration into something that's a hybrid of the two.

The Interactive Intelligence Interaction Mail places a dedicated server between the e-mail server/PBX and the client. The Interaction Mail Server is what the client accesses, from an e-mail client, telephone, or Web browser.

Figure 25-4. The Octel Unified Messenger client

Although this architecture provides a central point of failure like a standard server integration architecture, the e-mail server itself is still accessible if the Interaction Mail Server goes down.

Prices are competitive with integrated server architecture systems.

Outsourcing

You can also obtain unified messaging as a service, much like you obtain voice mail or paging services. Prices are quite affordable, and by all accounts the systems work well. Probably the best known service of this type is Wildfire, an extremely sophisticated voice mail system available for consumers or corporate use. Wildfire performs all the functions of a typical unified messaging phone service and is fully voice-activated. Full details about Wildfire can be found at www.wildfire.com.

Also, take a look at VoiceMall ESA at www.voicemall.com, which offers a similar service. Prices are low, with installation at $100 or less and access fees based on a per-minute schedule.

Telephony Standards and Protocols

Microsoft has been at the forefront of integrating voice and messaging technologies with its operating system for some time. Microsoft Windows 95/98 and Windows NT include technologies that enable unified messaging on the PC in the form of application programming interfaces (APIs).

Without delving too deeply into the technical details of each, here's a rundown of the four big Windows technologies that you'll run into during your implementation of a unified messaging system.

Note that there are probably a dozen additional standards for telephony and unified messaging, but most of them are relatively minor or have not yet gained acceptance, so they are not covered here.

Windows Telephony API (TAPI)

TAPI is an open standard designed to allow developers to create telephony applications for the PC, which can interact with a variety of phone systems. TAPI is the real guts of the Windows telephony interface.

TAPI supports a complete set of telephony features, and with TAPI, a developer can build telephone and voice messaging functions into just about any application. TAPI clients can also be managed centrally through Windows NT. TAPI is currently the only real standard for Windows-based telephony applications. (Support for Novell's server-centric TSAPI (Telephony Services API) has diminished greatly over the last few years.)

Coming with the release of Windows 2000 is the next revision of TAPI, version 3.0. TAPI 3.0 will upgrade the API by providing convergence of traditional telephony and IP, or Internet-based, telephony. TAPI 3.0 will provide a generic method for making telephone connections among any number of machines, regardless of the medium and protocol underlying the call.

TAPI 3.0 will support H.323 conferencing and IP multicast conferencing. It will be integrated with Active Directory and introduce the Component Object Model (COM) architecture to TAPI. *Quality of service* (QoS) features will also be added.

You can keep up with TAPI's development progress at www.microsoft.com/communications/tapiabout.htm.

Windows Message API (MAPI)

Also known as Windows Messaging API and XMAPI (Extended MAPI), MAPI is best known for allowing otherwise incompatible e-mail systems to work together. MAPI, however, is also responsible for providing connectivity between e-mail systems and voice messaging systems.

Windows Speech API (SAPI)

SAPI is responsible for allowing speech engines to run on Windows PCs. This provides speech recognition and text-to-speech features.

Unimodem

Unimodem is the Windows Universal Modem Driver, which simply translates TAPI function calls into commands that a computer's modem can recognize as answering and dialing codes.

Voice Profile for Internet Mail (VPIM)

VPIM is not only a protocol but is also a group, dedicated to establishing a standard profile built from Multipurpose Internet Mail Extensions (MIME) and Simple Mail Transfer Protocol (SMTP) to allow the interchange of voice and fax messages between voice mail systems and MIME-capable e-mail systems. The protocol also defines a Lightweight Directory Access Protocol (LDAP) directory service for voice messages. It was initiated in early 1996 and is on the cusp of becoming a true standard for unified messaging, pending ratification by the IETF.

The central focus of VPIM is to ultimately do away with the requirement of an e-mail address. With VPIM, all users can be centrally located and contacted through their telephone number, whether you are sending voice mail, a fax, a page, or an e-mail message. It's a very powerful concept that, if accepted, will revolutionize messaging as we know it.

VPIM is already supported in a number of unified messaging products and voice mail systems, including offerings from Lucent/Octel, Nortel, Centigram, Siemens Rolm, and many others. VPIM will solve the long-standing problem of interoperability among previously incompatible voice mail systems built by the above vendors. With VPIM, these systems can interchange messages over a TCP/IP network like the Internet and provide "intentional messaging" services, which let you send a voice mail message without having to call the person, listen to their message, then record your response.

Note that VPIM is not an API like TAPI or MAPI. It's a protocol that simply defines the way voice messages are interchanged. This way, an e-mail server is not tied to a specific set of development tools.

You can follow the ongoing development of VPIM at www.ema.org/vpimdir/index.htm.

Simple Computer Telephony Protocol (SCTP)

SCTP is another open protocol for building TCP/IP client/server telephony applications and for providing a common interface for digital telephone devices. SCTP is compatible with existing telephony APIs. It looks to be a minor player in the Internet telephony market, used to build such applications as Internet call waiting.

H.323

H.323 is an International Telecommunications Union (ITU) standard for providing audio, video, and data communications over TCP/IP local area networks. Its main function is in providing multimedia applications with standards-based interoperability through a common protocol.

H.323 is designed for any network that does not provide a guaranteed quality of service (QoS), notably standard Ethernet and Token Ring LANs, as opposed to Asynchronous Transfer Mode (ATM) networks.

H.323 is used predominantly in videoconferencing applications, which have special bandwidth requirements for keeping image and sound quality at a respectable level. H.323 is still a relatively new standard, and it has not really withstood the test of the market yet. You can get a good primer on H.323 at gw.databeam.com/h323/h323primer.html.

T.120

While H.323 is focused on providing videoconferencing services to LANs, T.120 is a companion standard designed for videoconferencing over the Internet. Like H.323, it is relatively new and relatively untested in the marketplace. You can get more information at www.databeam.com/Products/CCTS/t120primer/.

Session Initiation Protocol (SIP)

SIP is a protocol under development, designed to provide call forwarding and call transferring features to Internet telephony applications.

Implementation Tips

So, you're ready to try a unified messaging system? Here are some tips to keep in mind when selecting a solution and implementing it on your network.

Think About It

Unified messaging today is neither the most stable nor the most well-supported application in the world. Unified messaging is still a bit on the shaky side—never mind what vendors tell you. You need to decide whether the convenience offered by unified messaging outweighs the substantial cost of implementing it today, and if you can stand to wait even six months for a more robust solution.

Solid unified messaging systems start at about $100,000, so either way, you're going to be stuck with the solution you choose for a long time. It's certainly not something to implement on a whim.

Don't Go Proprietary

Don't listen to telecommunications vendors who tell you that their proprietary solution is a "de facto standard." When it inevitably comes time to connect that system to an IP network, it's going to require either an expensive upgrade or an entirely new system. Make sure whatever solution you purchase fully supports the latest revision of all relevant standards. Also, try to get free upgrades included in your purchase price as new standards emerge.

Hire a Consultant

Face it: You're not going to do this by yourself. It's doubtful that any unified messaging vendor will even let you try. Be prepared to pay and pay dearly for a consultant (usually the service arm of the vendor whose product you purchased) to do the installation for you and train you on its management.

Get a Deal

Vendors are dying to sell these systems, but there has, as yet, not been a mad rush to purchase them. Insist on big discounts from resellers, and get all the extras thrown in that you can. If they refuse, wait a month, and the price will come down anyway. But overall, vendors in this market space have much more flexibility to discount unified messaging systems in order to build an installed base of products.

At the same time, don't get the vendor or reseller on your bad side. After all, who's going to fix the system when it breaks?

What's Next?

Say it's 2003, and you're ready to perform an upgrade of your telecommunications infrastructure.

More likely than not, your next PBX will not be a proprietary solution from Lucent or Centigram; it will be a file server running Windows 2002 and a computer telephony application. Your voice mail and e-mail will probably run on this server as well.

Even if you stick with a proprietary (and more expensive PBX), it will probably be fully Internet-ready, able to place telephone calls over the Internet, and while you'll have the same choice of long-distance service providers, the calls will be much cheaper—especially international ones.

Eventually, maybe by 2010 to 2015, you'll have a plug in the wall that will provide telephone/videophone, interactive cable TV, and Internet access, regardless of where you are. Like an electrical socket, you'll just plug your laptop or television into the holes in the wall and expect it to work, automatically. The days of painful remote access configurations, cryptic long-distance arrangements, and a pocket full of calling cards will be over.

In theory, anyway. The promises of computer telephony integration and unified messaging are nothing short of revolutionary, but we have a long way to go. Still, the future looks bright for such developments.

For more speculation about the future of unified messaging, the hurdles that remain, and a comprehensive guide to what's been done so far, check out the Web site at www.computertelephony.org/.

APPENDIX

Keeping It Running

If this book has met its objectives, you now have a lot to keep you awake at night. We hope we've given you enough guidance to help you determine what's going on in your network. As well, we hope we've provided enough information about the choices you have for selecting each component, and have enabled you to make these selections, or at least put together a "short list" of suitable finalists for further investigation. Now the hard part begins: keeping all this running. The key to keeping it running is upgrades and enhancements. This appendix will give you pointers on planning and executing successful network projects.

UPGRADE AND ENHANCEMENT PROJECTS

To plan a project, you need to estimate costs. But before you can do that, you'll need to determine which segments of your network you want to upgrade. This can be your most difficult planning task, because you'll want the project to provide you with adequate resources for the foreseeable future, but not implement any more than you'll really need during that time because of the high costs associated with it. Here are a few guidelines to help you develop a good scope for your network conversion project:

▼ **Upgrade your network to see you through the next 18-24 months.** Upgrades intended to last less than that amount of time will be outdated nearly before they are complete. The future beyond 24 months is too unpredictable. Under no circumstances should you claim that no further upgrades will be required for more than two years—the networking industry is changing too fast to make such dangerous assertions!

■ **Whenever possible, upgrade your cable plant universally.** For example, if you're going to have to upgrade high-speed segments from Category 3 to Category 5 cable, go ahead and upgrade your whole network to Category 5. The incremental cost of upgrading cable is fairly low, and having a versatile cable plant will save you time and money in the future.

▲ **Upgrade the busiest 20 percent of your network.** The 80-20 rule usually applies in networking on the LAN, so upgrading the top 20 percent of bandwidth-starved segments should cover most of your problem areas.

Hardware Worksheet

The cost of equipment is probably the first and most obvious expense related to upgrading a network. What may not be so obvious, however, are the many costs directly and indirectly related to installing new hardware. The Hardware Worksheet, located at the end of this appendix, outlines the equipment and related costs you will have to consider, along with the quantity and the cost of each.

NOTE:　All of the worksheets discussed here appear at the end of this appendix.

Servers

When upgrading servers, be sure to contact your NOS vendor to find out exactly which network adapters and drivers are fully certified for the version of the NOS you now have. Remember, be sure that the version of the network operating system you currently have installed will support proposed applications and protocols. If it doesn't, a NOS upgrade—with all the attendant heartache—will be in order. Furthermore, a new version of the operating system—or even a high-speed NIC driver—may require other hardware upgrades, such as increased memory or disk space. Be sure to ask your vendors about system hardware requirements, and figure any upgrades into your cost estimate.

Hubs

The number of hubs you require depends on two things:

▼　How many ports you will be converting to a high-speed protocol

▲　The port density of the hubs you want to purchase

If you are purchasing stackable hubs, the smallest unit you can buy is a hub. Note that some stackable hubs require separate terminators, so be sure to include the cost of these terminators in your estimate.

If you have purchased or are planning to purchase a chassis-based unit, the smallest unit will be a chassis module. Be sure to include the cost of special cables and connectors required to attach new ports to your existing network.

Finally, remember to include the cost of any changes that you'll need to make in your wiring closet to accommodate the new hubs, such as additional racks and patch panels.

Routers

Your routers may require new physical interfaces, either internal or external, as well as software and firmware upgrades to work with a new protocol. They may even have to be replaced altogether. Some manual configuration will be necessary, so be sure to include all the associated costs.

Switches

You may need to purchase or upgrade existing switches. Upgrading your switches may involve high-speed interfaces or firmware upgrades. Be sure to quiz your vendor to make sure you know everything involved in preparing your switches for high-speed networking.

Workstations

Implementing upgrades at the workstation involves many of the same considerations as upgrading servers. Contact your workstation vendor to make sure the network adapters you have chosen are compatible. Select network adapters with PCI buses if at all possible. Also, make sure the workstations are running a version of the operating system that supports the network adapter driver, and that they have sufficient memory and hard disk storage to accommodate the operating system and drivers. And remember, to get the desired performance, you may need to replace the workstation altogether.

And a Smooth Road

Don't forget that you may need to upgrade your cable plant. The Hardware Worksheet will make sure you consider what kind of work will have to be done and the number of cable drops that will need this kind of work. Also, remember: New media will require new patch cables. This may seem insignificant at first, but it can add up to no small expense in most shops!

Service Cost Worksheet

You may need outside help to complete your upgrade. Use the Service Cost Worksheet at the end of this appendix when considering the cost of any outside service providers you may retain to help you with your project implementation. This will include contract programmers to help you enhance applications, network integrators to help you upgrade your servers and network operating system, as well as your switches and routers. Don't forget PC maintenance companies that can help you upgrade your desktop workstations. Finally, you may need to hire cabling contractors to help upgrade racks, risers, and patch panels in your wiring closets.

Staffing and Staff Development Worksheet

Hiring and/or training a staff to install and maintain a high-speed network is a significant expense. But networking technologies change rapidly and constantly, so chances are your current staff hasn't been adequately trained in some of the technologies you want to implement with your upgrade. Therefore, before you dive into a high-speed network implementation, you'll need to make sure that your staff has acquired the necessary skills both in troubleshooting and management. This means they need to learn not only how to physically connect devices to the network, but also to optimize drivers and applications, as well as operate management applications for the upgraded network.

Preparing your staff to handle these responsibilities includes sending them to courses and seminars, purchasing books and other reference materials, and possibly hiring temporary staff to keep your network running while your regular staff acquires expertise in the new networking products and technologies.

Sometimes developing existing staff isn't enough. You may even have to hire additional staff that are already experienced in the new technology. If that's the case, be sure to include recruiting and hiring costs into your implementation budget. The Staffing and Staff Development Worksheet can help you estimate your budget.

Time Estimate Worksheet

One of the hardest figures to estimate is that of time. Using the Time Estimate Worksheet, come up with an estimated time to upgrade each application, server, hub, router, workstation, and switch. Then, multiply that by the number of units of each piece of equipment you will convert.

Don't forget, the cost isn't limited to just time spent on the actual installation and configuration of your network project. A major expense of the project will be the costs of *downtime,* reduced productivity of everyone in your organization while systems are being optimized and the inevitable conversion problems are being solved, and reduced productivity of your staff while they become comfortable with the new equipment, software, and systems. Also, don't forget the opportunity cost associated with a network conversion—what won't get done well, or get done at all, while your staff is concentrating on completing the project.

Applications Worksheet

New applications are available all the time, and you will also want to upgrade and enhance existing applications. In addition, if you will be upgrading the network and/or desktop operating systems, application upgrades may be necessary or desirable to get the required performance and support of the operating system.

Live Fast, Die Young

Another issue to consider before undertaking a conversion to high-speed networking is the emotional cost. Whether and when it is worthwhile to begin a network upgrade depends a lot on the condition of your company and your department. Network upgrades can be expensive, laborious, time-consuming, and nerve-wracking projects. Therefore, if your company is in the midst of, say, a reorganization, a financial crisis, or an SEC audit, the stress of such a conversion will more than likely far outweigh its benefits. The same is true of your department. If you're having morale problems before you begin a networking conversion, you may not even have a department left when it's complete.

MORE PROJECT POINTERS

Now you have addressed every detail of the implementation plan. So what do you do after you have created a project work plan and budget?

First: Try Before You Buy

I can't stress this enough. All the vendor promises in the world notwithstanding, before you make your final selection of networking products, get the products into your network and test them under real conditions. I've seen too many products that looked great on the specifications sheets but failed miserably in the real network. Even if the product works out great, you'll probably uncover a detail or two about integrating it into your network that the sales literature didn't mention. For example, you may need to reconfigure the memory of—or even add memory to—your networked PCs to accommodate the network adapter. Or you may find that your routers can't be upgraded to be compatible with new protocols, and will have to be replaced altogether. These are things you won't necessarily discover in a vendor's demonstration. In fact, you may never discover them unless you get the products you plan to buy into your shop and put them through real-life testing.

TIP: In my experience, any vendor who promises that a network product has "seamless integration" and will be "transparent to the rest of the network"—especially if the vendor has never worked on my network—should be shown the door immediately.

Until you get the network products into your shop and discover all the details of installation, you won't be able to put together a comprehensive budget or schedule. So make this your first priority!

Second: Identify the Next Bottleneck

This is something you can do while you're testing equipment. As you probably know, improving network performance is simply a matter of moving the bottlenecks around. Right now, your network's bottleneck is inadequate bandwidth. When that is eased, where will the bottleneck be? Will it be underpowered servers? Decrepit workstations? At the same time you are making your pitch for a network upgrade, you should tell your management where the next slowdown will be and what will cause it. This will add to your credibility, and save you from discussions that begin, "You said if we put in this high-speed network, the network would speed up! What happened?"

Third: Make a Schedule

Using the information from the worksheets at the end of this appendix, create a schedule for the project. Determine the order in which the upgrades and installations will have to be done in your organization. Be sure to figure in ordering lead times and delivery delays. Then create a Gantt chart, like the one pictured in Figure A-1, showing dependencies and which steps have to be completed before others can begin. Assign beginning and ending dates.

TIP: You'll probably want to schedule network installation one building or one floor at a time.

Class Time

Consult with training companies or in-house instructors to create a schedule for training staff and network users. Timing is critical here. Training should take place close to the time of network implementation, or everyone will have forgotten what they learned by the time the network is in place. If you have a lot of people to train, you'll probably want to use outside training specialists even if you have in-house trainers, so that everyone can receive training shortly before the new network is put into service.

Fourth: Get Your Budget Approved

Now that you know everything you have to do and buy, how much it will cost, and how long it will take, it's time to get your final budget approved. Frequently, it's difficult for a network manager to justify to a non-technical management committee the expense of upgrading a network. You know it will increase performance, thus saving time and making network users more productive. Productivity, however, is a difficult thing to quantify. Indeed, a network upgrade may be helpful, even vital, to your organization. But given the reluctance of the powers that be to spend money on anything that won't show a tangible economic benefit, how do you convince them to approve the expenditures to build one?

The answer is deceptively simple: Put a price on it. Determine the following:

▼ How much the system really costs

■ How much money it will really save (or make)

▲ Whether the difference is worth it

You'll get a lot more attention when you present a purchase request in terms of money it can make or save your company than when you recommend it for convenience and ease of use. Telling your boss that a network upgrade will improve response time is one thing. Pointing out that having one is like getting an extra workday from each user each year is quite another.

Of course, this answer may be simple, but the means to accomplish it is a little more complicated. The task is to pinpoint the economic benefits of the improved network, calculate its exact cost, and determine whether the benefit justifies the cost. This requires not only technical expertise, but also business savvy and creative thinking. Let me give you a few pointers on how to translate benefits and costs into dollars and cents.

It's a Wonderful Life

The first step to putting a price on the benefit of a network enhancement is to take an objective look at life without the product—past, present, and future. Ask yourself what past problems the proposed network upgrade could have eased. For example, did the network in accounting slow to a standstill during year-end closing last January? Are your remote offices unable to start work on time each morning because the nightly data transfers from headquarters are taking too long to complete? Use these as concrete examples for your management of how the new network will be used in your organization.

Task	4/1/99	4/15/99	5/1/99	5/15/99	6/1/99
Order test components					
Network adapters	XXXXX				
Switches	XXXXX				
Patch cables	XXXXX				
Hubs	XXXXX				
Router interface cards	XXXXX				
Build test network		XXXXX			
Test protocol			XXXXX		
Final implementation decision				XXXXX	
Notify users of implementation decision					XXXXX
Order components					
Network adapters					
Switches					
Patch cables					
Hubs					
Router interface cards					
Install router interface cards					
Install switches in wiring closets					
Notify users of implementation schedule					
Floor 14					
Floor 15					
Floor 16					
Floor 17					
Floor 18					
Install network adapters					
Floor 14					
Floor 15					
Floor 16					
Floor 17					
Floor 18					
Cut over to new protocol					
Floor 14					
Floor 15					
Floor 16					
Floor 17					
Floor 18					

Figure A-1.   A Gantt chart for a network implementation project

6/15/99	7/1/99	7/15/99	8/1/99	8/15/99	9/1/99	9/15/99	10/1/99	10/15/99
XXXXX								
XXXXX								
XXXXX								
XXXXX								
XXXXX								
	XXXXX							
		XXXXX						
			XXXXX					
				XXXXX				
					XXXXX			
						XXXXX		
							XXXXX	
			XXXXX					
				XXXXX				
					XXXXX			
						XXXXX		
							XXXXX	
								XXXXX

Figure A-1.   A Gantt chart for a network implementation project *(continued)*

Next, ask yourself what will—or won't—happen in the future if you don't improve the network. Then figure out how that will affect your business. For example, survey your network users to find out how long it takes to complete a print job on a network printer. At the same time, ask them how much they expect their printing to increase over the next few quarters.

As another example, let's say that you manage a network with 2,500 users, and you find through your survey that on the average it takes users ten seconds to save a document. According to your research, the same task on the upgraded network would take two seconds. You also find, through your document management system, that the average network user saves 15 documents a day. "Eight seconds?" You say, "Big deal." A little math will show you that this is a very big deal indeed:

8 seconds × 15 documents × 250 workdays = 8.33 hours per year

This means that saving eight seconds per saved document amounts to saving a day's worth of work each year. Your friendly accounting department can help you put a dollar value on this. Suppose you find that the average salary of a network user is $35,000. A day's salary for an average network user would then be $140. Getting an extra day's work each year from all 2,500 users would mean an annual savings of $350,000. That should certainly get your manager's attention.

Doomsayer

Now that you have a feel for what not having the network upgrade is costing you, take a moment to play Cassandra. Get your known facts together, then conjure up the worst possible scene that could result from this. In our document saving example, for instance, assume that your company is actually paying a day's worth of overtime ($500,000 per year) for work that can't be done during regular business hours.

In another example, determine whether the bandwidth crunch on your network, coupled with increasing network usage, might cause work to slow to the point that important tax or SEC filing deadlines are missed. When you present visions like these to your management, you'll have their attention.

Considering the Alternative

Now it's time to concede that a network upgrade is not the only solution. There may be other ways to solve the problem. To have a persuasive pitch, you will have to acknowledge that there are alternatives and show that you have considered them. Then you have to reveal their inadequacies—if you can.

One of the problems with the alternatives that we have suggested is that most of them require much more maintenance and management than a high-speed network. Network segmentation in particular requires a great deal of configuration and reconfiguration as users are added and moved. As well, virtual networking requires expertise in the software and concepts of virtual networking, as well as time to maintain the virtual segments.

Too Much Is Not Enough

The biggest inadequacy of any of the networking alternatives is that there is never, ever enough bandwidth. Any means of squeezing a little more performance out of 10Mbps is truly a stopgap measure. As more users are added to the network, and PCs gain processing power, and more multimedia applications are put on networks, you will find that even a shared 100Mbps network may not provide sufficient bandwidth for long. One of the driving forces behind this seemingly unstoppable bandwidth drought is user expectations. As users are buying high-powered PCs for home, they will expect their work PCs—despite being networked—to match the response time of their supercharged standalone home PCs.

Therefore, giving your budget committee a short history lesson on the growth of networks, application packet sizes, PC processors, user expectations, and bandwidth requirements over the last three years should bring them around to reality.

The Price Is Right

Now it's time to put a complete price on the network project you want to implement. As you are now aware, the cost of a network upgrade is much more than the purchase price of the products. Ask yourself how the new protocol will affect client and server resources. Will additional hardware be required to install and run the system properly? Will you have to purchase annual support contracts? How will implementing the management system affect staffing? Overtime? Training? As we've mentioned, the worksheets at the end of this appendix will help you put together a detailed budget. Be honest with yourself when calculating these costs.

Benefit Analysis

After you evaluate the costs of the network improvement, you must assess its benefits. If you do build the network, how will it really benefit you? As we mentioned earlier, making your life easier isn't going to satisfy the budget committee. How is it going to save money? A product that cuts staffing and/or overtime, or that solves a significant operational or customer service problem, is going to get the budget dollars.

In my document-saving example, if the total cost of upgrading the network is $1,000,000 or less, the system will pay for itself in less than three years in time savings alone. After that, the network upgrade will be giving your company $350,000 worth of time each year.

Show Time

Now that you've gathered your facts, found the costs and shortcomings in your own solution, addressed the holes in your own logic, and built a case based on economic need and common sense, it's time to prepare your presentation. Start by telling your management how much the network upgrade will save the company. Then give your example of a past project that would have been done more cost-effectively if the network enhancement had been done. Next, present the worst-case scenario if the network isn't built, then conclude with a step-by-step explanation of the analysis you used to arrive at these conclusions. Finally, just in case your argument sparks enthusiasm, it's a good idea to have a high-level implementation plan on hand to give your management an idea of what will be involved.

You Can't Always Get What You Want

Your analysis has either produced a sound, justifiable, and hopefully unassailable case for upgrading the network, or a reasonable explanation of why the project just isn't feasible. In either instance, you win. Understanding why a purchase doesn't make business sense will build your credibility with your management just as much as knowing when it does. It also makes you aware of the types of systems and pricing that will make sense.

If your analysis shows that improving your network isn't a sound business move, don't give up. Instead, calculate a price at which the network would be a good buy. Then present that figure to your vendor (be fair—vendors have to make money, too). You never know, there may be room for negotiation. Even if there isn't, this will give your vendor information to take back to their manufacturers to let them know their products may be overpriced for their market.

This exercise will also give you more than a business case for upgrading your network. It will help you gain a broad perspective on how your network fits into your organization. It also encourages constant, close communication with other departments and an understanding of how they use the network and information about the network. This is the kind of perspective that will not only make you a better network manager, but also serve you well throughout your career.

Fifth: Set Expectations

As soon as you complete your implementation plan and schedule for your network upgrade, start setting appropriate expectations for your managers, your users, and your staff. Here are some tips:

▼ **Communicate.** Write a memo, hold meetings, post notices, and talk with everyone you meet in the hall about what you are doing and why. Explain it in excruciating detail. Tell them why it is necessary. Be a walking, talking seminar on building your network project. Even though some people may not understand everything you're saying, they will have an opportunity to grasp the enormity of the undertaking and perhaps be more sympathetic to any difficulties encountered as a result.

■ **Listen to their concerns about "another network project."** Everyone dreads having the network down, and it often seems that every major network upgrade or conversion is followed by a frustrating period of sporadic downtime while working out the "bugs." Some users may be anxious about the network project because they are about to begin demanding projects of their own. You should be aware of these projects and plan the network implementation accordingly. After talking with your users, you may even want to reschedule so that the network won't be "under construction" during a critical work period such as tax season at an accounting firm or a large trial at a law firm.

- ■ **Be very candid about how long the project will take.** You will gain nothing by being overly optimistic. If anything, overestimate the duration of the implementation.

- ■ **Let all concerned know where and when you are likely to encounter problems or delays.** At the same time, share your contingency plans for meeting important deadlines and keeping the work flowing even when the project isn't going as well as planned.

- ■ **Don't oversell the expected performance increases.** Obviously, you wouldn't be undertaking the project if you didn't think it was worthwhile. However, while you should be positive about the benefits of the network project, don't make anyone expect a miracle.

- ■ **Prepare your staff for long hours.** Be sure you have communicated very clearly exactly what this project is going to demand of them. Show them the schedule and the task assignments. Be sure everyone is committed to successful completion of the project. Then help them prepare for it.

TIP: Giving them some time off before the project begins may help ensure that they are fit, well-rested, and in good spirits at the outset. This will help the whole project to go more smoothly, to say the least.

- ▲ **Be prepared for cranky users.** No matter how carefully and thoroughly you communicate, there will no doubt be a user or two who becomes frustrated with the progress of the project and lashes out at you and/or your staff. Don't take it personally (no matter how personally it is aimed) and make sure your staff doesn't, either. Tell them that this is likely to happen, and instruct them to listen patiently to angry users, apologize for any inconvenience, tell the users what is being done, and walk away.

TIP: It might be wise to offer your staff an incentive—such as a bonus, a victory party, or some time off—or all of the above—when the project is completed.

To help you "put a pencil" to these potential expenses, we have prepared the worksheets at the end of the appendix. They outline the major cost components of a network upgrade and describe how to calculate the cash outlays associated with each. The actual prices for each of the specific protocols are discussed in the chapters covering those protocols.

SURVIVING

This appendix sounds more like you're preparing for war than for network management. However, it's not meant to scare you away from network maintenance and upgrades. In fact, its aim is to ensure that you come away from the project with a high-performance network and an intact career. The secret to a successful implementation is

▼ Doing your homework and carefully selecting which products and technologies to implement where

■ Carefully planning and scheduling the tasks and expenditures

▲ Preparing your staff, your users, and your management

Follow the guidelines laid out in this book, and you too can be King—or Queen—of the Information Superhighway!

Hardware Worksheet

Servers:

Equipment	No. of Units	Cost per Unit	Total
Network adapters			
NOS upgrades			
Memory upgrades			
Disk upgrades			
Driver upgrades			
Other hardware upgrades			
Total			

Hubs—Number of ports to upgrade:

Equipment	No. of Units	Cost per Unit	Total
New hubs			
Modules			
Chassis			
Total			

Routers:

Equipment	No. of Units	Cost per Unit	Total
New routers			
Router interfaces			
Firmware upgrades			
Software upgrades			
Total			

Hardware Worksheet *(continued)*

Switches—Number of switched ports needed:

Equipment	No. of Units	Cost per Unit	Total
New switches			
Switch upgrade modules			
Firmware upgrades			
Total			

Workstations:

Equipment	No. of Units	Cost per Unit	Total
New workstations			
Operating system upgrades			
Network adapters			
Memory			
Disk space			
Video cards			
Total			

Cable, media, and wiring closet:

Equipment	No. of Units	Cost per Unit	Total
New drops			
Upgraded drops			
Additional pair terminate			
Patch cables			
Connectors			
Terminators			
Racks			
Patch panels			
Total			

Service Cost Worksheet

Service	No. of Hours	Cost per Hour	Total
Contract programmers			
Client applications			
Server applications			
Management applications			
Network integrators			
Server upgrades			
Network operating system upgrades			
Cabling contractors			
Wiring closet upgrades			
Rack installation			
Riser wiring/installation			
Patch panel installation			
Total			

Staff Development Worksheet

Staff development costs:

Seminars	No. of Enrollees	Cost per Enrollee	Total
Management systems			
Cabling			
Switches			
Routers			
Hubs			
General protocol			
Total			

Courses	No. of Enrollees	Cost per Enrollee	Total
Management systems			
Cabling			
Switches			
Routers			
Hubs			
General protocol			
Total			

Books and Reference Materials	No. of Units	Cost per Unit	Total
Management systems			
Cabling			
Switches			
Routers			
Hubs			
General protocol			
Total			

Staffing Worksheet

Temporary Staff Costs	No. of Hours	Cost per Hour	Total
Network management			
Programming/ analyst			
Hardware maintenance			
Network administration			
Total			

New Staff Recruiting Costs	No. of Positions	Cost per Position	Total
Advertisements			
Search firm fees			
Orientation costs			
Total			

Time Estimate Worksheet

Installation Time	No. of Hours	Cost per Hour	Total
Servers			
Hubs			
Routers			
Switches			
Workstations			

Upgrades and Optimization	No. of Hours	Cost per Hour	Total
Servers			
Hubs			
Routers			
Switches			
Workstations			

Application Upgrades	No. of Hours	Cost per Hour	Total
Workstations			
Servers			
Network management			

Total

Time Estimate Worksheet *(continued)*

Segment	No. of People on Segment	Average Cost per Hour for Person on Segment	Estimated Downtime in Hours	Total Cost of Segment Downtime

What Won't Get Done

Total Downtime Lost

Application Worksheet

Client Applications	No. of Licenses	Cost per License	Total
Upgrade			
New			

Server Applications	No. of Licenses	Cost per License	Total
Upgrade			
New			

Management Applications	No. of Licenses	Cost per License	Total
Upgrade			
New			
Total			

Index

B

C

D

J

K

 ## L

N

 O

Q

R

S

T

U

 ## V

W

X

Z